COLLECTED WORKS OF

BERNARD LONERGAN

VOLUME 3

INSIGHT

COLLECTED WORKS
OF BERNARD
LONERGAN

INSIGHT:
A STUDY OF HUMAN
UNDERSTANDING

edited by
Frederick E. Crowe and
Robert M. Doran

τὰ μὲν οὖν εἴδη τὸ νοητικὸν ἐν τοῖς
φαντάσμασι νοεῖ.

Aristotle, *De anima*, III, 7, 431b 2

Published for Lonergan Research Institute
of Regis College, Toronto
by University of Toronto Press
Toronto Buffalo London

Insight: A Study of Human Understanding

Fifth edition, revised and augmented, of
Insight: A Study of Human Understanding,
first published by Longmans, Green & Co.,
London, 1957

© Bernard Lonergan Estate 1992
Printed in Canada

ISBN 0-8020-3454-3 (cloth)
ISBN 0-8020-3455-1 (paper)

Canadian Cataloguing in Publication Data

Lonergan, Bernard J.F. (Bernard Joseph Francis), 1904–84
    Collected works of Bernard Lonergan

    Vol. 3, 5th ed., rev. and aug. First ed. (1957).
    Partial contents: v. 3. Insight: a study of
    human understanding.
    Includes bibliographical references and index.
    ISBN 0-8020-3454-3 (v. 3 : bound)
    ISBN 0-8020-3455-1 (v. 3 : pbk.)

    1. Theology – 20th century. 2. Catholic Church.
    I. Crowe, Frederick E., 1915–   . II. Doran, Robert M., 1939–
    III. Lonergan Research Institute. IV. Title.

BX891.L595 1988   230   C88-093328-3

The Lonergan Research Institute
gratefully acknowledges the contribution of
DR. JOHN CHARLES BEER
given in honor of his brother, PETER BEER, S.J.,
founder in 1975 of the Australian branch of
the Toronto Lonergan Center,
toward publication of this volume
of the Collected Works of Bernard Lonergan.

Contents

Editors' Preface

This edition of *Insight: A Study of Human Understanding* may be called the fifth edition of the book first published by Longmans, Green & Co., London, in 1957. A second, students edition was published in 1958, with revision of several passages and the correction of a good number of minor mistakes; the pagination, however, remained the same from preface to end, the revisions having been tailored to replace exactly the deleted parts. In 1970 Philosophical Library, New York, published what they called a third edition, unchanged except for a publisher's foreword. In 1978 Harper & Row published a paperback edition which we may call the fourth; it was a reprint of the 1958 edition, but the whole preface was shifted back one page (and thus incidentally threw out a number of index references). There were several reprintings of all editions except the first.

The present edition is based on that of 1958, but we have made numerous revisions of the text (over 130), have expanded the footnote material, added editorial notes and other appendices, and reworked the index. The crucial changes for most readers are the revisions of the text, and we will presently declare our rationale in this area, but a short history of the way the book came to be written will be a useful preliminary.

It had its remote origin in lectures Bernard Lonergan gave at the Thomas More Institute in Montreal in the academic year of 1945–46.[1] They were entitled Thought and Reality and were largely philosophic,

---

1 Repeatedly, in the lectures and interviews of later years Lonergan spoke of the experience of those lectures and the assurance their reception

but the urgent need, as he experienced it in his own field, was for a viable method in theology, and a book on that topic is what he determined to write.[2]

At this time, however, he was just starting his series of *verbum* articles on Thomas Aquinas,[3] so he postponed the book till he finished that series in 1949. Lonergan had adopted as a motto the phrase of Leo XIII, *vetera novis augere et perficere* (to add to and perfect the old by means of the new); the *verbum* series was concerned with the *vetera*, as was his earlier series on divine grace in Thomas;[4] it was time now to add the *nova*, to come to the rescue of a theology in sore need of a method.

Three years later, in the fall of 1952, Lonergan was forced to modify his plan. His religious superiors had determined to bring him from Toronto, where he was then teaching, to the Gregorian University in Rome, he was convinced that he would get little writing done there, so he decided to 'round off' the work he had started and try to get it published.[5] The rounding off was finished by the summer of 1953, and in September of that year he left for Rome with three copies of the completed work.[6] The book went with unexpected rapidity through the

gave him that he had a book in his potential: for example, in the paper '*Insight* Revisited' (1974: 263–78, at 268 – for all such references in our preface see the appendix on Works of Lonergan Referred to). That he needed this assurance accords with a strange diffidence deep in Lonergan's character, hidden under a sometimes aggressive manner. See also note *b* to chapter 1 below.

2 '... my intention was an exploration of methods generally in preparation for a study of the method of theology' (1974: 268).

3 Published in *Theological Studies* (1946–49) as 'The Concept of *Verbum* in the Writings of St. Thomas Aquinas,' and in book form (1967) as *Verbum: Word and Idea in Aquinas*, ed. David Burrell (Notre Dame: University of Notre Dame Press).

4 Published in *Theological Studies* (1941–42) as 'St. Thomas' Thought on *Gratia operans*,' and in book form (1971) as *Grace and Freedom: Operative Grace in the Thought of St. Thomas Aquinas*, ed. J. Patout Burns (London: Darton, Longman & Todd).

5 '*Insight* Revisited' (1974: 268). This rounding off gives a basic perspective on *Insight*: though integral within its assigned limits – 'In constructing a ship or a philosophy one has to go the whole way' (p. 7 below) – it is not the finished book he had planned.

   Conversations Lonergan had with Frs Paul Dezza and Charles Boyer in the fall of 1952 were decisive at this time: both were 'clear and definite on point that no writing done at Greg' (1952–55: letter of December 23, 1952 – the 'Greg' is the Gregorian University).

6 *Caring about Meaning: Patterns in the Life of Bernard Lonergan*, ed. Pierrot

Roman censors, and later through those of Westminster in London.[7] There would be extensive revisions in several stages in 1954–55, typesetting would start in 1955, and a year later the galleys optimistically say 'First published 1956' – but in fact it was only on April 1st (he would later joke about this date) of 1957 that the book finally appeared.

The way Lonergan's thought unfolded as he wrote the book makes profitable study. The sources for study are extensive: two more sets of lectures, one of them again at Thomas More Institute in March–May 1951,[8] and one at Regis College, Toronto, in 1952–53;[9] two typescripts: Lonergan's autograph,[10] and the first carbon copy of the professionally typed text,[11] each with layers of revisions; sketches of ideas and tables of contents extant in the Archives; the first set of proofs (gal-

Lambert, Charlotte Tansey, Cathleen Going (Montreal, Thomas More Institute): 'I had two copies with me' on the boat (1982: 124). Two carbon copies surely, hence three in all. The first went to Longmans, Green and Co.; the second (first carbon), which Lonergan kept himself, is now in the Archives, the only copy extant except the autograph; the third, which he sent back to Canada in May 1954, eventually went to Philosophical Library, New York.

7 Ibid.: 'I got it through the censors of the Gregorian in Rome and the censors in Westminster in London.' It is not known who the Roman censors were, but Lonergan had asked Eric O'Connor and F. Crowe to write censor-style to Charles Boyer (1952–55: letter of October 25, 1953), and perhaps their reports were accepted as censorship. The 'Imprimi potest' was given in Rome on April 2, 1954, by the Rector of the Gregorian University, Fr P.M. Abellán; the Westminster Chancery is not mentioned in the 1957 edition, but that of 1958 carries the 'Nihil obstat' of Joannes M.T. Barton as 'Censor Deputatus.'

8 Intelligence and Reality (1951a: lectures); the lectures ran from March to May 1951, and Lonergan provided a copy of his own notes (29 pages) for his audience.

9 There is a very good set of notes taken by Thomas O'D. Hanley (1952–53: lectures), carefully dated November 11, 1952, to April 21, 1953; the plan is that of the book, but there is no lecture on chapter 5, and the series stops with objectivity and the dialectic of philosophy (chapter 14).

10 When Lonergan left Canada for Rome in 1953 he gave the autograph to Eric O'Connor (1982: 123), who turned it over circa 1975 to what was then the Lonergan Center of Regis College. It is now Batch IV of the Archives; the contents and those of Batch III (see the next note) have been catalogued by Philip McShane.

11 Lonergan kept this carbon copy till the early 1970s when he gave it to the Lonergan Center of Regis College. It is now Batch III of the Archives.

leys) with Lonergan's corrections;[12] and data from friends with whom he spoke or corresponded at the time. There is also a post-publication history in lectures and letters in which he explains his thought, in memories recorded later in conversations and interviews, and in the annotations on his personal copies of the book.[13] The whole fascinating story could itself become a volume; here we can give only a few headlines.

Lonergan's autograph, which we will call MSA, is filled with changes. On the pages he kept as final often a whole paragraph, or several lines of one, will be crossed out and followed by a new start; and for each page that he kept there could be as many as fifteen or twenty others previously scrapped.[14] The good copy prepared for the publishers, which we will call MSB, was typed by Beatrice Kelly (later White) of Montreal,[15] all but chapters 18 and 19, which were done by Bernard's

12 After Eric O'Connor's death in 1980, Edward Dowling, then Archivist of the Jesuits of Upper Canada, turned over to the Lonergan Research Institute anything in the O'Connor papers pertinent to its work; when Robert Croken came to catalogue these, the first proofs of *Insight* (galleys), with Lonergan's corrections, were found among them – very fortunately just in time for our present editing; there were page proofs for making the index, but these went back to the publisher (letter to F. Crowe from L.A. Carter, Longmans Production Department, November 27, 1956); Lonergan would, of course, have had the page proofs too, and seems to have made further changes at that stage.

13 We list in an appendix some of the lectures in which Lonergan explained his book. Several letters and interviews in which he responded to particular questions are a still untapped source. He annotated here and there a copy of the first edition and, more extensively, a copy of the third (hence in 1970 or later). In 1977 he responded to a questionnaire from Harper & Row with two packed pages of single-space typing (1991b); in his first approach to Longmans he had sent to them, along with the table of contents, 'five pages single spaced in outline of the general idea' (1952–55: letter of June 13, 1954), but this precious document does not seem to have survived. We will see some of this various wealth in our editorial notes.

14 When he went from Toronto to Rome in 1953, he left behind in his room at Regis College a stack two or three feet high of these discarded pages. They were not saved; historians of course were thereby spared a mountain of work, but deprived also of a valuable primary source on the genesis of *Insight*. There are in the Archives, however, besides the autograph, scattered pages in which Lonergan sketched his ideas and plans; much work is needed to determine the sequence of these sketches.

15 This was entirely a volunteer work on her part (nearly twenty years later she typed *Method in Theology*, but this time with appropriate compensation). The MSS here and there record her penciled questions;

Jesuit brother, Gregory.[16] MSB has its own share of revisions, with their own complex history. Some are simple matters of tidying up the MS, inserting subheadings, and so on – done, probably, in proofreading the typescript. Others were made in Rome; the Roman paper used is regularly a sufficient clue, but we have more accurate control through Lonergan's letters. Both MSA and MSB, then, refer to somewhat fluid entities. Our only other designation will be PT for the published text, with first or second edition specified when that is relevant.

The revisions made after September 1953 divide into roughly defined stages. There were scattered revisions (the addition of footnotes, the substitution of a page or so) as Lonergan fiddled with his text for most of a year before sending it to Longmans in May 1954. The first major change was a completely different preface, written as the result of conversations with T. Michael Longman in the summer of that year.[17] The next was a carefully listed set of further revisions, undated but sent apparently to Eric O'Connor by early October 1954 for incorporation into the second carbon, the dimmer parts of which were then being retyped for the American publisher that Longmans hoped to find.[18]

also suggestions, some of which Lonergan accepted. Her previous experience in typing scientific papers stood her in good stead when she came to chapters 1 to 5, and though we must correct her work in a number of places, we have the highest respect for her competence; the world of thought owes her an immense debt. She died in Montreal early in 1991.

16 A clue to Gregory's work is found in his use of Regiopolis College stationery (he was stationed there – in Kingston, Ontario – at the time), but there is more cogent evidence in a note of his still with the MS, and in a personal conversation with him. That Bernard enlisted his brother's help in typing argues to a rush period toward the end, as he tried to get the work done before leaving Toronto.

17 Rewriting of the preface seems to have preceded the undated list of revisions to be mentioned immediately in our text and in note 18; for some dates see below, our editorial note a to Lonergan's preface.

18 Lonergan had sent the second carbon of his work back to Canada in May 1954 (1952–55: letter of May 5, 1954). In September he asked about the possibility of having certain dimmer pages retyped (ibid.: letter of September 24, 1954). In October he reported that Eric O'Connor had taken on this task (ibid.: letter of October 16, 1954), and it seems that at this time he sent this undated list of revisions to O'Connor; the list is certainly prior to October 16 for it speaks of the new preface still to be sent, and that had been mailed from Rome by this date (ibid.). A few further but minor revisions followed a month later (ibid.: letter of November 9, 1954).

Meanwhile readers' reports had been submitted to Lonergan by the publishers, and so during the months November to March he rewrote some seventy pages of his typescript, sending it part by part to Eric O'Connor for criticism; when it was completed he sent O'Connor a detailed list of the pages to be removed from the previous text (MSB), and in our editing we had this list available along with the pages that had been removed and of course the new pages that were substituted.[19] Then there are the revisions made at the proofreading stage; and, finally, those made for the second edition of 1958.

Turning now to the stages in Lonergan's actual composition of the book, we may say in an overall view that the present chapters 1 to 13 were something like a unit and in the actual composition formed a kind of plateau reached by December of 1952, that within this 'unit' chapters 9 to 13 were the first ones written in final form (not so numbered at the time), and that chapters 14 to 20 were variously organized and reorganized in his planning and to some extent on paper, as he tried, in the last months of his Toronto period, to 'round off' his work in preparation for his transfer to Rome.

Thus twenty years later he declared: 'With chapter thirteen the book could end. The first eight chapters explore human understanding. The next five reveal how correct understanding can be discerned.'[20] This agrees perfectly with the plan of both sets of Thomas More Institute lectures, which also 'explore human understanding' (thought in 1945, intelligence in 1951) and then raise the question explicitly of the transi-

---

19 Lonergan's correspondence between October 1954 and April 1955 enables us to date these revisions. The most extensive changes (to be indicated in our editorial notes) are in chapters 1, 2, 3, and 5; they are due mainly to the report of George Temple, Sedleian Professor of Natural Philosophy at Oxford, who gave the publishers permission to forward his criticism to Lonergan; it is available now in the latter's archival papers.

 The criticism was a jolt to Lonergan, but did not embitter him. He wrote, 'Insight has hit a snag ... Nuisance, but hope to lick this problem.' He did speak, however, in the same letter of being ready to revise chapters 1 to 5 'or to scuttle most of it' (1952–55: letter of October 26, 1954). Three months later he reported completion of his revisions of the latter parts of chapters 1 and 2, adding, 'and, I think, they are much better from the viewpoint of the specialist reader' (1952–55: letter of January 25, 1955).

20 'Insight Revisited' (1974: 275).

tion from understanding to that which is, to being.[21] The account in 'Insight Revisited' continues: 'However ... if I went no further [than chapter 13], my work would be regarded as ... incapable of grounding a metaphysics ... A metaphysics could be possible and yet an ethics impossible. An ethics could be possible and yet arguments for God's existence impossible. In that fashion seven more chapters came to be written.'[22]

These are Lonergan's memories twenty years later, but contemporary with his 'rounding off' decision there is a letter adding precious details: 'About 12 chapters done. About 6 chapters to go.' It then lists the topics as follows: 'insight in maths, empirical science, common sense, knowing things, judgment; objectivity of insight; nature of metaphysics; God; dialectic of individual consciousness (Freud), of community (Marx), of objectivity (philosophies), of religion' (1952–55: letter of December 23, 1952).[23] The twelve completed chapters would almost certainly be the present chapters 1 to 13 (6 and 7 were originally a single chapter) and bring us to the objectivity of insight; but after that the titles listed bear little resemblance to those in the published book. It seems then that the six 'chapters to go' became the present chapters 14 to 20, and that from January through July Lonergan wrote all these, and added his Epilogue, along with a Preface and Introduction – a task of Hercules, surely.[24]

Regarding the order of writing within the first thirteen chapters, there is conflicting evidence. When he asked whether the dim pages in the second carbon copy could be retyped Lonergan remarked: 'I think ... that the poorest part is what was done first namely chapters 9–13'

21 Very clearly in Thought and Reality: 'Problem: – To effect the transition from subjective necessity that exists in our minds to the certainty that it is so' (1945–46: 26). There is a similar transition in the Regis College lectures: 'Do you know anything by insight?' followed by the underlined heading Insight as Knowledge (1952–53: 67, in lecture 14, about the end of March 1953).
22 'Insight Revisited' (1974: 275); see also 'An Interview with Fr. Bernard Lonergan, S.J.' (ibid.: 222), and Caring (1982: 70). External data on the actual composition of the last six or seven chapters are lacking, the Regis College lectures having ended on April 21, 1953, at chapter 14 (1952–53: 78).
23 Lonergan was answering a request for accounts of the lectures; 'no reportatio available,' he said, unaware perhaps of the Hanley notes.
24 Since the complete typescript of MSB was ready for reading by early August 1953 (see our editorial note f to Lonergan's Preface), the last of MSA must have gone to the typists some weeks earlier.

(1952–55: letter of September 24, 1954). This agrees in many ways with the state of his own typescript. For example, each of the chapters 9 to 13 has its own pagination, but then the pages are numbered cumulatively from 1 to 95 – that is, no pages at that time preceded them. Again, chapters 9 to 13 are done in single-space typing; so are chapters 1 to 5 and the first nine pages of chapter 6; then Lonergan shifts to double-space typing till the end of chapter 8 and, resuming it again after chapters 9 to 13, maintains double spacing for the rest of the book. This makes no sense if he wrote chapters 1 to 20 in that order, but makes evident sense if he started with single-spacing, then halfway through (after 9 to 13, 1 to 5, and part of 6) took pity on his typists and shifted to double-spacing. Other indications in the MSS point the same way.

Against this, however, there is an oral tradition: Thomas Daly and Robert Doran both report conversations in which Lonergan affirmed a different order: that chapters 1 to 5 came last (Fr Daly), that chapters 6 to 7 on common sense came before chapters 1 to 5 (Fr Doran). It could be that these are the confused memories thirty years later (the conversations took place in 1983 and 1984) of the shift from chapters 9–13 to chapters 1–5. But it is also possible that Lonergan had written an early draft of a chapter (or chapters) on common sense, then put it aside, and rewrote it completely when it came up in order after chapters 1 to 5.[25] What is certain is that the topics of chapter 7 had engaged him far back in his student days,[26] kept surfacing in the minor writings of his Montreal period of teaching, 1940–46,[27] and influenced his work on economics in 1942.[28]

25 This just might explain a peculiar pair of headings in the table of contents Lonergan drew up soon after completing chapters 9 to 13 (see the frontispiece of this volume). After listing those chapters, with the same titles and length that they have in the autograph, Lonergan adds 'Forms of Experience' (11 pages) and 'Critical Enlightenment' (12 pages); could these be a first draft of the present chapters 6 and 7? It is an intriguing suggestion, and would solve our little puzzle; unfortunately, neither item has come to light yet in the Archives.
26 The evidence for this is a set of papers Lonergan wrote, apparently between 1933 and 1938, and kept in part all his life (File 713 in his archival papers).
27 A number of reviews and articles that Lonergan wrote in this period (for *The Montreal Beacon* [later *The Canadian Register*, Quebec edition] and other journals) deal with economic, political, and social questions.
28 The first draft of Lonergan's essay on economics was written in 1942; he gave it to Eric Kierans who in turn gave it to the Lonergan Archives.

With this brief history (some points on the genesis of chapters 14 to 20 – omitted here – will be added in our editorial notes) we may turn to the present edition of the book, and to the principles and policies that guided our editing.

Of paramount importance is the problem of establishing the definitive text; it will perhaps surprise those who regard *Insight* as carved in stone to learn how often the materials presented us with choices. There are differences between MSA and MSB, which seem to be due to typing errors, as when A has 'definitive' and B has 'definite'; here we opt for MSA. Other cases are not so simple, as when A has 'cognitional,' B has 'conditional,' and Lonergan corrected the latter to 'unconditioned'; we suspect he did this without checking the autograph – again therefore we take MSA as his intent and our preferred reading. There are differences between the printed text and the two manuscripts, as when PT has 'his' and the MSS have 'this,' or when it has 'determine' and they have 'determinate,' or it has 'generally' and they have 'generically'; these look like typesetter's errors, and so we restored the MS reading. Sometimes also distinctive little features of Lonergan's style got lost; for example, he tended to write, 'It also is,' and this would become 'It is also'; or he wrote 'It easily is led,' and this became 'It is easily led' – inconsequential items, but we find Lonergan himself changing a text to conform to his order, and, for those who have an eye and ear for his style, that order seems worth restoring.[29]

We do not make a cast-iron rule of preferring the manuscripts to the printed text. We can check the changes Lonergan made on the galley proofs, superseding the MS readings; it is possible others were made on the page proofs, which we cannot check; and he may have made changes on the manuscript that went to the publisher while failing occasionally to copy them onto his carbon (which is all we now have). A complication in our work is the presence of marginal annotations that are not Lonergan's, but those of the typists, or perhaps censors, or readers to whom he submitted his manuscript. All this gives scope for numerous judgment calls.

---

29 The labor of studying the three texts – MSA, MSB, and PT – and comparing them, line by line, word by word, was undertaken by Robert Doran. His work turned up some 130 cases in which there seemed to be a slip between MSA and MSB or between MSB and PT – some of them of considerable importance for Lonergan's thought.

Besides restoring what we considered to be Lonergan's own language, we had to consider editorial 'correction' of his work – an awesome task in so monumental a work, but a responsibility we could not conscientiously avoid. Readers, however, will wish to control our editing; and so, apart from changes too simple to annotate – as when we moved an 'only' or an 'either' to its proper location, or brought the number of subject and predicate into agreement – we declared our 'corrections,' even quite trivial ones, in editorial notes.

We left alone some readings that purists might consider blemishes, for often they pertain to those distinctive touches we mentioned: Lonergan would use the word order of direct discourse for indirect ('determine ... what is the proportion'), or use 'both' for 'the two' ('the same meaning in both cases'), or 'all cannot' for 'not all can,' or 'between' for 'among,' or write 'has not and cannot establish,' and so on. Sayings quoted from memory remain with their mistakes; so does what now seems unnecessary repetition. We resisted too the temptation to tamper with less customary forms: his distinctive 'learnt' instead of 'learned,' 'upon' for 'on,' 'that' for 'who,' and others.[30] When he unwittingly made Cinderella walk backwards we allowed her the unusual exercise. With a few duly noted exceptions we cheerfully left such usages, 'blemishes' or not, as we found them (less cheerfully, his regular use of 'man' for the human race – on this point he wrote thirty years too soon).

Punctuation is another matter. Lonergan was not at his best in the use, for example, of commas, and so – cautiously, aware that commas can radically change the sense of a passage[31] – we exercised more editorial freedom here. In paragraphing too we changed some of his divisions. The use of quotation marks gave real difficulty, but two samples will indicate our policy; 'yes' and 'no' have become common nouns in Lonergan, and questions like 'What is it?' are part of his philosophic stock in trade; unless, then, there is question of their use by a real or fictive speaker (the famous worker who remarked 'Something happened'), we

30 Lonergan did consult friends on his English style, and some of their comments appear in MSB; for example, the line 'if the typical scientist's satisfaction in success is more sedate' (28 below) has the notation, 'too many sibilants,' quite possibly a comment of Patrick Plunkett, at that time a Jesuit professor of English literature at Guelph – he is thanked for his efforts in one draft of Lonergan's preface.

31 An excellent exercise for getting hold of *Insight*: remove all commas from a paragraph and try, a week later, to restore them.

use these and analogous terms and phrases without quotation marks. Greek words are transliterated. Our general usage in punctuation and related matters, as for volumes 4 and 5 of the Collected Works, is that of *The Chicago Manual of Style*. In spelling and syllabification we continue to follow the *Oxford American Dictionary*, making numerous changes from the British spelling of the first editions; but here again, we left some of Lonergan's personal touches alone: he would write 'unpractical,' 'unauthentic,' and so on – possibly a result of his study of Fowler's *Modern English Usage*.

We have numbered the footnotes (there were no numbers for them in previous editions); we also tried to locate references to Plato, Aristotle, Augustine, and Thomas Aquinas, but generally not those to familiar names in modern philosophy and science. For chapter divisions in the *Summa contra Gentiles* we counted paragraphs in the Leonine manual edition, as Lonergan himself was wont to do. Bibliographical data are given in full at the first mention of a work, but afterwards abbreviated. Footnotes that we added are put in square brackets; also additions that we made to Lonergan's footnotes, unless we are merely filling out the data. Some references he gave in the text we moved to footnotes.

We continue the use of letters to indicate our editorial notes. For *Insight* these notes fall into two classes; many of them explain changes we made in the text, and in these we chose to err on the side of more rather than fewer notes – they may at least reassure readers that we have not perpetrated printing errors in the relevant passages. Other notes are intended to facilitate research, and these continue the pattern established in previous volumes: they would illuminate Lonergan's meaning through data on his history, on the context in which he wrote, on parallel or contrasting points made in his other writings; but, due to the size of the book, this class was greatly reduced in number in *Insight*.

The same consideration of space restricted our references to the many interesting revisions made along the way, especially within MSA, but also in MSB and on the galleys; sometimes, however, we alert readers to their existence: that Lonergan pondered and rewrote a passage bears on our respect for his final wording. We do, however, publish the first-edition readings of the passages he revised for the second edition of his book in 1958. Also, to facilitate comparisons, we indicate in square brackets after each subtitle in our edition the corresponding pages of the second.

The editorial notes are joined by the usual appendices: a lexicon of Latin and Greek phrases, a list of Lonergan's works referred to in our editing, and (added for this volume) a list of the lectures he gave over the years in explanation of *Insight*.

It remains only to thank the many people who have contributed advice, information, or hours of labor to our work of editing, some of them in ways they may now have forgotten: Frank Braio, W. Norris Clarke, Edward Dowling, Robert Finlay, Michael Lapierre, Timothy Lynch, Jacques Monet, Elmer O'Brien, Desmond O'Grady, John Pungente, Quentin Quesnell, Giovanni Sala, and Michael Vertin; special thanks are owed to Philip McShane for his indispensable help in dealing with the first five chapters, and to the staff of the Lonergan Research Institute – Michael Shields, Marcela Dayao, Robert Croken, and Gregory Carruthers – for much tedious work in chasing footnotes, reading the proofs, and indexing the volume.

F.E.C. (for the editors)

This is a table of contents that Lonergan sketched at an early stage in the composition of *Insight*. It was filed with chapters 9 and 10 of the autograph (MSA) that he gave to Eric O'Connor when the professionally typed copy (MSB) was ready.

The seven headings from 'The Notion of Judgment' to 'Notion of Objectivity' correspond very closely to the titles of chapters 9 to 13 of the book, which we know to have been the first he wrote in definitive form. The page numbers given also correspond to the numbers for these chapters in the autograph.

We can only speculate on the content of the last two headings: 'Forms of Experience' and 'Critical Enlightenment'; as yet nothing has been noticed in the Archives that would provide a clue. As for the 92 pages that Lonergan added to his column of figures to give a total of 210 (indistinct on the margin), it would be a sheer guess to suggest a content; we have not found any sheaf or sheaves where the pages correspond to this figure.

INSIGHT:

A Study of Human Understanding

Preface[a]

In the ideal detective story the reader is given all the clues yet fails to spot the criminal. He may advert to each clue as it arises. He needs no further clues to solve the mystery. Yet he can remain in the dark for the simple reason that reaching the solution is not the mere apprehension of any clue, not the mere memory of all, but a quite distinct activity of organizing intelligence that places the full set of clues in a unique explanatory perspective.

By insight, then, is meant not any act of attention or advertence or memory but the supervening act of understanding. It is not any recondite intuition but the familiar event that occurs easily and frequently in the moderately intelligent, rarely and with difficulty only in the very stupid. In itself it is so simple and obvious that it seems to merit the little attention that commonly it receives. At the same time, its function in cognitional activity is so central that to grasp it in its conditions, its working, and its results is to confer a basic yet startling unity on the whole field of human inquiry and human opinion. Indeed, this very wealth of implications is disconcerting, and I find it difficult to state in any brief and easy manner what the present book is about, how a single author can expect to treat the variety of topics listed in the table of contents, why he should attempt to do so in a single work, and what good he could hope to accomplish even were he to succeed in his odd undertaking.

Still, a preface should provide at least a jejune and simplified answer to such questions, and perhaps I can make a beginning by saying that the aim of the work is to convey an insight into insight. Mathematicians seek insight into sets of elements. Scientists seek insight into ranges of phenomena. Men of common sense seek insight into concrete situations and practical affairs. But our concern is to reach the act of organizing intelligence that brings within a single perspective the insights of mathematicians, scientists, and men of common sense.

It follows at once that the topics listed in the table of contents are not so disparate as they appear on a superficial reading. If anyone wishes to become a mathematician or a scientist or a man of common sense, he will derive no direct help from the present work. As physicists study the shape of waves and leave to chemists the analysis of air and water, so we are concerned not with the objects understood in mathematics but with mathematicians' acts of understanding, not with objects understood in the various sciences but with scientists' acts of understanding, not with the concrete situations mastered by common sense but with the acts of understanding of men of common sense.

Further, while all acts of understanding have a certain family likeness, a full and balanced view is to be reached only by combining in a single account the evidence obtained from different fields of intelligent activity. Thus, the precise nature of the act of understanding is to be seen most clearly in mathematical examples; the dynamic context in which understanding occurs can be studied to best advantage in an investigation of scientific methods; the disturbance of that dynamic context by alien concerns is thrust upon one's attention by the manner in which various measures of common nonsense blend with common sense.

However, insight is not only a mental activity but also a constituent factor in human knowledge. It follows that insight into insight is in some sense a knowledge of knowledge. Indeed, it is a knowledge of knowledge that seems extremely relevant to a whole series of basic problems in philosophy. This I must now endeavor to indicate, even though I can do so only in the abrupt and summary fashion that leaves terms undefined and offers arguments that fall far short of proof.

First, then, it is insight that makes the difference between the tantalizing problem and the evident solution. Accordingly, insights seem to be the source of what Descartes named clear and distinct ideas, and on that showing insight into insight would be the source of the clear and distinct idea of clear and distinct ideas.

Secondly, inasmuch as it is the act of organizing intelligence, insight is an apprehension of relations. But among relations are meanings, for meaning seems to be a relation between sign and signified. Insight, then, includes the apprehension of meaning, and insight into insight includes the apprehension of the meaning of meaning.

Thirdly, in a sense somewhat different from Kant's, every insight is both a priori and synthetic. It is a priori, for it goes beyond what is merely given to sense or to empirical consciousness. It is synthetic, for it adds to the merely given an explanatory unification or organization. It seems to follow that insight into insight will yield a synthetic and a priori account of the full range of synthetic a priori components in our cognitional activity.

Fourthly, a unification and organization of other departments of knowledge is a philosophy. But every insight unifies and organizes. Insight into insight, then, will unify and organize the insights of mathematicians, scientists, and men of common sense. It seems to follow that insight into insight will yield a philosophy.

Fifthly, one cannot unify and organize knowing without concluding to a unification and organization of the known. But a unification and organization of what is known in mathematics, in the sciences, and by common sense is a metaphysics. Hence, in the measure that insight into insight unifies and organizes all our knowing, it will imply a metaphysics.

Sixthly, the philosophy and metaphysics that result from insight into insight will be verifiable. For just as scientific insights both emerge and are verified in the colors and sounds, tastes and odors, of ordinary experience, so insight into insight both emerges and is verified in the insights of mathematicians, scientists, and men of common sense. But if insight into insight is verifiable, then the consequent philosophy and metaphysics will be verifiable. In other words, just as every statement in theoretical science can be shown to imply statements regarding sensible fact, so every statement in philosophy and metaphysics can be shown to imply statements regarding cognitional fact.

Seventhly, besides insights there are oversights. Besides the dynamic context of detached and disinterested inquiry in which insights emerge with a notable frequency, there are the contrary dynamic contexts of the flight from understanding in which oversights occur regularly and one might almost say systematically. Hence, if insight into insight is not to be an oversight of oversights, it must include an insight into the principal devices of the flight from understanding.

Eighthly, the flight from understanding will be seen to be anything but a peculiar aberration that afflicts only the unfortunate or the perverse. In its philosophic form, which is not to be confused with its psychiatric, moral, social, and cultural manifestations, it appears to result simply from an incomplete development in the intelligent and reasonable use of one's own intelligence and reasonableness. But though its origin is a mere absence of full development, its consequences are positive enough. For the flight from understanding blocks the occurrence of the insights that would upset its comfortable equilibrium. Nor is it content with a merely passive resistance. Though covert and devious, it is resourceful and inventive, effective and extraordinarily plausible. It admits a vast variety of forms, and when it finds some untenable, it can resort to others. If it never refuses to supply superficial minds with superficial positions, it is quite competent to work out a philosophy so acute and profound that the elect strive in vain and for centuries to lay bare its real inadequacies.

Ninthly, just as insight into insight yields a clear and distinct idea of clear and distinct ideas, just as it includes an apprehension of the meaning of meaning, just as it exhibits the range of the a priori synthetic components in our knowledge, just as it involves a philosophic unification of mathematics, the sciences, and common sense, just as it implies a metaphysical account of what is to be known through the various departments of human inquiry, so also insight into the various modes of the flight from understanding will explain (1) the range of really confused yet apparently clear and distinct ideas, (2) aberrant views on the meaning of meaning, (3) distortions in the a priori synthetic components in our knowledge, (4) the existence of a multiplicity of philosophies, and (5) the series of mistaken metaphysical and antimetaphysical positions.

Tenthly, there seems to follow the possibility of a philosophy that is at once methodical, critical, and comprehensive. It will be comprehensive because it embraces in a single view every statement in every philosophy. It will be critical because it discriminates between the products of the detached and disinterested desire to understand and, on the other hand, the products of the flight from understanding. It will be methodical because it transposes the statements of philosophers and metaphysicians to their origins in cognitional activity, and it settles whether that activity is or is not aberrant by appealing, not to philosophers, not to metaphysicians, but to the insights, methods, and procedures of mathematicians, scientists, and men of common sense.

The present work, then, may be said to operate on three levels: it is a study of human understanding; it unfolds the philosophic implications of understanding; it is a campaign against the flight from understanding. These three levels are solidary. Without the first there would be no base for the second and no precise meaning for the third. Without the second the first could not get beyond elementary statements, and there could be no punch to the third. Without the third the second would be regarded as incredible, and the first would be neglected.

Probably I shall be told that I have tried to operate on too broad a front. But I was led to do so for two reasons. In constructing a ship or a philosophy one has to go the whole way; an effort that is in principle incomplete is equivalent to a failure. Moreover, against the flight from understanding half measures are of no avail. Only a comprehensive strategy can be successful. To disregard any stronghold of the flight from understanding is to leave intact a base from which a counteroffensive promptly will be launched.

If, however, these considerations are granted, it still will be urged that what I have attempted could be executed properly only by the organized research of specialists in many different fields. This, of course, I cannot but admit. I am far from competent in most of the many fields in which insights occur, and I could not fail to welcome the impressive assembly of talent and the comforting allocation of funds associated with a research project. But I was not engaged in what commonly is meant by research. My aim was neither to advance mathematics nor to contribute to any of the specialized branches of science but to seek a common ground on which men of intelligence might meet. It seemed necessary to acknowledge that the common ground I envisaged was rather impalpable at a time when neither mathematicians nor scientists nor men of common sense were notably articulate on the subject of insight. What had to be undertaken was a preliminary exploratory journey into an unfortunately neglected region. Only after specialists in different fields had been given the opportunity to discover the existence and significance of their insights could there arise the hope that some would be found to discern my intention where my expression was at fault, to correct my errors where ignorance led me astray, and with the wealth of their knowledge to fill the dynamic but formal structures I tried to erect. Only in the measure that this hope is realized will there be initiated the spontaneous collaboration that commonly must precede the detailed plans of an organized investigation.

There remains the question, What practical good[b] can come of this book? The answer is more forthright than might be expected, for insight is the source not only of theoretical knowledge but also of all its practical applications, and indeed of all intelligent activity. Insight into insight, then, will reveal what activity is intelligent, and insight into oversights will reveal what activity is unintelligent. But to be practical is to do the intelligent thing, and to be unpractical is to keep blundering about. It follows that insight into both insight and oversight is the very key to practicality.

Thus, insight into insight brings to light the cumulative process of progress. For concrete situations give rise to insights which issue into policies and courses of action. Action transforms the existing situation to give rise to further insights, better policies, more effective courses of action. It follows that if insight occurs, it keeps recurring; and at each recurrence knowledge develops, action increases its scope, and situations improve.

Similarly, insight into oversight reveals the cumulative process of decline. For the flight from understanding blocks the insights that concrete situations demand. There follow unintelligent policies and inept courses of action. The situation deteriorates to demand still further insights, and as they are blocked, policies become more unintelligent and action more inept. What is worse, the deteriorating situation seems to provide the uncritical, biased mind with factual evidence in which the bias is claimed to be verified. So in ever increasing measure intelligence comes to be regarded as irrelevant to practical living. Human activity settles down to a decadent routine, and initiative becomes the privilege of violence.

Unfortunately, as insight and oversight commonly are mated, so also are progress and decline.[c] We reinforce our love of truth with a practicality that is equivalent to an obscurantism. We correct old evils with a passion that mars the new good. We are not pure. We compromise. We hope to muddle through. But the very advance of knowledge brings a power over nature and over men too vast and terrifying to be entrusted to the good intentions of unconsciously biased minds. We have to learn to distinguish sharply between progress and decline, learn to encourage progress without putting a premium upon decline, learn to remove the tumor of the flight from understanding without destroying the organs of intelligence.

No problem is at once more delicate and more profound, more practical and perhaps more pressing. How, indeed, is a mind to become conscious of its own bias when that bias springs from a communal flight from understanding and is supported by the whole texture of a civilization? How can new strength and vigor be imparted to the detached and disinterested desire to understand without the reinforcement acting as an added bias? How can human intelligence hope to deal with the unintelligible yet objective situations which the flight from understanding creates and expands and sustains? At least we can make a beginning by asking what precisely it is to understand, what are the dynamics of the flow of consciousness that favors insight, what are the interferences that favor oversight, what, finally, do the answers to such questions imply for the guidance of human thought and action.

I must conclude. There will be offered in the introduction a more exact account of the aim and structure of this book. Now I have to make a brief acknowledgement of my manifold indebtedness, and naturally I am led to think in the first place of the teachers and writers who have left their mark upon me in the course of the twenty-eight years[d] that have elapsed since I was introduced to philosophy. But so prolonged has been my search, so much of it has been a dark struggle with my own flight from understanding, so many have been the half-lights and detours in my slow development, that my sincere gratitude can find no brief and exact yet intelligible expression. I turn, accordingly, to list more palpable benefactors:[e] the staff of l'Immaculée-Conception in Montreal where the parallel historical investigation[1] was undertaken; the staff of the Jesuit Seminary in Toronto where this book was written; the Rev. Eric O'Connor of Loyola College, Montreal, who was ever ready to allow me to draw upon his knowledge of mathematics and of science; the Rev. Joseph Wulftange, the Rev. Joseph Clark, the Rev. Norris Clarke, the Rev. Frederick Crowe, the Rev. Frederick Copleston, and the Rev. André Godin, who kindly read the typescript and by their diversified knowledge, encouraging remarks, and limited criticisms permitted me to feel that I was not entirely wrong; the Rev. Frederick Crowe, who has undertaken the tedious task of compiling an index.[f]

---

1 Bernard Lonergan, 'The Concept of *Verbum* in the Writings of St. Thomas Aquinas.' *Theological Studies* 7 (1946) 349–92; 8 (1947) 35–79, 404–44; 10 (1949) 3–40, 359–93. [In book form, *Verbum: Word and Idea in Aquinas*, ed. David B. Burrell (Notre Dame: University of Notre Dame Press, 1967) CWL 2.]

Introduction

The aim of the present work may be bracketed by a series of disjunctions. In the first place, the question is not whether knowledge exists but what precisely is its nature. Secondly, while the content of the known cannot be disregarded, still it is to be treated only in the schematic and incomplete fashion needed to provide a discriminant or determinant of cognitive acts. Thirdly, the aim is not to set forth a list of the abstract properties of human knowledge but to assist the reader in effecting a personal appropriation of the concrete dynamic structure immanent and recurrently operative in his own cognitional activities. Fourthly, such an appropriation can occur only gradually, and so there will be offered, not a sudden account of the whole of the structure, but a slow assembly of its elements, relations, alternatives, and implications. Fifthly, the order of the assembly is governed, not by abstract considerations of logical or metaphysical priority, but by concrete motives of pedagogical efficacy.

The program, then, is both concrete and practical, and the motives for undertaking its execution reside, not in the realm of easy generalities, but in the difficult domain of matters of fact. If at the end of the course the reader will be convinced of those facts, much will be achieved; but at the present moment all I can do is to clarify my intentions by stating my beliefs.

I ask, accordingly, about the nature rather than about the existence of knowledge because in each of us there exist two different kinds of knowledge. They are juxtaposed in Cartesian dualism with its rational *Cogito, ergo sum* and with its unquestioning extroversion to substantial extension.

They are separated and alienated in the subsequent rationalist and empiricist philosophies. They are brought together again to cancel each other in Kantian criticism. If these statements approximate the facts, then the question of human knowledge is not whether it exists but what precisely are its two diverse forms and what are the relations between them. If that is the relevant question, then any departure from it is, in the same measure, the misfortune of missing the point. But whether or not that is the relevant question can be settled only by undertaking an arduous exploratory journey through the many fields in which men succeed in knowing or attempt the task but fail.

Secondly, an account of knowing cannot disregard its content, and its content is so extensive that it mocks encyclopedias and overflows libraries; its content is so difficult that a man does well devoting his life to mastering some part of it; yet even so, its content is incomplete and subject to further additions, inadequate and subject to repeated future revisions. Does it not follow that the proposed exploratory journey is not merely arduous but impossible? Certainly it would be impossible, at least for the writer, if an acquaintance with the whole range of knowledge were a requisite in the present inquiry. But in fact our primary concern is not the known but the knowing. The known is extensive, but the knowing is a recurrent structure that can be investigated sufficiently in a series of strategically chosen instances. The known is difficult to master, but in our day competent specialists have labored to select for serious readers and to present to them in an adequate fashion the basic components of the various departments of knowledge. Finally, the known is incomplete and subject to revision, but our concern is the knower that will be the source of the future additions and revisions.

It will not be amiss to add a few corollaries, for nothing disorientates a reader more than a failure to state clearly what a book is not about. Basically, then, this is not a book on mathematics, nor a book on science, nor a book on common sense, nor a book on metaphysics; indeed, in a sense, it is not even a book about knowledge. On a first level, the book contains sentences on mathematics, on science, on common sense, on metaphysics. On a second level, the meaning of all these sentences, their intention and significance, are to be grasped only by going beyond the scraps of mathematics or science or common sense or metaphysics to the dynamic cognitional structure that is exemplified in knowing them. On a third level, the dynamic cognitional structure to be reached is not the transcendental ego of Fichtean speculation, nor the abstract pattern of relations verifiable in Tom and Dick and Harry, but the personally appropriated structure of one's own experiencing, one's own intelligent inquiry and insights, one's own critical reflection and judging and deciding. The crucial issue is an experimental issue, and the experiment will be performed not publicly but privately. It will consist in one's own rational self-consciousness clearly and distinctly taking possession of itself as rational self-consciousness. Up to that decisive achievement all leads. From it all follows. No one else, no matter what his knowledge or his eloquence, no matter what his logical rigor or his persuasiveness, can do it for you. But though the act is private, both its antecedents and its consequents have their public manifestation. There can be long series of marks on paper that communicate an invitation to know oneself in the tension of the duality of one's own knowing; and among such series of marks with an invitatory meaning the present book would wish to be numbered. Nor need it remain a secret whether such invitations are helpful or, when helpful, accepted. Winter twilight cannot be mistaken for the summer noonday sun.

In the third place, then, more than all else the aim of the book is to issue an invitation to a personal, decisive act. But the very nature of the act demands that it be understood in itself and in its implications. What on earth is meant by rational self-consciousness? What is meant by inviting it to take possession of itself? Why is such self-possession said to be so decisive and momentous? The questions are perfectly legitimate, but the answer cannot be brief.

However, it is not the answer itself that counts so much as the manner in which it is read. For the answer cannot but be written in words; the words cannot but proceed from definitions and correlations, analyses and inferences; yet the whole point of the present answer would be missed if a reader insisted on concluding that I must be engaged in setting forth lists of abstract properties of human knowing. The present work is not to be read as though it described some distant region of the globe which the reader never visited, or some strange and mystical experience which the reader never shared. It is an account of knowledge. Though I cannot recall to each reader his personal experiences, he can do so for himself and thereby pluck my general phrases from the dim world of thought to set them in the pulsing flow of life. Again, in such fields as mathematics and natural science it is possible to delineate with some accuracy the precise content of a precise insight; but the point of the delineation is not to provide the reader with a stream of words that he can repeat to others or with a set of terms and relations from which he can proceed to draw inferences and prove conclusions. On the contrary, the point here, as elsewhere, is appropriation; the point is to discover, to identify, to become familiar with, the activities of one's own intelligence; the point is to become able to discriminate with ease and from personal conviction between one's purely intellectual activities and the manifold of other, 'existential' concerns that invade and mix and blend with the operations of intellect to render it ambivalent and its pronouncements ambiguous.

At this juncture, however, many a potential reader will expostulate. The illustrations offered in the first five chapters do not lie within the orbit of his interests. Intelligence and reasonableness are marks common to all instances of Homo sapiens. But my initial concentration on mathematics and natural science seems unduly to narrow the effective range of the invitation that I issue to an appropriation of one's own rational self-consciousness.

Perhaps an explanation of the motives that guided my decision in this matter will serve not only to explain my procedure but also to enable each reader to estimate for himself the measure in which the earlier chapters have to be understood if he is to be in a position to profit from the book as a whole. In the first place, it is essential that the notion of insight, of the accumulation of insights, of higher viewpoints, and of their heuristic significance and implications not only should be grasped clearly and distinctly but also, insofar as possible, should be identified in one's own personal intellectual experience. The precise nature of such an identification will be clarified in the chapter on self-affirmation, for, as seems clear, it is both easy and common to conceive introspection and intellectual experience in a fashion that, when submitted to scrutiny, proves to be meaningless. Still, if that account of our awareness of the levels of consciousness is to be intelligible, it has to be preceded by a grasp, both precise and firm, of the successive types of activity that serve to mark and to define the successive levels of consciousness. In turn, if one's apprehension of those activities is to be clear and distinct, then one must prefer the fields of intellectual endeavor in which the greatest care is devoted to exactitude and in fact the greatest exactitude is attained. For this reason, then, I have felt obliged to begin my account of insight and its expansion with mathematical and scientific illustrations, and while I would grant that essentially the same activities can be illustrated from the ordinary use of intelligence that is named common sense, I also must submit that it would be impossible for common sense to grasp and say what precisely common sense happens to illustrate.

But further considerations are no less operative. For the present enterprise is concerned to unravel an ambiguity and to eliminate an ambivalence. St Augustine of Hippo narrates that it took him years to make the discovery that the name 'real' might have a different connotation from the name 'body.'[a] Or, to bring the point nearer home, one might say that it has taken modern science four centuries to make the discovery that the objects of its inquiry need not be imaginable entities moving through imaginable processes in an imaginable space-time. The fact that a Plato attempted to communicate through his dialogues, the fact that an Augustine eventually learnt from the writers whom, rather generically,[b] he refers to as Platonists, has lost its antique flavor and its apparent irrelevance to the modern mind. Even before Einstein and Heisenberg it was clear enough that the world described by scientists was strangely different from the world depicted by artists and inhabited by men of common sense. But it was left to twentieth–century physicists to envisage the possibility that the objects of their science were to be reached only by severing the umbilical cord that tied them to the maternal imagination of man.

As the reader will have divined, the relevance of mathematics and mathematical physics to the present investigation is not only the transference of their clarity and precision to the account of insight but also the significance of the transition from the old mechanism to relativity and from the old determinism to statistical laws. In earlier periods the thinker that would come to grips with his thinking could be aided by the dialogues of Plato, and on a more recondite level he could appeal to what M. Gilson would call the experiment of history[c] in ancient, medieval, and modern philosophy. But today there are at his disposal both the exactitude and the impressive scale of a complementary historical experiment that began with the blending of scientific principles and philosophic assumptions in Galileo and has ended with their sharp segregation in our own day. What a Plato labored to communicate through the effort in appropriation of his artistic dialogues, what the intelligence of an Augustine only slowly mastered in the throes of a religious conversion, what led a Descartes to a method of universal doubt and prompted a Kant to undertake a critique of pure reason, has cast a shadow, no less momentous but far more sharply defined, in the realm of exact science. Clearly, in a contemporary effort to resolve the duality in man's knowledge, it would be foolhardy to ignore, if not the most striking, at least the most precise element in the evidence available on the issue.

But there is also a third purpose that I hope to achieve through an appropriation of the modes of scientific thought.[d] For such thought is methodical, and the scientist pins his faith, not on this or that scientific system or conclusion, but on the validity of scientific method itself. But what ultimately is the nature and ground of method but a reflective grasp and specialized application of the object of our inquiry, namely, of the dynamic structure immanent and recurrently operative in human cognitional activity? It follows that empirical science as methodical not merely offers a clue for the discovery, but also exhibits concrete instances for the examination, of the larger, multiform dynamism that we are seeking to explore. Accordingly, it will be from the structural and dynamic features of scientific method that we shall approach and attempt to cast into the unity of a single perspective such apparently diverse elements as (1) Plato's point in asking how the inquirer recognizes truth when he reaches what, as an inquirer, he did not know,[1] (2) the intellectualist (though not the conceptualist[e]) meaning of the abstraction of form from material conditions, (3) the psychological manifestation of Aquinas's natural desire to know God by his essence,[2] (4) what Descartes was struggling to convey in his incomplete Regulae ad directionem ingenii, (5) what Kant conceived as a priori synthesis, and (6) what is named the finality of intellect in J. Maréchal's vast labor on Le point de départ de la métaphysique.[3]

I have been insisting on the gravity of the motives that led me to begin this essay in aid of self-appropriation with a scrutiny of mathematical physics. But if I am to avoid overstatement, I must hasten to add that the significance of the scrutiny is, so to speak, psychological rather than logical. For the present work falls into two parts. In the first part, insight is studied as an activity, as an event that occurs within various patterns of other related events. In the second part, insight is studied as knowledge, as an event that under determinate conditions reveals a universe of being. The first part deals with the question, What is happening when we are knowing? The second part moves to the question,[f] What is known when that is happening? Were there no psychological problem, the first·

1 [Lonergan may be referring to the questions raised in Meno, 80e–86c.]
2 [Thomas Aquinas, Summa theologiae, 1–2, q. 3, a. 8.]
3 [Joseph Maréchal, Le point de départ de la métaphysique, 5 vols. (Paris: Desclée de Brouwer, 1944–49).]

part could be reduced to sets of definitions and clarifications, for from a logical viewpoint the first judgment that occurs in the whole work is the judgment of self-affirmation in the eleventh chapter. But the hard fact is that the psychological problem exists, that there exist in man two diverse kinds of knowing, that they exist without differentiation and in an ambivalent confusion until they are distinguished explicitly and the implications of the distinction are drawn explicitly. The hard fact is that the personal psychological problem cannot be solved by the ordinary procedure of affirming the propositions that are true and denying the propositions that are false, for the true meaning of the true propositions always tends to be misapprehended by a consciousness that has not yet discovered its need of discovering what an Augustine took years and modern science centuries to discover.

It remains that something be said on the last two of the five disjunctions by which we proposed to bracket the aim of this book. As has been noted, we are concerned not with the existence of knowledge but with its nature, not with what is known but with the structure of the knowing, not with the abstract properties of cognitional process but with a personal appropriation of one's own dynamic and recurrently operative structure of cognitional activity. There is now to be explained the fourth disjunction, for the labor of self-appropriation cannot occur at a single leap. Essentially, it is a development of the subject and in the subject, and like all development it can be solid and fruitful only by being painstaking and slow.

Now it would be absurd to offer to aid a process of development and yet write as though the whole development were already an accomplished fact. A teacher of geometry may be convinced that the whole of Euclid is contained in the theory of the n-dimensional manifold of any curvature. But he does not conclude that Euclid is to be omitted from the elementary program and that his pupils should begin from the tensor calculus. For even though Euclid is a particular case, still it is the particular case that alone gives access to the general case. And even though Euclidean propositions call for qualification when the more general context is reached, still an effective teacher does not distract his pupils with qualifications they will understand only vaguely, when it is his business to herd them as best he can across the *pons asinorum*.

In similar fashion this book is written, not from above downwards, but from below upwards. Any coherent set of statements can be divided into definitions, postulates, and conclusions. But it does not follow that between the covers of a single book there must be a single coherent set of statements. For the single book may be written from a moving viewpoint, and then it will contain, not a single set of coherent statements, but a sequence of related sets of coherent statements. Moreover, as is clear, a book designed to aid a development must be written from a moving viewpoint. It cannot begin by presupposing that a reader can assimilate at a stroke what can be attained only at the term of a prolonged and arduous effort. On the contrary, it must begin from a minimal viewpoint and a minimal context; it will exploit that minimum to raise a further question that enlarges the viewpoint and the context; it will proceed with the enlarged viewpoint and context only as long as is necessary to raise still deeper issues that again transform the basis and the terms of reference of the inquiry; and clearly, this device can be repeated not merely once or twice but as often as may be required to reach the universal viewpoint and the completely concrete context that embraces every aspect of reality.

However, if this procedure alone is adapted to the aim of the present work, I must beg to stress once and for all that its implications are not to be overlooked. If Spinoza wrote his *Ethics* in what in his day was thought to be the geometric style, it is not to be inferred that I am endeavoring to walk in his footsteps, that I never heard of Gödel's theorem, that I am not operating from a moving viewpoint that successively sets up contexts only to go beyond them. If the inference is not to be made, the further implications of such an inference are not to be assumed. The premises from which my own position can be deduced are not complete in the first section of the first chapter when a brief description endeavors to fix the meaning of the name 'insight.' The context is enlarged but not completed when a study of mathematical development makes the notion of insight more precise. There is the broader context of a mathematicized world of events that has appeared by the end of the fifth chapter, but it has to be included within the still fuller context of the world of common sense to be depicted in chapters 6 and 7. The eighth chapter adds things, which, though previously disregarded, never were denied. The ninth and tenth chapters add reflection and judgment, which neither were excluded from earlier considerations nor, on the other hand, were they capable of making a systematic entry. In the eleventh chapter there occurs the first judgment of self-affirmation, but only in the twelfth chapter is it advanced that that judgment is knowledge, and only in the thirteenth is it explained in what sense such knowledge is to be named objective. The four chapters on metaphysics follow to sweep all that has been seen into the unity of a larger perspective, only to undergo a similar fate, first in the account of general transcendent knowledge, and again in the approach to special transcendent knowledge.

Clearly, then, if anyone were to offer to express my meaning within a briefer compass than I have been able to attain, he must bear in mind that earlier statements are to be qualified and interpreted in the light of later statements.

Nor is this all.[g] For already it has been pointed out that the present work is concerned with the known only in the schematic and incomplete fashion that is needed to clarify the nature, and affirm the existence, of different departments of knowing. This extremely general qualification has to be combined with the qualification of earlier statements by later, and, I suggest, the combination can be effected systematically in the following manner.

Gödel's theorem[h] is to the effect that any set of mathematical definitions and postulates gives rise to further questions that cannot be answered on the basis of the definitions and postulates. Consider, then, a series of sets of definitions and postulates, say $P, Q, R, \ldots$ such that if P is assumed there arise questions that can be answered only by assuming Q, if Q is assumed there arise questions that can be answered only by assuming R, and so forth. Then, besides the successive lower contexts $P, Q, R, \ldots$ there also is the upper context in which Gödel's theorem is expressed. Moreover, inasmuch as the theorem is quite general, the upper context is independent of the content of any particular contexts such as $P, Q, R, \ldots$ Finally, since there is no last lower context that is definitive, since R will demand a context S, and S a context T, and T a context U, and so on indefinitely, the really significant context is the upper context; all lower contexts $P, Q, R, S, T, U, \ldots$ are provisional; and they attain a definitive[i] significance only in the measure that they give access to the upper context.

Now let us go beyond Gödel's theorem, not in the direction of greater abstractness, but in the direction of greater concreteness, and not to greater concreteness on the side of the object (which is vast and difficult and open to further additions and revisions) but to greater concreteness on the side of the subject. Besides the *noêma* or *intentio intenta* or *pensée pensée* illustrated by the lower contexts $P, Q, R, \ldots$ and by the upper context that is Gödel's theorem, there also is the *noêsis* or *intentio inten-*

dens or *pensée pensante* that is constituted by the very activity of inquiring and reflecting, understanding and affirming, asking further questions and reaching further answers. Let us say that this noetic activity is engaged in a lower context when it is doing mathematics or following scientific method or exercising common sense. Then it will be moving towards an upper context when it scrutinizes mathematics or science or common sense in order to grasp the nature of noetic activity. And if it comes to understand and affirm what understanding is and what affirming is, then it has reached an upper context that logically is independent of the scaffolding of mathematics, science, and common sense. Moreover, if it can be shown that the upper context is invariant, that any attempt to revise it can be legitimate only if the hypothetical reviser refutes his own attempt by invoking experience, understanding, and reflection in an already prescribed manner, then it will appear that, while the *noêma* or *intentio intenta* or *pensée pensée* may always be expressed with greater accuracy and completeness, still the immanent and recurrently operative structure of the *noêsis* or *intentio intendens* or *pensée pensante* must always be one and the same.

In other words, not only are we writing from a moving viewpoint but also we are writing about a moving viewpoint. Not only are earlier statements to be qualified by later statements, but also the later qualification is to the effect that earlier statements tend to be mere scaffolding that can be subjected to endless revision without implying the necessity of any revision of one's appropriation of one's own intellectual and rational self-consciousness.

In the fifth place – to turn to the final disjunction – the order in which the moving viewpoint assembles the elements for an appropriation of one's own intellectual and rational self-consciousness is governed, not by considerations of logical or metaphysical priority, but by considerations of pedagogical efficacy.

Now this fifth disjunction would be superfluous if I could not anticipate that among potential readers there might be men already in possession of a logical or a metaphysical scheme of things. Accordingly, though it will be the constant rule of the present work to deal with issues in their proper generality and at their proper place and time, it seems necessary to depart for a moment from that rule to envisage some of the points on which logicians or metaphysicians are going to find it obvious that, on their already established criteria, I must be utterly on the wrong track.

From a logical viewpoint it might seem that enough has been said,[j] but two points merit special attention. In the course of chapter 14, or at least by chapter 17, the reader will be able to hold in a single coherent view the totality of contradictory positions on knowledge, objectivity, and reality. But such a perspective is dialectical or metalogical. It cannot be produced by the logical arts of definition, postulation, and inference. It can be mediated by a book only insofar as there is a communication of insights that in some remote fashion is analogous to the evocation of images or to the suggestion of feelings. Hence, particularly in our first ten chapters, which deal with the genesis of concepts and judgments, of terms and propositions, the only possible vehicle for the essential content of our analysis is a prelogical and even preconceptual mode of communication.

Secondly, our goal is insight into insight, and that goal is reached inasmuch as the insight that is sought rises upon a differentiated series of illustrative insights. But the illustrative insights have to be elementary. We cannot reproduce whole treatises, and if we could and did we should defeat our purpose. Hence our illustrations have to be simple insights stripped from their context of further complementary insights that correct, qualify, adjust, and refine. Now such stripping will pain specialist readers. If they miss our point entirely, it may even convince them that insight itself is as superficial as our illustrations. However, specialists have in their own understanding the remedy for their pain, for they always can bring to light the complementary insights by asking themselves *why* our illustrations are unsatisfactory. Moreover, if they do so, they can advance rapidly towards an insight into insight, while if they merely grumble that this set of words is wrong and that set misleading, they risk encouraging an oversight of insight and even a flight from understanding.

To turn from logical to metaphysical considerations[k] is to envisage a quite different circle of possible readers. Among contemporary scholastics there is a broad agreement on metaphysical issues, and at the same time a strongly contrasting divergence on epistemological questions. This disparity may lend my work an appearance of wrong-headedness, for instead of approaching what is doubtful from what is assured I begin from knowledge and reach metaphysics only as a conclusion.

I am far from certain,[l] however, that this is a correct perspective. The broad agreement of scholastics in metaphysics is matched by an equally broad agreement in epistemology, and the divergence of scholastic views in epistemology is matched by the no less impressive array of disputed questions in metaphysics. It follows that the real problem is to advance from a mere broad agreement in metaphysics and epistemology to a precise and detailed agreement in both, and to that end an obvious means is our attempt to reach a fresh and fuller view of the relevant facts.

To conclude, our aim regards (1) not the fact of knowledge but a discrimination between two facts of knowledge, (2) not the details of the known but the structure of the knowing, (3) not the knowing as an object characterized by catalogues of abstract properties but the appropriation of one's own intellectual and rational self-consciousness, (4) not a sudden leap to appropriation but a slow and painstaking development, and (5) not a development indicated by appealing either to the logic of the as yet unknown goal or to a presupposed and as yet unexplained ontologically structured metaphysics, but a development that can begin in any sufficiently cultured consciousness, that expands in virtue of the dynamic tendencies of that consciousness itself, and that heads through an understanding of all understanding to a basic understanding of all that can be understood.

The last phrase has the ring of a slogan, and happily enough it sums up the positive content of this work. *Thoroughly understand what it is to understand, and not only will you understand the broad lines of all there is to be understood but also you will possess a fixed base, an invariant pattern, opening upon all further developments of understanding.*

For the appropriation of one's own rational self-consciousness, which has been so stressed in this introduction, is not an end in itself[m] but rather a beginning. It is a necessary beginning, for unless one breaks the duality in one's knowing, one doubts that understanding correctly is knowing. Under the pressure of that doubt, either one will sink into the bog of a knowing that is without understanding, or else one will cling to understanding but sacrifice knowing on the altar of an immanentism, an idealism, a relativism. From the horns of that dilemma one escapes only through the discovery – and one has not made it yet if one has no clear memory of its startling strangeness – that there are two quite different realisms, that there is an incoherent realism, half animal and half human, that poses as a halfway house between materialism and idealism, and on the other hand that there is an intelligent and reasonable realism between which and materialism the halfway house is idealism.

The beginning, then, not only is self-knowledge and self-appropriation but also a criterion of the real. If to convince oneself that knowing is understanding, one ascertains that knowing mathematics is understanding and knowing science is understanding and the knowledge of common sense is understanding, one ends up not only with a detailed account of understanding but also with a plan of what there is to be known. The many sciences lose their isolation from one another; the chasm between science and common sense is bridged; the structure of the universe proportionate to man's intellect is revealed; and as that revealed structure provides an object for a metaphysics, so the initial self-criticism provides a method for explaining how metaphysical and antimetaphysical affirmations arise, for selecting those that are correct, and for eliminating those that patently spring from a lack of accurate self-knowledge. Further, as a metaphysics is derived from the known structure of one's knowing, so an ethics results from knowledge of the compound structure of one's knowing and doing; and as the metaphysics, so too the ethics prolongs the initial self-criticism into an explanation of the origin of all ethical positions and into a criterion for passing judgment on each of them. Nor is this all. Still further questions press upon one. They might be ignored if knowing were not understanding or if understanding were compatible with the obscurantism that arbitrarily brushes questions aside. But knowing is understanding, and understanding is incompatible with the obscurantism that arbitrarily brushes questions aside. The issue of transcendent knowledge has to be faced. Can man know more than the intelligibility immanent in the world of possible experience? If he can, how can he conceive it? If he can conceive it, how can he affirm it? If he can affirm it, how can he reconcile that affirmation with the evil that tortures too many human bodies, darkens too many human minds, hardens too many human hearts? Such are the questions of the last two chapters, but further comment on the answers offered there will be more intelligible in an epilogue than in an introduction.

As the reader shortly will discover, this is not an erudite work. Prior to all writing of history, prior to all interpretation of other minds, there is the self-scrutiny of the historian, the self-knowledge of the interpreter.[n] That prior task is my concern. It is a concern that has its origins and background, its dependences and affiliations. They might be worth recounting, but they would be worth recounting only because of the worth of the prior concern, and they would be interpreted correctly only if the prior concern were successful in accomplishing the prior task.

So it is that my references are few and unessential. In the analysis of empirical science I thought that it would be helpful to select a single book in which a reader could find an account of topics that arose; for this reason, then, and without any intention of suggesting some unique authoritativeness I regularly refer to Lindsay and Margenau's frequently reprinted *Foundations of Physics*.[4] Again, scattered throughout the work there occur bold statements on the views of various thinkers. May I express the hope that they will not cause too much annoyance? As the lengthy discussion of the truth of interpretation in chapter 17 will reveal, they can hardly pretend to be verdicts issued by the court of history, whose processes labor under much longer delays than the worst of the courts of law. Their primary significance is simply that of an abbreviated mode of speech that has a fair chance of communicating rapidly what otherwise could hardly be said at all. And perhaps to that primary meaning there could be added a suggestion that, in the measure that the principles of this work are accepted, the significance that we happen to have underlined may provide a starting point for further inquiry.

In the introduction to his *Treatise of Human Nature*, David Hume wrote that one does not conquer a territory by taking here an outpost and there a town or village but by marching directly upon the capital and assaulting its citadel. Still, correct strategy is one thing; successful execution is another; and even after the most successful campaign there remains a prolonged task of mopping up, of organization, and of consolidation. If I may be sanguine enough to believe that I have hit upon a set of ideas of fundamental importance, I cannot but acknowledge that I do not possess the resources to give a faultless display of their implications in the wide variety of fields in which they are relevant. I can but make the contribution of a single man and then hope that others, sensitive to the same problems, will find that my efforts shorten their own labor and that my conclusions provide a base for further developments.

4 [Robert Bruce Lindsay and Henry Margenau, *Foundations of Physics* (Woodbridge, CT: Ox Bow Press, 1981, reprint of 1936 [John Wiley and Sons] and 1957 [Dover Publications] editions).]

PART ONE

Insight as Activity

1

Elements

In the midst of that vast and profound stirring of human minds which we name the Renaissance, Descartes was convinced that too many people felt it beneath them to direct their efforts to apparently trifling problems. Again and again in his *Regulae ad directionem ingenii*, he reverts to this theme. Intellectual mastery of mathematics, of the departments of science, of philosophy is the fruit of a slow and steady accumulation of little insights. Great problems are solved by being broken down into little problems. The strokes of genius are but the outcome of a continuous habit of inquiry that grasps clearly and distinctly all that is involved in the simple things that anyone can understand.

I thought it well to begin by recalling this conviction of a famous mathematician and philosopher, for our first task will be to attain familiarity with what is meant by insight, and the only way to achieve this end is, it seems, to attend very closely to a series of instances all of which are rather remarkable for their banality.

1 A Dramatic Instance[a]   [3–6]

Our first illustrative instance of insight will be the story of Archimedes rushing naked from the baths of Syracuse with the cryptic cry 'Eureka!' King Hiero, it seems, had had a votive crown fashioned by a smith of rare skill and doubtful honesty. He wished to know whether or not baser metals had been added to the gold. Archimedes was set the problem and in the bath had hit upon the solution. Weigh the crown in water! Implicit in this directive were the principles of displacement and of specific gravity.

With those principles of hydrostatics we are not directly concerned. For our objective is an insight into insight. Archimedes had his insight by thinking about the crown; we shall have ours by thinking about Archimedes. What we have to grasp is that insight (1) comes as a release to the tension of inquiry, (2) comes suddenly and unexpectedly, (3) is a function not of outer circumstances but of inner conditions, (4) pivots between the concrete and the abstract, and (5) passes into the habitual texture of one's mind.[1]

First, then, insight comes as a release to the tension of inquiry. This feature is dramatized in the story by Archimedes' peculiarly uninhibited exultation. But the point I would make does not lie in this outburst of delight but in the antecedent desire and effort that it betrays. For if the typical scientist's satisfaction in success is more sedate, his earnestness in inquiry can still exceed that of Archimedes. Deep within us all, emergent when the noise of other appetites is stilled, there is a drive to know, to understand, to see why, to discover the reason, to find the cause, to explain. Just what is wanted has many names. In what precisely it consists is a matter of dispute. But the fact of inquiry is beyond all doubt. It can absorb a man. It can keep him for hours, day after day, year after year, in the narrow prison of his study or his laboratory. It can send him on dangerous voyages of exploration. It can withdraw him from other interests, other pursuits, other pleasures, other achievements. It can fill his waking thoughts, hide from him the world of ordinary affairs, invade the very fabric of his dreams. It can demand endless sacrifices that are made without regret though there is only the hope, never a certain promise, of suc-

---

1 A profusion of instances of insight is offered by E.D. Hutchinson in three articles originally published in *Psychiatry* and reprinted in *A Study of Interpersonal Relations*, ed. P. Mullahy (New York: Hermitage Press, 1949 [paperback edition, New York: Grove Press, 1957]). [The articles are entitled 'Varieties of Insight in Humans' (Mullahy 386–403); 'The Period of Frustration in Creative Endeavor' (Mullahy 404–20); and 'The Nature of Insight' (Mullahy 421–45). The articles appeared originally in *Psychiatry* 2 (1939) 323–32; 3 (1940) 351–59; and 4 (1941) 31–43. Two further articles by Hutchinson appear in the same series, but are not referred to by Lonergan, who seems to have consulted only Mullahy's book. The additional articles are 'The Period of Elaboration in Creative Endeavor,' *Psychiatry* 5 (1942) 165–76; and 'The Phenomenon of Insight in Relation to Religion,' *Psychiatry* 6 (1943) 347–57.]

cess. What better symbol could one find for this obscure, exigent, imperious drive, than a man, naked, running, excitedly crying, 'I've got it'?[b]

Secondly, insight comes suddenly and unexpectedly. It did not occur when Archimedes was in the mood and posture that a sculptor would select to portray 'The Thinker.' It came in a flash, on a trivial occasion, in a moment of relaxation. Once more there is dramatized a universal aspect of insight. For it is reached, in the last analysis, not by learning rules, not by following precepts, not by studying any methodology. Discovery is a new beginning. It is the origin of new rules that supplement or even supplant the old. Genius is creative. It is genius precisely because it disregards established routines, because it originates the novelties that will be the routines of the future. Were there rules for discovery, then discoveries would be mere conclusions. Were there precepts for genius, then men of genius would be hacks. Indeed, what is true of discovery also holds for the transmission of discoveries by teaching. For a teacher cannot undertake to make a pupil understand. All he can do is present the sensible elements in the issue in a suggestive order and with a proper distribution of emphasis. It is up to the pupils themselves to reach understanding, and they do so in varying measures of ease and rapidity. Some get the point before the teacher can finish his exposition. Others just manage to keep pace with him. Others see the light only when they go over the matter by themselves. Some, finally, never catch on at all; for a while they follow the classes, but sooner or later they drop by the way.

Thirdly, insight is a function, not of outer circumstances, but of inner conditions. Many frequented the baths of Syracuse without coming to grasp the principles of hydrostatics. But who bathed there without feeling the water, or without finding it hot or cold or tepid? There is, then, a strange difference between insight and sensation. Unless one is deaf, one cannot avoid hearing. Unless one is blind, one has only to open one's eyes to see. The occurrence and the content of sensation stand in some immediate correlation with outer circumstance. But with insight internal conditions are paramount. Thus, insight depends upon native endowment, and so with fair accuracy one can say that insight is the act that occurs frequently in the intelligent and rarely in the stupid. Again, insight depends upon a habitual orientation, upon a perpetual alertness ever asking the little question, Why? Finally, insight depends on the accurate presentation of definite problems. Had Hiero not put his problem to Archimedes, had Archimedes not thought earnestly, perhaps desperately, upon it, the baths of Syracuse would have been no more famous than any others.

Fourthly, insight pivots[c] between the concrete and the abstract. Archimedes' problem was concrete. He had to settle whether a particular crown was made of pure gold. Archimedes' solution was concrete. It was to weigh the crown in water. Yet if we ask what was the point to that procedure, we have to have recourse to the abstract formulations of the principles of displacement and of specific gravity. Without that point, weighing the crown in water would be mere eccentricity. Once the point is grasped, King Hiero and his golden crown become minor historical details of no scientific importance. Again the story dramatizes a universal aspect of insight. For if insights arise from concrete problems, if they reveal their value in concrete applications, nonetheless they possess a significance greater than their origins and a relevance wider than their original applications. Because insights arise with reference to the concrete, geometers use diagrams,[d] mathematicians need pen and paper, teachers need blackboards, pupils have to perform experiments for themselves, doctors have to see their patients, troubleshooters have to travel to the spot, people with a mechanical bent take things apart to see how they work. But because the significance and relevance of insight goes beyond any concrete problem or application, men formulate abstract sciences with their numbers and symbols, their technical terms and formulae, their definitions, postulates, and deductions. Thus by its very nature insight is the mediator, the hinge, the pivot. It is insight *into* the concrete world of sense and imagination. Yet what is known by insight, what insight adds to sensible and imagined presentations, finds its adequate expression only in the abstract and recondite formulations of the sciences.

Fifthly, insight passes into the habitual texture of one's mind. Before Archimedes could solve his problem, he needed an instant of inspiration. But he needed no further inspiration when he went to offer the king his solution. Once one has understood, one has crossed a divide. What a moment ago was an insoluble problem now becomes incredibly simple and obvious. Moreover, it tends to remain simple and obvious. However laborious the first occurrence of an insight may be, subsequent repetitions occur almost at will. This, too, is a universal characteristic of insight, and indeed it constitutes the possibility of learning. For we can learn inasmuch as we can add insight to insight, inasmuch as the new does not extrude the old but complements and combines with it. Inversely, inasmuch as the subject to be learnt involves the acquisition of a whole series of insights, the process of learning is marked by an initial period of darkness in which one gropes about insecurely, in which one cannot see where one is going, in which one cannot grasp what all the fuss is about; and only gradually, as one begins to catch on, does the initial darkness yield to a subsequent period of increasing light, confidence, interest, absorption. Then the infinitesimal calculus or theoretical physics or the issues of philosophy cease to be the mysterious and foggy realms they had seemed. Imperceptibly we shift from the helpless infancy of the beginner to the modest self-confidence of the advanced student. Eventually we become capable of taking over the teacher's role and complaining of the remarkable obtuseness of pupils that fail to see what, of course, is perfectly simple and obvious to those that understand.

2   Definition   [7–13]

As every schoolboy knows, a circle is a locus of coplanar points equidistant from a center. What every schoolboy does not know is the difference between repeating that definition as a parrot might and uttering it intelligently. So, with a sidelong bow to Descartes's insistence on the importance of understanding very simple things, let us inquire into the genesis of the definition of the circle.

2.1 The Clue   [7]

Imagine a cartwheel with its bulky hub, its stout spokes, its solid rim.
Ask a question. Why is it round?
Limit the question. What is wanted is the immanent reason or ground of the roundness of the wheel. Hence a correct answer will not introduce new data such as carts, carting, transportation, wheelwrights, or their tools. It will refer simply to the wheel.
Consider a suggestion. The wheel is round because its spokes are equal. Clearly, that will not do. The spokes could be equal yet sunk unequally into the hub and rim. Again, the rim could be flat between successive spokes.
Still, we have a clue. Let the hub decrease to a point; let the rim and spokes thin out into lines; then, if there were an infinity of spokes and all were exactly equal, the rim would have to be perfectly round; in-

versely, were any of the spokes unequal, the rim could not avoid bumps or dents. Hence we can say that the wheel necessarily is round inasmuch as the distance from the center of the hub to the outside of the rim is always the same.

A number of observations are now in order. The foregoing brings us close enough to the definition of the circle. But our purpose is to attain insight, not into the circle, but into the act illustrated by insight into the circle.

The first observation, then, is that points and lines cannot be imagined. One can imagine an extremely small dot. But no matter how small a dot may be, still it has magnitude. To reach a point, all magnitude must vanish, and with all magnitude there vanishes the dot as well. One can imagine an extremely fine thread. But no matter how fine a thread may be, still it has breadth and depth as well as length. Remove from the image all breadth and depth, and there vanishes all length as well.

2.2 Concepts   [8]

The second observation is that points and lines are concepts.

Just as imagination is the playground of our desires and our fears, so conception is the playground of our intelligence. Just as imagination can create objects never seen or heard or felt, so too conception can create objects that cannot even be imagined. How? By supposing. The imagined dot has magnitude as well as position, but the geometer says, 'Let us suppose it has only position.' The imagined line has breadth as well as length, but the geometer says, 'Let us suppose it has only length.'

Still, there is method in this madness. Our images and especially our dreams seem very random affairs, yet psychologists offer to explain them. Similarly, the suppositions underlying concepts may appear very fanciful, yet they too can be explained. Why did we require the hub to decrease to a point and the spokes and rim to mere lines? Because we had a clue – the equality of the spokes – and we were pushing it for all it was worth. As long as the hub had any magnitude, the spokes could be sunk into it unequally. As long as the spokes had any thickness, the wheel could be flat at their ends. So we supposed a point without magnitude and lines without thickness, to obtain a curve that would be perfectly, necessarily round.

Note, then, two properties of concepts. In the first place, they are constituted by the mere activity of supposing, thinking, considering, formulating, defining. They may or may not be more than that. But if they are more, then they are not merely concepts. And if they are no more than supposed or considered or thought about, still that is enough to constitute them as concepts. In the second place, concepts do not occur at random; they emerge in thinking, supposing, considering, defining, formulating; and that many-named activity occurs, not at random, but in conjunction with an act of insight.

2.3 The Image[e]   [8–9]

The third observation is that the image is necessary for the insight.

Points and lines cannot be imagined. But neither can necessity or impossibility be imagined. Yet in approaching the definition of the circle there occurred some apprehension of necessity and of impossibility. As we remarked, if all the radii are equal the curve must be perfectly round, and if any radii are unequal the curve cannot avoid bumps or dents.

Further, the necessity in question was not necessity in general but a necessity of roundness resulting from these equal radii. Similarly, the impossibility in question was not impossibility in the abstract but an impossibility of roundness resulting from these unequal radii. Eliminate the image of the center, the radii, the curve, and by the same stroke there vanishes all grasp of necessary or of impossible roundness.

But it is that grasp that constitutes the insight. It is the occurrence of that grasp that makes the difference between repeating the definition of a circle as a parrot might and uttering it intelligently, uttering it with the ability to make up a new definition for oneself.

It follows that the image is necessary for the insight. Inversely, it follows that the insight is the act of catching on to a connection between imagined equal radii and, on the other hand, a curve that is bound to look perfectly round.

2.4 The Question[f]   [9]

The fourth observation adverts to the question.

There is the question as expressed in words. Why is the wheel round?

Behind the words there may be conceptual acts of meaning, such as 'wheel,' 'round,' etc.

Behind these concepts there may be insights in which one grasps how to use such words as 'wheel,' 'round,' etc.

But what we are trying to get at is something different. Where does the 'Why?' come from? What does it reveal or represent? Already we had occasion to speak of the psychological tension that had its release in the joy of discovery. It is that tension, that drive, that desire to understand, that constitutes the primordial 'Why?' Name it what you please – alertness of mind, intellectual curiosity, the spirit of inquiry, active intelligence, the drive to know. Under any name, it remains the same, and is, I trust, very familiar to you.

This primordial drive, then, is the pure question. It is prior to any insights, any concepts, any words; for insights, concepts, words have to do with answers, and before we look for answers we want them; such wanting is the pure question.

On the other hand, though the pure question is prior to insights, concepts, and words, it presupposes experiences and images. Just as insight is into the concretely given or imagined, so the pure question is about the concretely given or imagined. It is the wonder which Aristotle claimed to be the beginning of all science and philosophy. But no one just wonders. We wonder about something.

2.5 Genesis   [10]

A fifth observation distinguishes moments in the genesis of a definition.

When an animal has nothing to do it goes to sleep. When a man has nothing to do he may ask questions. The first moment is an awakening to one's intelligence. It is release from the dominance of biological drive and from the routines of everyday living. It is the effective emergence of wonder, of the desire to understand.

The second moment is the hint, the suggestion, the clue. Insight has begun. We have got hold of something. There is a chance that we are on the right track. Let's see.

The third moment is the process. Imagination has been released from other cares. It is free to cooperate with intellectual effort, and its cooperation consists in endeavoring to run parallel to intelligent suppositions, while at the same time restraining supposition within some limits of approximation to the imaginable field.

The fourth moment is achievement. By their cooperation, by successive adjustments, question and insight, image and concept present a solid front. The answer is a patterned set of concepts. The image strains to approximate to the concepts. The concepts, by added conceptual determinations, can express their differences from the merely approximate image. The pivot between images and concepts is the insight. And setting the standard which insight, images, and concepts must meet is the question, the desire to know, that could have kept the process in motion by further queries had its requirements not been satisfied.

2.6 Nominal and Explanatory Definition[8]   [10–11]

A sixth observation distinguishes different kinds of definition. As Euclid defined a straight line as a line lying evenly between its extremes, so he might have defined a circle as a perfectly round plane curve. As the former definition, so also the latter would serve to determine unequivocally the proper use of the names 'straight line,' 'circle.' But in fact Euclid's definition of the circle does more than reveal the proper use of the name 'circle.' It includes the affirmation that in any circle all radii are exactly equal; and were that affirmation not included in the definition, then it would have had to be added as a postulate.

To view the same matter from another angle, Euclid did postulate that all right angles are equal. Let us name the sum of two adjacent right angles a straight angle. Then, if all right angles are equal, necessarily all straight angles will be equal. Inversely, if all straight angles are equal, all right angles must be equal. Now, if straight lines are really straight, if they never bend in any direction, must not all straight angles be equal? Could not the postulate of the equality of straight angles be included in the definition of the straight line, as the postulate of the equality of radii is included in the definition of the circle?

At any rate, there is a difference between nominal and explanatory definitions. Nominal definitions merely tell us about the correct usage of names. Explanatory definitions also include something further that, were it not included in the definition, would have to be added as a postulate.

What constitutes the difference? It is not that explanatory definitions suppose an insight while nominal definitions do not. For a language is an enormously complicated tool with an almost endless variety of parts that admit a far greater number of significant combinations. If insight is needed to see how other tools are to be used properly and effectively, insight is similarly needed to use a language properly and effectively.

Still, this yields, I think, the answer to our question. Both nominal and explanatory definitions suppose insights. But a nominal definition supposes no more than an insight into the proper use of language. An explanatory definition, on the other hand, supposes a further insight into the objects to which language refers. The name 'circle' is defined as a perfectly round plane curve, as the name 'straight line' is defined as a line lying evenly between its extremes. But when one goes on to affirm that all radii in a circle are equal or that all right angles are equal, one no longer is talking merely of names. One is making assertions about the objects which names denote.

2.7 Primitive Terms   [11–12]

A seventh observation adds a note on the old puzzle of primitive terms.

Every definition presupposes other terms. If these can be defined, their definitions will presuppose still other terms. But one cannot regress to infinity. Hence, either definition is based on undefined terms or else terms are defined in a circle so that each virtually defines itself.

Fortunately, we are under no necessity of accepting the argument's supposition. Definitions do not occur in a private vacuum of their own. They emerge in solidarity with experiences, images, questions, and insights. It is true enough that every definition involves several terms, but it is also true that no insight can be expressed by a single term, and it is not true that every insight presupposes previous insights.

Let us say, then, that for every basic insight there is a circle of terms and relations, such that the terms fix the relations, the relations fix the terms, and the insight fixes both. If one grasps the necessary and sufficient conditions for the perfect roundness of this imagined plane curve, then one grasps not only the circle but also the point, the line, the circumference, the radii, the plane, and equality. All the concepts tumble out together, because all are needed to express adequately a single insight. All are coherent, for coherence basically means that all hang together from a single insight.

Again, there can be a set of basic insights. Such is the set underlying Euclidean geometry. Because the set of insights is coherent, they generate a set of coherent definitions. Because different objects of definition are composed of similar elements, such terms as point, line, surface, angle keep recurring in distinct definitions. Thus, Euclid begins his exposition from a set of images, a set of insights, and a set of definitions; some of his definitions are merely nominal; some are explanatory; some are derived partly from nominally and partly from explanatorily defined terms.

2.8 Implicit Definition[h]   [12–13]

A final observation introduces the notion of implicit definition.

D. Hilbert has worked out foundations of geometry that satisfy contemporary logicians.[2] One of his important devices is known as implicit definition. Thus, the meaning of both point and straight line is fixed by the relation that two and only two points determine a straight line.

In terms of the foregoing analysis, one may say that implicit definition consists in explanatory definition without nominal definition. It consists in explanatory definition, for the relation that two points determine a straight line is a postulational element such as the equality of all radii in a circle. It omits nominal definition, for one cannot restrict Hilbert's point to the Euclidean meaning of position without magnitude. An ordered pair of numbers satisfies Hilbert's implicit definition of a point, for two such pairs determine a straight line. Similarly, a first-degree equation satisfies Hilbert's implicit definition of a straight line, for such an equation is determined by two ordered pairs of numbers.

The significance of implicit definition is its complete generality. The omission of nominal definitions is the omission of a restriction to the objects which, in the first instance, one happens to be thinking about. The exclusive use of explanatory or postulational elements concentrates attention upon the set of relationships in which the whole scientific significance is contained.

3   Higher Viewpoints   [13–19]

The next significant step to be taken in working out the nature of insight is to analyze development. Single insights occur either in isolation or in related fields. In the latter case, they combine, cluster, coalesce, into the mastery of a subject; they ground sets of definitions, postulates, deductions; they admit applications to enormous ranges of instances. But the matter does not end there. Still further insights arise. The short-

2 [David Hilbert, *The Foundations of Geometry*, trans. E.J. Townsend (La Salle, IL: Open Court, 1947). What is now the 'sole authorized' English edition, translated from the tenth German edition by Leo Unger, was published by Open Court in 1971, 3rd printing, 1987.]

comings of the previous position become recognized. New definitions and postulates are devised. A new and larger field of deductions is set up. Broader and more accurate applications become possible. Such a complex shift in the whole structure of insights, definitions, postulates, deductions, and applications may be referred to very briefly as the emergence of a higher viewpoint. Our question is, Just what happens?

Taking our clue from Descartes's insistence on understanding simple things, we select as our pilot instance the transition from arithmetic to elementary algebra. Moreover, to guard against possible misinterpretations, let us say that by arithmetic is meant a subject studied in grade school and that by elementary algebra is meant a subject studied in high school.[i]

3.1 Positive Integers   [13–14]

A first step is to offer some definition of the positive integers 1, 2, 3, 4, . . .

Let us suppose an indefinite multitude of instances of 'one.' They may be anything anyone pleases, from sheep to instances of the act of counting or ordering.

Further, let us suppose as too familiar to be defined the notions of 'one,' 'plus,' and 'equals.'

Then, there is an infinite series of definitions for the infinite series of positive integers, and it may be indicated symbolically by the following:

$$1 + 1 = 2$$

$$2 + 1 = 3$$

$$3 + 1 = 4$$

etc., etc., etc.[j] . . .

This symbolic indication may be interpreted in any of a variety of manners. It means one plus one equals two, or two is one more than one, or the second is the next after the first, or even the relations between classes of groups each with one, or two, or three, etc., members. As the acute reader will see, the one important element in the above series of definitions, is the etc., etc., etc. ... Without it the positive integers cannot be defined; for they are an indefinitely great multitude, and it is only insofar as some such gesture as etc., etc., etc. is really significant that an infinite series of definitions can occur. What, then, does the etc., etc. mean? It means that an insight should have occurred. If one has had the relevant insight, if one has caught on, if one sees how the defining can go on indefinitely, no more need be said. If one has not caught on, then the poor teacher has to labor in his apostolate of the obvious. For in defining the positive integers there is no alternative to insight.

Incidentally, it may not be amiss to recall what already has been remarked, namely, that a single insight is expressed in many concepts. In the present instance a single insight grounds an infinity of concepts.

3.2 Addition Tables   [14]

A second step will consist in making somewhat more precise the familiar notion of equality. Let us say that when equals are added to equals, the results are equal; that one is equal to one; and that, therefore, an infinite series of additional tables can be constructed.

The table for adding two is constructed by adding one to each side of the equations that define the positive integers. Thus,

From the table $2 + 1 = 3$

Adding one $2 + 1 + 1 = 3 + 1$

Hence from the table $2 + 2 = 4$

In like manner the whole table for adding two can be constructed. From this table, once it is constructed, there can be constructed a table for adding three. From that table it will be possible to construct a table for adding four. Etc., etc., etc., which again means that an insight should have occurred.

Thus, from the definitions of the positive integers and the postulate about adding equals to equals, there follows an indefinitely great deductive expansion.

3.3 The Homogeneous Expansion   [15]

A third step will be to venture into a homogeneous expansion. The familiar notion of addition is to be complemented by such further notions as multiplication, powers, subtraction, division, and roots. This development, however, is to be homogeneous, and by that is meant that no change is to be involved in the notions already employed.

Thus, multiplication is to mean adding a number to itself so many times, so that five by three will mean the addition of three fives. Similarly, powers are to mean that a number is multiplied by itself so many times, so that five to the third will mean five multiplied by five with the result multiplied again by five. On the other hand, subtraction, division, and roots will mean the inverse operations that bring one back to the starting point.

By a few insights, that need not be indicated, it will be seen that tables for multiplication and for powers can be constructed from the addition tables. Similarly, tables for subtraction, division, and roots can be constructed from the tables for addition, multiplication, and powers.

The homogeneous expansion constitutes a vast extension of the initial deductive expansion. It consists in introducing new operations. Its characteristic is that the new operations involve no modification of the old.

3.4 The Need of a Higher Viewpoint   [15]

A fourth step will be the discovery of the need of a higher viewpoint. This arises when the inverse operations are allowed full generality, when they are not restricted to bringing one back to one's starting point. Then, subtraction reveals the possibility of negative numbers, division reveals the possibility of fractions, roots reveal the possibility of surds. Further, there arise questions about the meaning of operations. What is multiplication when one multiplies negative numbers or fractions or surds? What is subtraction when one subtracts a negative number? Etc., etc., etc. Indeed, even the meaning of 'one' and of 'equals' becomes confused, for there are recurring decimals, and it can be shown that point nine recurring is equal to one.[3]

3.5 Formulation of the Higher Viewpoint   [16–17]

A fifth step will be to formulate a higher viewpoint.

Distinguish (1) rules, (2) operations, and (3) numbers.

Let numbers be defined implicitly by operations, so that the result of any operation will be a number, and any number can be the result of an operation.

3 Let $x = 0.\overline{9}$
then $10x = 9.\overline{9}$
hence $9x = 9$
and so $x = 1$.

Let operations be defined implicitly by rules, so that what is done in accord with rules is an operation.

The trick will be to obtain the rules that fix the operations which fix the numbers.

The emergence of the higher viewpoint is the performance of this trick. It consists in an insight that (1) arises upon the operations performed according to the old rules, and (2) is expressed in the formulation of the new rules.

Let me explain. From the image of a cartwheel we proceeded by insight to the definition of the circle. But while the cartwheel was imagined, the circle consists of a point and a line, neither of which can be imagined. Between the cartwheel and the circle there is an approximation, but only an approximation. Now the transition from arithmetic to elementary algebra is the same sort of thing. For an image of the cartwheel one substitutes the image of what may be named 'doing arithmetic'; it is a large, dynamic, virtual image that includes writing down, adding, multiplying, subtracting, and dividing numbers in accord with the precepts of the homogeneous expansion. Not all of this image will be present at once, but any part of it can be present, and when one is on the alert any part that happens to be relevant will pop into view. In this large and virtual image, then, there is to be grasped a new set of rules governing operations. The new rules will not be exactly the same as the old rules. They will be more symmetrical. They will be more exact. They will be more general. In brief, they will differ from the old much as the highly exact and symmetrical circle differs from the cartwheel.

What are the new rules? At school the rules for fractions were generalized; rules for signs were introduced; rules for equations and for indices were worked out. Their effect was to redefine the notions of addition, multiplication, powers, subtraction, division, and roots; and the effect of the redefinitions of the operations was that numbers were generated not merely by addition but by any of the operations.[k]

3.6 Successive Higher Viewpoints   [17]

The reader familiar with group theory will be aware that the definition of operations by rules, and of numbers – or more generally symbols – by operations is a procedure that penetrates deeply into the nature of mathematics. But there is a further aspect to the matter, and it has to do with the gradual development by which one advances through intermediate stages from elementary to higher mathematics. The logical analyst can leap from the positive integers to group theory, but one cannot learn mathematics in that simple fashion. On the contrary, one has to perform, over and over, the same type of transition as occurs in advancing from arithmetic to elementary algebra.

At each stage of the process there exists a set of rules that govern operations which result in numbers. To each stage there corresponds a symbolic image of doing arithmetic, doing algebra, doing calculus. In each successive image there is the potentiality of grasping by insight a higher set of rules that will govern the operations and by them elicit the numbers or symbols of the next stage. Only insofar as a man makes his slow progress up that escalator does he become a technically competent mathematician. Without it he may acquire a rough idea of what mathematics is about, but he will never be a master, perfectly aware of the precise meaning and the exact implications of every symbol and operation.

3.7   The Significance of Symbolism   [17–19]

The analysis also reveals the importance of an apt symbolism.

There is no doubt that, though symbols are signs chosen by convention, still some choices are highly fruitful while others are not. It is easy enough to take the square root of 1764. It is another matter to take the square root of MDCCLXIV. The development of the calculus is easily designated in using Leibniz's symbol dy/dx for the differential coefficient; Newton's symbol, on the other hand, can be used only in a few cases, and what is worse, it does not suggest the theorems that can be established.

Why is this so? It is because mathematical operations are not merely the logical expansion of conceptual premises. Image and question, insight and concepts all combine. The function of the symbolism is to supply the relevant image, and the symbolism is apt inasmuch as its immanent patterns as well as the dynamic patterns of its manipulation run parallel to the rules and operations that have been grasped by insight and formulated in concepts.

The benefits of this parallelism are manifold. In the first place, the symbolism itself takes over a notable part of the solution of problems, for the symbols, complemented by habits that have become automatic, dictate what has to be done. Thus, a mathematician will work at a problem up to a point and then announce that the rest is mere routine.

In the second place, the symbolism constitutes a heuristic technique: the mathematician is not content to seek his unknowns; he names them; he assigns them symbols; he writes down in equations all their properties; he knows how many equations he will need; and when he has reached that number he can say that the rest of the solution is automatic.

In the third place, the symbolism offers clues, hints, suggestions. Just as the definition of the circle was approached from the clue of the equality of the spokes, so generally insights do not come to us in their full stature: we begin from little hints, from suspicions, from possibilities; we try them out; if they lead nowhere, we drop them; if they promise success, we push them for all they are worth. But this can be done only if we chance upon the hints, the clues, the possibilities; and the effect of the apt symbolism is to reduce, if not entirely eliminate, this element of chance. Here, of course, the classical example is analytic geometry. To solve a problem by Euclidean methods, one has to stumble upon the correct construction. To solve a problem analytically, one has only to manipulate the symbols.

In the fourth place, there is the highly significant notion of invariance. An apt symbolism will endow the pattern of a mathematical expression with the totality of its meaning. Whether or not one uses the Latin, Greek, or Hebrew alphabet is a matter of no importance. The mathematical meaning of an expression resides in the distinction between constants and variables, and in the signs or collocations that dictate operations of combining, multiplying, summing, differentiating, integrating, and so forth. It follows that, as long as the symbolic pattern of a mathematical expression is unchanged, its mathematical meaning is unchanged. Further, it follows that if a symbolic pattern is unchanged by any substitutions of a determinate group, then the mathematical meaning of the pattern is independent of the meaning of the substitutions.

In the fifth place, as has already been mentioned, the symbolism appropriate to any stage of mathematical development provides the image in which may be grasped by insight the rules for the next stage.

4   Inverse Insight[1]   [19–25]

Besides direct insights, their clustering, and higher viewpoints, there exists the small but significant class of inverse insights. As direct, so also inverse insights presuppose a positive object that is presented by sense or represented by imagination. But while direct insight meets the spontaneous effort of intelligence to understand, inverse insight responds to a more subtle and critical attitude that distinguishes different degrees or levels or kinds of intelligibility. While direct insight grasps the point, or sees the solution, or comes to know the reason, inverse insight apprehends that in some fashion the point is that there is no point, or that the solution is to deny a solution, or that the reason is that the rationality of the real admits distinctions and qualifications. Finally, while the conceptual formulation of direct insight affirms a positive intelligibility though it may deny expected empirical elements, the conceptual formulation of an inverse insight affirms empirical elements only to deny an expected intelligibility.

Since the last phrase is crucial, let us attempt to elaborate it. By intelligibility is meant the content of a direct insight. It is the component that is absent from our knowledge when we do not understand, and added to our knowledge inasmuch as we are understanding in the simple and straightforward manner described in the earlier sections of this chapter. Now such an intelligibility may be already reached or it may be merely expected. To deny intelligibility already reached is not the result of inverse insight; it is merely the correction of a previous direct insight, the acknowledgment of its shortcomings, the recognition that it leaves problems unsolved. But to deny an expected intelligibility is to run counter to the spontaneous anticipations of human intelligence; it is to find fault not with answers but with questions. In a demonstrative science it is to prove that a question of a given type cannot be answered. In an empirical science it is to put forward a successful hypothesis or theory that assumes that certain questions mistakenly are supposed to require an answer. Finally, the occurrence of an inverse insight is not established by the mere presence of negative concepts: thus, 'not-red,' 'position without magnitude,' 'nonoccurrence' exclude respectively 'red,' 'magnitude,' 'occurrence'; but the latter terms refer to empirical components in our knowledge and not to the possibilities and necessities, the unifications and relations, that constitute the intelligibility known in direct insight.

While the general notion of inverse insight is fairly simple and obvious, I have been at some pains in presenting its characteristics because it is not too easy to set forth illustrations to the satisfaction of different groups of readers. Moreover, communication and discussion take place through concepts, but all insight lies behind the conceptual scene.

Hence, while there is always the danger that a reader will attend to the concepts rather than the underlying insight, this danger is augmented considerably when the point to be grasped by insight is merely that there is no point. To make matters worse, inverse insights occur only in the context of far larger developments of human thought. A statement of their content has to call upon the later systems that positively exploited their negative contribution. The very success of such later systems tends to engender a routine that eliminates the more spontaneous anticipations of intelligence, and then, to establish a key feature of an inverse insight, it may be necessary to appeal to the often ambiguous witness of history. In the midst of such complexity it very easily can happen that a reader's spontaneous expectation of an intelligibility to be reached should outweigh mere verbal admonitions to the contrary, and when that occurs illustrations of inverse insight can become very obscure indeed. Accordingly, while there is nothing difficult about the examples to follow, I have thought it wise to indulge in a preliminary elucidation of the obvious.

As a first example of inverse insight we shall take what the ancients named incommensurable magnitudes and the moderns call irrational numbers. In both cases there is a positive object indicated by the terms 'magnitude,' 'number.' In both cases there is a negative element indicated by the epithets 'incommensurable,' 'irrational.' Finally, in both cases the negation bears on the spontaneous anticipations of human intelligence. 'Incommensurable' denies the possibility of applying to certain magnitudes some type of measurement, and Aristotle viewed this denial as prima facie a matter of high surprise. Even more emphatically, 'irrational' denies a correspondence between certain numbers and human reason.

To indicate the relevant insight, let us ask why a surd is a surd. Essentially the question is parallel to the earlier question, Why is a cartwheel round? But while the earlier answer revealed an intelligibility immanent in the wheel, the present answer consists in showing that a surd cannot possess the intelligibility one would expect it to have.

Thus, the square root of two is some magnitude greater than unity and less than two. One would expect it to be some improper fraction, say m/n, where m and n are positive integers and by the removal of all common factors m may always be made prime to n. Moreover, were this expectation correct, then the diagonal and the side of a square would be respectively m times and n times some common unit of length. However, so far from being correct, the expectation leads to a contradiction. For if $\sqrt{2} = m/n$, then $2 = m^2/n^2$. But if m is prime to n, then m^2 is prime to n^2; and in that case m^2/n^2 cannot be equal to two or, indeed, to any greater integer. The argument is easily generalized, and so it appears that a surd is a surd because it is not the rational fraction that intelligence anticipates it to be.

A second example of inverse insight is the noncountable multitude. There is a positive object: multitude. There is a negative determination: noncountable. Moreover, when 'countable' is taken so broadly that all integers, all rational numbers, even all real algebraic numbers[4] demonstrably are countable multitudes, when further it can be shown that to remove a countable multitude from a noncountable multitude leaves a noncountable multitude, one spontaneously anticipates that the numbers between zero and unity must be a countable multitude. In fact it can be shown that the infinite decimals are a noncountable multitude, so that the algebraic fractions from zero to unity must be a negligible portion of the real[m] numbers in that interval.[n]

For a third example we turn to empirical science and consider the surprising part of Newton's first law of motion, namely, that a body continues in its existing state of uniform motion in a straight line unless that state is changed by external force.

In this statement and its context it is not too difficult to discern the three characteristics of the formulation of an inverse insight. For there is the positive object: a body continues to move at a uniform rate in a straight line. There is a negation: the continuance of the constant velocity depends not on the action of external force but on the absence of such action; for only as long as there is no acceleration does the velocity remain constant; and the moment the sum of the external forces differs from zero, there arises an acceleration. Finally, this negation of external force runs counter to the spontaneous anticipations of human intelligence, for spontaneously one thinks of uniform motion not as of a state like rest but as of a change that requires an external cause.

---

4 Algebraic numbers are the roots of algebraic equations with integral coefficients. For a generous exposition of the topic and its paradoxes see Abraham A. Fraenkel, *Abstract Set Theory* (Amsterdam: North-Holland Publishing Company, 1953) 43–75. For applications to the continuum, see 212–40. [There is a 1961 completely revised edition. The comparable pages are: algebraic numbers, 33–58; application to the continuum, 155–74.]

However, some readers may wish to refine on the issue. They will agree that the necessity of an external cause had been stressed by the Aristotelian theory of celestial movements, of projectiles, and of motion in a vacuum. But they will add that the Aristotelian view had been contradicted at least from the time of John Philoponus. On this contrary view projectiles were kept in motion not by any external force but by some internal principle or power or property or quality or other immanent ground. Finally, they will ask whether it is quite certain that Newton did not appeal to some innate power of matter to account for the continuance of inertial states.

Now clearly, Newtonian exegesis is not our present business. All we have to say is that inverse insight is not illustrated when explanation by external force is replaced by explanation in terms of some immanent power or property. For in that case there is merely the correction of an earlier direct insight by a later direct insight, and while the spontaneous anticipations of human intelligence are blocked in one direction, they are given an outlet in another.

Still, for purposes of illustration it may be permissible to block this second outlet without reopening the first. No doubt, when an external mover or force is denied, one may spontaneously think that there must be some innate quality that provides the real explanation. But while the assertion of an external mover or force can be tested experimentally, the assertion of some innate quality, of some *vis materiae insita*, can hardly be regarded as a scientific statement. If one affirms that, when acceleration is zero, then the sum of the relevant external forces is also zero, one's affirmation admits the ordinary tests. But if one goes on to add that the innate qualities of matter render the action of external forces superfluous, one is very likely to be reminded that scientists do not appeal to occult causes.

Now if this remonstrance is regarded as peremptory, we arrive at an example of inverse insight. There is the positive object of inquiry: bodies continue in their existing states of uniform motion. There is the negation: the continuance of uniform motion is not to be explained by any appeal to external forces. Finally, this negation is regarded as definitive for science, for science refuses to extrapolate from known laws to ulterior explanations in terms of vague qualities, properties, powers, and the like.

A fourth example of inverse insight may be derived from the basic postulate of the special theory of relativity. The postulate itself is that the mathematical expression of physical principles and laws is invariant under inertial transformations. To reach our illustration we have only to grasp the concrete meaning of the postulate whenever it is invoked by a physicist engaged in understanding any set of physical data.

For then the positive object of inquiry consists in the data inasmuch as they are considered (1) as referred to initial axes of coordinates, say K, and (2) as referred to other axes, say K', moving with a constant velocity relative to the axes K.

The negative element in the conception of the positive object is indicated by the word 'invariant.' It means that the transformation from one set of axes to another does not lead to any modification in the form of the mathematical expression of the appropriate physical principles and laws. But when the form of the mathematical expression undergoes no change, there is no change in the intelligibility that is expressed mathematically. When there is no change in the intelligibility, there is no change in the act of understanding that grasps the intelligibility and expresses it mathematically. Accordingly, the concrete meaning of the postulate is that, though there is a difference in the spatiotemporal standpoint from which the data are considered, still there is no difference in the act of understanding the data, no difference in the general intelligibility grasped in the data, and no difference in the form of the mathematical expression of the intelligibility.

Finally, it is quite common for there to exist differences either in data or in spatiotemporal standpoint without any corresponding difference in the act of understanding. But in most of such cases there is no occasion for an inverse insight since, while the empirical difference is assigned no intelligible counterpart, still no one expects that really there must be an intelligible counterpart. Thus, there is a notable empirical difference between large and small circles, yet no one expects different definitions of large circles and of small circles, or different theorems to establish the different properties of large and small circles. However, while similar instances are very numerous, the invariance postulated by special relativity is not among them. For that invariance implies a drastic revision of ordinary notions of space and of time, and against any such revision the spontaneous anticipations of human intelligence vigorously rebel.

Hence, to recapitulate the main point, when the basic postulate of special relativity is interpreted concretely in terms of (1) the data physicists consider, (2) the insights they enjoy, and (3) the form of the mathematical expression of the principles and laws reached by the insights, there arises the following explanatory syllogism:

When there is no difference in a physicist's insights, there should be no difference in the form of the mathematical expression of physical principles and laws.

But when an inertial transformation occurs, there is no difference in a physicist's insights.

Therefore, when an inertial transformation occurs, there should be no difference in the form of the mathematical expression of physical principles and laws.

The major premise postulates a correspondence between the insights of physicists and the form of the mathematical expression of physical principles and laws; in other words, it requires that the content of acts of understanding be reflected faithfully by the form of mathematical expressions. The minor premise contains our inverse insight: it denies a difference in insight that corresponds to the difference of an inertial transformation; in other words, it asserts for the whole of physics the defect of intelligibility in constant velocity that Newton asserted for mechanics by his first law of motion. The conclusion, finally, is true if the premises are true, but while the major premise may be regarded as a mere methodological rule, the minor premise is an assertion of empirical science and can be established only through the method of hypothesis and verification.

In conclusion, let us recall a point already mentioned. An inverse insight finds its expression only in some concomitant positive context. So the defect of intelligibility in constant velocity has been formulated in a whole series of different contexts. In the context of Eleatic philosophy, Zeno's paradoxes led to a denial of the fact of motion. In the context of his philosophy of being, Aristotle pronounced motion real yet regarded it as an incomplete entity, an infracategorial° object. In the context of mathematical mechanics, Newton asserted a principle of inertia. In the context of Clerk Maxwell's equations for the electromagnetic field, Lorentz worked out the conditions under which the equations would remain invariant under inertial transformations; FitzGerald explained Lorentz's success by supposing that bodies contracted along the direction of motion; Einstein found a no less general explanation in problems of synchronization and raised the issue to the methodological level of the transformation properties of the mathematical expression of physical principles and laws; finally, Minkowski systematized Einstein's position by introducing the four-dimensional manifold. No doubt, it would be a mistake to suppose that the same inverse insight was operative from Zeno to special relativity. But throughout there is a denial of intelligibility to local motion, and while the successive contexts differ notably in content and in value, at least they point in the same direction, and they illustrate the dependence of inverse insight on concomitant direct insights.

5   The Empirical Residue[P]   [25–32]

If inverse insights are relatively rare, they are far from being unimportant. Not only do they eliminate mistaken questions but also they seem regularly to be connected with ideas or principles or methods or techniques of quite exceptional significance. From the oddities of the mathematical continuum through the notions of correlation and limit there arises the brilliance of continuous functions and of the infinitesimal calculus. Similarly, the lack of intelligibility in constant velocity is linked with scientific achievements of the first order: the principle of inertia made it possible to conceive dynamics not as a theory of motions but as an enormously more compact and more powerful theory of accelerations; and the invariance of physical principles and laws under inertial transformations not only is an extremely neat idea but also has kept revealing its fruitfulness for the past fifty years.

To explore this significance, then, let us introduce the notion of an empirical residue that (1) consists in positive empirical data, (2) is to be denied any immanent intelligibility of its own, and (3) is connected with some compensating higher intelligibility of notable importance. In clarification of the first characteristic one may note that, inasmuch as a vacuum is merely an absence of data, it cannot be part of the empirical residue. In clarification of the second it is to be remembered that a denial of immanent intelligibility is not a denial of experience or description. Not only are elements in the empirical residue given positively but also they are pointed out, conceived, named, considered, discussed, and affirmed or denied. But though they are no less given than color or sound or heat, though they may be thought about no less accurately and talked about no less fluently, still they are not objects of any direct insight, and so they cannot be explained by transverse waves or longitudinal waves or molecular motion or any other theoretical construction that might be thought more apposite. Finally, in clarification of the third characteristic it is to be noted that inverse insight and the empirical residue are not exact correlatives. For inverse insight was not characterized by a connection with ideas, principles, methods, or techniques of exceptional significance.[q] Again, the empirical residue has not been characterized by the spontaneity of the questions for intelligence that are to be met by a denial of intelligibility.

This difference not only makes the empirical residue a broader category than inverse insight but also renders a discussion of it more difficult. For a great part of the difficulty in discovering the further positive aspects of experience that are to be denied intelligibility is that no one supposes them to possess intelligibility.

Thus, particular places and particular times pertain to the empirical residue. They are positive aspects of experience. Each differs from every other. But because no one ever asks why one place is not another or why one time is not another, people are apt to be puzzled when the question is put, to imagine that something different from such obvious foolishness must be meant, and to experience a variety of fictitious difficulties before arriving at the simple conclusion that (1) particular places and particular times differ as a matter of fact, and (2) there is no immanent intelligibility to be grasped by direct insight into that fact.

For example, one will begin by saying that obviously the position A differs from the position B because of the distance AB that separates them. But take three equidistant positions: A, B, C. Why are the distances AB, BC, CA different? One would be in a vicious circle if one doubled back and explained the difference of the distances by the difference of the positions. One cannot say that the distances differ in length for they are equal in length. But one may say that the distances differ because the directions differ. Still, why do the directions differ? And why are equal and parallel distances different distances? Now perhaps it will be urged that we are going too far, that some difference must be acknowledged as primitive, that everything cannot be explained. Quite so, but there is a corollary to be added. For what is primitive is not the content of some primitive insight but the content of some primitive experience to which no insight corresponds. Were it the content of some primitive insight, there would not be the conspicuous absence of a clearheaded explanation. But because the difference of particular places and the difference of particular times are given prior to any questioning and prior to any insight, because these given differences cannot be matched by any insights that explain why places differ and times differ, there has to be introduced the category of the empirical residue.

However, one may not surrender yet. For particular places and particular times can be united by reference frames; the frames can be employed to distinguish and designate every place and every time; and evidently such constructions are eminently intelligent and eminently intelligible. Now, no doubt, reference frames are objects of direct insight, but what is grasped by that insight is an ordering of differences that are not explained by the order but merely presupposed. So it is that different geometries grasped by different insights offer different intelligible orders for the differences in place or time that all equally presuppose and, quite correctly, none attempt to explain.

There is a further aspect to the matter. Because the differences of particular places and particular times involve no immanent intelligibility of their own, they do not involve any modification in the intelligibility of anything else. It is not mere difference of place but something different in the places that gives rise to different observations or different experimental results in different places. Similarly, it is not mere difference in time but something different at the time that gives rise to different observations and different experimental results at different times. Moreover, were that not so, every place and every time would have its own physics, its own chemistry, its own biology; and since a science cannot be worked out instantaneously in a single place, there would be no physics, no chemistry, and no biology. Conversely, because the differences of particular places and particular times pertain to the empirical residue, there exists the powerful technique of scientific collaboration. Scientists of every place and every time can pool their results in a common fund, and there is no discrimination against any result merely because of the place or merely because of the time of its origin.

Even more fundamental than scientific collaboration is scientific generalization. When chemists have mastered all of the elements, their isotopes, and their compounds, they may forget to be grateful that they do not have to discover different explanations for each of the hydrogen atoms which, it seems, make up about fifty-five per cent of the matter of our universe. But at least the fact that such a myriad of explanations is not needed is very relevant to our purpose. Every chemical element and every compound differs from every other kind of element or compound, and all the differences have to be explained. Every hydrogen atom differs from every other hydrogen atom, and no explanation is needed. Clearly, we have to do with another aspect of the empirical residue, and no less clearly, this aspect is coupled with the most powerful of all scientific techniques, generalization.

However, this issue has been booted about by philosophers ever since the Platonists explained the universality of mathematical and scientific knowledge by postulating eternal and immutable Forms or Ideas only to find themselves embarrassed by the fact that a single, eternal, immutable One could hardly ground the universal statement that one and one are two or, again, that a single, eternal, immutable Triangle would not suffice for theorems on triangles similar in all respects. So there arose, it seems, the philosophic problem of merely numerical difference, and connected with it there have been formulated cognitional theories based on a doctrine of abstraction. Accordingly, we are constrained to say something on these issues, and lest we appear to be attempting to dilute water, we shall do so as briefly as possible.

The assertion, then, of merely numerical difference involves two elements. On the theoretical side it is the claim that, when any set of data has been explained completely, another set of data similar in all respects would not call for a different explanation. On the factual side it is the claim that, when any set of data has been explained completely, only an exhaustive tour of inspection could establish that there does not exist another set of data similar in all respects.

The basis of the theoretical contention is that, just as the same act of understanding is repeated when the same set of data is apprehended a second time, so also the same act of understanding is repeated when one apprehends a second set of data that is similar to a first in all respects. Thus, the physicist offers different explanations for 'red' and 'blue'; he offers different explanations for different shades of 'red'; and he would discern no sense in the proposal that he should try to find as many different explanations as there are different instances of exactly the same shade of exactly the same color.

The factual contention is more complex. It is not an assertion that there exist different sets of data similar in all respects. It is not a denial of unique instances, that is, of instances that are to be explained in a manner in which no other instance in the universe is to be explained. It is not even a denial that every individual in the universe is a unique instance. On the contrary, the relevant fact lies in the nature of the explanations that are applicable to our universe. It is to the effect that all such explanations are made up of general or universal elements and that, while these general or universal elements may be combined in such a manner that every individual is explained by a different combination of elements, still such a combination is an explanation of a singular combination of common properties and not an explanation of individuality. For if the individuality of the individual were explained, it would be meaningless to suppose that some other individual might be understood in exactly the same fashion. On the other hand, because the individuality of the individual is not explained, it is only an exhaustive tour of inspection that can settle whether or not there exists another individual similar in all respects. Hence, even if there were reached a single comprehensive theory of evolution that explained and explained differently every instance of life on this planet, still in strict logic we should have to inspect all other planets before we could be absolutely certain that in fact there did not exist another instance of evolution similar in all respects.

In brief, individuals differ, but the ultimate difference in our universe is a matter of fact to which there corresponds nothing to be grasped by direct insight. Moreover, as scientific collaboration rests on the empirically residual difference of particular places and of particular times, so scientific generalization rests on the empirically residual difference between individuals of the same class. Just what the lowest class is has to be discovered by scientific advance in direct insight. Even if it should prove that in some sense there are as many classes as individuals, still we can know at once that that sense is not that the individuality of individuals is understood but merely that singular combinations of universal explanatory elements may be set in correspondence with singular combinations of common properties or aspects in each individual. For the content grasped in insight can be embodied no less in imagination than in sense; and whether there is more than one instance in sense can be settled only by an empirical tour of inspection.

Later we shall direct attention to further aspects of the empirical residue, for there exists a statistical method that rests on the empirically residual character of coincidental aggregates of events, and there is a dialectical method that is necessitated by the lack of intelligibility in man's unintelligent opinions, choices, and conduct. But perhaps enough has been said for the general notion to be clear, and so we turn to the allied topic of abstraction.

Properly, then, abstraction is not a matter of apprehending a sensible or imaginative gestalt; it is not a matter of employing common names just as it is not a matter of using other tools; finally, it is not even a matter of attending to one question at a time and meanwhile holding other questions in abeyance. Properly, to abstract is to grasp the essential and to disregard the incidental, to see what is significant and set aside the irrelevant, to recognize the important as important and the negligible as negligible. Moreover, when it is asked what is essential or significant or important and what is incidental, irrelevant, negligible, the answer must be twofold. For abstraction is the selectivity of intelligence, and intelligence may be considered either in some given stage of development or at the term of development when some science or group of sciences has been mastered completely.

Hence, relative to any given insight or cluster of insights the essential, significant, important consists (1) in the set of aspects in the data necessary for the occurrence of the insight or insights, or (2) in the set of related concepts necessary for the expression of the insight or insights. On the other hand the incidental, irrelevant, negligible consists (1) in other concomitant aspects of the data that do not fall under the insight or insights, or (2) in the set of concepts that correspond to the merely concomitant aspects of the data. Again, relative to the full development of a science or group of allied sciences, the essential, significant, important consists (1) in the aspects of the data that are necessary for the occurrence of all insights in the appropriate range, or (2) in the set of related concepts that express all the insights of the science or sciences. On the other hand, the incidental, irrelevant, negligible consists in the empirical residue that, since it possesses no immanent intelligibility of its own, is left over without explanation even when a science or group of sciences reaches full development.

Finally, to conclude this chapter on the elements of insight, let us indicate briefly what is essential, significant, important in its contents and, on the other hand, what is incidental, irrelevant, negligible. What alone is essential is insight into insight. Hence the incidental includes (1) the particular insights chosen as examples, (2) the formulation of these insights, and (3) the images evoked by the formulation. It follows that for the story of Archimedes the reader will profitably substitute some less resounding yet more helpful experience of his own. Instead of the definition of the circle he can take any other intelligently performed act of defining and ask why the performance is, not safe, not accurate, not the accepted terminology, but a creative stroke of insight. Instead of the transition from elementary arithmetic to elementary algebra one may review the process from Euclidean to Riemannian geometry. Instead of asking why surds are surds, one can ask why transcendental numbers are transcendental. Similarly, one can ask whether the principle of inertia implies that Newton's laws are invariant under inertial transformations, what inspired Lorentz to suppose that the electromagnetic equations should be invariant under inertial transformations, whether an inverse insight accounts for the basic postulate of general relativity, whether the differences of particular places or particular times are the same aspect of the empirical residue as the differences of completely similar hydrogen atoms. For just as in any subject one comes to master the essentials by varying the incidentals, so one reaches familiarity with the notion of insight by modifying the illustrations and discovering for oneself and in one's own terms the point that another attempts to put in terms he happens to think will convey the idea to a probably nonexistent average reader.

2

Heuristic Structures
of Empirical Method

In the previous chapter insight was examined in a static fashion. It was related to inquiry, to images, to empirical data, and to different types of positive and negative explanatory concepts. But if a set of fundamental notions has been introduced, no effort has been made to capture the essential dynamism of human intelligence. Now a first move must be made in this direction, and as empirical science is conspicuously and methodically dynamic, it will be well to begin by outlining the similarities and dissimilarities of mathematical and scientific insights.

1   Mathematical and Scientific Insights Compared[a]   [33–35]

1.1 Similarities   [33–34]

Galileo's determination of the law of falling bodies not only is a model of scientific procedure but also offers the attraction of possessing many notable similarities to the already examined process from the image of a cartwheel to the definition of the circle.

In the first place, the inquiry was restricted to the immanent intelligibility of a free fall. Just as we ruled out of consideration the purpose of cartwheels, the materials from which they are made, the wheelwrights that make them, and the tools that wheelwrights use, so also Galileo was uninterested in the final cause of falling, he drew no distinction between the different materials that fall, he made no effort to determine what agencies produce a fall.

Secondly, just as we started from a clue – the equality of the spokes – so too Galileo supposed that some correlation was to be found between the measurable aspects of falling bodies. Indeed, he began by showing the error in the ancient Aristotelian correlation that bodies fell according to their weight. Then he turned his attention to two measurable aspects immanent in every fall: the body traverses a determinate distance; it does so in a determinate interval of time. By a series of experiments he provided himself with the requisite data and obtained the desired measurements. Then he discovered that the measurements would satisfy a general rule: the distance traversed is proportional to the time squared. It is a correlation that has been verified directly and indirectly for over four centuries.

Thirdly, once we had defined the circle we found ourselves in a realm of the nonimaginable, of the merely supposed. Strangely, something similar happens when one formulates the law of falling bodies. It holds in a vacuum, and to realize a perfect vacuum is impossible. What can be established experimentally is that the more closely one approximates to the conditions of a vacuum, the more accurate the law of constant acceleration is found to be.

1.2 Dissimilarities   [34–35]

But besides similarities there also are differences, and these are perhaps more instructive. In reaching the definition of the circle, it was sufficient to take as our starting point the mere image of a cartwheel. There was no need for fieldwork. But to reach the law of falling bodies Galileo had to experiment. Climbing the tower of Pisa and constructing inclined planes were an essential part of his job, for he was out to understand, not how bodies are imagined to fall, but how in fact they fall.

Secondly, the data that give rise to insight into roundness are continuous, but the data that give rise to insight into the law of falling bodies are discontinuous. One can imagine the whole cartwheel or a whole loop of very fine wire. But no matter how many experiments one makes on falling bodies, all one can obtain is a series of separate points plotted on a distance-time graph. No doubt, it is possible to join the plotted points by a smooth curve, but the curve represents, not data that are known, but a presumption of what understanding will grasp.

Thirdly, the insight into the image of the wheel grasps necessity and impossibility: if the radii are equal, the curve must be round; if the radii drawn from the center are unequal, the curve cannot be round. But the insight into the discontinuous series of points on the graph consists in a grasp, not of necessity or impossibility, but simply of possibility. The simplest smooth curve could represent the law of falling bodies, but any of a vast range of more elaborate curves could equally well pass through all the known points.

Fourthly, once one catches on to the law of the circle, the insight and consequent definition exert a backward influence upon imagination. The geometer imagines dots but thinks of points; he imagines fine threads but thinks of lines. The thinking is exact and precise, and imagination does its best to keep pace. In like manner the empirical investigator will tend to endow his images with the closest possible approximation to the laws he conceives. But while his imagination will do its best, while his perceptions will be profoundly influenced by the habits of his imagination, nonetheless the data that are available for the ideal observer make no effort towards such conformity. They go their own way with their unanalyzed multiplicity and their refractoriness to measurements that are more than approximate.

Fifthly, as we have seen, higher viewpoints in mathematics are reached inasmuch as initial images yield insights, insights yield definitions and postulates, definitions and postulates guide symbolic operations, and symbolic operations provide a more general image in which the insights of the higher viewpoint are emergent. Now in empirical method there is a similar circle, but it follows a slightly different route. The operations that follow upon the formulation of laws are not merely symbolic. For the formulation expresses a grasp of possibility. It is a hypothesis. It provides a basis for deductions and calculations no less than mathematical premises do.[b] But it also provides a basis for further observations and experiments. It is such observation and experimentation, directed by a hypothesis, that sooner or later turns attention to data that initially were overlooked or neglected; it is attention to such further data that forces the revision of initial viewpoints and effects the development of empirical science.

The circuit, then, of mathematical development may be named immanent: it moves from images through insights and conceptions to the production of symbolic images whence higher insights arise. But the circuit of scientific development includes action upon external things: it moves from observation and experiment to tabulations and graphs, from these to insights and formulations, from formulations to forecasts, from forecasts to operations, in which it obtains fresh evidence either for the confirmation or for the revision of existing views.

2   Classical Heuristic Structures   [35–46]

In one respect this brief sketch must be completed at once. Quite airily, we have spoken of the initial clue. But just what is it? Where does it come from? Is it mere guesswork? One can be led on quite naturally to the definition of the circle, if one begins from a suspicion that a cart-wheel is round because its spokes are equal. Similarly, one can proceed in intelligible fashion to the determination of the law of falling bodies, provided one presumes initially that the law will be a correlation of measurable aspects of a free fall. But this only makes the origin of the clue or hint or suggestion or presumption all the more significant.

2.1   An Illustration from Algebra   [36]

With another bow, then, to Descartes's insistence on understanding extremely simple things, let us examine the algebraist's peculiar habit of solving problems by announcing, 'Let x be the required number.'

Thus, suppose that the problem is to determine when first after three o'clock the minute hand exactly covers the hour hand. Then one writes down, 'Let x be the number of minutes after three o'clock.' Secondly, one infers that while the minute hand moves over x minutes, the hour hand moves over $x/12$ minutes. Thirdly, one observes that at three o'clock the hour hand has a fifteen-minute start. Hence, $x = x/12 + 15$ = 16 4/11. The procedure consists in (1) giving the unknown a name or symbol, (2) inferring the properties and relations of the unknown, (3) grasping the possibility of combining these properties and relations to form an equation, and (4) solving the equation.[1]

2.2   'Nature'   [36–37]

Now let us generalize.

In every empirical inquiry there are knowns and unknowns. But the knowns are apprehended whether or not one understands: they are the

1 Because insight is into the presentations of sense or the representations of imagination, the third step in the solution of such problems is facilitated by drawing a diagram[c] and marking all relevant
quantities. In the present instance the equation becomes evident
on inspection when one has marked the three distances, x, $x/12$,
and 15.

data of sense. The unknowns, on the other hand, are what one will grasp by insight and formulate in conceptions and suppositions.

Accordingly, let us bestow a name upon the unknown. Rather, let us advert to the fact that already it has been named. For what is to be known by understanding these data is called their *nature*. Just as in algebra the unknown number is x until one finds out what the number is, so too in empirical inquiry the unknown to be reached by insight is named 'the nature of ...' Once Galileo discovered his law, he knew that the nature of a free fall was a constant acceleration. But before he discovered the law, from the mere fact that he inquired, he knew that a free fall possessed a nature, though he did not know what that nature was.

The first step in the generalization is, then, that just as the mathematician begins by saying, 'Let the required number be x,' so too the empirical inquirer begins by saying, 'Let the unknown be the nature of ...'

2.3 Classification and Correlation   [37–38]

Next, similars are similarly understood.

Hence, because individuality pertains to the empirical residue, one knows at once that the 'nature of ...' will be universal, that when one understands these data, then one will understand similar data in exactly the same fashion.

Accordingly, just as the mathematician follows up his naming of the unknown as x by writing down properties of x, so too the empirical inquirer follows up his declaration that he seeks the 'nature of ...' by noting that that 'nature of ...' must be the same for all similar sets of data.

But similarities[d] are of two kinds.

There are the similarities of things in their relations to us. Thus, they may be similar in color or shape, similar in the sounds they emit, similar in taste or odor, similar in the tactile qualities of the hot and cold, wet and dry, heavy and light, rough and smooth, hard and soft.

There also are the similarities of things in their relations to one another. Thus, they may be found together or apart. They may increase or decrease concomitantly. They may have similar antecedents or consequents. They may be similar in their proportions to one another, and such proportions may form series of relationships, such as exist between the elements in the periodic table of chemistry or between the successive forms of life in the theory of evolution.

Now sensible similarities, which occur in the relations of things to our senses, may be known before the 'nature of ...' has been discovered. They form the basis of preliminary classifications. They specify the 'nature of ...,' so that one states that one is seeking the nature of color, the nature of heat, the nature of change, the nature of life.

On the other hand, similarities that reside in the relations of things to one another are the proximate materials of insight into nature. Hence the empirical inquirer, to emphasize this fact, will say that his objective is not merely the 'nature of ...' but more precisely the unspecified correlation to be specified, the undetermined function to be determined.

The second step in the generalization is, then, that just as the mathematician states that he seeks an x which has such and such properties, so too the empirical inquirer states that he seeks a 'nature of ...,' where the nature antecedently is specified by a classification based on sensible similarity and consequently will be known when some indeterminate function is determined.

The reader will observe that Galileo differed from his Aristotelian opponents by taking this second step. The Aristotelians were content to talk about the nature of light, the nature of heat, etc. Galileo inaugurated modern science by insisting that the nature of weight was not enough; from sensible similarity, which resides in the relations of things to our senses, one must proceed to relations that hold directly between things themselves.

2.4 Differential Equations   [38–39]

Now the correlations and functions that relate things directly to one another are determined empirically by measuring, plotting measurements on graphs, and grasping in the scattered points the possibility of a smooth curve, a law, a formulation. But our present concern is with the antecedent heuristic clues. Accordingly, we recall[e] that, besides individuality, the continuum also pertains to the empirical residue, and as well, that just as the universal is reached by abstracting from the individual, so also the techniques of the infinitesimal calculus deal with the intelligibility reached by abstracting from the noncountable infinity of the continuum.

The third step, then, in our generalization is the observation that, where the mathematician says, 'Let x be the required number,' the empirical inquirer can say, 'Let some indeterminate function $f(x, y, z, \ldots)^f$ be the required function.' Further, just as the mathematician reaches x by making statements about it, so too the empirical inquirer can move towards the determination of his indeterminate function by writing down differential equations which it must satisfy.

This procedure is named by Lindsay and Margenau in their *Foundations of Physics* the 'Method of Elementary Abstraction.' They illustrate it by examining the general features of a fluid in motion. Thus, if the fluid is continuous, then at every point in the fluid there will be the velocity components u, v, w, and a density r. If the fluid is not vanishing,[g] then the excess rate of outflow over inflow with respect to any infinitesimal volume will equal the rate of decrease of density in that volume. Hence there may be derived the equation

$$\partial(ru)/\partial x + \partial(rv)/\partial y + \partial(rw)/\partial z = -\partial r/\partial t.$$

Further, if the motion is in only one direction, two of the terms on the left-hand side vanish. If the fluid is incompressible, so that the density does not vary in time, the term on the right-hand side becomes zero. If the fluid is also homogeneous, so that the density does not vary in space, then the density r vanishes from the expressions on the left-hand side. Finally, if the velocity components u, v, w are equal to the first partial derivatives of some function of the coordinates x, y, z, there arises Laplace's equation.

The foregoing equation of continuity can be combined with other equations based on similarly general considerations. Thus, by shifting from velocity and density to acceleration and pressure, three further differential equations can be obtained. By adding suitable assumptions and restrictions, there can be worked out the differential equation of a wave motion.[2]

What is happening?[h] Consider the algebraic procedure that we are generalizing, and observe the isomorphism. Where before we said, 'Let x be the required number,' now we say, 'Let the equation[i] $f(x, y, z, t) = 0$ be the required correlation.' Where before we noted that, while the minute hand moves over x minutes, the hour hand moves over $x/12$ minutes, now we work out a differential equation that expresses mathematically certain very general features of the data. Where before we

2 See Lindsay and Margenau, *Foundations of Physics* 29–48.

appealed to the fact that at three o'clock the hour hand had a fifteen-minute start, now we turn our attention to the boundary conditions that restrict the range of functions satisfying the differential equation.

2.5 Invariance [39–43]

Though a less inadequate account of the notion of invariance will be attempted in examining the notions of space and time in chapter 5, at least some mention of it should be made in the present outline of scientific clues and anticipations. Accordingly, we recall that the differences of particular places and particular times pertain to the empirical residue, and for that reason not only are scientific discoveries independent of the place and time of their origin but also they can claim to be equally and uniformly valid irrespective of merely spatiotemporal differences. Hence, for example, the formulae for chemical compounds not only have the same intelligibility and meaning but also exactly the same symbolic representation no matter what the place or time. However, physical principles and laws are involved in a difficulty. For they regard motions of one kind or another; motions are changes in place and time; places and times lead to reference frames constructed to include and designate all points and instants relatively to a particular origin and orientation. It follows that if physical principles and laws refer to motions, they also refer to the particular origin and orientation of some particular reference frame, and unless a special effort is made, change in the choice of reference frame may result in change in the statement of the principle or law. On the other hand, when a special effort is made, the mathematical expression of physical principles and laws undergoes no change in form despite changes in spatiotemporal standpoint, and then the mathematical expression is said to be invariant under some specified group of transformations.

Briefly, then, the meaning of invariance is that (1) all scientists expect their correlations and laws to be independent of merely spatiotemporal differences, (2) physicists are confronted with a special difficulty inasmuch as they have to use reference frames, and (3) physicists surmount their peculiar difficulty by expressing their principles and laws in mathematical equations that remain invariant under transformations of frames of reference.

However, to determine under which group of transformations invariance is to be achieved, some further principle has to be invoked, and in fact in different scientific theories different principles are invoked. Of these the most general is the principle of equivalence, which asserts that physical principles and laws are the same for all observers. Now at first sight this statement seems ambiguous. Does it mean that physical objects look the same from all observational standpoints? Or does it mean that physical principles and laws are simply and completely outside the range of seeing, hearing, touching, feeling, and all other direct and indirect acts of observing?

While some writers seem to favor the former view, there can be little doubt about Einstein's position. Moreover, that position follows quite plausibly from the premise that empirical science seeks not the relations of things to our senses but their relations to one another. For, as has been remarked, observations give way to measurements; measurements relate things to one another rather than to our senses; and it is only the more remote relations of measurements to one another that lead to empirical correlations, functions, laws. Now clearly if laws are reached by eliminating the relations of things to the senses of observers and by arriving at relations between the measured relations of things to one another, then there exists an extremely solid foundation for the affir- mation that principles and laws are the same for all observers because they lie simply and completely outside the range of observational activi- ties. It is, for example, not the appearance of colors but the general expla- nation in terms of wavelengths of light that is exactly the same no matter what may be the state of observers' eyes, the lighting by which they see, or the speed with which they may happen to be in relative motion.

Hence, if physical principles and laws are independent of any move- ment of observers, they should be equally independent of any similar movement of reference frames. But observers may be moving with any linear or angular velocity, provided the motion is continuous and pro- vided it involves no excursions into the imaginary sections of a manifold constructed by introducing complex numbers. It follows that physical principles and laws should be independent of similar movements of refer- ence frames. Accordingly, by the principle of equivalence the mathemati- cal expression of physical principles and laws is to be expected to be in- variant as long as transformation equations are continuous functions of real variables.

To implement this conclusion, which is no more than a general antici- pation based on cognitional theory, two further steps are required. First, the broad invariance that we have described has to be conceived precisely in terms of tensors. Secondly, appropriate empirical hypotheses have to be formulated and verified. But by those steps there are reached the general theory of relativity and the generalized theory of gravitation, and incidentally it may not be amiss to note that our remote anticipation offers a simple explanation for certain aspects of those theories. For what was anticipated was a nonrelatedness of abstract laws to observers. It follows that the consequences of the anticipation should not be verified (1) if the laws lose their abstract character through particularization,[3] or (2) if investigation concentrates on the frequencies of concrete events accessible to observers, as seems to be the case in quantum mechanics.

A less general anticipation of invariance is contained in the basic postulate of special relativity. Already in illustrating inverse insight we have had occasion to put this postulate in the form of an explanatory syllogism, in which the major premise expressed an anticipation of invariance and the minor premise enounced the defect of intelligibility in inertial transformations. On the present analysis, then, the difference between the anticipations represented respectively by general and by special relativity is that, while both expect invariant mathematical expression to result from the abstractness of principles and laws, general relativity implements this expectation by invoking a direct insight into the significance of measurements, but special relativity implements it by invoking an inverse insight into the insignificance of constant velocity.

The exact nature of this difference may be clarified by two further remarks. On the one hand, it does not prevent special relativity from being regarded as a particular case of general relativity, for general relativity does not attribute any significance to constant velocity, and special relativity primarily regards laws reached by relating measurements to one another. On the other hand, the difference is a difference not merely in degree but also in kind, for the anticipations of general relativity do not hold when the results of investigations include relations to observers, but the anticipations of special relativity do hold as long as the insignificance of constant velocity is extended to the whole of physics. So perhaps one may explain the fact that the anticipations of special relativity have been mated successfully with quantum mechanics.[4]

A third and still less general anticipation of invariance has been attributed retrospectively to Newtonian dynamics, and it is not difficult to grasp in terms of insight the justice of this view. For, as has been noted,

3 See ibid. 368.
4 See ibid. 501–14.

the defect in intelligibility known in inverse insight is formulated only by employing a positive context of concomitant direct insights. In particular, it has been remarked that the defect of intelligibility in constant velocity was expressed for mechanics by Newton in his first law of motion, but for physics generally by Einstein in the basic postulate of special relativity. Accordingly, one can move backwards from Einstein to Newton if (1) one holds fast to the defective intelligibility in constant velocity, and (2) one changes the concomitant context of direct insights in terms of which the inverse insight regarding constant velocity is expressed.

Now the relevant differences in the concomitant context are threefold. First, special relativity regards all physical principles and laws, but Newtonian dynamics is concerned primarily with mechanics. Secondly, special relativity is primarily a field theory, that is, it is concerned not with the efficient, instrumental, material, or final causes of events, but with the intelligibility immanent in data; but Newtonian dynamics seems primarily a theory of efficient causes, of forces, their action, and the reaction evoked by action. Thirdly, special relativity is stated as a methodological doctrine that regards the mathematical expression of physical principles and laws, but Newtonian dynamics is stated as a doctrine about the objects subject to laws.

From these differences it follows that what Einstein stated for physics in terms of the transformation properties of the mathematical expression of principles and laws, Newton stated for mechanics in terms of the forces that move bodies. In both cases what is stated is a negation of intelligibility in constant velocity. But the Einsteinian context makes the statement an affirmation of invariance despite inertial transformations, while the Newtonian context makes the statement an affirmation of continued uniform motion in a straight line despite the absence of external forces. Finally, as the Einsteinian statement may be regarded as a methodological rule governing the expression of physical principles and laws, so the Newtonian statement may be regarded as a general boundary condition complementing the laws that equate (1) force with rate of change[j] of momentum, and (2) action with an equal and opposite reaction.

2.6 Summary   [44–46]

Our concern has been the methodical genesis of insight. Scientists achieve understanding, but they do so only at the end of an inquiry.

Moreover, their inquiry is methodical, and method consists in ordering means to achieve an end. But how can means be ordered to an end when the end is knowledge and the knowledge is not yet acquired? The answer to this puzzle is the heuristic structure. Name the unknown. Work out its properties. Use the properties to direct, order, guide the inquiry.

In prescientific thought what is to be known inasmuch as understanding is achieved is named the 'nature of ...' Because similars are understood similarly, the 'nature of ...' is expected to be the same for all similar data, and so it is specified as the nature of light, the nature of heat, and so forth, by constructing classifications based on sensible similarity.

Scientific thought involves a more exact anticipation. What is to be known inasmuch as data are understood is some correlation or function that states universally the relations of things not to our senses but to one another. Hence the scientific anticipation is of some unspecified correlation to be specified, some indeterminate function to be determined; and now the task of specifying or determining is carried out by measuring, by tabulating measurements, by reaching an insight into the tabulated measurements, and by expressing that insight through some general correlation or function that, if verified, will define a limit on which converge the relations between all subsequent appropriate measurements.

This basic anticipation and procedure may be enriched in two further manners. First, functions are solutions of differential equations; but in many cases relevant differential equations can be deduced from very general considerations. Hence the scientist may anticipate that the function which is the object of his inquiry will be one of the solutions of the relevant differential equations. Secondly, the functions that become known in the measure that understanding is achieved are, both in origin and in application, independent of the differences of particular places and particular times. In such a science as physics this anticipation of independence becomes formulated as the invariance of principles and laws under groups of transformations, and different grounds are invoked to determine which group of transformations is to leave the mathematical expression of laws unchanged in form. So a direct insight into the significance of measurements yields the anticipations of general relativity; an inverse insight into the insignificance of constant velocity yields the anticipations of special relativity; and a restriction of this inverse insight to the context of Newtonian dynamics yields the anticipations that sometimes are named Newtonian relativity.

Such in brief are the anticipations constitutive of classical heuristic structure. The structure is named classical because it is restricted to insights of a type most easily identified by mentioning the names of Galileo, Newton, Clerk Maxwell, and Einstein. It is named heuristic because it anticipates insights of that type, and while prescinding from their as yet unknown contents, works out their general properties to give methodical guidance to investigations. It is named a structure because, though operative, it is not known explicitly until oversight of insight gives way to insight into insight.

In particular one should observe that classical heuristic structure has no suppositions except the minimal suppositions that insights of a certain type occur and that inquiry aiming at such insights may be not haphazard but methodical. Further, advertence to classical heuristic structure has no additional suppositions except the possibility of an insight that grasps the set of relations linking methodical inquiry with anticipated insights, data, similarities in data, measurements, curve fitting, indeterminate functions, differential equations, the principle of inertia, special relativity, and general relativity. If there has been communicated some grasp of such diverse objects within the unity of a single view, then there has been communicated an insight into the genesis of insight. No doubt, that is a very small thing. An insight is no more than an act of understanding. It may prove to be true or false, or to hold some intermediate position of greater or less probability. Still, it is solely the communication of that act of understanding that has been our aim, and if the reader has been concerned with anything else, he has done all that is necessary to miss the little we have had to offer in the present context.

A further observation is not without its importance. Precisely because our suppositions and our objective have been so restricted, our account of classical heuristic structure is essentially free from any opinion about corpuscles, waves, causality, mechanism, determinism, the uniformity of nature, truth, objectivity, appearance, reality. It follows immediately that if we venture to use the name 'classical,' we use it without being involved in any of the extrascientific views that historically have been associated with scientific discoveries and to a greater or less extent have influenced their interpretation. This point is, of course, of considerable importance at a time when a new statistical heuristic structure has grown enormously in prestige and it has become a matter of some obscurity whether the new approach conflicts with the assumptions of earlier science or merely with the extrascientific opinions of earlier scientists. Finally, if we may close this section on a still more general note, it is not perhaps rash to claim that an analysis of scientific procedures in terms of insight is also new, and that the value of such analysis cannot be tested except by working out its implications and confronting them, not with opinions on science based on other analyses, but solely with strictly scientific anticipations, procedures, and results.

3   Concrete Inferences from Classical Laws   [46–53]

Before advancing to a consideration of statistical heuristic structure, it will be well to ask just how far the full realization of classical anticipations would bring the scientist towards an adequate understanding of data. Accordingly, we ask about the range of concrete inferences from classical laws, and we do so all the more readily because discussions of this topic seem to have suffered from an oversight of insight.

For just as insight is a necessary intermediary between sets of measurements and the formulation of laws, so also it is needed in the reverse process that applies known laws to concrete situations. Hence a concrete scientific inference has not two but three conditions: it supposes information on some concrete situation; it supposes knowledge of laws; and it supposes an insight into the given situation. For it is only by the insight that one can know (1) which laws are to be selected for the inference, (2) how the selected laws are to be combined to represent the spatial and dynamic configuration of the concrete situation, and (3) what dimensions in the situation are to be measured to supply numerical values that particularize the selected and combined laws.

Further, such inferences can be carried out in two manners. While practical people wait for concrete situations to arise before attempting to work out their consequences, theoretical minds are given to anticipating ideal or typical cases and to determining how a deduction could be carried out in each case.

Now in these anticipatory concrete inferences a different type of insight comes into play. For in the practical inference the situation determines the relevant insight, and the insight determines the selection, combination, and particularization of laws. But in the anticipatory inference insight is creative and constructive. It is not hampered by any given situation. Rather it tends to be a free exploration of the potentialities of known laws, and its principal fruit is the formulation of ideal or typical processes that are dominated throughout by human intelligence. For in such processes the basic situation is any situation that satisfies the requirements of the constructive insight, and provided the process is closed off against all extraneous influence, every antecedent and consequent situation must assume the dimensions determined by the successive stages of the imaginative model.

Moreover, it can happen that such ideal or typical processes can be verified in a sequence of concrete situations, and then three very notable consequences follow. In the first place, some insight or some set of unified insights can grasp not only the process as a whole but also every event in the whole. Secondly, this single insight or single unified set can be expressed in a corresponding combination of selected laws, and any situation can be deduced from any other without any explicit consideration of intervening situations. Thirdly, when such processes exist and their laws are as yet unknown, their investigation enjoys a number of singular advantages. For the intelligible unity of the whole process implies (1) that data on any situation are equivalent to data on the whole process, (2) that if data are found to be significant in any situation, then similar data will be significant in every other situation, and (3) that the accuracy of reports on any situation can be checked by inferences from reports on other situations. Moreover, once initial difficulties are overcome and basic insights are reached, the investigation approaches a supreme moment when all data suddenly fall into a single perspective, sweeping yet accurate deductions become possible, and subsequent exact predictions regularly will prove to have been correct.

However, if the nature of statistical inquiry is to be understood, it is of considerable importance to grasp that a quite different type of process not only can be constructed but also probably can be verified. Accordingly, let us divide ideally constructed processes into systematic and nonsystematic. Let us define systematic processes by the already enumerated properties that, other things being equal, (1) the whole of a systematic process and its every event possess but a single intelligibility that corresponds to a single insight or single set of unified insights, (2) any situation can be deduced from any other without an explicit consideration of intervening situations, and (3) the empirical investigation of such processes is marked not only by a notable facility in ascertaining and checking abundant and significant data but also by a supreme moment when all data fall into a single perspective, sweeping deductions become possible, and subsequent exact predictions regularly are fulfilled.

Now whenever a group or series is constructed on determinate principles, it is always possible to construct a different group or series by the simple expedient of violating the determinate principles. But the group of systematic processes is constructed on determinate principles. Therefore, by violating the principles one can construct other processes that are nonsystematic.

It is to be noted that the construction of nonsystematic processes rests on the same knowledge of laws and the same creative intelligence as the construction of systematic processes. Hence, if one inclines to enlarge the group of systematic processes by postulating full knowledge of laws and an unlimited inventiveness, one must grant that the group of nonsystematic processes also is constructed from an equally full knowledge of laws and an equally unlimited (though perhaps perverse) inventiveness. Finally, though we do not know all laws, nonetheless we can form the general notion of the systematic process; and similarly, despite our ignorance of many laws, we also can form the general notion of the nonsystematic process.

For, in the first place, if nonsystematic process is understood, the understanding will be multiple. There will be no single insight, or single set of unified insights, that masters at once the whole process and all its events. The only correct understanding will be either a set of different insights or else a set of different unified sets. In the former case the different insights will not be unified intelligibly, and so they will not be related to one another in any orderly series or progression or grouping whatever. In the latter case the different sets of unified insights will have no higher intelligible unity, and so they will not be related to one another in any orderly series or progression or grouping whatever. Finally, let us say that a series, progression, grouping is orderly if the relations between the elements of the series, progression, grouping either (1) can be grasped by an insight that can be expressed in general terms, or (2) can be concluded from any single insight or any single set of unified insights.

Secondly, because different parts of the process are understood differently, there can be no single combination of selected laws that holds for the whole process. On the contrary, for every different insight or different set of unified insights there will be a different combination, and perhaps even a different selection, of laws. Again, just as the different insights or unified sets of insights, so the different selections and combinations will not satisfy any orderly series or progression or grouping whatever.

Thirdly, such nonsystematic process may be deducible in all its events. Let us suppose (1) the absence of extraneous interference, (2) full information on some one situation, (3) complete knowledge of all relevant laws, (4) correct insights into the basic situation, (5) sufficient skill in the manipulation of mathematical expressions, (6) correct insights into deduced situations, and (7) no restriction on the amount of time allowed for the deduction. Then, from the given situation the occurrence and the dimensions of the next significantly different situation can be deduced. Correct insights into the deduced data on this situation make it possible to deduce the occurrence and the dimensions of the third significantly different situation. Finally, since this procedure can be repeated indefinitely, and since there are no restrictions on the amount of time to be devoted to the deduction, it makes no difference how many significantly different situations there are.

Fourthly, in a number of manners nonsystematic process exhibits coincidental aggregates. For an aggregate is coincidental if (1) the members of the aggregate have some unity based on spatial juxtaposition or temporal succession or both, and (2) there is no corresponding unity on the level of insight and intelligible relation.

Now nonsystematic process as a whole possesses a spatiotemporal unity but has no corresponding unity on the level of insight or intelligible relation.

Again, the several insights by which the several parts of nonsystematic process are understood form another coincidental aggregate. For they are a multiplicity on the level of intelligibility, but they possess some unity from the spatiotemporal unity of the process.

Similarly, the succession of different premises by which different stages of nonsystematic process may be deduced are a third coincidental manifold. For they too are a multiplicity on the level of intelligibility, but they possess some unity from the spatiotemporal unity of the process.

Further, the basic situation of nonsystematic process must be a coincidental manifold. For it has unity by spatial juxtaposition; but it cannot be one on the level of insight and intelligible relation. If the basic situation were intelligibly one, then the deduction of the process from that intelligible unity would constitute an orderly grouping for the set of different insights and for the succession of different combinations of selected laws. But both the set of different insights and the succession of different combinations of selected laws are coincidental aggregates that cannot be unified by any orderly series or progression or grouping whatever. Therefore, the basic situation can be no more than a merely spatial unification of different intelligibilities that can be grasped only by a set of different and unrelated insights.

Similarly, if many different and unrelated insights are needed to understand the basic situation, the premises for a deduction from that situation cannot be a single unified combination of selected laws. And since a coincidental aggregate of premises will yield a coincidental aggregate of conclusions, it follows that every deducible situation, provided it is a total situation, also will be a coincidental aggregate. Further, it follows that, when a nonsystematic process happens to give rise to a systematic process (as in recent theories on the origin of planetary systems), then the total situation must divide into two parts, of which one happens to fulfil the conditions of systematic process and the other fulfils the requirement of other things being equal.

Finally, there emerges the rule for constructing nonsystematic processes. For a situation is 'random' if it is 'any whatever provided specified conditions of intelligibility are not fulfilled.' But nonsystematic process results from any basic situation provided it lacks intelligible unity from a definitive viewpoint. Therefore, the rule for constructing nonsystematic processes is to begin from any random basic situation.

Fifthly, if nonsystematic processes exist, then the difficulty of investigating their nature increases with the number and diversity of their several distinct and unrelated intelligibilities. Data on one situation are not equivalent to data on the whole process but are relevant only to one of many parts of the whole. Again, the types of data significant in one part will not be significant in disparate parts, and so several different inquiries must be undertaken. Thirdly, reports on one situation ordinarily cannot be checked by comparing them with inferences from reports on other situations. Fourthly, there is no supreme moment when all data fall into a single perspective, for there is no single perspective to be had. Fifthly, even when the laws involved in the process are thoroughly understood, even when current and accurate reports from usually significant centers of information are available, still such slight differences in matters of fact can result in such large differences in the subsequent course of events that deductions have to be restricted to the short run, and predictions have to be content with indicating probabilities. So, perhaps, it is that astronomers can publish the exact times of the eclipses of past and future centuries, but meteorologists need a constant supply of fresh and accurate information to tell us about tomorrow's weather.

Let us now pause to take our bearings. We began by noting that concrete inferences from classical laws suppose not only knowledge of laws and information on some basic situation but also an insight that mediates between the situation and general knowledge. We went on to distinguish between practical insights that apply laws to given situations and constructive insights that invent typical or ideal processes. We have been engaged in explaining that, just as constructive insight can devise systematic processes with all their beautiful and convenient properties, so also it can devise nonsystematic processes with a complete set of quite opposite properties. It remains that a few more general corollaries be added.

First, systematic process is monotonous, but nonsystematic process can be the womb of novelty. For the possibility of leaping deductively from any situation of a systematic process to any other situation rests on the fact that a systematic process is little more than a perpetual repetition of essentially the same story. On the other hand, the unfolding of a nonsystematic process has to be followed through its sequence of situations. Significant changes occur, and as they occur the relevant insights change. Hence, as will appear in chapter 4, within a large nonsystematic process there can be built a pyramid of schemes resting on schemes in a splendid ascent of novelty and creativeness.

Secondly, systematic process would seem to be reversible; that is, it would work equally well if, so to speak, the future were the past and the process ran backwards. For a systematic process is the expression of a single idea. Each successive situation is related to the next in accord with the dictates of the idea. Hence, to reverse the succession of dictates, so that the process begins from a last situation and moves backwards to a first, involves no new idea but merely a different and, it seems, equally workable application of the same idea. On the other hand, nonsystematic process may easily be irreversible. For it is not the unfolding of some single idea, and successive situations are not related in accord with the dictates of any single insight or any single set of unified insights. What is in control is not intelligence but any random basic situation, and the resulting coincidental sequence of coincidental situations easily includes both the emergence and the destruction of systematic processes. Hence, to expect nonsystematic process to be reversible is to expect destroyed systematic processes to reemerge from their ruins; again, it is to expect that reversed systematic processes will resolve into their origins at the right moment and in the right manner though no provision is made for that resolution.

Thirdly, the distinction between systematic and nonsystematic processes throws light on the precise meaning of closure. For there is an external closure that excludes outside interference. When it is applied to a systematic process, the whole course of events is mastered by intelligence with relative ease. But when it is applied to a nonsystematic process, then it merely leaves internal factors all the freer to interfere with one another.

Fourthly, whether world process is systematic or nonsystematic is a question to be settled by the empirical method of stating both hypotheses, working out as fully as one can the totality of their implications, and confronting the implications with the observable facts.

Fifthly, if world process proves to be nonsystematic, then it contains coincidental aggregates, and the word 'random' has an objective meaning. In that case, there would be some interpretation of statistical science as the science of what exists. In other words, in that case it would be false to say that statistical science must be a mere cloak for ignorance. Moreover, even if world process proves to be systematic, still that will be true only on empirical grounds and a posteriori; it follows that it cannot be true a priori that statistical science cannot be the science of what exists. On the present showing, then, there can be no valid theoretical arguments that establish that statistical science in every possible meaning of the term must be a mere cloak for ignorance.

4   Statistical Heuristic Structures[k]   [53–68]

4.1 Elementary Contrasts   [53–54]

Classical and statistical investigations exhibit marked differences that provide a convenient starting point for the present section.

In the first place, while classical investigation heads towards the determination of functions and their systematization, statistical investigation clings to concrete situations. Hence, while classical conclusions are concerned with what would be if other things were equal, statistical conclusions directly regard such aggregates of events as the sequences of occasions on which a coin is tossed or dice are cast, the sequences of situations created by the mobility of molecules in a gas, the sequences of generations in which babies are born, the young marry, and the old die.

Secondly, statistical inquiry attends not to theoretical processes but to palpable results. As Galileo sought the intelligibility immanent in a free fall, so Clerk Maxwell sought the intelligibility immanent in the electromagnetic field. But in a statistical investigation such theoretical analyses and constructions are set aside. The movement of dice observes perfectly the laws of mechanics, but the laws of mechanics are not premises in the determination of the probability of casting a 'seven.' Doctors commonly succeed in diagnosing the causes of death, but such causes are not studied in fixing death rates. The statistical scientist seems content to define events and areas, to count the instances of each defined class within the defined area, and to offer some general but rather vague view of things as a whole.

Thirdly, statistical science is empirical, but it does not endeavor to measure and correlate the spatial, temporal, and other variables that so fascinate classical investigators. Its attention is directed to *frequencies* that are straightforward numerical answers to the straightforward question, How often? Such frequencies may be *ideal* or *actual*, but while it is true that the ideal frequency or probability raises debatable issues, at least the *actual frequency* is a transparent report not of what should or might or will happen but of what in fact did happen. Such actual frequencies are *absolute* when they assign the actual number of events of a given kind within a given area during a given interval of time. However, since different areas commonly are not comparable, it is customary to proceed from absolute actual frequencies either to *rates*, say, per thousand of population or, when classes of events are alternative possibilities, to *relative actual frequencies* which are sets of proper fractions, say p/n, q/n, r/n, . . . where $n = p + q + r + . . .$

Fourthly, behind the foregoing rather superficial differences there is a profound difference in the mentality of classical and statistical inquirers. Had astronomers been content to regard the wandering of the planets as a merely random affair, the planetary system never would have been discovered. Had Joule been content to disregard small differences, the mechanical equivalent of heat would have remained unknown. But statistical inquirers make it their business to distinguish in their tables of frequencies between significant and merely random differences. Hence, while they go to great pains to arrive at exact numbers, they do not seem to attempt the obvious next step of exact explanation. As long as differences in frequency oscillate about some average, they are esteemed of no account; only when the average itself changes, is intellectual curiosity aroused and further inquiry deemed relevant.

4.2   The Inverse Insight   [54–58]

The existence of this radical difference in mentality demands an explanation, and the obvious explanation is the occurrence of something like an inverse insight. For an inverse insight has three characteristics:[1] it supposes a positive object of inquiry; it denies intelligibility to the object; and the denial runs counter to spontaneous anticipations of intelligence. But the differences named random are matters of fact: they occur in frequencies determined by counting the events in a given class in a given area during a given interval of time. Further, random differences are denied intelligibility, for, though statistical inquirers hardly would use such an expression, at least their deeds seem a sufficient witness to their thought. When differences are not random, further inquiry is in order; but when differences are random, not only is no inquiry attempted but also the very attempt would be pronounced silly. Finally, this denial of intelligibility is in open conflict with the anticipations of classical investigation. For classical precept and example tirelessly inculcate the lesson that no difference is to be simply neglected; and while one may doubt that this classical attitude is more spontaneous than its opposite, at least one can speak of a devaluated inverse insight that divides classical and statistical anticipations.

Further, while this devaluated inverse insight bears on the frequencies of events, it does not follow necessarily that the defect of intelligibility resides in single events. Indeed, it seems quite possible to acknowledge random differences in frequencies and at the same time to maintain that single events are determinate, that they are not random, even that they are deducible. At least the events must be determinate enough to be counted, for if they are not counted there are no frequencies and so no random differences in frequencies. Again, one can acknowledge random differences in death rates without suggesting that single deaths were random or that doctors were unable to perform successful diagnoses. Finally, if single events need not be random, they may be deducible. For if it is possible to argue from effect to cause, from consequent to antecedent, it should be equally possible to move from cause to effect, from determining antecedent to determined consequent.

It seems, then, that if we are to discover a *fully general* account of the meaning of random differences, we must look not to single events but to events as members of a group. So the question becomes, How can there be a defect in intelligibility in a group of events if each event singly is quite determinate, if none are random, and if one by one all may be deduced?

Fortunately, if not accidentally, our previous discussion of concrete inferences from classical laws offers a ready answer to this question. For knowledge of laws can be applied (1) to single events, (2) to systematic processes, and (3) to nonsystematic processes. Moreover, just as the assertion of random differences in frequencies need not imply that single events are indeterminate or random or that they are not deducible, so also in a nonsystematic process each event may be determinate, none need be random, and sometimes at least, if time were not money, all could be deduced. Again, just as the assertion of random differences springs from a devaluated inverse insight, so too does the notion of a nonsystematic process. For a nonsystematic process is as positive an object of inquiry as any process; it is nonsystematic inasmuch as it lacks the intelligibility that characterizes systematic process; and its properties are very surprising indeed when they are compared with what commonly Laplace is supposed to have meant when he claimed that any situation in world history could be deduced from any other.

The similarity of these two devaluated inverse insights provides an obvious clue, and to follow it up let us consider the four statements: (1) statistical inquiry is concerned with coincidental aggregates of events; (2) statistical inquiry investigates what classical inquiry neglects; (3) statistical inquiry finds an intelligibility in what classical inquiry neglects; and (4) this intelligibility is denied when random differences are affirmed.

First, statistical inquiry is concerned with coincidental aggregates of events. For it is not concerned with the intelligibly grouped events of systematic process: there are no statistics on the phases of the moon or on the transit of Venus, and there are no random differences in ordinary astronomical tables. Again, it is not concerned with events taken singly. For each single event amounts to just one more or less in tables of frequencies, and in general a difference of one more or one less may be regarded as random. Further, it is possible to discern random differences in some groups of events in which each event is determinate and deducible and no event is random. It remains, then, that the object of statistical inquiry is the coincidental aggregate of events, that is, the aggregate of events that has some unity by spatial juxtaposition or by temporal succession or by both but lacks unity on the level of insight and of intelligible relation. In other words, statistical inquiry is concerned with nonsystematic process.

Secondly, statistical inquiry investigates what classical inquiry neglects. For even if one grants that classical inquiry leads to the laws that explain every event, it remains that classical science rarely bothers to explain the single events of nonsystematic process, and still less does it offer any technique for the orderly study of groups of such events. Moreover, there are excellent reasons for this neglect. The deduction of each of the events of a nonsystematic process begins by demanding more abundant and more exact information than there is to be had. It proceeds through a sequence of stages determined by the coincidences of a random situation. It has to postulate unlimited time to be able to assert the possibility of completing the deduction. It would end up with a result that lacks generality, for, while the result would hold for an exactly similar nonsystematic process, it commonly would not provide a safe basis for an approximation to the course of another nonsystematic process with a slightly different basic situation. Finally, it would be preposterous to attempt to deduce the course of events for every nonsystematic process. Not only would the foregoing difficulties have to be surmounted an enormous number of times, but this Herculean labor would seem to be to no purpose. How could nonsystematic processes be classified? How could one list in an orderly fashion the totality of situations of all nonsystematic processes? Yet without such a classification and such a list, how could one identify given situations with situations contained in the extremely long deductions of the extremely large set of nonsystematic processes?

Thirdly, statistical inquiry finds an intelligibility in what classical inquiry neglects. So far we have been concerned to stress the defect of intelligibility in nonsystematic process. But a mere defect in intelligibility is not the basis of a scientific method. There is needed a complementary direct insight that turns the tables on the defect. Just as scientific generalization exploits the fact that individuality pertains to an empirical residue, just as the real numbers, the theory of continuous functions, and the infinitesimal calculus exploit the defect of intelligibility in the continuum, just as scientific collaboration is possible because particular places and particular times pertain to the empirical residue, just as the principle of inertia and the basic postulate of special relativity rest on an empirically residual aspect of constant velocity, so also statistical science is the positive advance of intelligence through the gap in intelligibility in coincidental aggregates of events.

Accordingly, besides the devaluated inverse insight that has been our concern hitherto, there is to be acknowledged in statistical science another basic moment that is positive and creative. Aristotle was quite aware of what we have named nonsystematic process, for he contended that the whole course of terrestrial events was just a series of accidents. But to this devaluated inverse insight he failed to add the further creative moment. Instead of discovering statistical method, he attempted to account for the manifest continuity of the terrestrial series of accidents by invoking the continuous influence of the continuously rotating celestial spheres.

Fourthly, it is this further intelligibility that is denied when random differences are affirmed. For if the statistical investigator deals with nonsystematic processes, he does not find the intelligibility of systematic process either in the differences he pronounces significant or in the differences he pronounces random. Again, to discover the intelligibility that statistical science finds in nonsystematic process, we must look to the differences pronounced significant. It follows that differences in frequencies of events are random when they lack not only the intelligibility of systematic process but also the intelligibility of nonsystematic process.

4.3 The Meaning of Probability   [58–62]

Still, the reader will be more interested in hearing what this intelligibility is than in being told that it is lacking in random differences. Its name, then, is probability, but to grasp the meaning of the name is to reach an explanatory definition.[m] Let us begin from the definition and then try to understand it.

Consider a set of classes of events, $P, Q, R, \ldots$ and suppose that in a sequence of intervals or occasions, events in each class occur respectively $p_1, q_1, r_1, \ldots p_2, q_2, r_2, \ldots p_i, q_i, r_i, \ldots$ times. Then, the sequence of relative actual frequencies of the events will be the series of sets of proper fractions $p_i/n_i, q_i/n_i, r_i/n_i, \ldots$ where $i = 1, 2, 3, \ldots$ and in each case $n_i = p_i + q_i + r_i + \ldots$ Now if there exists a single set of constant proper fractions, say $p/n, q/n, r/n, \ldots$ such that the differences $p/n - p_i/n_i, q/n - q_i/n_i, r/n - r_i/n_i, \ldots$ are always random, then the constant proper fractions will be the respective probabilities of the classes of events, the association of these probabilities with the classes of events defines a state, and the set of observed relative actual frequencies is a representative sample of the state.

The foregoing paragraph outlines a procedure in which the central moment is an insight. By that insight the inquirer abstracts from the randomness in frequencies to discover regularities that are expressed in constant proper fractions named probabilities. There results the solution of two outstanding methodological problems. Because the probabilities are to hold universally, there is solved the problem of reaching general knowledge of events in nonsystematic processes. Because states are defined by the association of classes of events with corresponding probabilities, there is bypassed the problem of distinguishing and listing nonsystematic processes. However, both the probabilities and the states they define are merely the fruits of insight. They are hypothetical entities whose existence has to be verified, and in fact becomes verified in the measure that subsequent frequencies of events conform to probable expectations. In turn, this need of verification provides a simple formulation for the notion of a representative sample. For a set of relative actual frequencies is a representative sample if the probabilities to which they lead prove to be correct. On the other hand, a set of relative actual frequencies is not a representative sample if the probabilities to which they lead run counter to the facts. It follows that the basic practical problem of statistical inquiry is the selection of representative samples, and indeed that its solution must depend not merely on a full theoretical development of statistical method but also on the general knowledge of individual investigators and on their insights into whatever specific issues they happen to be investigating.

Such, then, is the general context, but our concern must center on the insight by which intelligence leaps from frequencies to probabilities and by the same stroke abstracts from the randomness in frequencies. Now an insight is neither a definition nor a postulate nor an argument but a preconceptual event. Hence our aim must be to encourage in readers the conscious occurrence of the intellectual events that make it possible to know what happens when probability is grasped. First, then, we shall consider an easier insight that bears some general resemblance to insights into probability. Secondly, we shall consider an insight that occurs when a particular case of probability is understood. Thirdly, we shall move towards the general heuristic structure within which the notion of probability is developed and methods of determining its precise content are perfected.

In the first place, the mathematical notion of limit bears a general resemblance to the notion of probability. Accordingly, let us consider the simple sum

$$S = 1/2 + 1/4 + 1/8 + \ldots [\text{to } n \text{ terms}]$$

$$= 1 - 1/2^n$$

where, as n increases, S differs from unity by an ever smaller fraction, and so, by assigning n ever larger values, the difference between the sum S and unity can be made as small as one pleases. In the limit, then, when the number of terms in the series is infinite, the sum S is unity. However, one cannot write out an infinite number of terms; one cannot even conceive each of an infinite number of terms. Moreover, while it is contradictory to suppose that an unending series is ended, still one can understand the principle on which each fraction in the series is constructed, one can tell whether or not any fraction belongs to the series, one can conceive as many of the fractions as one pleases, and one can grasp that the more terms there are to the series, the nearer the sum is to unity. Finally, there is no contradiction in thinking or speaking of *all* the terms in the series, and one can see that there is no point in bothering about explicit conception of the remainder because it contains nothing that is not already understood. Now advertence to this absence of further intelligibility in the remainder is the abstractive aspect of the insight that claims the whole series to be understood sufficiently in its content and in its properties for it to be summed and for the sum to be equated with unity.

But, like a mathematical limit, a probability is a number. Like a limit, a probability is a number that cannot be reached from the data of a problem without the intervention of an insight. Again, just as the limit we considered lay beyond more terms than can be conceived, so a probability lies concealed within the random oscillations of relative actual frequencies. Finally, just as intelligence can reach a limit by grasping that there is nothing further to be understood in the unconceived infinite remainder of further terms, so also intelligence can reach probabilities by abstracting from the random oscillations of relative actual frequencies to discover a set of universally valid constants.

In the second place, to move closer to our quarry, let us analyze the tossing of a coin in the hope of generating the insight that pronounces the probability of 'heads' to be one-half. The result, then, of a toss is either of the alternatives, 'heads' or 'tails.' In any given instance the result might have been different if (1) the initial position of the coin had been different, or (2) different linear and angular momenta had been imparted to it, or (3) the motion had been arrested at a different point.

Let us name these three the determinants of the result and direct our attention to the set of possible combinations of determinants.

First, the set is very large. For any of a very large group of initial positions can be combined with any of a very large group of initial linear and angular momenta; and any of these combinations can be combined with any of a very large group of points of arrested movement.

Secondly, the set of possible combinations divides into two exactly equal parts. For whenever 'heads' results, 'tails' would have resulted if the coin had been turned over and exactly the same toss and catch had been executed. Similarly, whenever 'tails' results, 'heads' would have resulted if the coin had been turned over and exactly the same toss and catch had been executed.

Thirdly, every sequence of actual combinations is a random selection from the set of possible combinations. It is a selection inasmuch as it need not include all possible combinations. It is a random selection inasmuch as it may be any whatever, provided specified conditions of intelligibility are not fulfilled. Now intelligibility is to be excluded not from single tosses but from the sequence of tosses as a sequence. It is not to be excluded from single tosses, for there is no reason to suppose that tossing a coin involves a suspension of the laws of mechanics or of any similar science. It is to be excluded from the sequence as a sequence, for we have every reason to assert that a sequence of tosses is not a systematic process. Hence every sequence of actual combinations of determinants is a coincidental aggregate. It will possess the unity of a temporal succession. But while any single combination may be deducible from prior events, any sequence of combinations is deducible only from some prior coincidental aggregate; for the sequence cannot be orderly in the sense that there is some insight or some set of unified insights that can be expressed in general terms and can determine the exact content of the sequence.

Now the relative actual frequency of 'heads' is the fraction obtained by dividing the number of times 'heads' occurs on any given succession of tosses by the number of tosses in that succession. Clearly, this fraction can and often will differ from one-half. For the result of each toss is settled by the actual combination of determinants, and that combination may be any combination whatever. However, differences between relative actual frequencies and one-half must be a coincidental aggregate. For if they were not, they would form an orderly series; if the differences formed an orderly series, the results would have to form an orderly series; if the results formed an orderly series, the sequence of combinations of determinants would form an orderly series. *Ex hypothesi*, this conclusion is false; therefore, the supposition was false. Moreover, relative actual frequencies cannot help oscillating about one-half. For the set of possible combinations divides into two exactly equal parts; and every sequence of actual combinations is a random selection from the set of possible combinations. Now in a random selection of a sequence the sequence is stripped of all order, all regularity, all law; hence, while it can and will include runs of 'heads' and runs of 'tails,' it cannot possibly stick to one alternative to the exclusion of the other, and so relative actual frequency is bound to oscillate about one-half.

It has been shown that the relative actual frequencies of 'heads' (1) can and often do differ from one-half, but (2) only at random, and (3) in a manner that yields an oscillation about one-half as a center. Intelligence, then, can grasp a regularity in the frequencies by abstracting from their random features and by settling on the center about which they oscillate. That abstractive grasp of intelligibility is the insight that is expressed by saying that the probability of 'heads' is one-half.

However, it is only in games of chance that there can be discerned an antecedent symmetry in the set of possible combinations of determinants of events. In other instances probabilities have to be reached a posteriori, and to reach them a statistical heuristic structure has to be developed. To this issue we turn in the next subsection, not indeed in the hope of determining what precisely probability must be in all cases, but rather with the intention of grasping the underlying anticipations that inform statistical inquiry and are to be expected gradually to mount through trial and error, through theoretical discoveries and developing techniques, to some rounded methodological position such as already is enjoyed in classical investigations. In other words, besides the methodical genesis of scientific insights, there is the genesis of scientific method itself, and when a satisfactory account of the former is still a matter of obscure debates, a study of human understanding can draw no less profit from a consideration of the latter.

4.4 Analogy in Heuristic Structure   [63–66]

The present subsection is a protracted analogy. Under ten successive headings we shall recall distinctive features of classical heuristic structure, note their reason or ground, and in each case proceed to an analogous feature in a statistical heuristic structure.

First, then, there is the unspecified heuristic concept. For the goal of every inquiry is an act of understanding, and the basic device of methodical inquiry is to name the unknown that will become known when the anticipated act of understanding occurs. Hence, just as the classical inquirer seeks to know the 'nature of ...,' so the statistical inquirer will seek to know the 'state of ...'

Secondly, there is a specification of the heuristic concept by prescientific description. For all empirical inquiry presupposes some object that already is given but as yet is not understood; and every such object possesses its prescientific description that provides an initial specification for the heuristic concept. Hence, just as classical inquiry comes to know natures by understanding 'data of different kinds,' so statistical inquiry comes to know states by understanding 'ordinary and exceptional, normal and abnormal runs of events.'

Thirdly, linking the open heuristic concept with the prescientifically described object there is the heuristic theorem. Because similars are understood similarly, natures are linked with data classified by sensible similarity. So we speak of the nature of color or the nature of sound. Similarly, because a notable regularity is compatible with random differences in runs of events, states are linked with runs that despite occasional lapses are ordinary or normal, or again with runs that are pronounced exceptional or abnormal though they contain a few ordinary or normal elements. So we speak of the state of a person's health, brokers speak of the state of the market, and the President of the United States discourses on the state of the nation.

Fourthly, to effect a transformation of prescientific anticipations and descriptions, there has to be formulated an ideal of scientific explanation. Hence, just as the classical inquirer places knowledge of nature in the discovery and verification of determinate functional relations, so the statistical inquirer places knowledge of states in the association of sets of classes of events with corresponding sets of probabilities. In other words, just as the mysterious nature of gravity turns out to be for the scientist merely a constant acceleration, so the mysterious state of so-and-so's health turns out to be for the scientist a schedule of probabilities attached to a schedule of classes of events.

Fifthly, from the formulation of the precise scientific objective there follows the displacement of prescientific by scientific description. Thus, to determine functional relations measurement is added to observation, and mere sensible similarity gives way to similarities of conjunction and separation, of proportion and concomitant variation. In like manner, to determine sets of probabilities the adjectives 'ordinary' and 'exceptional,' 'normal' and 'abnormal' are replaced by actual counting of events and the consequent tabulation of rates or of relative actual frequencies.[n] Moreover, to justify this numerical accuracy, exact classifications are borrowed from classical science, and every resource is employed to delimit, as far as possible, internally homogeneous volume-intervals of events.

Sixthly, just as classical inquiry derives a general view of its possibilities from the mathematical investigation of functions and of spatiotemporal relations, so statistical inquiry finds similar guidance and orientation in the calculus of probabilities.

Seventhly, just as classical inquiry evolves practical techniques of curve fitting to aid the transition from measurements to functional relations, so statistical inquiry develops similar techniques to aid the transition from relative actual frequencies to probabilities.

Eighthly, just as classical inquiry proceeds not only from below upwards from measurements through curve fitting but also from above downwards from differential equations to their solutions, so also a comparable department of statistical inquiry has discovered that the solution of operator equations yields eigenfunctions and eigenvalues that serve both to select classes of events and to determine the respective probabilities of the selected classes.

Ninthly, just as classical discovery is a leap of constructive intelligence that goes beyond ascertained measurements to posit a functional relation on which the relations between all appropriate subsequent measurements should converge as on a limit, so also statistical discovery (as distinct from statistical information) is a leap of constructive intelligence that goes beyond ascertained relative actual frequencies to assign probabilities, where differences between probabilities and relative actual frequencies (1) should always be a coincidental aggregate, and (2) in each case should be eliminable by extending the investigation of that case.

Hence, just as classical laws are universal and constant while measurements are particular and subject to the variations introduced by extraneous influences, so statistical states are universal and constant though relative actual frequencies are particular and subject to random differences.

However, while both types of discovery are universal and so abstract, still they involve different types of abstraction. In both classical and statistical constructs there is abstraction from the empirically residual aspects of individuality, of the continuum, of particular places and times, and of constant velocity. But classical laws, at least in the determination of each law, also abstract from coincidental aggregates inasmuch as they demand the qualification 'other things being equal.' On the other hand, statistical states express an intelligibility immanent in coincidental aggregates, and to reach this intelligibility they abstract from the random differences in relative actual frequencies.

Tenthly, no less than the classical law, the statistical state has to be verified. For knowledge of states is derived from particular frequencies by a leap of constructive intelligence. That leap is neither the recognition of a fact nor the grasp of a necessity but simply an insight into possibility. The known frequencies are satisfied by the supposition of a state that universally is manifested by events of determinate classes occurring with determinate probabilities. But further investigation can compromise this result in a variety of manners. It may reveal an unsatisfactory classification of events, an underestimation of the complexity of the sequence of situations, a failure to reach representative samples. Then relative actual frequencies have to be ascertained on a more exact or broader basis, and the constructive leap has to be repeated in a new manner.

Still, though both classical and statistical hypotheses need verification, verification has not the same meaning in both cases. Because the relations between measurements converge on the functional relations that express classical laws, it is possible to substitute the numerical values determined by the measurements for the variables that are functionally related by the laws. In contrast, because relative actual frequencies differ at random from probabilities, it is not possible to deduce the probabilities from any fully determinate mathematical formula by substituting for the variables of the formula the fractions that correspond to relative actual frequencies.

The converse to this difference in the meaning of verification appears in the difference between classical and statistical predictions. Classical predictions can be exact within assignable limits, because relations between measurements converge on the functional relations that formulate classical laws. But because relative actual frequencies differ at random from probabilities, statistical predictions primarily regard the probabilities of events, and only secondarily determine the corresponding frequencies that differ at random from the probabilities. Hence, even when numbers are very great and probabilities high, as in the

kinetic theory of gases, the possibility of exceptions has to be acknowledged; and when predictions rest on a statistical axiomatic structure, as
in quantum mechanics, the structure itself seems to involve a principle
of indeterminacy or uncertainty.

4.5 Some Further Questions   [66–68]

Possible further questions abound. But as the shrewd reader will have
surmised, our purpose has been, not to work out definitive foundations
for statistical science, but to grasp in some fashion the statistical heuristic
structure that not only tackles specific problems but also develops its own
methods as it goes along, and thereby sets up an exigence for a succession of new and better foundations.°

I shall be asked whether probable events sooner or later occur. From
the viewpoint of empirical inquiry the answer seems to be affirmative.
If events are probable, they do not diverge systematically from their
probabilities. But if they occur neither sooner nor later, then there is
empirical evidence for the intervention of some systematic factor.

However, if with the mathematicians one envisages an infinity of occasions, then the qualifying phrase 'neither sooner nor later' admits so
broad a meaning that empirical evidence for a systematic factor never
can be reached. A common solution to this antinomy is to say that very
small probabilities are to be neglected, and this, I believe, can be defended by granting mathematical and denying empirical existence to the
assumed infinity of occasions. Logically, however, such a solution implies
that mathematical and scientific probability are distinct notions with
different implications, or perhaps it invites the development of a mathematical theory in which the field of occasions gradually expands.

Again, I may be asked for the operational meaning of the highly
theoretical coincidental aggregate. The answer is that the appropriate
operation occurs on the methodological level. Either a range of observations is to be subsumed under classical heuristic structure or it is to be
subsumed under statistical heuristic structure. On the former hypothesis
it will be possible to discover some orderly series, progression, or grouping. On the latter hypothesis no such series, progression, or grouping
exists. Both hypotheses can be formulated; their implications are to be
worked out; and the facts are to decide which hypothesis is, if not ultimate truth, at least the best available opinion at the given stage of
scientific development.

Finally, if probabilities must be verified, it also is true that there is a probability of verifications. But it is of no little importance to grasp that this second probability shares the name but not the nature of the first. For the first probability, apart from random differences, corresponds to the relative actual frequency of events. It is the regularity in the frequencies, and it is to be known by a leap of constructive intelligence that grasps the regularity by abstracting from the randomness. In contrast, the second probability is not some fraction that, apart from random differences, corresponds to the relative actual frequency of verifications. A preponderance of favorable tests does not make a conclusion almost certain; indeed, a very few contrary tests suffice to make it highly improbable. More fundamentally, the second probability is not known by a leap of constructive intelligence that abstracts from random differences, for such leaps never yield anything but hypotheses. As will appear in chapters 9 and 10, the second probability is known through acts of reflective understanding and judgment; it means that an affirmation or negation leads towards the unconditioned; and it is estimated, not by counting verifications and abstracting from random differences, but by criticizing verifications and by taking everything relevant into account.

For these reasons, then, we distinguish sharply between 'probably occurring' and 'probably true.' For the same reasons we refuse to identify 'certainty' in the sense of unit probability with 'certainty' in the sense of 'certainly verified.' It follows that we find it meaningless to represent by a fraction the probability of a verification. Similarly, we find it fallacious to argue that probable events are not certain events because probable judgments are not certain judgments. Indeed, that fallacy would wreck our analysis. Not only are there two meanings to probability and two meanings to certainty but also there are two manners in which some events of nonsystematic process can be investigated. Classical procedures would yield *particular*, probably verified conclusions about single events assigned a *unit* probability, where statistical procedures would yield *general*, probably verified conclusions about events as members of coincidental aggregates by assigning them *fractional* probabilities.

Before closing it may be well to add a word on the use of the terms 'classical' and 'statistical.' In contemporary physics it is customary to oppose 'classical' to 'quantum' and 'statistical' to 'mechanical.' So there arises the familiar division of classical mechanics (Newton), classical statistics (Boltzmann), quantum mechanics (Schrödinger, Heisenberg), and quantum statistics (Bose-Einstein, Fermi-Dirac). Clearly, however, the present study of heuristic structures demands not a fourfold but a two-fold division. Either intelligence anticipates the discovery of functional relations on which relations between measurements will converge, or else it anticipates the discovery of probabilities from which relative actual frequencies may diverge though only at random. The latter alternative has a fairly clear claim to the name 'statistical.' The former alternative is not limited to Newtonian mechanics, and in the opinion of many does not regard quantum mechanics. It is a mode of inquiry common to Galileo, Newton, Clerk Maxwell, and Einstein; it is as familiar to the chemist as to the physicist; it long was considered the unique mode of scientific investigation; it has been the principal source of the high repute of science. In such a work as the present no one, I trust, will be misled if so classical a procedure is named 'classical.'

5   **Survey**   [68–69]

Perhaps enough progress has been made for the rather novel orientation of this inquiry to come into better focus. We began from the description of a discovery to proceed to distinguish insights, their cumulation to higher viewpoints, and the significance of grasping that at times the point is that there is no point. In the present chapter we have moved not forward and outward to conclusions about objects but rather backward and inward to the subject's anticipations of insights that have not occurred and to the methodical exploitation of such anticipations. In that inward movement the reader can foresee the direction in which the whole work will advance. For our goal is not any scientific object, any universal and necessary truth, any primary propositions. Our goal is the concrete, individual, existing subject that intelligently generates and critically evaluates and progressively revises every scientific object, every incautious statement, every rigorously logical resting place that offers prematurely a home for the restless dynamism of human understanding. Our ambition is to reach neither the known nor the knowable but the knower. Chapter 1 spoke of the insights he seeks. Chapter 2 has introduced the heuristic structures that inform his seeking. Chapters 3 to 5 will consolidate this position. Chapters 6 and 7 will turn to the activities of more or less intelligent common sense. Chapter 8 will bring science and common sense together. Chapters 9 and 10 will tackle the problems of critical judgment and, incidentally, will explain to impatient readers what they have been about while we in the first eight chapters were attempting to communicate to them the necessary prior insights. Finally, chapters 11 to 17 will endeavor to grasp within a single view how the totality of views on knowledge, objectivity, and reality proceed from the empirical, intellectual, and rational consciousness of the concrete subject.

3

The Canons of
Empirical Method[a]

An examination of insight not only reveals the heuristic structures involved in empirical inquiry but also explains the rules or canons that govern the fruitful unfolding of the anticipations of intelligence.

Six canons will be presented, namely, (1) selection, (2) operations, (3) relevance, (4) parsimony, (5) complete explanation, (6) statistical residues. There is a canon of selection, for the empirical inquirer is confined to insights into the data of sensible experience. There is a canon of operations, for he aims at an accumulation of such insights, and the accumulation is reached, not in the mathematical circuit through insights, formulations, and symbolic images, but in the fuller circuit that adds observations, experiments, and practical applications. There is a canon of relevance, for pure science aims immediately at reaching the immanent intelligibility of data and leaves to applied science the categories of final, material, instrumental, and efficient causality. There is a canon of parsimony, for the empirical investigator may add to the data of experience only the laws verified in the data; in other words, he is not free to form hypotheses in the style of Descartes's vortices; but he must content himself with the laws and systems of laws exemplified by Newton's theory of universal gravitation and characterized generally by their verifiability. There is a canon of complete explanation: ultimately science must account for all data, and the account must be scientific; specifically, the old philosophic opinion that extension is a real and objective primary quality cannot dispense one from the task of determining empirically the correct geometry of experienced extensions and durations. Finally, there is a canon of statistical residues: though all data must be explained, one must not jump to the conclusion that all will be explained by laws of the classical type; there exist statistical residues, and their explanation is through statistical laws.

Before undertaking a fuller account of these canons, it may not be amiss to recall our viewpoint and purpose. The reader must not expect us to retail the history of the development of empirical method, nor look for descriptive accounts of what scientists do, nor anticipate an argument based on the authority of great names in science, nor hope for a summary of directives, precepts, and recipes to guide him in the practice of scientific investigation. Our aim still is an insight into the nature of insight. Our presumption is that empirical investigators are intelligent. Our supposition will be that the reader is already sufficiently familiar with scientific history and procedures,[b] authoritative pronouncements and practical directives. Our single purpose is to reveal the intelligible unity that underlies and accounts for the diverse and apparently disconnected rules of empirical method. Our concern is not what is done, or how it is done, but why. And our interest in seeking the reason why is not to extend methodology but to unify it, not to unify it that methodology may be improved but to unify it in the hope of exhibiting still more clearly and convincingly the fact and the nature of insight.

1   The Canon of Selection   [71–74]

First, there is a canon of selection.

If a correlation or hypothesis or law or probability expectation or theory or system pertains to empirical science, then (1) it involves sensible consequences, and (2) such consequences can be produced or at least observed.

Inversely, empirical method prescinds from all questions and answers that do not involve distinctive sensible consequences; and it discards all that involve such consequences logically yet fail to be confirmed by the results of observation or experiment.

The necessity of some canon of selection is obvious. Possible correlations, hypotheses, laws, probability expectations, theories, and systems form an indefinitely large group. They can be set up at will by the simple process of definition and postulation. But there is no reason why the empirical inquirer should investigate all the trees in this endless forest of possible thoughts, and so he needs some canon of selection.

The neatness of the canon of selection is no less clear. Not merely does it exclude at a stroke all the correlations and theories that cannot be relevant to empirical inquiry because they possess no sensible consequences. Also it operates progressively and cumulatively by discarding all the correlations and theories that possess sensible consequences by logical implication but have been tried and found wanting. Finally, the canon of selection has its positive aspect: besides ruling the irrelevant out of consideration, it directs the scientist's efforts to the issues that he can settle by the decisive evidence of observation and experiment.

However, the neatness and simplicity of the canon of selection can prove a trap for the unwary. If the canon demands sensible consequences, still it is satisfied when those consequences are so slight that only an expert equipped with elaborate apparatus can detect them. If the sensible consequences must be involved by the correlation or law or expectation, still grasping that implication may suppose a profound mastery of a field, a capacity to follow recondite and intricate mathematical operations, and the audacity necessary to form new primitive concepts and to follow long chains of abstract reasoning. Hence, besides the hodmen of science that gather the facts, there are also the architects of theories and systems. If no theory and no system pertains to empirical science unless it involves distinctive sensible consequences, still an appropriate division of labor may well result in some empirical inquirers devoting most of their time and energy to the development of concepts and postulates, theorems and corollaries. Finally, as the canon of selection is not to be misinterpreted as a mere charter for obtuseness, still less is it to be taken as a mere excuse for logical fallacy. Questions that do not satisfy the canon of selection do not arise within the confines of empirical science, but it does not follow immediately that they do not arise at all. Issues that cannot be settled by observation or experiment cannot be settled by empirical method, but it does not follow immediately that they cannot be settled at all.

1.1 *The Restriction to Sensible Data* [72]

Two further points call for consideration.

As we have formulated it, the canon of selection demands sensible consequences. But it may be urged that empirical method, at least in its essential features, should be applicable to the data of consciousness no less than to the data of sense. Now on this matter a great deal might be said, but the present is not the time for it. We have followed the common view that empirical science is concerned with sensibly verifiable laws and expectations. If it is true that essentially the same method could be applied to the data of consciousness, then respect for ordinary usage would require that a method which only in its essentials is the same be named a generalized empirical method.

1.2 What Are Sensible Data?   [73-74]

A more urgent issue is raised by the question, What are sensible data?

A datum of sense may be defined as the content of an act of seeing, hearing, touching, tasting, smelling. But the difficulty with that definition is that such contents do not occur in a cognitional vacuum. They emerge within a context that is determined by interests and preoccupations. Nor is this true merely of ordinary perceptions, of the milkmaid who laughed at Thales for falling into the well. It is more conspicuously true of the scientific Thales, so interested in the stars that he did not advert to the well. Accordingly, it would be a mistake to suppose that scientific observation is some mere passivity to sense impressions. It occurs within its own dynamic context, and the problem is to distinguish that cognitional orientation from the orientation of concrete living.

To be alive, then, is to be a more or less autonomous center of activity. It is to deal with a succession of changing situations; it is to do so promptly, efficaciously, economically; it is to attend continuously to the present, to learn perpetually from the past, to anticipate constantly the future. Thus the flow of sensations, as completed by memories and prolonged by imaginative acts of anticipation, becomes the flow of perceptions. It is of the latter, perceptual flow that we are conscious. It is only when the perceptual flow goes wrong that the mere sensation bursts into consciousness, as for example in the experience of trying to go down another step when already one has reached the floor.

Now what differentiates the perceptual flow in one man from that of another is found in the pattern of interests and objectives, desires and fears, that emphasize elements and aspects of sensible presentations, enrich them with the individual's associations and memories, and project them into future courses of possible fruitful activity. In some such fashion, it would seem, must be explained the differences in the perceptions of men and women, of people in different occupations, different climates, different stages in human history.

Hence to become a scientific observer is, not to put an end to perception, but to bring the raw materials of one's sensations within a new context. The interests and hopes, desires and fears, of ordinary living have to slip into a background. In their place the detached and disinterested exigences of inquiring intelligence have to enter and assume control. Memories will continue to enrich sensations, but they will be memories of scientific significance. Imagination will continue to prolong the present by anticipating the future, but anticipations with a practical moment will give way to anticipations that bear on a scientific issue. Just as the woodsman, the craftsman, the artist, the expert in any field acquires a spontaneous perceptiveness lacking in other men, so too does the scientific observer.

Still, there are differences in such developments, and to this fact the scientist alludes[c] when he insists that scientific observation is a matter of seeing just what there is to be seen, hearing exactly whatever sounds are sounded, and so forth. This claim cannot, I think, be taken literally, for the impartial and accurate observer, no less than anyone else, is under the dominance of a guiding orientation. Still, the claim does possess its elements of truth, for the guiding orientation of the scientist is the orientation of inquiring intelligence, the orientation that of its nature is a pure, detached, disinterested desire simply to know. For there is an intellectual desire, an eros of the mind. Without it there would arise no questioning, no inquiry, no wonder. Without it there would be no real meaning for such phrases as scientific disinterestedness, scientific detachment, scientific impartiality. Inasmuch as this intellectual drive is dominant, inasmuch as the reinforcing or inhibiting tendencies of other drives are successfully excluded, in that measure the scientific observer becomes an incarnation of inquiring intelligence, and his percepts move into coincidence with what are named the data of sense. Accordingly, it is not by sinking into some inert passivity but by positive effort and rigorous training that a man becomes a master of the difficult art of scientific observation.

2   The Canon of Operations   [74–76]

Secondly, there is a canon of operations.

Just as inquiry into the data of sense yields insights that are formulated in classical and statistical laws, so inversely the laws provide premises and rules for the guidance of human activity upon sensible objects.

Such activity in its turn brings about sensible change, to bring to light fresh data, raise new questions, stimulate further insights, and so generate the revision or confirmation of existing laws and in due course the discovery of new laws.

In the first instance, then, the canon of operations is a principle of cumulative expansion. Laws guide activities, which bring forth new laws, which guide further activities, and so forth indefinitely.

Secondly, the canon of operations is a principle of construction. Man knows best what man makes for himself, and so we began our study of insight by examining that elementary artifact, the cartwheel. But the development of science is followed by a technological expansion, by a vast increase of the things that man can make for himself and so can understand adequately because he has made them. Moreover, the more refined and resourceful technology becomes, the greater the frequency of the artificial synthesis of natural products. Thus nature itself becomes understood in the same fashion as man's own artifacts.

Thirdly, the canon of operations is a principle of analysis. Clearly, man can analyze the objects that he himself can construct. But it is no less true that he can also analyze objects which as yet he cannot manage to construct. For analysis is a mental construction, and where operational control fails, theoretical knowledge can step in to account for the failure of control, to identify the uncontrolled factors, to determine and measure their activity and influence, to discount their perturbing effect, and so to extrapolate to the law that would hold did they not interfere.

Fourthly, the canon of operations is a principle of cumulative verification. For laws guide operations successfully in the measure that they are correct. Hence, insofar as laws and their implications in a vast variety of situations are repeatedly found successful guides of operations, their initial verification is cumulatively confirmed.

Fifthly, the canon of operations provides a test of the impartiality and accuracy of observations. I do not mean that it makes intellectual detachment and disinterestedness superfluous, for, as is clear, the power of the totalitarian state can both corrupt the judge and pack the jury. But when a general conspiracy is absent, when ordinary good will can be presupposed, then the canon of operations sooner or later will exhibit on a grand scale in conspicuous failures even slight mistakes and oversights in observation.

Sixthly, the canon of operations is a principle of systematization. Insights yield simple laws, but simple laws are applicable only in pure cases. The law of a free fall holds in a vacuum. But operations do not occur in a vacuum. Hence one is driven to determine the law of air resistance and the laws of friction. Similarly, Boyle's law has to be complemented with Charles's and Gay-Lussac's, and all three need to be corrected by Van der Waals's formula. Thus the canon of operations is a perpetual recall from the abstract realm of laws to the complexity of the concrete, and so to the necessity of ever more laws. Nor is this all. A mere congeries of laws will not suffice. For if one is to operate upon the concrete, one must be able to employ at once several laws. To employ several laws at once, one must know the relations of each law to all the others. But to know many laws, not as a mere congeries of distinct empirical generalizations, but in the network of interrelations of each to all the others, is to reach a system.

Seventhly, the canon of operations is a source of higher viewpoints. Already attention has been drawn[1] to the difference between the circuit of the mathematician and the circuit of the empirical scientist. The mathematician mounts to higher viewpoints inasmuch as the symbolic representation of his previous terms and relations supplies the image in which insight grasps the rules of a more comprehensive systematization. But the empirical scientist advances to higher viewpoints, not solely by the construction of symbolic images, but more fundamentally by the expansiveness, the constructiveness, the analyses, the constant checking, and the systematizing tendencies of the canon of operations. In virtue of that canon, fresh data are ever being brought to light, to force upon scientific consciousness the inadequacies of existing hypotheses and theories, to provide the evidence for their revision, and in the limit, when minor corrections no longer are capable of meeting the issue, to demand the radical transformation of concepts and postulates that is named a higher viewpoint.

3　The Canon of Relevance　　　　　　　　　　　　　　　[76–78]

Thirdly, there is a canon of relevance.

The canon of selection and the canon of operations might be regarded as obverse and reverse of the same coin. Both are concerned with the elementary fact that the empirical inquirer is out to understand, not

1 Chapter 2, §1.2.

what he may imagine, but what he actually sees. The canon of relevance, on the other hand, aims at stating the type of understanding proper to empirical science.

Now it would be a mistake to say that the empirical scientist has no use whatever for final, material, instrumental, or efficient causes. Inasmuch as he praises the value and utility of science, he speaks of final causes. Inasmuch as he places that value and utility in the technological transformation of raw materials, he knows and acknowledges material and instrumental causes. Inasmuch as he accepts and acts upon the canon of operations, he is an efficient cause engaged in testing his knowledge by its consequences.

However, it is also clear that such types of causality lie not in the core but on the periphery of empirical science. They are the concern, not of pure but only of applied science. They have to do with the use to which science may be put rather than with the inner constituents of science itself.

The canon of relevance regards such inner constituents. It states that empirical inquiry primarily aims at reaching the intelligibility immanent in the immediate data of sense. Once that intelligibility is reached, one can go on to ask about the value or utility of such knowledge, about the tools that can be fashioned under its guidance, about the transformations of materials man can effect with such tools. But the first step, on which all others rest, is to grasp the intelligibility immanent in the immediate data of sense.

What precisely does the canon mean?

First, it presupposes that the same data can provide a starting point for different types of insight.

Secondly, it observes that questions about final, material, instrumental, and efficient causality automatically head one away from the data in hand. If I ask about the end of the cartwheel, I turn to carts and carting, and soon find myself involved in the economics of transportation. If I ask about the wood or iron of the cartwheel, the issue is shortly transposed to forestry and mining. If I ask about the wheelwright's tools, I am led on to discuss technology. If I inquire into the wheelwright himself, I am confronted with the sociology of the division of labor and with the psychology of the motivation of craftsmen.

Thirdly, it also observes that there is a further type of insight that arises immediately from the data. Such is the grasp that precedes and grounds the definition of the circle. Such was Galileo's insight formulated in the law of falling bodies. Such was Kepler's insight formulated in the laws of planetary motion. Such was Newton's insight formulated in the theory of universal gravitation. Such has been the point in the now well-established technique of measuring and correlating measurements. Such is the goal of the classical heuristic structure that seeks to determine some unknown function by working out the differential equations of which the unknown function will be a solution, and by imposing by postulation such principles as invariance and equivalence.

Fourthly, it notes that this intelligibility immanent in the immediate data of sense resides in the relations of things, not to our senses, but to one another. Thus, mechanics studies the relations of masses, not to our senses, but to one another; physics studies the relations of types of energy, not to our senses, but to one another; chemistry defines its elements, not by their relations to our senses, but by their places in the pattern of relationships named the periodic table; biology has become an explanatory science by viewing all living forms as related to one another in that complex and comprehensive fashion that is summarily denoted by the single word 'evolution.'

Fifthly, it notes that this intelligibility is hypothetical. It does not impose itself upon us, as does the multiplication table or the binomial[d] theorem. It announces itself as a possibility, as what could be the relevant correlation or function or law. Now the necessary must be, but the possible, though it can be, may in fact be or not be. Hence empirical science rests upon two distinct grounds: as insight grasping possibility, it is science; as verification selecting the possibilities that in fact are realized, it is empirical.

There is, then, an intelligibility immanent in the immediate data of sense; it resides in the relations of things, not to our senses, but to one another; it consists not in an absolute necessity, but in a realized possibility.

Ought there not to be introduced a technical term to denote this type of intelligibility? The trouble is that the appropriate technical term has long existed but also has long been misunderstood. For the intelligibility that is neither final nor material nor instrumental nor efficient causality is, of course, formal causality. But when one speaks of formal causality, some people are bound to assume that one means something connected with formal logic; others are bound to assume that one means merely the heuristic notion of the 'nature of ...,' the 'such as to ...,' the 'sort of thing that ...' If both of these misinterpretations are excluded, what we have called the intelligibility immanent in sensible data and residing in the relations of things to one another might be named more briefly formal causality, or rather, perhaps, a species of formal causality.

4   The Canon of Parsimony   [78–83]

Fourthly, there is a canon of parsimony.

It is at once obvious and difficult. It is obvious inasmuch as it forbids the empirical scientist to affirm what, as an empirical scientist, he does not know. It is difficult inasmuch as knowing exactly what one knows and what one does not know has been reputed, since the days of Socrates, a rare achievement. Nonetheless, some account of this fundamental canon must be attempted at once, even though its full meaning and implications can come to light only later.

On the previous analysis, then, empirical method involves four distinct elements, namely, (1) the observation of data, (2) insight into data, (3) the formulation of the insight or set of insights, and (4) the verification of the formulation.

Now the empirical investigator cannot be said to know what is not verified, and he cannot be said to be able to know the unverifiable. Because, then, verification is essential to his method, the canon of parsimony in its most elementary form excludes from scientific affirmation all statements that are unverified, and still more so all that are unverifiable. [e]

4.1   Classical Laws   [79–82]

Secondly, verification is of formulations, and formulations state (1) the relations of things to our senses, and (2) the relations of things to one another. It follows that formulations contain two types of terms which may be named, respectively, experiential conjugates and pure or explanatory conjugates.

Experiential conjugates are correlatives whose meaning is expressed, at least in the last analysis, by appealing to the content of some human experience.

Thus, 'colors' will be experiential conjugates when defined by appealing to visual experience; 'sounds' when defined by appealing to auditory experiences; 'heat' when defined by appealing to tactile experience; 'force' when defined by appealing to an experience of effort, resistance, or pressure.

It is clear enough that experiential conjugates satisfy the canon of parsimony. The fundamental set of such terms is verified, not only by scientists, but also by the secular experience of humanity. Scientists add further terms in virtue of their specific preoccupation, but as long as these terms satisfy the definition of the experiential conjugates, they will be in principle verifiable.

Pure or explanatory conjugates, on the other hand, are correlatives defined implicitly by empirically established correlations, functions, laws, theories, systems.

Thus, masses might be defined as the correlatives implicit in Newton's law of inverse squares. Then, there would be a pattern of relationships constituted by the verified equation; the pattern of relationships would fix the meaning of the pair of coefficients m_1, m_2; and the meaning so determined would be the meaning of the name 'mass.' In like manner, heat might be defined implicitly by the first law of thermodynamics, and the electric and magnetic field intensities E and H might be regarded as vector quantities defined by Maxwell's equations for the electromagnetic field.[2]

Now such pure conjugates satisfy the canon of parsimony. For the equations are or can be established empirically. And by definition pure conjugates mean no more than necessarily is implicit in the meaning of such verified equations.

There is, however, a difference between the mode of verifying pure conjugates and the mode of verifying experiential conjugates. For the experiential conjugate is either a content of experience, such as seeing red or touching extension, or else a correlative to such a content, for instance, red as seen or extension as touched, or finally, a derivative of such correlatives, as would be the red that could be seen or the extension that could be touched. On the other hand, the pure conjugate has its verification, not in contents of experience nor in their actual or potential correlatives, but only in combinations of such contents and correlatives. I see, for instance, a series of extensions, and alongside each I see a yardstick. From the series of combinations I obtain a series of measurements; from another series of combinations I obtain another series of measurements; from the correlation of the two series, together with the leap of insight, I am led to posit as probably realized some continuous function. Pure conjugates are the minimal correlatives im-

2 See on this point Lindsay and Margenau, *Foundations of Physics* 310.

plicit in such functions; and their verification finds its ground, not in experience as such, but only in the combination of combinations, etc., etc., etc., of experiences.

As the reader will have noted, the definitions of pure and experiential conjugates drop all mention of things whether related to one another or to our senses. The reason for this omission is that the notion of the 'thing'^{f} is highly ambiguous, and as yet we are unprepared to apply the canon of parsimony to it.^{3} However, though the notion of thing has been omitted, the point of the distinction between the relations of things to one another and to our senses remains. For in every experience one may distinguish between content and act, between the seen and the seeing, the heard and the hearing, the tasted and the tasting, and so forth. Let us represent, then, any series of experiences by the series of pairs AA', BB', CC', . . ., where the unprimed letters denote contents and primed letters denote the corresponding acts. Now correlations may be reached by combining the unprimed components A, B, C, . . ., or by combining the primed components A', B', C', . . ., or by combining both primed and unprimed components. In the first case, one will deal with the relations of contents to one another, and one will prescind from the corresponding acts; and in this fashion, without any mention of things, one deals with what hitherto has been named the relations of things to one another. In the second case, one will prescind from contents, and correlate acts to obtain a psychological or cognitional theory. In the third case, one will be employing experiential conjugates, and further information will be needed to settle whether one is working towards the goal of natural science or of cognitional theory.

Further, as this analysis reveals, there are only three basic alternatives. Either one's terms are experiential conjugates, or else they are pure conjugates based on combining contents alone, or finally they are a special case of pure conjugates based on combining acts alone. Still, theoretical analysis is one thing, and concrete practice is another. Thus, one would be inclined to say that physicists move easily and unconsciously back and forth between the use of experiential and pure conjugates. When they are called upon to define their terms, commonly they will suppose that definition comes at the beginning, and so offer definitions of experiential conjugates. On the other hand, methodologists and theorists of empirical science will be puzzled by the multiplicity of definitions

3 See chapter 8.

available in a mature science, and so they tend to disagree with one
another. Thus, E. Cassirer in his well-known *Substance and Function*[4]
emphasizes the relational and serial aspect of scientific terms. V. Lenzen
in his *Nature of Physical Theory*[5] emphasizes the genetic process that begins from experiential contents of force, heat, extension, duration, etc.,
to move through a process of redefinition towards terms implicitly defined by empirically established principles and laws. Finally, Lindsay and
Margenau in their *Foundations of Physics*, while they are more concerned
with ideas than concepts, may be said to exhibit a preference for terms
implicitly defined by equations.

For our purpose it would seem to be sufficient to reveal the materials
which scientists and theorists of science employ in different manners and
to show that these materials, despite incidental variations, satisfy the
canon of parsimony.

4.2 Statistical Laws   [82–83]

However, besides classical laws, there also are statistical laws; and since
the latter as well as the former are verifiable, it would seem that, besides
pure and experiential conjugates, one must also recognize events. When
the demonstrator in a lecture room propounds a law of nature and proceeds to illustrate it by an experiment, he does not inform his class that
the law will be refuted if the experiment does not work. On the contrary, he points out that the law retains its validity even if it happens that
the experiment is a failure. And members of the class may add interest
to the proceedings by determining the statistical law of the demonstrator's successes. The law of nature, then, is one thing. The event of its illustration is another. And such events are subject to laws of a different
type, which is named statistical.

What, then, is an event? The simplest answer is to say that it is a primitive notion too simple and obvious to be explained. Still, all primitive
notions, however simple and obvious, are related to other equally prim-

4 [Ernst Cassirer, *Substance and Function* and *Einstein's Theory of Relativity*,
   tr. William Curtis Swabey and Marie Collins Swabey (Chicago: London:
   The Open Court Publishing Company, 1923; New York: Dover Publica-
   tions, 1953).]
5 [Victor F. Lenzen, *The Nature of Physical Theory: A Study in Theory of
   Knowledge* (New York: J. Wiley & Sons; London: Chapman & Hall,
   1931).]

itive notions, and the set may be fixed by offering the data in which insight may grasp the relations.[g]

Let us begin, then, by formulating our answer. Events stand to conjugates as questions for reflection stand to questions for intelligence.

What is meant by a conjugate has been explained.

Moreover, knowledge of conjugates results from a process of inquiry, of asking questions; and the relevant questions all have the peculiarity that none of them can be answered appropriately by simply saying either yes or no. Thus, when one asks what is the 'nature of ...,' 'the sort of thing that ...,' the 'such as to ...,' the correlation to be specified, the indeterminate function to be determined, it is always meaningless to answer yes or no. One is called upon to state the nature, specify the correlation, determine the function, and that can be done only by achieving the insights that ground the formulation, first of experiential and later of pure conjugates.

But for every answer to a question for intelligence, there is a corresponding question for reflection; and all questions for reflection have the peculiarity that they can be answered appropriately simply by saying either yes or no. If I ask what a body is, I can also ask whether there are bodies. If I ask how bodies fall, I can also ask whether bodies fall. If I ask how bodies would fall in a vacuum, I can also ask whether any bodies ever fall in a vacuum. Generally, the enunciation of every law can be followed by the question for reflection that asks whether the law is verified, and the definition of every term can be followed by the question for reflection whether the defined exists or occurs. Inversely, whenever one asserts verification or existence or occurrence, one may be asked what is verified, what exists, what occurs.

Thus questions for intelligence and questions for reflection are universally concomitant and complementary.

There is a parallel concomitance and complementarity between conjugates and events. Without events, conjugates can be neither discovered nor verified. Without conjugates, events can be neither distinguished nor related. Such, I submit, is the elementary scheme in which insight can grasp what is meant by the otherwise puzzling name 'event.'

Now formulations that concern events satisfy the canon of parsimony. For probability expectations or statistical laws are formulations that answer the question for intelligence, How often? They concern events, for the frequency they assign is a frequency of events. Finally, the frequency assigned by a statistical law is verifiable; for the assigned frequency is an ideal frequency; it is distinct from the actual frequencies that can diverge from it in nonsystematic fashion; and it can be verified by appealing to those actual frequencies.

At this point our account of the canon of parsimony must be brought to a close. As the reader will have observed, attention has been confined to the positive aspects of the canon, to the experiential conjugates, the pure conjugates, and the events that are the terms of verifiable formulations. Whether things and their existence satisfy the canon is a further issue on which we have not touched. On the other hand, the negative or exclusive aspects of the canon, though they constitute its chief significance and utility, are too numerous to be mentioned and can best be dealt with incidentally when occasion arises.

5   The Canon of Complete Explanation   [84–86]

Fifthly, there is a canon of complete explanation.

The goal of empirical method is commonly stated to be the complete explanation of all phenomena or data.

In a sense, perseverance in the pursuit of this goal is assured by the canon of selection, especially when it is implemented by the canon of operations. Any particular investigator may overlook or ignore certain data. But his oversight or disregard will normally be corrected by other investigators substantiating their hypotheses and refuting those of their predecessors by appealing to hitherto neglected facts.

Nonetheless, a separate enunciation of this canon is relevant particularly at the present time, when a mistaken twist given to scientific method at the Renaissance finally is being overcome.

Where we distinguished between experiential and pure conjugates, Galileo distinguished between secondary and primary qualities. Secondary qualities were merely subjective appearances that arise in an animal's senses as a result of the action of other, primary qualities; such appearances were illustrated by color as seen, sounds as heard, heat as felt, tickling as experienced, and the like. Primary qualities, on the other hand, were the mathematical dimensions of the real and objective, of matter in motion. Hence, while we would place scientific progress in the movement from experiential to pure conjugates, Galileo placed it in the reduction of the merely apparent secondary qualities to their real and objective source in primary qualities.

The crucial difference between the two positions regards space and

time. For Galileo they were primary qualities, for there would be extension and duration if there were matter and motion, whether or not any
animals with their sensitive experiences existed. For us, on the other
hand, there is to be drawn the same distinction between extension and
duration as experiential and as pure conjugates as there is to be drawn
between the two formulations of colors or sound or heat or electric
phenomena.

As experiential conjugates, extensions and durations are defined as
correlatives to certain familiar elements within our experience.

As pure conjugates, extension and duration are defined implicitly by
the postulate that the principles and laws of physics are invariant under
inertial or, generally, under continuous transformations.

Thus, on our analysis, the space-time of relativity stands to the extensions and durations of experience in exactly the same relations as wavelengths of light stand to experiences of color, as longitudinal waves in air
stand to experience of sound, as the type of energy defined by the first
law of thermodynamics stands to experiences of heat, etc.

Moreover, in our analysis, this conclusion rests upon the canon of
complete explanation. All data are to be explained. The explanation of
data consists in a process from experiential conjugates towards pure
conjugates. Therefore, from extensions and durations as experienced,
there must be a process to extensions and durations as implicitly defined
by empirically established laws.

Further, as extension and duration, so also local movement has a
preliminary definition in terms of experiential conjugates and an explanatory definition in terms of pure conjugates. It was obvious and ex-
cusable for Galileo and Kepler and Newton to conceive local movement
in the two steps of determining a path or trajectory and then correlating points on the path with instants of time. After all, when a man
crosses the street, we see at once the whole distance that he traverses,
but we apprehend the duration of his movement as concomitant with
the duration of our watching. Nonetheless, this account of local movement can be no more than preliminary, for throughout it is in terms of
movement as related to us, as in terms of experiential conjugates. What
movement is, when movements are defined in terms of their relations
to one another, is another question. The answer to it will depend upon
the answer that determines extensions and durations as pure conjugates; and so it is that relativity mechanics conceives a velocity, not as
a function of three dimensions with time as a parameter, but as a func-

tion of four dimensions, of which three are spatial and the fourth temporal.

If we add the canon of parsimony to the canon of complete explanation, more fundamental objections to the Galilean theory of scientific explanation come to light.

Both experiential and pure conjugates are verifiable, and insofar as either are verified, they possess an equal claim upon reasonable affirmation. It follows that Galileo's repudiation of secondary qualities as mere appearance is a rejection of the verifiable as mere appearance.

Inversely, Galileo did not base his affirmation of the reality and objectivity of primary qualities upon a claim that these qualities, as he conceived them, were verifiable or verified. Accordingly, his affirmation was extrascientific. It did not satisfy the canon of parsimony; and today, if anyone were to try to bring the Galilean position into line with that canon, first of all he would have to settle an account with Einstein, who has made various proposals regarding the space-time of physics and has some grounds for supposing his line of thought verifiable and, to some extent, verified.

6   The Canon of Statistical Residues   [86–102]

Sixthly, there is a canon of statistical residues. It presupposes the existence of inquiry of the classical type, and from that premise it concludes to the existence of residues that call for statistical inquiry.

6.1 The General Argument   [86–87]

The basic distinction is between abstract system and particular cases. Both are objects of insight. But the particular case is the typical instance, presented by sense or imagination and understood by insight into the presentation. In contrast, the abstract system is neither sensible nor imaginable; it is a conceptual object constituted by terms and relations that, at least in the last resort, are defined implicitly.

Particular cases are relevant both to the genesis and to the application of abstract system. For the formulation of system comes at the end of a cumulative series of insights into different particular cases. Again, once abstract system is formulated, it can be applied to concrete situations only insofar as there occur insights into the situations as sensibly given; for without such insights there cannot be selected the relevant laws of abstract system, there cannot be determined the mode in which the laws combine in the concrete situation, and there cannot be substituted numerical values for the variables and undetermined constants of the general formulae.

Now let us suppose full knowledge of all classical principles and laws. Then we suppose full knowledge of abstract system: for principles and laws are relations; such relations necessarily involve the terms that they define implicitly; and abstract system consists in terms implicitly defined by the relations expressed in verified principles and laws.

However, if this full knowledge of abstract system is to be applied to the concrete universe, there will be needed a manifold of insights into particular cases. For, as was noted above, abstract system is applied to concrete situations only inasmuch[h] as insight into the situations selects the relevant laws, determines the mode of their combination, and substitutes numerical values for the variables and undetermined constants of the laws.

Still, the manifold of particular cases is enormous, and so there arises the question whether it can be cast into some ordered sequence. If it can, then knowledge of the sequence and of a few strategically chosen particular cases would suffice to transform mastery of abstract system into a scientific understanding of the universe. But if it cannot, if the manifold of particular cases does not form any kind of ordered sequence, then abstract system can be applied only to a limited range of particular cases, and new methods must be found if we are to reach an understanding of the concrete universe as a whole.

In fact, it can be shown that there do exist recurrent particular cases. For example, our planetary system is periodic; it is an individual set of masses; most of them are visible; and a relatively small number of concrete insights makes it possible to determine an indefinite sequence of particular cases.

On the other hand, while such schemes of recurrence are many not only in number but also in kind, still each presupposes materials in a suitable constellation that the scheme did not bring about, and each survives only as long as extraneous disrupting factors do not intervene. The periodicity of the planetary system does not account for its origin and cannot guarantee its survival.

Moreover, there does not seem to exist any universal scheme that controls the emergence and survival of the schemes that we know. Accordingly, in the last analysis we are driven to accept the second alternative. There does not exist a single ordered sequence that embraces the totality of particular cases through which abstract system might be applied to the concrete universe. In other words, though all events are linked to one another by law, still the laws reveal only the abstract component in concrete relations; the further concrete component, though mastered by insight into particular cases, is involved in the empirical residue from which systematizing intelligence abstracts; it does not admit general treatment along classical lines; it is a residue, left over after classical method has been applied, and it calls for the implementation of statistical method.

Such is the general argument, and a more detailed account of its meaning now has to be attempted.

6.2 The Notion of Abstraction [87–89]

A first task is to clarify the notion of abstraction. On a simple and common view, the abstract is an impoverished replica of the concrete. 'Red' means what is common to all instances of 'red.' 'Man' means what is common to all instances of 'man.' That is all there is to it.

Now with this view of abstraction, one can admit classical laws, and one can admit statistical laws, but one will be at a loss to determine some coherent manner in which both classical and statistical laws can be acknowledged. This may be shown as follows.

Let $A, B, C, \ldots$ denote sensible data, and let $a, a', a'', \ldots b, b', b'', \ldots c, c', c'', \ldots$ denote the totality of their impoverished replicas. Then there is no aspect of sensible data without its impoverished replica; inversely, the totality of sensible data can be constructed out of the totality of impoverished replicas.

Hence, if one admits some classical laws, one admits that some impoverished replicas are related systematically. Moreover, if one admits the classical laws as objective, there must be systematic relations not only between the impoverished replicas but also between the concrete aspects of sensible data to which they correspond. It follows that the classical laws can be objective only if they hold in the concrete. Finally, it will be only by denying the canon of complete explanation of all data that one can admit systematic relations between some impoverished replicas and deny systematic relations between others. It will follow that the only laws will be classical laws, and that statistical laws cannot be more than a cloak for ignorance.

Inversely, if one admits some statistical laws, then one denies systematic relations between some impoverished replicas. If the statistical laws are objective, there cannot be systematic relations between the corresponding aspects of sensible data. At least in those cases, classical laws are excluded. Moreover, to show that classical laws are not merely the macroscopic illusion resulting from a multitude of microscopic random occurrences, a correct theory of the abstract is needed; and in the present hypothesis, that correct theory is lacking.

What is, then, the correct theory?

So far from being a mere impoverishment of the data of sense, abstraction in all its essential moments is enriching. Its first moment is an enriching anticipation of an intelligibility to be added to sensible presentations: there is something to be known by insight. Its second moment is the erection of heuristic structures and the attainment of insight, to reveal in the data what is variously named as the significant, the relevant, the important, the essential, the idea, the form. Its third moment is the formulation of the intelligibility that insight has revealed. Only in this third moment does there appear the negative aspect of abstraction, namely, the omission of the insignificant, the irrelevant, the negligible, the incidental, the merely empirical residue. Moreover, this omission is neither absolute nor definitive. For the empirical residue possesses the universal property of being what intelligence abstracts from. Such a universal property provides the basis for a second set of heuristic procedures that take their stand on the simple premise that the nonsystematic cannot be systematized.

Now our whole effort has been to draw attention to the fact of insight, to the enriching moments on which abstraction follows. Accordingly, it is in this sense that we affirm classical laws to be abstract.[i] So far from being an impoverishment of sensible data, abstraction is an enrichment that goes beyond them. Because abstraction goes beyond the sensible field, the frontiers of the abstract are not coterminous with the frontiers of the experienced. Hence full and exact knowledge of the systems to be reached by abstraction by no means denies the existence of an empirical residue that is nonsystematic. Again, just as in abstraction we prescind from the empirical residue, so when we come to the concrete applications of abstract principles and laws, we are forced to take into account the nonsystematic conditions under which the systematic has its concrete realization.

6.3 The Abstractness of Classical Laws   [89–91]

In the second place, it may be well to recall that classical laws are ab-

stract (1) in their heuristic anticipation, (2) in the experimental techniques of their discovery, (3) in their formulation, and (4) in their verification.

They are abstract in their heuristic anticipation. For that anticipation
rests on the detached and disinterested drive of inquiry, and it consists
in a pure desire to understand. Hence the canon of relevance demands
that one seek the immanent intelligibility of the data; the canon of parsimony demands that one add to the data no more than the formulation
of what is grasped by understanding and verified; and the canon of
complete explanation demands that this parsimonious addition of intelligibility be effected for all data. Moreover, this anticipated enrichment
is seen to be universal: the nature to be known will be the same for all
data that are not significantly different, and the correlation to be specified is reached only if it holds for all parallel instances.

Secondly, classical laws are abstract in the experimental techniques of
their discovery. For the experimenter makes no pretence to deal with
concrete situations in their native complexity; on the contrary, he aims
overtly at reducing that complexity to a minimum, and so he does all he
can to bring the concrete into some approximation to an ideal, typical,
definable conjunction of materials and agents. Accordingly, as he begins
with an effort to secure materials from which all impurities have been
removed, so he ends with an argument that rests on their theoretical
definitions. As he begins by requiring instruments constructed in accord
with accurate specifications, so he ends by interpreting their performance on the basis of their ideal, often schematic, structure. He
measures, but he does so many times, and his accepted result is just the
probable mean of actual results. He reaches a conclusion with which
others agree, but the agreement makes allowance for the intrusion of
extraneous factors, and it acknowledges no more than a limited number
of significant decimal places. At every turn it seems apparent that the
concern of experiment is to determine, not the particular observable
qualities of the particular materials with which one deals, but a theoretical correlation between definable and abstract entities.

Thirdly, classical laws are abstract in their formulation. As laws, they
are correlations linking correlatives, and the correlatives are never the
unique data of some particular time and place. Indeed, they are not
even generalized data, but generalized combinations of combinations of
combinations of data. Nor may one suppose that the data taken in these
serial combinations uniquely determine what the law must be. For the

discontinuous set of observations represented, say, by points on a graph can be satisfied by any number of laws, of which the scientist chooses the one that, all things considered, he reputes to be the simplest. Enriching abstraction is still at work.

Fourthly, classical laws are abstract in their verification. For verification is reached, not by appealing to this or that isolated instance, but by securing as large and various a range of instances as both direct and indirect procedures make possible. It follows that what is verified is, not this or that particular proposition, but the general, abstract formulation that alone admits the large and various range of applications. Again, to repeat the argument from another viewpoint, what is verified is what can be refuted or revised. What can be refuted or revised is the general, abstract formulation. And so what is verified is the general, abstract formulation.

6.4 Systematic Unification and Imaginative Synthesis   [91–93]

In the third place, an objection must be met. Taken singly, classical laws are abstract. But what is true of single laws need not be true of the totality of laws. The single laws are abstract because they do not cover the totality of aspects of the data. But the totality of laws would cover that totality of aspects, and so the totality would be not abstract but concrete.

Now this objection may be merely a reversion to the assumption that abstraction yields merely an impoverished replica of sensible data. In that case, it has been met already. For the totality of aspects of data explained by the totality of classical laws will not include the aspects that we have named an empirical residue.[6] Even when all classical laws are known, individuality and continuity, particular place and particular time will not be explained but abstracted from.

However, the objection may be advanced by those that grant abstraction to be not impoverishing but enriching. They will point out that the canon of operations forces empirical inquiry to go beyond the mere aggregation of isolated laws to the development of systems. It is not enough to know the law of falling bodies, the law of air resistance, the law of friction. One also has to know how to apply these laws simultaneously if one is to solve practical problems. Hence the discovery of laws has to be accompanied by the discovery of correlations between laws,

6 See chapter 1, §5.

and no less of correlations between the correlations. There exists, then, a movement towards the systematic unification of classical laws, and as this unification is prompted by concrete problems, one may expect that, when all laws are known exactly and completely, there also will be known a systematic unification commensurate with world process in its concrete historical unfolding.

This consideration is, I think, impressive. But strangely enough, world process in its concrete historical unfolding rather conspicuously makes a large and generous use of the statistical techniques of large numbers and long intervals of time; it exhibits not a rigid but a fluid stability; it brings forth novelty and development; it makes false starts and suffers breakdowns. It would seem, then, that an understanding of the concrete unfolding of world process[j] will not be based exclusively on classical laws, however exactly and completely known, but in a fundamental manner will appeal to statistical laws.

Accordingly, the facts force us to a closer scrutiny of the argument from the systematic unification of laws, and the scrutiny brings to light an underlying ambiguity. It is one thing to attain a systematic unification; it is another to reach an imaginative synthesis. Thus, Riemannian geometry is a systematic unification, for it provides a single set of principles and techniques for dealing with n-dimensional manifolds of various curvatures. But Riemannian geometry is not an imaginative synthesis, for we cannot imagine more than three dimensions, and we normally imagine only flat surfaces. Again, Ptolemy and Copernicus possessed imaginative syntheses of celestial movements; but the laws of those movements were discovered by Galileo and Kepler, and the systematic unification of the laws was the achievement of Newtonian mechanics. To offer another example, nineteenth-century physicists made a notable series of efforts to construct an imaginable model of the ether.[7] But

7   See Edmund Whittaker, *A History of the Theories of Aether and Electricity* (Dublin: Dublin University Press; London: Longmans, 1911). [A new edition appeared in two volumes in 1953 (London, New York: Nelson), adding an account of twentieth-century theories and featuring a rewriting of the previously published material. This revised and augmented edition is reprinted by Tomash Publishers for American Institute of Physics, as part of a series, *The History of Modern Physics, 1800–1950*. Lonergan seems to have the wrong date (1911) for the original publication; indications are that the first edition was published in 1910. Lonergan's reference is to what now is the first volume of this work, and perhaps specifically to 'Models of Aether,' pp. 279–303.]

the fruit of their labors was a systematic set of equations verifiable in pointer readings. Today one may prefer Einstein, who clings to determinist views, or one may join the majority, who regard quantum mechanics as satisfactory. But neither alternative offers an imaginative synthesis. For Einstein offers a set of differential equations for a four-dimensional, curved manifold, and quantum mechanics, as it originated by giving up the attempt to carry through N. Bohr's model of the atom, so now it refuses to portray the objective process that leads up to observables.

There is, then, a difference between systematic unification and imaginative synthesis. Systematic unification is effected in the logical or conceptual order. It is attained when the totality of laws is reduced to minimum sets of defined terms and postulates, so that any law can be related to any other, and any aggregate of laws can be intelligibly combined and simultaneously employed. On the other hand, an imaginative synthesis is secured when images, informed by insight, are altered in accord with known laws. In this fashion one may imagine the sun, the planets, and their satellites in appropriate collocations, and understand their imagined movements in accord with mechanical laws. Clearly, such imaginative synthesis goes beyond the abstract content of the laws and supposes that certain bodies exist in certain relative positions with velocities less than the velocity of escape. One has passed from the tasks of pure science; one has introduced the suppositions and the facts that pertain to applied science. Now the ultimate attainment of a systematic unification of classical laws will not include particular matters of fact, and so that ultimate attainment cannot include an imaginative synthesis.

As systematic unification does not include imaginative synthesis, so it does not even guarantee its possibility. It is true enough that images are necessary for the emergence of insights, but the images may be not representative but symbolic, not pictures of the visible universe but mathematical notations on pieces of paper. Even if one supposed that, just as the image of the cartwheel approximates the definition of the circle, so some representative image approximated every classical law, nonetheless it would not follow that the aggregate of approximate images might somehow coalesce into a composite picture that approximated to the systematic unification of all laws.

The objection, then, breaks down on two points. In itself, it is inconclusive. Knowledge of all classical laws would be an understanding of the concrete only if it included a vast imaginative synthesis. It is true that empirical inquiry heads for a systematic unification of its laws. But there is no evidence that such a systematic unification ensures the possibility of any imaginative synthesis. Moreover, if the totality of classical laws provided an understanding of the concrete, statistical laws would be superfluous. But the conspicuous use of statistical techniques in world process shows that statistical laws are not superfluous in an understanding of our universe.

6.5 The Existence of Statistical Residues [93–97]

In the fourth place, an attempt must be made to indicate more precisely both the indeterminacy of abstract classical laws and the nature of the consequent statistical residues. Hence it will be argued (1) that classical laws hold in concrete instances only inasmuch as conditions are fulfilled, (2) that the conditions to be fulfilled form diverging series, and (3) that in the general case the patterns of such diverging series are a nonsystematic aggregate.

6.5.1 Classical Laws Conditional [93–94]

First, it is possible to apply classical laws to concrete situations and thereby reach conditioned predictions.

For example, if two motorcars are headed for the same spot, if their distances from the spot and their speeds are equal, then they will collide, provided they do not alter their directions or speeds, and provided that no obstacles force them to do so.

Similarly, in the general case, an event Z can be concluded from prior circumstances Y, provided some $P, Q, R, \ldots$ continue to occur and provided some $U, V, W, \ldots$ do not intervene.

Secondly, the necessity of positing conditions is universal. For the link between the antecedent circumstances and the consequent event rests on abstract classical laws. Just as the discovery of such laws rests on an experimental exclusion of extraneous factors, just as their verification stands despite contrary instances in which extraneous factors are not excluded, so when one returns from the abstract to concrete applications, the possible existence of extraneous factors has to be taken into account.

Thirdly, when the deduced or predicted event is fully determinate, then the conditions must be fulfilled right up to the occurrence of the event.

To return to the example of the two motorcars, it is one thing to infer or predict a collision, and it is quite another to infer or predict that a first contact will be between a very small area P on one car and a similar very small area Q on the other. If the cars are traveling at sixty miles an hour, and at the present instant they are just one inch apart, one might say that a collision is inevitable. No matter what happens in the remaining fraction of a second, there will be some impact. But under the same assumptions one cannot offer to drop all provisos and yet predict a first contact between specified small areas. For in the last fraction of a second there could occur some alteration of the speed or direction or swaying of either car; and that alteration would upset the prediction.

6.5.2 The Diverging Series of Conditions   [94–95]

Next, in the general case, conditions form a diverging series.

For in the general case, any event Z is deducible from antecedent circumstances Y, provided some P, Q, R, . . . continue to occur, and provided some U, V, W, . . . do not intervene.

It follows that the occurrence of the P, Q, R, . . . and the nonoccurrence of the U, V, W, . . . are similarly deducible.

It follows further that the occurrence of, say, P is conditioned by the occurrences A, B, C, . . . and the nonoccurrences G, H, I, . . . Similarly, there will be series of positive and negative conditions for Q, R, . . . and for U, V, W, . . . Similarly, each term in these series will have its series of positive and negative conditions, and so forth.

Such, then, is the diverging series of conditions. Any event Z will occur on the fulfilment of a set of conditions. Each condition in the set will be fulfilled on the fulfilment of its additional set of conditions. Since there are no unconditioned events, there are no unconditioned fulfilments of conditions. Since there are no unconditioned fulfilments of conditions, the diverging series has as many removes as one cares to explore. Finally, since each event ordinarily has several conditions, the series ordinarily diverges.

Certain further properties of the diverging series of conditions may be noted immediately.

Just as the series diverges when one goes back from an event Z to its antecedents, so it converges when one advances from the antecedents to the event. Accordingly, if one were to suppose that the concrete pattern of the diverging series had been worked out to some nth remove, and if one ascertained the fulfilment of all the conditions at that remove, then one's enormous labor would yield no more than the deduction of the event Z and the intervening occurrences and nonoccurrences.[k] So far from promising the deduction of all world situations from a single situation, this structure offers no more than the deduction of a converging series of events from as large a set of initial observations as one pleases.

Moreover, the conditions of any event Z, at any nth remove, are scattered in space and time. They are scattered in space, inasmuch as the occurrences and nonoccurrences conditioning the event Z, whether directly or indirectly, proximately or remotely, may be found in any direction and at any distance from the event Z. They are scattered in time, inasmuch as the influence from the condition to the conditioned is propagated with a finite velocity, and in different cases traverses either equal distances with unequal speeds or unequal distances with equal speeds.[l] Evidently, this scattering of the conditions makes it imperative to know beforehand the aggregate of concrete patterns of diverging series of conditions for events of all kinds; otherwise, one would not know which observations to make, and it would be only by luck that one hit upon those that were relevant.[m]

6.5.3 The Nonsystematic Aggregate of Diverging Series[n] [96–97]

It was shown in chapter 2 that coincidental aggregates can be investigated with scientific generality only by statistical methods. But statistical methods reveal states and probabilities. They tell us nothing about concrete patterns of diverging series of conditions for particular determinate events. It follows that if such concrete patterns are to be investigated with scientific generality then they must not be coincidental aggregates.

However, in the general case, concrete patterns of diverging series of conditions are coincidental aggregates. For any event, say Z, occurs if positive conditions P, Q, R, . . . occur and negative conditions U, V, W, . . . do not occur. What is true of Z is true of all its conditions. Nor in the general case can anything beyond the fulfilment of these conditions be required. On the other hand, to demand that the diverging series of conditions be not a coincidental aggregate is to add to the conditions necessary for the occurrence of Z; and to introduce such an addition is to depart from the general case and set up a particular case.

Further, even when particular cases exist, they cannot be explained completely along classical lines. For there exists a particular case if there exists an orderly sequence of sets of events such that, other things being equal, the events P_i result from the events P_{i-1} for all positive integral values of i from 2 to n,° where either n is as great a positive integer as one cares to assign or else there is a final set of events P_n that is similar in all respects to an initial set P_1. Clearly, the diverging series of conditions is brought to heel by any such scheme of perpetual continuity or of perpetual recurrence. Still, such a scheme holds only under the proviso that other things are equal, and the introduction of defensive mechanisms cannot eliminate the proviso since the mechanisms themselves will depend on classical laws. Moreover, as schemes cannot guarantee their own survival, so they cannot explain their own origin. For if there is a first instance of a set of events P_i, then there is no prior instance in the sequence or circle to account for the first instance; and if there is no first instance, then the origin of the sequence or circle, so far from being explained, is merely denied.

Still, it may be urged that perhaps world process as a whole is systematic, and so perhaps the total concrete pattern of diverging series of conditions is in fact orderly. But in the first place, this is merely a hypothesis. In the second place, it is an extremely doubtful hypothesis, for world process as a whole seems marked by the characteristically statistical devices of large numbers and long intervals of time. Finally, while this doubtful hypothesis implies that statistical method is ultimately mistaken, there is no difficulty in framing opposite hypotheses of equal value which, if true, would imply that ultimately classical method is mistaken.

In the present subsection (§ 6.5) we set out to indicate an exact meaning for both the indeterminacy of classical laws and the consequent canon of statistical residues. It has been argued that classical laws are indeterminate because they are abstract and so can become determinate premises for the deduction of determinate events only if sets of positive and negative conditions are fulfilled. Moreover, from this indeterminacy of the abstract there follows a canon of statistical residues, because in the general case such sets of conditions are coincidental aggregates, and coincidental aggregates can be investigated with scientific generality only by statistical methods.

In conclusion, two points may be noted. The root fallacy in determinist opposition to the objectivity of statistical knowledge is an oversight of insight. The determinist begins by overlooking the fact that a concrete inference from classical laws supposes an insight that mediates between the abstract laws and the concrete situation; and once that oversight occurs there is precluded a discovery of the difference between systematic processes and coincidental aggregates.

Secondly, our analysis prescinds from all questions regarding the intellectual capacity of Laplace's demon and other nonhuman beings. Clearly, such issues have no bearing on the nature of empirical science, or indeed of human understanding. Finally, this restriction seems contained in our definition of an orderly sequence; for a sequence is orderly if it can be mastered by an insight that can be expressed in general terms, and, it would seem, only human insights can be so expressed.

6.6 The General Character of Statistical Theories   [97–100]

The statistical heuristic structure worked out in chapter 2 (§ 4.4) may now be determined more fully in the light of the six canons of empirical method.

6.6.1 Events   [97]

First, then, statistical theories deal with events. For it is the event, the occurrence, the actual happening that cannot be settled by classical laws without the introduction of a concrete, nonsystematic manifold of further determinations.

6.6.2 Not Processes   [98]

Secondly, statistical theories will not analyze processes. For the processes that lead up to events fall under the patterns of diverging series of conditions. Such patterns form a nonsystematic aggregate, and the nonsystematic as such is not open to investigation.

6.6.3ᵖ Observable Events   [98]

The distinction between process and events raises a further question. For a process seems to be simply a continuum of events. On what principle, then, are some events in the continuum selected by a statistical theory? And on what ground are the rest of the events placed beyond the field of statistical knowledge?

Clearly, the selection is effected by the possibility of observation, and in this respect there is no difference between classical and statistical theory. A continuum of accurate measurements just cannot be achieved.

The difference arises in the meaning that may be assigned to continuous functions. Because classical theory can envisage concrete process, its continuous functions can be taken to refer to a continuum of events. Because statistical theory, insofar as we provide a meaning for it, prescinds from process, its continuous functions express merely the continuity of the ideal norm from which any observable events diverge nonsystematically.

6.6.4 Foundations [98]

The foregoing distinction between classical and statistical theories reaches back into the obscure region named foundations. A set of logical or mathematical premises acquires actual objective reference only through a philosophy or a verified scientific theory.[8] If the scientific theory is classical, the reference may be to concrete process. But if the scientific theory is statistical, then the acquired objective reference can be only to isolated events and their probabilities. Note, however, in qualification, that 'classical' for us is stripped of its associations with empiricist philosophy, while 'probability' stands within an open heuristic structure and receives its properties from the developing structure.

6.6.5 Use of Classical Concepts [98–99]

Scientifically significant statistical theory will define events by introducing the pure conjugates of classical laws.

For events must be defined if they are to be assigned any frequency but unity. In other words, only the defined type of event is not occurring always and everywhere.

The definition of events must be sought in conjugates. For the event corresponds to the yes in answer to a question for reflection, and the question for reflection has its content from an answer to a question for intelligence. By the canon of parsimony, verifiable answers to questions for intelligence are in terms of experiential or of pure conjugates.

But statistical investigations in terms of experiential conjugates contain no promise of scientific significance. For experience is within the reach

8 See below, chapter 10, §§ 7–8 [pp. 329–39].

of everyone, but a significant contribution to science rests upon knowledge of previous achievement. Such knowledge in one way or another involves pure conjugates, and so pure conjugates will be used in defining the events of scientifically significant statistical laws. Hence, quantum mechanics defines its observables by appealing to classical physics, which developed the notions of Cartesian coordinate, linear and angular momentum, energy, and so forth.

6.6.6 Images and Parsimony   [99]

The canon of parsimony excludes any problem concerning the picture of objects too small to be sensed. For the image as image can be verified only by the occurrence of the corresponding sensation. Thus, the visual image of a small ball can be verified only by seeing a small ball, and the visual image of a wave can be verified only by seeing a wave. When the sensations neither occur nor can occur, all that can be verified are certain equations and the terms implicitly defined by such equations.

It is to be noted that this conclusion rests on a divergence from Galilean assumptions. For on those assumptions, secondary qualities such as color, sound, heat, and the like are merely apparent; they are to be attributed not to objects but to our subjectivity. On the other hand, the mathematical dimensions of matter in motion are constitutive of the real and objective, so that to deny them[q] is to eliminate the object. Hence, on the Galilean view, electrons cannot be red or green or blue, hard or soft, hot or cold, but they must have dimensions either of little balls or of waves or of some other compatible set of primary qualities.

6.6.7 A Principle of Uncertainty   [99–100]

An axiomatic structure for statistical laws will involve an uncertainty principle.

For the concrete includes a nonsystematic component, and so the concrete cannot be deduced in its full determinacy from any set of systematic premises.

But an axiomatic structure is a set of systematic premises. Its implications reach to the concrete, for they regard statistical laws that deal with events, and events are always fully concrete.[r]

Therefore, the axiomatic structure for statistical laws must have some means of cutting short its implications before the full determinations of the concrete are reached.⁵ And any such means falls under the general case of an uncertainty principle.

On this analysis,⁶ then, indeterminacy is a general characteristic of statistical investigations. So, prior to the measured uncertainty of Heisenberg's equation, there was the unmeasured uncertainty inherent in classical statistics, in which predictions were unique but nonetheless were not expected to be correct in every case.⁹

Nor is this generality surprising. It runs parallel to the possibility of deducing Heisenberg's principle from a general axiomatic structure. It follows from the fact that the deduction of conclusions supposes systematic relations, so that if some relations are not systematic, the field of possible conclusions must be restricted.

6.7 Indeterminacy and the Nonsystematic   [100–102]

The foregoing account of the general character of statistical investigations must not be mistaken for a description of quantum mechanics. The canon of statistical residues is methodological. Its generality is not that of recent physics but of statistical method. Its basis lies, not in the conclusions of subatomic investigation, but in the analysis of the cognitional process that begins from data and inquiry, proceeds through insight and formulation, and recommences when experiments yield significantly new data. Its technical terms are derived, not from the usage that scientists have found suitable for their purposes, but from the exigences of a quite different study. Accordingly, as already we have had occasion to insist, only a further critical and creative effort can bring our conclusions into contact with the diverse interpretations of the results of contemporary physics.

For the canon of statistical residues involves three elements, and all three can be stated only in cognitional terms. The first element is the indeterminacy of the abstract: classical laws can be applied to concrete situations only by adding further determinations derived from the situations. The second element is the nonsystematic character of the further determinations. It does not mean that the further determinations are not related to one another by law; it means that the law is only an abstract part in a concrete relation of determinate numbers, magnitudes, relative positions, etc. It does not mean that these concrete relations cannot be mastered by insight into relevant presentations; it means that the con-

9 See Lindsay and Margenau, *Foundations of Physics* 398.

crete insight has a fuller object than the abstract formulation. It does not mean that no attempt can be made at a conceptual account of the concrete relations; it means that such a conceptual account bogs down in an unmanageable infinity of cases. It does not mean that concrete relations are never recurrent or that accurate prediction is never possible; it means that schemes of recurrence do not fall under some overarching scheme, that they are merely instances in which law triumphs over the empirical residue, that such triumphs of law do not occur in accord with some further classical law. The third element, finally, is the inverse insight: if the intelligibility of abstract system is not to be had, still generality is not to be renounced; for there is the generality of the ideal frequency of events, and from such an ideal frequency the nonsystematic cannot diverge in any systematic fashion.

Not only is the canon of statistical residues methodological but also it stands in a context of other canons that involve a transposition of current issues. A canon of relevance has fixed attention on what insight adds to data. A canon of parsimony has restricted scientific affirmation to defined types of verifiable propositions. A canon of complete explanation has placed space and time in much the same position as sensible qualities. Within that context there is no need to attempt to exorcize the images of the older determinists with the images of the new indeterminists. It is true enough that data are hazy, that measurements are not perfectly accurate, that measuring can distort the measured object. But those truths miss the methodological point. One can affirm them yet continue to misconceive classical laws. The law of falling bodies is not a statement of what would happen in a perfect vacuum; it is the statement of an element in an abstract system, and the complete system can be applied to any particular case. Again, Einstein's differential equations are not statements about positions and velocities in defiance of Heisenberg's principle; they are statements of the abstractness and so invariance of classical laws. The proper answer to the old determinism is an affirmation, not of an indeterminism on the same imaginative level, but of the indeterminacy of the abstract.

Finally, may we claim that this transposition hits the mark? Between indeterminism and probability the only apparent link is a common lack of precision and definiteness. But the indeterminacy of the abstract brings to light the nonsystematic character of the concrete. And the essence of probability is that it sets an ideal norm from which actual frequencies can diverge but not systematically.

4

The Complementarity
of Classical and Statistical
Investigations

A review of the main points that have been made will prove, perhaps, the most expeditious introduction to the problem of the present chapter.

Our study of human intelligence began from an account of the psychological aspects of insight. It turned to geometrical definitions as products of insight, and thence to the redefinitions that result from higher viewpoints. The argument then twisted to the queer type of insight that grasps that the understanding of given data or of the answer to a given question consists in understanding that there is nothing to be understood. Finally,[a] there was effected a generalization that acknowledged in all data an empirical residue from which intelligence always abstracts.

The second chapter switched to insights in the field of empirical science. After a brief contrast between mathematical and scientific developments of understanding, attention centered on the origin of the clues that form the first moment of insight. It was seen that, by inquiring, intelligence anticipates the act of understanding for which it strives. The content of that anticipated act can be designated heuristically. The properties of the anticipated and designated content constitute the clues intelligence employs to guide itself towards discovery. Finally, since there are not only direct insights that understand what is to be understood but also the queer type of insights that understand that there is nothing to be understood, heuristic structures fall into two groups, namely, the classical and the statistical. A classical heuristic structure is intelligent anticipation of the systematic-and-abstract on which the concrete converges. A statistical heuristic structure is intelligent anticipation of the systematic-and-abstract setting a boundary or norm from which the concrete cannot systematically diverge.

Of themselves, heuristic structures are empty. They anticipate a form that is to be filled. Now, just as the form can be anticipated in its general properties, so also can the process of filling be anticipated in its general properties. There exist, then, canons of empirical method. If insight is to be into data, there is a canon of selection. If insights into data accumulate in a circuit of presentations, insights, formulations, experiments, new presentations, there is a canon of operations. If applied science involves insights into materials, purposes, agents, and tools, then pure science, as prior to applied, will be concerned solely with the immanent intelligibility of data, and so will be subject to a canon of relevance. If pure science goes beyond the data inasmuch as it grasps their immanent intelligibility, still it adds to the data no more than that intelligible content; there results a canon of parsimony, which excludes any affirmation that goes beyond what can be verified in the data. If some data are to be understood, then all are to be understood; the scientific goal is the understanding of all phenomena, and so scientific method is subject to a canon of complete explanation; it follows that no exception is to be made for experienced extensions or for experienced durations; and this conclusion implies a shift from a Galilean to an Einsteinian viewpoint. Finally, though all data are to be explained, it remains that certain aspects of all data are explained in the queer fashion already noticed. There exist statistical residues, for the totality of the systematic is abstract, the abstract is applied to the concrete only by the addition of further determinations, and from the nature of the case the further determinations cannot be systematically related to one another.

Now this bare enumeration of the points that have been made in our first three chapters confronts us with a problem. Both the heuristic structures of science and the canons of empirical method involve a duality. Besides grasping the intelligibility immanent in data in a positive fashion, human intelligence also grasps a domination of the concrete by the abstract-and-systematic. However, though one admits this duality as a fact, one still may ask whether it is ultimate, whether classical and statistical inquiries are isolated or related procedures, whether they lead to isolated or related results. An answer to these questions is sought in the present chapter, and it falls into three parts.

First, it will be advanced that classical and statistical investigations are complementary as types of knowing. In their heuristic anticipations, in their procedures, in their formulations, in their differences of abstractness, in their verification, and in their domains of data, each will be shown to complement and to be complemented by the other.

Secondly, besides the complementarity in knowing, there is a complementarity in the to-be-known. Whether one likes it or not, heuristic structures and canons of method constitute an a priori. They settle in advance the general determinations, not merely of the activities of knowing, but also of the content to be known. Just as Aristotle's notions on science and method resulted in his cosmic hierarchy, just as the Galilean reduction of secondary to primary qualities necessitated a mechanist determinism, so too our simultaneous affirmation of both classical and statistical investigations involves a world view. What is that view?

Thirdly, there is a clarification that results from contrast. Accordingly, after endeavoring to determine the world view to which one commits oneself by accepting the heuristic structures and the canons of empirical method, there are set forth its differences from the world views of Aristotle, Galileo, Darwin, and contemporary indeterminists.

1   Complementarity in the Knowing   [105–15]

1.1 Complementary Heuristic Structures   [105]

First, the heuristic anticipations of classical and of statistical procedures are complementary. For the systematic and the nonsystematic are the contradictory alternatives of a dichotomy. Inquiry of the classical type is an anticipation of the systematic. Inquiry of the statistical type is an anticipation of the nonsystematic. Now the relations between data must be either systematic or nonsystematic. It follows that in any given case either the classical or the statistical anticipation must be correct.

Two corollaries follow.

The first is the openness of empirical method. The mere fact of inquiry is itself a presupposition, for it implies that there is something to be known by understanding the data. Still, this presupposition is inevitable, for it marks the difference between the scientific and the nonscientific attitudes to experience. Moreover, this presupposition is minimal. For it does not determine a priori whether any selected range of data is to be reduced to system in the classical fashion or, on the other hand, is to be accounted for by showing how the concrete diverges nonsystematically from systematic expectations.

The second corollary is the relevance of empirical method. For empirical method is a matter of trial and error, and the only way to settle whether a given aggregate of observations is or is not reducible to system is to formulate both hypotheses, work out their implications, and test the implications against observed results.

1.2 Complementary Procedures   [106–108]

Next, classical and statistical investigations are complementary procedures. For they separate systematically and nonsystematically related data, and the isolation of either type is a step towards the determination of the other.

With such separation everyone is familiar when it is effected physically by experimentation. As has been seen, the aim of the experimenter is to isolate a definable conjunction of elements and to exhibit their operations as they occur when uninfluenced by extraneous factors.

Again, physical separation is not always possible, and then one attempts to do by thought what one cannot achieve by deed. In this fashion, as soon as a science has made some progress, it invokes its known laws in seeking the determination of the unknown. Thus, once Boyle's law is known, one assumes it in determining Charles's law; once both are known, one assumes both in determining Gay-Lussac's law. Similarly in all departments, known laws are employed to guide experiment, to eliminate the consideration of what already has been explained, and to provide premises for the interpretation of observed results.

Moreover, such separation, whether physical or mental, is not confined to classical laws. All laws belong to a single complementary field. For this reason it has been possible to invoke the laws of probable errors and thereby to eliminate a nonsystematic component in observations and measurements. In like manner, Mendel's statistical laws of macroscopic genetic characters led to the postulation of microscopic entities named genes; to each gene was assigned, on the classical model, a single determinate effect and manifestation; genes with incompatible effects were classified as dominant and recessive; and so statistical combinations of classically conceived genes became the explanation of nonsystematic macroscopic phenomena.

The reader may be surprised that we lump together the laws of probable errors and the Mendelian laws of heredity. But from our viewpoint they belong together. In both cases a component in the data is brought under law. In both cases the discovery of the law grounds a mental separation of the component subject to the known law from other components still to be determined. In both cases this mental separation opens the way to the determination of further laws. In both cases, finally, it is the discovery of a statistical law that grounds the mental separation and that can lead to the discovery no less of classical than of statistical laws.

This complementarity of classical and statistical procedures has an important corollary. For the experimental physical exclusion of extraneous factors is not always possible. When it is not, there exists the alternative of discovering the law of the extraneous factor and then allowing for its influence in interpreting one's result. Now the corollary to which we would draw attention is that statistical laws can be employed in this fashion to the determination of classical laws. For knowledge of statistical laws enables one to separate mentally the nonsystematic component in the data, and so it leaves one free to investigate the remaining systematic component.

It will be asked, then, whether the statistical investigations of quantum mechanics may be expected to prepare the way for a later resurgence of classical thought in the field of subatomic physics.

This question is, I think, ambiguous. One may mean a return to the former type of classical thought with its imaginable models, its belief in the universal possibility of imaginative synthesis, its affirmation of a mechanist determinism, and its concept of explanation as the reduction of secondary to primary qualities. On the other hand, it is possible to speak of 'classical' thought in a transposed and analogous sense. In that case, one would grant to imagination a notable heuristic value, for images supply the materials for insights; but at the same time one would deny to unverified and unverifiable images any representative value; classical laws would be conceived as abstract, the abstraction would be conceived as enriching, and so full knowledge of classical laws would not preclude the existence of statistical residues.

Once this distinction is drawn, our answer to the foregoing question becomes obvious. In the light of the canons of complete explanation, of parsimony, and of statistical residues, we cannot expect any return to the older type of classical thought. Again, in the same light, we must expect quantum mechanics, if interpreted statistically, to open the way to a new development of 'classical' thought in a transposed and analogous sense. Indeed, Pauli's exclusion principle provides a premise for the determination of the states of electrons in atoms; and while changes of these states seem to occur statistically, still the series of states is as regular and systematic as the periodic table of chemical elements.[1] In like manner, one might note classical tendencies in the discovery of new subatomic entities over and above the more familiar electrons, protons, and neutrons.

1.3 Complementary Formulations   [108–10]

Thirdly, classical and statistical formulations are complementary. For classical formulations regard conjugates, which are verified only in events. And statistical formulations regard events, which are defined only by conjugates.

The dependence of classical upon statistical formulation comes to light when one probes into the meaning of the classical proviso 'other things being equal.' What are the other things? In what does their equality consist? These questions cannot be given an answer that is both detailed and systematic. For the proviso, which limits classical laws, is effectively any relevant pattern of a diverging series of conditions. Such series vary with circumstances, and the aggregate of patterns of such series is both enormous and nonsystematic. In other words, classical laws tell what would happen if conditions were fulfilled; statistical laws tell how often conditions are fulfilled; and so the phrase 'other things being equal' amounts to a vague reference to the statistical residues, which are the province of the complementary statistical laws.

The inverse dependence of statistical upon classical formulations comes to light when one asks which statistical investigations possess scientific significance. Thus, anyone would acknowledge a difference in such significance between determining the frequency of red hair in trombone players and, on the other hand, measuring the intensity of line spectra. In either case one arrives at a number that may be regarded as an actual frequency, but it is not apparent that in both cases one has an equal chance of contributing to the advance of science. For the advance of science is secured by operating in the light of present knowledge and towards the solution of well-formulated problems. As soon as any department of science has passed beyond its initial stages, it begins to desert the expressions of ordinary language and to invent technical terms of its own. Such technical terms have their origin in the correlations that

1 See Lindsay and Margenau, *Foundations of Physics* 488–93.

have been found significant; they are, or in some fashion they depend upon, what we have named pure conjugates. Accordingly, inasmuch as the statistical investigator proceeds in the light of acquired knowledge and towards the solution of well-formulated problems, he will be led to define events by appealing, directly or indirectly, to the pure conjugates that are implicit in classical laws.

However, the reader may ask whether this view can be regarded as definitive. It is true enough that the scientific classifications and definitions of the present are dependent on the discovery and formulation of classical laws. But may one not expect that a fuller development of statistical inquiry will result in the implicit definition of technical terms by statistical and not classical laws?

While there seem to be those that would answer this question affirmatively, I cannot see my way to agreeing with them. My reason runs as follows. The answer yes to a question for reflection obtains a determinate meaning only by reverting from the yes to the question and to its origin in the descriptive or explanatory answer to a question for intelligence. Now the event, the happening, the occurring corresponds to the bare yes. To say what happens, what occurs, one must raise a question that cannot be answered by a yes or a no. One must appeal either to the experiential conjugates of description or to the pure conjugates of explanation. On this showing, then, one cannot expect events to generate their own definitions any more than one can expect yes or no to settle what is affirmed or denied. Finally, if events cannot generate their own definitions, then frequencies of events cannot do so; for there seems no reason to expect that different types of events must have different numerical frequencies, or indeed that the numerical frequencies could serve to specify the kinds of events to which one wishes to refer.

There is, then, a complementarity of classical and statistical formulations. For if statistical formulations are to be significant contributions to the advance of science, they will appeal to the experiential and pure conjugates of classical classifications and definitions. Inversely, the conjugates of classical formulations are verifiable only in statistically occurring events, and their immanence in statistical residues is revealed by the proviso 'other things being equal.'

It may not be out of place to conclude this subsection by clarifying a slight puzzle. It is true enough that statistical laws also are immanent in statistical residues, and so hold under the general proviso 'other things being equal.' If 'P follows Q' has the probability p/q, still there are conditions for the occurrence of the occasion Q, and it is only when those conditions are fulfilled that the probability p/q is verifiable. The frequency of such fulfilment might be indicated by saying that 'Q follows R' has the probability q/r, so that one statistical law would be dependent on another. Still, this interdependence of statistical laws, while true enough, is beside our present point. It in no way invalidates the significant contention that the dependence of classical upon statistical formulations is revealed by the proviso 'other things being equal.'

1.4 *Complementary Modes of Abstraction*   [110–11]

Fourthly, there is a complementarity in modes of abstraction.

Classical heuristic procedure rests on the assumption that to some extent the relations between data are systematic, and it devotes its efforts to determine just what those systematic relations are.

Statistical heuristic procedure rests on an assumption of nonsystematic relations, and it aims at determining an ideal frequency from which actual frequencies may diverge but only nonsystematically.

In both cases the result obtained is abstract. For the classical law represents the systematic and prescinds from the nonsystematic. On the other hand, the statistical law represents, not the actual frequency of actual events, but the ideal frequency from which actual frequencies diverge.

Now while both types of law are abstract, still their modes of abstraction differ. The classical law is concerned simply with the systematic; it disregards the nonsystematic. The statistical law, on the contrary, assumes the nonsystematic as a premise. By itself, of course, such a premise could yield no conclusions such as the abstract, ideal, universal frequencies named probabilities. What concerns the statistical inquirer is, then, neither the purely systematic, nor the purely nonsystematic, but the systematic as setting ideal limits from which the nonsystematic cannot diverge systematically.

Clearly, these two modes of abstraction are complementary. In its first movement, inquiry aims at determining the systematic component in data; in its second movement, inquiry turns to the more concrete task of determining the manner in which the systematic component in data moderates the nonsystematic. The complete view results only from the combination of the two movements, and so the two are complementary.

There is another aspect to this complementarity. The systematic relations with which classical inquiry is concerned, mainly are the relations of things, not to our senses, but to one another. Insofar as the relations of things to one another are considered in the abstract and so as independent of their relations to our senses, there arises a principle of equivalence for all senses since all equally are abstracted from. On the other hand,[b] once one moves from classical to statistical inquiry, the foregoing interpretation of the principle of equivalence vanishes. It is true that, just as probability theory is not to be denied the convenience of continuous functions, so there is no a priori reason to deprive it of the advantage of full invariance. However, as will be recalled,[2] statistical theory deals with events selected from processes by the possibility of accurate measurement, and the continuity of its functions seems to refer, not to the continuity of concrete process but, so to speak, to the permanent availability of the ideal norms from which events diverge in nonsystematic fashion. As such norms, so their invariance lies outside the field of explanatory relations.

1.5 Complementarity in Verification   [111–12]

Fifthly, classical and statistical laws are complementary in their verification. This may be stated roughly by saying that classical laws determine what would happen if conditions were fulfilled, while statistical laws determine how often one may expect conditions to be fulfilled. However, a fuller account of this complementarity may be given by showing how the determination of either classical or statistical laws leaves room for the determination of the other.

Thus, if one were to suppose exact and complete knowledge of all classical laws, one would not preclude the possibility of the verification of statistical laws. For a set of classical laws, say P, would be exact and complete if there were no possibility of replacing them by some different set, say Q. Now there would be no possibility of replacing P by Q if there were no systematic divergence between the data and the set of laws P; for the sets P and Q differ as laws, and so differ systematically; and so the verification of the set Q in place of the set P supposes a systematic divergence between the set P and the data. Finally, though there is no systematic divergence between the set P and the data, there can be a nonsystematic divergence that would provide the field for the investigation and verification of statistical laws.

2 See above, chapter 3, §6.6.3 [pp. 121–22].

Again, as has been seen,[3] exact and complete knowledge of classical laws not merely can leave room for possible statistical investigation but also must do so. For such exact and complete knowledge would embrace all the systematic relations between determinate data; nonetheless, such knowledge would be abstract and so in need of further determinations to be applied to concrete instances; it follows that the further determinations cannot be systematically related to one another; and so there must be a field for statistical laws.

Finally, statistical investigations in their turn have no genuine tendency to totalitarian aspirations. For besides statistical predictions, there exist the fully accurate predictions that are exemplified by astronomy, and that rest on the existence of schemes of recurrence. Moreover, the intelligent manner of making these predictions is to analyze the schemes into their component classical laws. Copernicus corrected Ptolemy's imaginative scheme; Kepler corrected the circles of Copernicus; but it was Newton who worked out the underlying laws and Laplace who revealed the periodicity of the planetary system. From that discovery of laws the great movement of thought named modern science received its most powerful confirmation. It did so because it ended, at least for two centuries, the more common human tendency to speak, not of precise laws, but of the common run of events or the ordinary course of Nature. At the present moment, the profound significance of statistical laws is coming to light. But if this new movement is not to degenerate into the old talk about what commonly happens, it must retain its contact with the empirically established precision of classical formulations. For statistical laws are of no greater scientific significance than the definitions of the events whose frequencies they determine; unless these definitions are determined scientifically, statistical thought lapses into prescientific insignificance.

1.6 Complementarity in Data Explained   [112–14]

Sixthly, classical and statistical laws are complementary in their domains of data. By this is meant, not that some data are explained by classical laws and other data by statistical laws, but rather that certain aspects of all data receive the classical type of explanation while other aspects of the same data are explained along statistical lines.

---

3 See above, chapter 3, §§6.1–6.5 [pp. 109–21].

As has been seen,[4] the classical heuristic assumption is that similars are similarly understood. Consequently, preliminary classifications are based on similarity to sense. However, the scientist is interested in the relations of things, not to our senses, but to one another. Accordingly, the preliminary classifications are superseded by the emergence and development of technical terms that are derived, not from sensible similarity, but from similarities of constant or regularly varying proportion; and in the limit there are reached what we have named pure conjugates, that is, terms implicitly defined by the empirically established correlations in which they occur.

Still, to account for data as similar is not to account for data in all their aspects. Each datum is just this instance of the given. It emerges within a continuous manifold. It is in a particular place and at a particular time. It occurs rarely or frequently. Now these aspects of all data are disregarded in explanations of the classical type. The law of the lever tells us nothing about the frequency of levers, about the places where they are to be found, about the times at which they function. Hence explanations of the classical type have to be complemented by explanations of a further, different type.

Nor is it difficult to see, at least in some general fashion, that statistical laws can provide the complementary explanation. For the general form of the statistical law is that on p occurrences of the occasion P, there tend to be q occurrences of the event Q. Now the occasion P is itself an event or a combination of events. In either case it will possess its probability. In like manner, the occasions on which P is probable will have their probability, and so there arises an indefinite regress of probabilities from events of the type Q. More generally, for events of any type X, there are corresponding indefinite regresses of probabilities.

Now it is not immediately apparent that such regresses can be combined into a single view. But it suffices for present purposes to remark that, were such a combination possible, one would be on the way to attaining a statistical explanation of data in their numbers and in their spatiotemporal distribution. To invoke only the simplest considerations, low probabilities are offset by large numbers of occasions, so that what is probable only once on a million occasions is to be expected a million times on a million million occasions. In like manner, the rarity of occasions is offset by long intervals of time, so that if occasions arise only

4 See above, chapter 2, § 2.3 [pp. 61–62].

once in a million years, still they arise a thousand times in a thousand million years. At once there emerges the explanatory significance of statistical laws. Why are there in the world of our experience such vast numbers and such enormous intervals of time? Because probabilities are low, numbers have to be large; because occasions are rare, time intervals have to be long.

By itself, this is a very modest conclusion. Still, though the achievement is quite negligible, the potentialities are extremely significant. Statistical laws possess a capacity to generate explanation. Their heuristic assumption is simply that the nonsystematic cannot diverge systematically from the systematic. But this incapacity for systematic divergence, when combined with large numbers and long intervals of time, is equivalent to a positive tendency, to an intelligible order, to an effective thrust, that is no less explanatory than the rigorous conclusions based on classical laws. In other words, probability is one thing, and chance is another. Probability is an ideal norm that, for all its ideality, is concretely successful in the long run. Chance is merely the nonsystematic divergence of actual frequencies from the ideal frequencies named probabilities. Chance explains nothing. It pertains irretrievably to the merely empirical residue, to the aspects of data from which intelligence always abstracts. But probability is an intelligibility; it is, as it were, rescued from the merely empirical residue by the roundabout device in which inquiring intelligence sets up the heuristic anticipations of the statistical type of investigation.

1.7 Summary   [114–15]

We have been considering the complementarity of classical and statistical investigations as forms of knowing. We have found such complementarity to exist at each of the stages or components of the process of inquiry. There is the classical heuristic anticipation of the systematic; there is the complementary statistical heuristic anticipation of the nonsystematic. Next, to determine either a classical or a statistical law is to prepare the way for the determination of further laws of either type; for both classical and statistical laws pertain to a single complementary field, and to know either is to effect a mental separation between types of data that have been accounted for and types that still remain to be explained. Thirdly, there is a complementarity of formulations: the experiential and pure conjugates of classical laws can be verified only in events; the events occur only if other things are equal; and the failure to specify the other things amounts to an unconscious acknowledgment of the nonsystematic aggregate of patterns of diverging series of conditions; inversely, as conjugates are verified only in events, so events are defined only by conjugates, and statistical laws of events can possess scientific significance only in the measure that they employ definitions generated by classical procedures. Fourthly, there is a complementarity in modes of abstraction: classical laws regard the systematic in abstraction from the nonsystematic, the relations of things to one another in abstraction from their relations to our senses; but statistical laws consider the systematic as setting bounds to the nonsystematic, and they are confined to the observable events that include a relation to our senses. Fifthly, the two types of law are complementary in their verification: exact and complete knowledge of classical laws cannot successfully invade the field of statistical laws; and statistical investigations are confronted with regular recurrences that admit explanations of the classical type. Finally, there is complementarity in the aspects of data explained by the different types of laws: data as similar are explained on classical lines; but their numbers and their distributions become intelligible only by some synthesis of statistical considerations.

2 Complementarity in the Known   [115–28]

Just as the first part of this chapter was devoted to exhibiting the complementarity of classical and of statistical investigations from the viewpoint of knowing, so now the second part is to be directed to the determination of the corresponding complementarity from the viewpoint of what is to be known. For knowing and known, if they are not an identity, at least stand in some correspondence, and as the known is reached only through knowing, structural features of the one are bound to be reflected in the other. Aristotle's world view stemmed from his distinction between the necessary laws of the heavenly bodies and the contingent laws of things on this earth. Mechanist determinism had its scientific basis in the Galilean concept of explanation as the reduction of secondary to primary qualities. In similar fashion some parallel implication cannot be avoided by any fully conscious methodology, and so, if we are not to play the ostrich, we must face the question, What world view is involved by our affirmation of both classical and statistical laws?

2.1 General Characteristics of the View   [115–17]

Certain general characteristics of our position may be indicated immediately.

In the first place, it will be concerned with the intelligibility immanent in the universe of our experience. For it will be a conclusion from the structure of empirical method, and by the canon of relevance empirical method is confined to determining such immanent intelligibility. Hence we shall have nothing to say in this chapter about the end or purpose of this universe, about the materials from which it was fashioned, about the principal or instrumental agents responsible for it. Our efforts will be limited to determining the immanent design or order characteristic of a universe in which both classical and statistical laws obtain.

In the second place, our account of this design or order will be generic. A specific account would have to draw upon the content of the empirical sciences. It would have to appeal, not to classical and statistical laws in general, but to the precise laws that can be empirically established. Our account, on the other hand, will rest not on the results of scientific investigations but simply and solely upon the dynamic structure of inquiring intelligence. Accordingly, if in the course of the exposition any particular scientific conclusions are invoked, their function will be not determinative but merely illustrative. Just as mechanist determinism has been a world view that is independent of the precise content of classical laws, so too our objective is a similarly generic structure that is compatible not only with present classical and statistical laws but also with their future revisions.

In the third place, our account of the design or order of this universe will be relatively invariant. The content of the natural sciences is a variable. There has been the science of the Renaissance. There has been the science of the Enlightenment. There is the science of today. There will be the successive stages of scientific development in the future. But knitting together these diverse manifestations of scientific thought, generating each in turn only to bring forth the revision and transformation of each, there is the underlying invariant that loosely may be named scientific method and more precisely, I think, would be designated as the dynamic structure of inquiring intelligence. For, as has been seen, it is the desire to understand that results both in the heuristic structure of classical procedure and in the complementary structure of statistical investigation; and it is the nature of insight that accounts for the six canons of selection, operations, relevance, parsimony, complete explanation, and statistical residues, in accord with which the heuristic structures generate the series of scientific theories and systems. Now our premise is to be, not the variable contents of the sciences, but the invariant forms governing scientific investigation. It follows that the design of the universe to which we shall conclude will enjoy the invariance of the premise which we shall invoke.

Still, I have said that our account will be only relatively invariant, and the reason for this restriction is plain enough. For our appeal will be, not to the structure of the human mind itself, but only to our account of that structure. Just as the natural sciences are subject to revision, so too one may expect our account of inquiring intelligence to be subjected to rearrangements, modifications, and improvements. In the measure that such changes will affect the premises of the present argument, in the same measure they will also affect the conclusions. Accordingly, the world view to be presented will be invariant, inasmuch as it will be independent of changes in the content of the natural sciences; but it will be only relatively invariant, for it cannot be independent of revisions of our analysis of empirical method.

In the fourth place, our account of a world view within the limits of empirical science will not be complete in this chapter. In treating the canon of parsimony, we postponed the question of the validity of the notion of the thing. In a later chapter, that question will have to be met, and then a further complement to the present account will be added.

In the fifth place, our account will not claim to be deductive. Perhaps one might argue in strictly deductive fashion from the complementary structure of the knowing to the corresponding complementarity of the known. But if that procedure is possible, it also requires an elaboration that for present purposes would be excessive. Accordingly, our appeal will be to insight. We shall begin from the problem of showing how both classical and statistical laws can coalesce into a single unified intelligibility commensurate with the universe of our experience. Against this problem we shall set our clue, namely, the scheme of recurrence. On the one hand, the world of our experience is full of continuities, oscillations, rhythms, routines, alternations, circulations, regularities. On the other hand, the scheme of recurrence not only squares with this broad fact but also is related intimately both to classical and to statistical laws. For the notion of the scheme emerges in the very formulation of the canons of empirical method. Abstractly, the scheme itself is a combination of classical laws. Concretely, schemes begin, continue, and cease to function in accord with statistical probabilities. Such is our clue, our incipient insight. To develop it we shall consider (1) the notion of a conditioned series of schemes of recurrence, (2) the probability of a single scheme, (3) the emergent probability of a series of schemes, and (4) the consequent characteristics of a world order.

2.2 Schemes of Recurrence   [118–20]

The notion of the scheme of recurrence arose when it was noted that the diverging series of positive conditions for an event might coil around in a circle. In that case, a series of events A, B, C, . . . would be so related that the fulfilment of the conditions for each would be the occurrence of the others. Schematically, then, the scheme might be represented by the series of conditionals: If A occurs, B will occur; if B occurs, C will occur; if C occurs, . . . A will recur. Such a circular arrangement may involve any number of terms, the possibility of alternative routes, and in general any degree of complexity.

Two instances of greater complexity may be noted. On the one hand, a scheme might consist of a set of almost complete circular arrangements of which none could function alone yet all would function if conjoined in an interdependent combination. On the other hand, schemes might be complemented by defensive circles, so that if some event F tended to upset the scheme, there would be some such sequence of conditions as 'If F occurs, then G occurs; if G occurs, then H occurs; if H occurs, then F is eliminated.'

In illustration of schemes of recurrence the reader may think of the planetary system, of the circulation of water over the surface of the earth, of the nitrogen cycle familiar to biologists, of the routines of animal life, of the repetitive economic rhythms of production and exchange. In illustration of schemes with defensive circles, one may advert to generalized equilibria. Just as a chain reaction is a cumulative series of changes terminating in an explosive difference, so a generalized equilibrium is such a combination of defensive circles that any change within a limited range is offset by opposite changes that tend to restore the initial situation. Thus, health in a plant or animal is a generalized equilibrium; again, the balance of various forms of plant and animal life within an environment is a generalized equilibrium; again, economic process was conceived by the older economists as a generalized equilibrium.

However, we are concerned, not with single schemes, but with a conditioned series of schemes. Let us say that the schemes $P, Q, R, \ldots$ form a conditioned series if all prior members of the series must be functioning actually for any later member to become a concrete possibility. Then the scheme P can function though neither Q nor R exists; the scheme Q can function though R does not yet exist; but Q cannot function unless P is already functioning; and R cannot function unless Q is already functioning.

Thus, by way of a simple illustration, one may advert to the dietary schemes of animals. All carnivorous animals cannot live off other carnivorous animals. Hence a carnivorous dietary scheme supposes another, herbivorous dietary scheme, but inversely, there could be herbivorous animals without any carnivorous animals. Again, plants cannot in general live off animals; the scheme of their nourishment involves chemical processes; and that scheme can function apart from the existence of any animals. Finally, chemical cycles are not independent of physical laws, yet inversely, the laws of physics can be combined into schemes of recurrence that are independent of chemical processes.

Such in briefest outline is the notion of the conditioned series of schemes of recurrence. Let us seek a slight increase in precision by drawing a threefold distinction between (1) the possible seriation, (2) the probable seriation, and (3) the actual seriation.

The actual seriation is unique. It consists of the schemes that actually were, are, or will be functioning in our universe along with precise specifications of their places, their durations, and their relations to one another.

The probable seriation differs from the actual. For the actual diverges nonsystematically from probability expectations. The actual is the factual, but the probable is ideal. Hence, while the actual seriation has the uniqueness of the matter of fact, the probable seriation has to exhibit the cumulative ramifications of probable alternatives. Accordingly, the probable seriation is not a single series but a manifold of series. At each stage of world process there is a set of probable next stages, of which some are more probable than others. The actual seriation includes only the stages that occur. The probable seriation includes all that would occur without systematic divergence from the probabilities.

The possible seriation is still more remote from actuality. It includes all the schemes of recurrence that could be devised from the classical laws of our universe. It orders them in a conditioned series that ramifies not only along the lines of probable alternatives but also along lines of mere possibility or negligible probability. It is equally relevant to our universe and to any other universe subject to the same classical laws, no matter what its initial numbers, diversities, and distribution of elements.

Of the three seriations, then, the possible exhibits the greatest complexity and variety. It depends solely on a consideration of classical laws. It suffers from the indeterminacy of the abstract, and so exhibits the process of any universe with laws similar to ours. The probable seriation depends on statistical as well as classical laws, and indeed on the statistical laws that arise from the initial or basic situation of our world. Still, if it is not as abstract as the possible seriation, nonetheless it is ideal. For each moment of world history it assigns a most probable future course. But it also assigns a series of less probable courses, and it has to acknowledge that any of these may prove to be the fact. Finally, the actual seriation is unique, but it purchases its uniqueness by going beyond the field of all laws, classical and statistical, and entering the field of observation, in which alone nonsystematic divergences from probability are determinate.

2.3 The Probability of Schemes   [120–21]

Our outline of the notion of a conditioned series of schemes of recurrence supposes that one can attribute a probability to the emergence and to the survival of a scheme of recurrence. However, our account of probability has been in terms of the frequency, not of schemes, but of events. Have schemes any probability? If they have, is there a distinct probability for their emergence and another for their survival? Such questions must be met.

Consider a set of events of the types A, B, C, . . . and a world situation in which they possess respectively the probabilities p, q, r, . . . Then by a general rule of probability theory, the probability of the occurrence of all the events in the set will be the product pqr . . . of their respective probabilities.

Now let us add a further assumption. Let us suppose that the set of events A, B, C, . . . satisfies a conditioned scheme of recurrence, say K, in a world situation in which the scheme K is not functioning, but in virtue of the fulfilment of prior conditions could begin to function. Then, if A were to occur, B would occur. If B were to occur, C would occur. If C were to occur, . . . A would occur. In brief, if any of the events in the set were to occur, then, other things being equal, the rest of the events in the set would follow.

In this case we may suppose that the probabilities of the single events are respectively the same as before, but we cannot suppose that the probability of the combination of all events in the set is the same as before. As is easily to be seen, the concrete possibility of a scheme beginning to function shifts the probability of the combination from the product pqr . . . to the sum $p + q + r +$ . . . For in virtue of the scheme, it now is true that A and B and C and . . . will occur, if either A or B or C or . . . occurs; and by a general rule of probability theory, the probability of a set of alternatives is equal to the sum of the probabilities of the alternatives.

Now a sum of a set of proper fractions p, q, r, . . . is always greater than the product of the same fractions. But a probability is a proper fraction. It follows that, when the prior conditions for the functioning of a scheme of recurrence are satisfied, then the probability of the combination of events constitutive of the scheme leaps from a product of fractions to a sum of fractions.

There exists, then, a probability of emergence for a scheme of recurrence. That probability consists in the sum of the respective probabilities of all the events included in the scheme, and it arises as soon as the prior conditions for the functioning of the scheme are satisfied.

There also exists a probability for the survival of schemes that have begun to function. For, of itself, a scheme tends to assure its own perpetuity. The positive conditions for the occurrence of its component events reside in the occurrence of those events. Even negative conditions, within limited ranges, can be provided for by the development of defensive circles. Nonetheless, the perpetuity of a scheme is not necessary. Just as classical laws are subject to the proviso 'other things being equal,' so also are the schemes constituted by combinations of classical laws; and whether or not other things will continue to be equal is a question that admits an answer only in terms of statistical laws. Accordingly, the probability of the survival of a scheme of recurrence is the probability of the nonoccurrence of any of the events that would disrupt the scheme.

2.4 Emergent Probability [121–24]

There have been formulated the notion of a conditioned series of schemes of recurrence and, as well, the general sense in which one can speak of the probability of the emergence and the survival of single schemes. From these considerations there now comes to light the notion of an emergent probability. For the actual functioning of earlier schemes in the series fulfils the conditions for the possibility of the functioning of later schemes. As such conditions are fulfilled, the probability of the combination of the component events in a scheme jumps from a product of a set of proper fractions to the sum of those proper fractions. But what is probable, sooner or later occurs. When it occurs, a probability of emergence is replaced by a probability of survival; and as long as the scheme survives, it is in its turn fulfilling conditions for the possibility of still later schemes in the series.

Such is the general notion of emergent probability. It results from the combination of the conditioned series of schemes with their respective probabilities of emergence and survival. While by itself it is extremely jejune, it possesses rather remarkable potentialities of explanation. These must now be indicated in outline, and so we attempt brief considerations of the significance for emergent probability of spatial distribution, absolute numbers, long intervals of time, selection, stability, and development.

The notion of a conditioned series of schemes involves spatial concentrations. For each later set of schemes becomes possible in the places where earlier schemes are already functioning. Accordingly, the most elementary schemes, which are earliest in the series, can occur anywhere in the initial distribution of materials. But the second batch can occur only where the first have in fact occurred, the third can occur only where the second have in fact occurred, and so on. Moreover, since the realization of the schemes is in accord with the probabilities, which may be low, one cannot expect all possibilities to be actuated. Hence elementary schemes will not be as frequent as they could be, to narrow the possible basis for schemes at the second remove. These will not be as frequent as they could be, to narrow again the possible basis for schemes at the third remove, and so forth. It follows that, however widespread the realization of elementary schemes, there will be a succession of constrictions of the volumes of space in which later schemes can be found. Similarly, it follows that the points, so to speak, of greatest and least constriction occur where the probabilities of emergence of the next set of schemes are respectively the lowest and the highest. Finally, it follows that, since the latest schemes in the series have the greatest number of conditions to be fulfilled, their occurrence will be limited to a relatively small number of places.

Secondly, there is the significance of absolute numbers. For large numbers offset low probabilities. What occurs once on^c a million occasions is to be expected a million times on a million million occasions. Now the minimum probability pertains to the latest schemes in the series, for their emergence supposes the emergence of all earlier schemes. It follows that the lower the probability of the last schemes of the conditioned series, the greater must be the initial absolute numbers in which elementary schemes can be realized. In brief, the size of a universe is inversely proportionate to the probability of its ultimate schemes of recurrence.

Thirdly, there is the significance of long intervals of time. No matter how great the universe and how widespread the functioning of elementary schemes, there is an increasing concentration of the spatial volumes in which later schemes can be realized. Sooner or later the initial benefit of large numbers is lost by the successive narrowing of the basis for further developments. But at this point long intervals of time become significant. Just as a million million simultaneous possibilities yield a million probable realizations whose probability is one in a million, so also a million million successive possibilities yield a million probable realizations under the same expectation.

Fourthly, there is a selective significance attached to the distinction between probabilities of emergence and probabilities of survival. If both are low, the occurrence of the scheme will be both rare and fleeting. If both are high, the occurrences will be both common and enduring. If the probability of emergence is low and that of survival is high, the scheme is to be expected to be rare but enduring. Finally, in the opposite case, the expectation is that the scheme will be common but fleeting.

Fifthly, this selectivity has its significance for stability. The functioning of later schemes depends upon the functioning of earlier schemes, so that if the earlier collapse, then the later will collapse as well. It follows that the line of maximum stability would be of common and enduring schemes, while the line of minimum stability would be of rare and fleeting schemes.

Sixthly, no less than stability, the possibility of development must be considered. Unfortunately, these two can conflict. Schemes with high probabilities of survival tend to imprison materials in their own routines. They provide a highly stable basis for later schemes, but they also tend to prevent later schemes from emerging. A solution to this problem would be for the earlier, conditioning schemes to have a high probability of emergence but a low probability of survival. They would form a floating population on which later schemes could successively depend. Because their probability of survival was[d] low, they would readily surrender materials to give later schemes the opportunity to emerge. Because their probability of emergence was high, they would readily be available to fulfil the conditions for the functioning of later schemes.

Needless to say, the foregoing considerations are extremely rudimentary. They are limited to the emergent probability of any conditioned series of schemes of recurrence. They make no effort towards developing that notion in the direction of its application to the conditions of the emergence and survival of modes of living. However, while absolutely such a fuller exposition would be desirable, still it has no place in a merely generic account of world order. For the premise of a generic account is, not the content of the natural sciences, but the possibility and validity of their assumptions and method.

The point we are endeavoring to make, within the limits of our narrow premise, is that the notion of emergent probability is explanatory. Intelligent inquiry aims at insight. But classical laws alone offer no insight into numbers, distributions, concentrations, time intervals, selectivity, uncertain stability, or development. On the contrary, they abstract from the instance, the place, the time, and the concrete conditions of actual functioning. Again, statistical laws, as a mere aggregate, affirm in various cases the ideal frequency of the occurrence of events. They make no pretence of explaining why there are so many kinds of events, or why each kind has the frequency attributed to it. To reach explanation on this level, it is necessary to effect the concrete synthesis of classical laws into a conditioned series of schemes of recurrence, to establish that such schemes, as combinations of events, acquire first a probability of emergence and then a probability of survival through the realization of the conditioned series, and finally to grasp that, if such a series of schemes is being realized in accord with probabilities, then there is available a general principle that promises answers to questions about the reason for numbers and distributions, concentrations and time intervals, selectivity and uncertain stability, development and breakdowns. To work out the answers pertains to the natural sciences. To grasp that emergent probability is an explanatory idea is to know what is meant when our objective was characterized as a generic, relatively invariant, and incomplete account of the immanent intelligibility, the order, the design of the universe of our experience.

2.5 Consequences of Emergent Probability   [125–28]

There remains the task of working out the generic properties of a world process in which the order or design is constituted by emergent probability. This we shall attempt in two main steps. First, we shall summarize the essentials of the notion of emergent probability. Secondly, we shall enumerate the consequences of that notion to be verified in world process.

The essentials of the notion of emergent probability may be indicated in the following series of assertions.

(1) An event is what is to be known by answering yes to such questions as, Did it happen? Is it occurring? Will it occur?

(2) World process is a spatiotemporal manifold of events. In other words, there are many events, and each has its place and time.

(3) Events are of kinds. Not every event is a new species, else there could be neither classical nor statistical laws.

(4) Events are recurrent. There are many events of each kind, and all are not at the same time.

(5) There are regularly recurrent events. This regularity is understood inasmuch as combinations of classical laws yield schemes of recurrence. Schemes are circular relationships between events of kinds, such that if the events occur once in virtue of the circular relationships, then, other things being equal, they keep on recurring indefinitely.

(6) Schemes can be arranged in a conditioned series, such that the earlier can function without the emergence of the later, but the later cannot emerge or function unless the earlier already are functioning.

(7) Combinations of events possess a probability, and that probability jumps, first when a scheme becomes concretely possible in virtue of the fulfilment of its prior conditions, and secondly when the scheme begins actually to function.

(8) The actual frequencies of events of each kind in each place and at each time do not diverge systematically from their probabilities. However, actual frequencies may diverge nonsystematically from probabilities, and that nonsystematic divergence is chance. Accordingly, probability and chance are distinct and are not to be confused.

(9) Emergent probability is the successive realization in accord with

successive schedules of probability of a conditioned series of schemes of recurrence.

The consequent properties of a world process in which the design is emergent probability run as follows:

(1) There is a succession of world situations. Each is characterized (a) by the schemes of recurrence actually functioning, (b) by the further schemes that now have become concretely possible, and (c) by the current schedule of probabilities of survival for existing schemes and of probabilities of emergence for concretely possible schemes.

(2) World process is open. It is a succession of probable realizations of possibilities. Hence it does not run along the iron rails laid down by determinists, nor on the other hand is it a nonintelligible morass of merely chance events.

(3) World process is increasingly systematic. For it is the successive realization of a conditioned series of schemes of recurrence, and the further the series of schemes is realized, the greater the systematization to which events are subjected.

(4) The increasingly systematic character of world process can be assured. No matter how slight the probability of the realization of the most developed and most conditioned schemes, the emergence of those schemes can be assured by sufficiently increasing absolute numbers and sufficiently prolonging intervals of time. For actual frequencies do not diverge systematically from probabilities; but the greater the numbers and the longer the time intervals, the clearer the need for a systematic intervention to prevent the probable from occurring.

(5) The significance of the initial or basic world situation is limited to the possibilities it contains and to the probabilities it assigns its possibilities. By the initial world situation is meant the situation that is first in time; by the basic world situation is meant the partial prolongation through time of initial conditions, such as arises, for instance, in certain contemporary hypotheses of continuous creation.

In either case, what is significant resides in possibilities and their probabilities, for in all its stages world process is the probable realization of possibilities. While the determinist would desire full information, exact to the nth decimal place, on his initial or basic situation, the advocate of emergent probability is quite satisfied with any initial situation in which the most elementary schemes can emerge and probably will emerge in sufficient numbers to sustain the subsequent structure.

(6) World process admits enormous differentiation. It envisages the

totality of possibilities defined by classical laws. It realizes these possibilities in accord with its successive schedules of probabilities. And given sufficient numbers and sufficient time, even slight probabilities become assured.

(7) World process admits breakdowns. For no scheme has more than a probability of survival, so that there is for every scheme some probability of a breakdown; and since earlier schemes condition later schemes, a breakdown of the former entails the breakdown of the latter.

(8) World process includes blind alleys. For schemes with a high probability of survival have some probability of emergence. Insofar as they emerge, they tend to bind within their routines the materials for the possibility of later schemes, and so to block the way to full development.

(9) The later a scheme is in the conditioned series, the narrower is its distribution. For actual realization is less frequent than its concrete possibility; and each later set of schemes is concretely possible only where earlier, conditioning schemes are functioning.

(10) The narrower the basis for the emergence of each later set of schemes, the greater the need to invoke long intervals of time. For in this case the alternative of large numbers is excluded.

(11) The greater the probabilities of blind alleys and breakdowns, the greater must be the initial absolute numbers if the realization of the whole series of schemes is to be assured. For in this case the device of long time intervals might not be efficacious. Blind alleys with their inert routines could last for extremely long periods, and when they suffered breakdown,[e] they might result in another blind alley. Again, a situation which led to some development only to suffer breakdown might merely repeat this process more frequently in a longer interval of time. On the other hand, the effect of large initial numbers is to assure at least one situation in which the whole series of schemes will win through.

(12) The foregoing properties of world process are generic. They assume that there are laws of the classical type, but they do not assume the determinate content of any particular classical law. They assume that classical laws can be combined into the circular relationships of schemes, but they do not venture to analyze the structure of any scheme whatever. They assume that there are statistical laws, but there is no assumption of the determinate content of any statistical law.

Moreover,[f] these properties are relatively invariant. They rest on the scientist's necessary presupposition that there are classical and statistical laws to be determined. But they in no way prejudge the determination of those laws nor the manner in which they are to be combined to yield schemes of recurrence and their successive probabilities. It follows that the foregoing properties of world process cannot be upset by any amount of scientific work in the determination of classical or statistical laws.

Again, these properties are explanatory of world process. They reveal an order, a design, an intelligibility. For they account in generic fashion for numbers and time intervals, for distributions and concentrations, for blind alleys and breakdowns, for enormous differentiation, for increasing systematization, for stability without necessity, for assurance without determinism, for development without chance.

Finally, the intelligibility offered by the explanation is immanent in world process. It exhibits the inner design of world process as an emergent probability, and from that design it concludes to the outstanding generic features of the same process. Accordingly, since empirical method aims at such an immanent intelligibility, emergent probability is a view of world order within the limits of empirical method. As we began by inviting the reader to grasp the intelligibility immanent in the image of a cartwheel, so now we are inviting him to perform again the same kind of act. The only difference is that, for the image of the cartwheel, he now must substitute the main features of the universe of our experience.

3   Clarification by Contrast   [128–39]

There is a clarification of ideas through contrast with their opposites. As we have argued that an acceptance of both classical and statistical laws leads to some such world view as emergent probability, so now we have to see how different methodological positions result in different world views.

3.1 The Aristotelian World View   [129–30]

Aristotle recognized both natural laws and statistical residues. But his natural laws lumped together in primitive confusion not only classical laws and schemes of recurrence but also an element or aspect of statistical laws. His distinction was between the necessary and the contingent. The necessary was what always happens, as in the movements of the stars. The contingent was what usually happens; thus, usually heavy bodies fall to the earth, but sometimes they are propped up and so do not fall.

Not only did Aristotle fail to grasp the abstract laws of nature of the classical type, but explicitly he repudiated the possibility of a theory of probability. For him all terrestrial events were contingent. No doubt, effect follows from cause; but it does so only if some other cause does not intervene; and such intervention is a mere coincidence. It is true that any coincidence can be traced back to earlier coincidences, and that from the earlier coincidences one can regress to still earlier coincidences; but one can never get out of the category of the merely coincidental, and within that category there is nothing to be grasped by any science. Hence, while Aristotle recognized statistical residues and concrete patterns of diverging series of conditions, he had no theory of probability to bring them to heel within the field of scientific knowledge.

Still, Aristotle had no intention of allowing terrestrial process to bog down in a mere morass of coincidental interferences. To exorcize such entropy, he argued from seasonal variations to the influence of celestial bodies upon terrestrial activities. Because the sun and moon, the planets and stars, operated necessarily, because they operated from successively different positions, they supplied him with a sufficient ground and cause for the periodicity and perpetuity of terrestrial change. In this fashion there arose his notion of an eternal heaven, an eternal earth, and eternal cyclic recurrence.

Emergent probability differs from the Aristotelian world view because it rests on a different notion of science and of law. Classical laws are abstract. The alleged necessary movements of the heavens are merely schemes of recurrence that arose through the unfolding of probabilities and will survive in accord with probabilities. The regularities of terrestrial process are essentially similar, though here the schemes are more complex and the probabilities lower. Finally, eternal cyclic recurrence vanishes, and in its place there comes the successive realization, in accord with successive schedules of probabilities, of a conditioned series of ever more complex schemes of recurrence. It is not celestial necessity that assures the success of terrestrial process, but emergent probability that provides the design of all process; and that design is not an eternal cyclic recurrence, but the realization through probability of a conditioned series of ever more developed schemes.

3.2 The Galilean World View   [130–32]

Galileo discovered our law of falling bodies, but he failed to recognize its abstractness. Correctly, he grasped that explanation lies beyond description, that the relations of things to our senses must be transcended, that the relations of things to one another must be grasped, and that a geometrization of nature is the key tool in performing this task. Still, Galileo did not cast his methodological discoveries in the foregoing terms. Instead of speaking of the relations of things to our senses, he spoke of the merely apparent secondary qualities of things. Instead of speaking of the relations of things to one another, he spoke of their real and objective primary qualities, and these he conceived as the mathematical dimensions of matter in motion.

Thus Galilean methodology is penetrated with philosophic assumptions about reality and objectivity, and unfortunately those assumptions are not too happy. Their influence is evident in Descartes. Their ambiguities appear in Hobbes and Locke, Berkeley and Hume. Their final inadequacy becomes clear in Kant, where the real and objective bodies of Galilean thought prove to constitute no more than a phenomenal world.

Hitherto, on the other hand, our procedure has been to prescind severely from philosophic questions about reality and objectivity. In due course we shall have to meet them. But our present concern is the fact that Galilean laws of nature are not conceived in abstraction from sensible, or at least imaginable, elements, and consequently that the Galilean law stands in the field, not of our abstract classical laws, but rather of our schemes of recurrence, in which abstract laws and imaginable elements can combine.

From this concreteness of the conception of natural laws there follows a twofold consequence. On the one hand, there arises the hostility of incomprehension against statistical laws. On the other hand, there results a mechanistic view of the universe. For in the abstract, classical laws possess universality and necessity. The Galilean acknowledges this universality and necessity but cannot recognize its abstractness. For him it is attached immediately to imaginable particles or an imaginable ether or both. For him it is already concrete, and so it is not in need of further determinations to reach concreteness. For him the further determinations, which would be nonsystematically related to one another, simply do not exist. Accordingly, since he has no doubt of the existence of classical laws, he cannot but regard statistical laws as mere formulations of our ignorance. There is some vast aggregate of discrete or continuous but imaginable elements; they are subject to universal and necessary laws; and the business of the scientist is the hard task of determining those laws and so predicting what cannot but occur.

Moreover, within this context the negation of statistical laws involves mechanism. A machine is a set of imaginable parts, each of which stands in determinate systematic relations to all the others. In like manner, the universe implicit in Galilean methodology is an aggregate of imaginable parts, and each is related systematically to all the others. The sole difference is that, apart from the machine, there are other imaginable elements that can interfere with its operation, but apart from the universe of imaginable elements, what imaginable interventions can there arise? Mechanism accordingly becomes a determinism.

Until recently, this Galilean view had been dominant[g] in scientific circles. It easily survived the rather veiled implications of Darwinism. But it seems to have suffered a crippling wound from the overt claims of quantum mechanics. Our argument, however, moves on a different terrain. It appeals to Darwinism and to quantum mechanics only as illustrations of scientific intelligence. Its proper premises lie in the dynamic structure of empirical inquiry and in the canons that govern its unfolding. In that field it has noticed that abstraction is not impoverishing but enriching, that in the sense of enriching abstraction classical laws are abstract, that a systematic unification of classical laws does not imply the possibility of imaginative synthesis, that the concentration of systematic relationships in the abstract field leaves the further determinations needed for concrete applications nonsystematically related to one another. It follows that classical and statistical laws, so far from being opposed, are complementary. It follows that the regularities of our universe result, not from classical laws alone, but from the combination of such laws with suitable constellations of concrete circumstances. Finally, it follows that these schemes of recurrence – just as the machines that men make – emerge and function, survive and vanish, in accord with the successive schedules of probabilities for the realization of a conditioned series of schemes.

3.3 The Darwinian World View [132–34]

There are those that date the dawn of human intelligence from the publication of Darwin's *Origin of Species* in 1859. In fact, though the work does not contain any systematic statement of methodological foundations, it does present the outstanding instance of the employment of probability as a principle of explanation. For in the first place, Darwinism proposes to explain. It offers to tell why species differ, why they are found in their observable spatiotemporal distributions, why the numbers in each species increase, or remain constant, or diminish even to the point of extinction. In the second place, the explanation presents an intelligibility immanent in the data, grounded in similarities and differences, in numbers and their rates of change, in distributions over the surface of the earth and through the epochs of geology. In the third place, this immanent intelligibility differs radically from the immanent intelligibility offered, for instance, by Newton's theory of universal gravitation or Laplace's affirmation of a single mathematical formula by which a suitably endowed intelligence might deduce any world situation from complete information on a single situation. For the follower of Laplace cannot reach any determinate conclusions unless he is provided with fully accurate information on the basic situation. But the follower of Darwin is indifferent to the details of his basic situation, and he obtains his conclusions by appealing to the natural selection of chance variations that arise in any of a large variety of terrestrial processes from any of a large variety of initial situations.

It is not difficult to discern in Darwin's natural selection of chance variations a particular case of a more general formula. For it is not the single isolated variation but rather a combination of variations that is significant for the evolutionary process. Again, while such combinations of variations may be attributed to chance, in the sense that the biologist is concerned, not with efficient causality, but with an immanent intelligibility, still what is significant for evolution is the probability of emergence of such combinations of variations, and not the nonsystematic divergence from their probability which is our meaning of the name 'chance.' Finally, as chance variation is an instance of probability of emergence, so natural selection is an instance of probability of survival. Artificial selection is the work of the breeder, who mates the plants or animals possessing the characteristics he wishes to encourage. Natural selection is the work of nature, which gives a shorter life expectancy and so less frequent litters to the types that are less well equipped to fend for themselves. Still, nature effects this selection, not with the exact predictability of the changing phases of the moon, but only by a general tendency that admits exceptions and that increases in efficacy with the increase of numbers and the prolongation of time intervals. In a word, natural selection means survival in accord with the probabilities.

Moreover, these combinations of variations, which possess probabilities of emergence and of survival, are relevant to schemes of recurrence. For the concrete living of any plant or animal may be regarded as a set of sequences of operations. Such operations are of kinds; there are many of the same kind; and those of the same kind occur at different times. There are, then, in each set of sequences recurrent operations, and the regularity of the recurrence reveals the existence and functioning of schemes.

Within such schemes the plant or animal is only a component. The whole schematic circle of events does not occur within the living thing, but goes beyond it into the environment, from which sustenance is won and into which offspring are born. No doubt, the higher the type, the greater the complexity and the greater the proportion of significant events that occur within the animal. But this greater complexity only means that the larger circle connects a series of lesser and incomplete circles. The vascular circulation occurs within the animal, but it depends upon the digestive system, which depends upon the animal's capacity to deal with its environment, and in turn that capacity depends on the growth and nourishment secured by the vascular system.

Again, the plant or animal is a component for a range of schemes. Unlike the planets, which stick to their courses in the solar system, and like the electrons, which may be imagined to hop from one orbit to another, the plant or animal enters into any of a range of sets of alternative schemes. This range is limited by immanent structure and capacity. Still, though it is limited, it remains open to alternatives. For without change of structure or of basic capacity, the plant or animal continues to survive within some variations of temperature and pressure, of circumambient water or air, of sunlight and soil, of the floating population of other plants or animals on which it lives.

At this point, however, the differences between Darwinism and emergent probability begin to come to light. Emergent probability affirms a conditioned series of schemes of recurrence that are realized in accord with successive schedules of probabilities. Darwinism, on the other hand, affirms a conditioned series of species of things to be realized in accord with successive schedules of probability. The two views are parallel in their formal structures. They are related, inasmuch as species of living things emerge and function within ranges of alternative sets of schemes of recurrence. Nonetheless, there is a profound difference. For Darwinian probabilities of emergence and survival regard, not schemes of recurrence, but underlying potential components for any schemes within a limited range, and the Darwinian series of species is a sequence of higher potentialities that exhibit their development by their capacity to function in ever greater ranges of alternative sets of schemes.

This difference prompts us to recall that the present account of emergent probability did not aim at completeness. We had not raised the question, What are things? We had not determined whether there is an answer to that question that satisfies the scientific canon of parsimony. Accordingly, we presented emergent probability in the present chapter with the qualification that later, when the notion of thing has been investigated, there might be needed a further development of the analysis.

However, it may not be amiss to add at once that inquiry into the meaning of the name 'thing' will yield but a further manifestation of the dualism in uncritical thought. Just as mechanist determinism has involved an extrascientific world view, so also has Darwinism. Just as we have replaced the natural selection of chance variations by an emergent probability of schemes of recurrence, so in chapter 8 we shall find that a critical notion of the thing necessitates a still more significant departure from the unconscious philosophic assumptions of nineteenth-century science.[h]

3.4 Indeterminism[i]   [134–39]

By indeterminism is meant a contemporary tendency that owes its origin to the verified equations of quantum mechanics but goes beyond its source inasmuch as it pronounces on the nature of scientific knowledge and even on philosophic issues. While it is opposed radically to mechanical determinism, its positive features do not admit summary description, and perhaps our purpose will best be served by discussing successively a series of issues.

First, as Galileo distinguished between merely apparent secondary qualities and, on the other hand, the real and objective dimensions of matter in motion, so too there are indeterminists that offer a somewhat parallel disclosure of the nature of reality. The old distinction between the real and the apparent is retained, but now the real is microscopic and random, while the merely apparent is the macroscopic in which classical laws seem to be verified. However, we mention this issue only to decline an immediate discussion. Later in a philosophic context we shall attempt an explanatory account of the almost endless variety of views on reality and objectivity. For the present we shall have to be content with the canon of parsimony: the scientist may affirm what he can verify, and he may not affirm what he cannot verify.

Secondly, indeterminists tend to reject the old imaginable particles and waves and to favor some type of conceptual symbolism. Here again the issue is the precise nature of reality, but now, by appealing to the canon of parsimony, we can reach two conclusions. On the one hand, it would seem that the only possible verification of the imagined as imagined lies in a corresponding sensation; accordingly, if the particles are too small and the waves too subtle to be sensed as particles and waves, then the particles as imagined and the waves as imagined cannot be verified; and if they cannot be verified, they may not be affirmed by the scientist. On the other hand, it is possible to verify conceptual formulations if they possess sensible implications; for in the measure that an increasing number and variety of such implications are found to correspond to sensible experience, the verification of the conceptual formulation is approached. Thus, special relativity is said to be probable, not because many scientists feel that they have had a fairly good look at a four-dimensional space-time manifold, but because many scientists working on different problems have found procedures and predictions based on special relativity to be highly successful.

Thirdly, there occurs an argument from the haziness of data to the ultimate unverifiability of classical laws. While I do not believe it to be cogent, it is well worth attention. For it appeals to the criterion of verifiability; it rests on the solid fact of the haziness of data; and it does exclude misconceptions of the nature of classical laws.

To begin, the haziness of data is not to be denied. What of itself is determinate never is a datum and always is a concept. Of themselves, data may be said to be determinate materially or potentially; but they become determinate formally only in the measure that they are subsumed under concepts; and this process of subsumption can be prolonged indefinitely. Thus a greater formal determinateness of data is possible as long as scientific concepts can be revised to yield more precise objects for measurement, and as long as scientific techniques can be improved to make measurements more accurate. But as long as a greater formal determinateness is possible, the determinateness that actually is attained is conjoined with an unspecified remainder of merely potential determinateness. That unspecified remainder is the haziness of data, and it will be with us as long as new concepts and more accurate measurements are possible.

However, the haziness of data alone cannot prove the unverifiability of classical laws. Logically, it is impossible for a valid conclusion to contain a term that does not appear in the premises. More concretely, it could be true that, whenever data became more determinate formally, new classical laws were discovered; and in that case the haziness of data would prove, not that classical laws were unverifiable, but that existing classical laws were always due to be revised in favor of other classical laws.

One comes closer to the issue when one argues that classical laws are conceptual formulations, that they possess all the precision and formal determinateness of concepts, that they cannot be stripped of that precision and determinateness without ceasing to be classical laws. In contrast, data are irreducibly hazy. Because measurements never can be accurate to n decimal places, where n is as large as one pleases, classical laws never can be more than approximative. Their essential determinacy is in radical conflict with the haziness of data; and so classical laws essentially are unverifiable.

Now this argument is valid if classical laws are interpreted concretely. For on concrete interpretation classical laws are supposed to state relations between data, or between elements in strict correspondence with data. But there cannot be completely determinate relations between essentially hazy terms; and so, on concrete interpretation, classical laws must be regarded as no more than approximative.

Still, there is no need to interpret classical laws concretely. They can be statements of elements in abstract system where (1) the abstract system is constituted by implicitly defined relations and terms, (2) the abstract system is connected with data not directly but through the mediation of a complementary set of descriptive concepts, and (3) the laws of the abstract system are said to be verified inasmuch as they assign limits on which, other things being equal, vast varieties of data converge. On this showing, the completely determinate relations of classical laws are between the completely determinate terms they implicitly define. This closed structure is referred to data through a set of descriptive and so approximative concepts. Finally, the closed structure is proved relevant to data, not by exact coincidence, but by assigning the limits on which data converge.

Fourthly, the affirmation of convergence is also an admission of divergence. Is not that admission equivalent to the statement that ultimately classical laws are not verifiable?

Again, the issue is the precise nature of verification. It hardly would be claimed that any single law was not verified because it did not account for the whole of our experience. But what can hold for single laws also can hold for the totality of classical laws. The existence of the divergence proves that classical laws are not the whole of our explanatory knowledge. But though they are not the whole, they can be a part; and the classical laws that in fact are such a part are the ones that are verified in the sense that they assign the limits on which data do converge.

Fifthly, it is claimed that quantum mechanics is the more general theory and that it includes, say, Newtonian mechanics as a particular case.

Here I would suggest the relevance of a distinction between logical inclusion and concrete application. I see no reason for disputing the contention that Schrödinger's time equation can plausibly be simplified into Newton's second law of motion. But it need not follow that the simplification has no analogue in the world of events. On the contrary, it would seem that such an analogue would exist if schemes of recurrence were realized perfectly; and in that case it would seem difficult to maintain that the accuracy of basic observations was not the sole limit to the accuracy of predictions. More realistically, insofar as schemes are not realized perfectly or perfect realization cannot be ascertained, at least the reason for objective divagations or subjective ignorance would be assigned.

Sixthly, it may be argued that determinism must be true or false and that we seem to be dodging the issue. But if the disjunction is admitted, one finds oneself forced into philosophic questions. At least in the present context, our contention would be that the old determinism with its philosophic implications has to give way to a new, purely methodological view that consists in a developing anticipation of a determinate object.

Such a view would remain within the limits of empirical science. It would distinguish between an antecedent component of methodological assumptions and a consequent component of probably verified laws and frequencies. Both components would be regarded as variable. The antecedent component develops: initially it consists in such vague generalities as the assertion that there is a reason for everything; subsequently, as science advances, it takes on the increasing precision of ever more accurately differentiated heuristic structures. Again, the consequent component is subject to variation, for what is regarded as verified at any time may be called into question and subjected to revision. The concrete conjunction of the two components in the minds of scientists constitutes at any time their anticipations of a determinate object; and when the components are undergoing profound change, there naturally will be some uncertainty in their anticipations.

On this view the old determinism was mistaken not only because it was involved in philosophic issues but also because it failed to envisage the possibility of development in heuristic structures. It supposed the universal validity of a type of explanation that is possible only when schematic situations are realized perfectly. It overlooked the possibility of a type of explanation in which the probabilities of the nonschematic account for the emergence of the schematic.

Indeterminism is true as a negation of the old determinism. But it cannot escape the necessity of methodological assumptions and precepts; it cannot prevent their conjunction in thought with laws and frequencies that are regarded as verified; and so it cannot succeed even in delaying the day when, from a new viewpoint, scientific anticipations once more will envisage a determinate object to be known.

However, at the present time there is some difficulty in specifying in a universally acceptable fashion just what is the determinate object that science is to anticipate. A student of human knowledge can make suggestions that regard the antecedent component, and so I have offered a unified view that anticipates both the systematic and the nonsystematic without excluding in particular cases insight into concrete nonschematic situations. The possibility of concrete insight into the nonschematic situations of the subatomic order probably will be called into question on both practical and theoretical grounds. However, I do not propose to discuss this aspect of the issue, principally because it regards the consequent component of methodological anticipations, but also because I believe all discussions of concrete possibility to suffer from a radical ambiguity. For on any concrete issue further insight is always possible, and when it occurs, what previously seemed impossible turns out to be quite feasible after all.

4   Conclusion[j]   [139]

Let us bring this long chapter to an end. It began from the problem of apparent duality that arose from the existence of two types of insight, two heuristic structures, and two distinct methods of empirical investigation. There was no question of eliminating the duality, for the direct and the inverse types of insight both occur. There remained, then, the task of relating diverse procedures and results into a single whole. In a first section it was argued that classical and statistical investigations are complementary as cognitional activities. In a second section it was revealed how their results, whatever their precise content, can be combined into a single world view. In a third section this world view was contrasted with the Aristotelian, with that of mechanist determinism, with the Darwinian view, and with contemporary tendencies to affirm an indeterminism. In the course of the argument the problem of the thing, and with it the problem of objectivity, became increasingly apparent. But before tackling such large issues, it will be well to broaden the basis of our operations, and so we turn to the notions of space and time.

5

Space and Time

For a variety of reasons attention is now directed to the notions of space and time. Not only are these notions puzzling and so interesting, but they throw considerable light on the precise nature of abstraction, they provide a concrete and familiar context for the foregoing analyses of empirical science, and they form a natural bridge over which we may advance from our examination of science to an examination of common sense.

The present chapter falls into five sections. First of all, there is set forth a problem that is peculiar to physics as distinct from other natural sciences such as chemistry and biology. Secondly, there is worked out a descriptive account of space and time. Thirdly, an attempt is made to formulate their abstract intelligibility. Fourthly, there follows a discussion of rods and clocks. Finally, the concrete intelligibility of space and time is indicated.

1   The Problem Peculiar to Physics   [140–42]

1.1 Invariant and Relative Expressions   [140–41]

To formulate this problem, distinctions must be drawn (1) between propositions and expressions, and (2) between invariant and relative expressions.

For present purposes the distinctions between propositions and expressions will be indicated sufficiently by such illustrative statements as the following.

'It is cold' and '*Il fait froid*' are two expressions of the same proposition.

Again, '2 + 2 = 4' and '10 + 10 = 100' are respectively the decimal and binary expressions of the same proposition.

Now just as different expressions may stand for the same proposition, so the same expression under different circumstances may stand for different propositions. This fact leads to a distinction between invariant and relative expressions.

Expressions are named invariant if, when employed in any place or at any time, they stand for the same proposition.

Expressions are named relative if, when employed in different places or at different times, they stand for different propositions.

Thus, '2 + 2 = 4' stands for the same proposition no matter where or when it is uttered. It is invariant. On the other hand, 'John is here now' stands for as many different propositions as there are places in which it is uttered and times at which it is uttered. It is relative.

1.2 Their Ground in Abstraction [141]

It is not difficult to discern the reason why some expressions are invariant and others are relative. For if an expression stands for an abstract proposition, it contains no reference to any particular place or time; if it contains no reference to particular places or times, it contains no element that might vary with variations of the place or time of the speaker. Inversely, if an expression stands for a concrete proposition, it will contain a reference to a particular place or time, and so it will include an element that can vary with variations of the speaker's position and time.

The point may be illustrated by contrasting the use of the copula 'is' in the two expressions 'John is here' and 'Pure water is H_2O.' In the first expression, which stands for a concrete proposition, the copula is relative to the time of utterance; the grammatical present tense of the verb 'to be' has its proper force; and saying that John is here has no implication that John was or was not here, or that John will or will not be here. On the other hand, to say that pure water is H_2O is to utter an abstract law of nature; grammatically, the copula occurs in the present tense, but it is not intended to confine the force of the expression to the present time. For if really it is true that pure water is H_2O, then necessarily pure water was H_2O even before oxygen was discovered, and pure water will remain H_2O even after an atom bomb has eliminated anyone interested in chemistry. In brief, the copula 'is' in abstract expressions occurs not in the ordinary present tense but rather in an invariant tense that abstracts from particular times.[a]

1.3 Abstraction in Physics   [141–42]

Now if the invariance or relativity of expressions follows from the abstractness or concreteness of the propositions for which they stand, then, since all mathematical principles and all natural laws of the classical type are abstract, it follows that their appropriate expression must be invariant.

In fact, such invariance of expression is secured automatically in mathematics, in chemistry, and in biology. There never arose any tendency to write out the multiplication table or to state the binomial theorem differently in Germany and France, in the nineteenth or twentieth centuries. In like manner it would be impossible to find relative expressions for the hundreds of thousands of formulae for chemical compounds. Such statements simply contain no reference to space or time, and so cannot vary with variations of the speaker's position or epoch.

However, the science of physics does not enjoy the same immunity. It investigates local movements, and it cannot state their laws without some reference to places and times. Since the laws[b] contain a reference to places and times, they include an element that can vary with variations of the speaker's position and time. Accordingly, there arises a problem peculiar to physics. Just as ordinary language develops an invariant copula to express general truths, so too the physicist has to find spatiotemporal invariants if he is to employ the appropriate invariant expressions in stating laws of local motion.

2   The Description of Space and Time   [142–48]

Before tackling the problem peculiar to physics, it will be well to review the materials or data that are involved. Such a review is a task for description, and as we have seen, descriptions are cast in terms of experiential conjugates. Accordingly, we shall begin from elementary experiences, work out the resultant notions of space and time, and show how they necessarily involve the use of frames of reference and of transformations.

2.1 Extensions and Durations   [142–43]

There exist certain elementary and familiar experiences of looking, moving about, grasping, etc.

The experiences themselves have a duration. They occur, not all at once, but over time. Moreover, correlative to the duration of looking, there is the duration of what is looked at. Correlative to the duration of the moving, there is the duration of what is moved through or over. Correlative to the duration of the grasping, there is the duration of what is grasped. Descriptively, then, duration is either an immanent aspect or quality of an experience or a correlative aspect or quality of what is experienced.

While duration is commonly attributed both to the experience and to the experienced, extension is attributed only to the latter. The colors I see, the surfaces I grasp, the volumes through which I move, all have extension. But it would seem paradoxical to speak of the extension of the experience of seeing, of the experience of grasping, of the experience of moving. Descriptively, then, extensions are correlative to certain elementary and familiar experiences, but they are in the experienced and not in the experiencing.

2.2 Descriptive Definitions   [143–44]

Let us now define Space as the ordered totality of concrete extensions, and Time as the ordered totality of concrete durations. Further, let us give notice that henceforth, when Space and Time are written with capital letters, the words will be employed in accord with the foregoing definitions.

For besides the totalities of concrete extensions and concrete durations, there also are merely imaginary totalities. What a man experiences he also can imagine. As he experiences extension, he also imagines extension. As he experiences duration, he also imagines duration. Our concern is not with imaginary extensions or imaginary durations but with the concrete extensions and durations correlative to experience.

Immediately, however, there arises an obvious difficulty. For neither the totality of concrete extensions nor the totality of concrete durations falls within the experience of the human race, let alone the human individual. For this reason the definition refers, not to any totalities, but to ordered totalities. It is true enough that only a fragment of concrete extension and of concrete duration falls within human experience. Still, one can take that fragment as origin. Beyond the extension that is experienced, there is further extension; and since it is continuous with the extension of experience, it is not merely imagined. Similarly, beyond the duration of experience, there is further duration;[c] and since it is continuous with the duration of experience, it is not merely imagined.

There follows a simple criterion for distinguishing between the notion of concrete Space or Time and, on the other hand, merely imaginary space or time. Within concrete Space there is some extension that is correlative to experience; all other extension in Space is related to that concrete extension; and in virtue of that relation all other extension in Space is concrete. Similarly, a notion of concrete Time is constructed about a nucleus of experienced duration. On the other hand, merely imaginary space or time contains no part that is correlative to actual experience.

From the criterion, there follows a corollary. Imaginary space or time may or may not be structured about an origin. But notions of concrete Space or Time must be structured about an origin. For only fragments of concrete Space or Time enter into human experience, and so it is only by a relational structure to given extensions or durations that totalities of extensions or durations can be concrete. In other words, frames of reference are essential to the notions of Space and Time.

2.3 Frames of Reference   [144–45]

Frames of reference are structures of relations employed to order totalities of extensions and/or durations. They fall into three main classes: the personal, the public, and the special.

First, everyone has his personal reference frame. It moves when he moves, turns when he turns, and keeps its 'now' synchronized with his psychological present. The existence of this personal reference frame is witnessed by the correlation between the place and time of the speaker and, on the other hand, the meaning of such words as *here, there, near, far, right, left, above, below, in front, behind, now, then, soon, recently, long ago,* etc.

Secondly, there are public reference frames. Thus, men become familiar with the plans of buildings, the network of streets in which they move, the maps of their cities, countries, continents. Similarly, they are familiar with the alternation of night and day, with the succession of weeks and months, with the use of clocks and calendars. Now such relational schemes knit together extensions and durations. But they are not personal reference frames that shift about with an individual's movements. On the contrary, they are public, common to many individuals, and employed to translate the *here* and *now* of the personal reference frame into generally intelligible locations and dates. Finally, the difference between personal and public reference frames comes out clearly in the occurrence of such questions as, Where am I? What time is it? What is the date? Everyone is always aware that he is here and now. But further knowledge is required to correlate one's *here* with a place on a map and one's *now* with the reading of a clock or a calendar.

Thirdly, there are special reference frames. A basic position, direction, and instant are selected. Coordinate axes are drawn. Divisions on the axes are specified, and so any point at any instant can be denoted univocally as an (x, y, z, t).

Special reference frames may be mathematical or physical. They are mathematical if they order an imaginary space and time. They are physical if they order concrete Space and Time. The distinction is brought to light by selecting any (x, y, z, t) and asking where and when it is. For if the frame is physical, the answer will indicate some precise point in Space and some precise instant in Time. But if the frame is mathematical, the answer will be that any point-instant whatever will do.

2.4 Transformations   [145–46]

There can be as many distinct reference frames of any kind as there are possible origins and orientations.

From this multiplicity there follows the problem of transposing from statements relative to one reference frame to statements relative to another.

Solutions may be particular, and then they are obtained by inspection and insight. Thus, when two men face each other, one may observe that the region of Space to the right of one man is to the left of the other, and so one concludes that under such circumstances what for one is 'right' for the other is 'left.' In like manner, maps of different countries may be correlated by turning to the map of the continent that includes both countries, and clocks in different positions may be synchronized by appealing to the earth's spin.

Special reference frames admit a more general solution. Let the point

(x, y, z) in the frame K be identical with the point specified as (x', y', z') in the frame K'. From geometrical considerations it will be possible to find three equations relating x, y, and z, respectively, to x', y', and z', and further, to show that these equations hold for any point (x, y, z). In this fashion there are obtained transformation equations, and by the simple process of substitution any statement in terms of x, y, z can be transformed into a statement in terms of x', y', z'.

For example, the wave front of a light signal emitted from the origin of a frame K might be the sphere

$$x^2 + y^2 + z^2 = c^2t^2.$$

The equations for transforming from the frame K to a frame K' might be

$$x = x' - vt'; \; y = y'; \; z = z'; \; t = t'.$$

On substituting, one would obtain the equation of the wave front in the frame K', namely,

$$(x' - vt')^2 + y'^2 + z'^2 = c^2t'^2.$$

2.5 *Generalized Geometry*   [146–47]

In the foregoing consideration of transformations, the procedure in the special case was based upon geometrical considerations. It is worth noting that the inverse procedure is possible, that is, that from a consideration of transformations one can work out the general theory of geometries.

Consider any function of n variables, say,

$$F(x_1, x_2, \ldots) = 0 \tag{1}$$

and any n arbitrary transformation equations, say,

$$x_1 = x_1(x'_1, x'_2, \ldots)$$
$$x_2 = x_2(x'_1, x'_2, \ldots) \tag{2}$$

which on substitution yield the new function, say,

$$G(x'_1, x'_2, \ldots) = 0. \tag{3}$$

Let these mathematical expressions have a geometrical interpretation, so that the initial variables in x_i refer to positions along the axes of a coordinate system K, and the subsequent variables in x'_i refer to positions along the axes of another coordinate system K', and the transformation equations represent a shift from the reference frame K to the frame K'.

Now the mathematical expressions have the same meaning, stand for the same propositions, and require the same geometrical interpretation, if they have the same symbolic form. For the meaning of a mathematical expression resides, not in the material symbols employed, but in the form of their combination to indicate operations of adding, multiplying, and so forth.

Accordingly, when the symbolic form of a mathematical expression is unchanged by a transformation, the meaning of the expression is unchanged. But a transformation is a shift from one spatiotemporal standpoint to another, and when expressions do not change their meaning under such shifts, then, as we have seen above, the expressions are invariant, and the ground of that invariance is that the expressions stand for abstract and generally valid propositions.

Now the principles and laws of a geometry are abstract and generally valid propositions. It follows that the mathematical expression of the principles and laws of a geometry will be invariant under the permissible transformations of that geometry.

Such is the general principle, and it admits at least two applications. In the first application, one specifies successive sets of transformation equations, determines the mathematical expressions invariant under those transformations, and concludes that the successive sets of invariants represent the principles and laws of successive geometries. In this fashion one may differentiate Euclidean, affine, projective, and topological geometries.[1]

A second, slightly different application of the general principle occurs in the theory of Riemannian manifolds. The one basic law governing all such manifolds is given by the equation for the infinitesimal interval, namely,

$$ds^2 = \Sigma g_{ij} dx_i dx_j \ [i, j = 1, 2, \ldots n]$$

where $dx_1, dx_2, \ldots$ are differentials of the coordinates, where the coefficients g_{ij} are functions of the coordinates, and where in general there

---

1 See, for instance, the summary outline offered by Victor F. Lenzen, *The Nature of Physical Theory* 59–62.

are n^2 products under the summation. Since this equation defines the infinitesimal interval, it must be invariant under all permissible transformations. However, instead of working out successive sets of transformations, one considers any transformations to be permissible and effects the differentiation of different manifolds by imposing restrictions upon the coefficients. This is done by appealing to the tensor calculus. For tensors are defined by their transformation properties, and it can be shown that, in the present case, if the coefficients g_{ij} are any instance of a covariant tensor of the second degree, then the expression for the infinitesimal interval will be invariant under arbitrary transformations. It follows that there are as many instances of the Riemannian manifold, and so as many distinct geometries, as there are instances of covariant tensors of the second degree employed to specify the coefficients g_{ij}. Thus, in the familiar Euclidean instance, g_{ij} is unity when i equals j; it is zero when i does not equal j; and there are three dimensions. In Minkowski space the g_{ij} is unity or zero as before, but there are four dimensions, and x_4 equals ict. In the general theory of relativity the coefficients are symmetrical, so that g_{ij} equals g_{ji}; and in the generalized theory of gravitation the coefficients are antisymmetrical.

2.6 A Logical Note   [148]

It is to be observed that transformation equations, operations of transforming, the definition of tensors by their transformation properties, and the whole foregoing account of the differentiation of geometrical manifolds belong to higher-order statements.

For distinct reference frames assign different specifications to the same points and instants, and they assign the same specifications (numbers) to different points and instants. Accordingly, they must belong to different universes of logical discourse, else endless ambiguities would result. Now the relations between different universes of discourse can be stated only in a further, higher-order universe of discourse; in other words, the relations between different universes of discourse regard, not the things specified in those universes, but the specifications employed to denote the things. Thus, a transformation equation does not relate points or instants, but it does relate different ways of specifying the same points and instants. Similarly, such a property as invariance is a property, not of a geometrical entity, but of an expression regarding geometrical or other entities.

3   The Abstract Intelligibility of Space and Time   [148–60]

The argument began from a problem peculiar to physics. Because that science deals with objects in their spatial and temporal relations, the expression of its principles and laws does not automatically attain the invariance proper to such abstract propositions. However, as was shown in chapter 2, this difficulty can be turned to profit inasmuch as the physicist can posit a postulate of invariance and then employ that postulate as a heuristic norm in determining which expressions can represent physical principles and laws.

The second strand of the argument consisted in an outline of the descriptive notions of Space and Time. It began from experiences[d] of concrete extensions and durations, and it showed that we can form notions of all concrete extensions and of all concrete durations if, and only if, these totalities are ordered by frames of reference. Essentially, then, the descriptive notion of Space is of Space-for-us, and the descriptive notion of Time is of Time-for-us. Again, one might say that these notions necessarily contain, on the one hand, an empirical or material element, and on the other hand, an intelligible or formal element. The empirical or material element consists of concrete extensions and of concrete durations. The intelligible or formal element orders these materials into singular totalities. Moreover, without this intervention of ordering intelligence, the notion of Space cannot be both concrete and all-embracing, and similarly the notion of Time cannot regard the totality of concrete durations.

Still, these descriptive notions of Space and Time cannot contain the intelligibility that is explanatory of Space and Time. It is true that they contain an intelligible or formal component. But that component is the order of a reference frame, and reference frames are an infinity. They can be the intelligibility of Space-for-us and of Time-for-us, that is, they can be the manners in which we intelligently order extensions and durations in accord with the convenience of the moment. But they cannot be the immanent intelligibility that is explanatory of Space nor the immanent intelligibility that is explanatory of Time, for reference frames are infinite but correct explanations are unique.

However, this gives rise to a further problem. On the one hand, if we retain reference frames, we are dealing with infinities of formally different notions of Space and Time. On the other hand, if we drop reference frames, then our inquiry is confined either to merely imaginary space and time or else to the relatively few extensions and durations that fall within our experience. It is this dilemma that reveals the significance of transformations and invariance under transformations. For, while such considerations belong to a higher-order universe of discourse which directly regards not objects but expressions referring to objects, still they can serve to point the way to grasping the intelligibilities immanent in Space and in Time. Inasmuch as we say what we think, the properties of our expressions reflect the properties of our thoughts. Inasmuch as we think intelligently, the properties of our thoughts reflect the properties of our insights. In this fashion, the invariance of expression has already been traced to the abstractness of what is thought or meant, and at an earlier stage of the inquiry, the abstractness of classical laws was grounded on the enriching contribution of insight. Accordingly, we shall not be venturing into a new line of thought if we argue that the set of insights by which we grasp the intelligibility immanent in Space and Time will be the set that is formulated in spatial and temporal principles and laws invariant under transformations of reference frames.

Clearly enough, this conclusion gives no more than a generic answer to our question. It amounts to saying that the immanent intelligibility of Space and of Time will be formulated in one of the geometries that fall under the generalized notion of geometry. There remains the task of assigning the specific geometry that governs concrete extensions and concrete durations. Still, one has only to mention this task to be reminded that there is a problem peculiar to the empirical science of physics, that this problem arises in physics inasmuch as it is involved in spatial and temporal relations, and that the general form of its solution is to postulate the invariance of physical principles and laws.

3.1 The Theorem   [150–51]

It is time to turn from talk about what we propose to do and settle down to the work of doing it.

The abstract formulation of the intelligibility immanent in Space and in Time will be one of the possible sets of definitions, postulates, and inferences that systematically unify the relations of extensions and of durations. All such possible sets of definitions, postulates, and inferences are geometries. Therefore, the abstract formulation of the intelligibility immanent in Space and in Time will be a geometry.

The expression of the principles and laws of any geometry will be invariant. For principles and laws are independent of particular places and times, and so their proper expression cannot vary with variations of spatiotemporal standpoints.

Moreover, a geometry cannot refer to Space or to Time except through a reference frame. Accordingly, the invariance proper to the expression of geometrical principles and laws is an invariance under transformations of reference frames.

There follows at once the generic solution. The abstract formulation of the intelligibility of Space and Time consists in a set of invariants under transformations of reference frames. However, there is a range of such sets of invariants, and so there remains the task of determining the specific solution.

We note, accordingly, that the relevant intelligibility is immanent in concrete extensions and in concrete durations. It is an intelligibility that belongs not to the imagined but to the experienced. Now the empirical canon of complete explanation has already assigned to natural science the duty of doing for experienced extensions and durations exactly what is done for experienced colors, experienced sounds, experienced heat, experienced electromagnetic phenomena. Further, physics is the natural science on which this duty falls, as appears from its peculiar problem of invariance. Again, if the physicist solves his peculiar problem and arrives at an invariant expression of his principles and laws under transformations of reference frames, he cannot avoid reaching the specific solution which we are seeking. For the specific solution we are seeking is the set of invariants under transformations that is verifiable in experienced extensions and durations.

The abstract formulation, then, of the intelligibility immanent in Space and in Time is, generically, a set of invariants under transformations of reference frames, and specifically, the set verified by physicists in establishing the invariant formulation of their abstract principles and laws.[e]

A corollary may be added. The intelligibility immanent in Space and in Time is identical with the intelligibility reached by physicists investigating objects as involved in spatial and temporal relations. Hence, to eliminate the concrete objects of physics would be to eliminate the intelligibility of Space and of Time. Again, inasmuch as physical objects are involved differently in spatial and temporal relations, there result different intelligibilities of Space and of Time. This conclusion may be illustrated by the possibility of different types of tensors being employed to secure the covariance of different sets of physical principles and laws.

3.2 Euclidean Geometry   [151–52]

While the foregoing argument of itself says nothing for or against the verifiability of Euclidean geometry, still it supposes that Euclidean geometry is not the one and only true geometry, and it admits the possibility of other geometries being verifiable.

The supposition is, of course, far more fundamental than the admission. It is difficult not to find the inspiration of rationalism, which deduces everything else from alleged self-evident principles, in the notion that Euclid formulated the one and only true geometry. After all, the supreme rationalist wrote on his title page *Ethica ordine geometrico demonstrata*. Still, these high matters lie beyond the range of present considerations, though in due course we hope to meet this issue with a distinction between analytic propositions, which are not far from tautologies, and analytic principles, whose terms and relations are verifiable in the existent.

At any rate, present concern has to be confined to meeting claims that Euclidean geometry obviously is verified in concrete extensions and that ordinary notions of simultaneity obviously are verified in concrete durations.

Clearly, there is a sense in which these claims are true. It has been seen that one cannot form a notion of Space without invoking a frame of reference. It is plain that men form notions of Space, and no less that the frames of reference they construct satisfy Euclidean requirements. Similarly, one cannot form a notion of Time without introducing a frame of reference, and the frame ordinarily introduced is necessarily in complete accord with ordinary notions on simultaneity. Not for a moment would I dispute the contention that Euclidean geometry and the common view of simultaneity are both verifiable and verified in the descriptive notions men form of Space and Time.

However, after granting all that is obvious, we must now add that it is quite beside the point. The analysis of descriptive notions of Space and Time has its significance, but that significance is anthropological. It reveals how men commonly proceed from the extensions and durations of experience to the totalities named Space and Time. On the other hand, when we admit that Euclidean geometry might not be verifiable, we are speaking of a verification, not in human notions, but in concrete extensions and durations. We are not asking how men find it convenient to conceive Space and Time; we are asking how scientists may correctly explain Space and Time. Were the scientists in question the psychologists, one might appeal to what is obvious in the mentality of Western man. But the scientists in question happen to be physicists, and the data of consciousness, however clear, are not among the data proper to physics.

So much, then, for the sweeping claim that our conclusion must be wrong because its error is obvious. It remains that objections may be less sweeping, and these must now be met.

3.3 Absolute Space   [152–55]

The absolute space and the absolute time of Newtonian thought possess the twofold merit of exhibiting an 'obvious' view and of inviting criticism that goes to the root of the matter.

Suppose a penny to fall to the floor of a moving train, and ask for an account of the trajectory of the fall. Unfortunately, there are many accounts. Relatively to the floor, the trajectory is a vertical straight line. Relatively to the earth, it is a parabola. Relatively to the axes fixed in the sun, it is a more complicated curve that takes into account the spin and orbit of the earth's movements. Relatively to the receding nebulae, it contains still further components. But there is only one penny in question, and there is only one fall. Which, really, is the trajectory?

Newton would answer by distinguishing between true and apparent motion. Both are relative. But while apparent motion is relative to other bodies, such as the train, the earth, the sun, the nebulae, true motion is relative to an eternal set of immutable places named absolute space. If one thinks of apparent motion, one can say that the penny moves relatively to the train, the train relatively to the earth, the earth relatively to the sun, and the sun relatively to the nebulae. But if one thinks of true motion, one can say that, perhaps, the penny, the train, the earth, the sun, and the nebulae have a common velocity relatively to a set of eternal and immutable places.

Moreover, if Newton named his absolute space mathematical, he also considered it real. He admitted the difficulty of determining when there was a true motion. But he was far from acknowledging such a conclusion as impossible. On the contrary, he performed his famous bucket experiment to show that true motion relative to absolute space could be detected. A bucket of water was suspended from a twisted rope. The bucket spun, and for a while the surface of the water remained flat. The surface then hollowed out into a paraboloid. Eventually, the bucket ceased to spin, but the surface remained hollow. Finally, the surface became flat again. Now the hollowing of the surface of the water was due to the rotation of the water, and as this hollowing occurred both while the bucket was spinning and while the bucket was not spinning, it could not be merely an apparent motion relative to the bucket. Therefore, it was true motion relative to absolute space.

Let us now turn to criticism.

First of all, the bucket experiment does not establish the existence of an absolute space. From the experiment one might conclude that really and truly the water was rotating; for in the hollowing of the surface one might verify a centrifugal acceleration; and if there is a verified centrifugal acceleration, there is a verified motion. However, true motion in the sense of verified motion is one thing; and true motion in the sense of motion relative to absolute space is quite another. The bucket experiment does not establish true motion in this second sense. Indeed, the sole link between the experiment and absolute space lies in an equivocal use of the term 'true.'

Secondly, the Newtonian distinction between true and apparent motion involves the use of an extrascientific category. There are the data of experience. There are inquiries, insights, and formulations. There are verifications of formulations. But just as Galileo impugned given colors, sounds, heat, and the like as merely apparent, so Newton impugned as apparent the observable changes of relative position of observable bodies. Just as Galileo affirmed as real and objective the primary qualities that are mathematical dimensions of matter in motion, so Newton, after eliminating experienced motions as apparent, acknowledged as true the motions relative to a nonexperienced absolute space. What is this truth of true motion? Though Newton confused it with the truth of experiment and verification, it has to be something else; otherwise, there would be no confusion. What, then, is it?

A fuller account will be attempted when we treat the notion of objectivity. For the present it will suffice to recall that the Galilean assertion of the reality and objectivity of primary qualities was not in accord with the canon of parsimony but, as we have seen, extrascientific.[2] In simpler terms, Galileo's real and objective was the residue left in the popular

2 See chapter 3, §5 [pp. 107–9].

category of the 'really out there' after colors, sounds, heat, etc., had been eliminated. By parallel reasoning, Newton's absolute space was the 'really out there' but emptied not only of Galileo's secondary qualities but also of his own apparent motions. From this position to Kant's, it is an easy step. For Kant, as for his scientific predecessors, all sensible presentations were phenomenal. But while Newton secured a metaphysical status for his absolute space by naming it the divine sensorium,[3] Kant gave this empty 'really out there' a critical status by making it an a priori form of human sensibility.

Thirdly, Galileo, Newton, and Kant were looking for some sort of absolute, but they were looking in the wrong places. They sought the real as opposed to the apparent, only to end up with everything apparent, the notion of the real included. Let us follow a different tack. Then every content of experience will be equally valid, for all are equally given, and all equally are to be explained. Next, explanations result from enriching abstraction, and so they are abstract, and their proper expression must be invariant. Thirdly, not every explanation is equally correct; some can be verified, and some cannot. There follows at once the conclusion that the real, objective, true consists of what is known by formulating and verifying invariant principles and laws. Our account of Space is simply a particular case of that conclusion.

Fourthly, let us attempt to meet the problem of the trajectory of the penny. As we have seen, possible frames of reference are infinite; but in any determinate frame of reference, there is only one correct trajectory for the penny. Next, while some possible frames of reference are more convenient than others, still all are equally valid, and so there are many correct trajectories for the penny. Further, this involves no contradiction: just as what is to my right can be to your left, so the one fall of the one penny can be a straight line in one frame of reference and a parabola in another frame of reference; there would be a contradiction only if the same fall were both a straight line and a parabola in the same frame of reference.

3 See Edwin Arthur Burtt, *The Metaphysical Foundations of Modern Science* (Atlantic Highlands, NJ: Humanitas Press, 1980) 256–64. [Lonergan mentioned a 1925 edition published in London and New York. Indications are that the book was first published in 1924, and that a second revised edition appeared in 1932, but that the book was first published in the United States in 1952. The 1980 paperback is 'a reprint of second edition' by arrangement with Routledge & Kegan Paul, Ltd.]

Finally, this position is not unsatisfactory. As long as we are speaking of particular things at particular times in particular places, we cannot avoid employing relative expressions; for it is through our senses that we know the particular, and our senses are in particular places at particular times. On the other hand, invariant expression, which is independent of the spatiotemporal standpoint of particular thinkers, is a property of abstract propositions; it can be demanded only of the principles and laws of a science, and the trajectory of the fall of a particular penny is not a principle or a law in any science.

3.4 Simultaneity   [155–58]

The common view of simultaneity possesses, perhaps, a larger and more resolute following than Newton's absolute space. If two events are at the same time for any observer, then, we shall be told, they must be at the same time for every observer.

The first line of defence will be, no doubt, the principle of contradiction. The same events cannot be both at the same time and not at the same time. Therefore, to say that the same events are at the same time for one observer, and not at the same time for another, is simply to violate the principle of contradiction.

Still, this first line can be turned. What is 'now' for me writing is not 'now' for you reading. If the same event can be both now (for me) and not now (for you), it may be true that 'at the same time' belongs to the same class of relative terms as does 'now'; and if it does, then there is no more a contradiction in saying that events simultaneous for one observer are not simultaneous for another, than there is in saying that events of the present for one observer will be events of the past for another.

The issue is not the principle of contradiction. The issue is simply whether or not 'at the same time' is to be listed along with such relative terms as 'now' and 'soon,' 'here' and 'there,' 'right' and 'left.'

The simplest approach to the issue is to analyze elementary apprehensions of simultaneity. Already we have remarked that we experience duration both in the sense that the experiencing is over time and in the sense that the experienced endures through time. Now we have to add that these two aspects of the experience of duration stand in a certain order. Thus, when I watch a man crossing a street, I look out and inspect the distance that he traverses, but I cannot look out and inspect in the same manner the time he takes to cross. Nor is this surprising.

The whole distance traversed is there to be inspected all at once, but the duration of the traversing is there to be inspected, not all at once, but only in successive bits. Moreover, what is true of the traversing is also true of the inspecting; it too is, not all at once, but over time. If one supposed the possibility of a timeless inspecting, one might infer the inspection of a four-dimensional continuum in which both distances and durations were presented in exactly the same fashion. But when inspecting takes time, then the time of the inspecting runs concurrently with the time of the inspected.

Such remarks on the apprehension of durations seem relevant to an account of the apprehension of simultaneous durations. Instead of watching one man cross a street, I might watch two men crossing a street at the same time. Since it would be perfectly obvious that they were crossing at the same time, it should be equally obvious that there is some time that is one and the same. What time, then, obviously is the same? It must be the time of the watching. For in the first place, the watching has a duration, for it is not all at once. In the second place, the duration of the watching runs concurrently with the duration of what is watched. In the third place, when two movements are the object of one and the same watching, there are, in all, three durations, namely, one in each movement and one in the watching; but it is the duration of the watching that is apprehended as running concurrently both with the duration of one movement and with the duration of the other; and so it is the duration of the watching that is the one and same time at which both the movements are occurring.

This analysis is confirmed by a consideration of apprehensions of 'apparent' simultaneity. If you stand beside a man swinging a hammer, then the sight and the sound of the blow are at the same time. If you stand off at a distance of a few hundred feet, the sight of the blow is prior to the sound. In the first case, the sight and sound are at the same time. In the second case, the sight and the sound are not at the same time. Still, the blow is always the simultaneous source of both light waves and sound waves. The reason why there are different 'apparent' simultaneities must be that the 'appearance' of simultaneity has its ground in the duration immanent in the flow of consciousness.

Such seem to be the facts, and like the facts of relative motion, they give rise to a problem. Is one to follow Galileo and Newton and insist that, beyond the multiplicity of merely apparent simultaneities, there is a real, objective, and true simultaneity that is unique? If so, one can omit further mention of the observer, and one will end up with an absolute time that flows equably everywhere at once. It will not be the time of clocks, which run fast or slow. It will not be the time of the spinning earth, for under the action of the tides and the receding moon, that spin is decelerating. It will be an exact, constant velocity that at every point in the universe perpetually separates the present from the past and the future in precisely the same manner.

Still, this absolute time will not be what we have defined as Time. For Time, as we have defined it, is an ordered totality of concrete durations. It includes the concrete durations both of our experiencing and of what we experience. Through an ordering structure or reference frame it reaches out to embrace in a single totality all the other concrete durations which, though not experienced, are related to the concrete durations that are experienced. In contrast with this Time, absolute time simply lies outside experience. It meets the requirements of a mathematical ideal, and strangely enough, unlike other mathematical ideals, it is said to be 'really out there.' Rather, it once was thought to be really out there. For the Newtonian rejection of experienced durations as apparent time, in favor of a nonexperienced absolute time, promptly was followed by Kant's transformation of absolute time into an a priori form of human sensibility.

Nor is this the only complaint against the Newtonian procedure. As absolute space, so absolute time is a result of looking for the absolute where the absolute does not exist. If it were true that events simultaneous for one observer must be simultaneous for every other observer, then it would be true that expressions of simultaneity are invariant. But there is no reason to expect invariant expressions of simultaneity, for invariance results from abstractness, and no statement regarding the particular times of particular events is abstract. From the very structure of our cognitional apparatus, particulars are known through our senses, and our senses operate under spatiotemporal conditions. They cannot escape relativity, and so, if an absolute is wanted, it must be sought on the level of intelligence, which by abstraction from particulars provides a ground for invariant expressions.

3.5 Motion and Time   [158–59]

We have been speaking of the elementary durations and simultaneities of the personal reference frame. But besides personal reference frames there are public and special reference frames, and they call for a few remarks.

Aristotle defined time as the number and measure of local motion derived from successively traversed distances. Such is the time of the spinning earth and of clocks. 'Two o'clock' is a number, and 'two hours' is a measure. Both are reached from the local motion of the hands over the face of a dial.

However, there are many local motions, and every one successively traverses a series of distances. It follows that, though all do not yield numbers and measures indicating time, still all could do so. Objectively, then, and fundamentally there are many times.

This implication of the Aristotelian position was noted by Aquinas. However, it seemed to him not an important truth, but rather an objection to be answered. Time must be one, and so he appealed to the *primum mobile*, the outermost celestial sphere. There was only one such sphere, and it had only one local motion.[f] Moreover, as it grounded all other local motions both in the sky and on the earth, the time of its movement must be the ground of all other times.[4]

One will be inclined, I think, to agree that as long as Aristotle's *primum mobile* was supposed to exist, our universe was supplied with a single standard time. On the other hand, once Copernicus eliminated the Ptolemaic system, that standard time no longer was possible, and in its place there arose the problem of synchronization, of making many movements yield a single time for public and special reference frames.

Suppose, then, an aggregate of clocks scattered about the universe. Let their relative positions be constant, and let them be known in terms of some reference frame K. Let light signals be sent from the origin of coordinates to the clocks and reflected from the clocks back to the origin. Then a synchronization of clocks might be effected by laying down the rule

$$2t = t' + t''$$

where t is the reading of the distant clock when the light signal is received and reflected, and where t' and t'' are the readings of the clock at the origin when the light signal is emitted and when it returns.

However, synchronization by this rule would be successful only if the outward and the return journeys of the light signal took the same

4 See Thomas Aquinas, *In Aristotelis libros Physicorum*, IV, lect. 17, §§3, 4.

length of time. To satisfy this requirement, one might distinguish between basic and derived synchronizations and demand that the basic
synchronization take place with clocks that are at rest with respect to
the ether and in a reference frame that similarly is at rest. Then synchronization in moving frames would be the synchronization of their
clocks with the clocks of the basic frame, and there would follow for all
point-instants an observable time that conformed to the properties of
Newton's absolute time.

There is, however, one difficulty to this solution. One can in principle
suppose any number of reference frames exhibiting as many varieties of
relative motion as one pleases. One can supply each frame with clocks
that, relatively to the frame, are at rest. But a difficulty arises when one
attempts to select the frame that absolutely is at rest; and if one cannot
determine the basic synchronization, much less can one reach the derived synchronizations.

Still, there is an alternative. Instead of seeking the absolute in the field
of particular reference frames, one can seek it in the field of abstract
propositions and invariant expressions. Accordingly, one may postulate
that the mathematical expression of physical principles and laws be invariant under inertial transformations, and one may note that from the
postulate it follows that in all reference frames moving with a relative
uniform motion the velocity of light will be the same.[5]

3.6 The Principle at Issue[8]   [159–60]

Before closing this section, it will be well to set forth briefly the principles that have guided us in determining the abstract intelligibility of
Space and Time, and no less, to indicate the grounds that lead to different views.

Our position follows from our account of abstraction. Because the
principle or law is abstract, its expression cannot vary with variations of
spatiotemporal standpoint. On the other hand, because we know particulars through spatiotemporally conditioned senses, we know them
from some point and instant within Space and Time. It follows that
concrete places and times are apprehended only as relative to an observ-

---

5 For the consequent derivation of the Einstein-Lorentz transformation
and of Minkowski space, the reader may be referred to Lindsay and
Margenau, *Foundations of Physics* 333–55.

er, that their totalities can be embraced only through the device of reference frames, that reference frames will be many, and that transformations of reference frames can involve changes in the relativity of places
and times to observers. Accordingly, it would be a mistake to look for
the fixed or absolute on the level of particular places and times; the only
absolute relevant to Space and Time resides in the abstract propositions
whose expression remains invariant under permissible transformations
of reference frame.

On the other hand, opposed positions take their stand on the premise
that something fixed or absolute is to be acknowledged on the level of
sense. In the Aristotelian world view this was supplied by the outermost
celestial sphere, which bounded effective Space and, for Aquinas at least,
provided the universe with a standard time. Newton's absolute space and
absolute time were in the first instance imaginary mathematical constructions; but they were objectified through a confusion of the truth of
verification and the truth, prior to intelligence and thought, that resides
in a 'really out there'; finally, they were given a metaphysical status by
being connected with the omnipresence and the eternity of God. Kant
simplified this position by making Newton's empty space and time into
a priori forms of sensibility.

4   Rods and Clocks   [160–70]

On Galilean and Newtonian suppositions, measurements of distance and
of duration are invariant, so that if a measurement is correct in any
frame of reference, the same measurement must be correct in all frames
of reference that are permissible.

On the special theory of relativity the invariant is the four-dimensional
interval ds, where

$$ds^2 = dx^2 + dy^2 + dz^2 - c^2 dt^2.$$

Hence, if the value of ds is correct in any reference frame, the same
value must be correct in all permissible frames. On the other hand, the
values of the spatial components dx, dy, dz and the value of the temporal
component dt can be correct in one reference frame without therefore
being correct in other permissible frames. As is clear from the above
equation, the spatial and temporal components can assume any values[h]
compatible with the constancy of the interval ds.

Clearly enough, this theory necessitates some revision of earlier notions on measurable magnitudes, standard units, measuring, and measurement. For on the earlier view a measurement of a distance or duration is some single number valid in all reference frames. On the new view a measurement of a distance or a duration seems to be a series of numbers in correspondence with a series of reference frames.

Such a revision is not easy. Ordinarily people form their notions of measurements at a time when they take Newtonian presuppositions for granted. Later, when they are confronted with relativity, they are apt to be content to make obvious alterations without thinking things through to a fully coherent position. There results a piecemeal and inadequate revision of basic concepts, and this manifests itself in a parade of alleged Einsteinian paradoxes.

Our proposal is to attempt a thorough revision. First, we shall examine the elementary paradox that the measuring rods of one reference frame are both shorter and longer than those of another, and that the clocks of one frame run both slower and faster than those of another.[6] Secondly, we shall work out a generic notion of measurement that is independent of differences between Galileo and Einstein. Thirdly, we shall show how the same generic notion admits differentiation into the two different specific views.

4.1 The Elementary Paradox[i]   [161–64]

Consider the pair of point-instants P and Q, which in a frame of reference K have the coordinates (x_1, t_1) and (x_2, t_2), and in a frame K', moving with a relative constant velocity u, have the coordinates (x'_1, t'_1) and (x'_2, t'_2). Then by the Lorentz-Einstein transformation, writing

$$H = 1/(1 - u^2/c^2)^{1/2}$$

one easily obtains the equations

$$x'_2 - x'_1 = (x_2 - x_1)H - (t_2 - t_1)uH \qquad (1)$$

$$t'_2 - t'_1 = (t_2 - t_1)H - (x_2 - x_1)uH/c^2. \qquad (2)$$

It is to be noted that if either of the equations (1) and (2) can be obtained then both can be obtained. Moreover, by transforming in the opposite direction from K' to K, there are to be obtained two other equations similar to (1) and (2).

6 For an exposition see ibid. 339–42.

Now these equations admit both a spatial and a temporal application, and to each application three interpretations can be given. The spatial application is to suppose that P and Q are the simultaneous end positions of a standard rod of unit length in K so that

$$x_2 - x_1 = 1 \tag{3}$$

$$t_2 - t_1 = 0 \tag{4}$$

whence by equations (1) and (2)

$$x'_2 - x'_1 = H \tag{5}$$

$$t'_2 - t'_1 = -uH/c^2. \tag{6}$$

The temporal application is to suppose that P and Q are readings at successive seconds on a stationary standard clock in K so that

$$x_2 - x_1 = 0 \tag{7}$$

$$t_2 - t_1 = 1 \tag{8}$$

whence by equations (1) and (2)

$$x'_2 - x'_1 = -uH \tag{9}$$

$$t'_2 - t'_1 = H. \tag{10}$$

Accordingly, inasmuch as standard units of distance and of time are expected to transform invariantly, a problem of interpretation arises, and three answers may be given.

A first interpretation seems inspired by the Fitzgerald contraction. Since H is greater than unity, it is concluded from equations (3) and (5) that the standard rod in K' is shorter than the standard rod in K. Similarly, it is concluded from equations (8) and (10) that the unit of time in K' is shorter than the unit of time in K. Moreover, the opposite conclusions are reached from the equations obtained by transforming from K' to K. But quite apart from its paradox, this interpretation has the defect of saying very little about equations (4) and (6), (7) and (9).

A second interpretation begins by noting that in special relativity clocks are synchronized in each frame of reference by assuming, not that simultaneity is identical, but that the velocity of light is the same constant in all frames of reference. Accordingly, on this interpretation equations (5) and (6) are taken together, and at once it is apparent that a distance between simultaneous positions in K has been transformed into a distance between positions that are not simultaneous in K'. But even Cinderella's foot would seem large if one measured the distance between the tip of her toe at one instant and the back of her heel at another; and such is the view in K' of the standard unit of length in K. Similarly, equations (9) and (10) are taken together to reveal that what for K is a time interval on the same stationary clock, for K' is a difference in time between clocks in different positions. It follows that the difference in time given by equation (10) results not only from the difference in time given by equation (8) but also from the fact, underlying the transformation equations, that in every frame of reference, clocks in different positions are synchronized by assuming the velocity of light to be the same constant in all frames. Indeed, while one may find this method of synchronization to be strange, while one may even find it strange that there is any problem of synchronization, still, granted that initial oddity, there is no further oddity brought to light by equations (3) to (10) or by the similar equations obtained when one transforms from K' to K.

A third interpretation is in terms of Minkowski space. It asserts that, within the context of special relativity, it is a blunder to suppose that a difference of position is a merely spatial entity or that a difference of time is a merely temporal entity. Hence a standard rod is spatiotemporal: it is not merely a distance between two positions; it is a distance between a position x_1 at a time t_1 and a position x_2 at a time t_2. Similarly, a standard clock is spatiotemporal: it does not assign merely temporal differences; it assigns a difference between a time t_1 at a position x_1 and a time t_2 at a position x_2. Moreover, a unit on any standard rod determines one and the same invariant spatiotemporal interval for all frames of reference, namely, unity; and a unit on any standard clock determines one and the same invariant spatiotemporal interval for all frames of reference, namely, ic.[7] However, while standard rods and clocks determine the same spatiotemporal intervals for all frames of reference, still these invariant intervals divide differently into spatial and temporal components in different frames of reference. Hence one may distinguish between normal and abnormal frames by introducing the definitions:

7 This invariant interval s may be obtained from the equations
$$s^2 = (x_2 - x_1)^2 - c^2(t_2 - t_1)^2 = (x'_2 - x'_1)^2 - c^2(t'_2 - t'_1)^2.$$
Thus one will find that substitutions from equations (3) and (4) will yield the same result, unity, as substitutions from equations (5) and (6); similarly, substitutions from equations (7) and (8) will yield the same result ic as substitutions from equations (9) and (10).

A reference frame is normal to measurements if differences
of position have a temporal component that is zero and differences of time have a spatial component that is zero.

A reference frame is abnormal to measurements if differences
of position have a temporal component that is not zero and
differences of time have a spatial component that is not zero.

Operationally this means that reference frames, rods, clocks, and measurable objects should be relatively at rest if one's measuring is not to be
complicated by the ambiguities of the elementary paradox.

Finally, it may be noted that, while the first interpretation differs from
the other two, the second and third are compatible and complementary.
For the second explains the differences that arise on transforming units
of distance and time by remarking that, when the relative velocity is not
zero, the transformation equations cover over a peculiar technique in
synchronization, while the third interpretation systematizes the whole
matter by adverting to spatiotemporal invariants and by noting that
these invariants divide differently into spatial and temporal components
in different reference frames. It remains, however, that something be
said on the general notion of measurement presupposed by the second
and third interpretations.

4.2 The Generic Notion of Measurement   [164–67]

Empirical inquiry has been conceived as a process from description to
explanation. We begin from things as related to our senses. We end with
things as related to one another. Initial classifications are based upon
sensible similarities. But as correlations, laws, theories, systems are developed, initial classifications undergo a revision. Sensible similarity has
ceased to be significant, and definitions consist of technical terms that
have been invented as a consequence of scientific advance. In this
fashion biological classifications have felt the imprint of the theory of
evolution. Chemical compounds are defined by appealing to chemical
elements. Chemical elements are defined by their relations to one
another in a periodic table that has room for elements that as yet have
not been discovered or synthesized. The basic notions of physics are a
mass that is distinct from weight, a temperature that differs from the
intensity of the feeling of heat, and the electromagnetic vector fields.

Now the principal technique in effecting the transition from description to explanation is measurement. We move away from colors as seen, from sounds as heard, from heat and pressure as felt. In their place we determine the numbers named measurements. In virtue of this substitution we are able to turn from the relations of sensible terms, which are correlative to our senses, to the relations of numbers, which are correlative to one another. Such is the fundamental significance and function of measurement.

Further, in constructing these numerical relations of things to one another, there is introduced an almost necessary simplification of arrangement. If it would be theoretically possible, it would not be practicable to relate things to one another by stating separately the relations of each to all the others. The procedure that is both simpler and more systematic is to select one type of thing or magnitude, to relate all others directly to it, and to leave to deductive inference the relations of the others among themselves. Thus, instead of noting that Tom is 1/10 taller than Dick, Dick 1/20 shorter than Harry, and Harry 9/209 shorter than Tom, one selects some arbitrary magnitude as standard unit and measures Tom, Dick, and Harry, not in terms of one another, but in terms of feet or centimeters.

A standard unit, then, is a physical magnitude among other similar physical magnitudes. Its position of privilege is due to the systematic simplicity of implying the relations of each of these magnitudes to all the others by stating only the relations of all to some one.

In selecting and determining standard units there is a conventional, arbitrary element, and as well there is a far larger theoretical element. It is a matter of convention that the standard foot is the length between notches on a bar at a certain temperature in a given place. It is arbitrary that the foot happens to have the length it has, neither more nor less. On the other hand, the remaining aspects of the standard unit have their basis in presumed or acquired theoretical knowledge. What is length? Does length vary with temperature? Does length vary with change of place or of time? Does length vary with changes of frames of reference? These are relevant questions. If their answers rest on the results of empirical science, they are subject to revision when those results are revised. If their answers can be obtained only by appealing to the field of basic presuppositions and presumptions, they will be methodological and subject to the revisions of methodology.

The fundamental point to be grasped here is a point that already has been made. The absolute resides not on the level of sensible presentations but in the field of abstract propositions and invariant expressions. The constancy in time of the length of a standard metal bar cannot be ascertained by comparing its length yesterday with its length today; the field of observables is limited to the present place and time; today's length of the bar can be observed if today you are in the right place; but yesterday's length has passed out of the field of observables, and tomorrow's has not yet been ushered in. It remains that the constancy in time of the length of the bar is a conclusion based on general knowledge. One ascertains as best one can all the manners in which metal bars can change in length; one takes precautions to prevent the occurrence of any such changes in the standard; and one concludes that, as far as one knows, no such change has taken place. In other words, the constancy of the standard is a conclusion based upon the invariance of laws, and a revision of the laws will lead to a new determination of standard requirements.

This possible revision of standards sets a logical puzzle. How, one may ask, can one reach new laws except through measurements based on old standards? How can the new laws be correct if the old standards are wrong? How can incorrect laws lead to the correction of old standards? Behind such questions there lies a mistaken presupposition. Science does not advance by deducing new conclusions from old premises. Deduction is an operation that occurs only in the field of concepts and propositions. But the advance of science, as we have seen, is a circuit: from data to inquiry, from inquiry to insight, from insight to the formulation of premises and the deduction of their implications, from such formulation to material operations which yield fresh data and in the limit generate the new set of insights named a higher viewpoint. A basic revision, then, is a leap. At a stroke, it is a grasp of the insufficiency both of the old laws and of the old standards. At a stroke, it generates both the new laws and the new standards. Finally, by the same verification, it establishes that both the new laws and the new standards satisfy the data.

What holds for standards also holds for their use. It is necessary to define as accurately as possible the precise type of magnitude that is to be measured. It is necessary to define the precise procedure that leads from the measurable magnitude and the standard unit to the determination of the number named a measurement. At each stage in the development of a science, these definitions will be formed in the light of acquired or presumed knowledge. But at every subsequent stage, there is the possibility of further acquisitions and of new presumptions and so of a revision of the definitions. Such a revision involves, not the deduction of new conclusions from old premises, but a leap to fresh premises.

Such, then, is the generic notion of measurement. Clearly, it contains within itself the possibility of successive differentiations that result from revisions that occur in the abstract field of definitions, principles, and laws. We have now to turn our attention to the revision involved in the notions of spatial and temporal measurements by the special theory of relativity.

4.3 Differentiations of the Generic Notion of Measurement   [167–70]

Let us begin by distinguishing (1) size, (2) length, and (3) measurement.

By size will be meant magnitude apart from any geometrical conceptions. It is an elementary experiential conjugate, and it is to be characterized in terms of simple experiences.

Thus, spatial size may be indicated sufficiently by saying that it varies in two manners. It varies in an external fashion, inasmuch as the nearer it is, the bigger it looks. Also it varies in an internal fashion, inasmuch as it expands or contracts.

Temporal size similarly varies in two manners. There is the external variation named psychological time, which rushes by when we are interested and lags when we are bored. There are also internal differences between the sizes of durations: twenty years is a long time, even if one is not in prison; and a second is a short time, even if one is.

By length will be meant size as fitted into a geometrical construction.

Spatial length, at a first approximation, seems simply to be size in a single direction or dimension. Still, one does have to use some such expression as direction or dimension. This fact recalls, not only the analysis of size into length, breadth, and depth, but also the requirement that length has to be taken along a straight line or geodetic. Further, the ends of a straight line or geodetic are points, but the ends of a size are hardly just points; it follows that the size of the material object must have been submitted to some detailed geometrical analysis, so that boundaries of the size stand in some unique correspondence with points on a straight line. Finally, material objects may be varying internally in size, and they may be moving locally; an expanding or contracting object has a series of lengths at a series of instants; a moving object successively lies between two series of bounding positions; its length is not the distance between present and past bounding positions; and so it follows that the length of an object depends, not only on a geometry of space, but also upon determinations of the instant and of simultaneity.

The length of a duration can be determined only by adding mechanical to geometrical analysis. There has to be discovered some constant velocity or some regular periodicity. The spatial size traversed by the velocity has to be conceived in terms of length and divided into equal parts. Finally, while the length of a single duration may be determined by counting traversed parts or recurring periods, still there are many durations; they have to be related to one another in some fashion; and so there must be worked out some general determination of simultaneity or synchronization.

It has been noted that sizes differ in two manners: internally, in virtue of expansions and contractions, prolongations and curtailments; externally, in virtue of the relative position of our senses and the quality of our subjective states. The obvious advantage of the notion of length is that it eliminates merely external differences of size. Still, one must not jump to the conclusion that therefore length will prove invariant. As has been seen, determinations of length depend upon determinations of simultaneity, and it may be that simultaneity is not invariant. Again, determinations of length depend upon the supposition of some specific geometry, and it may happen that the specific geometry verified in Space and Time does not regard length as invariant.

There remains measurement. On Newtonian suppositions a measurement is a number that stands to unity as the length of the measured magnitude stands to the length of a standard unit. Thus, to say that a room is twenty feet long is to say that the length of the room stands to the length of a foot rule as the number 'twenty' stands to unity. Again, to say that a process lasts five seconds is to say that the length of the process stands to the length of a standard second as the number 'five' stands to unity. Finally, lengths are invariant under permissible transformations, and so measurements valid in one reference frame are valid in all permissible frames.

Now the transition[j] to the suppositions of special relativity may be effected very simply by noting an oversight in the foregoing account of measurement. Two rods, AP and BQ, are equal in length if, and only if, A coincides with B at the same time as P coincides with Q. In particular, if A coincides with B at one moment and P coincides with Q at another moment, relative motion could occur during the interval, and so equality could not be asserted. Similarly, two clocks, R and S, are synchronous if, and only if, readings taken at the same time agree. In particular, synchronization cannot be asserted on the ground that the readings from R at one series of moments agree with the readings from S at another series of moments.

Moreover, not only is an exact determination of the meaning of simultaneity an essential condition in measuring spatial and temporal differences but also, as has been seen, it cannot be presumed that that meaning is identical for all spatiotemporal standpoints. Indeed, since simultaneity is a relation between particular events occurring at particular times in particular places, it may be expected to be analogous to such notions as 'now' and 'here.'

Further, to escape the relativity of simultaneity, appeal must be made to some absolute. But the absolute in measurement, as the absolute in space and time, resides in the realm of principles and laws. For principles and laws, because they abstract from particular places and particular times, cannot vary with variations in place and time.

Hence the basic supposition of measurement in special relativity will coincide with its basic postulate that the mathematical expression of physical principles and laws is invariant under inertial transformations. It follows that the appropriate geometry into which sizes must be fitted to yield lengths will be Minkowski space. Further, it follows that the correct notion of simultaneity will be the notion implicit (1) theoretically in the Lorentz-Einstein transformation, and (2) operationally in the fact that in all reference frames clocks are synchronized by light signals, and the velocity of light is always the same constant.

Hence in special relativity the measurement of any spatial or temporal difference determines a spatiotemporal interval (1) that is invariant for all reference frames, but (2) that resolves into different spatial and temporal components in different relatively moving frames.

Further, a distinction may be drawn between normal and abnormal reference frames. For if a measured magnitude is purely spatial, in a normal frame it will have a temporal component that is zero, but in an abnormal frame it will have a temporal component that is not zero. Similarly, if a measured magnitude is purely temporal, in a normal frame it will have a spatial component that is zero, but in an abnormal frame it will have a spatial component that is not zero. It follows that in actual measuring only normal frames should be used if one is to avoid the complexity of discovering the temporal component in a spatial difference and the spatial component in a temporal difference.

It may be remarked that on the present analysis there seems to vanish the apparently arbitrary division of the universe into rods and clocks on the one hand and, on the other, everything else.[8] For the fundamental point is the relativity of simultaneity, and that relativity enters into the very notion of a determinate measurement. Hence, while measurements are relations between rods and clocks on the one hand and, on the other, all other spatial and temporal magnitudes, still there is no peculiarity in rods that is lacking in other spatial magnitudes, and there is no peculiarity in clocks that is lacking in other temporal magnitudes.

Finally, it is perhaps unnecessary to note that our account of measurement makes no attempt to treat either the notion of measurement implicit in general relativity or the problems that arise when the activity of measuring introduces a coincidental or nonsystematic element into the objects under investigation. No doubt these issues could not be omitted in a general treatment of the subject, but our purpose has been to reinforce the point that absolutes do not lie in the field of sensible particulars and to disassociate our account of the abstract intelligibility of Space and Time from the paradoxes that too readily have been supposed to be inherent in the special theory of relativity.

5   The Concrete Intelligibility of Space and Time   [170–72]

Space and Time have been defined as ordered totalities of concrete extensions and of concrete durations.

They are distinct from imaginary space and imaginary time, which are totalities of merely imagined extensions and of merely imagined durations. Moreover, the existence of this distinction reveals that notions of Space and Time begin from experienced extensions and experienced durations and employ reference frames to reach out and embrace the totality of other concrete extensions and concrete durations.

Since reference frames are an endless multiplicity, their intelligible order cannot be more than descriptive. If one would understand, not men's notions of Space and Time, but the intelligibility immanent in Space and Time, then one must advance from reference frames to the

8 See the autobiography in *Albert Einstein, Philosopher-Scientist*, ed. P.A. Schilpp, The Library of Living Philosophers (New York: Tudor, 1949 and 1951) 59.

geometrical principles and laws whose expression is invariant under transformations. Moreover, the geometry to be reached will coincide with the geometry determined by physicists in securing invariant expression for physical principles and laws.

However, such a geometry is abstract. It is abstract, not indeed in the sense that it is not verified (for what is wanted is a geometry verified by physicists), but in the sense that it consists in a set of abstract propositions and invariant expressions and that, while applicable to concrete extensions and durations, still it is applied differently from different spatiotemporal viewpoints. Thus, as long as men remain on the level of invariant expressions they are not considering any concrete extension and duration; inversely, as soon as men consider concrete extensions and durations, each views them differently. The endless multiplicity of different spatiotemporal standpoints and of different frames of reference, so far from being transcended, reappears with every return from the abstract to the concrete.

There is a parallel point to be made. The abstract intelligibility of Space and Time is coincident with the solution of a problem in physics. It is the intelligibility, not so much of Space and Time, as of physical objects in their spatiotemporal relations. May one not expect an intelligibility proper to Space and proper to Time?

Such, then, is the question envisaged by this section on the concrete intelligibility of Space and Time. What is wanted is an intelligibility grasped in the totality of concrete extensions and durations and, indeed, identical for all spatiotemporal viewpoints.

The answer is easily reached. One has only to shift from the classical type of inquiry which has been under consideration to the complementary statistical type. It has been argued that a theory of emergent probability exhibits generically the intelligibility immanent in world process. Emergent probability is the successive realization of the possibilities of concrete situations in accord with their probabilities. The concrete intelligibility of Space is that it grounds the possibility of those simultaneous multiplicities named situations. The concrete intelligibility of Time is that it grounds the possibility of successive realizations in accord with probabilities. In other words, concrete extensions and concrete durations are the field or matter or potency in which emergent probability is the immanent form or intelligibility.[k]

6

Common Sense and
Its Subject[a]

The illustrative basis of our study must now be broadened. In the previous five chapters, precision was our primary objective, and so our examples were taken from the fields of mathematics and physics. Still, the occurrence of insight is not restricted to the minds of mathematicians, when doing mathematics, and to the minds of physicists, when engaged in that department of science. On the contrary, one meets intelligence in every walk of life. There are intelligent farmers and craftsmen, intelligent employers and workers, intelligent technicians and mechanics, intelligent doctors and lawyers, intelligent politicians and diplomats. There is intelligence in industry and commerce, in finance and taxation, in journalism and public relations. There is intelligence in the home and in friendship, in conversation and in sport, in the arts and in entertainment. In every case, the man or woman of intelligence is marked by a greater readiness in catching on, in getting the point, in seeing the issue, in grasping implications, in acquiring knowhow. In their speech and action the same characteristics can be discerned as were set forth in describing the act that released Archimedes' 'Eureka!' For insight is ever the same, and even its most modest achievements are rendered conspicuous by the contrasting, if reassuring, occurrence of examples of obtuseness and stupidity.

1   Common Sense as Intellectual   [173–81]

The light and drive of intelligent inquiry unfolds methodically in mathematics and empirical science. In the human child it is a secret wonder that, once the mystery of language has been unraveled, rushes forth in a cascade of questions. Far too soon the questions get out of hand, and weary adults are driven to ever more frequent use of the blanket 'My dear, you cannot understand that yet.' The child would understand everything at once. It does not suspect that there is a strategy in the accumulation of insights, that the answers to many questions depend on answers to still other questions, that often enough advertence to these other questions arises only from the insight that to meet interesting questions one has to begin from quite uninteresting ones. There is, then, common to all men the very spirit of inquiry that constitutes the scientific attitude. But in its native state it is untutored. Our intellectual careers begin to bud in the incessant What? and Why? of childhood. They flower only if we are willing, or constrained, to learn how to learn. They bring forth fruit only after the discovery that, if we really would master the answers, we somehow have to find them out ourselves.

Just as there is spontaneous inquiry, so too there is a spontaneous accumulation of related insights. For questions are not an aggregate of isolated monads. Insofar as any question is followed by an insight, one has only to act, or to talk, or perhaps merely to think, on the basis of that insight, for its incompleteness to come to light and thereby generate a further question. Insofar as the further question is in turn met by the gratifying response of a further insight, once more the same process will reveal another aspect of incompleteness, to give rise to still further questions and still further insights. Such is the spontaneous process of learning. It is an accumulation of insights in which each successive act complements the accuracy and covers over the deficiency of those that went before. Just as the mathematician advances from images through insights and formulations to symbols that stimulate further insights, just as the scientist advances from data through insights and formulations to experiments that stimulate further insights, so too the spontaneous and self-correcting process of learning is a circuit in which insights reveal their shortcomings by putting forth deeds or words or thoughts, and through that revelation prompt the further questions that lead to complementary insights.

Such learning is not without teaching. For teaching is the communication of insight. It throws out the clues, the pointed hints, that lead to insight. It cajoles attention to drive away the distracting images that stand in insight's way. It puts the further questions that reveal the need of further insights to modify and complement the acquired store. It has grasped the strategy of developing intelligence, and so begins from the simple to advance to the more complex. Deliberately and explicitly, all this is done by professional teachers that know their job. But the point we would make is that it also is done, though unconsciously and implicitly, by parents with their offspring and by equals among themselves. Talking is a basic human art. By it each communicates to others what he knows, and at the same time provokes the contradictions that direct his attention to what he has overlooked. Again, far more impressive than talking is doing. Deeds excite our admiration and stir us to emulation. We watch to see how things are done. We experiment to see if we can do them ourselves. We watch again to discover the oversights that led to our failures. In this fashion the discoveries and inventions of individuals pass into the possession of many, to be checked against their experience, to undergo the scrutiny of their further questions, to be modified by their improvements. By the same token, the spontaneous collaboration of individuals is also the communal development of intelligence in the family, the tribe, the nation, the race. Not only are men born with a native drive to inquire and understand; they are born into a community that possesses a common fund of tested answers, and from that fund each may draw his variable share, measured by his capacity, his interests, and his energy. Not only does the self-correcting process of learning unfold within the private consciousness of the individual; for by speech, and still more by example, there is effected a sustained communication that at once disseminates and tests and improves every advance, to make the achievement of each successive generation the starting point of the next.

From spontaneous inquiry,[b] the spontaneous accumulation of related insights, and the spontaneous collaboration of communication, we have worked towards the notion of common sense as an intellectual development. Naturally enough, there will arise the question of the precise inventory of this public store. How does it define its terms? What are its postulates? What are the conclusions it infers from the premises? But if the question is obvious enough, the answer is more difficult. For the answer rests on one of those queer insights that merely grasps the false supposition of the question. Definitions, postulates, and inferences are the formulation of general knowledge. They regard, not the particular but the universal, not the concrete but the abstract. Common sense, unlike the sciences, is a specialization of intelligence in the particular and the concrete. It is common without being general, for it consists in a set of insights that remains incomplete until there is added at least one further insight into the situation in hand; and once that situation has passed, the added insight is no longer relevant, so that common sense at once reverts to its normal state of incompleteness. Thus, common sense may seem to argue from analogy, but its analogies defy logical formulation. The analogy that the logician can examine is merely an instance of the heuristic premise that similars are similarly understood. It can yield a valid argument only if the two concrete situations exhibit no significant dissimilarity. But common sense, because it does not have to be articulate, can operate directly from its accumulated insights. In correspondence with the similarities of the situation, it can appeal to an incomplete set of insights. In correspondence with the significant difference of situations, it can add the different insights relevant to each. Again, common sense may seem to generalize. But a generalization proposed by common sense has quite a different meaning from a generalization proposed by science. The scientific generalization aims to offer a premise from which correct deductions can be drawn. But the generalizations issued by common sense are not meant to be premises for deductions. Rather they would communicate pointers that ordinarily it is well to bear in mind. Proverbs are older far than principles, and like rules of grammar they do not lose their validity because of their numerous exceptions. For they aim to express, not the scientist's rounded set of insights that either holds in every instance or in none at all, but the incomplete set of insights which is called upon in every concrete instance but becomes proximately relevant only after a good look around has resulted in the needed additional insights. Look before you leap!

Not only does common sense differ from logic and from science in the meaning it attaches to analogies and generalizations. In all its utterances it operates from a distinctive viewpoint and pursues an ideal of its own. The heuristic assumptions of science anticipate the determination of natures that always act in the same fashion under similar circumstances, and as well the determination of ideal norms of probability from which events diverge only in a nonsystematic manner. Though the scientist is aware that he will reach these determinations only through a series of approximations, still he also knows that even approximate determinations must have the logical properties of abstract truth. Terms, then, must be defined unambiguously, and they must always be employed exactly in that unambiguous meaning. Postulates must be stated; their presuppositions must be examined; their implications must be explored. Automatically there results a technical language and a formal mode of speech. Not only is one compelled to say what one means and to mean what one says, but the correspondence that obtains between saying and meaning has the exact simplicity of such primitive utterances as 'This is a cat.'

Common sense, on the other hand, never aspires to universally valid knowledge, and it never attempts exhaustive communication. Its concern is the concrete and particular. Its function is to master each situation as it arises. Its procedure is to reach an incomplete set of insights that is to be completed only by adding on each occasion the further insights that scrutiny of the occasion reveals. It would be an error for common sense to attempt to formulate its incomplete set of insights in definitions and postulates and to work out their presuppositions and implications. For the incomplete set is not the understanding either of any concrete situation or of any general truth. Equally, it would be an error for common sense to attempt a systematic formulation of its completed set of insights in some particular case; for every systematic formulation envisages the universal, and every concrete situation is particular.

It follows that common sense has no use for a technical language and no tendency towards a formal mode of speech. It agrees that one must say what one means and mean what one says. But its correspondence between saying and meaning is at once subtle and fluid. As the proverb has it, a wink is as good as a nod. For common sense not merely says what it means; it says it to someone; it begins by exploring the other fellow's intelligence; it advances by determining what further insights have to be communicated to him; it undertakes the communication, not as an exercise in formal logic, but as a work of art; and it has at its disposal not merely all the resources of language but also the support of modulated tone and changing volume, the eloquence of facial expression, the emphasis of gestures, the effectiveness of pauses, the suggestiveness of questions, the significance of omissions. It follows that the only interpreter of commonsense utterances is common sense. For the relation between saying and meaning is the relation between sensible presentations and intellectual grasp, and if that relation can be as simple and exact as in the statement 'This is a cat,' it can also take on all the delicacy and subtlety, all the rapidity and effectiveness, with which one incarnate intelligence can communicate its grasp to another by grasping what the other has yet to grasp and what act or sound or sign would make him grasp it. Such a procedure, clearly, is logical, if by 'logical' you mean 'intelligent and reasonable.' With equal clearness, such a procedure is not logical, if by 'logical' you mean conformity to a set of general rules valid in every instance of a defined range; for no set of general rules can keep pace with the resourcefulness of intelligence in its adaptations to the possibilities and exigencies of concrete tasks of self-communication.

Just as the elliptical utterances of common sense have a deeper ground than many logicians and practically all controversialists have managed to reach, so too the plane of reality envisaged by commonsense meaning is quite distinct from the plane that the sciences explore. It has been said that the advance of science is from description to explanation, from things as related to our senses, through measurements, to things as related to one another. It is clear that common sense is not concerned with the relations of things to one another, and that it does not employ the technical terms that scientists invent to express those relations. Still, this obvious difference provides no premise for the inference that the object of scientific description is the same as the object of commonsense communication. It is true enough that both types of utterance deal with things^c as related to our senses. But also it is true that they do so from different viewpoints and with different ends. Scientific description is the work of a trained scientific observer. It satisfies the logician's demand for complete articulateness and exhaustive statement. It reveals the imprint of the scientist's anticipation of attainment of the pure conjugates that express the relations of things to one another. For, though scientific description deals with things as related to our senses, it does so with an ulterior purpose and under the guidance of a method that strains towards its realization.

Common sense, on the other hand, has no theoretical inclinations. It remains completely in the familiar world of things for us. The further questions by which it accumulates insights are bounded by the interests and concerns of human living, by the successful performance of daily tasks, by the discovery of immediate solutions that will work. Indeed, the supreme canon of common sense is the restriction of further questions to the realm of the concrete and particular, the immediate and practical. To advance in common sense is to restrain the omnivorous drive of inquiring intelligence and to brush aside as irrelevant, if not silly, any question whose answer would not make an immediately palpable difference. Just as the scientist rises in stern protest against the introduction into his field of metaphysical questions that do not satisfy his canon of selection, so the man of common sense (and nothing else) is ever on his guard against all theory, ever blandly asking the proponent of ideas what difference they would make, and if the answer is less vivid and less rapid than an advertisement, then solely concerned with thinking up an excuse for getting rid of the fellow. After all, men of common sense are busy. They have the world's work to do.

Still, how can the world's work be done either intelligently or efficiently, if it is done by men of common sense that never bother their heads a minute about scientific method? That question can be answered, I think, if we begin from another. Why is it that scientists need scientific method? Why must such intelligent men be encumbered with the paraphernalia of laboratories and the dull books of specialized libraries? Why should they be trained in observation and logic? Why should they be tied down by abstruse technical terms and abstract reasoning? Clearly it is because their inquiry moves off from the familiar to the unfamiliar, from the obvious to the recondite. They have to attend to things as related to us, in the manner that leads to things as related to one another. When they reach the universal relations of things to one another, they are straining beyond the native range of insight into sensible presentations, and they need the crutches of method to fix their gaze on things as neither sensibly given nor concrete nor particular.

Common sense, on the other hand, has no such aspirations. It clings to the immediate and practical, the concrete and particular. It remains within the familiar world of things for us. Rockets and space platforms are superfluous if you intend to remain on this earth. So also is scientific method superfluous in the performance of the tasks of common sense. Like the sciences, it is an accumulation of related insights into the data of experience. Like the sciences, it is the fruit of a vast collaboration. Like the sciences, it has been tested by its practical results. Still, there is a profound difference. For the sciences have theoretical aspirations, and common sense has none. The sciences would speak precisely and with universal validity, but common sense would speak only to persons and only about the concrete and particular. The sciences need methods to reach their abstract and universal objects; but scientists need common sense to apply methods properly in executing the concrete tasks of particular investigations, just as logicians need common sense if they are to grasp what is meant in each concrete act of human utterance. It has been argued that there exists a complementarity between classical and statistical investigations; perhaps it now is evident that the whole of science, with logic thrown in, is a development of intelligence that is complementary to the development named common sense. Rational choice is not between science and common sense; it is a choice of both, of science to master the universal, and of common sense to deal with the particular.

There remain to be mentioned the differentiations of common sense.[d] Far more than the sciences, common sense is divided into specialized departments. For every difference of geography, for every difference of occupation, for every difference of social arrangements, there is an appropriate variation of common sense. At a given place, in a given job, among a given group of people, a man can be at intelligent ease in every situation in which he is called upon to speak or act. He always knows just what is up, just the right thing to say, just what needs to be done, just how to go about it. His experience has taken him through the cycle of eventualities that occur in his milieu. His intelligence has ever been alert. He has made his mistakes, and from them he has learnt not to make them twice. He has developed the acumen that notices movements away from the familiar routine, the poise that sizes them up before embarking on a course of action, the resourcefulness that hits upon the response that meets the new issue. He is an embodiment of the ideal of common sense, yet his achievement is relevant only to its environment. Put him among others in another place or at another job, and until they become familiar, until he has accumulated a fresh set of insights, he cannot avoid hesitancy and awkwardness. Once more he must learn his way about, catch on to the tricks of a new trade, discern in little signs the changing moods of those with whom he deals. Such, then, is the specialization of common sense. At once, it adapts individuals in every walk of life to the work they have chosen or the lot that has befallen them, and no less, it generates all those minute differences of viewpoint and mentality that separate men and women, old and young, town and country, until in the limit one reaches the cumulative differences and mutual incomprehension of different strata of society, different nations, different civilizations, and different epochs of human history.

We have been endeavoring to conceive the intellectual component in common sense. Our effort began from spontaneous questions, spontaneous accumulations of insights, spontaneous collaboration in testing and improving them. Next, there was formulated the central notion of an habitual but incomplete set of insights that was completed with appropriate variations in each concrete set of circumstances that called for speech or action. It was shown that such an intellectual development not only aimed at mastering the concrete and particular but also achieved its aim in a concrete and particular manner that contrasted with the general rules of logic and the general methods of science, yet provided a necessary complement both for the concrete use of general techniques and the concrete application of general conclusions. Finally, attention was drawn to the differentiations of common sense which multiply, not by theoretical differences as do the departments of science,[e] but by the empirical differences of place and time, circumstance and environment.

2   The Subjective Field of Common Sense   [181–206]

If there is a parallel between a scientific and a commonsense accumulation of insights, there also exists a difference. Where the scientist seeks the relations of things to one another, common sense is concerned with the relations of things to us. Where the scientist's correlations serve to define the things that he relates to one another, common sense not merely relates objects to a subject but also constitutes relations of the subject to objects. Where the scientist is primarily engaged in knowing, common sense cannot develop without changing the subjective term in the object-to-subject relations that it knows.

There is, then, a subtle ambiguity in the apparently evident statement that common sense relates things to us. For who are we? Do we not change? Is not the acquisition of common sense itself a change in us? Clearly, an account of common sense cannot be adequate without an investigation of its subjective field. To this end we propose in the present section to introduce the notion of patterns of experience, to distinguish biological, aesthetic, intellectual, and dramatic patterns, to contrast the patterns of consciousness with the unconscious patterns of neural process, and finally, to indicate the connection between a flight from insight and, on the other hand, repression, inhibition, slips of the tongue, dreams, screening memories, abnormality, and psychotherapy.

2.1 Patterns of Experience   [181–82]

The notion of the pattern of experience may best be approached by remarking how abstract it is to speak of a sensation. No doubt, we are all familiar with acts of seeing, hearing, touching, tasting, smelling. Still, such acts never occur in isolation both from one another and from all other events. On the contrary, they have a bodily basis; they are functionally related to bodily movements; and they occur in some dynamic context that somehow unifies a manifold of sensed contents and of acts of sensing.

Thus, without eyes, there is no seeing; and when I would see with my eyes, I open them, turn my head, approach, focus my gaze. Without ears, there is no hearing; and to escape noise, I must move beyond its range or else build myself soundproof walls. Without a palate, there is no tasting; and when I would taste, there are involved movements of the body and arms, of hands and fingers, of lips and tongue and jaws. Sensation has a bodily basis, and functionally it is linked to bodily movements.

Nor is this all. Both the sensations and the bodily movements are subject to an organizing control. Besides the systematic links between senses and sense organs, there is, immanent in experience, a factor variously named conation, interest, attention, purpose. We speak of consciousness as a stream, but the stream involves not only the temporal succession of different contents but also direction, striving, effort. Moreover, this direction of the stream is variable. Thales was so intent upon the stars that he did not see the well into which he tumbled. The milkmaid was so indifferent to the stars that she could not overlook the well. Still, Thales could have seen the well, for he was not blind; and perhaps the milkmaid could have been interested in the stars, for she was human.

There are, then, different dynamic patterns of experience, nor is it difficult for us to say just what we mean by such a pattern. As conceived, it is the formulation of an insight; but all insight arises from sensitive or imaginative presentations, and in the present case the relevant presentations are simply the various elements in the experience that is organized by the pattern.

2.2 The Biological Pattern of Experience [182–84]

A plant draws its sustenance from its environment by remaining in a single place and by performing a slowly varying set of routines in interaction with a slowly varying set of things. In contrast, the effective environment of a carnivorous animal is a floating population of other animals that move over a range of places and are more or less well equipped to deceive or elude their pursuers. Both plant and animal are alive, for in both aggregates of events insight discerns an intelligible unity that commonly is formulated in terms of biological drive or purpose. But plants adapt slowly, animals rapidly, to changing situations; and if we endeavor to understand the sudden twists and turns both of fleeing quarry and pursuing beast of prey, we ascribe to them a flow of experience not unlike our own. Outer senses are the heralds of biological opportunities and dangers. Memory is the file of supplementary information. Imagination is the projection of courses of action. Conation and emotion are the pent-up pressure of elemental purposiveness. Finally, the complex sequence of delicately coordinated bodily movements is at once the consequence of striving and a cause of the continuous shift of sensible presentations.

In such an illustration insight grasps the biological pattern of experience. By such a pattern is not meant the visible or imaginative focus of attention offered by the characteristic shape and appearance of an animal. Nor again is the pattern reached by grasping that spatially and temporally distinct data all belong to a single living thing, for plants no less than animals are alive, and as yet we have not satisfied ourselves upon the validity of the notion of the thing. Rather, the pattern is a set of intelligible relations that link together sequences of sensations, memories, images, conations, emotions, and bodily movements; and to name the pattern biological is simply to affirm that the sequences converge upon terminal activities of intussusception or reproduction, or, when negative in scope, self-preservation. Accordingly, the notion of the pattern takes us beyond behaviorism, inasmuch as attention is not confined to external data; it takes us beyond a narrow positivism, inasmuch as the canon of relevance leads us to acknowledge that there is a content to insight; but it observes the canon of parsimony by adding no more than a set of intelligible relations to elements of experience.

A more informative characterization of the biological pattern of experience is to be obtained by comparing animals and plants. For conscious living is only a part of the animal's total living. As in the plant, so in the animal there go forward immanent vital processes without the benefit of any conscious control. The formation and nutrition of organic structures and of their skeletal supports, the distribution and neural control of muscles, the physics of the vascular system, the chemistry of digestion, the metabolism of the cell, all are sequences of events that fit into intelligible patterns of biological significance. Yet it is only when their functioning is disturbed that they enter into consciousness. Indeed, not only is a large part of animal living nonconscious, but the conscious part itself is intermittent. Animals sleep. It is as though the full-time business of living called forth consciousness as a part-time employee, occasionally to meet problems of malfunctioning, but regularly to deal rapidly, effectively, and economically with the external situations in which sustenance is to be won and into which offspring are to be born.

Thus extroversion is a basic characteristic of the biological pattern of experience. The bodily basis of the senses in sense organs, the functional correlation of sensations with the positions and movements of the organs, the imaginative, conative, emotive consequences of sensible presentations, and the resulting local movements of the body, all indicate that elementary experience is concerned, not with the immanent aspects of living, but with its external conditions and opportunities. Within the full pattern of living, there is a partial, intermittent, extroverted pattern of conscious living.

It is this extroversion of function that underpins the confrontational element of consciousness itself. Conation, emotion, and bodily movement are a response to stimulus; but the stimulus is over against[f] the response; it is a presentation through sense and memory and imagination of what is responded to, of what is to be dealt with. The stimulating elements are the elementary object; the responding elements are the elementary subject. When the object fails to stimulate, the subject is indifferent; and when nonconscious vital process has no need of outer objects, the subject dozes and falls asleep.

2.3 The Aesthetic Pattern of Experience [184–85]

There exists in man an exuberance above and beyond the biological account books of purposeful pleasure and pain. Conscious living is itself a joy that reveals its spontaneous authenticity in the untiring play of children, in the strenuous games of youth, in the exhilaration of sunlit morning air, in the sweep of a broad perspective, in the swing of a melody. Such delight is not, perhaps, exclusively human, for kittens play and snakes are charmed. But neither is it merely biological. One can well suspect that health and exercise are not the dominant motive in the world of sport; and it seems a little narrow to claim that good meals and fair women are the only instances of the aesthetic. Rather, one is led to acknowledge that experience can occur for the sake of experiencing, that it can slip beyond the confines of serious-minded biological purpose, and that this very liberation is a spontaneous, self-justifying joy.

Moreover, just as the mathematician grasps intelligible forms in schematic images, just as the scientist seeks intelligible systems that cover the data of his field, so too the artist exercises his intelligence in discovering ever novel forms that unify and relate the contents and acts of aesthetic experience.[1] Still, sense does not escape one master merely to fall into the clutches of another. Art is a twofold freedom. As it liberates experience from the drag of biological purposiveness, so it liberates intelligence from the wearying constraints of mathematical proofs, scientific verifications, and commonsense factualness. For the validation of the artistic idea is the artistic deed. The artist establishes his insights, not by proof or verification, but by skilfully embodying them in colors and shapes, in sounds and movements, in the unfolding situations and actions of fiction.[g] To the spontaneous joy of conscious living there is added the spontaneous joy of free intellectual creation.

The aesthetic and artistic also are symbolic.[h] Free experience and free creation are prone to justify themselves by an ulterior purpose or significance. Art then becomes symbolic,[i] but what is symbolized is obscure. It is an expression of the human subject outside the limits of adequate intellectual formulation or appraisal. It seeks to mean, to convey, to impart, something that is to be reached, not through science or philosophy, but through a participation, and in some fashion a reenactment of the artist's inspiration and intention. Prescientific and prephilosophic, it may strain for truth and value without defining them. Post-biological, it may reflect the psychological depths, yet by that very fact it will go beyond them.

Indeed, the very obscurity of art is in a sense its most generic meaning. Prior to the neatly formulated questions of systematizing intelligence, there is the deep-set wonder in which all questions have their source and ground. As an expression of the subject, art would show forth that wonder in its elemental sweep. Again, as a twofold liberation of sense and of intelligence, art would exhibit the reality of the primary object for that wonder. For the animals, safely sheathed in biological

1 Insight in musical composition is described by Susanne K. Langer, *Feeling and Form: A Theory of Art Developed from 'Philosophy in a New Key'* (New York: Charles Scribner's Sons, 1953) 120–32.

routines, are not questions to themselves. But man's artistry testifies to his freedom. As he can do, so he can be what he pleases. What is he to be? Why? Art may offer attractive or repellent answers to these questions,[j] but in its subtler forms it is content to communicate any of the moods in which such questions arise, to convey any of the tones in which they may be answered or ignored.

2.4 The Intellectual Pattern of Experience   [185–86]

The aesthetic liberation and the free artistic control of the flow of sensations and images, of emotions and bodily movements, not merely break the bonds of biological drive but also generate in experience a flexibility that makes it a ready tool for the spirit of inquiry. To the liveliness of youth, study is hard. But in the seasoned mathematician, sensitive process easily contracts to an unruffled sequence of symbolic notations and schematic images. In the trained observer, outer sense forgets its primitive biological functions to take on a selective alertness that keeps pace with the refinements of elaborate and subtle classifications. In the theorist intent upon a problem, even the subconscious goes to work to yield at unexpected moments the suggestive images of clues and missing links, of patterns and perspectives, that evoke the desiderated insight and the delighted cry 'Eureka!' In reflection, there arises a passionless calm. Memory ferrets out instances that would run counter to the prospective judgment. Imagination anticipates the shape of possibilities that would prove the judgment wrong. So deep is the penetration, so firm the dominance, so strange the transformation of sensitive spontaneity, that memories and anticipations rise above the threshold of consciousness only if they possess at least a plausible relevance to the decision to be made. For the stream of sensitive experience is a chameleon; and as its pattern can be biological or artistic, so too it can become the automatic instrument, or rather the vitally adaptive collaborator, of the spirit of inquiry.

No doubt, the frequency, intensity, duration, and purity of the intellectual pattern of experience are subject to great variation. For they depend upon native aptitude, upon training, upon age and development, upon external circumstance, upon the chance that confronts one with problems and that supplies at least the intermittent opportunity to work towards their solution. To be talented is to find that one's experience slips easily into the intellectual pattern, that one's sensitive spontaneity responds quickly and precisely to the exigencies of mind. Insights come readily. Exact formulation follows promptly. Outer sense pounces upon significant detail. Memory tosses out immediately the contrary instance. Imagination devises at once the contrary possibility. Still, even with talent, knowledge makes a slow, if not a bloody entrance. To learn thoroughly is a vast undertaking that calls for relentless perseverance. To strike out on a new line and become more than a weekend celebrity calls for years in which one's living is more or less constantly absorbed in the effort to understand, in which one's understanding gradually works round and up a spiral of viewpoints with each complementing its predecessor and only the last embracing the whole field to be mastered.

2.5 The Dramatic Pattern of Experience   [187–89]

If now we turn to ordinary human living, it is plain that we have to do with neither the biological nor the artistic nor the intellectual pattern of experience. Still, there is a stream of consciousness, and the stream involves not only succession but also direction. Conspicuous in this direction is a concern to get things done. But behind palpable activities, there are motives and purposes; and in them it is not difficult to discern an artistic, or more precisely, a dramatic component.

For human desires are not simply the biological impulses of hunger for eating and of sex for mating. Indeed, man is an animal for whom mere animality is indecent. It is true enough that eating and drinking are biological performances. But in man they are dignified by their spatial and psychological separation from the farm, the abattoir, the kitchen; they are ornamented by the elaborate equipment of the dining room, by the table manners imposed upon children, by the deportment of adult convention. Again, clothes are not a simple-minded matter of keeping warm. They are the colored plumes of birds as well as the furs of animals. They disguise as well as cover and adorn, for man's sensible and sensing body must not appear to be merely a biological unit. Sex, finally, is manifestly biological yet not merely so. On this point man can be so insistent that, within the context of human living, sex becomes a great mystery, shrouded in the delicacy of indirect speech, enveloped in an aura of romantic idealism, enshrined in the sanctity of the home.

Not only, then, is man capable of aesthetic liberation and artistic creativity, but his first work of art is his own living. The fair, the beautiful, the admirable is embodied by man in his own body and actions before it is given a still freer realization in painting and sculpture, in music and poetry. Style is the man^k before it appears in the artistic product. Still, if the style of living is more fundamental, it is also more constrained. For man's own body and actions cannot be treated as the painter treats his uncomplaining oils and the poet his verbal materials. As in the animal, so also in man, there exist the exigencies of underlying materials, and the pattern of experience has to meet these exigencies by granting them psychic representation and conscious integration. The biological cannot be ignored, and yet in man it can be transformed. The transformation varies with the locality, the period, the social milieu; but the occurrence of the variations only serves to reveal the existence of the variable. Men will claim that they work because they must live; but it is plain that they work so hard because they must make their living dignified. To lack that dignity is to suffer embarrassment, shame, degradation; it is to invite amusement, laughter, ridicule. Inversely, to grant free rein to man's impulse for artistically manifested dignity is to set so-called hardheaded industrialists and financiers to the task of stimulating artistic imagination with advertisements and of meeting its demands with the raw materials of the earth and with the technology of an age of science.

Such artistry is dramatic. It is in the presence of others, and the others too are also actors in the primordial drama that the theatre only imitates. If aesthetic values, realized in one's own living, yield one the satisfaction of good performance, still it is well to have the objectivity of that satisfaction confirmed by the admiration of others; it is better to be united with others by winning their approval; it is best to be bound to them by deserving and obtaining their respect and even their affection. For man is a social animal. He is born in one family only to found another of his own. His artistry and his knowledge accumulate over the centuries because he imitates and learns from others. The execution of his practical schemes requires the collaboration of others. Still, the network of man's social relationships has not the fixity of organization of the hive or the anthill; nor again is it primarily the product of pure intelligence devising blueprints for human behavior. Its ground is aesthetic liberation and artistic creativity, where the artistry is limited by biological exigence, inspired by example and emulation, confirmed by admiration and approval, sustained by respect and affection.

The characters in this drama of living are molded by the drama itself. As other insights emerge and accumulate, so too do the insights that govern the imaginative projects of dramatic living. As other insights are corrected through the trial and error that give rise to further questions and yield still further complementary insights, so too does each individual discover and develop the possible roles he might play, and under the pressure of artistic and affective criteria, work out his own selection and adaptation. Out of the plasticity and exuberance of childhood through the discipline and the play of education there gradually is formed the character of the man. It is a process in which rational consciousness with its reflection and criticism, its deliberation and choice, exerts a decisive influence. Still, there is no deliberation or choice about becoming stamped with some character; there is no deliberation about the fact that our past behavior determines our present habitual attitudes; nor is there any appreciable effect from our present good resolutions upon our future spontaneity. Before there can be reflection or criticism, evaluation or deliberation, our imaginations and intelligence must collaborate in representing the projected course of action that is to be submitted to reflection and criticism, to evaluation and decision. Already in the prior collaboration of imagination and intelligence, the dramatic pattern is operative, outlining how we might behave before others and charging the outline with an artistic transformation[1] of a more elementary aggressivity and affectivity. Ordinary living is not ordinary drama. It is not learning a role and developing in oneself the feelings appropriate to its performance. It is not the prior task of assembling materials and through insight imposing upon them an artistic pattern. For in ordinary living there are not first the materials and then the pattern, nor first the role and then the feelings. On the contrary, the materials that emerge in consciousness are already patterned, and the pattern is already charged emotionally and conatively.

2.6 Elements in the Dramatic Subject   [189–91]

The first condition of drama is the possibility of acting it out, of the subordination of neural process to psychic determinations. Now in the animals this subordination can reach a high degree of complexity to ensure large differentiations of response to nuanced differences of stimuli. Nonetheless, this complexity, so far from being an optional acquisition, seems rather to be a natural endowment and to leave the animal with a relatively small capacity for learning new ways and for mastering other than native skills. In contrast, man's bodily movements are, as it were, initially detached from the conative, sensitive, and emotive elements that direct and release them;[m] and the initial plasticity and indeterminacy ground the later variety. Were the pianist's arms, hands, and fingers locked from birth in natural routines of biological stimulus and response, they never could learn to respond quickly and accurately to the sight of a musical score. To take another illustration, the production of sound is a complicated set of correlated oscillations and movements; but the wailing and gurgling of infants develop through the prattle of children into articulate speech, and this vocal activity can be complemented with the visual and manual activities of reading and writing; the whole structure rests upon conventional signs, yet the endlessly complex correlations that are involved between the psychic and the neural have become automatic and spontaneous in a language that one knows.

Inverse to the control of the psychic over the neural are the demands of neural patterns and processes for psychic representation and conscious integration. Just as an appropriate schematic image specifies and leads to a corresponding insight, so patterns of change in the optic nerve and the cerebrum specify and lead to corresponding acts of seeing. What is true of sight is also true of the other outer senses, and though the matter is far from fully explored, one may presume that memory and imagination, conation and emotion, pleasure and pain, all have their counterparts in corresponding neural processes and originate from their specific demands.

It would be a mistake, however, to suppose that such demands are unconditional. Perceiving is a function not only of position relative to an object, of the intensity of the light, of the healthiness of eyes, but also of interest, anticipation, and activity. Besides the demands of neural processes, there also is the pattern of experience in which their demands are met; and as the elements that enter consciousness are already within a pattern, there must be exercised some preconscious selection and arrangement. Already we have noticed, in treating the intellectual pattern of experience, how the detached spirit of inquiry cuts off the interference of emotion and conation, how it penetrates observation with the abstruse classifications of science, how it puts the unconscious to work to have it bring forth the suggestions, the clues, the perspectives, that emerge at unexpected moments to release insight and call forth a delighted 'Eureka!' In similar fashion, the dramatic pattern of experience penetrates below the surface of consciousness to exercise its own domination and control, and to effect, prior to conscious discrimination, its own selections and arrangements. Nor is this aspect of the dramatic pattern either surprising or novel: there cannot be selection and arrangement without rejection and exclusion, and the function that excludes elements from emerging in consciousness is now familiar as Freud's censor.

Since, then, the demands of neural patterns and processes are subject to control and selection, they are better named demand functions. They call for some psychic representation and some conscious integration, but their specific requirements can be met in a variety of different manners. In the biological pattern of experience, where both unconscious vital process and conscious striving pursue the same end, there is, indeed, little room for diversification of psychic contents. But aesthetic liberation, artistic creativity, and the constant shifting of the dramatic setting open up vast potentialities. All the world's a stage, and not only does each in his time play many parts but also the many parts vary with changes of locality, period, and social milieu. Still, there are limits to this versatility and flexibility. The demand functions of neural patterns and processes constitute the exigence of the organism for its conscious complement; and to violate that exigence is to invite the anguish of abnormality.

2.7 Dramatic Bias [191–206]

Just as insight can be desired, so too it can be unwanted. Besides the love of light, there can be a love of darkness. If prepossessions and prejudices notoriously vitiate theoretical investigations, much more easily can elementary passions bias understanding in practical and personal matters. Nor has such a bias merely some single and isolated effect.[n] To exclude an insight is also to exclude the further questions that would arise from it, and the complementary insights that would carry it towards a rounded and balanced viewpoint. To lack that fuller view results in behavior that generates misunderstanding both in ourselves and in others. To suffer such incomprehension favors a withdrawal from the outer drama of human living into the inner drama of fantasy. This introversion, which overcomes the extroversion native to the biological pattern of experience, generates a differentiation of the persona that appears before others and the more intimate ego that in the daydream is at once the main actor and the sole spectator. Finally, the incomprehension, isolation, and duality rob the development of one's common sense of some part, greater or less, of the corrections and the assurance that result from learning accurately the tested insights of others and from submitting one's own insights to the criticism based on others' experience and development.

2.7.1 Scotosis   [191–92]

Let us name such an aberration of understanding a scotosis, and let us call the resultant blind spot a scotoma. Fundamentally, the scotosis is an unconscious process. It arises, not in conscious acts, but in the censorship that governs the emergence of psychic contents. Nonetheless, the whole process is not hidden from us, for the merely spontaneous exclusion of unwanted insights is not equal to the total range of eventualities. Contrary insights do emerge. But they may be accepted as correct, only to suffer the eclipse that the bias brings about by excluding the relevant further questions. Again, they may be rejected as incorrect, as mere bright ideas without a solid foundation in fact; and this rejection tends to be connected with rationalization of the scotosis and with an effort to accumulate evidence in its favor. Again, consideration of the contrary insight may not reach the level of reflective and critical consciousness; it may occur only to be brushed aside in an emotional reaction of distaste, pride, dread, horror, revulsion. Again, there are the inverse phenomena. Insights that expand the scotosis can appear to lack plausibility; they will be subjected to scrutiny; and as the subject shifts to and from his sounder viewpoint, they will oscillate wildly between an appearance of nonsense and an appearance of truth. Thus, in a variety of manners, the scotosis can remain fundamentally unconscious yet suffer the attacks and crises that generate in the mind a mist of obscurity and bewilderment, of suspicion and reassurance, of doubt and rationalization, of insecurity and disquiet.

2.7.2 Repression   [192–93]

Nor is it only the mind that is troubled. The scotosis is an aberration, not only of the understanding, but also of the censorship. Just as wanting an insight penetrates below the surface to bring forth schematic images that give rise to the insight, so not wanting an insight has the opposite effect of repressing from consciousness a scheme that would suggest the insight. Now this aberration of the censorship is inverse to it. Primarily, the censorship is constructive; it selects and arranges materials that emerge in consciousness in a perspective that gives rise to an insight; this positive activity has by implication a negative aspect, for other materials are left behind, and other perspectives are not brought to light; still, this negative aspect of positive activity does not introduce any arrangement or perspective into the unconscious demand functions of neural patterns and processes. In contrast, the aberration of the censorship is primarily repressive; its positive activity is to prevent the emergence into consciousness of perspectives that would give rise to unwanted insights; it introduces, so to speak, the exclusion of arrangements into the field of the unconscious; it dictates the manner in which neural demand functions are not to be met; and the negative aspect of its positive activity is the admission to consciousness of any materials in any other arrangement or perspective. Finally, both the censorship and its aberration differ from conscious advertence to a possible mode of behavior and conscious refusal to behave in that fashion. For the censorship and its aberration are operative prior to conscious advertence, and they regard directly not how we are to behave but what we are to understand. A refusal to behave in a given manner is not a refusal to understand; so far from preventing conscious advertence, the refusal intensifies it and makes its recurrence more likely; and, finally, while it is true that conscious refusal is connected with a cessation of the conscious advertence, still this connection rests, not on an obnubilation of intelligence, but on a shift of effort, interest, preoccupation. Accordingly, we are led to restrict the name 'repression' to the exercise of the aberrant censorship that is engaged in preventing insight.

2.7.3   Inhibition   [193–94]

The effect of the repression is an inhibition imposed upon neural demand functions. However, if we distinguish between demands for images and demands for affects, it becomes clear that the inhibition will not block both in the same fashion. For insights arise, not from the experience of affects, but rather from imaginative presentations. Hence, to prevent insights, repression will have to inhibit demands for images. On the other hand, it need inhibit demands for affects only if they are coupled with the undesired images. Accordingly, the repression will not inhibit a demand for affects if that demand becomes detached from its apprehensive component, slips along some association path, and attaches itself to some other apprehensive component. Inversely, when there emerges into consciousness an affect coupled with an incongruous object, then one can investigate association paths, argue from the incongruous to the initial object of the affect, and conclude that this combination of initial object and affect had been inhibited by a repression. Nor is this conclusion to be rejected as preposterous because the discovered combination of image and affect is utterly alien to conscious behavior. For the combination was inhibited precisely because it was alien. Insights are unwanted, not because they confirm our current viewpoints and behavior, but because they lead to their correction and revision. Inasmuch as the scotosis grounds the conscious affective attitudes of the persona performing before others, it also involves the repression of opposite combinations of neural demand functions; and these demands will emerge into consciousness with the affect detached from its initial object and attached to some associated and more or less incongruous object. Again, inasmuch as the scotosis grounds the conscious affective attitudes of the ego performing in his own private theatre, it also involves the repression of opposite combinations of neural demand functions; and in like manner these demands make their way into consciousness with the affect detached from its initial object and attached to some other more or less incongruous object. In a systematization of Jung's terminology, the conscious ego is matched with an inverse nonconscious shadow, and the conscious persona is matched with an inverse nonconscious anima. Thus the persona of the dispassionate intellectual is coupled with a sentimental anima, and an ego with a message for mankind is linked to a diffident shadow.°

2.7.4 Performance   [194–96]

Apprehension and affect are for operations, but as one would expect, the complex consequences of the scotosis tend to defeat the efforts of the dramatic actor to offer a smooth performance. To speak fluently or to play a musical instrument, one has to be able to confine attention to higher-level controls and to leave the infinite details of the execution to acquired habit. But the division of conscious living between the two patterns of the ego and persona can hamper attention to the higher-level controls and allow the sentiments of the ego or shadow to slip into the performance of the persona. Thus, a friend of mine who had been out of town asked me how my work was getting on. I answered with a dreaded didactic monologue on the connection between insight and depth psychology. His laudatory comment ended with the remark, 'Certainly, while I have been away, you have not been wasting my time.'ᴾ

Besides the waking performance of the dramatic actor, there is also the strange succession of fragmentary scenes that emerge in sleep. Then experience is not dominated by a pattern. Not only are there lacking the critical reflection and deliberate choosing that make waking consciousness reasonable, but also the preconscious activity of the censor, selecting and arranging neural demands, is carried out in a halfhearted and perfunctory manner. This relaxation of the censorship, however, not only accounts for the defective pattern of experience in dreamland but also explains the preponderant influence of the other determinant of conscious contents, namely, the neural demand functions. Claims ignored during the day become effective in sleep. The objects and affects of the persona and of the ego make an overt appearance, and with them mingle the covert affects of the shadow and the anima attached to their incongruous objects.

The basic meaning of the dream is its function. In the animal, consciousness functions as a higher technique for the effective prosecution of biological ends. In man, not only does it fulfil this purpose but also it provides the center for the operations of the self-constituting dramatic actor. Sleep is the negation of consciousness. It is the opportunity needed by unconscious vital process to offset without interference the wear and tear suffered by nerves during the busy day. Within this function of sleep lies the function of the dream. Not only have nerves their physical and chemical basis but also they contain dynamic patterns that can be restored to an easy equilibrium only through the offices of psychic representations and interplay. Besides restoring the organism, sleep has to knit up the raveled sleeve of care, and it does so by adding dreams, in which are met ignored claims of neural demand functions.

Functionally, then, the dream is a psychic flexibility that matches and complements the flexibility of neural demands. If consciousness is to yield to the preoccupations of the intellectual or of the dramatic actor, it cannot be simply a function of neural patterns and processes. Inversely, if neural demands ignored by consciousness are to be met without violating the liberation of the artistic, intellectual, or dramatic pattern of experience, then they find their opportunity in the dream.

There is a further aspect to this twofold flexibility. The liberation of consciousness is founded on a control of apprehensions; as has been seen, the censorship selects and arranges materials for insight, or in its aberration excludes the arrangements that would yield insight. Inversely, the imperious neural demands are not for apprehensive psychic contents but for the conations and emotions that are far more closely linked with activity; thus, while we imagine much as we please, our feelings are quite another matter. Accordingly, since the dream is the psychic safety valve for ignored neural demands, and since the imperious neural demands are affective rather than apprehensive, the dream will appear as a wish fulfilment. This statement, of course, must not be taken in the sense that the unconscious has wishes which are fulfilled in dreams, for wishing is a conscious activity. Nor again does it mean that the wishes fulfilled in dreams are those of the conscious subject, for inverse to the ego is the shadow and inverse to the persona is the anima. The accurate statement is that dreams are determined by neural demands for conscious affects, and the affects in question may be characteristic not only of the ego or the persona but also of the shadow or the anima. However, as has been seen, if the affects emergent in the dream are characteristic of the shadow or the anima, they emerge disassociated from their initial objects and attached to some incongruous object; and in this fact there now may easily be discerned a functional significance. The affects of the shadow and anima are alien to the conscious performer; were they to emerge into consciousness with their proper objects, not only would they interfere with his sleep but also they would violate his aesthetic liberation. The disguise of the dream is essential to its function of securing a balance between neural demands and psychic events while preserving the integrity of the conscious stream of experience.

Hence, to penetrate to the latent content of the dream is to bring to light a secret that, so to speak, has purposely been hidden. To equip an animal with intelligence constitutes not only the possibility of culture and of science but also the possibility of every abomination that has occurred in the course of human history. To affirm the latter human potentiality in abstract terms is somewhat unpleasant. To proceed syllogistically from the universal to the particular is distasteful. To assert that potentialities inherent in human nature exist in one's acquaintances, one's relatives, one's parents, oneself, is logical enough yet outrageous. Yet far more vivid than the utterance of such truths is their apprehension through insights into images that are affectively charged. In his waking hours

man may preclude the occurrence of such insights. Even if his unconscious patterns and processes have been so stimulated as to demand
them, the demand can be met in a dream in which the disassociation of
the affect from its proper object respects the immanent direction[q] of the
stream of consciousness.

A similar functional significance may be found in the formation of
screening memories. Of our childhood we are apt to remember only a
few vivid scenes, and when these are submitted to scrutiny and investigation, they are likely to prove mere fictions. Freud has divined such
false memories to be screens. Behind them are actions which later
understanding would view in a fashion unsuspected by the child that
performed them. If the memory of such actions is not to enter consciousness, it has to be repressed; if it is repressed, it undergoes the disassociation and recombination that result from inhibition. In this fashion
there is formed the false and screening memory that enables the dramatic actor to play his present role with all the more conviction because
he does not believe his past to differ too strikingly from his present.

2.7.5 A Common Problem   [196–99]

Our study of the dramatic bias has worked from a refusal to understand
through the series of its consequences. There result in the mind a scotosis, a weakening of the development of common sense, a differentiation
of the persona and the ego, an alternation of suspicion and reassurance,
of doubt and rationalization. There follow an aberration of the censorship, the inhibition of unwanted imaginative schemes, the disassociation
of affects from their initial objects and their attachment to incongruous
yet related materials, the release of affective neural demands in dreams,
and the functionally similar formation of screening memories.

However, if the account has made no explicit mention of sex, this
must not be taken to imply that the depth psychologists have been on
the wrong track. On the contrary, the peculiarities of sexual development make it the ordinary source of materials for the scotosis. Because
hunger and sex are vital, they constitute the areas in which experience
can be contracted from its dramatic to its biological pattern. But hunger
is present from birth, and its manifestations do not greatly change.
Sexual development, on the contrary, is prolonged, and indeed both
organic and psychological. From birth to puberty there occur successive
specializations of the neural demand functions; and their term is not

some free combination of movements, like playing the piano, but a naturally determined sequence of apprehensions, affects, and movements that admit only superficial modifications from the inventive dramatist. Interdependent with this change, there is a psychological transformation in which the affective and submissive attitudes of the child within the family give place to the man self-reliantly orientating himself in the universe and determining to found a family of his own.

During the course of this long and intricate process, there is room not only for waywardness motivated by strange pleasure but also for accidents, incomprehension, blunders, secretiveness. If adverse situations and mistakes occur at random, they can be offset by the excretory function of the dream, by the pressures and attractions of a healthy environment, by suitable and opportune instruction, by some form of inner acceptance of the drive to understanding and truth with its aesthetic and moral implications. If thy eye be single, thy whole body will be lightsome. On the other hand, one adverse situation can follow another; the error and waywardness of each previous occasion can make still more probable the mishandling of the next; a scotosis becomes established. As an aberration of the understanding, it stands in the way of the proper development of affective attitudes. As an aberration of the censorship, it loads the neural demand functions with inhibitions. Affective demands are shifted to incongruous dream objects. The incongruous objects may chance to function as do normal stimuli for affects, and waywardness may solidify the connection. The shadow and the anima can become organized as demands for integrated attitudes of love or hatred. Eventually, a point is reached where the immanently determined direction of the misled stream of consciousness is no longer capable of providing psychic representation and conscious integration for the distorted neural demand functions. Then neural demands assert themselves in waking consciousness through the inadequacies, compulsions, pains, and anxieties of the psychoneuroses. Dramatic living has forfeited its autonomy, and only through delusions can it pretend to its old mastery.

Still, before this point is reached, there can occur the intermediate phenomena studied by Freud in his *Totem and Taboo*.[2] It was remarked above that the dream provides release from the random repressions that

2 [Sigmund Freud, *Totem and Taboo*, The Standard Edition of the Complete Psychological Works of Sigmund Freud, vol. 13, ed. James Strachey (London: Hogarth Press, 1955).]

are more or less inevitable and that the development of scotosis results from the cumulative effect of successive adverse situations. Now, when adverse situations become the rule for most members of a society, then the society can survive only by providing a regular public equivalent for the dream. Such prophylactic group therapy will exist whenever unconscious needs are met in a disguised manner. Dr Stekel's description of the theatre as mass therapy[3] echoes Aristotle's statement that tragedy effects a catharsis of fear and pity.[4] Nor is the invention of such therapy in a primitive culture any more difficult than the invention of the cultural organization itself. For the constraints of the organization give rise to corresponding dreams; the relief afforded by the dreams can be noticed; this advertence may be given dramatic expression; the dramatic expression would meet in a disguised form the unconscious needs of the community; and if the dramatic expression is not included in the cultural organization, then the culture will not survive to be investigated by anthropologists.

This basic mechanism admits a series of applications that range from knowledge issuing forth in prophylactic purpose through successive stages of intellectual obnubilation to close approximations to abnormal phenomena. Man's capacity for art and science, psychology and philosophy, religion and morality operates in the primitive and in the uneducated without awareness of the differences between these departments and without any sharp distinction between them and underlying impulses or needs. In the complex phenomena of totemism, in the rites of the Mother Goddess, in the myths of the Sky Gods, there appear reflections not only of the social organization of hunters, agriculturalists, and parasitic nomads but also of human sexuality; nor did the Mosaic proscription of images prevent the backsliding lamented by the prophets, nor the mystical flight from sense of the Buddhists eliminate the earlier Brahminism, nor the rational criticism of the Greeks forestall popular hatred of the Christians.

Again, there is a nice distinction between the sensitive mechanism that enforces a taboo and the rational judgment that imposes a moral obligation. Freud was aware that his path would have been easier if he had

3 [Lonergan may be referring to chapter 17 of Wilhelm Stekel's book *Technique of Analytical Psychotherapy*, trans. Eden and Cedar Paul (New York: Liveright, 1950), the work of Stekel to which he will appeal shortly.]

4 [Aristotle, *Poetics*, 13 & 14.]

glozed over the more shocking elements in his discoveries; yet to take
the easier course would have involved not only a violation of his intellectual convictions but also a conquest of his moral feelings.[r] Still, such a
coincidence of conscience and moral feeling can be procured not only
by an adaptation of feeling to moral judgment but also by the determination of judgment in accord with the feelings instilled through
parental and social influence. Once feeling takes the lead, critical reflection can prevent an arbitrary extension of the moral code. But in the
primitive and in the child, not only is critical reflection undeveloped and
unequipped but also there is little capacity to distinguish between the
outer constraint of commands imposed through affection and fear, and
the inner implications through which reasonable judgment entails
reasonable living. Then moral feelings are free to develop according to
the psychological laws that link affects to successively associated objects.
The taboo not only operates but also tends to expand in much the same
fashion as the compulsion neurosis.

2.7.6 A Piece of Evidence[s]   [199–203]

It is not an easy matter to connect our outline of dramatic bias with the
evidence provided by specialists in the field of psychotherapy. Not only
are they not directly concerned with human intelligence but also the
scope of our work leaves no room for an account of the existence, on
the level of the sensitive psyche, of an initiating factor that operates in
a parallel fashion to the flight from understanding. It is true that later,
in the first section of chapter 17, an earlier exploration of genetic
method will have made it possible to offer some indications on this score.
But we must strike the iron while it is hot, and so we propose to prescind from all questions of causal origins and to view our account of
dramatic bias simply as a functional correlation. For if we cannot expect
the reader to believe that a flight from insight is the infantile beginning
of psychic trouble, we cannot but claim that there is some connection
between it and, on the other hand, repression and inhibition, the slips
of waking consciousness and the function of dreams, the aberrations of
religion and morality and, as a limit, the psychoneuroses. Moreover, our
claim would be more than Freud seems to have implied when, in his
History of the Psychoanalytic Movement, he prefaced his indictment of the
secessionists, Adler and Jung, with the remark that he had always asserted that repressions and the sustaining resistance *might* involve a sus-

pension of understanding.[5] Accordingly, we raise the question whether any specialists in the field of psychiatry offer any evidence for a correlation that links both psychic trouble with a flight from insight and psychic recovery with an intellectual illumination.

To this precise question an affirmative answer seems to be offered by Dr Wilhelm Stekel's *Technique of Analytic Psychotherapy*.[6] The work, which is thoroughly practical in conception and purpose, consistently considers analytic treatment as a retrospective education. Once the differential diagnosis has excluded both somatic disorder and the imminence of psychosis, the working hypothesis becomes the assumption that the analysand is the subject of a scotoma. A favorable prognosis requires that the patient's critical reflection and deliberate choice be allied with the analyst; but along with this rational attitude there exists a flight from knowledge that is to be cured by knowledge. During the analysis this flight continues to manifest itself in two manners named the resistance and the transference. Just as in the rest of his living the patient's understanding spontaneously finds measures of self-defence and thereby nourishes the scotoma, so in the intimate drama of the analysis the patient is engaged both in devising means to prevent the coming revelation, and at the same time in repressing the insights that would explain to him his own conduct. Such is the resistance; it is plausible, ingenious, resourceful; it adapts itself to each new situation; yet so far from being deliberate, it is at least fundamentally nonconscious. There is also the transference. The development of the scotoma has involved the repression of feelings of love or hatred for persons in the patient's milieu; this repression and the consequent inhibition mean that the patient is the subject of neural demands for affects that, however, are detached from their initial objects; the transference is the emergence into consciousness of these affects directed upon the person of the analyst.

Just as the disorder is linked with a refusal[t] to understand, so its cure is an insight, a 'lightning flash of illumination.'[7] Just as the refusal excluded not some single insight but an expanding series, so the cure

5 [Sigmund Freud, 'On the History of the Psycho-analytic Movement,' in The Standard Edition of the Complete Psychological Works of Sigmund Freud, vol. 14 (London: Hogarth Press, 1957). Freud's comments on the secession of Jung and Adler begin on p. 42.]
6 [See above, note 3, but Lonergan's own reference here was to the London edition, The Bodley Head, 1939.]
7 [Stekel, Technique of Analytical Psychotherapy 13.]

consists in the occurrence of at least the principal insights that were blocked. It is the re-formation of the patient's mentality. Moreover, these insights must occur, not in the detached and disinterested intellectual pattern of experience, but in the dramatic pattern in which images are tinged with affects. Otherwise the insights will occur but they will not undo the inhibitions that account for the patient's affective disorders; there will result a development of theoretical intelligence without a change in sensitive spontaneity. Finally, the patient is not to be thought capable of curing himself; for the cure consists precisely in the insights which arise from the schematic images that spontaneously the patient represses; and even if by an extraordinary effort of intellectual detachment the patient succeeded in grasping in part what he was refusing to understand, this grasp would occur in the intellectual pattern of experience and so would prove ineffectual; indeed, the effort would be likely to produce an obsession with analytic notions, and there would be some danger that such merely theoretical insight would tend to inoculate the patient against the benefit of a true analytical experience with its dramatic overtones.

The analyst, then, is needed. To perform the differential diagnosis, he must know medicine. Otherwise he will risk not merely ministering to the mind when the body is ill but also attempting to treat psychotics and so acquiring the reputation of driving people insane. Further, the analyst must himself be free from scotoma; a bias in his understanding of himself will also be a bias in his understanding of others; and this is all the more dangerous if he attempts to follow Dr Stekel's active therapy. This active therapy rests upon knowledge that is parallel in structure to common sense. As has been seen, common sense consists in a basic accumulation of insights to which must be added further insights derived from the situation in hand. Similarly, the analyst's knowledge has two parts. There is the basic accumulation derived from an academic formation and from personal experience. It consists in an understanding of the psychoneuroses or parapathies in their origins, their development, their results; it is a grasp of a vast manifold of possibilities; it involves an ability to proceed from a patient's biography and behavior, his dreams and associations, to a grasp of his precise flight from knowledge. However, that precise flight was the hidden component of an individual history; it possesses not merely typical features but also its own particular twists and turns; and it continues to be operative in the analytical situation. The analyst has to outwit the resistance. He has to discern the transference, be able to make capital of it, and know when to end it. He has to be able to wait for favorable opportunities, ready to take the initiative when the occasion calls for it, capable of giving up when he is defeated, and ingenious in keeping things going when he sees he can win. In this complicated and dangerous chess game, he is to be gaining insight into the patient's basic trouble, winning his confidence by the explanation and removal of superficial symptoms, and preparing the way for the discovery of the profound secret. Finally, he has to be able to end the analysis, stiffen the analysand to self-reliance, contribute what he can to the happy ending in which both need of the analyst and disturbing memories of the analysis pass away.

It is time to revert to our question. Does there exist empirical evidence for the assertion that the suspension of understanding is not merely a possible consequence but also a regular[u] factor in psychogenic disorder? Unfortunately, there are divisions among specialists in the field, and so, instead of giving a single answer, I must give two.

To those not disinclined to agree with Dr Stekel, one may say that there exists empirical evidence for a psychotherapeutic notion in the measure that the notion is operative in actual treatment, that it is operative in the treatment of all types of disorder rather than in a partial selection of types, that it survives prolonged and varied experience, that the survival contrasts with a readiness to drop unverified notions, that failures cannot be traced to the notion in question. Now Dr Stekel has attained an international position both as an analyst and as a writer of technical works; he is able to describe his *Technique of Analytic Psychotherapy* as the fruit of thirty years' experience;[8] in that book the analyst's working hypothesis is that the patient is suffering from a scotoma and the analyst's goal is to lead the patient towards a 'lightning flash of illumination'; this view dominates the whole treatment and is relevant to the whole class of parapathies or psychoneuroses; finally, there is a good deal of evidence for Dr Stekel's independence of mind and his readiness to abide by results.

However, there perhaps are those to whom Dr Stekel's favor for an opinion provides presumptive evidence that the opinion is erroneous or at least rash. To them I would point out that the present issue is not the validity of the whole of Dr Stekel's theory and practice but solely the existence of empirical evidence for a single correlation. I am not asking

8 [See ibid. xx.]

for the adoption of Dr Stekel's active method; I am not even urging that analytic treatment is desirable; my concern is restricted to a theoretical issue, and my question is whether or not evidence exists. It seems to me that a negative answer is impossible. Even if one prescinds entirely from Dr Stekel and his pupils, still there occur other analytic treatments in which the cure operates through knowledge.[9] But the knowledge in question is of a particular kind: it is not sensitive knowledge apart from organization through insights, for hypnosis is not a satisfactory method; it is not knowledge on the level of critical reflection and judgment, for delusions are not the principal characteristic of psychoneurosis; it is the intermediate factor that we have been investigating under the name of insight, and on the present theoretical level it makes no difference whether the patient be led to the insight by an active method or left to discover it for himself by a passive method.

2.7.7   A Note on Method   [203–206]

There is a final point to be made, and it regards the significance for depth psychology of recent developments in scientific methodology. At

9   Otto Fenichel (*Problems of Psychoanalytic Technique*, trans. David Bruns-
    wick, Albany, NY: *The Psychoanalytic Quarterly*, 1941) asks how it is that
    interpretation works (p. 52) and discusses the process in which the
    patient appropriates an interpretation (pp. 76–97). Gregory Zilboorg
    ('The Emotional Problem and the Therapeutic Role of Insight,' *The
    Psychoanalytic Quarterly*, 1952, 1–24) experiences difficulty in defining
    insight, grants that Freud's basic hope was an enlargement of our ca-
    pacity to understand, insists that therapeutically significant insight arises
    only as a consequence to psychic liberation. *A Study of Interpersonal Rela-
    tions*, ed. P. Mullahy (New York: Hermitage Press, 1949), included three
    papers on insight by E.D. Hutchinson [see above, chapter 1, note 1].
    From these papers Clara Thompson (*Psychoanalysis: Evolution and De-
    velopment*, with the collaboration of P. Mullahy, New York: Hermitage
    Press, 1951, 238–41) derives a definition of insight and applies it to a
    therapeutic process that ends with an illuminating moment in which
    previous thinking falls into perspective and sensitive spontaneity under-
    goes an effortless change. In *The Interpersonal Theory of Psychiatry* (New
    York: W.W. Norton, 1953), H.S. Sullivan speaks a number of times of a
    marvelous 'selective inattention' to what is significant (see the index
    under 'selective inattention') and depicts a patient suddenly seeing the
    point of a dream (338–39). In brief, there is an essential difference
    between the task of the teacher and the task of the psychotherapist; but
    teaching individuals something about themselves is a significant com-
    ponent in psychotherapy; and in the light of the present analysis of
    human knowledge successful teaching is a communication of insights.[v]

the turn of the century mechanist determinism was still the world view dominant in scientific circles. Freud's discovery and development of the notion of psychogenic disorder came at the ambiguous moment when the old outlook was about to dissolve, and as one might expect, the ambiguity of the moment forced ambiguity upon the interpretation of his work. Were mechanist determinism correct, then neither normality nor disorder could be psychogenic; Laplace's demon could calculate both from the world distribution of atoms in any basic situation; Freud could be said to introduce a new name and a new technique inasmuch as he dealt with collocations of atoms through their psychic appearances; but Freud could not be credited with the discovery of an autonomous science. On the other hand, if mechanist determinism is incorrect, the category of the psychogenic promptly assumes a profound significance. Let us attempt to clarify this point.

As we have seen, empirical science is the determination of correlations verified in observables.[10] Mechanism is the additional determination to invent what is neither a correlation nor verified nor observable. What is so invented is pronounced real and objective; and in comparison with this fictitious treasure, the observable becomes the merely apparent. Thus, in nineteenth-century physical theory, the ether is real and objective, and its properties resembling, say, a sponge-like vortex are what make electromagnetic equations true. Nor is this all. Because verified correlations are attributed to atoms or ether as imagined, they are not abstract but concrete; and once classical correlations are considered to be concrete, determinism follows, and the possibility of statistical laws, except as a confession of ignorance, rigorously is excluded.

Now Freud's own investigations threw some doubt on the scientific character of mechanist objectivation. He was aware of the importance of extroversion in the object-finding that pertains to the psychic side of sexual development. He could appeal to projection to account for the transformation of the unconscious ill will of primitives to deceased relatives, into the explicit ill will of the departed spirits to the bereaved mourners. But he had no intention of going back over the path traversed by Galileo and Descartes, Hobbes and Berkeley, Hume and Kant. Nor did the methodology of then contemporary science provide him

---

10 Here 'observable' denotes, not the physical variable of quantum mechanics, but simply what can be observed. [This note was added by Lonergan at the proof stage.]

with a canon of parsimony that restricted scientific affirmation to verified correlations and to observables. On the contrary, on many occasions Freud represents the outlook of his time and tends to regard observable psychic events as appearance and unobservable entities as reality. What precisely is the libido? Is it what is known either by observing nerves or by observing psychic events or by correlating these observables or by verifying these correlations? Or is it a construct that stands to Freud's verified correlations in much the same manner as the sponge-vortex ether once stood to electromagnetic equations? To resolve the ambiguity, if it can be resolved, would call for an investigation by a trained expert in the history of science.[11]

Again, Freud was professedly determinist. But insofar as determinism is operative in Freud's work, it amounts to the postulate that there is a reason for everything, even for numbers that one appears to select at random. But if one admits that some reasons are nonsystematic, that postulate becomes compatible with statistical laws; and if Laplace has failed to exclude probability from physics, there is little likelihood of its being excluded from psychology.

Still, whatever may have been Freud's involvement[w] in mechanist determinism, it remains that his scientific discovery was psychogenic disease. It is not science but a philosophy that pronounces conscious events to be appearance and some underlying ultimate to be reality. It is not science but a philosophy that confers upon atoms the exclusive role of ruling the course of conscious events. On the other hand, it is Freud's discovery that reveals the psychogenic to be more than an illusory name; and it is a sacrifice of mechanist determinism that opens the way to the recognition of the psychogenic as a genuine category.

For in the first place, an acknowledgment of the nonsystematic leads to an affirmation of successive levels of scientific inquiry. If the nonsystematic exists on the level of physics, then on that level there are coincidental manifolds that can be systematized by a higher chemical level

11 There is a long and nuanced chapter on 'Freud's Theory of Mind' in the first volume of Dr Ernest Jones's *The Life and Work of Sigmund Freud* (New York: Basic Books, 1953). Contrast the influence of contemporary physics in the relational concepts elaborated in *Culture and Personality*, ed. S. Stansfeld Sargent and Marian W. Smith (Proceedings of an Inter-disciplinary Conference held under the auspices of the Viking Fund, 14 East 71st Street, New York City, 7 and 8 November 1947. Published by the Viking Fund, New York, 1949, reprinted 1950. See pp. 9, 11, 13–30, 48–55, 175–94).

without violating any physical law. If the nonsystematic exists on the level of chemistry, then on that level there are coincidental manifolds that can be systematized by a higher biological level without violating any chemical law. If the nonsystematic exists on the level of biology, then on that level there are coincidental manifolds that can be systematized by a higher psychic level without violating any biological law. If the nonsystematic exists on the level of the psyche, then on that level there are coincidental manifolds that can be systematized by a higher level of insight and reflection, deliberation and choice, without violating any law of the psyche. In brief, an acknowledgment of the nonsystematic makes it possible to conceive (1) psychic health as a harmonious unfolding of a process that moves at once on distinct yet related levels, (2) psychic aberration as an orientation of the stream of consciousness in conflict with its function of systematizing underlying manifolds, and (3) analytic treatment as an effort to reorientate an aberrant stream of consciousness and to effect a release from unconscious obstructions with a psychic origin.

Again, an acknowledgment that the real is the verified makes it possible to affirm the reality no less of the higher system than of the underlying manifold. The chemical is as real as the physical; the biological as real as the chemical; the psychic as real as the biological; and insight as real as the psychic. At once the psychogenic ceases to be merely a name, for the psychic becomes a real source of organization that controls underlying manifolds in a manner beyond the reach of their laws.

By the same stroke there is laid the specter that at least popularly is associated with Freud's discoveries. For the latent content of the dream, so far from revealing the 'real' man, now merely exhibits potentialities that are rejected not only by waking but also by dreaming consciousness. Though the potentialities are for parricide and cannibalism, incest and suicide, still they are only potentialities, and commonly they are rejected. What has been found shocking or revolting is not the affirmation of the possibility of what, after all, does occur. It is the affirmation that under the disguise of a phenomenal consciousness there lurks a monster that is the reality of each of us and the effective master of our lives.

Finally, it is to be observed that, if this note on method draws upon previous discussion, it also is perhaps excessively proleptic. Only in chapter 8 shall we be in a position either to say what is meant by the thing, the man, the person, or to extend to things and persons the notion of emergent probability. Only in chapter 14 shall we be able to come to grips with the philosophic problems of reality and objectivity. Only in chapter 15 shall we be able to attempt a systematic account of genetic method. But if our present suggestions cannot avoid a conspicuous lack of precision and detail, perhaps they possess the pedagogical value of opening a perspective and promising a fuller though later scrutiny.

7

Common Sense as Object

The apparently modest and secure undertaking of common sense is to understand things in their relations to us. Unfortunately, we change; even the acquisition of common sense is a change in us; and so in the preceding section we attempted an investigation of the biological, aesthetic, artistic, intellectual, dramatic subject to which common sense relates things. But if the development of common sense is a change in its subject, still more obviously does it involve a change in its object. Common sense is practical. It seeks knowledge, not for the sake of the pleasure of contemplation, but to use knowledge in making and doing. Moreover, this making and doing involve a transformation of man and his environment, so that the common sense of a primitive culture is not the common sense of an urban civilization, nor the common sense of one civilization the common sense of another. However elaborate the experiments of the pure scientist, his goal is always to come closer to natural objects and natural relationships. But the practicality of common sense engenders and maintains enormous structures of technology, economics, politics, and culture, that not only separate man from nature but also add a series of new levels or dimensions in the network of human relationships. No less than the subjective, the objective field of common sense must be explored, for the development of common sense involves a change not only in us, to whom things are related, but also in the things which are related to us.

1   Practical Common Sense   [207–209]

In the drama of human living, human intelligence is not only artistic but also practical.[a] At first, there appears little to differentiate man from the beasts, for in primitive fruit-gathering cultures, hunger is linked to eating by a simple sequence of bodily movements. But primitive hunters take time out from hunting to make spears, and primitive fishers take time out from fishing to make nets. Neither spears nor nets in themselves are objects of desire. Still, with notable ingenuity and effort they are fashioned, because for practical intelligence desires are recurrent, labor is recurrent, and the comparatively brief time spent making spears or nets is amply compensated by the greater ease with which more game or fish is taken on an indefinite series of occasions.

Moreover, such an intervention of intelligence is itself recurrent. As products of human ingenuity, spears and nets illustrate not only the idea of the old mechanical arts but also the more recondite idea of modern technology. As pieces of material equipment, the same objects are initial instances of the idea of capital formation. Now the history of man's material progress lies essentially in the expansion of these ideas. As inventions accumulate, they set problems calling for more inventions. The new inventions complement the old only to suggest[b] further improvements, to reveal fresh possibilities, and eventually to call forth in turn the succession of mechanical and technological higher viewpoints that mark epochs in man's material progress. Moreover, this advance of practical intelligence is registered not merely in memory, and later in books, but more obviously in concrete products, in tools and buildings, in the ever increasing manifold of appurtenances of laborers, craftsmen, merchants, and carriers. Thus, in correspondence with each stage in the development of practical intelligence, there is a measure and structure of capital formation, that is, of things produced and arranged not because they themselves are desired but because they expedite and accelerate the process of supplying the goods and services that are wanted by consumers. Again, in correspondence with each advance of practical intelligence, there is a technological obsolescence of capital equipment. The old shops still have their shelves and counters; the old machines may suffer no material or mechanical defect. But the new models produce better goods more efficiently; and trade now walks on different streets.

The concrete realization of the succession of new practical ideas does not take place without human cooperation. It demands a division of labor, and at the same time it defines the lines along which labor is divisible. It invites men to specialize in the skillful use of particular tools and the expeditious performance of particular tasks. It calls forth some economic system, some procedure that sets the balance between the production of consumer goods and new capital formation, some method that settles what quantities of what goods and services are to be supplied, some device for assigning tasks to individuals and for distributing among them the common ·product.

As technology evokes the economy, so the economy evokes the polity. Most men get ideas, but the ideas reside in different minds, and the different minds do not quite agree. Of itself, communication only reveals the disparity. What is wanted is persuasion, and the most effective persuader becomes a leader, a chief, a politician, a statesman. For the problem of effective agreement is recurrent. Each step in the process of technological and economic development is an occasion on which minds differ, new insights have to be communicated, enthusiasm has to be roused, and a common decision must be reached. Beyond the common sense of the laborer, the technician, the entrepreneur, there is the political specialization of common sense. Its task is to provide the catalyst that brings men of common sense together. It is an incomplete accumulation of insights to be complemented and modified by the further insights that arise from the situation in hand. It involves some understanding of industry and of commerce but its special field is dealing with men. It has to discern when to push for full performance and when to compromise, when delay is wisdom and when it spells disaster, when widespread consent must be awaited and when action must be taken in spite of opposition. It has to be able to command attention and to win confidence, to set forth concretely the essentials of a case, to make its own decisions and secure the agreement of others, to initiate and carry through some section of that seriation of social responses meeting social challenges that Arnold Toynbee in his *Study of History* has so lavishly and brilliantly illustrated.[1]

2   The Dynamic Structure   [209–11]

As in the fields of physics, chemistry, and biology, so in the field of

1 [See Arnold J. Toynbee, *A Study of History*, vol. 3, *The Growth of Civilizations* (London: Oxford University Press, 1934), index, Challenge-and-Response; see the index also of vol. 6, *The Disintegration of Civilizations*, Part Two (1939) and of vol. 10, *The Inspiration of Historians* (1954).]

human events and relationships there are classical and statistical laws that combine concretely in cumulating sets of schemes of recurrence. For the advent of man does not abrogate the rule of emergent probability. Human actions are recurrent; their recurrence is regular; and the regularity is the functioning of a scheme, of a patterned set of relations that yields conclusions of the type: If an X occurs, then an X will recur. Children are born only to grow, mature, and beget children of their own. Inventions outlive their inventors and the memory of their origins. Capital is capital because its utility lies not in itself but in the acceleration it imparts to the stream of useful things. The political machinery of agreement and decision is the permanent yet self-adapting source of an indefinite series of agreements and decisions. Clearly, schemes of recurrence exist and function. No less clearly, their functioning is not inevitable. A population can decline, dwindle, vanish. A vast technological expansion, robbed of its technicians, would become a monument more intricate but no more useful than the pyramids. An economy can falter, though resources and capital equipment abound, though skill cries for its opportunity and desire for skill's product, though labor asks for work and industry is eager to employ it; then one can prime the pumps and make X occur; but because the schemes are not functioning properly, X fails to recur. As the economy, so too the polity can fall apart. In a revolution violence goes unchecked; laws lose their meaning; governments issue unheeded decrees; until from sheer weariness with disorder men are ready to accept any authority that can assert itself effectively. Yet a revolution is merely a passing stroke of paralysis in the state. There are deeper ills that show themselves in the long-sustained decline of nations, and in the limit in the disintegration and decay of whole civilizations. Schemes that once flourished lose their efficacy and cease to function; in an ever more rapid succession, as crises multiply and remedies have less effect, new schemes are introduced; feverish effort is followed by listlessness; the situation becomes regarded as hopeless; in a twilight of straitened but gracious living men await the catalytic trifle that will reveal to a surprised world the end of a once brilliant day.

Still, if human affairs fall under the dominion of emergent probability, they do so in their own way. A planetary system results from the conjunction of the abstract laws of mechanics with a suitable concrete set of mass-velocities. In parallel fashion there are human schemes that emerge and function automatically once there occurs an appropriate conjunction of abstract laws and concrete circumstances. But as human intelligence develops, there is a significant change of roles. Less and less importance attaches to the probabilities of appropriate constellations of circumstances. More and more importance attaches to the probabilities of the occurrence of insight, communication, persuasion, agreement,[c] decision. Man does not have to wait for his environment to make him. His dramatic living needs only the clues and the opportunities to originate and maintain its own setting. The advance of technology, the formation of capital, the development of the economy, the evolution of the state are not only intelligible but also intelligent. Because they are intelligible, they can be understood as are the workings of emergent probability in the fields of physics, chemistry, and biology. But because they also are increasingly intelligent, increasingly the fruit of insight and decision, the analogy of merely natural process becomes less and less relevant. What possesses a high probability in one country or period or civilization may possess no probability in another; and the ground of the difference may lie only slightly in outward and palpable material factors and almost entirely in the set of insights that are accessible, persuasive, and potentially operative in the community. Just as in the individual the stream of consciousness normally selects its own course out of the range of neurally determined alternatives, so too in the group commonly accessible insights, disseminated by communication and persuasion, modify and adjust mentalities to determine the course of history out of the alternatives offered by emergent probability.

Such is the high significance of practical common sense, and it will not be amiss, I believe, to pause and make certain that we are not misconceiving it. For the practical common sense of a group, like all common sense, is an incomplete set of insights that is ever to be completed differently in each concrete situation. Its adaptation is too continuous and rapid for it ever to stand fixed in some set of definitions, postulates, and deductions; even were it outfitted, like David in Saul's armor, with such a logical panoply, it could be validated neither in any abstract realm of relations of things to one another nor in all members of any class of concrete situations. As its adaptation is continuous, so its growth is as secret as the germination, the division, the differentiation of cells in seed and shoot and plant. Only ideal republics spring in full stature from the mind of man; the civil communities that exist and function know only a story of their origins, only an outline of their development, only an estimate of their present complexion. For the practical common sense operative in a community does not exist entire in the mind of any one man. It is parceled out among many, to provide each with an understanding of his role and task, to make every cobbler an expert at his last, and no one an expert in another's field. So it is that to understand the working of even a static social structure, one must inquire from many men in many walks of life, and as best one can, discover the functional unity that organically binds together the endlessly varied pieces of an enormous jigsaw puzzle.

3   Intersubjectivity and Social Order   [211–14]

Though I just spoke of a functional unity to be discovered, really there is a duality to be grasped. As intelligent, man sponsors the order imposed by common sense. But man is not a pure intelligence. Initially and spontaneously, he identifies the good with the object of desire, and this desire is not to be confused either with animal impulse or with egoistic scheming. Man is an artist. His practicality is part of his dramatic pursuit of dignified living. His aim is not for raw and isolated satisfactions. If he never dreams of disregarding the little matter of food and drink, still what he wants is a sustained succession of varied and artistically transformed acquisitions and attainments. If he never forgets his personal interest, still his person is no Leibnizian monad; for he was born of his parents' love; he grew and developed in the gravitational field of their affection; he asserted his own independence only to fall in love and provide himself with his own hostages to fortune. As the members of the hive or herd belong together and function together, so too men are social animals, and the primordial basis of their community is not the discovery of an idea but a spontaneous intersubjectivity.

Thus, primitive community is intersubjective. Its schemes of recurrence are simple prolongations of prehuman attainment, too obvious to be discussed or criticized, too closely linked with more elementary processes to be distinguished sharply from them. The bond of mother and child, man and wife, father and son, reaches into a past of ancestors to give meaning and cohesion to the clan or tribe or nation. A sense of belonging together provides the dynamic premise for common enterprise, for mutual aid and succor, for the sympathy that augments joys and divides sorrows. Even after civilization is attained, intersubjective community survives in the family with its circle of relatives and its accretion of friends, in customs and folkways, in basic arts and crafts and skills, in language and song and dance, and most concretely of all in the inner psychology and radiating influence of women. Nor is the abiding significance and efficacy of the intersubjective overlooked when motley states name themselves nations, when constitutions are attributed to founding fathers, when image and symbol, anthem and assembly, emotion and sentiment are invoked to impart an elemental vigor and pitch to the vast and cold technological, economic, and political structures of human invention and convention. Finally, as intersubjective community precedes civilization and underpins it, so also it remains when civilization suffers disintegration and decay. The collapse of imperial Rome was the resurgence of family and clan, feudal dynasty and nation.

Though civil community has its obscure origins in human intersubjectivity, though it develops imperceptibly, though it decks itself out with more primitive attractions, still it is a new creation. The time comes when men begin to ask about the difference between *physis* and *nomos*, between nature and convention. There arises the need of the apologue to explain to the different classes of society that together they form a functional unity and that no group should complain of its lot any more than a man's feet, which do all the walking, complain of his mouth, which does all the eating. The question may be evaded, and the apologue may convince, but the fact is that human society has shifted away from its initial basis in intersubjectivity[d] and has attempted a more grandiose undertaking. The discoveries of practical intelligence, which once were an incidental addition to the spontaneous fabric of human living, now penetrate and overwhelm its every aspect. For just as technology and capital formation interpose their schemes of recurrence between man and the rhythms of nature, so economics and politics are vast structures of interdependence invented by practical intelligence for the mastery not of nature but of man.

This transformation forces on man a new notion of the good. In primitive society it is possible to identify the good simply with the object of desire; but in civil community there has to be acknowledged a further component, which we propose to name the good of order. It consists in an intelligible pattern of relationships that condition the fulfilment of each man's desires by his contributions to the fulfilment of the desires of others, and similarly protect each from the object of his fears in the measure he contributes to warding off the objects feared by others. This good of order is not some entity dwelling apart from human actions and attainments. Nor is it any unrealized ideal that ought to be but is not. But though it is not abstract but concrete, not ideal but real, still it cannot be identified either with desires or with their objects or with their satisfactions. For these are palpable and particular, but the good of order is intelligible and all-embracing. A single order ramifies through the whole community to constitute the link between conditioning actions and conditioned results and to close the circuit of interlocked schemes of recurrence. Again, economic breakdown and political decay are not the absence of this or that object of desire or the presence of this or that object of fear; they are the breakdown and decay of the good of order, the failure of schemes of recurrence to function. Man's practical intelligence devises arrangements for human living; and in the measure that such arrangements are understood and accepted, there necessarily results the intelligible pattern of relationships that we have named the good of order.

In a simple yet inexorable fashion, this order originated by human invention and convention ceases to be an optional adjunct and becomes an indispensable constituent of human living. For the long-run effects of technological advance and new capital formation consist in some combination of increased population, reduced work, and improved living standards. In the course of a century the differences in all three respects may be so great that any return to an earlier state of affairs is regarded as preposterous and is to be brought about only by violence or disaster. But concomitant with the technological and the material development, there also takes place a complementary series of economic and political innovations. Each of these is motivated, to a greater or less extent, by the underlying technical and material changes; each, sooner or later, undergoes the adaptations demanded by subsequent changes; and so at any given moment all together present a united front that can be broken only by the destructive turmoil of a revolution or a conquest. Moreover, ideas have no geographical frontiers, and profits accrue to traders not only from domestic but also from foreign markets. Material and social progress refuses to be confined to a single country; like an incoming tide, first it reaches the promontories, then it penetrates the bays, and finally it pours up the estuaries. In an intricate pattern of lags and variations, new ideas spread over most of the earth to bind together in an astounding interdependence the fortunes of individuals living disparate lives in widely separated lands.

4   **The Tension of Community**   [214–16]

Intersubjective spontaneity and intelligently devised social order have their ground in a duality immanent in man himself. As intelligent, man is the originator and sponsor of the social systems within which, as an individual, he desires and labors, enjoys and suffers. As intelligent, man is a legislator, but as an individual, he is subject to his own laws. By his insights he grasps standard solutions to recurrent problems, but by his experience he provides the instances that are to be subsumed under the standard solutions. From the viewpoint of intelligence, the satisfactions allotted to individuals are to be measured by the ingenuity and diligence of each in contributing to the satisfactions of all; from the same high viewpoint the desires of each are to be regarded quite coolly as the motive power that keeps the social system functioning. But besides the detached and disinterested stand of intelligence, there is the more spontaneous viewpoint of the individual subjected to needs and wants, pleasures and pains, labor and leisure, enjoyment and privation. To each man his own desires, precisely because they are his own, possess an insistence that the desires of others can never have for him. To each man his own labors, because they are his own, have a dimension of reality that is lacking in his apprehension of the labors of others. To each man his own joys and sorrows have an expansive or contracting immediacy that others can know only through their own experience of joy and sorrow. Yet the ineluctable privacy of each one's experience provides no premise for a monadic theory of man. For the bonds of intersubjectivity make the experience of each resonate to the experience of others; and besides this elementary communion, there are operative in all a drive to understand and an insistence on behaving intelligently that generate and implement common ways, common manners, common undertakings, common commitments.

For this reason it would seem a mistake to conceive the sociological as simply a matter of external constraint. It is true enough that society constrains the individual in a thousand ways. It is true enough that the individual has but a slight understanding of the genesis and growth of the civilization into which he was born. It is true enough that many of the things he must do are imposed upon him in a merely external fashion. Yet within the walls of his individuality there is more than a Trojan horse. He has no choice about wanting to understand; he is committed not by any decision of his own but by nature to intelligent behavior; and as these determinants are responsible for the emergence of social orders in the past, so they account for their development, their maintenance, their reformation. Spontaneously every collapse is followed by a reconstruction, every disaster by a new beginning, every revolution by a new era. Commonly men want a different social order, but left to themselves they never consent to a complete anarchy.

There is, then, a radical tension of community. Intersubjective spontaneity and intelligently devised social order possess different properties and different tendencies. Yet to both by his very nature man is committed. Intelligence cannot but devise general solutions and general rules. The individual is intelligent, and so he cannot enjoy peace of mind unless he subsumes his own feelings and actions under the general rules that he regards as intelligent. Yet feeling and spontaneous action have their home in the intersubjective group, and it is only with an effort and then only in favored times that the intersubjective groups fit harmoniously within the larger pattern of social order.

Thus it is that in the history of human societies there are halcyon periods of easy peace and tranquility that alternate with times of crisis and trouble. In the periods of relaxed tension, the good of order has come to terms with the intersubjective groups. It commands their esteem by its palpable benefits; it has explained its intricate demands in some approximate yet sufficient fashion; it has adapted to its own requirements the play of imagination, the resonance of sentiment, the strength of habit, the ease of familiarity, the impetus of enthusiasm, the power of agreement and consent. Then a man's interest is in happy coincidence with his work; his country is also his homeland; its ways are the obviously right ways; its glory and peril are his own.

As the serenity of the good old days rests on an integration of common sense and human feeling, so the troubled times of crisis demand the discovery and communication of new insights and a consequent adaptation of spontaneous attitudes. Unfortunately, common sense does not include an inventory of its own contents. It does not reside whole and entire in a single mind. It cannot point to any recorded set of experiments for its justification. It cannot assert itself in any of the inflexible generalizations that characterize logic, mathematics, and science. Common sense knows, but it does not know what it knows nor how it knows nor how to correct and complement its own inadequacies. Only the blind and destructive blows inevitable in even a partial breakdown of social order can impress on practical common sense that there are limits to its competence and that, if it would master the new situation, it must first consent to learn. Still, what is to be learnt? The problem may baffle what experts are available. A theoretical solution need not lead automatically to its popular presentation. Even when that is achieved, the reorientation of spontaneous attitudes will remain to be effected. The time of crisis can be prolonged, and in the midst of the suffering it entails and of the aimless questioning it engenders, the intersubjective groups within a society tend to fall apart in bickering, insinuations, recriminations, while unhappy individuals begin to long for the idyllic simplicity of primitive living in which large accumulations of insights would be superfluous and human fellow-feeling would have a more dominant role.

5   The Dialectic of Community   [217–18]

The name 'dialectic' has been employed in a variety of meanings. In Plato, it denoted the art of philosophic dialogue and was contrasted with eristic. In Aristotle, it referred to an effort to discover clues to the truth by reviewing and scrutinizing the opinions of others. For the schoolmen, it became the application of logical rules to public disputation. Hegel employed the word to refer to his triadic process from the concept of being to the Absolute Idea. Marx inverted Hegel and so conceived as dialectical a nonmechanical materialist process. Summarily, then, dialectic denotes a combination of the concrete, the dynamic, and the contradictory; but this combination may be found in a dialogue, in the history of philosophic opinions, or in historical process generally.

For the sake of greater precision, let us say that a dialectic is a concrete unfolding of linked but opposed principles of change. Thus there will be a dialectic if (1) there is an aggregate of events of a determinate character, (2) the events may be traced to either or both of two principles, (3) the principles are opposed yet bound together, and (4) they are modified by the changes that successively result from them. For example, the dramatic bias described above[2] was dialectical. The contents and affects emerging into consciousness provide the requisite aggregate of events of a determinate kind; these events originate from two principles, namely, neural demand functions and the exercise of the constructive or repressive censorship; the two principles are linked as patterned and patterning; they are opposed inasmuch as the censorship not only constructs but also represses, and again inasmuch as a misguided censorship results in neglected neural demands forcing their way into

2 Chapter 6, § 2.7.

consciousness; finally, change is cumulative, for the orientation of the censorship at any time and the neural demands to be met both depend on the past history of the stream of consciousness.

Now as there is a dialectic of the dramatic subject, so also there is a larger dialectic of community. Social events can be traced to the two principles of human intersubjectivity and practical common sense. The two principles are linked, for the spontaneous, intersubjective individual strives to understand and wants to behave intelligently; and inversely, intelligence would have nothing to put in order were there not the desires and fears, labors and satisfactions, of individuals. Again, these linked principles are opposed, for it is their opposition that accounts for the tension of community. Finally, these linked and opposed principles are modified by the changes that result from them; the development of common sense consists in the further questions and insights that arise from the situations produced by previous operations of practical common sense; and the alternations of social tranquility and social crisis mark successive stages in the adaptation of human spontaneity and sensibility to the demands of developing intelligence.

In two manners this dialectic of community differs from the dialectic of the dramatic subject. First, there is a difference in extent, for the dialectic of community regards the history of human relationships, while the inner dialectic of the subject regards the biography of an individual. Secondly, there is a difference in the level of activity, for the dialectic of community is concerned with the interplay of more or less conscious intelligence and more or less conscious spontaneity in an aggregate of individuals, while the dialectic of the subject is concerned with the entry of neural demands into consciousness. Accordingly, one might say that a single dialectic of community is related to a manifold of individual sets of neural demand functions through a manifold of individual dialectics. In this relationship the dialectic of community holds the dominant position, for it gives rise to the situations that stimulate neural demands, and it molds the orientation of intelligence that preconsciously exercises the censorship. Still, as is clear, one must not suppose this dominance to be absolute, for both covertly and overtly neural demands conspire with an obnubilation of intelligence, and what happens in isolated individuals tends to bring them together and so to provide a focal point from which aberrant social attitudes originate.

This raises the basic question of a bias in common sense. Four distinct aspects call for attention. There is the already mentioned bias arising from the psychological depths, and commonly it is marked by its sexual overtones. There also are the individual bias of egoism, the group bias with its class conflicts, and a general bias that tends to set common sense against science and philosophy. On these three something must now be said.

6   Individual Bias   [218–22]

There is a rather notable obscurity in the meaning of the terms 'egoism' and 'altruism.' When a carnivorous animal stalks and kills its prey, it is not properly egoistic; for it is simply following its instincts, and in general for animals to follow their instincts is for them to secure the biological ends of individual and specific survival. By parity of reasoning, when a female animal fosters its young, it too is following its instincts; though it contributes to a general biological end, still it does so rather by the scheming of nature than by altruism in its proper sense. Finally, if animal spontaneity is neither egoistic nor altruistic, it seems to follow that the same must be said of human spontaneity; men are led by their intersubjectivity both to satisfy their own appetites and to help others in the attainment of their satisfactions;ᶜ but neither type of activity is necessarily either egoistic or altruistic.

There is a further aspect to the matter. In his *Ethics* Aristotle asked whether a good friend loved himself. His answer was that while true friendship excluded self-love in the popular sense, nonetheless it demanded self-love in a higher sense; for a man loves himself if he wants for himself the finest things in the world, namely, virtue and wisdom; and without virtue and wisdom a man can be a true friend neither to himself nor to anyone else.[3] Accordingly, as Aristotle's answer suggests, when one turns from the realm of spontaneity to that of intelligence and reasonableness, one does not find that egoism and altruism provide ultimate categories. For intelligence and reasonableness with their implications automatically assume the ultimate position; and from their detached viewpoint there is set up a social order in which, as in the animal kingdom, both taking care of oneself and contributing to the well-being of others have their legitimate place and necessary function.

Nonetheless, it remains that there is a sense in which egoism is always

3 [Aristotle, *Ethics*, IX, 8. This text of Aristotle was discussed more at length in 'Finality, Love, Marriage.' See CWL 4, § 2.3 *Friendship*, p. 25.]

wrong and altruism its proper corrective. For man does not live exclusively either on the level of intersubjectivity or on the level of detached intelligence. On the contrary, his living is a dialectical resultant springing from those opposed but linked principles; and in the tension of that union of opposites, the root of egoism is readily to be discerned. For intelligence is a principle of universalization and of ultimate synthesis; it understands similars in the same manner; and it gives rise to further questions on each issue until all relevant data are understood. On the other hand, spontaneity is concerned with the present, the immediate, the palpable; intersubjectivity radiates from the self as from a center, and its efficacy diminishes rapidly with distance in place or time. Egoism is neither mere spontaneity nor pure intelligence but an interference of spontaneity with the development of intelligence. With remarkable acumen one solves one's own problems. With startling modesty one does not venture to raise the relevant further questions, Can one's solution be generalized? Is it compatible with the social order that exists? Is it compatible with any social order that proximately or even remotely is possible?

The precise nature of egoistic interference with intellectual process calls for attention. It is not to be thought that the egoist is devoid of the disinterestedness and detachment of intelligent inquiry. More than many others, he has developed a capacity to face issues squarely and to think them through. The cool schemer, the shrewd calculator, the hardheaded self-seeker are very far from indulging in mere wishful thinking. Without the detachment of intelligence, they cannot invent and implement stratagems that work. Without the disinterestedness of intelligence, they cannot raise and meet every further question that is relevant within their restricted terms of reference. Nor can one say that egoism consists in making intelligence the instrument of more elementary desires and fears. For as long as the egoist is engaged upon his problems, the immanent norms of intelligent inquiry overrule any interference from desire or fear; and while the egoist refuses to put the still further questions that would lead to a profound modification of his solution, still that refusal does not make intelligence an instrument but merely brushes it aside.

Egoism, then, is an incomplete development of intelligence. It rises above a merely inherited mentality. It has the boldness to strike out and think for itself. But it fails to pivot from the initial and preliminary motivation provided by desires and fears to the self-abnegation involved in allowing complete free play to intelligent inquiry. Its inquiry is reinforced by spontaneous desires and fears; by the same stroke it is restrained from a consideration of any broader field.

Necessarily, such an incompleteness of development is an exclusion of correct understanding. Just as in the sciences intelligence begins from hypotheses that prove insufficient and advances to further hypotheses that successively prove more and more satisfactory, so too in practical living it is through the cumulative process of further questions and further insights that an adequate understanding is reached. As in the sciences, so also in practical living, individuality pertains to the empirical residue, so that there is not one course of action that is intelligent when I am concerned and quite a different course when anyone else is involved. What is sauce for the goose is sauce for the gander. But egoistic emancipation rests on a rejection of merely proverbial wisdom yet fails to attain the development of personal intelligence that would reestablish the old sayings.

Thus, the golden rule is to do to others as you would have them do to you. One may object that common sense is never complete until the concrete situation is reached, and that no two concrete situations are identical. Still, it does not follow that the golden rule is that there is no golden rule. For the old rule did not advocate identical behavior in significantly different situations; on the contrary, it contended that the mere interchange of individual roles would not by itself constitute a significant difference in concrete situations.

Nor is the egoist totally unaware of his self-deception. Even in the bias and scotosis of the dramatic subject, which operates preconsciously, there is a measure of self-suspicion and disquiet. In the egoist there are additional grounds for an uneasy conscience, for it is not by sheer inadvertence but also by a conscious self-orientation that he devotes his energies to sizing up the social order, ferreting out its weak points and its loopholes, and discovering devices that give access to its rewards while evading its demands for proportionate contributions. As has been insisted already, egoism is not spontaneous, self-regarding appetite. Though it may result automatically from an incomplete development of intelligence, it does not automatically remain in that position. There have to be overcome both the drive of intelligence to raise the relevant further questions that upset egoistic solutions and, as well, the spontaneous demands of intersubjectivity, which, if they lack the breadth of a purely intellectual viewpoint with its golden rule, at least are commonly broader in their regard for others than is intelligent selfishness. Hence it is that, however much the egoist may appreciate the efforts of philosophers to assure him that intelligence is instrumental, he will be aware that, in his cool calculations, intelligence is boss and that, in his refusal to consider further questions, intelligence is not made into a servant but merely ruled out of court. Again, however much he may reassure himself by praising the pragmatists, still he suffers from the realization that the pragmatic success of his scheming falls short of a justification; for prior to the criteria of truth invented by philosophers, there is the dynamic criterion of the further question immanent in intelligence itself. The egoist's uneasy conscience is his awareness of his sin against the light. Operative within him there is the eros of the mind, the desire and drive to understand; he knows its value, for he gives it free rein where his own interests are concerned; yet he also repudiates its mastery, for he will not grant serious consideration to its further relevant questions.

7   Group Bias   [222–25]

As individual bias, so also group bias rests on an interference with the development of practical common sense. But while individual bias has to overcome normal intersubjective feeling, group bias finds itself supported by such feeling. Again, while individual bias leads to attitudes that conflict with ordinary common sense, group bias operates in the very genesis of commonsense views.

Basically, social groups are defined implicitly by the pattern of relations of a social order, and they are constituted by the realization of those dynamic relations. In its technological aspect the social order generates the distinctions between scientists and engineers, technicians and workers, skilled and unskilled labor. In its economic aspect it differentiates the formation of capital from the production of consumer goods and services, distinguishes income groups by offering proportionate rewards to contributions, and organizes contributors in hierarchies of employees, foremen, supervisors, superintendents, managers, and directors. In its political aspect it distinguishes legislative, judicial, diplomatic, and executive functions with their myriad ramifications, and it works out some system in which the various offices are to be filled and the tasks performed.

However, in the dialectic of community there is the operation not only of practical common sense but also of human intersubjectivity. If human intelligence takes the lead in developments, still its products do not function smoothly until there is effected a suitable adaptation of sensitive spontaneity. In a school, a regiment, a factory, a trade, a profession, a prison, there develops an ethos that at once subtly and flexibly provides concrete premises and norms for practical decisions. For in human affairs the decisive factor is what one can expect of the other fellow. Such expectations rest on recognized codes of behavior; they appeal to past performance, acquired habit, reputation; they attain a maximum of precision and reliability among those frequently brought together, engaged in similar work, guided by similar motives, sharing the same prosperity or adversity. Among strangers we are at a loss what to say or do. The social order not only gathers men together in functional groups but also consolidates its gains and expedites its operations by turning to its own ends the vast resources of human imagination and emotion, sentiment and confidence, familiarity and loyalty.

However, this formation of social groups, specifically adapted to the smooth attainment of social ends, merely tends to replace one inertial force with another. Human sensitivity is not human intelligence, and if sensitivity can be adapted to implement easily and readily one set of intelligent dictates, it has to undergo a fresh adaptation before it will cease resisting a second set of more intelligent dictates. Now social progress is a succession of changes. Each new idea gradually modifies the social situation to call forth further new ideas and bring about still further modifications. Moreover, the new ideas are practical; they are applicable to concrete situations; they occur to those engaged in the situations to which they are to be applied. However, while the practical common sense of a community may be a single whole, its parts reside separately in the minds of members of social groups, and its development occurs as each group intelligently responds to the succession of situations with which it immediately deals. Were all the responses made by pure intelligences, continuous progress might be inevitable. In fact, the responses are made by intelligences that are coupled with the ethos and the interests of groups, and while intelligence heads for change, group spontaneity does not regard all changes in the same cold light of the general good of society. Just as the individual egoist puts further questions up to a point, but desists before reaching conclusions incompatible with his egoism, so also the group is prone to have a blind spot for the insights that reveal its well-being to be excessive or its usefulness at an end.

Thus group bias leads to a bias in the generative principle of a developing social order. At a first approximation, one thinks of the course of social change as a succession of insights, courses of action, changed situations, and fresh insights. At each turn of the wheel, one has to distinguish between fresh insights that are mere bright ideas of no practical moment and, on the other hand, the fresh insights that squarely meet the demands of the concrete situation. Group bias, however,[f] calls for a further distinction. Truly practical insights have to be divided into operative and inoperative; both satisfy the criteria of practical intelligence; but the operative insights alone go into effect for they alone either meet with no group resistance or else find favor with groups powerful enough to overcome what resistance there is.

The bias of development involves a distortion. The advantage of one group commonly is disadvantageous to another, and so some part of the energies of all groups is diverted to the supererogatory activity of devising and implementing offensive and defensive mechanisms. Groups differ in their possession of native talent, opportunities, initiative, and resources; those in favored circumstances find success the key to still further success; those unable to make operative the new ideas that are to their advantage fall behind in the process of social development. Society becomes stratified; its flower is far in advance of average attainment; its roots appear to be the survival of the rude achievement of a forgotten age. Classes become distinguished, not merely by social function, but also by social success; and the new differentiation finds expression not only in conceptual labels but also in deep feelings of frustration, resentment, bitterness, and hatred.

Moreover, the course of development has been twisted. The social order that has been realized does not correspond to any coherently developed set of practical ideas. It represents the fraction of practical ideas that were made operative by their conjunction with power, the mutilated remnants of once excellent schemes that issued from the mill of compromise, the otiose structures that equip groups for their offensive and defensive activities. Again, ideas are general, but the stratification of society has blocked their realization in their proper generality. Ideas possess retinues of complementary ideas that add further adjustments and improvements; but these needed complements were submitted to the sifting of group interests and to the alterations of compromise.

Still, this process of aberration creates the principles for its own reversal. When a concrete situation first yields a new idea and demands its realization, it is unlikely that the idea will occur to anyone outside the group specialized in dealing with situations of that type. But when some ideas of a coherent set have been realized, or when they are realized in a partial manner, or when their realization does not attain its proper generality, or when it is not complemented with a needed retinue of improvements and adjustments, then there is no need to call upon experts and specialists to discover whether anything has gone wrong, nor even to hit upon a roughly accurate account of what can be done. The sins of group bias may be secret and almost unconscious. But what originally was a neglected possibility, in time becomes a grotesquely distorted reality. Few may grasp the initial possibilities; but the ultimate concrete distortions are exposed to the inspection of the multitude. Nor has the bias of social development revealed the ideas that were neglected without also supplying the power that will realize them. For the bias generates unsuccessful as well as successful classes; and the sentiments of the unsuccessful can be crystallized into militant force by the crusading of a reformer or a revolutionary.

The ensuing conflict admits a variety of forms. The dominant groups may be reactionary or progressive or any mixture of the two. Insofar as they are reactionary, they are out to block any correction of the effects of group bias, and they employ for this purpose whatever power they possess in whatever manner they deem appropriate and effective. On the other hand, insofar as they are progressive, they make it their aim both to correct existing distortions and to find the means that will prevent their future recurrence. Now to a great extent the attitude of the dominant groups determines the attitude of the depressed groups. Reactionaries are opposed by revolutionaries. Progressives are met by liberals. In the former case the situation heads towards violence. In the latter case there is a general agreement about ends with disagreement about the pace of change and the mode and measure of its execution.

8   General Bias [225–42]

To err is human, and common sense is very human. Besides the bias of the dramatic subject, of the individual egoist, of the member of a given class or nation, there is a further bias to which all men are prone. For men are rational animals, but a full development[g] of their animality is both more common and more rapid than a full development of their intelligence and reasonableness. A traditional view credits children of seven years of age with the attainment of an elementary reasonableness. The law regards as a minor anyone under twenty-one years of age. Experts in the field of public entertainment address themselves to a mental age of about twelve years. Still more modest is the scientific attitude that places man's attainment of knowledge in an indefinitely removed future. Nor is personal experience apt to be reassuring. If everyone has some acquaintance with the spirit of inquiry and reflection, few think of making it the effective center of their lives; and of that few, still fewer make sufficient progress to be able to withstand other attractions and persevere in their high purpose.

The lag of intellectual development, its difficulty, and its apparently meager returns bear in an especial manner on common sense. It is concerned with the concrete and particular.[h] It entertains no aspirations about reaching abstract and universal laws. It easily is led[i] to rationalize its limitations by engendering a conviction that other forms of human knowledge are useless or doubtfully valid. Every specialist runs the risk of turning his specialty into a bias by failing to recognize and appreciate the significance of other fields. Common sense almost invariably makes that mistake; for it is incapable of analyzing itself, incapable of making the discovery that it too is a specialized development of human knowledge, incapable of coming to grasp that its peculiar danger is to extend its legitimate concern for the concrete and the immediately practical into disregard of larger issues and indifference to long-term results.

8.1 The Longer Cycle   [226–28]

This general bias of common sense combines with group bias to account for certain features of the distorted dialectic of community. As has been noted, at each turn of the wheel of insight, proposal, action, new situation, and fresh insight, the tendency of group bias is to exclude some fruitful ideas and to mutilate others by compromise. Now fruitful ideas are of several kinds. They may lead to technical and material improvements, to adjustments of economic arrangements, or to modifications of political structure. As one might expect, technical and material improvements are less subject to the veto of dominant groups than are changes in economic and political institutions. Again, when we shift to the second phase of the distorted dialectic, the resonant demands of the unsuccessful are for material well-being; and when the clamor goes up for economic or political change, such change is apt to be viewed simply as a necessary means for attaining more palpably beneficial ends.

Accordingly, there arises a distinction between the shorter cycle, due to group bias, and the longer cycle, originated by the general bias of common sense. The shorter cycle turns upon ideas that are neglected by dominant groups only to be championed later by depressed groups. The longer cycle is characterized by the neglect of ideas to which all groups are rendered indifferent by the general bias of common sense. Still, this account of the longer cycle is mainly negative; to grasp its nature and its implications, we must turn to fundamental notions.

Generically, the course of human history is in accord with emergent probability; it is the cumulative realization of concretely possible schemes of recurrence in accord with successive schedules of probabilities. The specific difference of human history is that among the probable possibilities is a sequence of operative insights by which men grasp possible schemes of recurrence and take the initiative in bringing about the material and social conditions that make these schemes concretely possible, probable, and actual. In this fashion man becomes for man the executor of the emergent probability of human affairs. Instead of being developed by his environment, man turns to transforming his environment in his own self- development. He remains under emergent probability, inasmuch as his insights and decisions remain probable realizations of concrete possibilities, and inasmuch as earlier insights and decisions determine later possibilities and probabilities of insight and decision. Still, this subjection to emergent probability differs from the subjection of electrons or of evolving species. For in the first place, insight is an anticipation of possible schemes, and decision brings about the concrete conditions of their functioning instead of merely waiting for such conditions to happen; moreover, the greater man's development, the greater his dominion over circumstances, and so the greater his capacity to realize possible schemes by deciding to realize their conditions. But there is also a second and profounder difference. For man can discover emergent probability; he can work out the manner in which prior insights and decisions determine the possibilities and probabilities of later insights and decisions; he can guide his present decisions in the light of their influence on future insights and decisions; finally, this control of the emergent probability of the future can be exercised not only by the individual in choosing his career and in forming his character, not only by adults in educating the younger generation, but also by mankind in its consciousness of its responsibility to the future of mankind. Just as technical, economic, and political development gives man a dominion over nature, so also the advance of knowledge creates and demands a human contribution to the control of human history.

So far from granting common sense a hegemony in practical affairs, the foregoing analysis leads to the strange conclusion that common sense has to aim at being subordinated to a human science that is concerned, to adapt a phrase from Marx, not only with knowing history but also with directing it. For common sense is unequal to the task of thinking on the level of history. It stands above the scotosis of the dramatic subject, above the egoism of the individual, above the bias of dominant and of depressed but militant groups that realize only the ideas they see to be to their immediate advantage. But the general bias of common sense prevents it from being effective in realizing ideas, however appropriate and reasonable, that suppose a long view or that set up higher integrations or that involve the solution of intricate and disputed issues. The challenge of history is for man progressively to restrict the realm of chance or fate or destiny and progressively to enlarge the realm of conscious grasp and deliberate choice. Common sense accepts the challenge, but it does so only partially. It needs to be guided but it is incompetent to choose its guide. It becomes involved in incoherent enterprises. It is subjected to disasters that no one expects, that remain unexplained even after their occurrence, that can be explained only on the level of scientific or philosophic thought, that even when explained can be prevented from recurring only by subordinating common sense to a higher specialization of human intelligence.

This is not the whole story. The general bias of common sense involves sins of refusal as well as of mere omission. Its complacent practicality easily twists to the view that, as insistent desires and contracting fears necessitate and justify the realization of ideas, so ideas without that warrant are a matter of indifference. The long view, the higher integration, the disputed theoretical issue fall outside the realm of the practical; it may or may not be too bad that they do; but there is no use worrying about the matter; nothing can be done about it; indeed, what could be done about it probably would not be done. Now I am far from suggesting that such practical realism cannot adduce impressive arguments in its favor. Like the characters in Damon Runyon's stories, politicians and statesmen are confined to doing what they can. Nonetheless, if we are to understand the implications of the longer cycle, we must work out the consequences of such apparently hardheaded practicality and realism.

8.2 Implications of the Longer Cycle   [228-32]

Already we have explained the nature of the succession of higher viewpoints that characterize the development of mathematics and of empirical science. Now we must attend to the inverse phenomenon, in which
each successive viewpoint is less comprehensive than its predecessor. In
each stage of the historical process, the facts are the social situation
produced by the practical intelligence of the previous situation. Again,
in each stage practical intelligence is engaged in grasping the concrete
intelligibility and the immediate potentialities immanent in the facts.
Finally, at each stage of the process, the general bias of common sense
involves the disregard of timely and fruitful ideas; and this disregard not
only excludes their implementation but also deprives subsequent stages
both of the further ideas to which they would give rise and of the correction that they and their retinue would bring to the ideas that are
implemented. Such is the basic scheme, and it has three consequences.

In the first place, the social situation deteriorates cumulatively. For
just as progress consists in a realization of some ideas that leads to the
realization of others until a whole coherent set is concretely operative,
so the repeated exclusion of timely and fruitful ideas involves a cumulative departure from coherence. The objective social situation possesses
the intelligibility put into it by those that brought it about. But what is
put in, less and less is some part of a coherent whole that will ask for its
completion, and more and more it is some arbitrary fragment that can
be rounded off only by giving up the attempt to complete the other
arbitrary fragments that have preceded or will follow it. In this fashion
social functions and enterprises begin to conflict; some atrophy and
others grow like tumors; the objective situation becomes penetrated with
anomalies; it loses its power to suggest new ideas and, once they are
implemented, to respond with still further and better suggestions. The
dynamic of progress is replaced by sluggishness and then by stagnation.
In the limit, the only discernible intelligibility in the objective facts is an
equilibrium of economic pressures and a balance of national powers.

The second consequence is the mounting irrelevance of detached and
disinterested intelligence. Culture retreats into an ivory tower. Religion
becomes an inward affair of the heart. Philosophy glitters like a gem
with endless facets and no practical purpose. For man cannot serve two
masters. If one is to be true to intellectual detachment and disinterestedness, to what can be intelligently grasped and reasonably affirmed, then

one seems constrained to acknowledge that the busy world of practical affairs offers little scope to one's vocation. Intelligence can easily link culture, religion, philosophy to the realm of concrete living only if the latter is intelligible. But concrete living has become the function of a complex variable; like the real component of such a function, its intelligibility is only part of the whole. Already we have spoken of an empirical residue from which understanding always abstracts; but the general bias of common sense generates an increasingly significant residue that (1) is immanent in the social facts, (2) is not intelligible, yet (3) cannot be abstracted from if one is to consider the facts as in fact they are. Let us name this residue the social surd.

The third consequence is the surrender of detached and disinterested intelligence. There is the minor surrender on the level of common sense. It is an incomplete surrender, for common sense always finds a profoundly satisfying escape from the grim realities of daily living by turning to men of culture, to representatives of religion, to spokesmen for philosophy. Still, the business of common sense is daily life. Its reality has to be faced. The insights that accumulate have to be exactly in tune with the reality to be confronted and in some measure controlled. The fragmentary and incoherent intelligibility of the objective situation sets the standard to which commonsense intelligence must conform. Nor is this conformity merely passive. Intelligence is dynamic. Just as the biased intelligence of the psychoneurotic sets up an ingenious, plausible, self-adapting resistance to the efforts of the analyst, so men of practical common sense become warped by the situation in which they live, and regard as starry-eyed idealism and silly unpracticality any proposal that would lay the axe to the root of the social surd.

Besides this minor surrender on the level of common sense, there is the major surrender on the speculative level. The function of human intelligence, it is claimed, is not to set up independent norms that make thought irrelevant to fact, but to study the data as they are, to grasp the intelligibility that is immanent in them, to acknowledge as principle or norm only what can be reached by generalization from the data. There follow the need and the development of a new culture, a new religion, a new philosophy; and the new differs radically from the old. The new is not apriorist, wishful thinking. It is empirical, scientific, realistic. It takes its stand on things as they are. In brief, its many excellences cover its single defect. For its rejection of the normative significance of detached and disinterested intelligence makes it radically uncritical. It possesses no standpoint from which it can distinguish between social achievement and the social surd. It fails to grasp that an excellent method for the study of electrons is bound to prove naive and inept in the study of man. For the data on man are largely the product of man's own thinking; and the subordination of human science to the data on man is the subordination of human science to the biased intelligence of those that produce the data. From this critical incapacity there follow the insecurity and the instability of the new culture, religion, philosophy. Each new arrival has to keep bolstering its convictions by attacking and denouncing its predecessors. Nor is there any lack of new arrivals, for in the cumulative deterioration of the social situation there is a continuous expansion of the surd, and so there is an increasing demand for further contractions of the claims of intelligence, for further dropping of old principles and norms, for closer conformity to an ever growing manmade incoherence immanent in manmade facts.

It is in this major surrender of intellectual detachment that the succession of ever less comprehensive viewpoints comes to light. The development of our Western civilization, from the schools founded by Charlemagne to the universities of today, has witnessed an extraordinary flowering of human intelligence in every department of its activity. But this course of human progress has not been along a smooth and mounting curve. It has taken place through the oscillations of the shorter cycle, in which social groups become factions, in which nations go to war, in which the hegemony passes from one center to another to leave its former holders with proud memories and impotent dreams. No less does it exhibit the successive lower viewpoints of the longer cycle. The medieval synthesis through the conflict of church and state shattered into the several religions of the Reformation. The wars of religion provided the evidence that man has to live not by revelation but by reason. The disagreement of reason's representatives made it clear that, while each must follow the dictates of reason as he sees them, he also must practice the virtue of tolerance to the equally reasonable views and actions of others. The helplessness of tolerance to provide coherent solutions to social problems called forth the totalitarian, who takes the narrow and complacent practicality of common sense and elevates it to the role of a complete and exclusive viewpoint. On the totalitarian view every type of intellectual independence, whether personal, cultural, scientific, philosophic, or religious, has no better basis than nonconscious myth. The time has come for the conscious myth that will secure man's total sub-

ordination to the requirements of reality. Reality is the economic development, the military equipment, and the political dominance of the
all-inclusive state. Its ends justify all means. Its means include not merely
every technique of indoctrination and propaganda, every tactic of economic and diplomatic pressure, every device for breaking down the moral
conscience and exploiting the secret affects of civilized man, but also the
terrorism of a political police, of prisons and torture, of concentration
camps, of transported or extirpated minorities, and of total war. The
succession of less comprehensive viewpoints has been a succession of
adaptations of theory to practice. In the limit, practice becomes a theoretically unified whole, and theory is reduced to the status of a myth that
lingers on to represent the frustrated aspirations of detached and disinterested intelligence.

8.3 Alternatives of the Longer Cycle   [232–34]

What is the subsequent course of the longer cycle generated by the
general bias of common sense? Insofar as the bias remains effective,
there would seem to be only one answer. The totalitarian has uncovered
a secret of power. To defeat him is not to eliminate a permanent temptation to try once more his methods. Those not subjected to the temptation by their ambitions or their needs will be subjected to it by their fears
of danger and by their insistence on self-protection. So in an uneasy
peace, in the unbroken tension of a prolonged emergency, one totalitarianism calls forth another. On an earth made small by a vast human
population, by limited natural resources, by rapid and easy communications, by extraordinary powers of destruction, there will arise sooner or
later the moment when the unstable equilibrium will seem threatened
and the gamble of war will appear the lesser risk to some of the parties
involved. If the war is indecisive, the basic situation is unchanged. If it
is totally destructive, the longer cycle has come to its end. If there results
a single world empire, then it inherits both the objective stagnation of
the social surd and the warped mentality of totalitarian practicality; but
it cannot whip up the feverish energy of fear or of ambition; it has no
enemy to fight; it has no intelligible goal to attain.

Common sense, on the other hand, has no use for any theoretical
integration, even for the totalitarian integration of commonsense practicality. It will desert the new empire for the individual or group
interests that it understands. This centrifugal tendency will be augment-

ed by the prepossessions and prejudices, the resentments and hatreds, that have been accumulating over the ages; for every reform, every revolution, every lower viewpoint overstates both the case in its own favor and the case against those it would supersede; from each generation to the next there are transmitted not only sound ideas but also incomplete ideas, mutilated ideas, enthusiasms, passions, bitter memories, and terrifying bogies. In this fashion the objective social surd will be matched by a disunity of minds all warped but each in its private way. The most difficult of enterprises will have to be undertaken under the most adverse circumstances, and under the present hypothesis that the general bias of common sense remains effective, one cannot but expect the great crises that end in complete disintegration and decay.

Still, on the assumption of emergent probability, nothing is inevitable. Indeed, the essential logic of the distorted dialectic is a reversal. For dialectic rests on the concrete unity of opposed principles; the dominance of either principle results in a distortion, and the distortion both weakens the dominance and strengthens the opposed principle to restore an equilibrium. Why, then, is it that the longer cycle is so long? Why is the havoc it wreaks so deep, so extensive, so complete? The obvious answer is the difficulty of the lesson that the longer cycle has to teach. Nor are we quite without hints or clues on the nature of that lesson. On the contrary, there is a convergence of evidence for the assertion that the longer cycle is to be met, not by any idea or set of ideas on the level of technology, economics, or politics, but only by the attainment of a higher viewpoint in man's understanding and making of man.

In the first place, the general bias of common sense cannot be corrected by common sense, for the bias is abstruse and general, and common sense deals with the particular. In the second place, man can discover how present insights and decisions influence through emergent probability the occurrence of future insights and decisions; as he can make this discovery, so he can use it, not only in shaping individual biographies and educating children in the image of their parents and of the state authorities, but also in the vastly more ambitious task of directing and in some measure controlling his future history. In the third place, the longer cycle of Western civilization has been drawing attention repeatedly to the notion of a practical theory of history. It was conceived in one manner or another by Vico in his *Scienza nuova*, by Hegel, and by Marx. It has exercised a conspicuous influence on events through the liberal doctrine of automatic progress, through the Marxian doctrine of class war, through the myths of nationalist totalitarianism. In the fourth place, a remedy has to be on the level of the disease; but the disease is a succession of lower viewpoints that heads towards an ultimate nihilism; and so the remedy has to be the attainment of a higher viewpoint.

As there is evidence for the necessity of a higher viewpoint, so also there is some evidence on its nature. Inquiry and insight are facts that underlie mathematics, empirical science, and common sense. The refusal of insight is a fact that accounts for individual and group egoism, for the psychoneuroses, and for the ruin of nations and civilizations. The needed higher viewpoint is the discovery, the logical expansion, and the recognition of the principle that intelligence contains its own immanent norms and that these norms are equipped with sanctions which man does not have to invent or impose. Even in the sphere of practice, the last word does not lie with common sense and its panoply of technology, economy, and polity; for unless common sense can learn to overcome its bias by acknowledging and submitting to a higher principle, unless common sense can be taught to resist its perpetual temptation to adopt the easy, obvious, practical compromise, then one must expect the succession of ever less comprehensive viewpoints, and in the limit the destruction of all that has been achieved.

8.4 Reversal of the Longer Cycle   [234–36]

What is the higher principle? Since we have not as yet discussed such notions as truth and error, right and wrong, human science and philosophy, culture and religion, our immediate answer can be no more than a series of notes.

In the first place, there is such a thing as progress, and its principle is liberty. There is progress, because practical intelligence grasps ideas in data, guides activity by the ideas, and reaches fuller and more accurate ideas through the situations produced by the activity. The principle of progress is liberty, for the ideas occur to the man on the spot, their only satisfactory expression is their implementation, their only adequate correction is the emergence of further insights; on the other hand, one might as well declare openly that all new ideas are taboo, as require that they be examined, evaluated, and approved by some hierarchy of officials and bureaucrats; for members of this hierarchy possess authority and power in inverse ratio to their familiarity with the concrete situations in which the new ideas emerge; they never know whether or not the new idea will work; much less can they divine how it might be corrected or developed; and since the one thing they dread is making a mistake, they devote their energies to paper work and postpone decisions.

However, while there is progress and while its principle is liberty, there also is decline and its principle is bias. There is the minor principle of group bias, which tends to generate its own corrective. There is the major principle of general bias, and though it too generates its own corrective, it does so only by confronting human intelligence with the alternative of adopting a higher viewpoint or perishing. To ignore the fact of decline was the error of the old liberal views of automatic progress. The far more confusing error of Marx was to lump together both progress and the two principles of decline under the impressive name of dialectical materialism, to grasp that the minor principle of decline would correct itself more rapidly through class war, and then to leap gaily to the sweeping conclusion that class war would accelerate progress. What in fact was accelerated was major decline, which in Russia and Germany leaped to fairly thorough brands of totalitarianism. The basic service of the higher viewpoint will be a liberation from confusion through clear distinctions. Progress is not to be confused with decline; the corrective mechanism of the minor principle of decline is not to be thought capable of meeting the issues set by the major principle.

Secondly, as there are sciences of nature, so also there is a science of man. As the sciences of nature are empirical, so also the science of man is empirical; for science is the resultant of an accumulation of related insights, and scientific insights grasp ideas that are immanent not in what is imagined but in what is given. If the sciences of nature can be led astray by the blunder that the objective is, not the verified, but the 'out there,' so also can the human sciences; but while this blunder in physics yields no more than the ineptitude of Galileo's primary qualities and Newton's true motion, it leads zealous practitioners of scientific method in the human field to rule out of court a major portion of the data and so deny the empirical principle. Durkheimian sociology and behaviorist psychology may have excuses for barring the data of consciousness, for there exist notable difficulties in determining such data; but the business of the scientist is not to allege difficulties as excuses but to overcome them, and neither objectivity in the sense of verification nor the principle of empiricism can be advanced as reasons for ignoring the data of consciousness. Further, as mathematics has to deal not only with direct intelligibilities but also with such inverse instances as primes, surds, imaginaries, continua, and infinities, as the physicist has to employ not only the classical procedures and techniques that deal with the systematic but also the statistical procedures and techniques that take into account the nonsystematic, so also human science has to be critical. It can afford to drop the nineteenth-century scientific outlook of mechanist determinism in favor of an emergent probability. It can profit by the distinction between the intelligible emergent probability of prehuman process and the intelligent emergent probability that arises in the measure that man succeeds in understanding himself and in implementing that understanding. Finally, it can be of inestimable value in aiding man to understand himself and in guiding him in the implementation of that understanding, if, and only if, it can learn to distinguish between progress and decline, between the liberty that generates progress and the bias that generates decline. In other words, human science cannot be merely empirical; it has to be critical; to reach a critical standpoint, it has to be normative. This is a tall order for human science as hitherto it has existed. But people looking for easy tasks had best renounce any ambition to be scientists; and if mathematicians and physicists can surmount their surds, the human scientist can learn to master his.

8.5 Culture and Reversal   [236–38]

In the third place, there is culture. The dramatic subject, as practical, originates and develops capital and technology, the economy and the state. By his intelligence he progresses, and by his bias he declines. Still, this whole unfolding of practicality constitutes no more than the setting and the incidents of the drama. Delight and suffering, laughter and tears, joy and sorrow, aspiration and frustration, achievement and failure, wit and humor stand, not within practicality but above it. Man can pause and with a smile or a forced grin ask what the drama, what he himself is about. His culture is his capacity to ask, to reflect, to reach an answer that at once satisfies his intelligence and speaks to his heart.

    Now if men are to meet the challenge set by major decline and its longer cycle, it will be through their culture that they do so. Were man a pure intelligence, the products of philosophy and human science would be enough to sway him. But as the dialectic in the individual and in society reveals, man is a compound-in-tension of intelligence and intersubjectivity, and it is only through the parallel compound of a culture that his tendencies to aberration can be offset proximately and effectively.

The difficulty is, of course, that human aberration makes an uncritical culture its captive. Mario Praz in *The Romantic Agony*[4] has found that depth psychology throws an unpleasantly penetrating light upon romanticism. Nor is the ooze of abnormality anything more than a secondary symptom, for the expanding social surd of the longer cycle is not matched by a succession of less comprehensive viewpoints, without the services of a parallel series of cultural transformations. Opinions and attitudes that once were the oddity of a minority gradually spread through society to become the platitudes of politicians and journalists, the assumptions of legislators and educators, the uncontroverted nucleus of the common sense of a people. Eventually, they too become antiquated; they are regarded as the obstinacy of an old guard that will not learn; their influence is restricted to backwaters immune to the renewing force of the main current of human thought and feeling. Change succeeds change. Indiscriminately, each of the new arrivals rests upon the good it brings, upon the opposite defects of the old, and upon a closer harmony with the fact of the social surd. In the limit, culture ceases to be an independent factor that passes a detached yet effective judgment upon capital formation and technology, upon economy and polity. To justify its existence, it had to become more and more practical, more and more a factor within the technological, economic, political process, more and more a tool that served palpably useful ends. The actors in the drama of living become stagehands; the setting is magnificent; the lighting superb; the costumes gorgeous; but there is no play.

Clearly, by becoming practical, culture renounces its one essential function, and by that renunciation condemns practicality to ruin. The general bias of common sense has to be counterbalanced by a representative of detached intelligence that both appreciates and criticizes, that identifies the good neither with the new nor with the old, that, above all else, neither will be forced into an ivory tower of ineffectualness by the social surd nor, on the other hand, will capitulate to its absurdity.

Marx looked forward to a classless society and to the withering of the state. But as long as there will be practical intelligence, there will be

---

4 [Mario Praz, *The Romantic Agony*, tr. Angus Davidson (New York: Meridian, 1960; originally published by Oxford University Press, 1933, with a second edition in 1951.)]

technology and capital, economy and polity. There will be a division of labor and a differentiation of functions. There will be the adaptation of human intersubjectivity to that division and differentiation. There will be common decisions to be reached and to be implemented. Practical intelligence necessitates classes and states, and no dialectic can promise their permanent disappearance. What is both unnecessary and disastrous is the exaltation of the practical, the supremacy of the state, the cult of the class. What is necessary is a cosmopolis that is neither class nor state, that stands above all their claims, that cuts them down to size, that is founded on the native detachment and disinterestedness of every intelligence, that commands man's first allegiance, that implements itself primarily through that allegiance, that is too universal to be bribed, too impalpable to be forced, too effective to be ignored.

8.6 Cosmopolis   [238–42]

Still, what is cosmopolis? Like every other object of human intelligence, it is in the first instance an X, what is to be known when one understands. Like every other X, it possesses some known properties and aspects that lead to its fuller determination. For the present, we must be content to indicate a few of these aspects and to leave until later the task of reaching conclusions.

First, cosmopolis is not a police force. Before such a force can be organized, equipped, and applied, there is needed a notable measure of agreement among a preponderant group of men. In other words, ideas have to come first, and at best force is instrumental. In the practical order of the economy and polity, it is possible, often enough, to perform the juggling act of using some ideas to ground the use of force in favor of others, and then using the other ideas to ground the use of force in favor of the first. The trouble with this procedure is that there is always another juggler that believes himself expert enough to play the same game the other way by using the malcontents held down by the first use of force to upset the second set of ideas and, as well, using malcontents held down by the second use of force to upset the first set of ideas. Accordingly, if ideas are not to be merely a façade, if the reality is not to be merely a balance of power, then the use of force can be no more than residual and incidental. But cosmopolis is not concerned with the residual and incidental. It is concerned with the fundamental issue of the historical process. Its business is to prevent practicality from being shortsightedly practical and so destroying itself. The notion that cosmopolis employs a police force is just an instance of the shortsighted practicality that cosmopolis has to correct. However, I am not saying that there should not be a United Nations or a world government; I am not saying that such political entities should not have a police force; I am saying that such political entities are not what is meant by cosmopolis. Cosmopolis is above all politics. So far from being rendered superfluous by a successful world government, it would be all the more obviously needed to offset the tendencies of that and any other government to be shortsightedly practical.

Secondly, cosmopolis is concerned to make operative the timely and fruitful ideas that otherwise are inoperative. So far from employing power or pressure or force, it has to witness to the possibility of ideas being operative without such backing. Unless it can provide that witness, then it is useless. For at the root of the general bias of common sense and at the permanent source of the longer cycle of decline, there stands the notion that only ideas backed by some sort of force can be operative. The business of cosmopolis is to make operative the ideas that, in the light of the general bias of common sense, are inoperative. In other words, its business is to break the vicious circle of an illusion: men will not venture on ideas that they grant to be correct, because they hold that such ideas will not work unless sustained by desires or fears; and inversely, men hold that such ideas will not work, because they will not venture on them and so have no empirical evidence that such ideas can work and would work.

Thirdly, cosmopolis is not a busybody. It is supremely practical by ignoring what is thought to be really practical. It does not waste its time and energy condemning the individual egoism that is in revolt against society and already condemned by society. It is not excited by group egoism, which in the short run generates the principles that involve its reversal. But it is very determined to prevent dominant groups from deluding mankind by the rationalization of their sins; if the sins of dominant groups are bad enough, still the erection of their sinning into universal principles is indefinitely worse; it is the universalization of the sin by rationalization that contributes to the longer cycle of decline; it is the rationalization that cosmopolis has to ridicule, explode, destroy. Again, cosmopolis is little interested in the shifts of power between classes and nations; it is quite aware that the dialectic sooner or later upsets the shortsighted calculations of dominant groups; and it is quite free from the nonsense that the rising star of another class or nation is going to put a different human nature in the saddle. However, while shifts of power in themselves are incidental, they commonly are accompanied by another phenomenon of quite a different character. There is the creation of myths. The old regime is depicted as monstrous; the new envisages itself as the immaculate embodiment of ideal human aspiration. Catchwords that carried the new group to power assume the status of unquestionable verities. On the bandwagon of the new vision of truth there ride the adventurers in ideas that otherwise could not attain a hearing. Inversely, ideas that merit attention are ignored unless they put on the trappings of the current fashion, unless they pretend to result from alien but commonly acceptable premises, unless they disclaim implications that are true but unwanted. It is the business of cosmopolis to prevent the formation of the screening memories by which an ascent to power hides its nastiness; it is its business to prevent the falsification of history with which the new group overstates its case; it is its business to satirize the catchwords and the claptrap and thereby to prevent the notions they express from coalescing with passions and resentments to engender obsessive nonsense for future generations; it is its business to encourage and support those that would speak the simple truth though simple truth has gone out of fashion. Unless cosmopolis undertakes this essential task, it fails in its mission. One shift of power is followed by another, and if the myths of the first survive, the myths of the second will take their stand on earlier nonsense to bring forth worse nonsense still.

Fourthly, as cosmopolis has to protect the future against the rationalization of abuses and the creation of myths, so it itself must be purged of the rationalizations and myths that became part of the human heritage before it came on the scene. If the analyst suffers from a scotoma, he will communicate it to the analysand; similarly, if cosmopolis itself suffers from the general bias of common sense in any of its manifestations, then the blind will be leading the blind and both will head for a ditch. There is needed, then, a critique of history before there can be any intelligent direction of history. There is needed an exploration of the movements, the changes, the epochs of a civilization's genesis, development, and vicissitudes. The opinions and attitudes of the present have to be traced to their origins, and the origins have to be criticized in the light of dialectic. The liberal believer in automatic progress could praise all that survives; the Marxist could denounce all that was and praise all that would be; but anyone that recognizes the existence both of intelligence and of bias, both of progress and of decline, has to be critical, and his criticism will rest on the dialectic that simply affirms the presuppositions of possible criticism.

Perhaps enough has been said on the properties and aspects of our X named cosmopolis for a synthetic view to be attempted. It is not a group denouncing other groups; it is not a superstate ruling states; it is not an organization that enrolls members, nor an academy that endorses opinions, nor a court that administers a legal code. It is a withdrawal from practicality to save practicality. It is a dimension of consciousness, a heightened grasp of historical origins, a discovery of historical responsibilities. It is not something altogether new, for the Marxist has been busy activating the class consciousness of the masses, and before him the liberal had succeeded in indoctrinating men with the notion of progress. Still, it possesses its novelty, for it is not *simpliste*. It does not leap from a fact of development to a belief in automatic progress nor from a fact of abuse to an expectation of an apocalyptic utopia reached through an accelerated decline. It is the higher synthesis of the liberal thesis and the Marxist antithesis. It comes to minds prepared for it by these earlier views, for they have taught man to think historically. It comes at a time when the totalitarian fact and threat have refuted the liberals and discredited the Marxists. It stands on a basic analysis of the compound-intension that is man; it confronts problems of which men are aware; it invites the vast potentialities and pent-up energies of our time to contribute to their solution by developing an art and a literature, a theatre and a broadcasting, a journalism and a history, a school and a university, a personal depth and a public opinion, that through appreciation and criticism give men of common sense the opportunity and help they need and desire to correct the general bias of their common sense.

Finally, it would be unfair not to stress the chief characteristic of cosmopolis. It is not easy. It is not a dissemination of sweetness and light, where sweetness means sweet to me, and light means light to me. Were that so, cosmopolis would be superfluous. Every scotosis puts forth a plausible, ingenious, adaptive, untiring resistance. The general bias of common sense is no exception. It is by moving with that bias rather than against it, by differing from it slightly rather than opposing it thoroughly, that one has the best prospect of selling books and newspapers, entertainment and education. Moreover, this is only the superficial difficulty. Beneath it lies the almost insoluble problem of settling clearly and exactly what the general bias is. It is not a culture but only a compromise that results from taking the highest common factor of an aggregate of cultures. It is not a compromise that will check and reverse the longer cycle of decline. Nor is it unbiased intelligence that yields a welter of conflicting opinions. Cosmopolis is not Babel, yet how can we break from Babel?ʲ This is the problem. So far from solving it in this chapter, we do not hope to reach a full solution in this volume. But, at least, two allies can be acknowledged. On the one hand, there is common sense, and in its judgments, which as yet have not been treated, common sense tends to be profoundly sane. On the other hand, there is dialectical analysis; the refusal of insight betrays itself; the Babel of our day is the cumulative product of a series of refusals to understand; and dialectical analysis can discover and expose both the series of past refusals and the tactics of contemporary resistance to enlightenment.

9   **Conclusion**   [242–444]

It is time to end this study of common sense. In the first section of chapter 6 there was worked out the parallel between common sense and empirical science: both are developments of intelligence. Next, attention centered on the differences between empirical science, which relates things to one another, and common sense, which relates things to us. It was seen that the relations grasped by common sense stand between two variables: on the one hand, common sense is a development of the subject to which things are related; on the other hand, common sense effects a development in the things to which we are related. Moreover, both developments are subject to aberration; besides the progressive accumulation of related insights, there is the cumulative effect of refusing insights. In the subjective field, such refusal tends to be preconscious; it heads towards psychoneurotic conflict; it is opposite to the subject's rational judgment and deliberate choice, which, accordingly, can provide the analyst with his opportunity. In the objective field, the refusal is rationalized by a distinction between theory and practice; it heads both to social conflict and to social disintegration; it is to be opposed both by the commonsense view that practicality is for man and not man for practicality, and on a more recondite level, by the principle, implicit in dialectic, that practice succeeds in diverging from theory by taking the short view and refusing to raise and face further relevant questions.

Our account of common sense has led us to touch on many issues, but our concern is not these issues, which function illustratively, but the fact and the nature of insight. Within the perspectives of the present work, there is no point to a full and accurate account of the fields of psychology and of sociology. The topic is insight. To exhibit its nature and its implications, one has to venture into every department in which human intelligence plays a significant role. Still, that venture is essentially a limited venture. For it is enough for our purpose to show that the notion of insight is indispensable in an adequate view, that it explains both the high esteem in which common sense is commonly held and the limitatations to which it is subject, that this explanation can begin from independent and apparently disparate premises and, within the larger context that they yield, succeed in hitting off the thought of the average man, the problem of his affects, and the dialectic of his history.[k]

Further, though our topic is common sense, still it has not been the whole of common sense. Besides intelligence, there are operative in common sense both judgment and choice with their implications of truth and error and of right and wrong. These higher components of common sense will receive some attention later. The foregoing study has been concerned with common sense as an accumulation of related insights.

A final observation has to do with method. From the beginning we have been directing attention to an event that occurs within consciousness. Accordingly, our method has not been the method of empirical science, which draws its data from the field of sensible presentations. However, we have had occasion to speak of a generalized empirical method that stands to the data of consciousness as empirical method stands to the data of sense. In the present chapter,[1] the nature of this generalized method has come to light. As applied solely to the data of consciousness, it consists in determining patterns of intelligible relations that unite the data explanatorily. Such are the biological, artistic, dramatic, and intellectual forms of experience; moreover, our previous studies of mathematical and of scientific thought would regard particular cases of the intellectual form of experience; and similar differentiations could be multiplied. However, generalized method has to be able to deal, at least comprehensively, not only with the data within a single consciousness but also with the relations between different conscious subjects, between conscious subjects and their milieu or environment, and between consciousness and its neural basis. From this viewpoint, dialectic stands to generalized method as the differential equation to classical physics, or the operator equation to the more recent physics. For dialectic is a pure form with general implications; it is applicable to any concrete unfolding of linked but opposed principles that are modified cumulatively by the unfolding; it can envisage at once the conscious and the nonconscious either in a single subject or in an aggregate and succession of subjects; it is adjustable to any course of events, from an ideal line of pure progress resulting from the harmonious working of the opposed principles, to any degree of conflict, aberration, breakdown, and disintegration; it constitutes a principle of integration for specialized studies that concentrate on this or that aspect of human living, and it can integrate not only theoretical work but also factual reports; finally, by its distinction between insight and bias, progress and decline, it contains in a general form the combination of the empirical and the critical attitudes essential to human science.

It is perhaps unnecessary to insist that dialectic provides no more than the general form of a critical attitude. Each department has to work out its own specialized criteria, but it will be able to do so by distinguishing between the purely intellectual element in its field and, on the other hand, the inertial effects and the interference of human sensibility and human nerves. Moreover, just as our study of insight has enabled us to formulate on a basis of principle a large number of directives that already had been established through mathematical and scientific development – I am thinking of higher viewpoints, the significance of symbolism, of functions, of differential equations, of invariance, of equivalence, of probability – so we may hope that a fuller study of man's mind will provide us with further general elements relevant to determining a far more nuanced yet general critical viewpoint.

To this end the present chapters on common sense are contributory. May we note before concluding that, while common sense relates things to us, our account of common sense relates it to its neural basis and relates aggregates and successions of instances of common sense to one another.

8

Things

So far we have been dodging the question, What is a thing? Now that question must be faced. The first two sections will be devoted to determining what in general a thing is and what a thing commonly but mistakenly is supposed to be. In the third section, we tackle the problem of the differentiation of things on the generic level and from an explanatory viewpoint. In the fourth, we ask whether there are things within things. In the fifth, we extend emergent probability to include an account, not of the origin of things, but of the immanent intelligibility of their numbers, differences, distributions, concentrations, developments, and breakdowns. In the sixth, we attempt an explanatory formulation of the notion of species.

1   The General Notion of the Thing   [245–50]

Since the notion of a thing involves a new type of insight, we had best begin by recalling the main features of the old and now familiar type. It rested upon the presence or absence of laws governing the relations between data. Thus, experiential conjugates were reached by grasping the correlation between such terms as 'red as seen' and 'seeing red,' or 'heat as felt' and 'feeling heat.' Similarly, explanatory conjugates were reached by grasping the higher and more remote correlations that link and implicitly define, say, masses or the electromagnetic field vectors. On the other hand, probabilities were reached by arguing from the absence of system in the relations between data.

This attention to law and system led to a consideration of data, not in the totality of their concrete aspects, but only from some abstractive viewpoint. To employ an experiential conjugate is to prescind from all aspects of data except some single quality such as 'red' or 'hot.' To employ an explanatory conjugate is to turn attention away from all directly perceptible aspects and direct it to a nonimaginable term that can be reached only through a series of correlations of correlations of correlations. To speak of a probability is to suppose a process of reasoning that rests, not directly on what is given, nor positively on what can be understood in the given, but indirectly and negatively on what follows from a lack of system in the given.

Now the notion of a thing is grounded in an insight that grasps, not relations between data, but a unity, identity, whole in data; and this unity is grasped, not by considering data from any abstractive viewpoint, but by taking them in their concrete individuality and in the totality of their aspects. For if the reader will turn his mind to any object he names a thing, he will find that object to be a unity to which belongs every aspect of every datum within the unity. Thus, the dog Fido is a unity, and to Fido is ascribed a totality of data whether of color or shape, sound or odor, feeling or movement. Moreover, from this grasp of unity in a concrete totality of data there follow the various characteristics of things.

Thus, things are conceived as extended in space, permanent in time, and yet subject to change. They are extended in space, inasmuch as spatially distinct data pertain to the unity at any given instant. They are permanent in time, inasmuch as temporally distinct data pertain to the same unity. They are subject to change, inasmuch as there is some difference between the aggregate of data at one instant and the aggregate of data on the same unity at another instant.

Again, things possess properties and are subject to laws and to probabilities. For the very data that, taken concretely, are understood as pertaining to a single thing may also be taken abstractly and so may lead to a grasp of experiential conjugates, explanatory conjugates, and probabilities. Because the data are the same, there results an obvious relation between the insights and between the consequent concepts. This relation is expressed by saying that the conjugates are properties of the thing and that the probabilities regard the occurrence of changes in the thing.

Again, the same relation is involved in what is named attribution. The concrete unity embraces a totality of aspects. From various abstractive viewpoints, other notions apart from the notion of the thing are to be reached. But because the same set of aspects yields both the notion of the thing and the other notions, the latter are related to the former, and the relation, considered logically, is named attribution. Thus, to say that Fido is black or that he is a nuisance is to conceive both a unity in a totality of aspects and some aspect out of the totality, and then to attribute the latter to the former.

Again, Aristotle's syllogism aimed at putting an intelligible order into the attributes of things. In a given totality of data there is grasped a unity named the moon. In the same totality there is grasped a regular series of luminous shapes named the phases of the moon. In the regular series of phases one may grasp that the surface of the moon cannot be flat and must be spherical. Aristotle would name the moon the subject, its phases the middle term, and its sphericity the predicate. He would note that the middle term accounts for the attribution of the predicate to the subject. He would draw attention to the difference between a *causa essendi* and a *causa cognoscendi*: the phases are the reason why we know the moon is spherical; but the sphericity is the reason why the borrowed light of the sun is reflected from the moon in the regular series of shapes named phases.

Again, without the notion of the thing there can be no notion of change. For a change is not just a newly observed datum, nor the substitution of one datum for another, nor the creation of a datum that previously did not exist. Moreover, there are no changes in the realm of abstractions, for every abstraction is eternally whatever it is defined to be. If there is change, there has to be a concrete unity of concrete data extending over some interval of time, there has to be some difference between the data at the beginning and at the end of the interval, and this difference can be only partial, for otherwise there would occur not a change but an annihilation and a new creation.

As the notion of the thing is necessary for the notion of change, so also is it necessary for the continuity of scientific thought and development. For scientific development involves a succession of explanatory systems. Each of such systems serves to define implicitly a set of conjugate terms that through a series of correlations of correlations can be linked with concrete data. Still, this succession of systems with their implications does not suffice to constitute scientific thought. For the systems have to be discovered in data and verified in data; they cannot be discovered and verified in any data whatever; neither can they be discovered and verified in the data which they themselves select, for then a number of incompatible systems would be equally verifiable for each would satisfy equally well the data it selected. Accordingly, scientific thought needs, not only explanatory systems, but also descriptions that determine the data which explanations must satisfy. Moreover, scientific thought needs the notion of the thing, which has as its properties both experiential and explanatory conjugates, which remains identical whether it is described or explained, which by its identity demands a coherent explanation or set of explanations that is verifiable in the easily ascertainable data of the thing as described.

Thus the thing is the basic synthetic construct of scientific thought and development. It embraces in a concrete unity a totality of spatially and temporally distinct data. It possesses as its qualities and properties the experiential conjugates that can be determined by observation. It is subject to change and variation inasmuch as its data at one time differ from its data at another. Through observations of qualities, things are classified by their sensible similarities. Through measurements of changes, there are reached classical laws and statistical frequencies. Such laws and frequencies are subject to revision, and the revision is effected by showing that the earlier view does not satisfy completely the data on the thing as described. Finally, not only experiential conjugates, explanatory conjugates, and probabilities of events are verifiable; the construct of the thing is itself verifiable; for the ancient list of four elements – earth, water, fire, and air – has been rejected, and the new list of the periodic table has been established on the scientific ground of hypothesis and verification; both the old list and the new are lists of kinds of things.

Further, things are said to exist. Earlier we distinguished between questions that admit the simple answers yes and no, and questions that do not. It is meaningless to answer either yes or no to the question, What is a thing? On the other hand, that answer is quite appropriate when one asks whether there are any things. Now existence may be defined as what is known inasmuch as an affirmative answer is given to the question, Are there things? Accordingly, existence stands to the thing as event or occurrence stands to the conjugate. For the existence of the thing is known by verifying the notion of the thing, as the occurrence is known by verifying the conjugate. Moreover, general knowledge of things, like knowledge of conjugates, is reached by classical procedures, but general knowledge of existence, like knowledge of occurrence, is obtained through statistical laws. Thus, the definitions of chemical elements and compounds are of the classical type, but predictions of successful analysis or synthesis in nature or in the laboratory have to be based on probabilities.

May it be noted, once and for all, that regularly the foregoing meaning is to be attributed to our use of the terms 'exist,' 'existence,' 'existential'? Only when the context demands it are these words to be given the meaning they bear in existentialist philosophy.

Again, all existing things are particular, but we may think of them in general, and then we abstract from their particularity. One reaches the notion of the thing by grasping a unity in individual data; but once the notion is reached, one can think and speak both of things in general and of things of determinate kinds specified by their conjugates or properties. Moreover, from such general considerations one can revert to the particular, and that reversal may occur in any of three manners. The simplest case arises when one reverts to a particular thing whose data here and now are given; then by a simple shift of attention one moves from 'thing' or 'things' to 'this thing' or 'these things.' The second case occurs when the particular thing to which one reverts does not lie in the field of observation; then a spatiotemporal frame of reference has to be invoked to provide the link between the data given here and now and the data relevant to the particular thing in question; through the use of such a frame of reference, one comes to think and speak of 'that thing' or 'those things.' The third case arises within the confines of fully explanatory science, which deals with things, not as related to our senses, but as related to one another. Clearly, there are data on things only inasmuch as they are related to our senses; it follows that there can be no appeal to data as long as one considers things themselves, things as explained, things as related to one another, things as equivalent for all observers inasmuch as one prescinds from all observers. Nonetheless, we think and speak of things themselves as existing, and only particulars exist. What, then, is the ground of the individuality of the thing itself? The Aristotelian solution to this problem would be to posit a prime matter that stands to the intelligible unity or form of the thing as data stand to insight; just as data as given are prior to all insight and so prior to all distinction and relation or unification, so prime matter is conceived as a constituent of reality that is presupposed by form and so, of itself, is not a thing nor a quantity nor a quality nor a relation nor a place nor a time nor any other positively conceivable object.[1]

As yet, however, we cannot attempt to say what possible meaning could be assigned the phrase 'constituent of reality.' But it is worth noting that the problem of the individuality of things themselves is neither unique nor isolated. As has been seen, when there is no possibility of observation, there is no possibility of a verifiable image; for the imagined as imagined can be verified only when what is imagined also can be sensed. Accordingly, there are no verifiable images for subatomic elements. But if subatomic elements cannot be imagined, then atoms cannot be imagined, for one cannot imagine a whole as made up of non-imaginable parts. It follows that no thing itself, no thing as explained, can be imagined. If atoms cannot be imagined, then by parity of reasoning, molecules cannot be imagined. If molecules cannot be imagined, then neither can cells. If cells cannot be imagined, then neither can plants. Once one enters upon the way of explanation by relating things to one another, one has stepped out of the path that yields valid representative images. No doubt, I can imagine the plant as seen, as related to my senses, as described. But if I apply the full principle of equivalence and prescind from all observers, then I also prescind from all observables. As the electron, so also the tree, insofar as it is considered as a thing itself, stands within a pattern of intelligible relations and offers no foothold for imagination. The difference between the tree and the electron is simply that the tree, besides being explained, also can be observed and described, while the electron, though it can be explained, cannot be directly observed and can be described adequately only in terms of observables that involve other things as well. For the present, however, we must be content to note that the thing itself sets problems which as yet we are not prepared to tackle.

2   Bodies   [250–54]

The name 'thing' has been employed in a very precise meaning. It denotes a unity, identity, whole; initially it is grasped in data as individual; inasmuch as it unifies spatially and temporally distinct data, it is extended and permanent; inasmuch as the data it unifies also are understood

1 [On matter as ground of individuation, see Aristotle, *Metaphysics*, VIII, 2; for this definition of prime matter, see ibid., VII, 3, 1029a 19–21.]

through laws, conjugates become its properties, and probabilities govern its changes; finally, things exist, and only particulars exist, though the particularity, and indeed the reality, of things themselves give rise to disconcerting problems.

Now there may be men that employ the name 'body' in exactly the same meaning as we have assigned to the name 'thing.' But men are not pure intelligences. They are animals; they live largely under the influence of their intersubjectivity; they are guided by a common sense that does not bother to ask nice questions on the meaning of familiar names. Accordingly, it would not be rash to suspect that their usage of the name 'thing' does not quite coincide with the account we have given; and it is to follow up this suspicion that in the present section we turn our attention to the notion of a body or, rather, of a 'body,' where the quotation marks denote some divergence from the notion to be reached by intelligence and reasonableness.

To begin from a clear-cut instance in which there is no need to suppose either intelligence or reasonableness, let us consider a kitten. It is awake, and its stream of consciousness flows in the biological pattern. Such consciousness is a higher technique for attaining biological ends. It may be described as orientated toward such ends and as anticipating means to the ends. Moreover, the means lie in external situations, and so the anticipation is extroverted. The kitten's consciousness is directed outwards towards possible opportunities to satisfy appetites. This extroversion is spatial: as it is by the spatial maneuvers of moving its head and limbs that the kitten deals with means to its end, so the means also must be spatial, for otherwise spatial maneuvers would be inept and useless. The extroversion is also temporal: present data are distinct from the memories that enrich them; they are no less distinct from the imagined courses of future action to which they lead. Finally, the extroversion is concerned with the 'real': a realistic painting of a saucer of milk might attract a kitten's attention, make it investigate, sniff, perhaps try to lap; but it could not lead to lapping, and still less to feeling replete; for the kitten, painted milk is not real.

Let us now characterize a 'body' as an 'already out there now real.' 'Already' refers to the orientation and dynamic anticipation of biological consciousness; such consciousness does not create but finds its environment; it finds it as already constituted, already offering opportunities, already issuing challenges. 'Out' refers to the extroversion of a consciousness that is aware, not of its own ground, but of objects distinct

from itself. 'There' and 'now' indicate the spatial and temporal determinations of extroverted consciousness. 'Real,' finally, is a subdivision
within the field of the 'already out there now': part of that is mere appearance; but part is real; and its reality consists in its relevance to biological success or failure, pleasure or pain.

As the reader will have surmised, the terms 'body,' 'already,' 'out,'
'there,' 'now,' 'real' stand for concepts uttered by an intelligence that is
grasping, not intelligent procedure, but a merely biological and nonintel-
ligent response to stimulus. In other words, the point to the preceding
paragraphs is not to suggest that a kitten can understand and describe
its spontaneity but, on the contrary, to indicate through human concepts
the elements in a nonconceptual 'knowing.'

Again, as the reader once more will have surmised, our interest in
kittens is rather limited. For the point we wish to make is that not a few
men mean by 'thing' or 'body,' not simply an intelligible unity grasped
in data as individual, but also an 'already out there now real' which is as
accessible to human animals as to kittens. When Galileo pronounced
secondary qualities to be merely subjective, he meant that they were not
'already out there now real.' When the decadent Aristotelians and, generally, people that rely on good common sense insist that secondary
qualities obviously are objective, they mean that they are 'already out
there now real.' When Descartes maintained that material substance
must be identical with spatial extension, his material substance was the
'already out there now real.' When Kant argued that primary and secondary qualities are merely phenomenal, he meant that for him the
reality of the 'already out there now real' was mere appearance. Our
own position, as contained in the canon of parsimony, was that the real
is the verified; it is what is to be known by the knowing constituted by
experience and inquiry, insight and hypothesis, reflection and verification. Our present point is that, besides knowing in that rather complex
sense, there is also 'knowing' in the elementary sense in which kittens
know the 'reality' of milk.

It is not difficult to set forth the differences between the two types of
knowing. The elementary type is constituted completely on the level of
experience; neither questions for intelligence nor questions for reflection
have any part in its genesis; and as questions do not give rise to it, neither can they undo it; essentially it is unquestionable. On the other
hand, in fully human knowing experience supplies no more than
materials for questions; questions are essential to its genesis; through

questions for intelligence it moves to accumulations of related insights which are expressed or formulated in concepts, suppositions, definitions, postulates, hypotheses, theories; through questions for reflection it attains a further component, which hitherto has been referred to as verification and presently will have to be examined more closely in a series of chapters on judgment, its suppositions, and its implications.

Both types of knowing possess their validity. One cannot claim that one is concerned with mere appearance while the other is concerned with reality. For elementary knowing vindicates its validity by the survival, not to mention the evolution, of animal species. On the other hand, any attempt to dispute the validity of fully human knowing involves the use of that knowing, and so, if the attempt is not to be frustrated by its own assumptions, it must presuppose that validity.

The problem set by the two types of knowing is, then, not a problem of elimination but a problem of critical distinction. For the difficulty lies, not in either type of knowing by itself, but in the confusion that arises when one shifts unconsciously from one type to the other. Animals have no epistemological problems. Neither do scientists, as long as they stick to their task of observing, forming hypotheses, and verifying. The perennial source of nonsense is that, after the scientist has verified his hypothesis, he is likely to go a little further and tell the layman what, approximately, scientific reality looks like! Already we have attacked the unverifiable image; but now we can see the origin of the strange urge to foist upon mankind unverifiable images. For both the scientist and the layman, besides being intelligent and reasonable, also are animals. To them as animals, a verified hypothesis is just a jumble of words or symbols. What they want is an elementary knowing of the 'really real,' if not through sense, at least by imagination.

As is apparent, we are back at the notion of dialectic. There are two types of knowing. Each is modified by its own development. They are opposed, for one arises through intelligent and reasonable questions and answers, and the other does not. They are linked together in man, who at once is an animal, intelligent, and reasonable. Unless they are distinguished sharply by a critical theory of knowledge, they become confused, to generate aberrations that afflict not only scientific thought but far more conspicuously the thought of philosophers. Further development of this point must be left to the chapter on the method of metaphysics, but perhaps enough has been said to justify the following conclusions.

(1) By a thing is meant an intelligible concrete unity. As differentiated

by experiential conjugates and commonsense expectations, it is a thing for us, a thing as described. As differentiated by explanatory conjugates and scientifically determined probabilities, it is a thing itself, a thing as explained.

(2) The notion of thing satisfies the canon of parsimony. For it adds to data only what is grasped by intelligence and reasonably is affirmed. Indeed, not only does it satisfy the canon of parsimony but it seems necessary to scientific thought, both because it is presupposed by the necessary notion of change, and because the scientist has to possess a construct that combines both descriptive and explanatory knowledge.

(3) By a 'body' is meant primarily a focal point of extroverted biological anticipation and attention. It is an 'already out there now real,' where these terms have their meaning fixed solely by elements within sensitive experience and so without any use of intelligent and reasonable questions and answers.

(4) By a 'body' is meant secondarily any confusion or mixture of elements taken both from the notion of a thing and from the notion of a 'body' in its primary meaning.

(5) As Newton and Kant, so we also speak of things themselves. But for us the thing itself has the meaning defined above. For Newton it seems to have been a 'body.' For Kant it also seems to have been a 'body,' though with the difference that it was inaccessible to scientific knowledge.

(6) Ernst Cassirer's work *Substance and Function*[2] contains a polemic against the notion of the thing. I would say that his strictures are valid against the notion of 'body' but would claim his argument to be inefficacious against the notion of thing. It is true that the development of explanatory science tends to eliminate the notion of 'body'; on the other hand, if explanatory science were to eliminate the notion of thing, it would cut its communications with the data in which it has to be discovered and verified.[3]

2 [Ernst Cassirer, *Substance and Function* and *Einstein's Theory of Relativity*. Part 1 is entitled 'The Concept of Thing and the Concept of Relation.']

3 There exists a parallel duality and ambiguity in the notion of oneself. Corresponding to 'body' there is 'my body.' Corresponding to things that are understood and verified, there is the intelligently and rationally conscious subject to be considered in chapter 11. According to H.S. Sullivan, *The Interpersonal Theory of Psychiatry* 136–41, the notion of 'my body' has its origins in the infantile activity of thumb sucking. This activity meets a need, since the energy available for taking in food ex-

3   Genus as Explanatory   [254–57]

Mechanist determinism is bound to conceive all things as of a single kind. For mechanism posits things as instances of the 'already out there now real'; determinism makes every event completely determined by laws of the classical type; and the combination of the two views leaves no room for a succession of ever higher systems, for mechanism would require the higher component to be a 'body,' and determinism would exclude the possibility of the higher component modifying lower activities.

On the other hand, the notion of the thing as an intelligible concrete unity differentiated by experiential and explanatory conjugates clearly implies the possibility of different kinds of things. Moreover, since explanatory conjugates are defined by their relations to one another, there is the possibility of distinct sets of such conjugates. There follows the notion of the explanatory genus. Consider a genus of things T_i, with explanatory conjugates C_i, and a second genus of things T_j, with explanatory conjugates C_i and C_j, such that all conjugates of the type C_i are defined by their relations to one another, and similarly, all conjugates of the type C_j are defined by their relations to one another. Then, since C_i and C_j differ, there will be two different systems of terms and relations; as the basic terms and relations differ, all logically derived terms and relations will differ, so that by logical operations alone there is no transition from one system to the other.

Now it seems that such explanatory genera exist. The laws of physics hold for subatomic elements; the laws of physics and chemistry hold for chemical elements and compounds; the laws of physics, chemistry, and biology hold for plants; the laws of physics, chemistry, biology, and sensitive psychology hold for animals; the laws of physics, chemistry,

---

ceeds the need for food. It meets a need in an exceptional manner: both mouth and thumb are both sensing and sensed. Finally, it occurs at the infant's own behest without the labor of crying for mother's help. In such a fashion, clearly, there can arise an empirical consciousness of a center of power and self-satisfaction. No less clearly, the empirically conscious self is just as intractable within a field theory of interpersonal relations as the old-style atom within modern physical theory; and so, as Cassirer attacked the notion of thing, Sullivan attacks the delusion of unique individuality. Both views have the same merit and, I suggest, the same defect.

biology, sensitive psychology, and rational psychology hold for men. As one moves from one genus to the next, there is added a new set of laws which defines its own basic terms by its own empirically established correlations. When one turns from physics and chemistry to astronomy, one employs the same basic terms and correlations; but when one turns from physics and chemistry to biology, one is confronted with an entirely new set of basic concepts and laws.

No doubt, a mechanist would have to claim that biology does not differ essentially from astronomy. He would argue that biology introduces its special terms and laws merely as a matter of convenience, that biology deals not with a new genus of things but with extremely complex macroscopic products of the same old things. Already we have stated the case against mechanism and determinism, and so we have only to indicate how the possibility of new genera arises.

Consider, then, a genus of things T_i, with explanatory conjugates C_i, and a consequent list of possible schemes of recurrence S_i. Suppose there occurs an aggregate of events E_{ij} that is merely coincidental when considered in the light of the laws of the things T_i and of all their possible schemes of recurrence S_i. Then, if the aggregate of events E_{ij} occurs regularly, it is necessary to advance to the higher viewpoint of some genus of things T_j, with conjugates C_i and C_j, and with schemes of recurrence S_j. The lower viewpoint is insufficient, for it has to regard as merely coincidental what in fact is regular. The higher viewpoint is justified, for the conjugates C_j and the schemes S_j constitute a higher system that makes regular what otherwise would be merely coincidental.

Accordingly, if the laws of subatomic elements have to regard the regular behavior of atoms as mere patterns of happy coincidences, then there is an autonomous science of chemistry. If the laws of chemistry have to regard the metabolism and division of cells as mere patterns of happy coincidences, then there is an autonomous science of biology. If the laws of biology have to regard the behavior of animals as mere patterns of happy coincidences, then there is an autonomous science of sensitive psychology. If the laws of sensitive psychology have to regard the operations of mathematicians and scientists as mere patterns of happy coincidences, then there is an autonomous science of rational psychology. Nor does the introduction of the higher autonomous science interfere with the autonomy of the lower; for the higher enters into the field of the lower only insofar as it makes systematic on the lower level what otherwise would be merely coincidental.

As has been remarked, the succession of sciences corresponding to the succession of higher genera does not admit any purely logical transition. Each of these main departments has its own basic terms defined implicitly by its own empirically established correlations. Still, this negation of a logical transition must not be interpreted as a negation of any transition whatever. For logical operations are confined to the field of concepts and definitions, hypotheses and theories, affirmations and negations. This field is only part of the larger domain that includes as well sensitive presentations and imaginative representations, inquiry and insight, reflection and critical understanding. Within this larger domain, the successive departments of science are related, for the laws of the lower order yield images in which insight grasps clues to laws of the higher order. In this fashion, the Bohr model of the atom is an image that is based on subatomic physics yet leads to insights into the nature of atoms. Again, the chemistry of the cell can yield an image of catalytic process in which insight can grasp biological laws. Again, an image of the eye, optic nerve, and cerebrum can lead to insights that grasp properties of the psychic event 'seeing,' and so the oculist can make one see better, and more generally the surgeon can make one feel better. Finally, it is with respect to sensed and imagined objects that the higher levels of inquiry, insight, reflection, and judgment function.

This linking of the main departments of science runs parallel to the notion of successive higher viewpoints outlined in our first chapter. Just as elementary arithmetic and elementary algebra are distinct systems, with different rules yielding different operations and different operations yielding different numbers, so the main departments of science are distinct systems without logical transitions from one to the other. Just as the image of 'doing arithmetic' leads to the insights that ground algebra, so images based on the lower science lead to insights that ground elements of the higher science. Finally, it is because new insights intervene that the higher science is essentially different from the lower.

Naturally, the reader will be inclined to view these images as pictures of reality. In this fashion intelligence is reduced to a pattern of sensations; sensation is reduced to a neural pattern; neural patterns are reduced to chemical processes; and chemical processes to subatomic movements. The force of this reductionism, however, is proportionate to the tendency to conceive the real as a subdivision of the 'already out there now.' When that tendency is rejected, reductionism vanishes. The real becomes the verified, and one can argue in the opposite direction that, since there is no verifiable image of the subatomic, there can be no verifiable image of objects composed of subatomic elements. The verifiably imagined is restricted to the sensibly given. One has to be content with reasonable affirmations of intelligently conceived terms and relations. On that showing, the function of the transition images is simply heuristic; such images represent, perhaps only symbolically, the coincidental manifold that becomes systematic when subsumed within the higher genus.

To conclude, let us remark that we have been concerned merely to reveal the possibility of genera of things and their compatibility with the sciences as they exist. A much longer investigation would be needed to prove that in fact there are such genera. We are convinced that the longer inquiry can be omitted safely enough, for the contention that things are all of one kind has rested, not on concrete evidence, but on mechanist assumption.

4   Things within Things   [258–59]

Once things are recognized to be of different kinds, there arises the obvious question whether there are things within things. Are electrons things within atoms, atoms things within compounds, compounds things within cells, cells things within animals, animals things within men?

The difficulty against an affirmative answer is that the thing is an intelligible unity grasped in some totality of data. It follows that if any datum pertains to a thing, every aspect of the datum pertains to that thing. Hence, no datum can pertain to two or more things, for if in all its aspects it pertains to one thing, there is no respect in which it can pertain to any other.

The difficulty against a negative answer is that the laws of the lower science can be verified in things pertaining to a higher genus. If the laws of the electron are observed in the atom, it would seem that electrons exist, not only in a free state, but also within atoms. If the laws of the chemical compound are observed within the living cell, it would seem that chemical compounds exist, not only in their free state, but also within cells.

Strangely, it is the argument against a negative answer that has the weak point. The fact that the laws of the lower order are verified in the higher genus proves that the conjugates of the lower order exist in things of the higher genus. But it is one thing to prove that conjugates of the lower order survive within the higher genus; it is quite another to prove that things defined solely by the lower conjugates also survive. To arrive at conjugates, abstractive procedures are normal; one considers events under some aspects and disregards other aspects of the same events. But to arrive at a thing, one must consider all data within a totality, and one must take into account all their aspects. It follows that one cannot consider the aggregate of events E_{ij} insofar as they satisfy the laws of the lower order, and then conclude to the existence of things of the lower order. For this would be to abstract from the aspect of the aggregate that cannot be accounted for on the lower viewpoint and that justifies the introduction of the higher viewpoint and the higher genus. Accordingly, if there is evidence for the existence of the higher genus, there cannot be evidence for things of lower genera in the same data.

Naturally enough, the reader will be inclined to ask what happens to the things of the lower order. But perhaps a moment's reflection will recall that there is quite a difference between things and 'bodies.' If the objects of the lower order were 'bodies,' then it would be mere mystification to claim that they do not exist within higher genera. Our claim does not regard alleged 'bodies.' It is the simple statement of fact that in an object of a higher order, there is an intelligible concrete unity differentiated by conjugates of both the lower and the higher order, but there is no further intelligible concrete unity to be discerned in the same data and to be differentiated solely by conjugates of some lower order. In other words, just as the real is what is to be known by verified hypothesis, so also change is what is to be known through correct, successive, and opposed affirmations.

5   Things and Emergent Probability   [259-62]

Our account of the objective implications of the use of both classical and statistical procedures was cast in the form of a world view. There now arises the question, previously omitted, whether there is an emergent probability of things as well as of schemes of recurrence. Our answer will consist in a discussion of the suppositions or postulates of an affirmative answer.

A first, logical postulate will be that, if there exist conjugates C_j of a higher order, then there will exist things T_j of the same higher order. This postulate is named logical because it follows necessarily from our account of the notion of a thing. For the evidence for the conjugates C_j

will be found in concrete data; in the same data there will be evidence for some thing that is to be differentiated by the conjugates verified in the same data; hence there cannot be conjugates of a higher order without things of the same order.

A second, probability postulate will be that, if there exist things T_i differentiated by conjugates C_i and functioning in schemes S_i, then there exists the possibility, and as well there will be some probability, of a nonsystematic occurrence of the aggregate of events E_{ij} that would occur regularly only if things of a higher order existed. There exists this possibility, for none of the events in the aggregate exceeds the capacity of the things T_i. There exists some probability for an isolated occurrence of each of the events in the aggregate, for each is concretely possible. From the theory of probability it follows necessarily that there will be some probability for a nonsystematic occurrence of the combination of all the events in the aggregate.

A third, evolutionary postulate will be that, if nonsystematically there occur suitable aggregates of events E_{ij}, then there will emerge conjugates C_j of a higher order to make the recurrence of the aggregates systematic. By the first, logical postulate, there will follow the existence of things T_j of the higher order. By emergent probability there will arise schemes of recurrence S_j that depend upon the classical laws that define the new conjugates C_j.

It must be noted that this evolutionary postulate is to be understood within the limits of possible empirical science. It states what happens on the fulfilment of determinate conditions. It is relevant to an understanding of the generic immanent intelligibility of the order of this universe. It is relevant only to an account of such immanent intelligibility; as empirical science, it prescinds from efficient, instrumental, and final causes, which refer to distinct types of intelligibility and lie beyond the qualifications of empirical method either to affirm or to deny.

Further, it may be observed that the evolutionary postulate, as stated, is equivalent to the old axiom *Materiae dispositae advenit forma*.[a] In the postulate and in the old axiom, there are involved exactly the same components, namely, a lower order of things, the occurrence of a suitable disposition in the lower order, and the emergence of a component that pertains to a higher order. It follows that the evidence for the axiom, which consists in certain obvious facts of transformation, generation, and nutrition, is also evidence for the postulate. Finally, while there are differences between the context of the axiom and the context of the postulate, these differences do not appear to be significant. For the context of the axiom involves efficient and final causes, to which we can attend in due course, and the context of the postulate involves probabilities, whose scientific import was not grasped until recently.

The fourth, sequential postulate would effect the extension of emergent probability to things. It affirms the possibility of a conditioned series of both things and schemes of recurrence realized cumulatively in accord with successive schedules of probabilities. Thus the sequential postulate presupposes the other three; it adds an affirmation of the possibility of applying the other three postulates over and over so that one could begin from the simplest things and proceed to the most complex. On the other hand, the sequential postulate affirms no more than a possibility. It does not claim that human science has reached the stage of complete and definitive knowledge that would be necessary to state fully the total sequence of emerging things and schemes. Accordingly, the sequential postulate is methodological; it is not some hypothesis of empirical science but rather an assumption that can generate an almost endless stream of hypotheses; it is not a scientific theory that can be verified or refuted, for it is far too general to be tested in that fashion; it is an approach, a heuristic assumption, that can be worked out in an enormous number of different manners and that can be tested empirically only through such specific determinations and applications.

It follows that the validity of the sequential postulate rests simply on the validity of inquiring intelligence. Just as we endeavor to understand smaller aggregates of data, so also we seek the intelligibility immanent in the universe of data. Just as the rejection of all inquiry is a total obscurantism, so the rejection of this or that inquiry is a partial obscurantism. For all data are equally data; all are materials for understanding; and as it is impossible to exclude all understanding, so it is incoherent to attempt insight in some cases and to refuse to attempt it in others that do not significantly differ. Now if there is to be known an intelligibility immanent in the universe of data, then it will regard things no less than events and schemes of recurrence; for things are to be grasped in data; their numbers and differentiation, their distribution and concentrations, their emergence and survival give rise to questions that require an answer. One does not escape that requirement by appealing to divine wisdom and divine providence, for that appeal reinforces the rejection of obscurantism and provides another argument for affirming an intelligible order immanent in the visible universe. Nor can a satisfactory answer be given by the necessity of determinists, for statistical residues are a fact, or by the chance of indeterminists, for chance is a residual defect of intelligibility, or by the eternally recurrent cycles of the Aristotelians, for these cycles are based on a mistaken overestimate of the influence of the celestial spheres. In a word, the sequential postulate seems to stand without a serious competitor in the field.

Four postulates have been outlined. Together they effect the extension of emergent probability, so that it regards the differentiation, numbers, distribution, development, survival, and disintegration of things as well as of schemes of recurrence. Moreover, the extended affirmation, no less than the original, is generic and methodological. It rests on the principle that data are to be understood, that understanding grasps concrete unities, systematic relations, and nonsystematic probabilities of existence and occurrence. It affirms that inquiry moves in a determinate direction and that this direction implies an emergent probability of things and schemes. At that point it stops, for it leaves to those competent in specialized departments the task of working out precise statements on the unfolding of generalized emergent probability.

6   Species as Explanatory   [262–67]

As there are classifications based on the relations of things to our senses, so also there are classifications based on the relations of things to one another. The latter classifications are explanatory, and they imply not only explanatory genera but also explanatory species.

The key notion in the explanatory species is that any lower species of things T_i, with their conjugates C_i and their schemes S_i, admit a series of coincidental aggregates of events, say $E_{ijm}, E_{ijn}, E_{ijo}, \ldots$ which stand in correspondence with a series of conjugates $C_{jm}, C_{jn}, C_{jo}, \ldots$ of a higher genus of things T_j.

For example, let T_i stand for the subatomic elements, C_i for the terms implicitly defined by the laws governing such elements, S_i for all the combinations of laws that yield schemes of recurrence for subatomic events. Then the terms of the series E_{ijx} stand for a sequence of aggregates of subatomic events, where each aggregate is merely coincidental from the viewpoint of subatomic laws and schemes. Such coincidental aggregates can be represented by symbolic images, and in such images there are clues leading to insights that pertain to the higher viewpoint of chemistry. Such insights form two levels. A first level yields the series of relations constitutive of the periodic table; these relations define implicitly the conjugates C_{jx}; such conjugates both differentiate the chemical elements which are the things T_j, and stand as the higher system that makes systematic the coincidental aggregates E_{ijx}. A second level yields the multitudinous series of chemical compounds, where combinations of aggregates E_{ijx} yield new and larger aggregates E_{ijy} that become systematic under the conjugates C_{jy}.

Again, let T_i now stand for the chemical elements and compounds, C_i for the conjugates implicitly defined by their laws, S_i for the schemes of recurrence that can be explained by chemical laws. Let the terms of the series E_{ijx} stand for aggregates of chemical processes, where each aggregate is merely coincidental from the chemical viewpoint. Such coincidental manifolds can be imagined symbolically, and in them there will be clues leading to insights that pertain to the higher viewpoint of biology. Again, the insights occur on two levels. Aggregates E_{ijx} vary with different kinds of cell; aggregates of aggregates, say E_{ijy}, vary with different kinds of multicellular living things. The things T_j are the series of biological species. They are higher systems that make systematic the coincidental aggregates E_{ijx}, E_{ijy}. The terms defined by the relations of the higher systems are the conjugates C_{jx}, C_{jy}, which vary with variations in the type of the aggregates of processes E_{ijx}, E_{ijy}.

Though the same formal structure yields both the chemical and the biological species, the greater complexity of the latter necessitates their markedly dynamic characteristics. An inspection of the periodic table reveals some elements to be extremely inert, others to be highly unstable, some to possess fewer and others more numerous capacities for combination. It follows that chemical elements and compounds will not be all equally suitable for the aggregates of processes to be systematized biologically. Moreover, in a universe in which concrete events are never more than probable, the higher biological system will have the function not merely of systematizing what otherwise would be coincidental but also of extruding what has become inept and intussuscepting fresh materials. Again, the fulfilment of the twofold function will be only probable, and so there follows a third function: of reproduction, of starting up a new instance of the system in fresh materials. Again, the system can shift its ground; instead of maintaining and reproducing a single cell, it can maintain and reproduce an ordered manifold of cells; and this shift involves a new dimension of growth and differentiation in the functions of the system. Thus the biological species are a series of solutions to the problem of systematizing coincidental aggregates of chemical processes. Minor changes in the underlying aggregates yield variations within the species; major changes that are surmounted successfully yield new types of solution and so new species. The existence of a series of such major changes is the biological content of the sequential postulate of generalized emergent probability.

The third application of the key notion takes the biological organism as its lower level and animal sensitivity as its higher system. Already something has been said of the biological pattern of experience and of its correspondence with underlying neural demand functions. The higher conjugates C_{jx} now are defined implicitly by the laws of psychic stimulus and psychic response, and these conjugates make systematic otherwise merely coincidental aggregates of neural events E_{ijx}. However, these neural events occur within an already constituted nervous system, which in great part would have no function if the higher psychic system did not exist to inform it.

In this fashion we are confronted with a basic fact which a mechanistic viewpoint has tended to overlook and to obscure, namely, that immanent intelligibility or constitutive design increases in significance as one mounts from higher to still higher systems. The periodic table of chemical elements is dominated by atomic numbers and atomic weights that are explained by underlying subatomic entities. A first degree of freedom appears in the vast diversity of chemical compounds, in which patterned aggregates of aggregates render subatomic limitations indirect. A second degree of freedom appears in the multicellular plant: each cell is an aggregate of aggregates; and the plant not only is an aggregate of cells but also it is the aggregate determined by its own laws of development and growth. A third degree of freedom appears in the animal, in which the second degree is exploited to provide the materials for the higher system of biological consciousness. In other words, because the multicellular structure is an immanently controlled aggregate of aggregates of aggregates of aggregates, there is the possibility of an organic nervous system that stands in correspondence with a still higher psychic system. Hence, while the chemical elements appear as dominated by the manifolds that they systematize, a multicellular structure is dominated by an idea that unfolds in the process of growth, and this idea can itself be subordinated to the higher idea of conscious stimulus and conscious response. While chemical compounds and unicellular entities systematize aggregates that, at least initially, are put together nonsystematically, multicellular formations systematize aggregates that they themselves assemble in systematic fashion. There follows an enormous shift of emphasis and significance from the materials to be systematized to the conditioned series of things and schemes that represents possibilities of systematizing. No doubt, plants and animals cannot emerge without the initial aggregation of chemicals in their initial cell or without an environment in which there are the possible and probable schemes of recurrence in which they function. Yet the fulfilment of these necessary conditions seems to differ enormously from the developed plant or animal; and the ground of the difference is that development has its ultimate basis, not in outer conditions or events, but in the realm of intelligible possibility.

Accordingly, emergent probability has quite different implications from the gradual accumulation of small variations that is associated with the name of Darwin. The fundamental element in emergent probability is the conditioned series of things and schemes; that series is realized cumulatively in accord with successive schedules of probabilities; but a species is not conceived as an accumulated aggregate of theoretically observable variations; on the contrary, it is an intelligible solution to a problem of living in a given environment, where the living is a higher systematization of a controlled aggregation of aggregates of aggregates of aggregates, and the environment tends to be constituted more and more by other living things. This notion of the intelligibility of species differs greatly from Plato's eternal Forms or even from Aristotle's alleged transference of Forms from their noetic heaven into things. Still, it does not take the notion of species out of the realm of the intelligible and place it in some aggregation of sensible qualities. Though later species are solutions to concrete problems in concrete circumstances, though they are solutions that take into account and, as it were, rise upon previous solutions, still a solution is the sort of thing that insight hits upon and not the sort that results from accumulated observable differences.

There is a further point to be made. An explanatory account of animal species will differentiate animals not by their organic but by their psychic differences. No doubt, there are many reasons for considering the study of animals to pertain not to psychology but to biology. In the first place, animal consciousness is not accessible to us. Secondly, an indirect study of an animal's psyche through its behavior is difficult, for what is significant is not any instance of behavior but the range of different modes of behavior relative to another range of significant different circumstances. Thirdly, an indirect study of the psyche through its neural basis is blocked by the peculiar difficulty of a correspondence that relates, not conjugates defined by a single system of laws, but distinct higher and lower systems of conjugates. Fourthly, it is far easier to describe organs and functions. Fifthly, such descriptive work may be reconciled more easily with the notion that science deals with 'bodies.' Still, science deals not with 'bodies' but with the intelligible unities of things; it describes, but it does so in order to move on towards explanation; and its business is not to follow some line of least resistance but to triumph in surmounting apparently insoluble difficulties. In brief, the alleged reasons are excuses. Against them stands a fact: the animal pertains to an explanatory genus beyond that of the plant; that explanatory genus turns on sensibility; its specific differences are differences of sensibility; and it is in differences of sensibility that are to be found the basis for differences of organic structure, since that structure, as we have seen, possesses a degree of freedom that is limited, but not controlled, by underlying materials and outer circumstances.

The fourth application of the key notion brings us to man. As sensitive appetite and perception are a higher system of the organic, so inquiry and insight, reflection and judgment, deliberation and choice are a higher system of sensitive process. The content of images provides the materials of mathematical understanding and thought; the content of sensible data provides the materials of empirical method; the tension between incompletely developed intelligence and imperfectly adapted sensibility grounds the dialectics of individual and social history.

Already we have noted the aesthetic liberation of human experience from the confinement of the biological pattern and the further practical liberation of human living that is brought about inasmuch as man grasps possible schemes of recurrence and fulfils by his own action the conditions for their realization. Now we must proceed to the root of these liberations. They rest on two facts. On the one hand, inquiry and insight are not so much a higher system as a perennial source of higher systems, so that human living has its basic task in reflecting on systems and judging them, deliberating on their implementation and choosing between possibilities. On the other hand, there can be in man a perennial source of higher systems because the materials of such systematization are not built into[b] his constitution. For an animal to begin a new mode of living, there would be needed not only a new sensibility but also a new organism. An animal species is a solution to the problem of living, so that a new solution would be a new species; for an animal to begin to live in quite a new fashion, there would be required not only a modification of its sensibility but also a modification of the organism that the sensibility systematizes. But in man a new department of mathematics, a new viewpoint in science, a new civilization, a new philosophy has its basis, not in a new sensibility but simply in a new manner of attending to data and of forming combinations of combinations of combinations of data. Seeing and hearing, tasting and smelling, imagining and feeling are events with a corresponding neural basis; but inquiring and understanding have their basis, not in a neural structure, but in a structure of psychic contents. Sensation supposes sense organs; but understanding is not another type of sensation with another sense organ; it operates with respect to the content of sensation and imagination; it represents a still further degree of freedom. A multicellular formation is an immanently directed aggregation of aggregates of aggregates of aggregates. Sensibility is a higher system of otherwise coincidental events in the immanently directed aggregation. Intelligence is the source of a sequence of systems that unify and relate otherwise coincidental aggregates of sensible contents. Just as the famous experiments on sea urchins reveal the immanent direction of the aggregation of aggregates of aggregates of aggregates, so the constructive and repressive censorship exercised preconsciously by intelligence reveals a still higher immanent direction that controls the sensible and imaginative contents that are to emerge into consciousness.

Man, then, is at once explanatory genus and explanatory species. He is explanatory genus, for he represents a higher system beyond sensibility. But that genus is coincident with species, for it is not just a higher system but a source of higher systems. In man there occurs the transition from the intelligible to the intelligent.

7   Concluding Summary   [267-70]

Frequently in the course of reading earlier chapters, the reader may have wondered, to the point of impatience and annoyance, why we did not begin from the simple and obvious notion of the thing. Now, perhaps, he will grant not only that that notion is neither as simple nor as obvious as it seems but also that things, since they are concrete syntheses both of the object and of the subject, cannot be treated until there are assembled the elements to be synthesized.

The basic difficulty is from the side of the subject. He is involved in a dialectical tension, and he can be made aware of the fact only after he has grasped what is meant and what is not meant by inquiry, insight, and conception as opposed to sensible data and schematic images. Accordingly, our first task was to clarify the nature of insight, and to it we devoted our first five chapters. On that foundation we constructed, first, a pure theory of common sense, and secondly, an account of its dialectical involvement. Only then could we hope to distinguish effectively between things and 'bodies,' between the intelligible unities to be grasped when one is within the intellectual pattern of experience and, on the other hand, the highly convincing instances of the 'already out there now real' that are unquestioned and unquestionable not only for animals but also for the general bias of common sense.

If that distinction has been drawn effectively, still it does not follow that the reader will always find it convincing. For the distinction is a work of intelligence operating in the intellectual pattern of experience. No one can hope to live exclusively in that pattern. As soon as anyone moves from that pattern to the dramatic pattern of his intercourse with others or the practical pattern of his daily tasks, things as intelligible unities once more will take on for him the appearance of unreal speculation, while 'bodies' or instances of the 'already out there now real' will resume the ascendancy that they acquired without opposition in his infancy. Accordingly, the attainment of a critical position means not merely that one distinguishes clearly between things and 'bodies' but also that one distinguishes between the different patterns of one's own experience and refuses to commit oneself intellectually unless one is operating within the intellectual pattern of experience. Inversely, it is the failure to reach the full critical position that accounts for the endless variety of philosophic positions so rightly lamented by Kant; and it is by a dialectical analysis, based on the full critical position, that one can hope to set up a philosophy of philosophies in the fully reflective manner that at least imperfectly was initiated by Hegel and still is demanded by modern needs. But clearly enough, these points can be developed only after we have answered questions on the nature of rational consciousness, of critical reflection, of judgment, of the notions of being and objectivity.

To revert from these high matters, which belong to later chapters, we turn from the dialectical involvement of the thing as subject to the thing as object. Things are concrete intelligible unities. As such, all are alike.

Still, they are of different kinds, not merely when described in terms of their relations to us, but still more so when explained in terms of their relations to one another. For there is a succession of higher viewpoints; each is expressed in its own system of correlations and implicitly defined conjugates; and each successive system makes systematic what otherwise would be merely coincidental on the preceding viewpoint. In this fashion one proceeds from the subatomic to the chemical, from the chemical to the biological, from the biological to the sensitive, and from the sensitive to the intelligent. Moreover, emergent probability is extended to realize cumulatively, in accord with successive schedules of probabilities, a conditioned series not only of schemes of recurrence but also of things. The conditioned series reveals not only an increasing systematization of events but also an increasing liberation of serial possibilities from limitations and restrictions imposed by previous realizations. Plants and, still more so, animals function, not in this or that scheme of recurrence, but in any of ever increasing ranges of schemes. Man invents his own schemes and produces by his labor and his conventions the conditions for their actuality. Again, there is an immanent direction, in the aggregation of aggregates in the multicellular formations, that is exploited by plants and animals; there is a similar immanent direction exercised by the censorship over contents to emerge into consciousness; and so, in the limiting case of man, the intelligible yields to the intelligent, and the higher system is replaced by a perennial source of higher systems.

This view of the thing is opposed by other views. The uncritical mechanist supposes that things are 'bodies' and that the unities and systems grasped by intelligence are merely subjective contents of merely subjective activities. No doubt, if subjectivity is simply the opposite of 'body,' then what is grasped by intelligence is merely subjective. But it is not quite so clear that 'objectivity' and 'body' are convertible terms. The uncritical realist would dispute our account of explanatory genera and species; on his view the empirical scientist understands, not reality but phenomena; beyond the unities and relations grasped by the scientist there is a deeper reality, a metaphysical essence, apprehended by philosophic intuition. But what is this philosophic intuition? I have looked for it and failed to find it. I know no reason for affirming its occurrence, and I know no reason for refusing to identify the alleged metaphysical essence with the already quite precisely defined notion of 'body.'

Besides the uncritical mechanists and the uncritical realists, there is a variety of more or less critical positions. Before we tackle them, let us ask ourselves a rather pertinent question. All along we have been concerned with insight, with what it is to understand. But among the more conspicuous properties of understanding is its liability to incompleteness, inadequacy, error. What we have ventured to say about mathematics, empirical science, common sense, things, may be quite coherent and intelligible. Still, that is not enough. Is it correct? Are things so? Have we been offering mere airy speculations?

Our answer is threefold. With regard to what has been put forward, it is quite enough for our purpose that what has been said is coherent and intelligible; for our purpose has been to reveal the nature of insight and to indicate its basic role in human knowledge; the fact that there are other views more coherent and more intelligible as well as more satisfactory than our own on mathematics and empirical method, on common sense and things, will not change our account of insight but confirm it. Secondly, there has been raised the second type of question, Is it so? Such are the questions, not of intelligent inquiry, but of critical reflection. It is to such questions and to the possibility of answering them that the following chapters are devoted. Thirdly, just as an account of insight is an account of method and so an account of what method cannot but yield at the term of inquiry, so also an account of critical reflection and the possibility of judgment will reveal unavoidable judgments. Those unavoidable judgments will be our answer to the question whether we are indulging in airy speculation or not.

9

The Notion of Judgment

A first determination of the notion of judgment is reached by relating it to propositions.

For present purposes it will suffice to distinguish (1) utterance, (2) sentence, and (3) proposition, in the following summary manner.

If you say, 'The king is dead,' and I say, 'The king is dead,' then there are two utterances but only one sentence.

If you say, 'Der König ist tot,' and I say, 'The king is dead,' then there are two utterances and two sentences but only one proposition.

Similarly, if you write in decimal notation, '2 + 2 = 4,' and I write in binary notation, '10 + 10 = 100,' again there are two utterances and two sentences but only one proposition.

Further, it will be supposed that utterances may be spoken, written, or merely imagined, and that the imagining may be visual, auditory, or motor; again, grammarians distinguish declarative, interrogative, optative, and exclamatory sentences, but of these only the declarative corresponds to the proposition.

Now with regard to propositions there are two distinct mental attitudes: one may merely consider them, or one may agree or disagree with them. Thus, what I write I also affirm; but what you are reading you may neither affirm nor deny but merely consider.

A proposition, then, may be simply an object of thought, the content of an act of conceiving, defining, thinking, supposing, considering.

But a proposition also may be the content of an act of judging; and then it is the content of an affirming or denying, an agreeing or disagreeing, an assenting or dissenting.

A second determination of the notion of judgment is reached by relating it to questions.

Questions fall into two main classes. There are questions for reflection, and they may be met by answering yes or no. There are questions for intelligence, and they may not be met by answering yes or no.

Thus, one may ask, 'Is there a logarithm of the square root of minus one?' This is a question for reflection. It is answered correctly by saying 'Yes.' On the other hand, though it would be a mistake to answer 'No,' still that answer would make sense. But if one asks, 'What is the logarithm of the square root of minus one?' there is no sense in answering either yes or no. The question is not for reflection but for intelligence. The only appropriate answer is to show that the square root of minus one results from raising a given base to a certain power.

Our second determination of the notion of judgment is, then, that judging is answering yes or no to a question for reflection.

A third determination of the notion of judgment is that it involves a personal commitment. As de la Rochefoucauld remarked, 'Everyone complains of his memory but no one of his judgment.'[1] One is ready to confess to a poor memory because one believes that memory is not within one's power. One is not ready to confess to poor judgment because the question for reflection can be answered not only by yes or no but also by 'I don't know'; it can be answered assertorically or modally, with certitude or only probability; finally, the question as presented can be dismissed, distinctions introduced, and new questions substituted. The variety of possible answers makes full allowance for the misfortunes and shortcomings of the person answering, and by the same stroke it closes the door on possible excuses for mistakes. A judgment is the responsibility of the one that judges. It is a personal commitment.

However, just what a person is, or what responsibility is, or why the person is responsible for his judgments are further questions that cannot be considered as yet. We now observe the fact and leave explanation to more appropriate occasions.

On the basis of the foregoing determinations we next attempt to relate

1 [A fairly exact quotation of Maxim 89 in François, Duc de la Rochefoucauld (1613–1680), *Reflections, or Sentences and Moral Maxims*, 5th ed., as given by John Bartlett, *Familiar Quotations* (Boston, Toronto: Little, Brown & Co., 1955) 265.]

judgment to the general structure of our cognitional process. We distinguish a direct and an introspective process, and in both of these we
distinguish three levels: a level of presentations, a level of intelligence,
and a level of reflection.

Hitherto, our inquiry has centered on the level of intelligence. It consists in acts of inquiry, understanding, and formulation. Thus, the question, What is it? leads to a grasp and formulation of an intelligible
unity-identity-whole in data as individual. The question, Why? leads to
a grasp and formulation of a law, a correlation, a system. The question,
How often? leads to a grasp and formulation of an ideal frequency from
which actual frequencies nonsystematically diverge.[a]

Our account of the classical and statistical phases of empirical method,
of the notion of the thing, of explanatory abstraction and system has
been concerned with the level of intelligence in cognitional process.

However, this level of intelligence presupposes and complements
another level. Inquiry presupposes elements in knowledge about which
inquiry is made. Understanding presupposes presentations to be understood. Formulation expresses not only what is grasped by understanding
but also what is essential to the understanding in the understood. This
prior level was described in the chapter on common sense.[b] It is the level
of presentations. Its defining characteristic is the fact that it is presupposed and complemented by the level of intelligence, that it supplies, as
it were, the raw materials on which intelligence operates, that, in a word,
it is empirical, given indeed but merely given, open to understanding
and formulation but by itself not understood and in itself ineffable.

Thirdly, the level of intelligence, besides presupposing and complementing an initial level, is itself presupposed and complemented by
a further level of reflection.

The formulations of understanding yield concepts, definitions, objects
of thought, suppositions, considerations. But man demands more. Every
answer to a question for intelligence raises a further question for reflection. There is an ulterior motive to conceiving and defining, thinking
and considering, forming suppositions, hypotheses, theories, systems.
That motive appears when such activities are followed by the question,
Is it so? We conceive in order to judge. As questions for intelligence,
What? and Why? and How often? stand to insights and formulations, so
questions for reflection stand to a further kind of insight and to judgment. It is on this third level that there emerge the notions of truth and
falsity, of certitude and the probability that is not a frequency but a

quality of judgment. It is within this third level that there is involved the personal commitment that makes one responsible for one's judgments. It is from this third level that come utterances to express one's affirming or denying, assenting or dissenting, agreeing or disagreeing.

It will be useful to represent schematically the three levels of cognitional process.

   I. Data. Perceptual Images.   Free Images.   Utterances.
  II. Questions for Intelligence. Insights.   Formulations.
 III. Questions for Reflection.   Reflection.   Judgment.

The second level presupposes and complements the first. The third level presupposes and complements the second. The exception lies in free images and utterances, which commonly are under the influence of the higher levels before they provide a basis for inquiry and reflection. Further, by questions for intelligence and reflection are not meant utterances or even conceptual formulations; by the question is meant the attitude of the inquiring mind that effects the transition from the first level to the second, and again the attitude of the critical mind that effects the transition from the second level to the third. Finally, the scheme is anticipatory inasmuch as the nature of reflection comes up for discussion only in the next chapter.

Now, as has been remarked, the three levels of the cognitional process operate in two modes. Data include data of sense and data of consciousness. Data of sense include colors, shapes, sounds, odors, tastes, the hard and soft, rough and smooth, hot and cold, wet and dry, and so forth. The direct mode of cognitional process begins from data of sense, advances through insights and formulations to reach reflection and judgment. Thus, empirical science pertains to the direct mode of cognitional process. On the other hand, the data of consciousness consist of acts of seeing, hearing, tasting, smelling, touching, perceiving, imagining, inquiring, understanding, formulating, reflecting, judging, and so forth. As data, such acts are experienced; but as experienced, they are not described, distinguished, compared, related, defined, for all such activities are the work of inquiry, insight, and formulation. Finally, such formulations are, of themselves, just hypotheses; they may be accurate or inaccurate, correct or mistaken; and to pronounce upon them is the work of reflection and judgment. Thus the three levels of the direct mode of cognitional process provide the data for the introspective mode; and as the direct mode, so also the introspective unfolds on the three

levels: an initial level of data, a second level of understanding and formulation, and a third level of reflection and judgment.

The foregoing offers an analysis of cognitional process. A whole is
divided into different levels; on each level different kinds of operation
are distinguished and related; each level is related to the others; and two
modes of the whole process are contrasted. But analysis prepares the
way for synthesis. Accordingly, we have now to ask how the various
elements come together to constitute knowing. As yet, we are unprepared to answer the Kantian question that regards the constitution of
the relation of knowing subject and known object. Our concern is the
more elementary question of the unification of the contents of several
acts into a single known content.

To this the general answer has already been indicated. Contents of
different acts come together inasmuch as the earlier are incomplete
without the later while the later have nothing to complete without the
earlier. Questions for intelligence presuppose something to be understood, and that something is supplied by the initial level. Understanding
grasps in given or imagined presentations an intelligible form emergent
in the presentations. Conception formulates the grasped idea along with
what is essential to the idea in the presentations. Reflection asks whether
such understanding and formulation are correct. Judgment answers that
they are or are not.

The cognitional process is thus a cumulative process: later steps presuppose earlier contributions and add to them. However, not all additions have the same significance. Some are merely provisional, as are
free images. Some put together in a new mode the contributions of
previous acts; thus, abstract formulation puts generally what insight
grasps in a particular presentation. Finally, some constitute, as it were,
the addition of new dimensions in the construction of the full cognitional content; and it is this addition of a new dimension that forms the
basis of the distinction between the three levels of presentation, intelligence, and reflection.

From this viewpoint one may distinguish between the proper and the
borrowed content of judgment.

The proper content of a judgment is its specific contribution to cognitional process. This consists in the answers yes or no.

The borrowed content of a judgment is twofold. There is the direct
borrowed content that is found in the question to which one answers yes
or no; and there is the indirect borrowed content that emerges in the

reflective act linking question and answer, that claims the yes or no to be true and, indeed, either certainly or only probably true.

Thus, the direct borrowed content of the judgment, I am writing, is the question, Am I writing? The proper content of that judgment is the answer, Yes, I am. The indirect borrowed content of the same judgment is the implicit meaning 'It certainly is true that I am writing.'

Again, from the same viewpoint, the judgment may be described as the total increment in cognitional process.

Every element in that process is at least a partial increment. It makes some contribution to knowing. But the judgment is the last act in the series that begins from presentations and advances through understanding and formulation ultimately to reach reflection and affirmation or denial. Thus, the proper content of judgment, the yes or no, is the final partial increment in the process. But this proper content is meaningless apart from the question it answers. With the question it forms an integrated whole. But the question takes over a formulation from the level of intelligence, and that formulation draws upon both insight and presentation. It follows that the judgment as a whole is a total increment in cognitional process, that it brings to a close one whole step in the development of knowledge.

Finally, there is the contextual aspect of judgment. Though single judgments bring single steps in inquiries to their conclusion, still the single steps are related to one another in a highly complex fashion.

The most general aspects of cognitional context are represented by logic and dialectic. Logic is the effort of knowledge to attain the coherence and organization proper to any stage of its development. Dialectic, on the other hand, rests on the breakdown of efforts to attain coherence and organization at a given stage, and consists in bringing to birth a new stage in which logic again will endeavor to attain coherence and organization.

From the viewpoint of the logical ideal, every term has one and only one precise meaning, every relation of every term to every other term is set down in an unequivocal proposition, the totality of propositions is neatly divided into primitive and derived, the derived may all be obtained by the rules of inference from a minimum number of primitive propositions, no proposition contradicts any other, and finally the employment of the principle of excluded middle does not introduce undefined or false suppositions, as does the question, Have you or have you not stopped beating your wife?

Now the pursuit of the logical ideal, so far from favoring a static immobility, serves to reveal the inadequacy of any intermediate stage in the development of knowledge. The more deeply it probes, the more effectively it forces the cognitional process to undergo a radical revision of its terms and postulates and so to pursue the logical ideal from a new base of operations. However, such revision has its limits, for there is no revision of revisers themselves. They are subject to the general conditions of beginning from presentations, advancing through insights and formulations, to terminate with reflections and judgments. Their insights are acts of grasping concrete unities, systematic regularities, or ideal frequencies. Their judgments are personal commitments to a yes or no; both answers cannot be given to the same question; and under ideal conditions either one of the two answers has to be given. The simple fact of the uniformity of nature in revisers provides both logic and dialectic with an immutable ultimacy.

Within the general schemes of logic and dialectic, the contextual aspect of judgment appears in three manners.

There is the relation of the present to the past. Thus, past judgments remain with us. They form a habitual orientation, present and operative, but only from behind the scenes. They govern the direction of attention, evaluate insights, guide formulations, and influence the acceptance or rejection of new judgments. Previous insights remain with us. They facilitate the occurrence of fresh insights, exert their influence on new formulations, provide presuppositions that underlie new judgments whether in the same or in connected or in merely analogous fields of inquiry. Hence, when a new judgment is made, there is within us a habitual context of insights and other judgments, and it stands ready to elucidate the judgment just made, to complement it, to balance it, to draw distinctions, to add qualifications, to provide defence, to offer evidence or proof, to attempt persuasion.

Secondly, there are the relations within the present. Existing judgments may be found to conflict, and so they release the dialectical process. Again, though they do not conflict, they may not be completely independent of each other, and so they stimulate the logical effort for organized coherence.

Thirdly, there are the relations of the present to the future. The questions we answer are few compared to the questions that await an answer. Knowing is a dynamic structure. If each judgment is a total increment consisting of many parts, still it is only a minute contribution towards the whole of knowledge. But further, our knowing is dynamic in another sense. It is irretrievably habitual. For we can make but one judgment at a time, and one judgment cannot bring all we know into the full light of actual knowing. A judgment may be very comprehensive and so bear witness to the depth and breadth of our perspectives. It may be very concrete and so reveal our grasp of nuance and detail. But it cannot be both comprehensive and concrete. All we know is somehow with us; it is present and operative within our knowing; but it lurks behind the scenes, and it reveals itself only in the exactitude with which each minor increment to our knowing is effected. The business of the human mind in this life seems to be, not contemplation of what we know, but relentless devotion to the task of adding increments to a merely habitual knowledge.

10

Reflective Understanding

Like the acts of direct and introspective understanding, the act of reflective understanding is an insight. As they meet questions for intelligence, it meets questions for reflection. As they lead to definitions and formulations, it leads to judgments. As they grasp unity, or system, or ideal frequency, it grasps the sufficiency of the evidence for a prospective judgment.

When Archimedes shouted his 'Eureka!' he was aware of a significant addition to his knowledge, but it is not likely that he would have been able to formulate explicitly just what a direct insight is. Similarly, we perform acts of reflective understanding, we know that we have grasped the sufficiency of the evidence for a judgment on which we have been deliberating, but without prolonged efforts at introspective analysis we could not say just what occurs in the reflective insight. What we know is that to pronounce judgment without that reflective grasp is merely to guess; again, what we know is that, once that grasp has occurred, then to refuse to judge is just silly.

Accordingly, the present section will be an effort to determine what precisely is meant by the sufficiency of the evidence for a prospective judgment. There is presupposed a question for reflection, Is it so? There follows a judgment, It is so. Between the two there is a marshaling and weighing of evidence. But what are the scales on which evidence is weighed? What weight must evidence have if one is to pronounce a yes or a no?

Unfortunately, the more complex judgments become, the more complex is the analysis of the grounding act of reflective understanding. The whole answer cannot be given at once, and partial answers are incomplete. Hence, we shall begin from a very general statement and then illustrate its meaning from the form of deductive inference. Next, we shall turn to the concrete judgments of everyday life, and consider in turn concrete judgments of fact, judgments on the correctness of insights into concrete situations, and finally the occurrence of analogies and generalizations. In the third place, there will be considered the judgments of empirical science, the radical difference of such judgments from those of ordinary living, the nature of scientific generalization and verification, and what is meant by the probability of scientific opinions. Fourthly, analytic propositions and principles are distinguished and their criteria investigated. Fifthly, the nature of mathematical judgments is considered. Finally, we may add that philosophic judgments are not treated in this chapter, for they can be examined satisfactorily only after further elements in the problem have been set forth.

1   The General Form of Reflective Insight   [280–81]

To grasp evidence as sufficient for a prospective judgment is to grasp the prospective judgment as virtually unconditioned.

Distinguish, then, between the formally and the virtually unconditioned. The formally unconditioned has no conditions whatever. The virtually unconditioned has conditions indeed, but they are fulfilled.

Accordingly, a virtually unconditioned involves three elements, namely, (1) a conditioned, (2) a link between the conditioned and its conditions, and (3) the fulfilment of the conditions. Hence a prospective judgment will be virtually unconditioned if (1) it is the conditioned, (2) its conditions are known, and (3) the conditions are fulfilled. By the mere fact that a question for reflection has been put, the prospective judgment is a conditioned: it stands in need of evidence sufficient for reasonable pronouncement. The function of reflective understanding is to meet the question for reflection by transforming the prospective judgment from the status of a conditioned to the status of a virtually unconditioned; and reflective understanding effects this transformation by grasping the conditions of the conditioned and their fulfilment.

Such is the general scheme, and we proceed to illustrate it from the form of deductive inference. Where A and B each stand for one or more propositions, the deductive form is

If A, then B
But A
Therefore B.

For instance

If X is material and alive, X is mortal
But men are material and alive
Therefore, men are mortal.

Now the conclusion is a conditioned, for an argument is needed to support it. The major premise links this conditioned to its conditions, for it affirms 'If A, then B.' The minor premise presents the fulfilment of the conditions, for it affirms the antecedent A. The function, then, of the form of deductive inference is to exhibit a conclusion as virtually unconditioned. Reflective insight grasps the pattern, and by rational compulsion there follows the judgment.

However, deductive inference cannot be the basic case of judgment, for it presupposes other judgments to be true. For that reason we have said that the form of deductive inference is merely a clear illustration of what is meant by grasping a prospective judgment as virtually unconditioned. Far more general than the form of deductive inference is the form of reflective insight itself. If there is to be a deduction, the link between the conditioned and its conditions must be a judgment, and the fulfilment of the conditions must be a further judgment. But judgments are the final products of cognitional process. Before the link between conditioned and conditions appears in the act of judgment, it existed in a more rudimentary state within cognitional process itself. Before the fulfilment of conditions appears in another act of judgment, it too was present in a more rudimentary state within cognitional process. The remarkable fact about reflective insight is that it can make use of those more rudimentary elements in cognitional process to reach the virtually unconditioned. Let us now see how this is done in various cases.

2   Concrete Judgments of Fact   [281–83]

Suppose a man to return from work to his tidy home and to find the windows smashed, smoke in the air, and water on the floor. Suppose him to make the extremely restrained judgment of fact, 'Something happened.' The question is, not whether he was right, but how he reached his affirmation.

The conditioned will be the judgment that something happened.

The fulfilling conditions will be two sets of data: the remembered data of his home as he left it in the morning; the present data of his home as he finds it in the evening. Observe that the fulfilling conditions are found on the level of presentations. They are not judgments, as is the minor premise of syllogisms. They involve no questions for intelligence nor insights nor concepts. They lie simply on the level of past and present experience, of the occurrence of acts of seeing and smelling.

The link between the conditioned and the fulfilling conditions is a structure immanent and operative within cognitional process. It is not a judgment. It is not a formulated set of concepts, such as a definition. It is simply a way of doing things, a procedure within the cognitional field.

The general form of all such structures and procedures has already been outlined in terms of the three levels of presentations, intelligence, and reflection. Specializations of the general form may be exemplified by the classical and statistical phases of empirical method, by the notion of the thing, and by the differences between description and explanation. However, such accounts of the general form and its specializations pertain to introspective analysis. Prior to such an investigation and formulation, the structures and procedures exist and operate; nor, in general, do they operate any better because the analysis has been effected.

Now in the particular instance under consideration, the weary worker not only experiences present data and recalls different data but by direct insights he refers both sets of data to the same set of things, which he calls his home. The direct insight, however, fulfils a double function. Not merely are two fields of individual data referred to one identical set of things but a second level of cognitional process is added to a first. The two together contain a specific structure of that process, which we may name the notion of knowing change. Just as knowing a thing consists in grasping an intelligible unity-identity-whole in individual data, so knowing change consists in grasping the same identity or identities at different times in different individual data. If the same thing exhibits different individual data at different times, it has changed. If there occurs a change, something has happened. But these are statements. If they are affirmed, they are judgments. But prior to being either statements or judgments, they exist as unanalyzed structures or procedures immanent and operative within cognitional process. It is such a structure that links the conditioned with the fulfilling conditions in the concrete judgment of fact.

The three elements have been assembled. On the level of presentations there are two sets of data. On the level of intelligence there is an insight referring both sets to the same things. When both levels are taken together, there is involved the notion of knowing change. Reflective understanding grasps all three as a virtually unconditioned to ground the judgment 'Something happened.'

While our illustrative instance was as simple as it could be, still it provides the model for the analysis of more complex instances of the concrete judgment of fact. The fulfilling conditions may be any combination of data from the memories of a long life, and their acquisition may have involved exceptional powers of observation. The cognitional structure may suppose the cumulative development of understanding exemplified by the man of experience, the specialist, the expert. Both complex data and a complex structure may combine to yield a virtually unconditioned that introspective analysis could hardly hope to reproduce accurately and convincingly. But the general nature of the concrete judgment of fact would remain the same as in the simple case we considered.

However, the reader is probably asking how we know whether the insights that constitute the pivot of such structures are themselves correct. To this point we have now to turn.

3   Insights into Concrete Situations   [283–87]

Direct and introspective insights arise in response to an inquiring attitude. There are data to be understood; inquiry seeks understanding; and the insight arises as the relevant understanding. But a mere bright idea is one thing, and a correct idea is another. How do we distinguish between the two?

The question is asked, not in its full generality, but with respect to concrete situations that diverge from our expectations and by that divergence set us a problem. Thus, to retain our former illustration, the man on returning home might have said, 'There has been a fire.' Since there no longer was any fire, that judgment would suppose an insight that put two and two together. Our question is on what grounds such an insight could be pronounced correct.

First, then, observe that insights not only arise in answer to questions but also are followed by further questions. Observe, moreover, that such further questions are of two kinds. They may stick to the initial issue, or they may go on to raise distinct issues. 'What started the fire?' 'Where is my wife?' Observe, thirdly, that the transition to distinct issues may result from very different reasons; it may be because different interests supervene to draw attention elsewhere; but it may also be because the initial issue is exhausted, because about it there are no further questions to be asked.

Let us now distinguish between vulnerable and invulnerable insights. Insights are vulnerable when there are further questions to be asked on the same issue. For the further questions lead to further insights that certainly complement the initial insight, that to a greater or less extent modify its expression and implications, that perhaps lead to an entirely new slant on the issue. But when there are no further questions, the insight is invulnerable. For it is only through further questions that there arise the further insights that complement, modify, or revise the initial approach and explanation.

Now this reveals a law immanent and operative in cognitional process. Prior to our conceptual distinction between correct and mistaken insights, there is an operational distinction between invulnerable and vulnerable insights. When an insight meets the issue squarely, when it hits the bull's eye, when it settles the matter, there are no further questions to be asked, and so there are no further insights to challenge the initial position. But when the issue is not met squarely, there are further questions that would reveal the unsatisfactoriness of the insight and would evoke the further insights that put a new light on the matter.

Such, then, is the basic element in our solution. The link between the conditioned and its conditions is a law immanent and operative in cognitional process. The conditioned is the prospective judgment, 'This or that direct or introspective insight is correct.' The immanent law of cognitional process may be formulated from our analysis: Such an insight is correct if there are no further pertinent questions.

At once it follows that the conditions for the prospective judgment are fulfilled when there are no further pertinent questions.

Note that it is not enough to say that the conditions are fulfilled when no further questions occur to me. The mere absence of further questions in my mind can have other causes. My intellectual curiosity may be stifled by other interests. My eagerness to satisfy other drives may refuse the further questions a chance to emerge. To pass judgment in that case is to be rash, to leap before one looks.

As there is rash judgment, so also there is mere indecision. As the mere absence of further questions in my mind is not enough, so it is too much to demand that the very possibility of further questions has to be excluded. If in fact there are no further questions, then in fact the insight is invulnerable; if in fact the insight is invulnerable, then in fact the judgment approving it will be correct.

But how is one to strike this happy balance between rashness and indecision? How is one to know when it is reached? Were there some simple formula or recipe in answer to such questions, then men of good judgment could be produced at will and indefinitely. All we can attempt is an analysis of the main factors in the problem and an outline of the general nature of their solution.

In the first place, then, one has to give the further questions a chance to arise. The seed of intellectual curiosity has to grow into a rugged tree to hold its own against the desires and fears, conations and appetites, drives and interests that inhabit the heart of man. Moreover, every insight has its retinue of presuppositions, implications, and applications. One has to take the steps needed for that retinue to come to light. The presuppositions and implications of a given insight have to knit coherently with the presuppositions and implications of other insights. Its possibilities of concrete application have to enter into the field of operations and undergo the test of success or failure. I do not mean, of course, that concrete living is to pursue this logical and operational expansion in the explicit, deliberate, and elaborate manner of the scientific investigator. But I do mean that something equivalent is to be sought by intellectual alertness, by taking one's time, by talking things over, by putting viewpoints to the test of action.

In the second place, the prior issue is to be noted. Behind the theory of correct insights, there is a theory of correct problems. It was to dodge this prior issue that we supposed a concrete situation that diverges from our expectations and by that divergence defines a problem. In other words, there has been postulated an inquirer that understands the background of the situation and so knows what is to be expected; there also has been postulated a problem that exists, that is accurately defined by the divergence of the situation from current expectations, that in turn provides a definition of the pertinence of any further questions.

Now this amounts to saying that good judgment about any insight has to rest on the previous acquisition of a large number of other, connected, and correct insights. But before attempting to break this vicious circle, let us assure ourselves of the fact of its existence. Children ask endless questions; we have no doubt about their intellectual curiosity; but so far from crediting them with good judgment, we do not suppose them to reach the age of reason before their seventh year. Young men and women have the alertness of mind that justifies their crowding into schools and universities, but the law doubts the soundness of their judgment and regards them as minors, while Aristotle denied they had enough experience to study ethics with profit.[1] Nor is there merely the initial difficulty of acquisition, but as well there is the subsequent necessity of keeping in touch. The man that returns to a field of commerce or industry, to a profession or a milieu in which once he was completely at home may try to carry on from where he left off. But unless from mistakes and minor ineptitudes he learns to be more wary, he is merely inviting blunders and disaster. Good judgment about concrete insights presupposes the prior acquisition of an organized set of complementary insights.

In the third place, then, there is the process of learning. It is the gradual acquisition and accumulation of insights bearing on a single domain. During that process one's own judgment is in abeyance. It is being developed and formed but it has not yet reached the maturity needed for its independent exercise. For the gradual acquisition and accumulation of insights are not merely a matter of advancing in direct or introspective understanding. At the same time, intellectual curiosity is asserting itself against other desires. At the same time, the logical retinues of presuppositions and implications of each insight are being expanded, either to conflict and provoke further questions or else to mesh into coherence. At the same time, operational possibilities are envisaged, to be tested in thought experiments, to be contrasted with actual practice, to be executed in ventures that gradually increase in moment and scope to enlighten us by failures and to generate confidence through success.

So it is the process of learning that breaks the vicious circle. Judgment on the correctness of insights supposes the prior acquisition of a large number of correct insights. But the prior insights are not correct because we judge them to be correct. They occur within a self-correcting process in which the shortcomings of each insight provoke further questions to yield complementary insights. Moreover, this self-correcting process tends to a limit. We become familiar with concrete situations; we know what to expect; when the unexpected occurs, we can spot just what

1 [Aristotle, *Ethics*, I, 3, 1095a 2–12.]

happened and why, and what can be done to favor or to prevent such a recurrence; or, if the unexpected is quite novel, we know enough to recommence the process of learning, and we can recognize when, once more, that self-correcting process reaches its limit in familiarity with the concrete situation and in easy mastery of it.

In the fourth place, rashness and indecision commonly have a basis in temperament. Apart from occasional outbursts, that we view as out of character, the rash man nearly always is quite sure, and the indecisive man regularly is unable to make up his mind. In such cases it is not enough to point out that learning is a self-correcting process that tends to a limit or that, while the limit is not marked with a label, still its attainment is revealed by a habitual ability to know just what is up. For unless a special effort is made to cope with temperament itself, the rash man continues to presume too quickly that he has nothing more to learn, and the indecisive man continues to suspect that deeper depths of shadowy possibilities threaten to invalidate what he knows quite well.

Finally, we note that we leave to another occasion a discussion of the philosophic opinions that no one ever can be certain. Our immediate purpose is to explain the facts. Human judgments and refusals to judge oscillate about a central mean. If the precise locus of that divide can hardly be defined, at least there are many points on which even the rash would not venture to pronounce and many others on which even the indecisive would not doubt. What, then, is the general form of such certitude of ignorance and such certitude of knowledge?

Our answer is in terms of the virtually unconditioned. There occurs a reflective insight in which at once one grasps (1) a conditioned, the prospective judgment that a given direct or introspective insight is correct, (2) a link between the conditioned and its conditions, and this on introspective analysis proves to be that an insight is correct if it is invulnerable and it is invulnerable if there are no further pertinent questions, and (3) the fulfilment of the conditions, namely, that the given insight does put an end to further pertinent questioning and that this occurs in a mind that is alert, familiar with the concrete situation, and intellectually master of it.

4   Concrete Analogies and Generalizations   [287–89]

Two brief corollaries have to be drawn.

An argument from analogy assumes that some concrete situation A is correctly understood. It argues that some other similar situation B is to be understood in the same fashion.

A generalization makes the same assumption, to argue that any other similar situation X is to be understood in the same fashion.

In both cases what is at work is the law, immanent and operative in cognitional process, that similars are similarly understood. Unless there is a significant difference in the data, there cannot be a difference in understanding the data. This point has already been made in discussing the heuristic procedure of the classical phase of empirical method. Clearly enough, it holds not merely for regularities, rules, laws, correlations, but also for ideal frequencies and for things. A second look does not necessarily mean one is looking at a second thing. A second actual frequency does not necessarily mean that one will establish a second ideal frequency. If there is to be a second thing or a second ideal frequency, an appropriate difference in the data has to be supposed.

In the simplest possible manner, then, our analysis resolves the so-called problem of induction. It makes the transition from one particular case to another, or from a particular case to the general case, an almost automatic procedure of intelligence. We appeal to analogies and we generalize because we cannot help understanding similars similarly. This solution, be it noted, squares with the broad fact that there is no problem of teaching men to generalize. There is a problem of teaching them to frame their generalizations accurately; indeed, the whole point of the analogy is that it absolves one from that conceptual task and the complexities it involves. There is, above all, a problem of preventing men from generalizing on insufficient grounds, and very easily such grounds are merely putative.

For if our view makes generalization an easy matter, it also clips the generalizer's wings. There must be a correct insight with respect to the basic situation. Before similars can be similarly understood, there is needed an act of understanding; and if that act is mistaken in the first instance, it will be equally mistaken in the second. But, as we have seen, to know one's insights are correct presupposes a process of learning and the attainment of familiarity and mastery. Further, the analogous or the general situation must be similar. If there is any significant dissimilarity, then further pertinent questions arise, to complement, to modify, perhaps to revise, the basic insight. Finally – and this is the real catch – what differences are significant? My familiarity and mastery of the initial situation enables me to tell whether further questions there are pertinent. Another's familiarity and mastery of the analogous situation would enable him to tell whether further questions are pertinent in that situation. But unless the two situations are similar in all respects, my familiarity with one does not enable me to tell whether or not further questions arise when my insight is transferred to the other.

To conclude, analogy and generalization are essentially valid procedures, but when their basis is an insight into a concrete situation, the conditions of their proper use can become so stringent as to render them almost useless. It is this fact that grounds the suspicion with which men greet arguments from analogy and generalizations. But at the same time, there is a compensating factor that arises from human collaboration in the process of learning. To this we have now to turn our attention.

5   Commonsense Judgments   [289–99]

Common sense is that vague name given to the unknown source of a large and floating population of elementary judgments which everyone makes, everyone relies on, and almost everyone regards as obvious and indisputable. Though some repetition will be involved,[a] three points, I think, call for our attention: (1) the source of these judgments, (2) their proper object or field, and (3) their relation to empirical science.

5.1 The Source of Commonsense Judgments   [289–91]

The proximate ground and source of commonsense judgments lies in the procedures just described of concrete judgments of fact, judgments on the correctness of insights into concrete situations, and concrete analogies and generalizations. The remote source is more complex. One has to envisage these procedures carried out, not by isolated individuals, but by members of families, of tribes, of nations, over the face of the earth for generation after generation. One has to take into account the diffusion of judgments by communication and their transmission by tradition. Finally, one has to note that there results not merely an enlargement but also a unification and transformation of the self-correcting process of learning.

If I may repeat myself, besides the hard way of finding things out for oneself, there is the comparatively easy way of learning from others. Archimedes had to rack his brains to discover what every schoolboy can be taught. For teaching is a vast acceleration of the process of learning. It throws out the clues, the pointed hints, that lead to insights; it cajoles attention to remove the distracting images that obstruct them; it puts the further questions that reveal the need of further insights to complement and modify and transform the acquired store; it grasps the seriation of acts of understanding to begin from the simple and work towards the more complex. But what is done explicitly and deliberately by professional teachers also is done implicitly and unconsciously by parents with their children and by equals among themselves. Talking is a basic human art; by it each reveals what he knows and provokes from others the further questions that direct his attention to what he had overlooked. More general and more impressive than talking is doing: deeds excite our admiration and stir us to emulation; we watch to see how things are done; we experiment to see if we can do them ourselves; we watch again to discover the oversights that led to our failures. Thus it is that what anyone discovers passes into the possession of many, to be checked against their experience and to be confronted with the test of their further questions. Thus too it is that the discoveries of different individuals enter into single, cumulative series; that the later presuppose and improve upon the earlier; and that the starting point of each generation is where its predecessor left off.

The remote source, then, of commonsense judgments is a collaboration. The self-correcting process of learning goes on in the minds of individuals, but the individual minds are in communication. The results reached by one are checked by many, and new results are added to old, to form a common fund from which each draws his variable share measured by his interests and his energy.

There is another side to the story. It is human to err, and commonsense judgments are very human. They rest upon the self-correcting process of learning as transformed by communication and collaboration. But men share not only in intellectual curiosity but also in more earthy passions and prejudices. The mixed character of human drives can generate a common deviation from the pure product of intelligence and even a common dishonesty in refusing to acknowledge the effective pertinence of further pertinent questions. So it is that we find each tribe and nation, each group and class, prone to develop its own brand of common sense and to strengthen its convictions by pouring ridicule upon the common nonsense of others. From the contradictory varieties of common sense, men have appealed to the common consent of the human race. But one may well doubt that such a procedure goes quite to the root of the matter. If one must suspect the collaboration of groups and classes, of tribes and nations, it does not follow that one cannot suspect the collaboration of mankind. Error is not primarily a class product or a national product. It is human. The group or class, the tribe or nation only gives a more specific twist to the mixed motives of human effort. Undertake to select the judgments on which all men agree, and you have no guarantee either that when all men agree they will do so from the pure and detached motives of intelligence and reason, or indeed that you yourself in your investigation and selection have operated exclusively from that unmixed drive.

The collaboration named common sense not only offers enormous benefits and advantages but it also intertwines them with more than a danger of deviation and aberration. Nor do we ourselves stand outside this collaboration as spectators. We were born into it. We had no choice but to become participants, to profit by its benefits, and to share in its errors. We have no choice about withdrawing from it, for the past development of one's own intellect can no more easily be blotted out than the past growth of one's body, and future development will have to take place under essentially the same conditions and limitations as that of the past. There is, then, a fundamental problem, and how it is to be met we cannot discuss at once. Our immediate objective has to be confined to discerning the field or domain within which common sense might be expected to operate successfully. This brings us to our second topic.

5.2 The Object of Commonsense Judgments [291–93]

Already a distinction has been drawn between description and explanation. Description deals with things as related to us. Explanation deals with the same things as related among themselves. The two are not totally independent, for they deal with the same things, and as we have seen, description supplies, as it were, the tweezers by which we hold things while explanations are being discovered or verified, applied or revised. But despite their intimate connection, it remains that description and explanation envisage things in fundamentally different manners. The relations of things among themselves are, in general, a different field from the relations of things to us. There is an apparent overlapping only when we consider the relations of men among themselves; and then the different procedures of description and explanation prevent the overlapping from being more than apparent, for description is in terms of the given while explanation is in terms of the ultimates reached by analysis.

Not only are description and explanation distinct, but there are two main varieties of description. There are the ordinary descriptions that can be cast in ordinary language. There are also scientific descriptions for which ordinary language quickly proves inadequate and so is forced to yield its place to a special technical terminology. Nor is it difficult to discern behind these linguistic differences a more fundamental difference. Both ordinary and scientific description are concerned with things as related to us, but both are not concerned with the same relations to us. The scientist selects the relations of things to us that lead more directly to knowledge of the relations between things themselves. Ordinary description is free from this ulterior preoccupation. As it begins, so also it ends with human apprehensions and interests as its center.

There exists, then, a determinate field or domain of ordinary description. Its defining or formal viewpoint is the thing as related to us, as it enters into the concerns of man. Its object is what is to be known by concrete judgments of fact, by judgments on the correctness of insights into concrete situations, by concrete analogies and generalizations, and by the collaboration of common sense. It is as much an object of knowledge as any other, for it is reached by beginning from the level of presentations, by advancing through inquiry, insights, and formulation, by culminating in the critical inquiry of reflective understanding, the grasp of the unconditioned, and the rationally compelled pronouncement of judgment. To anticipate a later vocabulary, the domain of ordinary description is a section of the universe of being, of what intelligently is grasped and reasonably is affirmed. How much of that section really is reached by ordinary description is of course a further question. At least it is something to know the goal at which it aims, and that has been our restricted topic.

But before going on to our third topic, it may be well to preclude possible misconceptions. First, then, the human collaboration that results in a common sense involves belief. The analysis of belief cannot as yet be undertaken. But the type of belief that is essential in this collaboration resembles that of the pupil, who believes his teacher only that later he himself may understand and be able to judge for himself. It resembles that of the scientist, who does not insist on exploring for himself all the blind alleys down which his predecessors wandered but is content to test their final results either directly by repeating experiments, or more commonly by operating on the principle that, if those results were erroneous, the error would be revealed indirectly in the experiments he himself does perform. Hence it is that a man pronouncing a common-sense judgment is convinced that he is uttering, not what someone else told him, but what he himself knows.

Secondly, the human collaboration that results in a common sense is under the dominance of practical considerations and pragmatic sanctions. The further questions that arise and are considered pertinent do not come from any theoretical realm, and the tests that are employed move within the orbit of human success and failure. Still that dominance, so far from vitiating the results, is dictated by the object to be known, by the thing as it is related to us and as it enters into the concerns of men. It was a philosophic school that invented the notion that ideas are true because they happen to work. Despite its practicality, common sense is convinced that ideas work only if they are true. Nor is this surprising, for the practical further question is a further question that leads to the modification or revision of an insight; and the pragmatic criterion of success is the absence of the failure that would reveal the necessity of thinking things out afresh.

Thirdly, the human collaboration that results in a common sense is subject to the deviations and aberrations that have their root in the mixed motives of man. But it is only insofar as I myself share in those mixed motives that my understanding and my judgment will suffer the same bias and fall in line with the same deviations and aberrations. As long as I share in them, my efforts at correction and selection will be just as suspect as the judgments I wish to eliminate. It is only when I go to the root of the matter and become efficaciously critical of myself that I can begin to become a reliable judge; and then that becoming will consist in the self-correcting process of learning which has already been described.

5.3 Commonsense Judgment and Empirical Science   [293–99]

Our third main topic was the relation of common sense to science, and our fundamental assertion is that the two regard distinct and separate fields. Common sense is concerned with things as related to us. Science is concerned with things as related among themselves. In principle, they cannot conflict, for if they speak about the same things, they do so from radically different viewpoints.

When I say that in principle they cannot conflict, I mean of course that in fact they can and do. To eliminate actual conflict, it is necessary to grasp the principle and to apply it accurately.

The basic difficulty has been to grasp the principle. The scientists of the Renaissance were quite aware that there was some difference in principle, but they expressed it by a distinction between primary and secondary qualities. Science is concerned with things and their primary qualities, that is, with things as they really are. Common sense is concerned with things, with their primary qualities, and most of all with their secondary qualities, that is, mainly with things as they merely appear. On this showing, knowledge is science, and where common sense diverges from science, partly it is the darkness of ignorance and error, partly it is the twilight soon to be replaced by a scientific dawn. Naturally enough such exclusive pretensions were met by opposite pretensions equally exclusive, and the debate raged on a mistaken issue. Today, I think, we can be not only cooler but also wiser about the whole matter. As has been argued in earlier chapters, it is necessary to distinguish within knowledge between separate yet complementary domains. There is a comprehensive, universal, invariant, nonimaginable domain; its object is the thing-itself, with differences in kind defined by explanatory conjugates, and with differences in state defined by ideal frequencies. There is also an experiential, particular, relative, imaginable domain; its object is the thing-for-us, with differences in kind defined by experiential conjugates,[b] and with differences in state defined by expectations of the normal. The former field, of empirical science, is to be reached only by abstracting from the empirical residue. The latter field includes the empirical residue; it views things in their individuality, their accidental determinations, their arbitrariness, their continuity.

The significance of this distinction appears in logic as the separation of two universes of discourse. To put the matter concretely, let us take illustrative propositions and consider the three cases of (1) ignoring the distinction of the domains, (2) denying the distinction of the domains, and (3) accepting the distinction of the domains.

First, if one ignores the distinction of the domains, then one has the problem of choosing between the propositions

The planets move in approximately elliptical orbits with the sun at their focus.
The earth is at rest, and the sun rises and sets.

Secondly, if one denies the distinction of the domains, one is committed to the more rigorous choice between the propositions

> From every viewpoint, the planets move in elliptical orbits with the sun at their focus.
> From every viewpoint, the earth is at rest and the sun rises and sets.

Thirdly, if one affirms the distinction of the domains, then one will reject all four of the preceding propositions to assert both of the following:

> From the viewpoint of explanation, the planets move in approximately elliptical orbits with the sun at their focus.
> From the viewpoint of ordinary description, the earth is at rest and the sun rises and sets.

On this third position there result two separate universes of discourse. All the affirmations of empirical science contain the qualifying reservation 'from the viewpoint of explanation.' Similarly, all the affirmations of common sense contain the qualifying reservation 'from the viewpoint of ordinary description.' Automatically, all logical conflict is eliminated, for the qualifying reservations prevent the propositions of one universe from contradicting the propositions of the other.

Underlying this logical separation there will be more fundamental methodological differences. Both ordinary description and empirical science reach their conclusions through the self-correcting process of learning. Still, they reach very different conclusions because, though they use essentially the same process, they operate with different standards and criteria. What is a further pertinent question for empirical science is not necessarily a further pertinent question for ordinary description. Inversely, what is a further pertinent question for ordinary description is not necessarily a further pertinent question for empirical science. It is this fundamental difference in the criterion of the relevance of further questions that marks the great divide between a scientific attitude and a commonsense attitude. Because he aims at ultimate explanation, the scientist has to keep asking why until ultimate explanation is reached. Because the layman aims at knowing things as related to us, as entering into the domain of human concerns, his questioning ceases as soon as further inquiry would lead to no immediate appreciable difference in the daily life of man. Hence it is that the layman is attempting to impose his criteria on the scientist when he asks him what he is doing and follows that up with the further question, What is the good of it? For if the practical question can be put to engineers and technologists and medical doctors, its only effect upon pure science would be to eliminate all further progress. Inversely, the pure scientist is attempting to impose his criteria upon common sense when he interprets a practical attitude as a lack of interest in truth; it is, indeed, a lack of interest in the truth that the scientist seeks, but that is not the sole domain in which truth is to be learned. Reflective understanding can reach the virtually unconditioned, to pronounce correct judgments of concrete fact and to discern correct insights into concrete situations. Without those basic judgments, science has no starting point, and equally, the glorious achievements of applied science cannot be truly affirmed.

The difference of the domains appears not only in different criteria of the pertinence of further questions but also in the difference of the terms employed and in the possibilities they respectively offer for logical deduction. Because ordinary description is concerned with things-for-us, it derives its terms from everyday experience; because the elements of daily experience are constant, the terms of ordinary description are constant; visible shapes and the spectrum of colors, the volume, pitch, and tone of sounds, the hot and cold, wet and dry, hard and soft, slow and swift, now and then, here and there do not shift in meaning with the successive revisions of scientific theories; the concrete unities that are men and animals and plants, the regularities of nature and the expectations of a normal course of events form a necessary and unchanged basis and context into which applied science introduces its improvements.

Inversely, because science seeks knowledge of the things as related among themselves, because such relations lie outside our immediate experience, because the ultimates in such relations are to be reached only when ultimate explanation is reached, each great forward step of scientific knowledge involves a more or less profound revision of its fundamental terms. Again, because science is analytic and abstractive, its terms are exact; because its correlations purport to be generally valid, they must be determined with utmost precision; because its terms are exact and its correlations general, it must be ready to bear the weight of a vast superstructure of logical deductions in which each conclusion must be equally exact and valid generally.

On the other hand, as we have seen, ordinary description must be perpetually on its guard against analogies and generalizations; for, though similars are similarly understood, still concrete situations rarely are similar, and the synthesis of an aggregate of concrete situations is not itself a concrete situation. Because things fall away from the polestar in the northern hemisphere, it does not follow that they will do so in the southern. Because within the range of human vision the earth is approximately flat, it does not follow that the integration of all such views will be a flat surface. The procedure of sound common sense is, not to generalize nor to argue from analogy, but to retain the insights gained in former experience and to add the complementary insights needed in fresh situations. The collaboration of common sense aims, not at establishing general truths, but at building up a core of habitual understanding that is to be adjusted by further learning in each new situation that arises.

Common sense, then, has its own specialized field or domain. It has its own criteria on the relevance of further questions. It has its own basically constant vocabulary, its proper universe of discourse, and its own methodological precepts of keeping to the concrete, of speaking in human terms, of avoiding analogies and generalizations and deductions, of acknowledging that it does not know the abstract, the universal, the ultimate. Precisely because it is so confined, common sense cannot explicitly formulate its own nature, its own domain, its own logic and methodology. These it has to learn, if it would limit properly its pronouncements, but it has to learn them in its own shrewd fashion through instances and examples, fables and lessons, paradigms and proverbs, that will function in future judgments not as premises for deductions but as possibly relevant rules of procedure. Finally, because common sense has to be acquired, it is not possessed equally by all. It has its adept pupils who make mistakes, indeed, but also learn by them. Within their familiar field they are masters, and as well they know that their mastery ends when they step beyond its limits. Above all they know that they must master their own hearts, that the pull of desire, the push of fear, the deeper currents of passion are poor counselors, for they rob a man of that full, untroubled, unhurried view demanded by sure and balanced judgment.

If the domains of science and common sense are distinct, so also they are complementary. If one must recognize the differences in their objects, their criteria, their universes of discourse, their methodological precepts, one must also insist that they àre the functionally related parts within a single knowledge of a single world. The intelligibility that science grasps comprehensively is the intelligibility of the concrete with which common sense deals effectively. To regard them as rivals or competitors is a mistake, for essentially they are partners, and it is their successful cooperation that constitutes applied science and technology, that adds inventions to scientific discoveries, that supplements inventions with organizations, knowhow, and specialized skills.

But if common sense itself, once it is supplied with its appropriate evidence, has little difficulty in recognizing this fact, theorists of science can hardly be credited with an equal perspicacity. Misled by a confusion between the heuristic and the representative functions of imagination, they assumed that the business of science was to paint a picture of the really real. If, as we have argued, such a picture is essentially unverifiable and gratuitous, it cannot coincide with the verifiable pictures of common sense. If from this conflict the theorists of science proceeded to conclude that common sense must be some brutish survival, that it was in need of being instructed in lofty tones on the far superior virtues and techniques of the scientist, one cannot be surprised that common sense retaliated with its jokes on the ineptitude of the theorists and professors and with its quietly imperious demand that, if they were to justify their existence, they had best continue to provide palpable evidence of their usefulness. But such opposition, I would contend, does justice neither to common sense nor to science; it has no better basis than a mistaken theory; and it had best be written off as an error incidental to an age of transition. During the past four centuries, empirical science has emerged and developed, to set us the twofold problem both of determining its nature and of working out the proper adjustment of the complementary functions of common sense. If such large problems cannot be solved in short order, one should not infer that they cannot be solved at all.

To conclude, common sense is one thing and commonsense judgments are another. Common sense is common and specific. It is a specialized domain of knowledge with a proper universe of discourse, proper criteria on the pertinence of further questions, and proper methodological precepts. Operation within that domain is basically and fundamentally a communal collaboration in the self-correcting process of learning. The fruit of that collaboration is a habitual core of accumulated insights into concrete situations and into the procedures needed to complement and adjust that core before one can pass judgment on further concrete situations. Hence it is that commonsense judgments are issued, not by some public authority named common sense, but only by individual judges in their own individual situations. Further, they can be known to be correct only by the individual judges in the individual situations, for no one else is in possession of the evidence as it is given, and no one else is informed with the familiarity and mastery that result from the self-correcting process of learning within that situation. I can be certain that I am writing this, and you can be certain that you are reading it. But it is quite another matter for you to be certain that I am correct in affirming that I am writing, as it will be quite another matter for me to be certain that you are correct in affirming that you are reading. The common element in common sense is not some list of general truths about which all men can agree; it is not some list of particular truths about which all men can agree; but it is a collaboration in the erection of a basic structure by which, with appropriate adjustments, each individual is enabled to fill out his individual list of particular truths. Finally, each of those particular pronouncements occurs inasmuch as reflective understanding grasps the virtually unconditioned in the manner described in the sections on concrete judgments of fact and on judgments on the correctness of insights into concrete situations.

6   Probable Judgments   [299–304]

When the virtually unconditioned is grasped by reflective understanding, we affirm or deny absolutely. When there is no preponderance of evidence in favor of either affirmation or denial, we can only acknowledge our ignorance. But between these extremes there is a series of intermediate positions, and probable judgments are their outcome.

This probability of judgment differs from the probability investigated in studying statistical method. As has been seen, the probable expectation answers a question for intelligence by assigning an ideal frequency from which actual events nonsystematically diverge. But the probable judgment answers a question for reflection, and though it anticipates a divergence between the judgment and actual fact, still the ground of this anticipation lies, not in a nonsystematic element in the facts, but in the incompleteness of our knowledge. Hence judgments about things, about correlations, and about probability expectations may be certain and may be only probable.

Probable judgments differ from guesses. In both cases knowledge is incomplete. In both cases reflective understanding fails to reach the virtually unconditioned. But the guess is a nonrational venture beyond the evidence that resembles the nonsystematic aspect of events. On the other hand, the probable judgment results from rational procedures. Though it rests on incomplete knowledge, still there has to be some approximation towards completeness. Though it fails to reach the virtually unconditioned, still it has to be closing in upon that exigent norm. Thus one may say that guesses are probably true only in the statistical sense of diverging nonsystematically from true judgments, but probable judgments are probably true in the nonstatistical sense of converging upon true judgments, of approaching them as a limit.

It is the nature of this approximation, approach, convergence that constitutes the problem of the probable judgment. What precisely can be meant by such metaphors? If anything is meant, then how can it be known? No one, surely, makes a probable judgment when he can make a certain judgment; yet how can the probable be known to approach the certain when the certain is unknown?

Fortunately, such paradox is not as acute as it may seem. We seek the truth because we do not know it. But though we do not know it, still we can recognize it when we reach it. In like manner we also are able to recognize when we are getting near it. As we have seen, the self-correcting process of learning consists in a sequence of questions, insights, further questions, and further insights that moves towards a limit in which no further pertinent questions arise. When we are well beyond that limit, judgments are obviously certain. When we are well short of that limit, judgments are at best probable. When we are on the borderline, the rash are completely certain and the indecisive full of doubts. In brief, because the self-correcting process of learning is an approach to a limit of no further pertinent questions, there are probable judgments that are probably true in the sense that they approximate to a truth that as yet is not known.

Directly, the foregoing analysis regards the probability of judgments on the correctness of insights into concrete situations. Indirectly, it can be extended to all other probable judgments. Thus, concrete judgments of fact involve some insight that links the level of presentations with the question for reflection, and so the probability of such concrete judgments may be reduced to the probability of the correctness of the insight they involve. Did something happen? Something did happen if the same set of things exhibits different data at different times. An insight is required to grasp the identity of the things, and such an identification may be certain or probable. But the data exhibited at different times either differ or do not differ. If no difference is detected, there is no ground whatever for asserting change. If any difference is detected, there are the grounds for asserting change. If you do not remember accurately the former data, then you just do not know whether or not there was a change. If you are inclined to think that the former data were different, then the issue shifts. What inclines you to think so? Any reason that can be offered will suppose some insight into the objective course of events or into the habits of your memory, and it is that insight that gives rise to probability. More complex cases call for a more complex analysis, but the general lines of the analysis will be the same.

This brings us to the probability of the empirical sciences. Two questions arise: Why are their conclusions no more than probable? In what sense are their conclusions an approximation to what is true and certain? Discussion of analytic propositions is deferred to the next section, and so we have to consider the empirical sciences in their generalizations and in their particular judgments of fact.

Since similars cannot but be similarly understood, generalization itself offers no difficulty. If the particular case is understood correctly, then every similar case will be understood correctly. If the problem of induction arose because the rest of the particular cases were not inspected, then that problem would be insoluble because the rest of the particular cases never are inspected; were they, there would be no generalization. In fact, the problem of induction arises because the particular case may not be properly understood; and it is solved by seeking that correct understanding.

Still, seeking is one thing and finding another. Empirical science gets its start by hitting off significant correlations. The correlations implicitly define abstract correlatives. But precisely because they are abstract, the return to the concrete is greeted with further questions. The law of the lever is simplicity itself. But to have an independent measurement of weights, one needs the law of the spring. To test the law accurately, one needs the theorem on centers of gravity. To formulate the law, one needs the geometry of perpendiculars. Automatically one has embarked upon a vectorial representation of forces, an assumption of Euclidean geometry, a theory of the application of forces at a point, a parallel investigation of the tension of wires, and a certain amount of dabbling with gravitation. Further questions arise. Not only do they arise from the concrete problems set by tension and gravitation. What is far more significant is the presence of the highly abstract theorems and procedures. Can every force be represented by a vector? Are all forces applied at a point? Did Euclid have the last word? The initial abstraction allows one to return to the concrete only after the exploration of successively widening circles of inquiry. Statics is mastered only to raise the problems of kinetics. Kinetics is mastered only to reveal that thermal and electromagnetic phenomena may be the antecedents or the consequents of local movements. One begins to get the lot in line and to feel that the future of physics is a matter of determining accurately a few more decimal points when along come a Planck and an Einstein with their further questions.

The generalization of classical laws, then, is no more than probable because the application of single laws raises further questions that head towards the systematization of a whole field. In turn, such systematization is no more than probable until the limit of no further pertinent questions is reached. But that limit is not reached, first, if there may be further, unknown facts that would raise further questions to force a revision, or secondly, if there may be further, known facts whose capacity to raise such further questions is not grasped.

Similar considerations render the generalization of statistical laws no more than probable. For statistical laws presuppose some classification of events. One is not going to advance quantum theory by investigating baseball averages. Hence definitive statistical laws suppose definitive classifications. The future discovery of new kinds or of new subdivisions of subatomic elements will invite a revision of the statistical laws. Similarly, more accurate investigations may lead to the discernment within the statistical law of a systematic element that can be abstracted in classical form to leave a new statistical residue.

If empirical generalizations are no more than probable, what about the particular facts that ground them? Here a distinction seems necessary. Insofar as such facts are expressed in the terms of ordinary description, they fall under the criteria of the concrete judgment of fact. Insofar as they are relevant to the establishment[c] of a scientific theory, they come under the control of empirical method. What has to be observed is, not the percept with its spontaneous integration into the processes of sensitive living, but the sheer datum that is stripped of non-scientific memories, associations, and anticipations. Again, measurements must conform to the best available rules and utilize the best available instruments. Finally, the observables have to be the terms defined by the theoretical structure, and as this structure is subject to revision, so also are its definitions. Hence one may say that empirical science is solidly grounded in fact in virtue of its concrete judgments, and at the same time one may add that technical developments and theoretical advance can render such facts more or less obsolescent.

But if empirical science is no more than probable, still it truly is probable. If it does not attain definitive truth, still it converges upon truth. This convergence, this increasing approximation, is what is meant by the familiar phrase 'the advance of science.' Questions yield insights that are expressed in hypotheses; the testing of hypotheses raises further questions that generate complementary insights and more satisfactory hypotheses. For a while the process advances in widening circles; then the coherence of system begins to close in; investigation turns from fresh ventures in new fields to the labor of consolidation, of working out implications fully, of settling issues that leave the general view unchanged. The self-correcting process of learning is palpably approaching a limit.

An ulterior question may be raised. Is scientific progress indefinite? Does the self-correcting process of learning reach one limit only to discover, sooner or later, that there are further developments to be effected? If I am unable to answer this question directly, still certain observations seem relevant.

First, the advance of science through increasing accuracy would seem to head towards a limit. A measurement is not a point but an interval, not simply a number but a number plus or minus some quantity determined by a theory of errors. Hence increasing accuracy has to result from the invention of new techniques and instruments, and while such inventions may go well beyond our present anticipations, still we have no reason to expect an infinite series of them. Once such possibilities become exhausted, the canon of selection[d] comes into play. Empirical method settles only the theoretical differences that imply sensible differences. If a second theory supplants a first by advancing from the second decimal place to the fourth, and a third supplants the second by advancing from the fourth decimal place to the sixth, it does not follow that there can be some nth theory established by advancing from $2n$ decimals to $(2n + 2)$, where n is as large a number as you please.

Secondly, as the advance of science has a lower limit in the field of presentations, so also it has an upper limit in the basic structure of the human mind. Theories can be revised if there is a reviser. But to talk about revising the revisers is to enter a field of empty speculation in which the name 'revision' loses its determinate meaning. Moreover, theorists take advantage of this fact. Thus, the foundations of logic are placed in the inevitabilities of our processes of thought. Nor is logic a unique example. As we have already indicated, the theory of relativity in its basic postulate rests upon a structural feature of our cognitional process. Now if the invariants governing mental process imply invariants in our theoretical constructions, there will follow an upper limit to the variation of theoretical constructions and a possibility of mapping out in advance the alternatives between which theoretical effort has to choose. To this topic we return in investigating what will be named the elements or categories[e] of the range of proportionate being.

In conclusion, it may be noted that these considerations confirm the positive probability of the conclusions of empirical science. For those conclusions are probable inasmuch as the self-correcting process of learning is approaching a limit. Our argument was based upon the immanent tendency of the process itself to a limit, inasmuch as each great stage of scientific development heads for the closed coherence of system, and each successive system grips the facts with greater nuance and accuracy over wider expanses of data. Still, this immanent tendency receives confirmation if there exist external limitations to the process itself. For they too point to the possibility of some system, as yet unknown, that increasingly is determined inasmuch as it will have to meet the requirement of verification in a body of fact that is increasingly large and increasingly organized.

7   Analytic Propositions and Principles   [304–309]

A proposition[f] is what is proposed either for consideration or for affirmation. An analysis of propositions is reached by distinguishing what is meant from acts of meaning and from sources of meaning. Any cognitional activity is a source of meaning.[g] Conceiving, judging, and uttering are three quite different acts of meaning. Finally, as sources lead to acts, so acts refer to terms of meaning, to what is meant.

Terms of meaning may be divided in two ways. There is the basic distinction between what is meant when one affirms or denies, and on the other hand, what is meant when one merely considers, supposes, defines. Again, in utterances there is the obvious distinction between the incomplete meaning of a word and the complete meaning of a sentence. So one is led to distinguish (1) partial terms of meaning, (2) rules of meaning, (3) formal terms of meaning, and (4) full terms of meaning.

The full term of meaning is what is affirmed or denied.

The formal term of meaning is what could be affirmed or denied but in fact is merely supposed or considered.

The partial term of meaning is what is meant by a word or by a phrase.

Rules of meaning govern the coalescence of words and phrases into the complete sense that may be supposed or considered, affirmed or denied.

There results at once a particular case of the virtually unconditioned. A formal term of meaning provides the conditioned. The definitions of its partial terms provide the fulfilling conditions. And the rules of meaning provide the link between the conditions and the conditioned. Such propositions are termed analytic.

Thus, if A is defined by a relation R to B, and B is defined by the converse relation R' to A, then by the rules of meaning it follows that there cannot be an A without the relation R to B, and that there cannot be a B without the relation R' to A. Such conclusions resting on definitions and rules of meaning are analytic propositions.

Now, since the analytic proposition is an instance of the virtually unconditioned, reflective understanding will find in it its proper object and thereby ground a judgment. There then arises a further question, What precisely is the meaning or force or implication of such a judgment?

It would seem that its meaning is not assertoric but hypothetical. If there occur suppositions or judgments containing significant terms in the same sense as they are assigned in the analytic proposition, then such suppositions or judgments must be consistent with the analytic proposition; moreover, when that condition and other logical requirements are met, there follow valid inferences. On the other hand, the mere fact that a proposition is analytic offers no guarantee that its terms in their defined sense occur in any supposition or judgment apart from the affirmation of the analytic proposition.

It follows that analytic propositions remain in sterile isolation unless there accrues to them some form of validation. This will consist in the occurrence of the same terms in their defined sense in some other supposition or judgment; and the precise nature of the validation will depend upon the nature of the added supposition or judgment.

There also follows the explanation of the fact that analytic propositions can be produced more or less at will and indefinitely. Partial terms of meaning are a vast multitude, and further partial terms can be supplied by the art of definition. Rules of meaning provide a principle of selection of the partial terms that will coalesce into analytic propositions. And if this seems to require too much ingenuity, the task can be simplified by using symbols instead of words and by defining them by their relations in propositions. But significant increments of knowledge are not to be obtained by mere ingenuity, and in fact the analytic proposition, by itself, is not a significant increment of knowledge; without the fulfilment of further conditions it remains in isolation and fails to enter fruitfully into the texture of knowing.

Hence we are in substantial agreement with the contemporary view that mere analytic propositions are tautologies. The use of the term 'tautology' would seem to be incorrect, but the general meaning of the statement is sound. However, it may not be out of place to add that the present point was made centuries ago. Aquinas advanced that conclusions depend upon principles and that principles depend upon their terms; but he was not ready to accept any terms whatever; he added that proper terms are selected by wisdom,[2] and by wisdom he meant an accumulation of insights that stands to the universe as common sense stands to the domain of the particular, incidental, relative, and imaginable.

Let us now turn from analytic propositions to analytic principles.

By an analytic principle is meant an analytic proposition of which the partial terms are existential; further, the partial terms of an analytic proposition are existential if they occur in their defined sense in judgments of fact, such as the concrete judgment of fact or the definitively established empirical generalization.

Further, since such analytic principles are hard to come by, we shall also speak of two mitigated cases.

The provisional analytic principle is an analytic proposition of which the terms are probably existential, that is, they occur in probable empirical generalizations.

The serially analytic principle is an analytic proposition of which the terms are serially existential; what is meant by the serially existential will be clarified in our next section on mathematical judgments.

It may be remarked that the analytic principle also connotes in its

2 Thomas Aquinas, *Summa theologiae*, 1–2, q. 66, a. 5, ad 4m.

terms not only an existential reference but also a basic, primitive character. I think this feature will be found to follow from the defined requirements, for as we shall proceed to argue, analytic principles lie pretty well outside the reach of common sense and empirical science.

They lie outside the reach of common sense because analytic principles are universal and common sense regards the particular. Common sense makes concrete judgments of fact, and it passes judgment on the correctness of insights into concrete situations. But in neither case does it employ terms in the sense assigned them by abstract definitions. As Socrates discovered, the average man does not define; he is suspicious of the search for definitions; and when that pursuit brings out the inference that he does not know what he is talking about, he is rather resentful.

The fact would seem to be that the structure of commonsense meanings is much the same as the structure of common sense itself. There is a communal collaboration that yields a habitual core of understanding and, as well, a range of concepts and linguistic terms in ordinary use. But just as the common core of understanding has to be adjusted by complementary insights into the present concrete situation before judgment occurs, so also common concepts and terms receive their ultimate complement of meaning from those complementary insights.

'This is a dog.' 'What do you mean by a *dog*?' The question supposes that the term 'dog' has a precise meaning outside the series of statements in which it occurs. But in fact what comes first is the series of statements, and what comes only later, and then only if one goes in for analysis, is the determination of the precise meaning of the single, partial term. What the average man means by a dog is (1) what he would with certainty pronounce to be a dog in any concrete situation with which he is familiar, (2) what he could learn to be a dog, and (3) what he would be willing to believe is a dog.

Hence it is that a dictionary is constructed, not by the Socratic art of definition, but by the pedestrian, inductive process of listing sentences in which each word occurs in good usage.

It may be objected that one cannot make a brick house without first making bricks. But one is only arguing from a false analogy if one claims that the mind develops in the same fashion as the wall of a house is built. Prior to concepts there are insights. A single insight is expressed only by uttering several concepts. They are uttered in conjunction, and reflection pronounces whether the insight and so the conjunction is correct. The isolation and definition of concepts is a subsequent procedure, and common sense does not undertake it.

Because we have denied that common sense reaches analytic principles, it is not to be inferred that the average man has no principles. Analytic principles suppose analysis; analysis supposes accurate conceptualization. But prior to analysis, to concepts, to judgments, there are the native endowments of intelligence and reasonableness and the inherent structures of cognitional process. These are the real principles on which the rest depend. Moreover, all understanding has its universal aspect, for similars are similarly understood. But it is one thing to exploit this universal aspect in a professional manner; it is another to exploit the intelligibility, which is by itself universal, by adding further intelligibilities until one comes to grips with concrete situations. The latter line of development we have named common sense, so that by definition common sense deals with the particular. Again, the latter line of development is conspicuous in the average man. But what else the average man knows, and how he knows it, are further questions. As has been remarked already, one cannot treat all issues at the same time.

Next, analytic principles lie outside the reach of empirical science. It is true, of course, that every insight yields several concepts linked together through the insight; it also is true that the empirical scientist formulates definitions, postulates, and inferences; but the trouble is that the empirical scientist knows his insights not as certainly correct but only as probable. Hence his defined terms, in the sense they are defined, are as much subject to revision as the probable judgments of fact that contain them and validate them.

Thus, consider the assertions: (1) water probably is H_2O; (2) what I mean by water is H_2O; (3) this water contains impurities; (4) there are two kinds of water, heavy and ordinary.

The first is an empirical conclusion. The second is a definition. The third is a concrete judgment of fact; its meaning is that this sample is water in the sense of the empirical conclusion but it is not solely water in the sense of the definition. The fourth introduces a new basis of definition that has its ground in fresh experimental work. Now both the initial definition and the later definitions yield analytic propositions, namely, that what does not satisfy certain specifications is not pure water, or it is not pure water of molecular weight eighteen, or it is not pure heavy water. Moreover, none of these are merely analytic propositions; they are not the sort of thing that can be produced at will and indefinitely. On the other hand, they are not strictly analytic principles, for though their terms possess validating judgments of fact, still those judgments are subject to revision, and indeed the discovery of heavy water has already forced such a revision.

Generally one may say that the advance of empirical science is an instance of the advance of the self-correcting process of learning. But in this instance the previous insights yield correlations, definitions, and inferences. It is in terms of such formulations that are framed the further questions that will complement and modify the previous insights by later insights. In like manner the later insights receive their formulation, which is presupposed by the further questions that lead to a still fuller understanding. Now in this process the successive formulations have three distinct aspects. First, they are the expression of insights that grasp the intelligible form of data; thus they are probable empirical conclusions. Secondly, they are the presupposition of the further questions that lead to further insights; from this viewpoint they are provisional analytic principles. Thirdly, they are revised in the light of the further insights and so cease to be probable empirical conclusions and provisional analytic principles, to pass into the limbo of the analytic propositions, whose terms have no existential reference.[3]

8   Mathematical Judgments   [309–15]

In mathematical thought one may readily discern the difference between operations on the level of intelligence and operations on the level of reflection.

The level of intelligence is the level of discovery and invention, of catching on and learning, of grasping problems and coming to grasp their solutions, of seeing the point made in each of a series of mathematical statements and then seeing how the successive points hang together.

The level of reflection is the complementary process of checking. One understands, and now one wishes to know whether what is understood is also correct. One has grasped the point, and one asks whether it is

---

3 The reader interested in further illustrations of this process will find numerous examples in Arthur Pap's *The A Priori in Physical Theory* (New York: King's Crown Press, 1946). [Transferred by editors from text to footnote.]

right. One has seen how the successive steps hang together, and one is out to make sure that what hangs together is really cogent.

Now the process of checking can be developed into an elaborate technique. What is checked becomes a whole department of mathematics. Definitions are worked out. Postulates are added. From the definitions and postulates it is shown that all the conclusions of the department can be reached by the rigorous procedure of deductive inference.

But what is the goal of checking? Clearly, it is to marshal the evidence in the shape in which reflective understanding can grasp the virtually unconditioned and so ground rational judgment. Insofar as the checking reduces conclusions to premises, there is the virtually unconditioned of the form of deductive inference. Insofar as the definitions and postulates coalesce into a self-justifying meaning, there is the virtually unconditioned of analytic propositions. Both of these types of the virtually unconditioned have already been considered, and so for us the problem of mathematical judgment consists in determining what else is required for such judgment.

First of all, something else is required. For if the premises of mathematical thought are analytic propositions, still not all analytic propositions are mathematical premises. Analytic propositions can be produced at will and indefinitely. But the premises of mathematical thought are to be reached only through the discoveries of genius and the labor of learning what genius has grasped. Further, it does happen that abstruse regions of mathematics are occasionally pulled out of their cold and airy regions to become the tools of empirical hypotheses and theories and to share with such formulations the probable existential reference that they possess. But prior to a probable existential reference or isomorphism there is a possible existential reference or isomorphism; before a department of mathematics can be applied, it must possess an inherent possibility of being applied. What, then, is that inherent possibility? And what is its criterion?

Secondly, we have to undertake an examination of mathematics to determine what this further element is and what its criterion is. Let us say, then, that there is a mathematical series, that each term in the series is a department of mathematics, that each department consists (1) of rules governing and so defining operations, and (2) of operations proceeding from some terms to others and so relating and defining them.

Further, we may presuppose each department of mathematics to be formalized, that is, to be stated in a set of definitions, postulates, and

deductions. Finally, we shall presuppose that there are other formalizations, equally rigorous, equally elegant, but in fact not members of the
mathematical series. Our problem thus becomes the question, In the
light of our general analysis of knowledge, how is one to recognize some
formalizations as mathematical and others as not mathematical?

Our answer contains three elements, and it will be convenient to refer
to them respectively as the material element, the formal element, and
the actual element.

The material element is what we have named the empirical residue.
There are aspects of data from which understanding always abstracts.
Such have been seen to be the individual, the continuum, particular
places and times, and the nonsystematic divergence of actual frequency
from probable expectations.

The formal element may be designated by abstraction as enriching. It
has been seen that insight goes beyond images and data by adding intelligible unities and correlations and frequencies, which, indeed, contain
a reference to images or data but nonetheless add a component to knowledge that does not exist actually on the level of sense or imagination.

Finally, the actual element lies in the conjunction of the material and
the formal elements.

By the mathematician, the formal element commonly is viewed as
dynamic. There is a laborious process named 'learning mathematics.' It
consists in gradually acquiring the insights that are necessary to understand mathematical problems, to follow mathematical arguments, to
work out mathematical solutions. This acquisition occurs in a succession
of higher viewpoints. One department of mathematics follows upon
another. Logically they are discontinuous, for each has its own definitions, postulates, and inferences. But intellectually they are continuous,
inasmuch as the symbolic representation of operations in the lower field
provides the images in which intelligence grasps the idea of the new
rules that govern operations in the higher field.

However, this expansion of intelligence does not seem to be completely free. Not only is there the link between higher viewpoints and
preceding lower viewpoints, but also there is a bias from the particular
to the general, from the part to the totality, from the approximate to the
ideal. If there exist concrete instances of one, two, three, the mathematician explores the totality of positive integers, of real numbers, of complex numbers, of ordered sets. If there exist edges and surfaces, the
mathematician works out not merely one geometry but the total series

of possible geometries. If there are various fields in which it seems mathematics may be applied, the mathematician sets out to explore the whole of each region in which the fields occur.

Again, besides its preference for the general, the complete, the ideal, the development of mathematical thought also seems restricted by its material element. By this I do not mean that the mathematician is confined to individuals that exist, to continua that exist, to places and times that exist, to nonsystematic divergences that occur, or to any other actual elements in the empirical residue that may be discovered through the introduction of new techniques of abstraction. For it is quite clear that mathematical thought in its pursuit of the general and complete and ideal reveals a profound unconcern for the existent. Still, it does seem to be true that the empirical residue does supply mathematics with samples of the type of stuff on which mathematical ideas confer intelligibility and order. For unless the mathematician is investigating the pure intelligibilities that Aquinas identified with angels,[4] there must be some mathematical matter; and since there are other sciences that deal with data as of determinate kinds, there remains for the mathematician the empirical residue of all data.

If we have succeeded in characterizing the material and formal elements of mathematics, there remains the question of the significance of their conjunction. Briefly, this may be indicated by recalling that we found the heuristic structures of empirical method to operate in a scissors-like fashion. Not only is there a lower blade that rises from data through measurements and curve fitting to formulae, but also there is an upper blade that moves downward from differential and operator equations and from postulates of invariance and equivalence. Moreover, it is no secret that the upper blade owes its effectiveness to the labors of mathematicians. But what is the possibility of that upper blade?

To grasp the answer to that question, two complementary tendencies have to be envisaged at once. On the one hand, there is the movement of empirical science from description to explanation, from proper domains of data to systems of laws that implicitly define the terms they relate; and at the end of this movement there is the ideal goal that is to be attained when all aspects of data except the empirical residue will have their intelligible counterpart in systems of explanatory conjugates and ideal frequencies. On the other hand, there is the movement of mathematical thought

4 [*Summa theologiae*, 1, q. 50, aa. 1–2.]

that begins from the empirical residue and endeavors to explore the totality of manners in which enriching abstraction can confer intelligibility upon any materials that resemble the empirical residue. Clearly, these two movements are complementary. For the mathematician begins from the empirical residue with which the empirical scientist would end; and if the mathematical exploration of intelligible systems is thorough, then it is bound to include the systems of explanatory conjugates that the empirical sciences will verify in their respective domains.

Let us now revert to our distinction between outright analytic principles, provisional analytic principles, and serially analytic principles. All are analytic propositions, i.e., instances of the virtually unconditioned in which the conditioned is linked to its conditions by syntactical rules and the conditions are fulfilled by defining terms. None are mere analytic propositions that are obtained by devising any definitions or syntactical rules that one pleases. For the terms and relations of outright analytic principles occur, in their defined sense, in certain judgments of fact. The terms and relations of provisional analytic principles occur, in their defined sense, in probable judgments of fact. Finally, the terms and relations of serially analytic principles ground the deductive expansions that explore completely, generally, and ideally the total range of fields to which outright and provisional analytic principles give access in a particular, fragmentary, or approximate manner.

Next, it seems possible to identify the basic propositions of mathematics with serially analytic principles. For there is a material element in mathematical thought, and it bears some similarity to the empirical residue in the data of the empirical sciences. Again, there is a formal element in mathematical thought, and it tends towards a general, complete, and ideal account of the manners in which enriching abstraction can add intelligibility and order to the material element. But the empirical sciences are in search of the intelligibility and order that, when combined with the empirical residue in the data of their several domains, will provide a complete and definitive explanation of those data. It follows that the mathematician is concerned to establish generally, completely, and ideally the range of possible systems that include verifiable scientific systems as particular, fragmentary, or approximate cases.

Thirdly, if the basic propositions of mathematics are serially analytic principles, then we have the answer to our principal question that asked the difference between free formalizations and mathematical formalizations.

Fourthly, there readily follows an account of the possibility of isomorphism between mathematical relations and the relations of the empirical sciences. Both sets of relations are products of enriching abstraction, and both possess a relevance to the empirical residue in data.

Finally, it seems appropriate to add a note on the difference between the foregoing account of the field of mathematics and current views. Commonly, it would be agreed that mathematics is based on mere analytic propositions, and it would be explained that, if one disregards merely arbitrary definitions and syntactical rules, one can distinguish[h] (1) logic, which deals with such relations as 'and,' 'or,' 'if ... then,' (2) mathematics, which deals with relations of equivalence or congruence in individuals and sets, and (3) a more general subject, call it 'mathesis,' which deals with rules common to logic and to mathematics.

The principal difference in our approach is that it goes behind concepts and affirmations to the grounding acts of direct and reflective understanding. From this feature there follows its dynamic character, for it contains an invitation to mathematicians to explore the possibility of setting up the series of deductive expansions that would do as much for other empirical sciences as has been done for physics. On the other hand, while we have emphasized a relation between mathematics and empirical science, it must be insisted that we have not done so by restricting materially the field of mathematics. The mathematician remains free to take as his materials anything that resembles the empirical residue. He is free to discover further additions to the residue that at present is known. He is free to explore with full generality, completeness, and ideality the enrichments that the exercise of human intelligence can add. Yet his creations will remain serially existential, for they will exhibit the series of systems to some of which the empirical scientist will be able to say 'Yes.'

9   Summary   [315–16]

Prospective judgments are propositions (1) that are the content of an act of conceiving, thinking, defining, considering, or supposing, (2) that are subjected to the question for reflection, to the critical attitude of intelligence, and (3) that thereby are constituted as the conditioned.

There is sufficient evidence for a prospective judgment when it may be grasped by reflective understanding as virtually unconditioned. Hence sufficient evidence involves (1) a link of the conditioned to its conditions, and (2) the fulfilment of the conditions. These two elements are supplied in different manners in different cases.

In formal inference the link is provided by the hypothetical premise 'If the antecedent, then the consequent.' The fulfilment is the minor premise.

In judgment on the correctness of insights, the link is that the insight is correct if there are no further pertinent questions, and the fulfilment lies in the self-correcting process of learning reaching its limit in familiarity and mastery.

In judgments of fact the link is the correct insight or set of insights, and the fulfilment lies in present and/or remembered data.

In generalizations the link is the cognitional law that similars are similarly understood, and the fulfilment lies in such similarity that further pertinent questions no more arise in the general case than in the correctly understood particular case.

In probable judgments the link is that insights are correct when there are no further pertinent questions, and the fulfilment is some approximation of the self-correcting process of learning to its limit of familiarity and mastery.

In analytic propositions the link lies in rules of meaning that generate propositions out of partial terms of meaning, and the fulfilment is supplied by the meanings or definitions of the terms.

Analytic propositions become analytic principles when their terms are existential; and terms are existential when they occur in definitive factual judgments.

Provisional analytic principles are analytic propositions whose terms are probably existential.

Serially analytic principles are the analytic propositions from which follow the ranges of systems of which some in some fashion exist.

PART TWO

Insight as Knowledge

11

Self-affirmation of the Knower

It is time to turn from theory to practice. Judgment has been analyzed. Its grounds in reflective understanding have been explored. Clearly the next question is whether correct judgments occur, and the answer to it is the act of making one.

Since our study has been of cognitional process, the judgment we are best prepared to make is the self-affirmation of an instance of such a process as cognitional. By the 'self' is meant a concrete and intelligible unity-identity-whole. By 'self-affirmation' is meant that the self both affirms and is affirmed. By 'self-affirmation of the knower' is meant that the self as affirmed is characterized by such occurrences as sensing, perceiving, imagining, inquiring, understanding, formulating, reflecting, grasping the unconditioned, and affirming.

The affirmation to be made is a judgment of fact. It is not that I exist necessarily, but merely that in fact I do. It is not that I am of necessity a knower, but merely that in fact I am. It is not that an individual performing the listed acts really does know, but merely that I perform them and that by 'knowing' I mean no more than such performance.

As all judgment, self-affirmation rests upon a grasp of the unconditioned. The unconditioned is the combination of (1) a conditioned, (2) a link between the conditioned and its conditions, and (3) the fulfilment of the conditions. The relevant conditioned is the statement 'I am a knower.' The link between the conditioned and its conditions may be cast in the proposition 'I am a knower, if I am a concrete and intelligible unity-identity-whole, characterized by acts of sensing, perceiving, imagining, inquiring, understanding, formulating, reflecting, grasping the unconditioned, and judging.' The fulfilment of the conditions is given in consciousness.

The conditioned offers no difficulty. It is merely the expression of what is to be affirmed. Similarly, the link offers no difficulty; the link itself is a statement of meaning; and the conditions which it lists have become familiar in the course of this investigation. The problematic element, then, lies in the fulfilment of the conditions, and we proceed to indicate what is meant and not meant by consciousness and by the fulfilment of conditions.

1   The Notion of Consciousness [320–21]

First, consciousness is not to be thought of as some sort of inward look. People are apt to think of knowing by imagining a man taking a look at something, and further, they are apt to think of consciousness by imagining themselves looking into themselves. Not merely do they indulge in such imaginative opinions but also they are likely to justify them by argument. Knowing, they will say, is knowing something; it is being confronted by an object; it is the strange, mysterious, irreducible presence of one thing to another. Hence, though knowing is not exclusively a matter of ocular vision, still it is radically that sort of thing. It is gazing, intuiting, contemplating. Whatever words you care to employ, consciousness is a knowing, and so it is some sort of inward looking.

Now, while consciousness is a factor in knowing, and while knowing is an activity to which a problem of objectivity is annexed, still it is one thing to give an account of the activity, and it is something else to tackle the problem of objectivity. For the present we are concerned simply with an account of the activity, and so we have defined the knower, not by saying that he knows something, but solely by saying that he performs certain kinds of acts. In like manner, we have not asked whether the knower knows himself; we ask solely whether he can perform the act of self-affirmation. Hence, while some of our readers may possess the rather remarkable power of looking into themselves and intuiting things quite clearly and distinctly, we shall not base our case upon their success. For after all, there may well exist other readers that, like the writer, find looking into themselves rather unrewarding.

Secondly, by consciousness we shall mean that there is an awareness immanent in cognitional acts. Already a distinction has been drawn between act and content: for instance, between seeing and color, hearing and sound, imagining and image, insight and idea. To affirm consciousness is to affirm that cognitional process is not merely a procession of contents but also a succession of acts. It is to affirm that the acts differ radically from such unconscious acts as the metabolism of one's cells, the maintenance of one's organs, the multitudinous biological processes that one learns about through the study of contemporary medical science. Both kinds of acts occur, but the biological occur outside consciousness, and the cognitional occur within consciousness. Seeing is not merely a response to the stimulus of color and shape; it is a response that consists in becoming aware of color and shape. Hearing is not merely a response to the stimulus of sound; it is a response that consists in becoming aware of sound. As color differs from sound, so seeing differs from hearing. Still, seeing and hearing have a common feature, for in both occurrences there is not merely content but also conscious act.

By the conscious act is not meant a deliberate act; we are conscious of acts without debating whether we will perform them. By the conscious act is not meant an act to which one attends; consciousness can be heightened by shifting attention from the content to the act, but consciousness is not constituted by that shift of attention, for it is a quality immanent in acts of certain kinds, and without it the acts would be as unconscious as[a] the growth of one's beard. By the conscious act is not meant that the act is somehow isolated for inspection, nor that one grasps its function in cognitional process, nor that one can assign it a name, nor that one can distinguish it from other acts, nor that one is certain of its occurrence.

Does, then, 'conscious act' mean no more than 'cognitional act'? A distinction has to be drawn. First, I do not think that only cognitional acts are conscious. Secondly, there are those that would define 'seeing' as 'awareness of color' and then proceed to argue that in seeing one was aware of color but of nothing else whatever, that 'awareness of color' occurs but that a concomitant 'awareness of awareness' is a fiction. This, I think, does not accurately reflect the facts. If seeing is an awareness of nothing but color and hearing is an awareness of nothing but sound, why are both named 'awareness'? Is it because there is some similarity between color and sound? Or is it that color and sound are disparate, yet with respect to both there are acts that are similar? In the latter case, what is the similarity? Is it that both acts are occurrences, as metabolism is an occurrence? Or is it that both acts are conscious? One may quarrel with the phrase 'awareness of awareness,' particularly if one imagines awareness to be a looking and finds it preposterous to talk about looking at a look. But one cannot deny that, within the cognitional act as it occurs, there is a factor or element or component over and above its content, and that this factor is what differentiates cognitional acts from unconscious occurrences.

2   Empirical, Intelligent, and Rational Consciousness[b]   [322–24]

By consciousness is meant an awareness immanent in cognitional acts. But such acts differ in kind, and so the awareness differs in kind with the acts. There is an empirical consciousness characteristic of sensing, perceiving, imagining. As the content of these acts is merely presented or represented, so the awareness immanent in the acts is the mere givenness of the acts. But there is an intelligent consciousness characteristic of inquiry, insight, and formulation. On this level cognitional process not merely strives for and reaches the intelligible, but in doing so it exhibits its intelligence; it operates intelligently. The awareness is present but it is the awareness of intelligence, of what strives to understand, of what is satisfied by understanding, of what formulates the understood, not as a schoolboy repeating by rote a definition, but as one that defines because he grasps why that definition hits things off. Finally, on the third level of reflection, grasp of the unconditioned, and judgment, there is rational consciousness. It is the emergence and the effective operation of a single law of utmost generality, the law of sufficient reason, where the sufficient reason is the unconditioned. It emerges as a demand for the unconditioned and a refusal to assent unreservedly on any lesser ground. It advances to grasp of the unconditioned. It terminates in the rational compulsion by which grasp of the unconditioned commands assent.

Empirical consciousness needs, perhaps, no further comment, for by it we illustrated the difference between conscious and unconscious acts. Intelligent and rational consciousness, on the other hand, may be clarified by a contrast. In their different manners both common sense and positive science view the material world as subject to intelligible patterns and as governed by some law of causality. To confine our attention to what man knows best, namely, his own artifacts, there is discernible in them an intelligible design, and their existence has its ground in the labor of production. But before the design is realized in things, it was invented by intelligence; before the sequence of productive operations was undertaken, it was affirmed as worth while for some sufficient or apparently sufficient reason. In the thing there is the intelligible design, but in the inventor there was not only the intelligibility on the side of the object but also intelligent consciousness on the side of the subject. In the thing there is the groundedness that consists in its existence being accounted for by a sequence of operations, but in the entrepreneur there was not only the groundedness of his judgment in the reasons that led to it but also the rational consciousness that required reasons to reach judgment.

Intelligence and intelligibility are the obverse and reverse of the second level of knowing: intelligence looks for intelligible patterns in presentations and representations; it grasps such patterns in its moments of insight; it exploits such grasp in its formulations and in further operations equally guided by insights. In like manner, reasonableness and groundedness are the obverse and reverse of the third level of knowing. Reasonableness is reflection inasmuch as it seeks groundedness for objects of thought; reasonableness discovers groundedness in its reflective grasp of the unconditioned; reasonableness exploits groundedness when it affirms objects because they are grounded. In man's artifacts there are the reverse elements of the intelligibility and groundedness, but there are not the obverse elements of intelligence and reasonableness. The obverse elements pertain to cognitional process on its second and third levels; they do not pertain to the contents emergent on those levels, to the idea or concept, to the unconditioned or affirmed; on the contrary, they characterize the acts with which those contents are coupled, and so they are specific differentiations of the awareness of consciousness. Clear and distinct conception not only reveals the intelligibility of the object but also manifests the intelligence of the subject. Exact and balanced judgment not only affirms things as they are but also testifies to the dominance of reasonableness in the subject.

Still, it may be asked, 'Am I really conscious of intelligence and reasonableness?' The question, I think, is misleading. It suggests that there is a type of knowing in which intelligence and reasonableness come up for inspection. But what is asserted is not that you can uncover intelligence by introspection, as you can point to Calcutta on a map. The assertion is that you have conscious states and conscious acts that are intelligent and reasonable. Intelligent and rational consciousness denote characters of cognitional process, and the characters they denote pertain not to the contents but to the proceeding. It is repugnant to me to place astrology and astronomy, alchemy and chemistry, legend and history, hypothesis and fact, on exactly the same footing. I am not content with theories, however brilliantly coherent, but insist on raising the further question, Are they true? What is that repugnance, that discontent, that insistence? They are just so many variations on the more basic expression that I am rationally conscious, that I demand sufficient reason, that I find it in the unconditioned, that I assent unreservedly to nothing less, that such demanding, finding, self-committing occur, not like the growth of my hair, but within a field of consciousness or awareness.

Again, if at moments I can slip into a lotus land in which mere presentations and representations are juxtaposed or successive, still that is not my normal state. The Humean world of mere impressions comes to me as a puzzle to be pieced together. I want to understand, to grasp intelligible unities and relations, to know what's up and where I stand. Praise of the scientific spirit that inquires, that masters, that controls, is not without an echo, a deep resonance within me, for in my more modest way I too inquire and catch on, see the thing to do and see that it is properly done. But what are these but variations on the more basic expression that I am intelligently conscious, that the awareness characteristic of cognitional acts on the second level is an active contributing to the intelligibility of its products? When I listen to the story of Archimedes and when I read the recital of a mystical experience, there is a marked difference. What a mystic experiences I do not know. But though I never enjoyed so remarkable an insight as Archimedes, still I do know what it is to miss the point and to get the point, not to have a clue and then to catch on, to see things in a new light, to grasp how they hang together, to come to know why, the reason, the explanation, the cause. After Archimedes shouted, 'I've got it,' he might well be puzzled by the question whether he was conscious of an insight. Still, there can be no doubt that he was conscious of an increment of knowledge, an increment that he had wanted very much. Did he want the king's favor? Did he want to enhance his reputation? Perhaps, but at a deeper and more spontaneous level, he wanted to know how to do something; he wanted to solve a problem; he wanted to understand; his consciousness was on the second level, where it seeks the intelligible and follows up partial insights with further questions until there comes the final crowning insight that ends questioning and satisfies intelligent consciousness.

3   The Unity of Consciousness   [324-25]

In the fourth place, there are unities of consciousness. Besides cognitional contents there are cognitional acts; different kinds of acts have different kinds of awareness: empirical, intelligent, rational. But the contents cumulate into unities: what is perceived is what is inquired about; what is inquired about is what is understood; what is understood is what is formulated; what is formulated is what is reflected on; what is reflected on is what is grasped as unconditioned; what is grasped as unconditioned is what is affirmed. Now just as there are unities on the side of the object, so there are unities on the side of the subject. Conscious acts are not so many isolated, random atoms of knowing, but many acts coalesce into a single knowing. Not only is there a similarity between my seeing and your hearing, inasmuch as both acts are conscious; there also is an identity involved when my seeing and my hearing or your seeing and your hearing are compared. Moreover, this identity extends all along the line. Not only is the percept inquired about, understood, formulated, reflected on, grasped as unconditioned, and affirmed, but also there is an identity involved in perceiving, inquiring, understanding, formulating, reflecting, grasping the unconditioned, and affirming. Indeed, consciousness is much more obviously of this unity in diverse acts than of the diverse acts, for it is within the unity that the acts are found and distinguished, and it is to the unity that we appeal when we talk about a single field of consciousness and draw a distinction between conscious acts occurring within the field and unconscious acts occurring outside it.

One might go further and argue that, were the unity of consciousness not given, then it would have to be postulated. For many contents on diverse levels cumulate into a single known. But how can that occur? How can images be derived from sensations? How can inquiry be about percepts? How can insight be into images? How can definition draw upon both images and the ideas grasped in insight? How can reflecting be about formulations? How can the grasp of the unconditioned be obtained by combining the conditioned that is thought and the fulfilment that is sensed? How can each judgment emerge in a context of other judgments that determine its meaning, complement it, qualify it, defend it, so that it is but a single increment within a far vaster knowing? I cannot inquire into your experience or reflect on your thoughts. But if there were no 'I,' how could there be a 'my experience' with respect to which a 'my inquiry' occurred, or 'my thoughts' with respect to which 'my reflection' occurred? If there were not one consciousness, at once empirical, intelligent, and rational, how could rational judgment proceed from an unconditioned grasped in the combination of thought and sensible experience?

4   The Unity as Given   [326–28]

Still, if the unity of consciousness would have to be postulated on the hypothesis that it were not given, it remains that it is given. By this, of course, I do not mean that it is the object of some inward look. What is meant is that a single agent is involved in many acts, that it is an abstraction to speak of the acts as conscious, that, concretely, consciousness pertains to the acting agent. Seeing and hearing differ inasmuch as one is an awareness of color and the other an awareness of sound. Seeing and hearing are similar inasmuch as each is an awareness. But the similarity between my seeing and your hearing is an abstract indication of consciousness, which, as it is given, is primarily an identity uniting my seeing and my hearing or your seeing and your hearing.

We have been engaged in determining what precisely is meant by consciousness. We have contended that it is not some inward look but a quality of cognitional acts, a quality that differs on the different levels of cognitional process, a quality that concretely is the identity immanent in the diversity and the multiplicity of the process. However, one cannot insist too strongly that such an account of consciousness is not itself consciousness. The account supposes consciousness as its data for inquiry, for insight, for formulation, for reflection, for grasp of the unconditioned, for judgment. But giving the account is the formulating and the judging, while the account itself is what is formulated and affirmed. Consciousness as given is neither formulated nor affirmed. Consciousness is given independently of its being formulated or affirmed. To formulate it does not make one more conscious, for the effect of formulation is to add to one's concepts. To affirm it does not make one more conscious, for the effect of affirmation is to add to one's judgments. Finally, as consciousness is not increased by affirming it, so it is not diminished by denying it, for the effect of denying it is to add to the list of one's judgments and not to subtract from the grounds on which judgments may be based.

This remark brings us to our second topic. We proposed to say what was meant and not meant by consciousness. We also proposed to say what was meant and not meant by the experiential fulfilment of con-- ditions for the affirmation of the conditioned. By such experiential fulfilment,[c] then, one does not mean the conditioned, nor the link be- tween the conditioned and its conditions, nor the conditions as formu- lated, let alone as affirmed. One does mean that the conditions which are formulated also are to be found in a more rudimentary state within cognitional process. Just as inquiry brings about the advance from the perceived and not understood to the perceived and understood, so there is a reverse shift by which one moves from the perceived and under- stood to the merely perceived. It is this reverse shift that commonly is meant by verification. If from a more general theory I obtain the for- mula $PV = 64$, then I can infer that when P is 2, 4, 8, 16, 32, V will have theoretically the values 32, 16, 8, 4, 2. By setting up suitable apparatus and securing appropriate conditions defined by the theory, I can ad- vance from theoretical inference to an experimental check. The results of the experiment may be expressed in a series of propositions, such as the statement that, when P was approximately 2, V was approximately 32; but such a series of statements, however accurate, is not what was given by the experiment. The statements represent judgments of fact; the judgments rest on grasping the unconditioned; the grasp rests on formulations and visual experiences. The experiment gives neither state- ments nor judgments nor reflective understanding nor formulations but only visual experiences. The experiment gives not visual experiences as described but visual experiences on the level of merely seeing. That P is 2 when the needle on a dial stands at a certain place is a judgment. That V is 32 when certain dimensions of an object coincide with certain dimensions of a measuring rod is another judgment. All that is seen is the needle in a position on the dial or the dimensions of an object stand- ing in coincidence with numbered units on a rod. Nor is it this descrip- tion that is seen, but only what is so described. In brief, verification is an appropriate pattern of acts of checking; acts of checking are reversals from formulations of what would be perceived to the corresponding but more rudimentary cognitional contents of acts of perceiving or sensing. In the formulation there always are elements derived from inquiry, insight, conceiving. But in virtue of the checking one can say that the formulation is not pure theory, that it is not merely supposed or merely postulated or merely inferred, that its sensible component is given.

Now just as there is reversal to what is given sensibly, so there is reversal to what is given consciously. Just as the former reversal is away from the understood as understood, the formulated as formulated, the affirmed as affirmed, and to the merely sensed, so also the latter reversal is from the understood, formulated, affirmed as such, to the merely given. Hence in the self-affirmation of the knower the conditioned is the statement 'I am a knower.' The link between the conditioned and its conditions is cast in the proposition 'I am a knower if I am a unity performing certain kinds of acts.' The conditions as formulated are the unity-identity-whole to be grasped in data as individual and the kinds of acts to be grasped in data as similar. But the fulfilment of the conditions in consciousness is to be had by reverting from such formulations to the more rudimentary state of the formulated, where there is no formulation but merely experience.

5   Self-affirmation   [328]

From preliminary clarifications, we turn to the issue. 'Am I a knower?' Each has to ask the question of himself. But anyone who asks it is rationally conscious. For the question is a question for reflection, a question to be met with a yes or no; and asking the question does not mean repeating the words but entering the dynamic state in which dissatisfaction with mere theory manifests itself in a demand for fact, for what is so. Further, the question is not any question. If I ask it, I know what it means. What do I mean by 'I'? The answer is difficult to formulate, but strangely, in some obscure fashion, I know very well what it means without formulation, and by that obscure yet familiar awareness, I find fault with various formulations of what is meant by 'I.' In other words, 'I' has a rudimentary meaning from consciousness, and it envisages neither the multiplicity nor the diversity of contents and conscious acts but rather the unity that goes along with them. But if 'I' has some such rudimentary meaning from consciousness, then consciousness supplies the fulfilment of one element in the conditions for affirming that I am a knower. Does consciousness supply the fulfilment for the other conditions? Do I see, or am I blind? Do I hear, or am I deaf? Do I try to understand, or is the distinction between intelligence and stupidity no more applicable to me than to a stone? Have I any experience of insight, or is the story of Archimedes as strange to me as the account of Plotinus's vision of the One? Do I conceive, think, consider, suppose, define, formulate, or is my talking like the talking of a parrot? I reflect, for I ask whether

I am a knower. Do I grasp the unconditioned, if not in other instances, then in this one? If I grasped the unconditioned, would I not be under the rational compulsion of affirming that I am a knower, and so either affirm it or else find some loophole, some weakness, some incoherence, in this account of the genesis of self-affirmation? As each has to ask these questions of himself, so too he has to answer them for himself. But the fact of the asking and the possibility of the answering are themselves the sufficient reason for the affirmative answer.

6   Self-affirmation as Immanent Law   [329–32]

The foregoing account of self-affirmation stresses its positive aspect. It is a judgment of fact, and so it rests heavily upon the experiential component in knowing. Still, it is a singular type of judgment for it possesses a variety of overtones. I might not be, yet if I am, I am. I might be other than I am, yet in fact I am what I am. The contingent, if you suppose it as a fact, becomes conditionally necessary, and this piece of elementary logic places the merely factual self-affirmation in a context of necessity.

Am I a knower? The answer yes is coherent, for if I am a knower, I can know that fact. But the answer no is incoherent, for if I am not a knower, how could the question be raised and answered by me? No less, the hedging answer 'I do not know' is incoherent. For if I know that I do not know, then I am a knower; and if I do not know that I do not know, then I should not answer.

Am I a knower? If I am not, then I know nothing. My only course is silence. My only course is not the excused and explained silence of the sceptic, but the complete silence of the animal that offers neither excuse nor explanation for its complacent absorption in merely sensitive routines. For if I know nothing, I do not know excuses for not knowing. If I know nothing, then I cannot know the explanation of my ignorance.

It is this conditional necessity of contingent fact that involves the talking sceptic in contradiction. If enthusiasm for the achievement of Freud were to lead me to affirm that all thought and affirmation is just a byproduct of the libido, then since I have admitted no exceptions, this very assertion of mine would have to be mere assertion from a suspect source. If second thoughts lead me to acknowledge an exception, they lead me to acknowledge the necessary presuppositions of the exception. By the time that list has been drawn up and accepted, I am no longer a sceptic.

Still, the Aristotelian prescription of getting the sceptic to talk derives its efficacy not only from the conditional necessity of contingent fact but also from the nature, the natural spontaneities and natural inevitabilities, that go with that fact. Why is it that the talking sceptic does not talk gibberish? Why is it that one can count on his being nonplussed by self-contradiction? It is because he is conscious, empirically, intelligently, and rationally. It is because he has no choice in the matter. It is because extreme ingenuity is needed for him not to betray his real nature. It is because, were his ingenuity successful, the only result would be that he had revealed himself an idiot and lost all claim to be heard.

This aspect of the matter deserves further attention. Cognitional process does not lie outside the realm of natural law. Not merely do I possess the power to elicit certain types of acts when certain conditions are fulfilled, but also with statistical regularity the conditions are fulfilled and the acts occur. I cannot escape sensations, percepts, images. All three keep occurring during my waking hours, and the images often continue during my sleep. No doubt, I can exercise a selective control over what I sense, perceive, imagine. But the choice I cannot make effective is to sense nothing, perceive nothing, imagine nothing. Not only are the contents of these acts imposed upon me, but also consciousness in some degree is inseparable from the acts. Nor is that consciousness merely an aggregate of isolated atoms; it is a unity.

If I cannot escape presentations and representations, neither can I be content with them. Spontaneously I fall victim to the wonder that Aristotle named the beginning of all science and philosophy.[1] I try to understand. I enter, without questioning, the dynamic state that is revealed in questions for intelligence. Theoretically there is a disjunction between 'being intelligent' and 'not being intelligent.' But the theoretical disjunction is not a practical choice for me. I can deprecate intelligence; I can ridicule its aspirations; I can reduce its use to a minimum; but it does not follow that I can eliminate it. I can question everything else, but to question questioning is self-destructive. I might call upon intelligence for the conception of a plan to escape intelligence, but the effort to escape would only reveal my present involvement, and strangely enough, I would want to go about the business intelligently, and I would want to claim that escaping was the intelligent thing to do.

---

1 [Aristotle, *Metaphysics*, I, 1, 980a 21 – a favorite reference of Lonergan; see also p. 34 above.]

As I cannot be content with the cinematographic flow of presentations and representations, so I cannot be content with inquiry, understanding, and formulation. I may say I want not the quarry but the chase, but I am careful to restrict my chasing to fields where the quarry lies. If, above all, I want to understand, still I want to understand the facts. Inevitably, the achievement of understanding, however stupendous, only gives rise to the further question, Is it so? Inevitably, the progress of understanding is interrupted by the check of judgment. Intelligence may be a thorough-bred exulting in the race; but there is a rider on its back; and without the rider the best of horses is a poor bet. The insistence that modern science envisages an indefinite future of repeated revisions does not imply an indifference to fact. On the contrary, it is fact that will force the revisions, that will toss into the wastebasket the brilliant theories of previous under-standing, that will make each new theory better because it is closer to the facts. But what is fact? What is that clear, precise, definitive, irrevocable, dominant something that we name fact? The question is too large to be settled here. Each philosophy has its own view on what fact is and its con-sequent theory on the precise nature of our knowledge of fact. All that can be attempted now is to state what we happen to mean by knowing fact.

Clearly, then, fact is concrete as is sense or consciousness. Again, fact is intelligible: if it is independent of all doubtful theory, it is not independ-ent of the modest insight and formulation necessary to give it its preci-sion and its accuracy. Finally, fact is virtually unconditioned: it might not have been; it might have been other than it is; but as things stand, it pos-sesses conditional necessity, and nothing can possibly alter it now. Fact, then, combines the concreteness of experience, the determinateness of accurate intelligence, and the absoluteness of rational judgment. It is the natural objective of human cognitional process. It is the anticipated unity to which sensation, perception, imagination, inquiry, insight, formulation, reflection, grasp of the unconditioned, and judgment make their several, complementary contributions. When Newton knew that the water in his bucket was rotating, he knew a fact, though he thought that he knew absolute space. When quantum mechanics and relativity posit the un-imaginable in a four-dimensional manifold, they bring to light the not too surprising fact that scientific intelligence and verifying judgment go be-yond the realm of imagination to the realm of fact. Just what that realm is, as has been said, is a difficult and complicated problem. Our present concern is that we are committed to it. We are committed, not by knowing what it is and that it is worth while, but by an inability to avoid experience, by the subtle conquest in us of the eros that would understand, by the inevitable aftermath of that sweet adventure when a rationality identical with us demands the absolute, refuses unreserved assent to less than the unconditioned, and when that is attained, imposes upon us a commitment in which we bow to an immanent Ananké.

Confronted with the standard of the unconditioned, the sceptic despairs. Set before it, the products of human understanding are ashamed. Great are the achievements of modern science; by far are they to be preferred to earlier guesswork; yet rational consciousness finds that they approximate indeed to the unconditioned but do not attain it; and so it assigns them the modest status of probability. Still, if rational consciousness can criticize the achievement of science, it cannot criticize itself. The critical spirit can weigh all else in the balance, only on condition that it does not criticize itself. It is a self-assertive spontaneity that demands sufficient reason for all else but offers no justification for its demanding. It arises, fact-like, to generate knowledge of fact, to push the cognitional process from the conditioned structures of intelligence to unreserved affirmation of the unconditioned. It occurs. It will recur whenever the conditions for reflection are fulfilled. With statistical regularity those conditions keep being fulfilled. Nor is that all, for I am involved, engaged, committed. The disjunction between rationality and nonrationality is an abstract alternative but not a concrete choice. Rationality is my very dignity, and so closely to it do I cling that I would want the best of reasons for abandoning it. Indeed, I am so much one with my reasonableness that, when I lapse from its high standards, I am compelled either to repent my folly or to rationalize it.

Self-affirmation has been considered as a concrete judgment of fact. The contradiction of self-negation has been indicated. Behind that contradiction there have been discerned natural inevitabilities and spontaneities that constitute the possibility of knowing, not by demonstrating that one can know, but pragmatically by engaging one in the process. Nor in the last resort can one reach a deeper foundation than that pragmatic engagement. Even to seek it involves a vicious circle; for if one seeks such a foundation, one employs one's cognitional process; and the foundation to be reached will be no more secure or solid than the inquiry utilized to reach it. As I might not be, as I might be other than I am, so my knowing might not be and it might be other than it is. The ultimate basis of our knowing is not necessity but contingent fact, and the fact is established, not prior to our engagement in knowing, but simultaneously with it. The sceptic, then, is not involved in a conflict with absolute necessity. He might not be; he might not be a knower. Contradiction arises when he utilizes cognitional process to deny it.

7 Description and Explanation [332–35]

There is a further aspect to the matter. Is the self-affirmation that has been outlined descriptive of the thing-for-us or explanatory of the thing-itself? We have spoken of natural inevitabilities and spontaneities. But did we speak of these as they are themselves or as they are for us?

Unfortunately, there is a prior question. The distinction that was drawn earlier between description and explanation was couched in terms that sufficed to cover the difference in the fields of positive science. But human science contains an element not to be found in other departments. Both the study of man and the study of nature begin from inquiry and insight into sensible data. Both the study of man and the study of nature can advance from the descriptive relations of the object to the inquirer, to the explanatory relations that obtain immediately between objects. Just as the physicist measures, correlates measurements, and implicitly defines correlatives by the correlations, so too the student of human nature can forsake the literary approach, to determine economic, political, sociological, cultural, historical correlations. But the study of man also enjoys through consciousness an immediate access to man, and this access can be used in two manners.

The initial use is descriptive. In this fashion we began from an account of an event named insight. We pointed out that it was satisfying, that it came unexpectedly, that its emergence was conditioned more by a dynamic inner state of inquiry than by external circumstance, that while the first emergence was difficult, repeated occurrence was easy and spontaneous, that single acts of insight accumulate into clusters bearing on a single topic, that such clusters may remain without exact formulation, or may be worked out into a systematic doctrine. Naturally enough, this general description of insight was presupposed and utilized when we came to examine it more closely; and this closer examination was in turn presupposed in our account of explanatory abstraction and explanatory system and in our study of empirical method. Moreover, since data, percepts, and images are prior to inquiry, insight, and formulation, and since all definition is subsequent to inquiry and insight, it was necessary to define data, percepts, and images as the materials presupposed and complemented by inquiry and insight, and further, it was necessary to distinguish between them by contrasting the formulations of empirical science with those of mathematics and the formulations of both of these with the formulations of common sense. Finally, the analysis of judgment and the account of reflective understanding consisted in relating these acts to each other, and to the formulations of understanding, and to the fulfilment provided by experience.

As the reader will discern, the initial procedure of description gradually yielded to definition by relation; and the defining relations obtained immediately between different kinds of cognitional state or act. But definition by this type of relation is explanatory, and so descriptive procedure was superseded by explanatory.

There are, then, two types of description and two types of explanation. If the inquirer starts from the data of sense, he begins by describing but goes on to explain. Again, if he starts from the data of consciousness, he begins by describing and goes on to explain. Still, there is an important difference between the two types of explaining. For explanation on the basis of sense can reduce the element of hypothesis to a minimum but it cannot eliminate it entirely. But explanation on the basis of consciousness can escape entirely the merely supposed, the merely postulated, the merely inferred.

First, explanation on the basis of sense can reduce hypothesis to a minimum. This, of course, is the point of the principle of relevance. Galileo's law of falling bodies does not merely suppose or postulate distance or time or the measurements of either. It does not merely suppose or postulate the correlation between distance and time; for there is some relation between the two inasmuch as a falling body falls farther in a longer time; and the actual measurements ground a numerical determination of that relation. Moreover, what holds for the law of falling bodies holds for the other laws of mechanics. If one pleases, one may contend that the use of inquiry, insight, formulation, and consequent generalization is mere supposition or mere postulation; but at least it is not the type of mere supposition that the empirical scientist systematically avoids or that he seriously fears will be eliminated in some more intelligent method of inquiry to be devised and accepted in the future. To reach the element of mere supposition that makes any system of mechanics subject to future revision, one must shift attention from single laws to the set of primitive terms and relations which the system employs in formulating all its laws. In other words, one has to distinguish between, say, mass as defined by correlations between masses and, on the other hand, mass as enjoying the position of an ultimate mechanical concept. Any future system of mechanics will have to satisfy the data that now are covered by the notion of mass. But it is not necessary that every future system of mechanics will have to satisfy the same data by employing our concept of mass. Further developments might lead to the introduction of a different set of ultimate concepts, to a consequent reformulation of all laws, and so to a dethronement of the notion of mass from its present position as an ultimate of mechanical system. Hence, while empirical method can reduce the hypothetical to a minimum, it cannot eliminate it entirely. Its concepts as concepts are not hypothetical, for they are defined implicitly by empirically established correlations. Nonetheless, its concepts as systematically significant, as ultimate or derived, as preferred to other concepts that might be empirically reached, do involve an element of mere supposition. For the selection of certain concepts as ultimate occurs in the work of systematization, and that work is provisional. At any time a system is accepted because it provides the simplest account of all the known facts. But at the same time it is acknowledged that there may be unknown yet relevant facts, that they might give rise to further questions that would lead to further insights, and that the further insights might involve a radical revision of the accepted system.

Secondly, explanation on the basis of consciousness can escape this limitation. I do not mean, of course, that such explanation is not to be reached through the series of revisions involved in the self-correcting process of learning. Nor do I mean that, once explanation is reached, there remains no possibility of the minor revisions that leave basic lines intact but attain a greater exactitude and a greater fulness of detail. Again, I am not contending here and now that human nature and so human knowledge are immutable, that there could not arise a new nature and a new knowledge to which present theory would not be applicable. What is excluded is the radical revision that involves a shift in the fundamental terms and relations of the explanatory account of the human knowledge underlying existing common sense, mathematics and empirical science.

8   The Impossibility of Revision   [335–36]

The impossibility of such revision appears from the very notion of revision. A revision appeals to data. It contends that previous theory does not satisfactorily account for all the data. It claims to have reached complementary insights that lead to more accurate statements. It shows that these new statements either are unconditioned or more closely approximate to the unconditioned than previous statements. Now, if in fact revision is as described, then it presupposes that cognitional process falls on the three levels of presentation, intelligence, and reflection; it presupposes that insights are cumulative and complementary; it presupposes that they head towards a limit described by the adjective 'satisfactory'; it presupposes a reflective grasp of the unconditioned or of what approximates to the unconditioned. Clearly, revision cannot revise its own presuppositions. A reviser cannot appeal to data to deny data, to his new insights to deny insights, to his new formulation to deny formulation, to his reflective grasp to deny reflective grasp.

The same point may be put in another manner. Popular relativism is prone to argue that empirical science is the most reliable form of human knowledge; but empirical science is subject to indefinite revision; therefore, all human knowledge is equally subject to indefinite revision. Now such argument is necessarily fallacious. One must definitively[d] know invariant features of human knowledge before one can assert that empirical science is subject to indefinite revision; and if one definitively[e] knows invariant features of human knowledge, then one knows what is not subject to revision. Moreover, as is obvious, such knowledge surpasses empirical science at least in the respect that it is not subject to revision.

9   Self-affirmation in the Possibility of Judgments of Fact

[336–39]

The same conclusion may be reached by setting forth the a priori conditions of any possible judgment of fact. For any such judgment can be represented by a yes or no in answer to a question, Is it so? The answer will be rational, that is, it will rest on known sufficient reason. Moreover, the answer will be absolute: yes utterly excludes no, and no utterly excludes yes. Hence, since the known sufficient reason for an absolute answer must itself be absolute and known, the yes or no must rest on some apprehension or grasp of the unconditioned. Now the judgment of fact is not to the effect that something must be so or could not be otherwise; it merely states that something is so; hence the unconditioned that grounds it will be not formally but only virtually unconditioned. The first condition, then, of any possible judgment of fact is the grasp of (1) a conditioned, (2) a link between the conditioned and its conditions, and (3) the fulfilment of the conditions. It is such a grasp that effects the transition from the question, Is it so? to a rational, absolute answer.

But this first requirement presupposes other requirements. The 'it' of the judgment of fact is not a bare 'it.' On the contrary, it is the conditioned, known as conditioned, that through the fulfilment of its conditions is grasped as virtually unconditioned. Prior to the question for reflection, there must be a level of activity that yields the conditioned as conditioned, the conditioned as linked to its conditions. But this is a level of intelligence, of positing systematic unities and systematic relations. Moreover, it will be a freely developing level; for without free development questions of fact would not arise. The only instances of the conditioned that would be envisaged would be instances with the conditions fulfilled. In that case the answer would always be an automatic yes; and if the answer were always an automatic yes, there would be no need to raise any questions of fact. Still, though there is free development of systematic unities and relations, such development cannot occur in some pure isolation from the fulfilling conditions. Were there such isolation, it would be impossible to tell whether or not conditions were fulfilled; and if that were impossible, then judgments of fact could not occur. This yields the second condition of judgment of fact. It is a level of intellectual activity that posits systematic unities and relations (1) with some independence of a field of fulfilling conditions, and (2) with reference to such a field.

But this second requirement presupposes a third. There must be a field of fulfilling conditions. More exactly, since conditions are simultaneous with what they condition, there must be a prior field containing what can become fulfilling conditions. Of themselves, they will be neither conditioning nor conditioned; they will be merely given.

Finally, possibility is concrete. Logicians may say that a 'mountain of gold' is possible if there is no intrinsic contradiction involved in supposing such a mountain. But, in fact, a mountain of gold is possible only if the means are available for acquiring enough gold to make a mountain, for transporting it to a single place, for heaping it up in the fashion of a mountain, and for keeping it there long enough for the golden mountain to exist for some minimum interval of time. Similarly, any possible judgment of fact would be some concrete judgment. The conditions of its possibility include the conditions of bringing together its diverse components. There must be, then, a concrete unity-identity-whole that experiences the given, that inquires about the given to generate the free development of systematic unities and relations, that reflects upon such developments and demands the virtually unconditioned as its ground for answering yes or no. It is this concrete unity that asks, Is it so? It is this concrete unity that initiates the free development by asking about the given, What is this? Why is it? How often does it exist or happen? It is this concrete unity that grasps and formulates the conditioned as conditioned and that appeals to the given to grasp the virtually unconditioned and to affirm it rationally and absolutely.

There remains a corollary. Judgments of fact may be not only possible. They may actually occur. But if any judgment of fact occurs, there must be as well the occurrence of its conditions. Hence, if there is any judgment of fact, no matter what its content, there also is a concrete unity-identity-whole that experiences some given, that inquires, understands, and formulates, that reflects, grasps the unconditioned, and so affirms or denies. Finally, such a concrete unity-identity-whole is a thing-itself, for it is defined by an internally related set of operations, and the relations may be experientially validated in the conscious and dynamic states (1) of inquiry leading from the given to insight, (2) of insight leading to formulation, (3) of reflection leading from formulation to grasp of the unconditioned, and (4) of that grasp leading to affirmation or denial.

From the corollary there results our prior contention. There cannot occur a revision without the occurrence of some judgment of fact. But if there occurs any judgment of fact, there occur the dynamic states in which may be validated experientially the relations that define the conjugate terms by which the thing-itself that knows is differentiated.

What is the source of this peculiarity of cognitional theory? It is that other theory reaches its thing-itself by turning away from the thing as related to us by sense or by consciousness, but cognitional theory reaches its thing-itself by understanding itself and affirming itself as concrete unity in a process that is conscious empirically, intelligently, and rationally. Moreover, since every other known becomes known through this process, no known could impugn the process without simultaneously impugning its own status as a known.

10 Contrast with Kantian Analysis[f]   [339–42]

We have performed something similar to what a Kantian would name a transcendental deduction. Accordingly, we shall be asked to explain the fact that our deduction yields different results from Kant's.

A first difference is that Kant asked the a priori conditions of the possibility of experience in the sense of knowing an object. We have distinguished two issues: there is the problem of objectivity, and from this we have carefully prescinded not only in the present section but also in all earlier sections; there also is the prior problem of determining just what activities are involved in knowing, and to this prior problem we have so far confined our efforts. Hence we asked, not for the conditions of knowing an object, but for the conditions of the possible occurrence of a judgment of fact. We have asked for the conditions of an absolute and rational yes or no viewed simply as an act. We have not asked on what conditions there would be some fact that corresponded to the yes. We have not even asked what meaning such correspondence might have.

A second difference lies in the distinction between thing-for-us and thing-itself. Kant distinguished these as phenomenon and noumenon. Just what he meant is a matter of dispute, but at least it is clear that the distinction pertained to his formulation of a theory of objectivity. Moreover, it seems to me to be probable enough that the historical origin of the Kantian distinction is to be sought in the Renaissance distinction of primary and secondary qualities, where the former pertained to the real and objective things themselves while the latter pertained to the subject's apprehension of them. In any case, our distinction is neither the Renaissance nor the Kantian distinction. It is simply a distinction between description and explanation, between the kind of cognitional activities that fix contents by indicating what they resemble and, on the other hand, the kind that fix contents by assigning their experientially validated relations. A thing is a concrete unity-identity-whole grasped in data as individual. Describe it, and it is a thing-for-us. Explain it, and it is a thing-itself. Is it real? Is it objective? Is it anything more than the immanent determination of the cognitional act? These are all quite reasonable questions. But as yet we answer neither yes nor no. For the moment, our answer is simply that objectivity is a highly complex issue and that we shall handle it satisfactorily only if we begin by determining what precisely cognitional process is. No doubt, there are objections that may be urged against this procedure; but the objections too will be handled satisfactorily only after the prior questions are answered.

A third difference regards universal and necessary judgments. They stand in the forefront of the Kantian critique, which was largely engaged in the problem of transcending Hume's experiential atomism. But in our analysis they play a minor role. A universal and necessary judgment may be merely the affirmation of an analytic proposition, and such analytic propositions may be mere abstract possibilities without relevance to the central context of judgments that we name knowledge. Our emphasis falls on the judgment of fact that itself is an increment of knowledge and, as well, contributes to the transition from the analytic proposition to the analytic principle, that is, to the universal and necessary judgment whose terms and relations are existential in the sense that they occur in judgments of fact.

A fourth difference regards the immediate ground of judgment. Kant formulated this ground by setting forth his schematism of the categories. There is a proper use of the category Real if there occurs a filling of the empty form of Time. There is a proper use of the category Substance if there is a permanence of the Real in Time. However, Kant's schematism is not regarded as one of his happiest inventions. In any case we have argued that by their very genesis concepts are united with data. Inquiry is about the data of sense or of consciousness. Insight is into the data of inquiry. Concepts and theories are the products of insight and have to be checked against the data. Moreover – and this is the essential difference – the process of checking reveals in human knowledge, beyond experience and understanding, a third, distinct, constitutive level that is both self-authenticating and decisive. It is self-authenticating: rational reflection demands and reflective understanding grasps a virtually unconditioned; and once that grasp has occurred, one cannot be reasonable and yet fail to pass judgment. Again, the third level is alone decisive: until I judge, I am merely thinking; once I judge, I know; as insight draws the definite object of thought from the hazy object of experience, so judgment selects the objects of thought that are objects of knowledge. Finally, as will appear in chapters 12 and 13, to know means to know being, and to know being includes knowing objects and subjects.

Now because the third level is self-authenticating, reason and its ideal, the unconditioned, cannot be left in the dubious and merely supervisory role assigned them by Kant. Because it is constitutive and alone decisive, the one criterion in our knowledge is rational judgment; and this rules out the vestigial empiricism so often denounced in Kantian thought. Still, our unconditioned is only virtual; it is only what is so in fact; and the universal relevance of fact in this sense[2] both corrects pre-Kantian

---

2 See above, pp. 355–56. [Transferred by editors from text to footnote.]

rationalism and excludes post-Kantian idealism. Finally, our realism, while not intuitive, will be immediate; cognitional analysis is needed not to know being but to know knowledge.[8]

A fifth difference has to do with consciousness. Kant acknowledged an inner sense that corresponds roughly to what we have named empirical consciousness, namely, the awareness that is immanent in acts of sensing, perceiving, imagining, desiring, fearing, and the like. Besides this acknowledgment of inner sense, Kant deduced or postulated an original synthetic unity of apperception as the a priori condition of the 'I think' accompanying all cognitional acts. On the other hand, Kantian theory has no room for a consciousness of the generative principles of the categories; the categories may be inferred from the judgments in which they occur; but it is impossible to reach behind the categories to their source. It is precisely this aspect of Kantian thought that gives the categories their inflexibility and their irreducible mysteriousness. It is the same aspect that provided Fichte and Hegel with their opportunity to march into the unoccupied territory of intelligent and rational consciousness. The dynamic states named inquiry and reflection do occur. Inquiry is generative of all understanding, and understanding is generative of all concepts and systems. Reflection is generative of all reflective grasp of the unconditioned, and that grasp is generative of all judgment. If the Kantian proscribes consideration of inquiry and reflection, he lays himself open to the charge of obscurantism. If he admits such consideration, if he praises intelligent curiosity and the critical spirit, then he is on his way to acknowledge the generative principles both of the categories Kant knew and of the categories Kant did not know.

The foregoing list of differences account for the divergence between Kant's conclusion and our own. They are differences in the problem under consideration, in the viewpoint from which it is considered, in the method by which it is solved. More fundamentally there are differences about questions of fact, for our self-affirmation is, as we have insisted and may be pardoned for repeating, primarily and ultimately a judgment of fact. The orthodox Kantian would refer to our stand as mere psychologism, as an appeal to the empirical that can yield no more than a provisional probability. But our retort is simple enough. Without judgments of fact one cannot get beyond mere analytic propositions. Further, though self-affirmation is no more than a judgment of mere fact, still it is a privileged judgment. Self-negation is incoherent. One has only to inquire and reflect, to find oneself caught in the spontaneities and inevitabilities that supply the evidence for self-affirmation. One has only to make a single judgment of fact, no matter what its content, to involve oneself in a necessary self-affirmation. Finally, cognitional theory differs from other theory; for other theory reaches explanation only by venturing into the merely supposed; but cognitional theory reaches explanation without any such venture; and since it contains no merely hypothetical element, it is not subject to radical revision.

11   Contrast with Relativist Analysis   [342–47]

From Kantian we turn to relativist thought. The initial question in the present section was whether correct judgments occur. Our account of self-affirmation directly contradicts the relativist contention that correct judgments do not occur. Though the arguments for our position have been given, it will not be amiss to indicate where the relativist would disagree and why.

First, relativist thought is largely devoted to a refutation of empiricism. Correctly it insists that human knowing cannot be accounted for by the level of presentations alone. There is as well the level of intelligence, of grasping and formulating intelligible unities and systematic relations. Without this second level of activities, there is indeed a given but there is no possibility of saying what is given.

Secondly, just as the relativist insists on the level of intelligence against the empiricist, so we insist on the level of reflection against the relativist. Human knowing is not merely theory about the given; there are also facts; and the relativist has not and cannot establish that there are no facts, for the absence of any other fact would itself be a fact.

Thirdly, just as the empiricist could have nothing to say if, in fact, he did not utilize operations on the level of intelligence, so also the relativist does not confine himself strictly to the levels of presentations and of intelligence. He is quite familiar with the notion of the unconditioned. He regards the unconditioned as the ideal towards which human knowing tends. But he supposes that this ideal is to be reached through understanding. If the universe in its every part and aspect were thoroughly understood, there could be no further questions; everything would be conceived exactly as it ought to be;[h] on every possible topic a man could say just what he meant and mean just what he said. On the other hand, short of this comprehensive coherence, there can be no sure footing. There is understanding, but it is partial; it is joined with incomprehension; it is open to revision when present incomprehension yields to future understanding; and so intimately are all things related that knowledge of anything can be definitive only when everything is known.

Fourthly, the relativist is able to follow up this general view by facing concrete issues. Is this a typewriter? Probably, yes. For practical purposes, yes. Absolutely? The relativist would prefer to be clear about the precise meaning of the name 'typewriter'; he would like to be told just what is meant by the demonstrative 'this'; he would be grateful for an explanation of the meaning of the copula 'is.' Your simple question is met by three further questions; and if you answer these three, your answers will give rise to many more. If you are quick and see that you are starting on an infinite series, you may confront the relativist with a rounded system. But the relativist is also a smart fellow. He will point out that ordinary people, quite certain that this is a typewriter, know nothing of the system on which you base their knowledge. Nor is this all. For human knowledge is limited; systems have their weak points; and the relativist will pounce upon the very issues on which a defender of the system would prefer to profess ignorance.

Fifthly, not only will the relativist make it plain that there are further questions until everything is known, but also he will explain why this is so. A relation is named internal to an object when, without the relation, the object would differ radically. Thus, we have spoken of inquiry and insight. But by inquiry we have not meant some pure wonder; we have meant a wonder about something. Similarly, by insight we have not meant a pure understanding but an understanding of something. Inquiry and insight, then, are related internally to materials about which one inquires and into which one gains insight. Now, if one supposes that the whole universe is a pattern of internal relations, clearly it follows that no part and no aspect of the universe can be known in isolation from any other part or aspect; for every item is related internally to every other; and to prescind from such relations is to prescind from things as they are and to substitute in their place other, imaginary objects that simply are not. If, then, one asks the relativist to explain why questions run off to infinity, he has a ready answer. The universe to be known by answering questions is a tissue of internal relations.

Sixthly, if the foregoing fairly represents the relativist position, it also reveals its oversights. Questions are of two kinds. There are questions for intelligence asking what this is, what that means, why this is so, how frequently it occurs or exists. There also are questions for reflection that ask whether answers to the former type of question are correct. Next, the unconditioned that is required for judgment is not the comprehensive coherence that is the ideal of understanding, that grounds answers to all questions of the first type. On the contrary, it is a virtually unconditioned that results from the combination of a conditioned with the fulfilment of its conditions. Further, a judgment is a limited commitment; so far from resting on knowledge of the universe, it is to the effect that, no matter what the rest of the universe may prove to be, at least this is so. I may not be able to settle borderline instances in which one might dispute whether the name 'typewriter' would be appropriate. But at least I can settle definitively[i] that this is a typewriter. I may not be able to clarify the meaning of 'is,' but it is sufficient for present purposes to know the difference between 'is' and 'is not'; and that, I know. I am not very articulate when it comes to explaining the meaning of 'this,' but if you prefer to use 'that,' it will make no difference provided we both see what we are talking about. You warn me that I have made mistakes in the past. But your warning is meaningless if I am making a further mistake in recognizing a past mistake as a mistake. And in any case, the sole present issue is whether or not I am mistaken in affirming this to be a typewriter. You explain to me that my notion of a typewriter would be very different if I understood the chemistry of the materials, the mechanics of the construction, the psychology of the typist's skill, the effect on sentence structure resulting from the use of a machine in composing, the economic and sociological repercussions of the invention, its relation to commercial and political bureaucracy, and so forth. But may I not explain to you that all these further items, however interesting and significant, are to be known through further judgments, that such further judgments, so far from shifting me from my present conviction that this is a typewriter, will only confirm me in it, that to make those further judgments would be rather difficult if, at the start, I could not be certain whether or not this is a typewriter?

Seventhly, however, the questions that are answered by a pattern of internal relations are only questions that ask for explanatory system. But besides things-themselves and prior to them in our knowing, there are things-for-us, things as described. Moreover, the existents and occurrences in which explanatory systems are verified diverge nonsystematically from the ideal frequencies that ideally would be deduced from the explanatory systems. Again, the activity of verifying involves the use of description as an intermediary between the system defined by internal relations and, on the other hand, the presentations of sense that are the fulfilling conditions. Finally, it would be a mistake to suppose that explanation is the one true knowledge; not only does its verification rest on description but also the relations of things to us are just as much objects of knowledge as are the relations of things among themselves.

Eighthly, the relativist invents for himself a universe that consists merely of explanatory system because he conceives the unconditioned as the ideal of understanding, as the comprehensive coherence towards which understanding tends by asking what and why. But as we have seen, the criterion of judgment is the virtually unconditioned. Each judgment is a limited commitment. So far from pronouncing on the universe, it is content to affirm some single conditioned that has a finite number of conditions which in fact are fulfilled. No doubt, were the universe simply a vast explanatory system, knowledge of the conditions of any conditioned would be identical with knowledge of the universe. But in fact the universe is not simply explanatory system; its existents and its occurrences diverge nonsystematically from pure intelligibility; it exhibits an empirical residue of the individual, the incidental, the continuous, the merely juxtaposed, and the merely successive; it is a universe of facts, and explanatory system has validity in the measure that it conforms to descriptive facts.

Ninthly, the relativist argument from unending further questions is more impressive than conclusive. Human knowing does not begin from previous knowing but from natural spontaneities and inevitabilities. Its basic terms are not defined for it in some knowing prior to knowing; they are fixed by the dynamic structure of cognitional process itself. The relativist asks what is meant by the copula 'is' and the demonstrative 'this.' But neither he nor anyone else is given to confusing 'is' with 'is not' or 'this' with 'not this'; and that basic clarity is all that is relevant to the meaning of the affirmation 'This is a typewriter.' A cognitional theorist would be called upon to explain such elementary terms; he would do so by saying that 'is' represents the yes that occurs in judgment and that is anticipated by such questions as 'Is it?' 'What is it?' Similarly, a theorist would explain 'this' as the return from the field of conception to the empirical residue in the field of presentations. But questions relevant to cognitional theory are not relevant to every instance of knowing. They are not universally relevant because, in fact, there is no operational obscurity about the meanings that cognitional theory elucidates. Again, they are not universally relevant, because such elementary meanings are fixed, in a manner that surpasses determination by definition, with the native immutability of the dynamic structures of cognitional process.

Tenthly, as human knowing begins from natural spontaneity, so its initial developments are inarticulate. As it asks what and why without being given the reason for its inquiry, so also it sets off on the self-correcting process of learning without the explicit formulations that rightly would be required in an explanatory system. Single insights are partial. Spontaneously they give rise to the further questions that elicit complementary insights. Were the universe purely an explanatory system, the minor clusters of insights reached by what is called common sense would not head for a limiting position of familiarity and mastery in which evidently it is silly to doubt whether or not this is a typewriter. But in fact, the universe to be known by answering questions is not pure explanatory system. In fact, insights do head for limiting positions of familiarity and mastery. In fact, as everyone knows very well, it is silly to doubt whether or not this is a typewriter. The relativist would beg me to advert to the enormous difference in my notion of the typewriter were I to understand fully the chemistry of its materials, the mechanics of its construction, the psychology of the typist's skill, the twist given literary style by composing on a typewriter, the effect of its invention on the development of commercial and political bureaucracy, and so forth. But granted such an enrichment of my knowledge to be possible and desirable, nonetheless it is further knowledge to be obtained by further judgments; and since the enrichment is explanatory, since explanatory knowledge rests on descriptive knowledge, not only must I begin by knowing that this is a typewriter, not only must I advance by learning how similar other machines must be if they are to be named typewriters, but also I can attain valid explanation only insofar as my descriptions are exact.

Eleventhly, it is quite true that I can be mistaken. But that truth presupposes that I am not making a further mistake in acknowledging a past mistake as a mistake. More generally, judgments of fact are correct or incorrect, not of necessity, but merely in fact. If this is something, still it might be nothing at all. If it is a typewriter, still it might be something else. Similarly, if I am correct in affirming it to be a typewriter, it is not a pure necessity, but merely a fact, that I am correct. To ask for the evidence that excludes the possibility of my being mistaken in affirming this to be a typewriter is to ask too much. Such evidence is not available, for if I am correct, that is merely fact. But if that evidence is not available, still less is there the evidence that will exclude the possibility of error in all judgments of fact. Errors are just as much facts as are correct judgments. But the relativist is in conflict with both categories of fact. For him nothing is simply true, for that is possible only when comprehensive coherence is reached; for him, nothing is simply wrong, for every statement involves some understanding and so some part of what he names truth. In the last analysis, just as the empiricist tries to banish intelligence, so the relativist tries to banish fact and with it what everyone else names truth.

12

The Notion of Being

If the main lines of cognitional process have been set down, it remains that certain fundamental and pervasive notions have still to be clarified. Among them, in the first place, is the notion of being. It is a tricky topic, and perhaps the most satisfactory procedure will be to begin from a definition.

1   A Definition   [348–50]

Being, then, is the objective of the pure desire to know.

By the desire to know is meant the dynamic orientation manifested in questions for intelligence and for reflection. It is not the verbal utterance of questions. It is not the conceptual formulation of questions. It is not any insight or thought. It is not any reflective grasp or judgment. It is the prior and enveloping drive that carries cognitional process from sense and imagination to understanding, from understanding to judgment, from judgment to the complete context of correct judgments that is named knowledge. The desire to know, then, is simply the inquiring and critical spirit of man. By moving him to seek understanding, it prevents him from being content with the mere flow of outer and inner experience. By demanding adequate understanding, it involves man in the self-correcting process of learning in which further questions yield complementary insights. By moving man to reflect, to seek the unconditioned, to grant unqualified assent only to the unconditioned, it prevents him from being content with hearsay and legend, with unverified hypotheses and untested theories. Finally, by raising still further questions for intelligence and reflection, it excludes complacent inertia; for if the questions go unanswered, man cannot be complacent; and if answers are sought, man is not inert.

Because it differs radically from other desire, this desire has been named pure. It is to be known, not by the misleading analogy of other desire, but by giving free rein to intelligent and rational consciousness. It is, indeed, impalpable, but also it is powerful. It pulls man out of the solid routine of perception and conation, instinct and habit, doing and enjoying. It holds him with the fascination of problems. It engages him in the quest of solutions. It makes him aloof to what is not established. It compels assent to the unconditioned. It is the cool shrewdness of common sense, the disinterestedness of science, the detachment of philosophy. It is the absorption of investigation, the joy of discovery, the assurance of judgment, the modesty of limited knowledge. It is the relentless serenity, the unhurried determination, the imperturbable drive of question following appositely on question in the genesis of truth.

This pure desire has an objective. It is a desire to know. As mere desire, it is for the satisfaction of acts of knowing, for the satisfaction of understanding, of understanding fully, of understanding correctly. But as pure desire, as cool, disinterested, detached, it is not for cognitional acts and the satisfaction they give their subject, but for cognitional contents, for what is to be known. The satisfaction of mistaken understanding, provided one does not know it as mistaken, can equal the satisfaction of correct understanding. Yet the pure desire scorns the former and prizes the latter; it prizes it, then, as dissimilar to the former; it prizes it not because it yields satisfaction but because its content is correct.

The objective of the pure desire is the content of knowing rather than the act. Still, the desire is not itself a knowing, and so its range is not the same as the range of knowing. Initially in each individual, the pure desire is a dynamic orientation to a totally unknown. As knowledge develops, the objective becomes less and less unknown, more and more known. At any time the objective includes both all that is known and all that remains unknown, for it is the goal of the immanent dynamism of cognitional process, and that dynamism both underlies actual attainment and heads beyond it with ever further questions.

What is this objective? Is it limited or unlimited? Is it one or many? Is it material or ideal? Is it phenomenal or real? Is it an immanent content or a transcendent object? Is it a realm of experience, or of thought, or of essences, or of existents? Answers to these and to any other questions have but a single source. They cannot be had without the functioning of the pure desire. They cannot be had from the pure desire alone. They are to be had inasmuch as the pure desire initiates and sustains cognitional process. Thus, if it is true that A is, that A is one, and that there is only A, then the objective of the pure desire is one. But if it is true that A is, that B is, that A is not B, then the objective is many. Which, you ask, is true? The fact that you ask, results from the pure desire. But to reach the answer, desiring is not enough; answers come only from inquiring and reflecting.

Now our definition was that being is the objective of the pure desire to know. Being, then, is (1) all that is known, and (2) all that remains to be known. Again, since a complete increment of knowing occurs only in judgment, being is what is to be known by the totality of true judgments. What, one may ask, is that totality? It is the complete set of answers to the complete set of questions. What the answers are remains to be seen. What the questions are awaits their emergence. Meaningless or incoherent or illegitimate questions may be possible, but how they are to be defined is a further question. The affirmation in hand is that there exists a pure desire to know, an inquiring and critical spirit, that follows up questions with further questions, that heads for some objective which has been named being.

Our definition of being, then, is of the second order. Other definitions determine what is meant. But this definition is more remote for it assigns, not what is meant by being, but how that meaning is to be determined. It asserts that if you know, then you know being; it asserts that if you wish to know, then you wish to know being; but it does not settle whether you know or what you know, whether your wish will be fulfilled or what you will know when it is fulfilled.

Still, though our definition is of the second order, it is not simply indeterminate. For neither the desire to know nor knowing itself is indeterminate. Inasmuch as knowing is determinate, we could say that being is what is to be known by true judgments. Inasmuch as the desire to know ever goes beyond actual knowledge, we could say that being is what is to be known by the totality of true judgments. Hence being has at least one characteristic: it is all-inclusive. Apart from being there is nothing. Again, being is completely concrete and completely universal.

It is completely concrete: over and above the being of any thing, there is nothing more of that thing. It is completely universal: apart from the realm of being, there is simply nothing.

2　An Unrestricted Notion   [350–52]

One may wonder just how all-inclusive being is. That wonder may be formulated in a variety of manners. But no matter how it is formulated, no matter whether it can be formulated, it can serve only to show how all-inclusive being is. For the wonder is inquiry. It is the desire to know. Anything it can discover or invent, by that very fact is included in the notion of being. Hence the effort to establish that being is not all-inclusive must be self-defeating; for at the root of all that can be affirmed, at the root of all that can be conceived, is the pure desire to know; and it is the pure desire, underlying all judgment and formulation, underlying all questioning and all desire to question, that defines its all-inclusive objective.

Nonetheless, it may not be amiss to illustrate this principle concretely. It will be said that there is much we do not know. No doubt, our ignorance is great, but we know that fact by raising questions that we do not answer; and being is defined not only by the answers we give but also by the questions we ask. Next, it will be said that there is much it would be futile for us to try to learn. No doubt, the proximately fruitful field of inquiry is restricted. But we know that fact by distinguishing between the questions we can hope soon to answer and those that as yet we are not prepared to tackle; and being is defined, not only by the questions we can hope to answer, but also by the questions whose answer we have to postpone.

Thirdly, it will be objected by many that they have no desire to know everything about everything. But how do they know that they do not already know everything about everything? It is because so many questions can be asked. Why do they not effectively will to know everything about everything? Because it is so troublesome to reach even a few answers that they are completely disheartened by the prospect of answering all the questions they could ask.

The attack may be made from the opposite flank. The trouble is that the definition of being is too inclusive. Questions can be meaningless, illusory, incoherent, illegitimate. Trying to answer them does not lead to knowledge of anything. Now, no doubt, there are mistaken questions that lead nowhere. But mistaken questions are formulated questions. Being has been defined, not as the objective of formulated questions, but as the objective of the pure desire to know. Just as that desire is prior to any answer, and it itself is not an answer,[a] so too it is prior to any formulated question, and it itself is not a formulation. Moreover, just as the pure desire is the intelligent and rational basis from which we discern between correct and incorrect answers, so also it is the intelligent and rational basis from which we discern between valid and mistaken questions. In brief, the pure desire to know, whose objective is being, is the source not only of answers but also of their criteria, and not only of questions but also of the grounds on which they are screened. For it is intelligent inquiry and reasonable reflection that just as much yield the right questions as the right answers.[b]

More fundamental misgivings may arise. If one pleases, one may define being as what is to be known through the totality of true judgments. But is being really that? Might it not be something entirely different? The questions arise. They may be valid or mistaken. If they are mistaken, they are to be ignored. If they are valid, then our misgivings are without foundation. For the being that might be totally different turns out to be exactly what we are talking about. If we ask whether it might be, we ask; and the being we are talking about is whatever we ask about.[c]

Again, might there not be an unknowable? If the question is invalid, it is to be ignored. If the question is valid, the answer may be yes or no. But the answer 'yes' would be incoherent, for then one would be knowing that the unknowable is; and the answer 'no' would leave everything knowable and within the range of being.

Other doubts may arise, but instead of chasing after them one by one, it will be better to revert to our initial theorem. Every doubt that the pure desire is unrestricted serves only to prove that it is unrestricted. If you ask whether X might not lie beyond its range, the fact that you ask proves that X lies within its range. Or else, if the question is meaningless, incoherent, illusory, illegitimate, then X turns out to be the mere nothing that results from aberration in cognitional process.

Not only, then, is judgment absolute, not only does it rest upon a grasp of the unconditioned, not only does reflection set the dichotomy 'Is it or is it not?' But at the root of cognitional process there is a cool, detached, disinterested desire to know, and its range is unrestricted. Being is the anything and everything that is the objective of that desire.

3   A Spontaneous Notion   [352–56]

If we have explained what we mean by being, we must now ask what the notion of being is.

In the first place, a distinction has to be drawn between the spontaneously operative notion and, on the other hand, theoretical accounts of its genesis and content. The spontaneously operative notion is invariant; it is common to all men; it functions in the same manner no matter what theoretical account of it a man may come to accept. On the other hand, theoretical accounts of the content and genesis of the notion are numerous; they vary with philosophic contexts, with the completeness of a thinker's observations, with the thoroughness of his analysis. First, we shall give our account of the spontaneously operative notion, and then we shall add a few notes on other theoretical accounts of it.

On the supposition of our analysis of cognitional process, it is easy enough to conclude that the spontaneously operative notion of being has to be placed in the pure desire to know. For, first of all, men are apt to agree that things are, whether or not we know them, and moreover that there are many things that are known only incompletely or even not at all. The notion of being, then, extends beyond the known. Secondly, being is known in judgment. It is in judgment that we affirm or deny, and until we are ready to affirm or deny, we do not yet know whether or not any X happens to be. Still, though being is known only in judging, the notion of being is prior to judging. For prior to any judgment there is reflection, and reflection is formulated in the question, Is it? That question supposes some notion of being, and strangely enough, it is prior to each instance of our knowing being. Not only, then, does the notion of being extend beyond the known but also it is prior to the final component of knowing when being is actually known. Thirdly, there are objects of thought. I can think of a horse, and no less I can think of a centaur. I can think of the best available scientific opinion on any subject, and no less I can think of all the previous opinions that in their day were the best available on the same subject. In one sense, they are all equivalent, for as long as one is merely thinking, merely considering, merely supposing, one deals merely with the conditioned, and it makes no difference whether or not its conditions are fulfilled. Thinking, then, prescinds from existing. But if it prescinds from existing, does it not prescind from being? And if it prescinds from being, is not all thinking about nothing? The trouble with this argument is that thinking also prescinds from not existing. If I think of a centaur or of phlogiston, I prescind from the fact that they do not exist; hence, if prescinding from existing is prescinding from being, prescinding from nonexistence is prescinding from not being; if prescinding from being proves that I am thinking of nothing, then prescinding from not being proves that I am thinking of something.

Now this type of consideration has led many thinkers to suppose that being is one thing and existing is another, that horses and centaurs, electrons and phlogiston equally are, but horses and electrons exist while centaurs and phlogiston do not exist. Still, that conclusion does not satisfy the facts, for apart from the oddity of asserting that the nonexistent is, there is the oversight of the dynamism of cognitional process. In a sense, thinking prescinds from existing and not existing, for it is not thinking but judging that determines whether or not anything exists. In another sense, thinking does not prescind from existing and not existing, for thinking is purposive; we think to get our concepts straight; we wish to get our concepts straight that we may be able to judge; so far from prescinding from existing and not existing, thinking is for the purpose of determining whether or not what is thought does exist.

It follows that the notion of being goes beyond the merely thought, for we ask whether or not the merely thought exists. No less, it follows that the notion of being is prior to thinking, for were it not, then thinking could not be for the purpose of judging, for the purpose of determining whether or not the merely thought exists. The notion of being, then, is prior to conception and goes beyond it; and it is prior to judgment and goes beyond it. That notion must be the immanent, dynamic orientation of cognitional process. It must be the detached and unrestricted desire to know as operative in cognitional process. Desiring to know is desiring to know being; but it is merely the desire and not yet the knowing.[d] Thinking is thinking being; it is not thinking nothing; but thinking being is not yet knowing it. Judging is a complete increment in knowing; if correct, it is a knowing of being; but it is not yet knowing being, for that is attained only through the totality of correct judgments.

Still, how can an orientation or a desire be named a notion? A fetal eye is orientated towards seeing; but a fetal eye does not see, and it has no notion of seeing; a notion arises only insofar as understanding discerns future function in present structure. Hunger is orientated towards food and eating; it is a desire; it lies within empirical consciousness; but a notion arises only insofar as the orientation of hunger is understood. Purposive human action is orientated towards some end or product; cognitional elements provide the rule and guide of such action; but the cognitional elements are prior to the action; they are constituted, not by the action itself, but by the planning that precedes it.

It remains that none of these instances is exactly parallel to the relation between the desire to know and cognitional process. For the desire to know is not unconscious, as is the fetal eye, nor empirically conscious, as is hunger, nor a consequence of intellectual knowledge, as are deliberation and choice. The desire to know is conscious intelligently and rationally; it is inquiring intelligence and reflecting reasonableness. Simply as desire, it is orientation, without as yet involving any cognitional content or notion. Still, intelligence as obverse looks for the intelligible as reverse. Reasonableness as obverse looks for the grounded as reverse. More fundamentally, the looking for, the desiring, the inquiring-and-reflecting is an obverse that intelligently and rationally heads for an unrestricted objective named being. Were that heading unconscious, there would be an orientation towards being but there would be no desire to know being and no notion of being. Were that heading empirically conscious, there would be an orientation towards being and a felt desire to know being, but there would be no notion of being. In fact, the heading is intelligent and rational, and so there is not only an orientation towards being, not only a pure desire to know being, but also a notion of being.

Let us try to catch this notion, this intention of being, in the act. We speak of abstraction, and commonly we mean a direction of attention to some aspects of the given with a concomitant neglect of other aspects. The geometer considers the circle as a plane figure obeying a certain rule; he disregards the size, the color, the inexactitude, of the figure he draws or imagines; still more does he disregard other and more loosely connected aspects of the given. But that is not all. He disregards all other questions in geometry, all other departments of mathematics, all other fields of science, all other human occupations to which he could turn his hand. He considers only the circle. He abstracts from everything else. He does so intelligently, for though the objective of his desire is unrestricted, still he can move towards it only by concentrating on one element at a time. Again, as intelligence abstracts, so reflection prescinds. If I am to judge whether or not this is a typewriter, I have to prescind from all that is not relevant to that issue. I have to know all that is relevant. If I were a relativist, I would have to know the universe to know all that is relevant to that single judgment. Even though I am not a relativist, even though I find that many conditioned propositions become virtually unconditioned on the fulfilment of a manageable number of conditions, still this restriction of the relevant is accompanied by an acknowledgment of a universe of irrelevances.

Finally, as intelligence concentrates on the significant to abstract from all else, as reflection concentrates on the relevant to prescind from all else, so further questions and further issues arise neither as a surprise nor as a new beginning. The abstracting and the prescinding were provisional; they were only moments in a larger process. Nor is that larger process merely the object of introspective analysis. Immanent within it and operative of it lies an intelligent and rational consciousness that unrestrictedly intends a correspondingly unrestricted objective named being, or the all, or everything about everything, or the concrete universe. Just as the notion of the intelligible is involved in the actual functioning of intelligence, just as the notion of the grounded is involved in the actual functioning of reasonableness, so the notion of being is involved in the unrestricted drive of inquiring intelligence and reflecting reasonableness.

4   An All-pervasive Notion   [356–57]

Hence it is that the notion of being is all-pervasive: it underpins all cognitional contents; it penetrates them all; it constitutes them as cognitional.

It underpins all cognitional contents. Without the pure desire to know, sensitive living would remain in its routine of perception and conation, instinct and habit, emotion and action. What breaks that circuit and releases intellectual activity is the wonder Aristotle described as the beginning of all science and philosophy. But that wonder is intelligent inquiry. It selects data for insight, and by that selecting it underpins even the empirical component in our knowing. Still more obviously, all ideas and all concepts are responses to the desire to understand, and all judgments are responses to the demand for the unconditioned.

Secondly, the notion of being penetrates all cognitional contents. It is the supreme heuristic notion. Prior to every content, it is the notion of the to-be-known through that content. As each content emerges, the 'to-be-known through that content'ᵉ passes without residue into the 'known through that content.' Some blank in universal anticipation is filled in, not merely to end that element of anticipation, but also to make the filler a part of the anticipated. Hence, prior to all answers, the notion of being is the notion of the totality to be known through all answers. But once all answers are reached, the notion of being becomes the notion of the totality known through all answers.

Thirdly, the notion of being constitutes all contents as cognitional. Experiencing is only the first level of knowing: it presents the matter to be known. Understanding is only the second level of knowing: it defines the matter to be known. Knowing reaches a complete increment only with judgment, only when the merely experienced has been thought and the merely thought has been affirmed. But the increment of knowing is always completed in the same fashion. Experience is a kaleidoscopic flow. Objects of thought are as various as the inventiveness of human intelligence. But the contribution of judgment to our knowing is ever a mere yes or no, a mere 'is' or 'is not.' Experience is for inquiring into being. Intelligence is for thinking out being. But by judgment being is known, and in judgment what is known is known as being. Hence knowing is knowing being, yet the known is never mere being, just as judgment is never a mere yes apart from any question that 'yes' answers.

5   The Core of Meaning   [357–59]

As the notion of being underpins all contents and penetrates them and constitutes them as cognitional, so also it is the core of meaning.

For present purposes it will suffice to distinguish (1) sources of meaning, (2) acts of meaning, (3) terms of meaning, and (4) the core of meaning.[f]

Any element of knowledge may serve as a source of meaning. Hence, sources of meaning include data and images, ideas and concepts, the grasp of the unconditioned and judgment, and no less, the detached and unrestricted desire to know.

Acts of meaning are of three kinds. They are (1) formal, (2) full, (3) instrumental. The formal act of meaning is an act of conceiving, thinking, considering, defining, supposing, formulating. The full act of meaning is an act of judging. The instrumental act of meaning is the implementation of a formal or of a full act by the use of words or symbols in a spoken, written, or merely imagined utterance.

Terms of meaning are what is meant. They are formal or full. Formal terms of meaning are what is conceived, thought, considered, defined, supposed, formulated. Full terms of meaning are what is affirmed or denied.

Now the all-inclusive term of meaning is being, for apart from being there is nothing. Inversely, the core of all acts of meaning is the intention of being.

Thus, any given judgment pertains to a context of judgments, and it is from the context that the meaning of the given judgment is determined. But why is the meaning of the given judgment a function[g] of a context of other judgments? Because any judgment is but an increment in a whole named knowledge; because the meaning of the judgment is but an element in the determination of the universal intention of being.

Again, judgments may be true or false. The true judgment affirms what is and denies what is not. In the true judgment there is harmony between what is intended and what is meant. But in the false judgment there is conflict between intention and meaning. The false judgment as a judgment intends being; it intends to affirm what is and to deny what is not. But the false judgment as false is a failure to carry out its intention as a judgment. It affirms what is not and denies what is. It means not what is but only what would be, were it not false but true; again, in its negative form, it means, not what is not, but what would not be, were it not false but true.

Perhaps it is this internal conflict that has led some to the conclusion that a false judgment is meaningless. But such a conclusion seems astoundingly false. Were the false judgment meaningless, there would be nothing to be false. The false judgment is false precisely because it means a state of affairs that is the opposite of the state one intends to affirm, namely, the state that truly is.

On the level of conception there is a similar but less conspicuous contrast between meaning and its core, which is the intention of being. Horses and unicorns, electrons and phlogiston may be equally valid as formal terms of meaning. One can suppose them, or consider them, or define them, and that is all that is required of the formal term of meaning. Still, horses and electrons seem preferable as formal terms to unicorns and phlogiston. Absolutely, one can think of the latter, but there is something idle, something superfluous, something futile, about such thinking. The reason for this is that thinking is a moment in the unfolding of the pure desire to know; though the thought as thought is merely a formal term of meaning, though the unicorn is just as valid a formal term as is the horse, still we do not merely think. Our thinking is purposive. It is a tentative determination of the all-inclusive notion of being. It not merely thinks the object of thought but also anticipates the object of judgment. It not merely means the formal term of meaning but also looks ahead to the full term. Because the unicorn and phlogiston are known to be unsuccessful determinations of being, they are formal terms in which the core of meaning, the intention of being, has become uninterested.

Finally, in view of the prevalence of empiricist theories of meaning, a few words may be added on instrumental acts. Ordinary instrumental acts, such as spoken or written words or symbols, offer no special interest. But the empiricist emphasizes ostensive acts, such as demonstrative pronouns and adjectives and, of course, gestures. The reason for this emphasis may be readily grasped if one distinguishes between the function of gestures in any theory of meaning and the function gestures acquire in virtue of empiricist affirmations. In any theory of meaning an ostensive act is an instrumental act of meaning; it presupposes formal or full acts of meaning, inasmuch as one knows what one means; and it refers to formal or full terms of meaning, inasmuch as all meaning refers to a meant. Again, in any theory of meaning the ostensive act is operative inasmuch as it succeeds in drawing another's attention to a sensible source of meaning, so that by drawing on that source, by understanding, and by reflecting, he may reach the appropriate formal or full term of meaning that is meant. But in empiricist opinion the ostensive act has a third function; for the empiricist identifies the valid field of full terms of meaning (that is, the universe of being) with the range of sensible presentations; hence, for the empiricist, the ostensive act indicates not merely a source of meaning but also a full term of meaning. Whether or not this empiricist modification of the general theory of meaning is correct will depend on the question whether or not the set of propositions that enunciate empiricism is to be pronounced true or false.

6   A Puzzling Notion   [359–64]

Before going on to consider other accounts of the notion of being, it will be well to deal with a series of puzzles that seem to have a common root. Just as other concepts, the notion of being is represented by instrumental acts that are the name 'being' and the verb 'to be.' By mistaken analogy it is inferred that the notion of being resembles concepts in their other aspects. But in fact the notion of being is unique; for it is the core of all acts of meaning; and it underpins, penetrates, and goes beyond all other cognitional contents. Hence it is idle to characterize the notion of being by appealing to the ordinary rules or laws of conception. What has to be grasped is its divergence from such rules and laws, and to descend to details, a series of questions will be briefly considered.

First, does the notion of being result from the expression or formulation of an act of understanding?

Other concepts result from some insight either into the use of their names, or into things-for-us, or into things-themselves. The notion of being penetrates all other contents, and so it is present in the formulation of every concept. It cannot result from an insight into being, for such an insight would be an understanding of everything about everything, and such understanding we have not attained. It is, as has been said, the orientation of intelligent and rational consciousness towards an unrestricted objective.

Secondly, has the notion of being an essence, or is it an essence?

As other concepts result from acts of understanding, as acts of understanding consist in grasping what from some viewpoint is essential, other concepts are essences. Moreover, as other concepts are complete prior to the question for reflection that asks whether or not any such essence is, other concepts are merely essences and prescind from existence or actuality. But the notion of being does not result from an understanding of being; it does not rest on the grasp of what from some viewpoint is essential; and so the notion of being is not the notion of some essence. Further, the notion of being remains incomplete on the level of intelligence; it moves conception forward to questions for reflection; it moves beyond single judgments to the totality of correct judgments; and so it does not prescind from existence and actuality.

Thirdly, can the notion of being be defined?

It cannot be defined in any ordinary manner, for it underpins and penetrates and goes beyond the content of every definition. However, it does possess certain definite characteristics. For it regards the unrestricted objective of our knowing, the concrete universe, the totality of all that is. Moreover, it is determinate inasmuch as the structure of our knowing is determinate, and so it can be defined at a second remove by saying that it refers to all that can be known by intelligent grasp and reasonable affirmation. On the other hand, such definition does not settle which questions are appropriate to our knowing or which answers are correct. It leaves the materialist free to claim that to be is to be material. Equally, it allows the empiricist to claim that to be is to be experienced, the idealist to insist that to be is to be thought, the phenomenalist to explain that to be is to appear, and so forth.

Fourthly, how can one notion have such diverse meanings?

Because it is determinate only at a second remove. The notion of being is the notion of what is to be determined by correct judgments. If the strategic correct judgments are that matter exists and nothing but matter exists, then the materialist is right. If the strategic correct judgments are that there is appearance and nothing but appearance, then the phenomenalist is right. Similarly, if the propositions enunciating other positions are correct, then being is as such positions declare. The notion of being does not determine which position is correct; it merely determines that the intelligently grasped and reasonably affirmed is being.

Fifthly, has the notion of being any presuppositions or properties?

Other concepts are determinate essences, and so they have presuppositions and implications. If X is not an animal, then X is not a man. If X is a man, then X is mortal. But the notion of being is not the notion of some essence. It becomes determined only as correct judgments are made, and it reaches its full determination only when the totality of correct judgments are made. However, the making of judgments is a determinate process, and one does not have to make all judgments to grasp the nature of that process. It is this fact that makes cognitional theory a base of operations for the determination of the general structure of the concrete universe.

Sixthly, is the notion of being univocal or analogous?

Concepts are said to be univocal when they have the same meaning in all applications, and they are said to be analogous when their meaning varies systematically as one moves from one field of application to another. The notion of being may be named univocal inasmuch as it underpins all other contents; for in that respect it is the one desire to know, and it regards one unrestricted objective that is the concrete universe. Again, the notion of being may be named analogous inasmuch as it penetrates all other contents; in this fashion it is said that *esse viventium est vivere*, the being of living things is being alive. Finally, the notion of being may be said to be neither univocal nor analogous, for this distinction regards concepts, while the notion of being both underpins and goes beyond other contents. It may be noted, however, that what frequently enough is meant by the analogy of being is precisely what we mean by saying that the notion of being underpins, penetrates, and goes beyond other contents.

Seventhly, is the notion of being abstract?

For a notion to be abstract it must possess a determinate content and abstract from other contents. The notion of being abstracts from nothing whatever. It is all-inclusive. [h] Its content is determined by the totality of correct judgments.

However, there is a still larger totality of possible judgments; within it there are strategic sets that serve to define the general character of the concrete universe in accord with the varying viewpoints of different philosophies. Such strategic sets have already been illustrated; for example, there is matter and nothing but matter, or there is appearance and nothing but appearance, or there is thought and nothing but thought, or the structure of our knowing is determinate and so the structure of being proportionate to our knowing is determinate.

Now in virtue of such strategic sets of judgments it is possible to distinguish between the general character of the concrete universe and, on the other hand, the concrete universe in all its details. Clearly enough, a determination of the general character of the concrete universe is an abstract view of being, for it considers not the whole of being as a whole but the whole of being as fixed by some strategic part or aspect.

In this fashion one reaches a general meaning for the phrase 'being as being.' But to determine what being as being is in any particular philosophy, one has to examine the strategic judgments of that philosophy; and to determine what is the correct meaning of being as being, one has to examine the strategic judgments of the correct philosophy.

Eighthly, is the notion of being a genus or species or difference?

Inasmuch as the notion of being is prior to all other cognitional contents, it is like a genus awaiting division by the addition of differences. [i] But inasmuch as the notion of being anticipates, penetrates, and includes all other contents, it differs from the genus, which is a determinate content quite distinct from the content of its differences. Thus, being can be divided into red, green, and blue beings; and color can be divided into red, green, and blue colors. But the concept of red has a content or element of content absent in the concept of color, and so it differentiates the genus by adding to it from without. On the other hand, the concept of red has no content and no element of content absent in the notion of being; it cannot differentiate being by adding to it from without, for without being, apart from being, there is simply nothing. Finally, the notion of being not only underpins and penetrates all other contents but also complements them inasmuch as the yes of judgment constitutes them as actually cognitional[j] and so endows them with an actual objective reference.

Ninthly, when one thinks without as yet judging, one is thinking either of being or of nothing. If one is thinking of being, then one does not need to judge in order to know being. If one is thinking of nothing, then all thought must be identical, for it always deals with the same nothing.

When one thinks, conceives, considers, supposes, or defines, one does so with respect to being. Hence we accept the first alternative. What one thinks of is being. Still, to think of being is one thing, to know being is another. To think of being is to operate on the second level of cognitional process; it is to be on the way towards a complete increment of knowing; but it is not to have reached anything more than a partial increment that can be completed only by judging.

Tenthly, the notion of being is the notion of the concrete universe. But universal propositions are abstract, and nonetheless they may be affirmed in judgment. Either, then, judgment is not about being, or else being is not concrete.

The notion of being is the notion of the concrete in the same manner as it is of the universe. It is of the universe because questions end only when there is nothing more to be asked. It is of the concrete, because until the concrete is reached, there remain further questions. Hence it is not the single judgment but the totality of correct judgments that equates with the concrete universe that is being.

The problem of the universal proposition may be met by distinguishing between the formal and the material aspects of the analytic proposition. Formally, an analytic proposition is (1) a conditioned, (2) linked to its conditions by the laws governing the coalescence of the partial instrumental meanings of words into the complete instrumental meaning of the sentence, and (3) having its conditions fulfilled by the meanings or definitions of the words it employs. Materially, analytic propositions differ inasmuch as the terms and relations employed (1) may be known to occur in concrete judgments of fact, (2) may not be known to occur in concrete judgments of fact, or (3) may be known not to occur in concrete judgments of fact.

Formally, every analytic proposition regards the concrete universe inasmuch as syntactical laws are factual aspects of the coalescence of partial into complete instrumental meanings. Materially, some analytic propositions regard the concrete universe either in fact, as in the first case, or tentatively, as in the second.

7   Theories of the Notion of Being   [364–74]

A distinction has been drawn between the spontaneously operative notion of being, common to all men, and theoretical accounts of that notion, which differ from one philosophy to another. Our own theoretical account has been given. It remains that further clarifications be sought by contrasting it with some of the views that have been proposed by others.

For Parmenides, Being was one, without origin or end, homogeneous and indivisible, immovable and unchangeable, full and spherical. [1]

The genesis of this position would seem to be as follows. Parmenides eliminated the alternative of blank negation, and so was left with the alternative of affirming. Affirmation may be reasonably grounded, and then it is the Way of Truth, or it may lack reasonable grounds, and then it is the Way of Seeming. Parmenides arrived at his notion of being by following the Way of Truth.

What does the choice of reasonable affirmation imply being to be? If one accepts any affirmation, one has also to accept the correct statement of the meaning, suppositions, and consequences of that affirmation. Every judgment is in need of a context, and without affirming the context the affirmation of the initial judgment loses its meaning. Thus reasonable affirmation has to be the affirmation of a set of judgments which form a single whole, and so the affirmed is a corresponding single whole.

What is this single whole that is affirmed to be? The proper answer is to set to work inquiring and reflecting with respect to the whole of experience. The whole to be known corresponds to the totality of correct judgments. But Parmenides took a shorter route. He did not advert to the fact that being admits no more than a definition of the second order. He treated the notion of being as though it were a concept like

1 See F.M. Cornford, *Plato and Parmenides* (London: Routledge and Kegan Paul, 1939) 28–52.

'man' or 'circle.' He supposed that it was a determinate essence with determinate suppositions and determinate consequences. Because being is, it cannot be not-being, nor becoming, nor ceasing to be. Inversely, neither not-being nor becoming nor ceasing to be is being, and so all three[k] must be nothing. Again, being cannot be differentiated; what differs from being is not being; and what is not being is nothing. Again, since there are no differences within being, there can be no motion or change within being. Finally, emptiness, the void, is nothing; being is not nothing, and so it cannot be emptiness; therefore, it is full. Etc.

Plato's Forms were projections into a noetic heaven of what transcends ordinary sensitive experience. The Forms, then, are the ideal objectives of (1) aesthetic experience, (2) the insights of the mathematician and physicist, (3) the unconditioned of reflective understanding, (4) moral conscience, and (5) intelligently and reasonably purposive living. They are a confused bag, and, as it seems, the *Parmenides* marks the turning point in which the necessity of drawing distinctions and setting up a more comprehensive theory becomes evident.

In the *Sophist* the philosopher is described as heading through rational discourse for the Idea of Being.[2] It is acknowledged that the isolation of each Form from all the others would eliminate the possibility of discourse, which lies in the conjunction of distinct Forms or categories.[3] There is, then, a commingling or participation among the Forms,[4] and there is a Form of Not-being just as much as of the Great or the Fair.[5]

The inadequacy of this position lies in its failure to distinguish between the level of intelligence and the level of reflection. Without that distinction, the unconditioned of judgment is surreptitiously attributed to mere objects of thought, to transform them into eternal Forms, and inversely, the 'is' and 'is not' by which judgment posits the unconditioned can have a meaning only if they too are supposed to be Forms. There results an aggregate of Forms, each radically and eternally distinct from all the others. Still, they are to be reached only through rational discourse, and if discourse is to refer to them, then there must be a commingling on their part to correspond to the synthetic element[l] in discourse. What is this commingling of distinct Forms? It would seem

2 Plato, *Sophist*, 254a. [This and the next three notes have been transferred by editors from text to footnotes.]
3 Ibid. 259e.
4 Ibid. 259a.
5 Ibid. 258c.

better, before trying to answer so difficult a question, to determine whether or not the question really arises. In fact, we would argue, it does not. Until judgment is reached, the increment of knowing is incomplete. Before judgment is reached, the synthetic element is already present in knowing. All that judgment adds to the question for reflection is the yes or no, the 'is' or 'is not.' What is affirmed or denied may be a single proposition or the whole set of propositions constitutive of a hypothesis, for either may be regarded as conditioned, and either may be grasped as virtually unconditioned. Judgment, then, is not a synthesis of terms but the unconditioned positing of such a synthesis. Corresponding to judgment there is not a synthesis of Forms but the absolute of fact. Platonism is magnificent in its devotion to the pure desire to know. But its failure to grasp the nature of judgment resulted in a deviation from the concrete universe of fact to an ideal heaven.

Aristotle clung to the Platonist definition of judgment as a synthesis.[6] Still, he distinguished sharply between questions for intelligence (What is it? Why is it so?) and questions for reflection (Is it? Is it so?)[7] with the result that he had a sane and clearheaded respect for fact without reaching its exact implications. He would not have agreed with the empiricist that places fact, not in the virtually unconditioned, but in the sensible fulfilment through which the conditioned becomes grasped as unconditioned. But you would put him a question he had not adequately considered, if you asked him whether the virtually unconditioned was a third component in our knowing or, on the other hand, merely a rubber stamp of approval attached to the conceptual unification of its sensible and intelligible components.

This unresolved ambiguity appears both in his methodology and in his metaphysics. For him the supreme question was the question of existence. Still, it was a question that was already answered in descriptive knowing; that answer had to be presupposed in the search for explanation; and the function of explanation was simply to determine what things are and why they have the properties they possess. The intrinsically hypothetical character of explanation and its need of a further, verifying judgment of existence were overlooked. Again, Aristotle asks what being is. That question expresses the demand for understanding, for knowledge of the cause. Quite naturally, Aristotle answers that the

6 Ibid. 263; Aristotle, *De anima*, III, 6, 430a 26.
7 *Posterior Analytics*, II, 1, 89b 22–38.

cause of being is its immanent form.[8] Primarily, being is what is constituted by a substantial form or, on second thoughts, by the combination of substantial form and matter. Secondarily, being is what is constituted by accidental forms; 'white,' 'heat,' 'strength' are not nothing, though they are not simply what is meant by being. Again, being is the collection of existing substances with their properties and incidental modifications; but though being denotes the factually existent, still existing is no more than the reality of substantial forms along with their mainly immanent suppositions and consequences.[9]

Quite plainly this position is going to give rise to a problem of the unity of the notion of being. Aristotle broke with his Parmenidean and Platonist antecedents by identifying being with the concrete universe as in fact it is known to be. But Aristotle did not break with their supposition that the notion of being was a conceptual content. He asked what being is. In other words, he supposed that being is some conceptual content, and he demanded what act of understanding occurred prior to the formulation of that content. But, as we have seen, being can be defined by us only indirectly, and so Aristotle was unable to assign any specific act of understanding that resulted in the conceptual content of being. However, the conspicuous type of acts of understanding is the insight that grasps intelligible form emergent in sensible data; and so Aristotle assigned the ontological principle 'form' as the ground of being in things and the cognitional act of grasping form as the insight from which originates the conceptual content 'being.'

In this fashion, medieval scholasticism inherited a problem. Is the notion of being one or is it many? If it is one, is its unity the unity of a single content or is it the unity of a function of variable contents?

Henry of Ghent seems to have held that the unity of being is merely the unity of a name. God is, and I am. In both cases, being is affirmed. But the realities affirmed are simply disparate.

Duns Scotus contended that, besides the unity of the name, there is

---

8 *Metaphysics*, VII, 17. [Transferred by editors from text to footnote.]
9 See Suzanne Mansion, *Le jugement d'existence chez Aristote* (Louvain: Editions de l'Institut Supérieur de Philosophie, 1946; 2nd ed., revised and augmented, 1976); Joseph Owens, *The Doctrine of Being in the Aristotelian Metaphysics: A Study in the Greek Background of Mediaeval Thought* (Toronto: Pontifical Institute of Mediaeval Studies, 1951; a second, revised edition was published in 1963 and a third, further revised edition in 1978).

also a unity of content. If no part or aspect of you is by identity a part or aspect of me, still neither of us is nothing. There is, then, some minimal conceptual content that positively constitutes what is expressed negatively by the negation of nothing. What it is cannot be declared by appealing to other positive contents, for it is one of the ultimate atoms of thought; it is simply simple. Still, one can approach it by noting that Socrates supposes man, man supposes animal, animal supposes living material substance, and substance supposes a something that is even less determinate and less exclusive. The concept of being is the concept with least connotation and greatest denotation. Moreover, it is essentially abstract. What it denotes is never just being, but either the infinite or some finite mode of being, where the mode is to be viewed not as some further and distinct content but rather as an intrinsic variation of basic, indeterminate content.[10]

Thomas de Vio Caietanus was no more satisfied with the Scotist view than Scotus himself had been satisfied with that of Henry of Ghent. If a single name without a single meaning will not do, neither will a single meaning that as single seems restricted to the order of thought. Accordingly, Cajetan worked out his theory of the unity of a function of variable contents. Just as 'double' denotes indifferently the relation of 2 to 1, 4 to 2, 6 to 3, and so forth, so 'being' denotes indifferently the proportion of essence to existence or, as we might say, the proportion between what is formulated by thought and what is added to it by judgment. On this position the notion of being always includes some conceptual content, but it may include any; again, being in act will never be known without some affirmative judgment, but the affirmation is never mere affirmation nor the affirmation of an indeterminate content: it is always the affirmation of some determinate content, and any affirmable determinate content will do. In brief, Cajetan can grant that atomic conceptual contents are many and disparate; he can deny the Scotist view that there is some common factor, some positive counterpart of 'not nothing,' of absolutely universal denotation; and yet by his theory of the unity of a function of variable contents, he can possess not only a single name 'being' and a single notion of being, but

10 See Allan B. Wolter, The Transcendentals and Their Function in the Metaphysics of Duns Scotus (St. Bonaventure, NY: The Franciscan Institute, 1946); André Marc, L'Idée de l'être chez saint Thomas et dans la scolastique postérieure (Paris: Beauchesne, 1933), Archives de Philosophie 10 (Cahier 1): 31–49.

also a single notion that is applicable to anything that in fact is known to exist.[11]

It is to be noted that, if Scotus stands for the Parmenidean and Platonist suppositions from which Aristotle did not free himself, Cajetan stands for the main orientation of Aristotelian thought but succeeds in doing so only by going beyond it. If conceptual contents are products of acts of understanding that grasp forms emergent in sensible presentations, one may well expect such contents to be a disparate multiplicity. Hence Aristotle answered the question, What is being? not by assigning a conceptual content but by assigning the ground of being in the general object of understanding: form. Since forms are many, it follows that the ground of being is a variable; further, it follows that if the notion of being is to be one, then its unity will have to be the unity of a function of variable contents. What, then, are the variables within the single function? One of them is form. At first sight, the obvious candidate for the other is matter. Still, if it were selected, it would follow that Aristotle's immaterial substance would not belong to the universe of being. To maintain the Aristotelian position in its integrity, it was necessary to make the second variable the virtually unconditioned grasped by reflective understanding and affirmed in judgment; this in the general case is existence, actuality, fact, that combines with pure form or the compound of form and matter to constitute a being in act.

Brilliant as it is, Cajetan's position has its shortcomings. It envisages an aggregate of concrete beings, each of which is constituted by essence and existence. It offers as the unity of the notion of being the relation or proportion of what is conceived to its being affirmed. But it does not elucidate how that relation emerges in our knowledge as a single notion; and it gives no clue to account for the fact that by 'being' we mean, not only this and that being, but everything, totality, the universe. In brief, Cajetan seems to have been more interested in explaining the unity of the notion of being than the notion itself.

To complete Cajetan's position, it is necessary to go back to his master, St Thomas Aquinas. For Aquinas, as for Aristotle, human intellect is a potential omnipotence, a *potens omnia facere et fieri*. But Aquinas could exploit that affirmation in a manner that would have startled Aristotle, and while he did not distinguish explicitly between the *intentio intendens*

11 Marc, *L'Idée* ... 50–66.

or notion of being and the *intentio intenta* or concept of being, still he was remarkably aware of the implications of that distinction.

First, he recognized an unrestricted desire to know. As soon as we learn of God's existence, we wish to understand his nature, and so by our nature we desire what by our nature we cannot achieve.[12]

Secondly, from the unrestrictedness of intellect there follows the determination of its object. Because intellect is *potens omnia fieri*, its object is *ens*.[13]

Thirdly, for the same reason an intellect fully in act must be infinite act, and so a finite intellect must be potential.[14]

Fourthly, being is per se and naturally known to us,[15] and it cannot be unknown to us.[16] Avicenna had interpreted Aristotle's agent intellect as some separate immaterial substance. Aquinas found it immanent within us because, he argued, the light of intelligence in each of us performs the functions Aristotle ascribed to agent intellect.[17] Augustine had advanced that our knowledge of truth originated not from without but from within us, yet not simply from within us but in some illumination in which we consulted the eternal grounds and norms of things. Aquinas explained that we consult the eternal ground and norms, not by taking a look at them, but by having within us a light of intelligence that is a created participation of the eternal and uncreated light.[18]

Fifthly, though being is naturally known, though our intellects are created participations of uncreated light, still there is no valid ontological argument for the existence of God.[19] God's knowledge of being is a priori; he is the act of understanding that grasps everything about everything; but we advance towards knowledge by asking the explanatory question, *Quid sit?* and the factual question, *An sit?*

In such positions it is easy to discern not only the justification of

---

12 Thomas Aquinas, *Summa theologiae*, 1, q. 12; 1–2, q. 3, a. 8; *Summa contra Gentiles*, 3, cc. 25–63. [This and notes 13–19 are transferred by editors from text to footnotes.]
13 *Summa theologiae*, 1, q. 79, a. 7.
14 *Summa theologiae*, 1, q. 79, a. 2; *Summa contra Gentiles*, 2, c. 98.
15 *Summa contra Gentiles*, 2, c. 83, §31; see Bernard Lonergan, 'The Concept of *Verbum* ...,' *Theological Studies* 8 (1947) 43–44 [*Verbum* 56].
16 Thomas Aquinas, *De veritate*, q. 11, a. 1, ad 3m.
17 *Summa contra Gentiles*, 2, c. 77, §5.
18 *Summa theologiae*, 1, q. 84, a. 5.
19 *Summa theologiae*, 1, q. 2, a. 1.

Cajetan's theory of analogy but also the elements which that theory tends to overlook. Prior to conception and to judgment, there is the dynamic orientation of intelligent and rational consciousness with its unrestricted objective. This orientation is man's capacity to raise questions and thereby to generate knowledge. Immanent within man, it is a spark of the divine. Cognate to God, still it is knowing, not in act but in sheer potency. As it is the common root of intelligent grasp and reasonable judgment, so also it is the root of the relation or proportion between the conceived essence and the affirmed existence. As its objective is unrestricted, so it regards not only single compounds of essence and existence but also the universe, totality, infinity.

It has been noted how Cajetan saves the main orientation of Aristotelian thought by going beyond it, and though this involves still more metaphysics, it may be added how Aquinas does so. Aristotle asked what being is. But *what* is just a disguised *why*. What the question really asks for is the ground of being, and so Aristotle answered by indicating substantial form as the immanent cause of each being. But since his substantial form was not some unique and separate Platonic Idea, his answer gave rise to the problem of the unity of the notion of being. Now if Aquinas were to ask the same question, his answer would be that God is the ground of being; God's own being is self-explanatory and necessary; by the Aristotelian theorem of the identity of knower and known, God's being is identical with God's understanding; by that single act of understanding, God understands himself, and so he understands his own power, and so he understands all that by that power could be produced. God, then, is the act of understanding that grasps everything about everything. The content of the divine act of intellect is the idea of being, and so, precisely because our intellects are potential, they can define being only at a second remove as whatever is to be known by intelligent grasp and reasonable affirmation.

Again, both the position of Cajetan and the position of Scotus stand within the field accessible to the logician. By going behind that field to its dynamic basis, one can find the ground not only of Cajetan's proportion but also of Scotus's minimal content. What is it that is common to every conceptual content? It is that all are underpinned and penetrated by the pure desire's intention of its unrestricted objective. The Scotist notion of being is reached by distinguishing between the penetrating intention of being and the penetrated conceptual content; from instance to instance the conceptual content differs; but in every instance, there is the anticipating, enveloping, penetrating intention, and that is what the Scotist alleges to be a common factor in all contents.

Still, if the intention of being is a common factor in all conceptual contents, it is also a dynamic factor that goes beyond them. To set aside this dynamism is to nullify not only what lies beyond the conceptual contents but also the intention of being itself. In a famous little treatise Aquinas had remarked, *Essentia dicitur secundum quod per eam et in ea ens habet esse.*[20] It is in and through essences that being has existence. Hence, being apart from essence is being apart from the possibility of existence; it is being that cannot exist; but what cannot exist is nothing, and so the notion of being apart from essence is the notion of nothing.

It will be worth grasping why Scotus felt he could escape this conclusion while Hegel felt that he could not avoid it. Scotus felt he could avoid it because he conceived knowing, not as process that reaches a complete increment in judgment, but as taking a look. When Scotus separated his notion of being from other conceptual contents, he also separated that notion from the possibility of judgment. Still, that separation did not imply for Scotus a separation from the possibility of knowing, for he viewed knowing, not as ultimately constituted by judging, but as essentially a matter of looking. He would grant that there was no look in which the seen was solely the common content that he named being. But he would insist that that common content was included in the object of every intellectual intuition, and still more would he insist[m] that a look at nothing, an intuition of nothing, was absurd. In brief, for the Scotist, being is an aspect of the real at which intellect looks; the theory of modes and the distinction between quidditative and denominative being are efforts to blow this aspect up to the dimensions of the whole. For the Thomist, on the other hand, being is the whole of what intelligence anticipates; it is the objective of an unrestricted, dynamic orientation; it is whatever intelligent grasp and reasonable affirmation will determine; and so the notion of being is open to all the incomplete and partial moments from which cognitional process suffers without ever renouncing its all-inclusive goal.

Five hundred years separate Hegel from Scotus. As will appear from our discussion of the method of metaphysics, that notable interval of time was largely devoted to working out in a variety of manners the possibilities of the assumption that knowing consists in taking a look.

20 [Thomas Aquinas, *De ente et essentia*, c. 1.]

The ultimate conclusion was that it did not and could not. If the reader does not himself accept that conclusion as definitive, certainly Hegel did, and so Hegel could not take advantage of the Scotist escape from the identification of the notion of being with the notion of nothing. But Hegel was boxed on the other side as well. He effectively acknowledged a pure desire with an unrestricted objective. But he could not identify that objective with a universe of being, with a realm of factual existents and occurrences. For being as fact can be reached only insofar as the virtually unconditioned is reached; and as Kant had ignored that constitutive component of judgment, so Hegel neither rediscovered nor reestablished it. The only objective Hegel can offer the pure desire is a universe of all-inclusive concreteness that is devoid of the existential, the factual, the virtually unconditioned. There is no reason why such an objective should be named being. It is, as Hegel named it, an Absolute Idea. It is the all-inclusive summit of the pure desire's immanent dialectical process from position through opposition to sublation that yields a new position to recommence the triadic process until the Absolute Idea is reached.

Now if the intention that is the pure desire has neither a Scotist reality on which it can look back nor a Thomist universe of existents to which it can look forward, nonetheless in psychological fact it underpins and penetrates all conceptual contents. It constitutes, then, a common factor in all conceptual contents; it can be distinguished from them, for it is identical with none of them; yet, as distinguished from them, it becomes indistinguishable from the notion of nothing; for the only ground of the latter distinction would be that it looked back or forward to something.

It is interesting to note that, if the foregoing succeeds in fixing fundamental features of Hegel's thought, by that very fact it shows that on Hegelian criteria Hegelianism is mistaken. Hegel's System is not afraid of facts: it explains any fact alleged against it by showing it to be a manifestation of an incomplete viewpoint included within the System. Hegel's System is not afraid of contradictions: it explains any contradiction alleged against it by revealing what opposed and incomplete viewpoints, accounted for by the System, yield the alleged contradictory terms. The only thing the System has to fear is that it itself should be no more than some incomplete viewpoint, and in fact that is what it is. Hegel aimed at rehabilitating the speculative reason that Kant had dethroned. But the basis of the Kantian attack was that the unconditioned is not a constitutive component of judgment. A complete rehabilitation of human rational consciousness will show that the unconditioned is a constitutive component of judgment. This, Hegel did not do. His viewpoint is essentially the viewpoint of a thinker who does not and cannot regard the factual as unconditioned, who cannot acknowledge any factually fixed points of reference, who cannot advance by distinguishing the definitively certain, the more or less probable, and the unknown. Hegel's range of vision is enormous; indeed, it is unrestricted in extent. But it is always restricted in content, for it views everything as it would be if there were no facts. It is a restricted viewpoint that can topple outwards into the factualness of Marx or inwards into the factualness of Kierkegaard. It is a viewpoint that is transcended automatically by anyone that, in any instance, grasps the virtually unconditioned and affirms it.[21]

For this reason, we placed the discussion of self-affirmation prior to the discussion of the notion of being. Self-affirmation is the affirmation of the knower, conscious empirically, intelligently, rationally. The pure desire to know is a constituent element both of the affirming and of the self that is affirmed. But the pure desire to know is the notion of being as it is spontaneously operative in cognitional process, and being itself is the to-be-known towards which that process heads.

21 It is not to be inferred that my attitude towards Hegel[n] is merely negative. In fact, characteristic features in the very movement of his thought have their parallels in the present work. As his *Aufhebung* both rejects and retains, so also in their own fashion do our higher viewpoints. As he repeatedly proceeds from *an sich*, through *für sich*, to *an und für sich*, so our whole argument is a movement from the objects of mathematical, scientific, and commonsense understanding, through the acts of understanding themselves, to an understanding of understanding. [This note was added by Lonergan at the proof stage.]

13

The Notion of Objectivity

Human knowing is cyclic and cumulative. It is cyclic inasmuch as cognitional process advances from experience through inquiry and reflection to judgment, only to revert to experience and recommence its ascent to another judgment. It is cumulative, not only in memory's store of experiences and understanding's clustering of insights, but also in the coalescence of judgments into the context named knowledge or mentality.

This complexity of our knowing involves a parallel complexity in our notion of objectivity. Principally the notion of objectivity is contained within a patterned context of judgments which serve as implicit definitions of the terms 'object,' 'subject.' But besides this principal and complete notion, there also are partial aspects or components emergent within cognitional process. Thus, there is an experiential aspect of objectivity proper to sense and empirical consciousness. There is a normative aspect that is contained in the contrast between the detached and unrestricted desire to know and, on the other hand, merely subjective desires and fears. Finally, there is an absolute aspect that is contained in single judgments considered by themselves inasmuch as each rests on a grasp of the unconditioned and is posited without reservation.

1 The Principal Notion   [375–77]

Principally, the notion of objectivity is contained in a patterned context of judgments. For one may define as object any A, B, C, D, . . . where, in turn, A, B, C, D, . . . are defined by the correctness of the set of judgments

> A is; B is; C is; D is; . . .
>
> A is neither B nor C nor D nor . . .
>
> B is neither C nor D nor . . .
>
> C is neither D nor . . .

Again, one may define a subject as any object, say A, where it is true that A affirms himself as a knower in the sense explained in the chapter on self-affirmation.

The bare essentials of this notion of objectivity are reached if we add to the judgments already discussed – I am a knower, This is a typewriter – the further judgment that I am not this typewriter. An indefinite number of further objects may be added by making the additional appropriate positive and negative judgments. Finally, insofar as one can intelligently grasp and reasonably affirm the existence of other knowers besides oneself, one can add to the list the objects that also are subjects.

The properties of the principal notion of objectivity have now to be noted. First, as has already been remarked, the notion resides in a context of judgments; without a plurality of judgments that satisfy a definite pattern, the notion does not emerge. Secondly, there follows an immediate corollary: the principal notion of objectivity, as defined, is not contained in any single judgment, and still less in any experiential or normative factor that occurs in cognitional process prior to judgment. Thirdly, the validity of the principal notion of objectivity is the same as the validity of the set of judgments that contain it; if the judgments are correct, then it is correct that there are objects and subjects in the sense defined, for the sense defined is simply the correctness of the appropriate pattern of judgments.

Fourthly, to turn to certain broader aspects of the principal notion, judgments in the appropriate pattern commonly are made and commonly are regarded as correct. It follows that commonly people will know objects and subjects and that commonly they will be surprised that any doubt should be entertained about the matter. On the other hand, it does not follow that people will commonly be able to give a lucid account of their knowledge of objects and subjects. For the lucid account employs the somewhat recondite art of implicit definition, and at the same time people are apt to jump to the conclusion that so evident a matter as the existence of objects and subjects must rest on something as obvious and conspicuous as the experiential aspect of objectivity. Hence, on the one hand, they will say that the typewriter is an object because they see it or feel it; on the other hand, however, they will admit they would not consider the typewriter an object if they knew it to be true either that there was no typewriter at all or that what they named a typewriter was identical with everything else.

Fifthly, the principal notion of objectivity is closely related to the notion of being. Being is what is to be known through the totality of correct judgments. Objectivity in its principal sense is what is known through any set of judgments satisfying a determinate pattern. In brief, there is objectivity if there are distinct beings, some of which both know themselves and know others as others. Moreover, the notion of being explains why objectivity in its principal sense is to be reached only through a pattern of judgments. For the notion of being becomes determinate only insofar as judgments are made; prior to judgment, one can think of being but one cannot know it; and any single judgment is but a minute increment in the process towards knowing it. Again, being is divided from within; apart from being there is nothing; it follows that there cannot be a subject that stands outside being and looks at it; the subject has to be before he can look; and once he is, then he is not outside being but either the whole of it or some part. If he is the whole of it, then he is the sole object. If he is only a part, then he has to begin by knowing a multiplicity of parts (A is; B is; A is not B) and add that one part knows others ('I' am A).

Sixthly, the principal notion of objectivity solves the problem of transcendence. How does the knower get beyond himself to a known? The question is, we suggest, misleading. It supposes the knower to know himself and asks how he can know anything else. Our answer involves two elements. On the one hand, we contend that, while the knower may experience himself or think about himself without judging, still he cannot know himself until he makes the correct affirmation, 'I am,' and then he knows himself as being and as object. On the other hand,[a] we contend that other judgments are equally possible and reasonable, so that through experience, inquiry, and reflection there arises knowledge of other objects both as beings and as being other than the knower. Hence we place transcendence, not in going beyond a known knower, but in heading for being, within which there are positive differences and, among such differences, the difference between object and subject. Inasmuch as such judgments occur, there are in fact objectivity and transcendence; and whether or not such judgments are correct is a distinct question to be resolved along the lines reached in the analysis of judgment.

2   Absolute Objectivity   [377–80]

Besides the principal notion of objectivity, there also are the partial aspects of experiential, normative, and absolute objectivity. It will be convenient to begin from the last of the three.

The ground of absolute objectivity is the virtually unconditioned that is grasped by reflective understanding and posited in judgment. The formally unconditioned, which has no conditions at all, stands outside the interlocked field of conditioning and conditioned terms;[b] it is intrinsically absolute. The virtually unconditioned stands within that field; it has conditions; it itself is among the conditions of other instances of the conditioned; still its conditions are fulfilled; it is a de facto absolute.

Because the content of the judgment is an absolute, it is withdrawn from relativity to the subject that utters it, the place in which he utters it, the time at which he utters it. Caesar's crossing of the Rubicon was a contingent event occurring at a particular place and time. But a true affirmation of that event is an eternal, immutable, definitive validity. For if it is true that he did cross, then no one whatever at any place or time can truly deny that he did.

Hence it is in virtue of absolute objectivity that our knowing acquires what has been named its publicity. For the same reason that the unconditioned is withdrawn from relativity to its source, it also is accessible not only to the knower that utters it but also to any other knower.

Again, it is the absolute objectivity of the unconditioned that is formulated in the logical principles of identity and contradiction. The principle of identity is the immutable and definitive validity of the true. The principle of contradiction is the exclusiveness of that validity. It is, and what is opposed to it is not.

Further, absolute objectivity pertains to single judgments as single. As has been argued, the principal notion of objectivity is constituted only by a suitable constellation of judgments. But each judgment in such a constellation is an absolute, and moreover, it is an absolute in virtue of its own affirmation of the unconditioned. The validity of the principal notion is a derived validity resting on the set of absolutes it involves. But the absolute aspect of objectivity has its ground in the single judgment to which it pertains. It is quite compatible with the affirmation that there is but one being, that there is no object except the affirming subject; accordingly, the absolute aspect of objectivity does not imply any subject-object relation; it constitutes the entry of our knowing into the realm of being, but by itself it does not suffice to posit, distinguish, and relate beings. However, this insufficiency arises, not from some defect of absolute objectivity, nor because the posited beings, their distinction, and their relations are not all unconditioned, but because several judgments are needed to posit, to distinguish, and to relate.

It is important not to confuse the absolute objectivity of any correct judgment with the invariance proper to the expression of universal judgments. Both universal and particular judgments, if correct, are absolutely objective. But the former are expressed invariantly because the expression is independent of variations in spatiotemporal reference frames, while the latter are expressed relatively because their expression does not enjoy such independence. However, the variation of the expression presupposes and reveals the absolute objectivity of what is expressed. Because 'I am here now' has absolute objectivity, there is an identical truth to be repeated only by employing the different words, 'He was there then.'

Again, absolute objectivity has no implications of an absolute space or of an absolute time. If it is true that space is, then what is absolute is the truth and not the space. Whether the space is absolute or relative is a further question. If it is true that space consists of an infinite set of immovable and empty places, then space is absolute. If it is true that space is not such a set, then space is relative. Which is correct? At least the issue cannot be settled by appealing to the fact that a true judgment posits an unconditioned.

Further, as Zeno argued, to affirm that something or other is does not imply that it is within space. If it did, one could ask whether or not the space (within which it is) is. If space is not, it is nothing, and to affirm things within nothing is meaningless. If, however, it is, then since 'to be' is 'to be within space,' the question recurs; if 'X is' means 'X is within space,' it would seem to follow that 'space is' means that 'space is within space'; the second space cannot be identical with the first, else it would not contain it; and if it is distinct, then it can be only by being within a further space, and so on indefinitely.

The same argument holds for being within time. If 'to be' is 'to be at some time,' then either there is time or there is not. If there is not, then 'to be at some time' is really a mere 'to be.' If there is time, then it has to be at some time, and that at some time, and so forth to infinity.

Interpretations of being or of absolute objectivity in terms of space and time are mere intrusions of imagination. Absolute objectivity is simply a property of the unconditioned; and the unconditioned, as such, says nothing about space or time. If one's imagination makes the use of the preposition 'within' imperative, then one may say that every judgment is within a context of other judgments and that every unconditioned is within a universe of being. Then 'space is' by being within the universe of being, and 'time is' by being within the universe of being, where 'to be within the universe of being' is 'to be unconditioned along with other instances of the unconditioned.'

3   Normative Objectivity   [380–81]

The second of the partial aspects of objectivity is the normative. It is objectivity as opposed to the subjectivity of wishful thinking, of rash or excessively cautious judgments, of allowing joy or sadness, hope or fear, love or detestation, to interfere with the proper march of cognitional process.

The ground of normative objectivity lies in the unfolding of the unrestricted, detached, disinterested desire to know. Because it is unrestricted, it opposes the obscurantism that hides truth or blocks access to it in whole or in part. Because it is detached, it is opposed to the inhibitions of cognitional process that arise from other human desires and drives. Because it is disinterested, it is opposed to the well-meaning but disastrous reinforcement that other desires lend cognitional process only to twist its orientation into the narrow confines of their limited range.

Normative objectivity is constituted by the immanent exigence of the pure desire in the pursuit of its unrestricted objective. A dynamic orientation defines its objective. No less, it defines the means towards attaining its objective. Not only does the pure desire head for the universe of being, but also it does so by desiring to understand and by desiring to grasp the understood as unconditioned. Hence, to be objective, in the normative sense of the term, is to give free rein to the pure desire, to its questions for intelligence, and to its questions for reflection. Further, it is to distinguish between questions for intelligence that admit proximate solutions and other questions of the same type that, at present, cannot be solved. Similarly, it is to distinguish between sound questions and, on the other hand, questions that are meaningless or incoherent or illegitimate. For the pure desire not only desires; it desires intelligently and reasonably; it desires to understand because it is intelligent, and it desires to grasp the unconditioned because it desires to be reasonable.

Upon the normative exigences of the pure desire rests the validity of all logics and all methods. A logic or method is not an ultimate that can be established only by a hullabaloo of starry-eyed praise for Medieval Philosophy or for Modern Science, along with an insecure resentment of everything else. Logic and method are intelligent and rational; their grounds are not belief nor propaganda nor the pragmatic utility of atom bombs and nylon stockings; their grounds are the inner exigence of the pure desire to know. They are to be accepted insofar as they succeed in formulating that dynamic exigence; and they are to be revised insofar as they fail.

In various manners this dependence has already been noted. Thus, the logical principles of identity and contradiction result from the unconditioned and the compulsion it exercises upon our reasonableness. The principle of excluded middle possesses ultimate but not immediate validity: it possesses ultimate validity because, if a judgment occurs, it must be either an affirmation or a denial; it does not possess immediate validity, for with respect to each proposition, rational consciousness is presented with the three alternatives of affirmation, of negation, and of seeking a better understanding and so a more adequate formulation of the issue. Again, the procedures of empirical method in its classical and statistical phases have been accounted for by the pure desire's movement towards understanding, towards an understanding that regards not only things as related to us by our senses but also things as related functionally among themselves, towards an understanding that presupposes data to admit systematization in the classical phase and in other respects to be nonsystematic and so necessitate a statistical phase. Finally, precepts regarding judgment can be derived from the general requirement of the unconditioned and from the special circumstances of different kinds of judgments, which may be primitive or derived, theoretical or concrete, descriptive or explanatory, certain or probable.

4   **Experiential Objectivity**   [381–83]

The third partial aspect of objectivity is the experiential. It is the given as given. It is the field of materials about which one inquires, in which one finds the fulfilment of conditions for the unconditioned, to which cognitional process repeatedly returns to generate the series of inquiries and reflections that yield the contextual manifold of judgments.

Further, the given is unquestionable and indubitable. What is constituted by answering questions can be upset by other questions. But the given is constituted apart from questioning; it remains the same no matter what the result of questioning may be; it is unquestionable in the sense that it lies outside the cognitional levels constituted by questioning and answering. In the same fashion the given is indubitable. What can be doubted is the answer to a question for reflection; it is a yes or a no. But the given is not the answer to any question; it is prior to questioning and independent of any answers.

Again, the given is residual and, of itself, diffuse. It is possible to select elements in the given and to indicate them clearly and precisely. But the selection and indication are the work of insight and formulation, and the given is the residue that remains when one subtracts from the indicated (1) the instrumental act of meaning by which one indicates, (2) the concepts expressed by that instrumental act, (3) the insights on which the concepts rest. Hence, since the given is just the residue, since it can be selected and indicated only through intellectual activities, of itself it is diffuse; the field of the given contains differences, but insofar as they simply lie in the field, the differences are unassigned.

Again, the field of the given is equally valid in all its parts but differently significant in different parts.

It is equally valid in all its parts in the sense that there is no screening prior to inquiry. Screening is the fruit of inquiry. It takes place once inquiry has begun.

It is differently significant in different parts in the sense that some parts are significant for some departments of knowledge and other parts for other departments. The physicist has to disregard what he merely imagines, merely dreams, merely derives from his personal equation. The psychologist has to explain imagination, dreaming, and personal equations. Hence, once inquiry begins, the first step is the screening that selects the relevant field of the given.

We are employing the name 'given' in an extremely broad sense. It includes not only the veridical deliverances of outer sense but also images, dreams, illusions, hallucinations, personal equations, subjective bias, and so forth. No doubt, a more restricted use of the term would be desirable if we were speaking from the limited viewpoint of natural science. But we are working at a general theory of objectivity, and so we have to acknowledge as given not only the materials into which natural science inquires but also the materials into which the psychologist or methodologist or cultural historian inquires.

There is a profounder reason. Our account of the given is extrinsic. It involves no description of the stream of sensitive consciousness. It involves no theory of that stream. It discusses neither the contribution of the empirically conscious subject nor the contribution of other 'outside' agents. It simply notes that reflection and judgment presuppose understanding, that inquiry and understanding presuppose materials for inquiry and something to be understood. Such presupposed materials will be unquestionable and indubitable, for they are not constituted by answering questions. They will be residual and diffuse, for they are what is left over once the fruits of inquiry and reflection are subtracted from cognitional contents.

Now such unquestionable and indubitable, residual and diffuse materials for inquiry and reflection must be regarded as equally valid in all their parts. Were they all invalid, there could be neither inquiry nor reflection, and so no reasonable pronouncement that they are invalid. Were some valid and others invalid, there would have to be a reasonably affirmed principle of selection; but such a principle can be grasped and reasonably affirmed only after inquiry has begun. Prior to inquiry there can be no intelligent discrimination and no reasonable rejection.

There is a still deeper reason.[c] Why is the given to be defined extrinsically? Because all objectivity rests upon the unrestricted, detached, disinterested desire to know. It is that desire that sets up the canons of normative objectivity. It is that desire that gives rise to the absolute objectivity implicit in judgment. It is that desire that yields the constellation of judgments that implicitly define the principal notion of distinct objects in the universe of being, some of which know others. Experiential objectivity has to rest on the same basis, and so the given is defined, not by appealing to sensitive process, but by the pure desire regarding the flow of empirical consciousness as the materials for its operation.

5   Characteristics of the Notion   [383–84]

An account has been given of a principal notion of objectivity and of its three partial aspects: the experiential, the normative, and the absolute.

However, there also exists subjectivity, and the reader may be inclined to find in the present section a full confirmation of a suspicion that he has for some time entertained, namely, that we have failed to place our finger on what really is objective,[d] that we are confusing with the objective either in part or in whole what really is subjective. To deal with this problem will call for a further and rather complex investigation, but before we go on to it, let us note the more general characteristics of the notion of objectivity that has just been outlined.

First of all, despite its complexity, it can be the notion of objectivity that common sense presupposes and utilizes. The principal notion is implicit within a suitable pattern of judgments; it arises automatically when the judgments that happen to be made fall within such a pattern. The absolute aspect is implicit in judgment for, as we have argued at length, judgment affirms the unconditioned that reflective understanding grasps. The normative aspect is not any set of rules that has to be invented; it results from the intelligent inquiry and the reflective reasonableness that are the unfolding of the pure desire to know. Finally, the experiential aspect, while it may appear to do violence to common-sense expectations, is fully in accord with scientific practice, which claims to be an extension and refinement of common sense.

Secondly, the notion of objectivity that has been outlined is a minimal notion. There arises the question, What is objectivity? If the answer is to be intelligent and reasonable, then the pure desire and its normative exigences must be respected. Moreover, there must be materials into which intelligence inquires and on which reasonableness reflects. Further, if there is a definitive answer, the unconditioned and so the absolute will be attained. Finally, if the question and answer have a point, there will be other judgments which, if they occur in an appropriate pattern, will yield the principal notion.

Thirdly, our notion of objectivity begs no questions. Just as our notion of being does not decide between empiricism and rationalism, positivism and idealism, existentialism and realism, but leaves that decision to the content of correct judgments that are made, so also our notion of objectivity is equally open. If judgments occur in the appropriate pattern, then it involves a plurality of knowing subjects and known objects. If in effect there is only one true judgment, say, the affirmation of the Hegelian Absolute Idea, our notion of objectivity undergoes no formal modification. If true judgments are never reached, there arises the relativist position that acknowledges only experiential and normative objectivity.

Only on the supposition that inquiry and reflection, intelligence and reasonableness have nothing to do with objectivity, is our notion invalidated. But in that case there does not arise the question, What is objectivity?

14

The Method of Metaphysics

1   The Underlying Problem^a

[385–90]

It is not difficult to set antitheses against the conclusions of the preceding three chapters. Against the objectivity that is based on intelligent inquiry and critical reflection, there stands the unquestioning orientation of extroverted biological consciousness and its uncritical survival not only in dramatic and practical living but also in much of philosophic thought. Against the concrete universe of being, of all that can be intelligently grasped and reasonably affirmed, there stands in a prior completeness the world of sense, in which the 'real' and the 'apparent' are subdivisions within a vitally anticipated 'already out there now.' Against the self-affirmation of a consciousness that at once is empirical, intellectual, and rational, there stands the native bewilderment of the existential subject, revolted by mere animality, unsure of his way through the maze of philosophies, trying to live without a known purpose, suffering despite an unmotivated will, threatened with inevitable death and, before death, with disease and even insanity.

The peculiarity of these antitheses is not to be overlooked. They are not mere conflicting propositions. They are not pure logical alternatives, of which one is simply true and the other is utterly false. But in each case both the thesis and the antithesis have their ground in the concrete unity-in-tension that is man. For human consciousness is polymorphic. The pattern in which it flows may be biological, aesthetic, artistic, dramatic, practical, intellectual, or mystical. These patterns alternate; they blend or mix; they can interfere, conflict, lose their way, break down. The intellectual pattern of experience is supposed and expressed by our intellectual pattern of experience is supposed and expressed by our account of self-affirmation, of being, and of objectivity. But no man is born in that pattern; no one reaches it easily; no one remains in it permanently; and when some other pattern is dominant, then the self of our self-affirmation seems quite different from one's actual self, the universe of being seems as unreal as Plato's noetic heaven, and objectivity spontaneously becomes a matter of meeting persons and dealing with things that are 'really out there.'

Not merely are the antitheses based on the polymorphic fact of a protean consciousness, but initially there is the bewildering fact without the clear antitheses. To reach that sharp formulation, it was necessary for us to begin from insight, to study its functioning in mathematics, in empirical science, and in common sense, to turn to reflective understanding and judgment, and throughout to avoid involvement in obviously pressing problems on the nature of knowledge, of reality, and of the relation between them. Even in unfolding the process that ends in self-affirmation, we were unprepared to say whether affirming the self was knowing the self. Affirming the self became knowing the self inasmuch as knowing being was seen to be affirming it; and knowing being became objective knowing through a grasp of the nature of experiential, normative, absolute, and the consequent principal objectivity.

If a clear and sharp formulation of the antitheses occurs only at the end of a long and difficult inquiry, still that inquiry today is prepared and supported in a manner unattainable in earlier centuries. The development of mathematics, the maturity of some branches of empirical science, the investigations of depth psychology, the interest in historical theory, the epistemological problems raised by Descartes, by Hume, and by Kant, the concentration of modern philosophy upon cognitional analysis, all serve to facilitate and to illumine an investigation of the mind of man. But if it is possible for later ages to reap the harvest of earlier sowing, still before that sowing and during it there was no harvest to be reaped.

It is not too surprising, then, that the philosophies have been many, contradictory, and disparate. For surprise merely expresses the mistaken assumption that the task of philosophy lies in the observation or utterance of some simple entity by some simple mind. In fact, the mind is polymorphic; it has to master its own manifold before it can determine what utterance is, or what is uttered, or what is the relation between the two; and when it does so, it finds its own complexity at the root of antithetical solutions. From the welter of conflicting philosophic definitions

and from the babel of endless philosophic arguments, it has been concluded that the object of philosophy either does not exist or cannot be
attained. But this conclusion disregards two facts. On the one hand, the
philosophers have been men of exceptional acumen and profundity. On
the other hand, the many, contradictory, disparate philosophies can all
be contributions to the clarification of some basic but polymorphic fact;
because the fact is basic, its implications range over the universe; but
because it is polymorphic, its alternative forms ground diverse sets of
implications.

Such is the view to be developed in the present account of the
method[b] of philosophy. As in our remarks on mathematics, on empirical
science, and on common sense, so also here, the one object of our inquiry is the nature and fact of insight. Philosophers and philosophies
engage our attention inasmuch as they are instances and products of
inquiring intelligence and reflecting reasonableness. It is from this viewpoint that there emerges a unity not only of origin but also of goal in
their activities; and this twofold unity is the ground for finding in any
given philosophy a significance that can extend beyond the philosopher's
horizon and, even in a manner he did not expect, pertain to the permanent development of the human mind.

The possibility of contradictory contributions to a single goal is, in its
main lines, already familiar to the reader. Besides the direct insights that
grasp the systematic, there are also the inverse insights that deal with the
nonsystematic. As both types of insight are needed by the mathematician, the empirical scientist, the depth psychologist, and the theorist of
history, so also both types are needed by the philosopher. Moreover,
inasmuch as the philosopher employs both direct and inverse insights in
his survey and estimate of the philosophic process, his mind and grasp
become the single goal in which contradictory contributions attain their
complex unity. Finally, the heuristic structure of that unity admits determination through the principle that positions invite development and
counterpositions invite reversal. This principle we now must explain.

First, in any philosophy it is possible to distinguish between its cognitional theory and, on the other hand, its pronouncements on metaphysical, ethical, and theological issues. Let us name the cognitional
theory the basis, and the other pronouncements the expansion.

Secondly, there are two aspects to the basis. On the one hand, cognitional theory is determined by an appeal to the data of consciousness
and to the historical development of human knowledge. On the other

hand, the formulation of cognitional theory cannot be complete unless some stand is taken on basic issues in philosophy.

Thirdly, the inevitable philosophic component immanent in the formulation of cognitional theory will be either a basic position or else a basic counterposition.

It will be a basic position (1) if the real is the concrete universe of being and not a subdivision of the 'already out there now'; (2) if the subject becomes known when it affirms itself intelligently and reasonably and so is not known yet in any prior 'existential' state; and^c (3) if objectivity is conceived as a consequence of intelligent inquiry and critical reflection, and not as a property of vital anticipation, extroversion, and satisfaction.

On the other hand, it will be a basic counterposition if it contradicts one or more of the basic positions.

Fourthly, any philosophic pronouncement on any epistemological, metaphysical, ethical, or theological issue will be named a position if it is coherent with the basic positions on the real, on knowing, and on objectivity; and it will be named a counterposition if it is coherent with one or more of the basic counterpositions.

Fifthly, all counterpositions invite reversal. For any lack of coherence prompts the intelligent and reasonable inquirer to introduce coherence. But counterpositions, though coherent with one another, though the insertion of their symbolic equivalents into an electronic computer would not lead to a breakdown, nonetheless are incoherent with the activities of grasping them intelligently and affirming them reasonably. For these activities contain the basic positions; and the basic positions are incoherent with any counterposition. One can grasp and accept, propose and defend a counterposition; but that activity commits one to grasping and accepting one's grasping and accepting; and that commitment involves a grasp and acceptance of the basic positions. The only coherent way to maintain a counterposition is that of the animal; for animals not only do not speak but also do not offer excuses for their silence.

Sixthly, all positions invite development. For they are coherent not only with one another but also with the activities of inquiring intelligence and reflective reasonableness; because these activities are coherent with existing attainment, their exercise is possible; because existing attainment is incomplete, further development is invited.

A simple example will clarify the meaning of the foregoing abstract statements. Let us say that Cartesian dualism contains both a basic position and a basic counterposition. The basic position is the *cogito, ergo sum*, and as Descartes did not endow it with the clarity and precision that are to be desired, its further development is invited by such questions as, What is the self? What is thinking? What is being? What are the relations between them? On the other hand, the basic counterposition is the affirmation of the *res extensa*; it is real as a subdivision of the 'already out there now'; its objectivity is a matter of extroversion; knowing it is not a matter of inquiry and reflection. This counterposition invites reversal, not merely in virtue of its conjunction with the other component in Cartesian thought, but even when posited by itself in anyone's thought. Thus, Hobbes overcame Cartesian dualism by granting reality to the *res cogitans* only if it were another instance of the *res extensa*, another instance of matter in motion. Hume overcame Hobbes by reducing all instances of the 'already out there now real' to manifolds of impressions linked by mere habits and beliefs. The intelligence and reasonableness of Hume's criticizing were obviously quite different from the knowledge he so successfully criticized. Might one not identify knowledge with the criticizing activity rather than the criticized materials? If so, Cartesian dualism is eliminated by another route. One is back at the thinking subject, and at the term of this reversal one's philosophy is enriched not only by a stronger affirmation of the basic position but also by an explicit negation of the basic counterposition.

In the light of the dialectic, then, the historical series of philosophies would be regarded as a sequence of contributions to a single but complex goal. Significant discoveries, because they are not the prerogative of completely successful philosophers, are expressed either as positions or as counterpositions. But positions invite development, and so the sequence of discoveries expressed as positions should form a unified, cumulative structure that can be enriched by adding the discoveries initially expressed as counterpositions. On the other hand, since counterpositions invite reversal, a free unfolding of human thought should tend to separate the discovery from its author's bias in the measure that its presuppositions are examined and its implications tested.

However, the dialectic itself has a notable presupposition, for it supposes that cognitional theory exercises a fundamental influence in metaphysics, in ethics, and in theological pronouncements. This presupposition merits exploration. In the present chapter, then, an attempt will be made to define metaphysics, to state its method, and to clarify the method by contrasting it with other methods. In subsequent chapters the method will be articulated by an outline of metaphysics, a sketch of ethics, and a presentation of transcendent knowledge.

2 A Definition of Metaphysics [390–96]

Just as the notion of being underlies and penetrates and goes beyond all other notions, so also metaphysics is the department of human knowledge that underlies, penetrates, transforms, and unifies all other departments.

It underlies all other departments, for its principles are neither terms nor propositions, neither concepts nor judgments, but the detached and disinterested drive of the pure desire to know and its unfolding in the empirical, intellectual, and rational consciousness of the self-affirming subject. From the unfolding of that drive proceed all questions, all insights, all formulations, all reflections, all judgments; and so metaphysics underlies logic and mathematics, the various sciences and the myriad instances of common sense.

It penetrates all other departments. For other departments are constituted by the same principles[d] as metaphysics. They are particular departments inasmuch as they are restricted to some particular viewpoint and field. Yet despite the restrictions that make them particular, all departments spring from a common source and seek a common compatibility and coherence, and in both these respects they are penetrated by metaphysics.

It transforms all other departments. For the consciousness of man is polymorphic, and it ever risks formulating its discoveries not as positions but as counterpositions. Common sense is subject to a dramatic bias, an egoistic bias, a group bias, and a general bias that disregards the complex theoretical issues in which it becomes involved and their long-term consequences from which it blindly suffers. Scientists are not just scientists but also men of common sense; they share its bias insofar as their specialty does not correct it; and insofar as their specialty runs counter to the bias of common sense, they find themselves divided and at a loss for a coherent view of the world. Metaphysics springs from the pure desire to know; it is free from the restrictions of particular viewpoints; it distinguishes positions from counterpositions in the whole of knowledge; it is a transforming principle that urges positions to fuller development and, by reversing counterpositions, liberates discoveries from the shackles in which at first they were formulated.

It unifies all other departments. For other departments meet particular ranges of questions, but it is the original, total question, and it moves to the total answer by transforming and putting together all other answers. Metaphysics, then, is the whole in knowledge but not the whole of knowledge. A whole is not without its parts, nor independent of them, nor identical with them. So it is that, while the principles of metaphysics are prior to all other knowledge, still the attainment of metaphysics is the keystone that rests upon the other parts and presses them together in the unity of a whole.

From the foregoing account, it would appear that metaphysics can exist in three stages or forms. In its first stage, it is latent. Empirical, intellectual, and rational consciousness are immanent and operative in all human knowing; from them spring both the various departments of knowledge and the attempts that are made to reverse counterpositions and to attain coherence and unity; but the common source of all knowledge is not grasped with sufficient clarity and precision; the dialectical principle of transformation is not a developed technique; and efforts at unification are haphazard and spasmodic. In its second stage, metaphysics is problematic. The need of a systematic effort for unification is felt; studies of the nature of knowledge abound; but these very studies are involved in the disarray of the positions and counterpositions that result from the polymorphic consciousness of man. In its third stage, metaphysics is explicit. Latent metaphysics, which always is operative, succeeds in conceiving itself, in working out its implications and techniques, and in affirming the conception, the implications, and the techniques.

What is this explicit metaphysics? It will simplify matters enormously if, in the present chapter, we prescind from the complicated and disputed question of the possibility of man's knowing what lies beyond the limits of human experience. Accordingly, we introduce the notion of proportionate being. In its full sweep, being is whatever is to be known by intelligent grasp and reasonable affirmation. But being that is proportionate to human knowing not only is to be understood and affirmed but also is to be experienced. So proportionate being may be defined as whatever is to be known by human experience, intelligent grasp, and reasonable affirmation.

Now let us say that explicit metaphysics is the conception, affirmation, and implementation of the integral heuristic structure of proportionate being. The meaning and implications of this statement have now to be explored.

First, what is meant by an integral heuristic structure? To begin by assembling the elements of the answer, conceptual contents may be primitive or derived; the derived are defined by appealing to the primitive; the primitive are fixed inasmuch as terms and relations proceed from a single understanding, with the relations settled by the terms and the terms settled by the relations. However, prior to the understanding that issues in answers, there are the questions that anticipate answers; and as has been seen, such anticipation may be employed systematically in the determination of answers that as yet are unknown; for while the content of a future cognitional act is unknown, the general characteristics of the act itself not only can be known but also can supply a premise that leads to the act. A heuristic notion, then, is the notion of an unknown content, and it is determined by anticipating the type of act through which the unknown would become known. A heuristic structure is an ordered set of heuristic notions. Finally, an integral heuristic structure is the ordered set of all heuristic notions.

In illustration, one may point to the definition of proportionate being. It is whatever is to be known by human experience, intelligent grasp, and reasonable affirmation. The definition does not assign the content of any experience, of any understanding, of any affirmation. Yet it does assign an ordered set of types of acts, and it implies that every proportionate being is to be known through such an ordered set. Accordingly, the definition is an instance of a heuristic structure; but it is not an instance of an integral heuristic structure, for it does not exhaust the resources of the human mind in anticipating what it is to know.

Secondly, if the integral heuristic structure of proportionate being were conceived, affirmed, and implemented, then latent metaphysics would become explicit. For latent metaphysics is the dynamic unity of empirical, intellectual, and rational consciousness as underlying, penetrating, transforming, and unifying the other departments of knowledge. But an integral heuristic structure of proportionate being would perform these offices in an explicit manner. As heuristic, it would underlie other knowledge. As the questions which other knowledge answers, it would penetrate other fields. As dialectical, it would transform these answers. As integral, it would contain in itself the order that binds other departments into a single intelligible whole.

Thirdly, such an explicit metaphysics would be progressive. For heuristic notions and structures are not discovered by some Platonic recall of a prior state of contemplative bliss. They result from the resourcefulness of human intelligence in operation. They are to be known only by an analysis of operations that have become familiar and are submitted to examination. Just as the other departments of knowledge advance by discovering new methods, so metaphysics advances by adding these discoveries to its account of the integral heuristic structure of proportionate being.

Fourthly, such an explicit metaphysics would be nuanced. It would be a whole of many parts, and different parts would possess varying degrees of clarity and precision, of evidence and inevitability. It follows that not all parts could be affirmed with the same confidence, that some could be regarded as certain, others as highly probable, others as recommended by the lack of alternatives, others as doubtful and in need of further confirmation.

Fifthly, such a metaphysics would be factual. Proportionate being is not the merely possible nor need it be absolutely necessary. It is what in fact is, and the science that views it as a whole can be content to ascertain what in fact is true. Moreover, the various empirical sciences and the myriad instances of common sense aim at no more than knowing what in fact is so; but metaphysics is their unification; as a principle, it precedes them; but as an attainment, it follows upon them, emerges from them, depends upon them; and so, like them, it too will be factual.

Sixthly, the dependence of such a metaphysics upon the sciences and upon common sense would be the dependence, neither of a conclusion on premises nor of an effect upon its cause, but of a generating, transforming, and unifying principle upon the materials that it generates, transforms, and unifies. Metaphysics does not undertake either to discover or to teach science; it does not undertake either to develop or to impart common sense; it does not pretend to know the universe of proportionate being independently of science and common sense; but it can and does take over the results of such distinct efforts, it works them into coherence by reversing their counterpositions, and it knits them into a unity by discerning in them the concrete prolongations of the integral heuristic structure which it itself is.

Seventhly, such a metaphysics, once it had surmounted its initial difficulties, would be stable. It would admit incidental modifications and improvements, but it could not undergo the revolutionary changes to which the empirical sciences are subject. For a science is open to revolutionary change inasmuch as it is possible to reach a higher viewpoint and consequently to alter the content of its primitive terms and relations. But it is possible to reach a higher viewpoint only within the framework of inquiring and critical intelligence; there is not, in human knowledge, any possible higher viewpoint that goes beyond that framework itself and replaces intelligent inquiry and critical reflection by some surrogate; and the viewpoint of metaphysics is constituted by nothing less than inquiring intelligence and critical reflection. Moreover, a higher viewpoint can alter the content of primitive terms and relations only if that content is some determinate object of thought or affirmation. The Aristotelian, the Galilean, the Newtonian, and the Einsteinian accounts of the free fall of heavy bodies are all open to revision, for all are determinate contents. On the other hand, a merely heuristic account is not open to revision. One cannot revise the heuristic notion that the nature of a free fall is what is to be known when the free fall is understood correctly; for it is that heuristic notion that is both antecedent to each determinate account and, as well, subsequent to each and the principle of the revision of each. Accordingly, since metaphysics is the integral heuristic structure of proportionate being, since it is a structure that is coincident with inquiring intelligence and critical reflection, metaphysics is not open to revolutionary change.

Eighthly, metaphysics primarily regards being as explained, but secondarily it includes being as described. Primarily, it regards being as explained, for it is a heuristic structure, and a heuristic structure looks to what is to be known when one understands. Secondarily, it includes being as described. For explanation is of things as related to one another; description is of things as related to us; and so, since we are things, the descriptive relations must be identical with some of the explanatory relations.

It is to be noted that the inclusion of descriptive relations in metaphysics is implicit, general, mediated, and intellectual. It is implicit, for explicitly metaphysics regards things as explained. It is general, for metaphysics is just a heuristic structure, and so only in the most general fashion can it determine which explanatory relations are identical with descriptive relations. It is mediated, inasmuch as metaphysics unifies the sciences and common sense and through them it can determine more precisely which explanatory relations also are descriptive. Finally, the inclusion is intellectual, for it occurs on the level of intelligence and judgment and not on the level of sense. Just as thinking of the thermodynamic equations will not make anyone feel warmer or cooler, so the metaphysics of heat will be incapable of producing the experience of heat as felt. Similarly, no metaphysics, even if it regards mathematical science as superficial and undertakes to uphold the distinctive reality of quality, will be able to impart to a blind man the experience of color as seen or to a deaf man the experience of sound as heard.

Incidentally, once this last point is grasped, it would seem that metaphysical attempts to uphold the distinctive reality of sensible quality have nothing to uphold. For if metaphysics cannot reproduce the sensed as sensed, it can uphold sensible quality only by assigning some corresponding intelligibility. But mathematical science already offers a corresponding intelligibility, and though the materials of mathematical intelligibility are quantitative or, more accurately, ordinable, mathematical intelligibility is not itself quantitative. The difference between a trigonometric and an exponential function is not a difference in size; it is a difference in intelligible law governing relations between continuously ordinable elements.

A corollary of wider interest regards the ten categories commonly ascribed to Aristotle. They are descriptive. A naturalist will assign the genus, species, and instance (substance) of an animal, its size and weight (quantity), its color, shape, abilities, propensities (quality), its similarities to other animals and its differences from them (relation), its performance and susceptibilities (action and passion), its habitat and seasonal changes (place and time), its mode of motion and rest (posture), and its possession of such items as claws, talons, hooves, fur, feathers, horns (habit). But metaphysics, as it is being conceived, is a heuristic structure that regards being as explained and only implicitly, generally, mediately, and intellectually includes being as described. It follows that Aristotle's ten categories, though they regard proportionate being, nonetheless do not pertain to the constitutive structure of metaphysics.[1]

Perhaps enough has been said to clarify what we mean by metaphysics. The detached and disinterested desire to know and its unfolding in inquiry and reflection not only constitute a notion of being but also impose a normative structure upon man's cognitional acts. Such a structure provides the relations by which unknown contents of the acts can be defined heuristically. This heuristic structure is immanent and operative in all human knowing, but initially it is latent, and the polymor-

1 In Aristotelian terms, metaphysics is a science; a science is knowledge through causes; and causes are not the ten categories but the end, the agent, the matter, and the form. [This note was added by Lonergan at the proof stage.]

phism of human consciousness makes it problematic as well. Nonetheless, it can be conceived, affirmed, and implemented, and from that implementation there follow a transformation and an integration of the sciences and of the myriad instances of common sense. But knowing is knowing being. So the integral heuristic structure of proportionate being, as determined by the sciences and common sense, is knowledge of the organizing structure of proportionate being. As has been said, such a metaphysics is progressive, nuanced, factual, formally dependent on cognitional theory and materially dependent on the sciences and on common sense, stable, and in its outlook explanatory.

There remains the clarification that results from a discussion of method, and to this we now turn our attention.

3   Method in Metaphysics   [396–401]

A method is a set of directives that serve to guide a process towards a result. The result at which we are aiming is the explicit metaphysics outlined in the previous section. It would consist in a symbolic indication of the total range of possible experience, in a set of acts of insight that unify such experience, and in a grasp of the virtually unconditioned issuing in a reasonable affirmation of the unified view.

This result can exist only in the empirical, intellectual, and rational consciousness of the self-affirming subject. Metaphysics, then, is not something in a book but something in a mind. Moreover, it is produced not by a book but only by the mind in which it is. Books can serve to supply the stimulus for a set of precise visual experiences, to issue through experiences an invitation to acts of insight, to lead through the insights to a grasp of the virtually unconditioned. But books cannot constitute the visual experiences, nor necessitate the insights, nor impose the attainment of the high moment of critical reflection that through the unconditioned reaches judgment. Further, the subject that is envisaged is not some general or transcendental or absolute subject; from the viewpoint of the writer it is any particular subject that can experience, can inquire intelligently, can reflect critically; but from the viewpoint of the reader the particular subject is the subject that he or she is. No one can understand for another or judge for another. Such acts are one's own and only one's own. Explicit metaphysics is a personal attainment.

Particular subjects are many. Their respective histories and attainments are diverse. Their outlooks on the universe are disparate. Yet despite their multiplicity, their diversity, their disparateness, they, as they actually are, constitute the starting point for the process that leads to explicit metaphysics. There is no use addressing minds that could be or should be but in fact are not, if one would encourage the genesis of explicit metaphysics in the minds that are. Just as metaphysics can exist only in a mind and can be produced only by the mind in which it is to be, so also metaphysics can begin only in minds that exist, and it can proceed only from their actual texture and complexion. Bluntly, the starting point of metaphysics is people as they are.

Between this starting point and the goal, there is the process. It is a process from latent through problematic to explicit metaphysics. People as they are cannot^e avoid experience, cannot put off their intelligence, cannot renounce their reasonableness. But they may never have adverted to these concrete and factual inevitabilities. They may be unable to distinguish between them sharply, or discern the immanent order that binds them together, or find in them the dynamic structure that has generated all their scientific knowledge and all their common sense, or acknowledge in that dynamic structure a normative principle that governs the outcome of all inquiry, or discover in themselves other equally dynamic structures that can interfere with the detached and disinterested unfolding of the pure desire to know, or conclude to the polymorphism of their subjectivity and the untoward effects it can have upon their efforts to reach a unified view of the universe of proportionate being.

The process, then, to explicit metaphysics is primarily a process to self-knowledge. It has to begin from the polymorphic subject in his native disorientation and bewilderment. It cannot appeal to what he knows, for as yet he has not learnt to distinguish sharply and effectively between the knowing men share with animals, the knowing that men alone possess, and the manifold blends and mixtures of the two that are the disorientation and ground the bewilderment of people as they are. Since an appeal to disorientated knowledge would only extend and confirm the disorientation, the appeal must be to the desire that is prior to knowledge, that generates knowledge, that can effect the correction of miscarriages in the cognitional process. Still, it cannot be taken for granted that the subject knows his own desire and its implications; were there such knowledge, the disorientation would be remedied already; and so the initial appeal is to the desire, not as known, but as existing and operative. The first directive, then, is to begin from interest, to excite it, to use its momentum to carry things along. In other words, the method of metaphysics primarily is pedagogical: it is headed towards an end that is unknown and as yet cannot be disclosed; from the viewpoint of the pupil, it proceeds by cajoling or forcing attention and not by explaining the intended goal and by inviting an intelligent and reasonable cooperation. So it was that without mentioning metaphysics, we studied the fact and the nature of insight in mathematics, in the empirical sciences, in common sense, in judgments on mathematics, on the empirical sciences, and on the myriad concrete and particular objects of common sense. So too we examined self-affirmation and the notions of being and of objectivity. So too we began to talk about the dialectic of philosophy. In the measure in which we have been successful, the reader will know what is meant by insight, what is meant by reasonableness, how both differ from the internal and external experience that they presuppose, how all three form a patterned orientation that differs from other orientations that commonly are more familiar and more frequent. In the measure that such self-knowledge has been reached, it is possible to leave pedagogy and to discuss method; and so we find ourselves discussing method.

A method, as was remarked, is a set of directives that guide a process to a result. But the result can exist only in a self-affirming subject, and the process can be produced only by the subject in which the result is to exist. It follows that the directives of the method must be issued by the self-affirming subject to himself. The initial pedagogical stage was to enable the subject to issue the proper directives; and the present discussion of method has to be the subject's own determination of the directives he is to issue.

The method, then, of metaphysics is dictated by the self-affirming subject in the light of his pedagogically acquired self-knowledge. For that self-knowledge is dynamic. It has revealed the source of disorientation and bewilderment. Spontaneously it moves towards the attainment of reorientation and integration.

The reorientation is to be effected in the field of common sense and of the sciences. On the one hand, these departments of the subject's knowledge and opinion are not to be liquidated. They are the products of experience, intelligence, and reflection, and it is only in the name of experience, intelligence, and reflection that self-knowledge issues any directives. As they are not to be liquidated, so they are not to be taken apart and reconstructed, for the only method for reaching valid scientific views is the method of science, and the only method for attaining common sense is the method common sense already employs. As metaphysicians neither teach science nor impart common sense, so they cannot revise or reconstruct either science or common sense. Still, this is not the whole story. For it would be excessively naive for the self-knowing subject to suppose that his scientific knowledge and his common sense are purely and simply the product of experience, intelligent inquiry, and critical reflection. The subject knows the polymorphism of his own consciousness; he knows how it generates a dramatic, an egoistic, a group, and a general bias in common sense; he knows how it intrudes into science confused notions on reality, on objectivity, and on knowledge. While, then, science and common sense are to be accepted, the acceptance is not to be uncritical. There are precise manners in which common sense can be expected to go wrong; there are definite issues on which science is prone to issue extrascientific opinions; and the reorientation demanded and effected by the self-knowledge of the subject is a steadily exerted pressure against the common nonsense that tries to pass for common sense and against the uncritical philosophy that pretends to be a scientific conclusion.

As the subject's advertence to the polymorphism of his consciousness leads to a transforming reorientation of his scientific opinions and his common sense, so his advertence both to his detached and disinterested desire to know and to the immanent structure of its unfolding leads to an integration of what is known and of what is to be known of the universe of proportionate being. It is in this integration that metaphysics becomes explicit; and to forestall misapprehension and misinterpretation, let us attempt to state as clearly as we can the nature of the transition from latent to explicit metaphysics.

First, then, in its general form, the transition is a deduction. It involves a major premise, a set of primary minor premises, and a set of secondary minor premises.

Secondly, the major premise is the isomorphism that obtains between the structure of knowing and the structure of the known. If the knowing consists of a related set of acts and the known is the related set of contents of these acts, then the pattern of the relations between the acts is similar in form to the pattern of the relations between the contents of the acts. This premise is analytic.

Thirdly, the set of primary minor premises consists of a series of affirmations of concrete and recurring structures in the knowing of the self-affirming subject. The simplest of these structures is that every instance of knowing proportionate being consists of a unification of experiencing, understanding, and judging. It follows from the isomorphism of knowing and known that every instance of known proportionate being is a parallel unification of a content of experience, a content of understanding, and a content of judgment.

Fourthly, the set of secondary minor premises is supplied by reorientated science and common sense. From the major and the primary minor premises there is obtained an integrating structure; but from the secondary minor premises there are obtained the materials to be integrated. Again, from the major and the primary minor premises there is obtained a well-defined and definitive set of questions to be answered; from the secondary minor premises there is obtained the fact of answers and their frequency.

Fifthly, this use of the above premises effects a transition from a latent to an explicit metaphysics. For in any case, cognitional activity operates within heuristic structures towards goals that are isomorphic with the structures. If this basic feature of cognitional activity is overlooked, metaphysics is latent. If this feature is noted, if the structures are determined, if the principle of isomorphism is grasped, then the latent metaphysics to which everyone subscribes without knowing he does so ceases to be latent and becomes explicit.

Sixthly, the method is not essential to obtaining the results. There is nothing to prevent an intelligent and reasonable man from beginning with the set of secondary minor premises, from discovering in them the structures that they cannot escape, and from generalizing from the totality of examined instances to the totality of possible instances. In fact, this has been the procedure of the Aristotelian and Thomist schools, and as will appear, their results largely anticipate our own.

Seventhly, however, there is much to be gained by employing the method. Aristotelian and Thomist thought has tended to be, down the centuries, a somewhat lonely island in an ocean of controversy. Because of the polymorphism of human consciousness, there are latent in science and common sense not only metaphysics but also the negation of metaphysics; and only the methodical reorientation of science and common sense puts an end, at least in principle, to this permanent source of confusion. Further, without the method it is impossible to assign with exactitude the objectives, the presuppositions, and the procedures of metaphysics; and this lack of exactitude may result in setting one's aim too low or too high, in resting one's case on alien or insecure foundations, in proceeding to one's goal through unnecessary detours.

Finally, the misconceptions in which metaphysics thus becomes involved may rob it of its validity and of its capacity for development; what should provide an integration for the science and the common sense of any age risks taking on the appearance of a mummy that would preserve for all time Greek science and medieval common sense.

To recapitulate, the goal of the method is the emergence of explicit metaphysics in the minds of particular men and women. It begins from them as they are, no matter what that may be. It involves a preliminary stage that can be methodical only in the sense in which a pedagogy is methodical; that is, the goal and the procedure are known and pursued explicitly by a teacher but not by the pupil. The preliminary stage ends when the subject reaches an intelligent and reasonable self-affirmation. Such self-affirmation is also self-knowledge. It makes explicit the pursuit of the goal that has been implicit in the pure desire to know. From that explicit pursuit there follow the directives, first, of reorientating one's scientific knowledge and one's common sense, and secondly, of integrating what one knows and can know of proportionate being through the known structures of one's cognitional activities.

4   The Dialectic of Method in Metaphysics[f]   [401–30]

A method can direct activity to a goal only by anticipating the general nature of the goal. But the only question to be settled in metaphysics is the general nature of the goal of knowledge, for all questions of detail have to be met by the sciences and by common sense. Accordingly, it would seem that every method in metaphysics must be involved in the fallacy of begging the question. By the mere fact of settling upon a method, one presupposes as settled the very issue that metaphysics proposes to resolve.

This difficulty reveals the significance of the distinction we have drawn between latent and explicit metaphysics. For latent metaphysics is an anticipation of the goal of knowledge that is present and operative independently of any metaphysical inquiry. Inasmuch as metaphysical inquiry aims at making latent metaphysics explicit, it proceeds not from arbitrary assumptions about the goal of knowledge, which would involve it in the fallacy of begging the question, but from matters of fact that any inquirer can verify in his own empirical, intelligent, and rational consciousness.

There is, however, a further aspect to the matter. Because the results obtained in the empirical sciences commonly are far less general than the methods they employ, scientists are not troubled to any notable extent by a predetermination of their results by their choice of method. In metaphysics, however, methods and results are of equal generality and tend to be coincident. It follows that differences[8] in metaphysical positions can be studied expeditiously and compendiously by examining differences in method. Moreover, such a study is not confined to tabulating the correlations that hold between different methods and different metaphysical systems. For there is only one method that is not arbitrary, and it grounds its explicit anticipations on the anticipations that, though latent, are present and operative in consciousness. Finally, besides the correlations between methods and systems, besides the criticism of methods based on the latent metaphysics of the human mind, there is the dialectical unfolding of positions inviting development and counterpositions inviting reversal. It is to this dialectic of metaphysical methods that attention now is to be directed, not of course in the full expansion that would be possible only in a survey of the whole history of philosophy, but in the articulation of its basic alternatives and with the modest purpose of indicating the outlines of a heuristic scheme for historical investigations.

4.1 Deductive Methods   [402–408]

Any metaphysical system eventually assumes the form of a set of propositions. The propositions can be divided into primitive and derived, and a logical technique can establish that if the primitive propositions are accepted, then the derived must also be accepted. The problem, then, of a deductive method is to select correctly the primitive propositions.

A first alternative is to assert that one's primitive propositions are universal and necessary truths. Since they are not deduced, they commonly will be claimed to be self-evident. However, a dialectic of method need not scrutinize this claim, for the properties of universal and necessary truths turn out to be sufficiently significant.

If the primitive propositions are universal, then they are abstract. They may refer to existing objects, but they do not assert the existence of any object, unless the universal is supposed to exist. This conclusion is confirmed by such keen logicians as Duns Scotus and William of Ockham, both of whom felt compelled to complement their abstract systems with the affirmation of an intuition of the existing and present as existing and present.

Further, if the primitive propositions are necessary, then they hold not merely for this universe but also for any possible world. It follows that the metaphysical system has no particular reference to this universe, for it holds equally for any universe. Again, it follows that the metaphysical system does not aim at integrating the empirical sciences and common sense; for both the empirical sciences and common sense are content to ascertain what in fact is so; but the deductive system in question has no interest in any contingent truth no matter how general or how comprehensive it may be.

Let us now inquire which truths can be regarded as universal and necessary. Clearly, all analytic propositions meet the above requirements. For they suppose nothing but the definitions of their terms and the rules of syntax that govern the coalescence of the terms into propositions. Provided that one does not affirm either the existence of the terms or the existence of operations in accord with the syntactical rules, one can have at one's disposal an indefinitely large group of truths that are universal and necessary, that affirm no existent, and that are equally valid in every possible world. On the other hand, the metaphysical system in question cannot be based on analytic principles, for the transition from the analytic proposition to the analytic principle is through a concrete judgment[h] of fact affirming that the terms as defined occur in a concrete existing universe.

It follows that the abstract metaphysics of all possible worlds is empty. Historically, however, this emptiness was discovered by a different route. For the medieval theologians that explored this type of system acknowledged the existence and the omnipotence of God; the only possible restriction upon divine omnipotence, and so the only restriction on the range of possible worlds, lay in the principle of contradiction. Their metaphysics dealt with all possible worlds, and so it dealt simultaneously with every possible instance of the noncontradictory. Not only did this object prove extremely tenuous and elusive, but it soon became apparent that the one operative principle in their thought was the principle of contradiction. Moreover, this principle ran counter to their affirmation of an intuition of the existing and present as existing and present. For it would be contradictory to affirm and deny some occurrence of the intuition; it would be contradictory to affirm and deny the existence of some object; but there is no apparent contradiction in affirming the occurrence of the intuition and denying the existence of its object. If no contradiction is involved, then in some possible world there would occur intuitions of the existence of what did not exist; and as Nicholas of Autrecourt perceived, neither analytic propositions nor intuitions can assure one that the possibility of illusory intuitions is not realized in this world.

The alternative to the abstract deduction that turns out to be empty is, of course, a concrete deduction. The existent does not lie outside the deductive system but from the start is included within it. Instead of operating vainly with analytic propositions, one proposes to operate fruitfully with analytic principles, whose terms in their defined sense refer to what exists.

Now it is characteristic of a deduction that conclusions follow necessarily from the premises. It follows that a concrete deduction is possible only if an objective necessity binds the existent that is concluded to,[i] to the existent referred to in the premises. For without this objective necessity logically impeccable inferences would arrive at possibly false conclusions.

Now there are many metaphysical systems that reveal how this objective necessity might be conceived. Thus, a monist would affirm the existence of a single reality with a set of necessary attributes and modes; and clearly enough his chain of syllogisms could be applied validly to a universe conceived in this fashion. Again, emanationist doctrines begin from a necessary being from which proceed necessarily all other beings; the application of a syllogistic chain would be more difficult in this case but there is no point in haggling over the matter. In the third place, one might suppose that God exists necessarily but is bound morally to create the best of all possible worlds; and so in a fashion one would secure a universe for concrete deductivist thought.

However, it is one thing to conceive a variety of universes; it is another to know whether any one of them exists. If one affirms this universe to be monist, because that is the conclusion of one's concrete deduction, it will be pointed out that one's choice of method amounted to begging the question; for the choice of concrete deduction makes it inevitable that one conclude to a monism or an emanationism or an optimism or a mechanist determinism; and so one's argument could be relevant only to discovering which of this limited range of alternatives was the most satisfactory. Clearly, the real issue is to determine, not what follows once the method of concrete deduction is assumed, but whether or not that method is to be employed.

Accordingly, if abstract deduction is empty, concrete deduction sets a prior question. Moreover, since the metaphysical question is the general nature or structure of the universe, the prior question, it seems, must regard the mind that is to know the universe. In this fashion one is led to ask what kind of mind would be needed if the universe is to be known by concrete deduction. Or, to give the issue its more concrete form, what are the constitutive conditions of such a concrete deduction as Newton's *Mathematical Principles of Natural Philosophy*?

Since the deducing can be performed satisfactorily by an electronic computer, the problem may be limited to the origin of the requisite premises. These premises, it would seem, must be both synthetic and a priori. They must be synthetic, for analytic propositions lack both relevance and significance: they lack relevance, for they regard all possible worlds but are isolated from the actual world; they lack significance, for they are obtained by studying the rules of syntax and the meanings of words, and clearly that procedure does not yield an understanding of this universe. Again, the required premises must be a priori: they are not to be known merely by taking a look at what is there to be seen, for what is there to be seen is particular, and no amount of mere looking endows it with the significance that explains the existing universe. The possibility, then, of a concrete deduction such as Newton's coincides with the possibility of synthetic a priori premises. But this possibility implies that the mind must be, not a mirror that simply reflects reality, but a sort of factory in which the materials supplied by outer and inner sense are processed into appropriate syntheses. Finally, if the mind is a factory of this type, it is capable of performing concrete deductions of the scientific type, but it does not seem at all capable of performing concrete deductions of the metaphysical type.

Various objections have been raised against such a deduction of the possibility of concrete deduction, but the most fundamental seems to be that the problem is not envisaged in its full generality. It is not enough to account for Newton's deduction alone or for Einstein's deduction alone. What has to be accounted for is a series of concrete deductions, none of which is certain and each of which is the best available scientific opinion of its time. The mind is not just a factory with a set of fixed processes; rather it is a universal machine tool that erects all kinds of factories, keeps adjusting and improving them, and eventually scraps them in favor of radically new designs. In other words, there is not some fixed set of a priori syntheses. Every insight is an a priori synthesis;[j] insight follows on insight to complement and correct its predecessor; earlier accumulations form viewpoints to give place to higher viewpoints; and above the succession of viewpoints, there is the activity of critical reflection with its demand for the virtually unconditioned and its capacity to estimate approximations to its rigorous requirement.

Now there are those who would prefer a simpler solution, and they point out that Kant overlooked the medieval theory of abstraction. The oversight, however, is multiple, for there were different medieval theories; and at least two of them merit our attention.

Certainly Duns Scotus would have rejected the Kantian notion of the a priori for the very reasons that led him to reject the Aristotelian and Thomist view that intellect apprehends the intelligible in the sensible and grasps the universal in the particular. After all, what is presented by sense or imagination is not actually intelligible or actually universal. But objective knowing is a matter of taking a look at what actually is there to be seen. If, then, intellect apprehends the intelligible in the sensible and the universal in the particular, its apprehension must be illusory, for it sees what is not there to be seen. Nonetheless, we do know what is intelligible and universal. To account for this fact without violating his convictions on extroversion as the model of objectivity, Scotus distinguished a series of steps in the genesis of intellectual knowledge. The first step was abstraction; it occurs unconsciously; it consists in the impression upon intellect of a universal conceptual content. The second step was intellection: intellect takes a look at the conceptual content. The third step was a comparison of different contents, with the result that intellect saw which concepts were conjoined necessarily and which were incompatible. There follows the deduction of the abstract metaphysics of all possible worlds, and to it one adds an intuition of the existing and present as existing and present, to attain knowledge of the actual world.

Aristotle and Aquinas both affirmed the fact of insight as clearly and effectively as can be expected. As they considered the sensible as seen to be only potentially in the object, so they considered the intelligible as understood to be only potentially in the image. Similarly, they considered both faculties to operate infallibly, but they affirmed this infallibility not absolutely but only as a rule (per se).[2] Finally, truth and error lie not on the level of questions for intelligence but on the level of questions for reflection; and prior to the judgment,[k] which is true or false, there occurs a scrutiny in which the proposed judgment is reduced to its sources in the data of sense and the activities of intellect.

Again, Aristotle and Aquinas affirmed self-evident principles that result necessarily from the definitions of their terms. But Aquinas, at least, had a further requirement; it was not enough for the principles to result necessarily from any terms whatever; the terms themselves needed some validation, and this office was attributed to the judicial habit or virtue named wisdom. What, then, is wisdom? In its higher form, Aquinas considered it a gift of the Holy Spirit and connected it with mystical experience. In its lower form, Aquinas identified it with Aristotle's first philosophy defined as the knowledge of all things in their ultimate causes. Clearly enough, the problem of metaphysical method demands a third form of wisdom. For the problem is not to be solved by presupposing a religion, a theology, or mystical experience. Similarly, the problem is not to be solved by presupposing a metaphysics, for what is wanted is the wisdom that generates the principles on which the metaphysics is to rest. But it does not seem that Aquinas treated explicitly the third type of wisdom. He was concerned to present the universe from the explanatory viewpoint that relates things to one another. From that viewpoint the human subject is just one being among others; and the human subject's knowledge is a relating of one type of being to others. So Thomist cognitional theory[l] is cast explicitly in metaphysical terms; and one cannot be surprised that the Thomist theory of basic judgments similarly has metaphysical suppositions. Finally, if, as I have argued elsewhere,[3] there is to be pieced together from Thomist writings a sufficient number of indications and suggestions to form an adequate account of wisdom in cognitional terms, it cannot be denied that the polymorphism of human consciousness interferes with the performance of

2 Nor is it difficult to surmise what the per se infallibility of insight is. One cannot misunderstand what one imagines; misunderstanding is the fault, not of intelligence but of imagination, which can exhibit what is not and can fail to exhibit all that is; hence, when we attempt to correct a misunderstanding, we point out what we think is misrepresented or overlooked by imagination; and when we acknowledge a misunderstanding, we add that we had not adverted to this or that.

3 [See Bernard Lonergan, *Verbum*, esp. pp. 66–75.]

this delicate operation; after all, G. van Riet needed over six hundred pages to outline the various types of Thomist epistemology that have been put forward in the last century and a half.[4]

Our consideration of deductive methods in metaphysics found abstract deduction to be empty, and concrete deduction to stand in need of a prior inquiry. This prior inquiry was not conducted with sufficient generality by Kant, nor with sufficient discrimination by Scotus. Finally, its possibility was implied by Aquinas, but the varieties of Thomist interpretation are as much in need of a prior inquiry as anything else. It would seem, then, that at least one positive conclusion can be drawn, namely, that deductive method alone is not enough. The fascination exerted by this method lies in its apparent promise of automatic results that are independent of the whims and fancies of the subject. The deducing proceeds in accord with a rigorous technique; the primitive premises are guaranteed by a self-evidence that claims to exercise an objective compulsion to which the subject must submit if he is not to be guilty of a lapse in intellectual probity. In fact, however, it is not so easy to leave the subject outside one's calculations, and so we now must turn to directive methods that aim to guide the metaphysical enterprise by guiding the subject that undertakes it.

4.2 Universal Doubt   [408–11]

In its simplest form the method of universal doubt is the precept 'Doubt everything that can be doubted.' Let us begin by attempting to determine the consequences of following out this precept, by applying rigorously its criterion of indubitability.

First, all concrete judgments of fact are to be excluded. For while they rest on invulnerable insights, still the invulnerability amounts to no more than the fact that further relevant questions do not arise. A criterion of indubitability is more exigent. It demands the impossibility of further relevant questions, and in concrete judgments of fact such impossibility neither exists nor is apprehended.

Secondly, both empirical science and common sense are excluded. For both aim at ascertaining what in fact is so, and neither succeeds in reach-

---

4 [Georges van Riet, *L'épistémologie thomiste: Recherches sur le problème de la connaissance dans l'école thomiste contemporaine* (Louvain: Éditions de l'Institut Supérieur de Philosophie, 1946).]

ing the indubitable. No doubt, it would be silly to suppose that there are further relevant questions that would lead to the correction of the insights grounding bare statements of fact or elementary measurements. But that is beside the point, for the question is not what certainly is true or false but what indubitably is true or false; and indubitability requires not the fact but the impossibility of further relevant questions.

Thirdly, the meaning of all judgments becomes obscure and unsettled. For the meaning of a judgment can be clear and precise only if one can assign a clear and precise meaning to such terms as reality, knowledge, objectivity. A clear and precise meaning can be assigned to such terms only if one succeeds in clarifying the polymorphic consciousness of man. Such a clarification can be effected by a lengthy, difficult, and delicate inquiry into the facts of human cognitional activity. But if one excludes all concrete judgments of fact, one excludes the clarification, and so one is bound to regard the meaning of every judgment as obscure and unsettled.

Fourthly, all mere suppositions satisfy the criterion of indubitability. For the mere supposition excludes the question for reflection, and doubt becomes possible only after the question for reflection arises. Thus, if you suppose that A is B, and I ask whether A really is B, you are entitled to point out that you are merely supposing A to be B, and that my question tries to put an end to mere supposing. On the other hand, there is no possibility of doubting whether or not A is B until that question arises, and so all mere suppositions are indubitable. It follows that all analytic propositions are indubitable, inasmuch as they rest on rules of syntax and on definitions of terms, and all such rules and definitions are regarded as mere suppositions. On the other hand, analytic principles are not indubitable, for they require concrete judgments of fact in which occur the defined terms in their defined sense; and, as has been seen, all concrete judgments of fact are excluded by the criterion of indubitability.

Fifthly, the existential subject survives, for the existential subject is the subject as prior[m] to the question, Am I? The criterion of indubitability does not eliminate the experienced center of experiencing, the intelligent center of inquiry, insight, and formulations, the rational center of critical reflection, scrutiny, hesitation, doubt, and frustration. Indeed, the method of universal doubt presupposes the existence of this center and imposes frustration upon it. One can argue that before I can doubt, I must exist, but what does the conclusion mean? What is the 'I'? What is existing? What is the meaning of affirming? All these questions can be given answers that are correct in fact. But as long as the criterion of indubitability remains in force, they cannot be given any clear or precise answer, for that would suppose a clarification of the polymorphism of human consciousness.

Sixthly, not even the criterion of indubitability is indubitable. It is clear enough that one makes no mistake in accepting the indubitable. It is not at all clear that one makes no mistake in rejecting everything that in fact is true. But the criterion of indubitability excludes all concrete judgments of fact, no matter how true and certain they may be. Therefore, the criterion of indubitability is not itself indubitable. It follows that the frustrated existential subject practicing universal doubt cannot console himself with the thought that there is anything rational about his doubting.

Seventhly, every assignable reason for practicing universal doubt is eliminated by a coherent exercise of the doubt. Thus, one might adopt the method of universal doubt in the hope of being left with premises for a deduction of the universe; but the exercise of the doubt removes all premises and leaves only mere suppositions; moreover, even if it left some premises, it would question the validity of the project of deducing the universe, for it is not indubitable that the universe can be deduced. Again, one might adopt the method of universal doubt because one felt the disagreement of philosophers to reveal their incompetence and to justify the use of a violent remedy; but the exercise of the doubt leaves nothing for philosophers to disagree about, and as well it leaves open to suspicion the assumption that their disagreement stems from their incompetence; for it is conceivable that philosophic process is dialectical, with positions inviting development and counterpositions inviting reversal.

Eighthly, the method of universal doubt is a leap in the dark. If we have been able to determine a list of precise consequences of universal doubt, we also have presupposed our account of the structure of human knowledge and of the polymorphism that besets it. But that account is not indubitable. At most, it is true as a matter of fact. Accordingly, to accept the criterion of indubitability is to deprive oneself of the means of ascertaining what precisely that criterion implies; and to accept a criterion without being able to determine its precise implications is to make a leap in the dark.

Ninthly, while the consequences of universal doubt will come to light in the long run, the proximate results of the method will be arbitrary and illusory. Proximate results will be arbitrary, for the exact implications of the method are unknown. Moreover, proximate results will be illusory, for doubting affects, not the underlying texture and fabric of the mind, but only the explicit judgments that issue from it. One can profess in all sincerity to doubt all that can be doubted, but one cannot abolish at a stroke the past development of one's mentality, one's accumulation of insights, one's prepossessions and prejudices, one's habitual orientation in life. So one will have little difficulty in seeing that the views of others are very far from being indubitable; at the same time, because the doubt is applied arbitrarily, one's own rooted convictions not merely will survive but also will be illuminated with the illusory splendor of having passed unscathed through an ordeal that the views of others could not stand. Accordingly, it will be only in the long run that the full implications of universal doubt will come to light, when the method has been applied by many persons with quite different initial convictions.

However, if I believe that universal doubt was practiced more successfully by Hume than by Descartes, and perhaps more successfully by the existentialists and some of the logical positivists than by Hume, I must also recall that my topic has been, not the concrete proposal entertained by Descartes, but the consequences of interpreting literally and applying rigorously the precept 'Doubt everything that can be doubted.' Clearly enough, the implications of that precept fail to reveal the profound originality and enduring significance of Descartes, for whom universal doubt was not a school of scepticism but a philosophic program that aimed to embrace the universe, to assign a clear and precise reason for everything, to exclude the influence of unacknowledged presuppositions. For that program we have only praise, but we also believe that it should be disassociated from the method of universal doubt, whether that method is interpreted rigorously or mitigated in a fashion that cannot avoid being arbitrary.

Finally, it should be noted that a rejection of universal doubt implies a rejection of the excessive commitment with which it burdens the philosophic enterprise. The only method to reach the conclusions of science is the method of science. The only method to reach the conclusions of common sense is the method of common sense. Universal doubt leads the philosopher to reject what he is not equipped to restore. But philosophers that do not practice universal doubt are not in that predicament, and it is only a mistaken argument from analogy that expects of them a validation of scientific or commonsense views.

4.3 Empiricism [411–16]

A second method that offers to guide the subject issues the precept 'Observe the significant facts.' Unfortunately, what can be observed is merely a datum; significance accrues to data only through the occurrence of insights; correct insights can be reached only at the term of a prolonged investigation that ultimately reaches the point where no further relevant questions arise; and without the combination of data and correct insights that together form a virtually unconditioned, there are no facts. Such, I believe, is the truth of the matter, but it is an extremely paradoxical truth, and the labor of all the pages that precede can be regarded as a sustained effort both to clarify the nature of insight and judgment and to account for the confusion, so natural to man, between extroversion and objectivity. For man observes, understands, and judges, but he fancies that what he knows in judgment is not known in judgment and does not suppose an exercise of understanding but simply is attained by taking a good look at the 'real' that is 'already out there now.' Empiricism, then, is a bundle of blunders, and its history is their successive clarification.

In its sublimest form, the observation of significant facts occurs in St Augustine's contemplation of the eternal reasons. For years, as he tells us, St Augustine was unable to grasp that the real could be anything but a body. When with neo-Platonist aid he got beyond that view, his name for reality was *veritas*; and for him truth was to be known, not by looking out, nor yet by looking within, but rather by looking above, where in an immutable light men consult and contemplate the eternal reasons of things. It is disputed, of course, just how literally St Augustine intended this inspection of the eternal to be understood. Aquinas insisted that the uncreated light grounds the truth of our judgments, not because we see that light, but because our intellects are created participations of it. But if St Augustine's meaning is doubtful, there is less doubt about a group of nineteenth-century Catholics known as ontologists, who believed that the only way to meet Kant's claim that the unconditioned is, not a constitutive element in judgment, but a merely regulative ideal, was to issue under Augustinian auspices the counterclaim that the notion of being was an obscure intuition of God.

As there is an empiricism on the level of critical reflection, so there is an empiricism on the level of understanding. The Scotist theory of abstraction was outlined above, and as was said, its second step consists in intellect taking a look at a conceptual content produced in the intellect by the unconscious cooperation of the intellective and the imaginative powers of the soul. Moreover, such intellectual empiricism reaches far beyond the confines of the Scotist school. The objective universals of Platonist thought seem to owe their origin to the notion that, as the eye of the body looks upon colors and shapes, so there is a spiritual eye of the soul that looks at universals, or at least recalls them. Finally, the Aristotelian and Thomist traditions are not without their ambiguities. Though Aristotle acknowledged the fact of insight and Aquinas added to Aristotle a transposition of Augustinian thought on judgment and of neo-Platonist thought on participation and being, still Aristotle's physics probably is a study of 'bodies,' and until recently Thomist commentators have tended almost universally to ignore Aquinas's affirmation of insight and to take it for granted that, while Aquinas obviously differed from Scotus in the metaphysical analysis of cognitional process, still the psychological content of his doctrine was much the same as that of Scotus.

The conflict between objectivity as extroversion and intelligence as knowledge has provided a fundamental theme in the unfolding of modern philosophy. Cartesian dualism was the juxtaposition of the rational affirmation *Cogito, ergo sum* and of the 'already out there now real' stripped of its secondary qualities and of any substantiality distinct from spatial extension. While Spinoza and Malebranche attempted to swallow the dualism on the rationalist side, Hobbes reduced thinking to an unprivileged instance of matter in motion. The Cambridge Platonists endeavored to accept Hobbes's conception of the real as 'out there now' and yet to affirm God as supremely real because his omnipresence was the reality of space and his eternity was the reality of time. Berkeley sought the same end by a different route; he granted secondary qualities to be mere appearance, and concluded that primary qualities with still greater certainty were mere appearance; being then was being perceived, and so reality shifted from apparent 'bodies' to the cognitional order. Finally, Hume brought analysis to bear effectively on the issue; our knowing involves not only elements but also unities and relations; the elements consist in a manifold of unrelated sense impressions; the unities and relations have no better foundation than our mental habits and beliefs; whatever may be the practical utility of our knowledge, at least it cannot pretend to philosophic validity.

If it is merely confusion of thought that interprets objectivity in terms of extroversion, Kant's Copernican revolution was a half-hearted affair.

He pronounced both primary and secôndary qualities to be phenomena. He made absolute space and absolute time a priori forms of outer and inner sense. He regarded the things themselves of Newtonian thought to be unknowable. But he was unable to break cleanly from the basic conviction of animal extroversion that the 'real' is the 'already out there now.' Though unknowable, Newton's things themselves were somehow known to produce impressions on our senses and to appear. The category of reality was to be employed by understanding when there occurred some filling in the empty form of time. The category of substance was identified with the permanence of reality in time. However convinced Kant was that 'taking a look' could not be valid human knowing, he devoted his energies to showing how it could seem to be knowing and in what restricted sense it could be regarded as valid. Nor is the anomaly of his position surprising. If the schematism of the categories comes within striking distance of the virtually unconditioned, still Kant failed to see that the unconditioned is a constituent component in the genesis of judgment, and so he relegated it to the role of a regulative ideal of systematizing rationality. But once extroversion is questioned, it is only through man's reflective grasp of the unconditioned that the objectivity and validity of human knowing can be established. Kant rightly saw that animal knowing is not human knowing; but he failed to see what human knowing is. The combination of that truth and that failure is the essence of the principle of immanence that was to dominate subsequent thought.

Cartesian dualism had been a twofold realism, and both the realisms were correct; for the realism of the extroverted animal is no mistake, and the realism of rational affirmation is no mistake. The trouble was that, unless two distinct and disparate types of knowing were recognized, the two realisms were incompatible. For rational affirmation is not an instance of extroversion, and so it cannot be objective in the manner proper to the 'already out there now.' On the other hand, the flow of sensible contents and acts is neither intelligent nor reasonable, and so it cannot be knowledge of the type exhibited by science and philosophy. The attempt to fuse disparate forms of knowing into a single whole ended in the destruction of each by the other; and the destruction of both forms implied the rejection of both types of realism. The older materialism and sensism were discredited, but there was room for positivism and pragmatism to uphold the same viewpoint in a more cultured tone. German idealism swung through its magnificent arc of dazzling systems to come to terms with reality in relativism and neo-Kantian analysis. But if a century and a half have brought forth no solution, it would seem necessary to revert to the beginning and distinguish two radically distinct types of knowing in the polymorphic consciousness of man.

For I do not think that E. Husserl's phenomenology does provide a solution. Scientific description can be no more than a preliminary to scientific explanation. But Husserl begins from relatedness-to-us, not to advance to the relatedness of terms to one another, but to mount to an abstract looking from which the looker and the looked-at have been dropped because of their particularity and contingence. The vitality of animal extroversion is attenuated from sensitive perception to intuition of universals, and from intuition of universals to the more impalpable inspection of formal essences (approximately, scholastic transcendentals). As objects increase in generality and purity, subjects shrink to intentional acts. With remarkable acuteness and discrimination there are uncovered, described, compared, and classified the pure forms of noetic experience terminating in noematic contents. But the whole enterprise is under the shadow of the principle of immanence, and it fails to transcend the crippling influence of the extroversion that provides the model for the pure ego. In brief, phenomenology is a highly purified empiricism, and it did not take long for it to topple over into an existentialism that describes, not the abstract possibility of description, but men as they are.

But description is not enough. If it claims simply to report data in their purity, one may ask why the arid report should be added to the more lively experience. If it pretends to report the significant data, then it is deceived, for significance is not in data but accrues to them from the occurrence of insight. If it urges that it presents the insights that arise spontaneously, immediately, and inevitably from the data, one must remark that the data alone are never the sole determinants of the insights that arise in any but an infantile mind, and that beyond the level of insight there is the level of critical reflection with its criterion of the virtually unconditioned. If it objects that at least one must begin by describing the facts that are accessible to all, one must insist that knowledge of fact rests on a grasp of the unconditioned and that a grasp of the unconditioned is not the starting point but the end of inquiry. Moreover, if one hopes to reach this end in an inquiry into knowledge, then one had better not begin with the assumption that knowing is 'something there to be looked at and described.' For knowing is an organically integrated activity: on a flow of sensitive experiences, inquiry intelligently generates a cumulative succession of insights, and the significance of the experiences varies concomitantly with the cumulation of insights; in memory's store of experiences and in the formulation of accumulated insights, reflection grasps approximations towards the virtually unconditioned and attainments of it, to issue into probable and certain judgments of fact. To conceive knowing one must understand the dynamic pattern of experiencing, inquiring, reflecting; and such understanding is not to be reached by taking a look. To affirm knowing it is useless to peer inside, for the dynamic pattern is to be found not in this or that act but in the unfolding of mathematics, empirical science, common sense, and philosophy; in that unfolding must be grasped the pattern of knowing, and if one feels inclined to doubt that the pattern really exists, then one can try the experiment of attempting to escape experience, to renounce intelligence in inquiry, to desert reasonableness in critical reflection.

In brief, empiricism as a method rests on an elementary confusion. What is obvious in knowing is, indeed, looking. Compared to looking, insight is obscure, and grasp of the unconditioned is doubly obscure. But empiricism amounts to the assumption that what is obvious in knowing is what knowing obviously is. That assumption is false, for if one would learn mathematics or science or philosophy or if one sought commonsense advice, then one would go to a man that is intelligent and reasonable rather than to a man that is stupid and silly.

4.4 Commonsense Eclecticism [416–21]

The third of the methods that would guide the philosopher to his goal is commonsense eclecticism. If it rarely is adopted by original thinkers, it remains the inertial center of the philosophic process. From every excess and aberration men swing back to common sense, and perhaps no more than a minority of students and professors, of critics and historians ever wander very far from a set of assumptions that are neither formulated nor scrutinized.

As has been seen, however, common sense is a variable.[n] The common sense of one age is not that of another; the common sense of Germans is not that of Frenchmen; the common sense of Americans is not that of Englishmen and still less that of Russians. Roman Catholics have their common sense, Protestants theirs, Moslems theirs, and agnostics a fourth variety. Clearly such variations preclude hard and fast rules, yet general tendencies are not too difficult to discern. For commonly a distinction is drawn between the activities of theoretical understanding, which not undeservedly are to be distrusted, and the pronouncements of prephilosophic reflection, which ground human sanity and human cooperation and therefore must be retained.

Theoretical understanding, then, seeks to solve problems, to erect syntheses, to embrace the universe in a single view. Neither its existence, nor its value, nor the remote possibility of its success is denied. Still, common sense is concerned not with remote but with proximate possibilities. It lauds the great men of the past, ostensibly to stir one to emulation, but really to urge one to modesty. It remarks that, if there are unsolved problems – and no doubt there are – at least men of undoubted genius have failed to solve them. It leaves to be inferred that, unless one is a still greater genius, then one had best regard such problems as practically insoluble. But emphatically it would not discourage anyone inclined to philosophy. A recognition of one's limitations need not prevent one from studying philosophy, from teaching it, from contributing to reviews, from writing books. One can become learned in the history of philosophy. One can form one's reasoned judgments about the views of others. By taking care not to lose the common touch, by maintaining one's sense of reality, by cultivating balance and proportion, one can reach a philosophic viewpoint that is solidly reliable and, after all, sufficiently enlightened. For opinions are legion; theories rise, glow, fascinate, and vanish; but sound judgment remains. And what is sound judgment? It is to bow to the necessary, to accept the certain, merely to entertain the probable, to distrust the doubtful, to disregard the merely possible, to laugh at the improbable, to denounce the impossible, and to believe what Science says. Nor are these precepts empty words, for there are truths that one cannot reject in practical living, there are others which it would be silly to doubt, there are claims to truth that merit attention and consideration, and each of these has its opposites. List the lot, draw out their implications, and you will find that you already possess a sound philosophy that can be set down in a series of propositions confirmed by proofs and fortified by answers to objections.

Such, approximately, is the program of commonsense eclecticism, and I must begin by clarifying which of its many aspects I shall single out for comment and criticism. The present topic is the method of philosophy.

On commonsense eclecticism as a practical attitude, as a pedagogy, as a style in composing textbooks, as a technique in discussing issues, I have no remarks to make. But I began by pointing out that one's method in philosophy predetermines what one's philosophy will be, and now I have to examine what is the philosophy or lack of philosophy to which one commits oneself by adopting commonsense eclecticism as a method.

In the first place, attention must be drawn to the difference between the foregoing eclecticism and my own concessions to common sense. In the method outlined after defining metaphysics, common sense no less than science was called upon to supply secondary minor premises in the argument; for the aim was to integrate science and common sense, and an integration is not independent of its materials. However, before being invited to play this subsidiary role, both science and common sense were to be subjected to a reorientation which they did not control; in particular, the liability of common sense to dramatic, egoistic, group, and general bias had been noted; the ambiguities of such terms as reality, knowledge, and objectivity had been examined; and only a criticized and chastened common sense was entrusted with no more than a subsidiary philosophic role. The method of commonsense eclecticism not only dispenses with such criticism and reorientation but also allows uncriticized common sense to settle by its practicality the aim of philosophy and to measure naively the resources at the philosopher's disposal. Let us attempt to expand these points briefly.

Secondly, then, commonsense eclecticism brushes aside the aim of philosophy. For that aim is the integrated unfolding of the detached, disinterested, and unrestricted desire to know. That aim can be pursued only by the exercise of theoretical understanding, and indeed only by the subtle exercise that understands both science and common sense in their differences and in their complementarity. But commonsense eclecticism deprecates the effort to understand. For it, problems are immutable features of the mental landscape, and syntheses are to be effected by somebody else who, when he has finished his system, will provide a name for merely another viewpoint.

Thirdly, commonsense eclecticism denies the vital growth of philosophy. It restricts significant activity to men of genius, and it takes it for granted that they are very few and very rare. But within the context of the philosophic process, every discovery is a significant contribution to the ultimate aim. If it is formulated as a position, it invites the development of further coherent discovery. If it is formulated as a counterposition, it invites the exploration of its presuppositions and implications and it leads to its own reversal, to restore the discovery to the cumulative series of positions and to enlighten man on the polymorphism of his consciousness. This activity of discovery, of developing positions and of reversing counterpositions, is not restricted to the men of genius of whom common sense happens to have heard. It results from all competent and conscientious work, and like natural growth it goes forward without attracting widespread attention. So far from being the product of genius, it produces genius. For the genius is simply the man at the level of his time, when the time is ripe for a new orientation or a sweeping reorganization; and it is not the genius that makes the time ripe, but the competent and conscientious workers that slowly and often unconsciously have been developing positions and heading towards the reversal of counterpositions. But commonsense eclecticism brushes all this aside with a homily on the acknowledgment of one's personal limitations. The exercise of theoretical understanding is to be left to men of genius, and common sense will see to it that no effort is made to prepare their way and no comprehension is available to greet their achievements.

Fourthly, while commonsense eclecticism discourages the effort to understand, it encourages a wide exercise of judgment. But this is to overlook the fact that understanding is a constitutive component in knowledge, that before one can pass judgment on any issue, one has to understand it. Nor is the requisite understanding to be estimated by average attainment, by the convictions of common sense, by the beliefs of a given milieu, but solely by that absence of further relevant questions that leads to a reflective grasp of the virtually unconditioned. Unless one endeavors to understand with all one's heart and all one's mind, one will not know what questions are relevant or when their limit is approached. Yet eclecticism, while discouraging understanding, urges one to paw through the display of opinions in the history of philosophy and to discriminate between the necessary and the certain, the probable and the doubtful, the possible, the improbable, and the impossible.

The fallacy of this procedure is, of course, that it fails to grasp the limitations of common sense. The proper domain of common sense is the field of particular matters of fact; it is that field, not as a single whole, but divided up and parceled out among the men and women familiar with its several parts; it is such a part, not in its basic potentialities, nor in its underlying necessities, nor in its accurately formulated actuality, but simply in its immediate relevance to human living in the mode and fashion of such living in each region and each age. One can entrust common sense with the task of a juror; one cannot ask it to formulate the laws of a country, to argue cases in its courts, to decide on issues of procedure, and to pass sentence on criminals. One does not have to be a scientist to see the color of litmus paper or to note the position of a needle on a dial; but one cannot rely on mere common sense to devise experiments or to interpret their results. Similarly in philosophy, if one presupposes an independently established set of philosophic concepts and positions, then common sense can provide the factual boundary conditions that decide between theoretical alternatives. But it is vain to ask common sense to provide the philosophic concepts, to formulate the coherent range of possible positions, to set the questions that can be answered by an appeal to commonly known facts. By deprecating theoretical understanding and by encouraging a wide exercise of judgment, commonsense eclecticism does what it can to make philosophy obtuse and superficial.

Fifthly, commonsense eclecticism cannot be critical. Not only is common sense a variable but also it is subject to a dramatic, an egoistic, a group, and a general bias. Once the aim of philosophy is brushed aside, once the resources of its natural growth are ignored, once a vain program of incompetent judgment is established, not only common sense but also its bias are in charge, and they are there to stay. Distinct philosophies emerge for the changing tastes and fashions of racial, economic, regional, national, cultural, religious, and antireligious groups and even subgroups. Spice and originality are added by the special brands of common sense peculiar to psychoneurotics, assertive egoists, and aspiring romanticists. And if human society tires of muddling through one crisis into another, then there arises the temptation that the only means to attain an effective community of norms and directives is to put the educational system, the press, the stage, the radio, and the churches under the supervision of a paternal government, to call upon social engineers to channel thought and condition feeling, and to hold in reserve the implements that discipline refractory minds and tongues. For commonsense eclecticism is incapable of criticizing common sense. It is not by discouraging theoretical understanding that the polymorphism of human consciousness can be grasped, and it is not by appealing to what common sense finds obvious that the correct meaning of such terms as reality, knowledge, and objectivity is to be reached.

4.5 Hegelian Dialectic°   [421–23]

Whether one considers the deductive methods that offer to function automatically or the guiding methods that rest on the conviction that the subject cannot be ignored, one is forced to the conclusion that philosophic method must concern itself with the structure and the aberrations of human cognitional process. Abstract deduction yields to concrete; the use of concrete deduction raises the question of its own possibility; and that possibility is found to lie in the genesis of a wisdom that is prior to metaphysics. Universal doubt heads for the same emptiness as abstract deduction; empiricism seeks the concrete in the obvious manner that proves mistaken in almost every respect; and a commonsense use of judgment leaves philosophy obtuse, superficial, and divided. Might one not conclude, then, that the method of philosophy lies in this very process that turns positions into their contradictories only to discover in such reversal a new position that begets its opposite to bring to birth a third position with similar consequences until through successive repetitions the totality of positions and opposites forms a dialectical whole? Such, approximately, was Hegel's inspiration, and since I venture to employ his term 'dialectic' I feel constrained to list the differences that separate his notion from my own.

In the first place, then, Hegelian dialectic is conceptualist, closed, necessitarian, and immanental. It deals with determinate conceptual contents; its successive triadic sets of concepts are complete; the relations of opposition and sublation between concepts are pronounced necessary; and the whole dialectic is contained within the field defined by the concepts and their necessary relations of opposition and sublation. In contrast, our position is intellectualist, open, factual, and normative. It deals not with determinate conceptual contents but with heuristically defined anticipations. So far from fixing the concepts that will meet the anticipations, it awaits from nature and from history a succession of tentative solutions. Instead of binding these solutions by necessary relations, it regards them as products of a cumulative succession of insights, and it claims that the succession follows neither a unique nor a necessary path; for identical results can be reached by different routes, and besides valid developments there are aberrations. Finally, the appeal to heuristic structures, to accumulating insights, to verdicts awaited from nature and history, goes outside the conceptual field to acts of understanding that rise upon experiences and are controlled by critical reflection; and so instead of an immanental dialectic that embraces all positions and their opposites, ours is a normative dialectic that discriminates between advance and aberration.

The foregoing differences have a common source. Hegel endeavors to pour everything into the concept; we regard concepts as byproducts of the development of understanding, and place understanding itself in an intermediate role between experience and critical reflection. It follows that what Hegel is bound to regard as conceptual we can interpret quite differently. Thus, Hegel's notion of being is a minimum conceptual content that topples over into nothing, but our notion of being is the all-inclusive heuristic anticipation issuing from an unrestricted desire to know. Hegel's dialectical opposition is a contradiction within the conceptual field, but our dialectical opposition is the conflict between the pure desire to know and other human desires. Hegel's sublation is through a reconciling third concept, but our development is both the accumulation of insights moving to higher viewpoints and the reversal of the aberrations that were brought about by the interference of alien desire. Hegel's absolute is a terminal concept that generates no antithesis to be sublated in a higher synthesis; we recognize a manifold of instances of the virtually unconditioned, and through them attain knowledge of proportionate being in its distinctions and relations. Hegel's concrete is an integrated whole of determinate conceptual contents, but our concrete is a prospective totality to be known by answering correctly the totality of questions for intelligence and for reflection. Hence it is that Hegel's dialectic is a universal and undifferentiated tool: it is relevant in the same manner within logic, within nature or science, and within the realm of spirit. Our dialectic is a restricted and differentiated tool: it is relevant to human knowledge and to human activities that depend upon knowledge; it admits separate application to psychoneural problems, to the historical expansion of practical common sense, to the diversity of philosophic methods and systems; but it does not lie within logic but rather regards the movement from one logically formalized position to another; and it has no relevance to purely natural process.

Finally, from a genetic standpoint, Hegel's dialectic has its origins in the Kantian reversal both of the Cartesian realism of the *res extensa* and of the Cartesian realism of the *res cogitans*; but where Kant did not break completely with extroversion as objectivity, inasmuch as he acknowledged things themselves that, though unknowable, caused sensible impressions and appeared, Hegel took the more forthright position that extroverted consciousness was but an elementary stage in the coming-to-be of mind; where Kant considered the demand of reflective rationality for the unconditioned to provide no more than a regulative ideal that, when misunderstood, generates antinomies, Hegel affirmed an identification of the real with a rationality that moved necessarily from theses through antitheses to higher syntheses until the movement exhausted itself by embracing everything; where Kant had restricted philosophy to a critical task, Hegel sought a new mode, distinct from Cartesian deductivism, that would allow philosophy to take over the functions and aspirations of universal knowledge. In contrast, we affirm the realism of the *res cogitans* for human knowing and the realism of the *res extensa* for elementary knowing;[P] while the two realities as realities may be coincident, the two knowings must be distinguished and kept apart; and it is failure to keep them apart that originates the component of aberration in our dialectic of philosophy. Hence we break completely from mere extroverted consciousness, not because it is illusory, but because it is confusing and philosophically irrelevant. At the same time, a more thorough and precise account of human knowing enables us to eliminate the rigidity of the Kantian a priori, to uncover a grasp of the unconditioned as essential to judgment, to identify the notion of being with the drive of intelligent inquiry and critical reflection, to define metaphysics by the integral heuristic structure of this drive, and so to conceive philosophy as universal knowledge without infringing upon the autonomy either of empirical science or of common sense. Finally, as will appear shortly, this procedure yields a metaphysics that brings to contemporary thought the wisdom of the Greeks and of the medieval schoolmen as reached by Aristotle and Aquinas, but purged of every trace of antiquated science, formulated to integrate not only the science of the present but also of the future, and elaborated in accord with a method that makes it possible to reduce every dispute in the field of metaphysical speculation to a question of concrete psychological fact.

4.6 Scientific Method and Philosophy   [423–30]

As there is nothing to prevent a scientist from being a man of common sense, so there is nothing to prevent him from being a philosopher. Indeed, the scientist's dedication to truth and his habituation to the intellectual pattern of experience are more than a propaedeutic to philosophy; and if every mind by its inner unity demands the integration of all it knows, the mind of the scientist will be impelled all the more forcibly to proceed to that integration along a course that is at once economical and effective.

In the past the philosophic appetite of scientists was satisfied commonly enough[q] with a scientific monism. The philosophies were regarded as misguided efforts to attain the knowledge that science alone can bestow. Common sense was considered as mere ignorance that the advance of science and the legal enforcement of universal education soon would eliminate. In this fashion the integration of human knowledge was identified with the unification of the sciences, and that unification was obtained by the simple device of proclaiming that objectivity was extroversion, knowing was taking a look, and the real was a subdivision of the 'already out there now.' It followed that the universe consisted of imaginable elements linked together in space and time by natural laws; because the elements were imaginable, the universe was mechanist; because the laws were necessary, the mechanism was determinist. Mechanics, then, was the one science, and thermodynamics, electromagnetism, chemistry, biology, psychology, economics, politics, and history were just so many provisional macroscopic views of a microscopic reality. Finally, to add a note on method, it was unsuspected that there was involved an extrascientific supposition in the pronouncement on the meaning of objectivity, knowledge, and reality. That was far too obvious to be questioned. It followed that to doubt mechanist determinism was to doubt the validity of the sciences, and so doubters were summoned to explain which of the methods or conclusions of the sciences they thought to be mistaken.

From the incubus of this fallacy, the more recent development of the sciences has been effecting a salutary liberation. Darwin introduced a type of explanation that had its basis not in necessary laws but in probabilities. Freud, despite his involvement in mechanist determinism, established the concept of psychogenic disease. Einstein removed the space and time in which the imaginable elements were imagined to reside. Quantum mechanics removed from science the relevance of any image of particles, or waves, or continuous process. No less than his predecessors, the contemporary scientist can observe and experiment, inquire and understand, form hypotheses and verify them. But unlike his predecessors, he has to think of knowledge, not as taking a look, but as experiencing, understanding, and judging; he has to think of objectivity, not as mere extroversion, but as experiential, normative, and tending towards an absolute; he has to think of the real, not as a part of the 'already out there now,' but as the verifiable. Clearly, the imagined as imagined can be verified only by actual seeing, and so there is no verifiable image of the elements of mechanism. Moreover, what science does verify does not lie in any particular affirmations, which are never more than approximate; what science verifies is to be found in general affirmations, on which ranges of ranges of particular affirmations converge with an accuracy that increases with the precision of measurements and with the elimination of probable errors.

Still, this is only one aspect of the matter. Scientific monism not only identified science with philosophy but also concluded that the method of science must be the method of philosophy. While this implication cannot be challenged as long as its premise stands, the breakdown of the premise cannot be expected to transform the long-established habits of mind that were generated and nourished by the conclusion. Only through a positive accumulation of new insights can scientists be expected to grasp the differences between the methods of empirical science and the method that must be followed if the detached and disinterested desire to know is to attain an integrated view of the universe. Accordingly, though most of the present book bears on this issue, it will not be amiss, I think, to indicate and to explain briefly the differences of method that commonly lead scientists to find philosophy baffling, repellent, or absurd.

The basic difference is that scientific method is prior to scientific work and independent of particular scientific results, but philosophic method is coincident with philosophic work and so stands or falls with the success or failure of a particular philosophy. This difference leads the scientist to conclude that it is nonsense to talk about a philosophic method and that the plain fact is that philosophy has no method at all. Now there is no use disputing about names, but there is[r] a point to understanding just where differences lie. At least in a generalized sense, there is a method if there is an intelligible set of directives that lead from a starting point that may be assumed to a goal that is to be obtained. In this generalized sense, both science and philosophy possess method. In a specialized sense, there is a method if the same intelligible set of directives will lead to a variety of different goals. In this specialized sense, science has a method and philosophy has not. The first reason for this difference is that there are many particular sciences and each of them deals with a variety of objects, but there is only one integrated view of one universe and there is only one set of directives that lead to it. The second reason for the difference is that the sciences are concerned to assign determinate conceptual contents to fill empty heuristic structures, so that the same method leads successively to a series of different determinations; on the other hand, philosophy obtains its integrated view of a single universe, not by determining the contents that fill heuristic structures, but by relating the heuristic structures to one another. Because of these differences in their objectives, scientific method stands to scientific conclusions as a genetic universal to generated particulars, but philosophic method stands to philosophic conclusions as the genesis to the attainment of a single all-inclusive view.

In the second place, scientists are repelled by the failure of philosophers to reach a single, precise, universally accepted, technical language. They point out the simplicity of this device and the enormous benefits it has conferred on science. They lament the obtuseness of philosophers in overlooking so necessary a procedure, and they deplore their wrong-headedness in clinging to equivocal and even literary usage. Perhaps, however, they will grant that the desired technical language of philosophy must be compatible with the problems of philosophy. It would be absurd to demand that modern chemists express their thought in terms of Aristotle's four elements, and similarly it would be absurd to provide philosophers with a language that was incapable of expressing their thought. Further, the polymorphism of human consciousness seems relevant to the problems of philosophy, for philosophy is concerned with knowledge, reality, and objectivity, and these terms take on different meanings as consciousness shifts from one pattern or blend of patterns of experience to another. But the meaning of every other term changes with changes in the meaning of the terms 'knowledge,' 'reality,' 'objectivity,' for the function of all language is to express presumptive knowledge of presumptive reality and affirm or deny the objectivity of the knowledge.

Accordingly, the fundamental task in working out an appropriate technical language for philosophy would be to explore the range of meanings that may be assumed by the basic variables: knowledge, reality, and objectivity. There would follow the complementary task of selecting the range of different combinations of particular values of the three basic variables and of showing how each combination modified the meaning of the remaining terms of philosophy. This, of course, would be a lengthy procedure, and allowance would have to be made for differences of opinion on the manner in which variations in the basic combinations modified the meaning of the remaining terms.

Finally, two further points must be mentioned. There would be the problem of discovering what logicians call the meta-language in which one would express with technical accuracy just what is meant by the polymorphism of human consciousness and by different meanings in the ranges of the basic variables. There also would be the difficulty of explaining to people as they are before they begin philosophy just what is meant by the terms and syntax of this meta-language, and at the same time of convincing them, as well as those with philosophic opinions of a different color and shade, that the polymorphism of human consciousness is the one and only key to philosophy. It would seem that this preliminary task would have to be conducted in literary language despite its equivocations; and as the performance of the preliminary task has to be adapted continuously to the changing mentality of successive generations, it seems unlikely that a philosophy which integrates the personal knowledge of living and changing minds will ever be able to wrap itself completely in the restful cocoon of a technical language. In brief, while enormous advantages are to be derived from a technical language in exploiting what is already known, the problems of contemporary philosophy are not problems of exploitation.

A third difficulty of scientists, when they turn to philosophic problems, is psychological. We are accustomed to think of scientists as pioneers in a novel and daring adventure of exploration, but the fact is that modern science has had four centuries in which to develop a traditionalist mentality. Again, there is a screening ambiguity to contemporary usage of the word 'belief.' If a moron reads in his newspaper that energy is equal to the product of the mass by the square of the velocity of light, we are not inclined to say that his acceptance is mere belief, for after all what Science says is not belief but knowledge. However, if we care to be accurate, the difference between knowledge and belief lies not in the object but in the attitude of the subject. Knowing is affirming what one correctly understands in one's own experience. Belief is accepting what we are told by others on whom we reasonably rely.

Now every conclusion of science is known by several scientists, but the vast and cumulative collaboration of the scientific tradition would be impossible if every conclusion of science had to be known by every scientist. For each science is an extensive array of elements of information and correlation, and the scientific attitude is not to spend one's life checking over what was settled by one's predecessors but to proceed from this basis to further discoveries.

The theoretical and practical training of a scientist aims at bringing him abreast of present knowledge and enabling him to carry on the work. He must understand how information was acquired, what type of evidence went to the determination of definitions, formulae, constants, systems, how he might test and, if need should arise, successfully challenge past or current views. But no effort is made to enable each scientist to recapitulate within his own experience, understanding, and reflection the whole development of the science. On the contrary, the effort that is made is to convince him how reasonably he may rely on past results; on the one hand, there are the specimens of scientific method that he witnesses in class demonstrations and, more intimately, in his own laboratory work; and on the other hand, there is the general argument that whatever is wrong in any accepted view will come to light sooner or later, not by reliving the past, but by using it as a premise for further investigation. Belief, then, is an essential moment in scientific collaboration. It is variable in its extent. It is provisional. It is subject to checking and control. It is quite reasonable. But the reasonableness of belief does not make it knowledge, and the extent to which belief is essential in the scientific tradition disposes and conditions the minds of scientists in a manner that ill equips them for philosophy.

For while philosophy has had its traditional schools from, it seems, the days of Pythagoras, still the schools have proliferated. Instead of a single tradition with distinct departments as in science, philosophy has been a cumulative multiplication of distinct and opposed traditions. Nor is there anything surprising about this contrast. For in science a single method operates towards a variety of different goals, but in philosophy a single all-inclusive goal is sought by as many different methods as arise from different orientations of the historically developing but polymorphic consciousness of man. Hence, while a scientist is reasonable in entering into the scientific tradition and carrying on its work, a philosopher cannot be reasonable on the same terms; he has to become familiar with different traditions; he has to find grounds for deciding between them; and it is the reasonableness of that decision on which will rest the reasonableness of his collaboration within any single tradition.

It follows that, while the reasonableness of each scientist is a consequence of the reasonableness of all, the philosopher's reasonableness is grounded on a personal commitment and on personal knowledge. For the issues in philosophy cannot be settled by looking up a handbook, by appealing to a set of experiments performed so painstakingly by so-and-so, by referring to the masterful presentation of overwhelming evidence in some famous work. Philosophic evidence is within the philosopher himself. It is his own inability to avoid experience, to renounce intelligence in inquiry, to desert reasonableness in reflection. It is his own detached, disinterested desire to know. It is his own advertence to the polymorphism of his own consciousness. It is his own insight into the manner in which insights accumulate in mathematics, in the empirical sciences, in the myriad instances of common sense. It is his own grasp of the dialectical unfolding of his own desire to know in its conflict with other desires that provides the key to his own philosophic development and reveals his own potentialities to adopt the stand of any of the traditional or of the new philosophic schools. Philosophy is the flowering of the individual's rational consciousness in its coming to know and take possession of itself. To that event its traditional schools, its treatises, and its history are but contributions; and without that event they are stripped of real significance.

It is this aspect of personal development and personal commitment that the scientist turning to philosophy is, perhaps, most likely to overlook. Spontaneously, he will be attracted by the range of recent philosophies that rest on the successive attempts to formulate a symbolic logic, for a deductivism offers the security of an impersonal and automatically expanded position. Spontaneously, he will seek a new integration of the sciences in works written by individual scientists or by commissions of scientists, for he is accustomed to believing scientists and hopes for a new philosophy that can be named not philosophy but science. In the light of his antecedents, such tendencies are explained easily enough, but the explanation does not reveal them to be reasonable. As has been seen, the attractions of deductivism have been felt before, and abstract deductivism proved to be empty, concrete deductivism turned out to beg the question, and transcendental deductivism revealed itself too crude an instrument to deal with the complexity of developing intelligence. Nor can any hope be entertained that the unification of the sciences will be effected correctly because it is the work of scientists. They are not made of a different clay from mere philosophers. They are not exempt from the polymorphism of human consciousness. They are not to be expected to escape involvement in the ambiguities that reside in such terms as knowledge, reality, objectivity.

To conclude, philosophy has been fertilized repeatedly by scientific achievement. But it would seem a mistake to expect that philosophy should conform to the method, to the linguistic technique, or to the group mentality of the scientist. The contribution of science and of scientific method to philosophy lies in a unique ability to supply philosophy with instances of the heuristic structures which a metaphysics integrates into a single view of the concrete universe.

15

Elements of Metaphysics

As the preceding chapter outlined a program, so the present chapter turns to its execution. We have to make explicit the latent metaphysics of the human mind, and the first step is to establish its elements. There are six of them:[a] central potency, central form, central act, conjugate potency, conjugate form, and conjugate act. In the light of earlier chapters, it will be a relatively brief task to distinguish and relate them. But the prevalence of counterpositions made it seem inadvisable, if not impossible, to tackle the problem of genetic method until we were able to employ our basic metaphysical concepts; and so the present chapter owes its length and any complexity it may possess to the necessity of clarifying the notion of development and of outlining the heuristic structure of genetic method both in general and as applied to the organism, to the psyche, to intelligence, and to the combination of all three in man.

1   Potency, Form, and Act   [431–34]

Metaphysics has been conceived as the integral heuristic structure of proportionate being. It envisages an indefinitely remote future date when the whole domain of proportionate being will be understood. It asks what can be known here and now of that future explanation. It answers that, though full explanation may never be reached, at least the structure of that explanatory knowledge can be known at once.

For proportionate being is whatever is to be known by experience, intelligent grasp, and reasonable affirmation. While there are three components in that knowing, still only one of them is an unknown. The content of intelligent grasp of proportionate being necessarily remains unknown until full explanation is reached. But the content of reasonable affirmation is known already, for it is a virtually unconditioned yes. And the content of experience that survives in fully explanatory knowledge also is known already, for it is the intellectually patterned experience of the empirical residue; and already we know that experience is in its intellectual pattern when it is dominated by the detached and disinterested desire to know; similarly, we already have determined that the empirical residue lies in the individuality, the continuity, the coincidental conjunctions and successions, and the nonsystematic divergence from intelligible norms, which are to be known by experiencing and only by experiencing.

Accordingly, let us introduce the terms 'potency,' 'form,' and 'act.'

'Potency' denotes the component of proportionate being to be known in fully explanatory knowledge by an intellectually patterned experience of the empirical residue.

'Form' denotes the component of proportionate being to be known, not by understanding the names of things, nor by understanding their relations to us, but by understanding them fully in their relations to one another.

'Act' denotes the component of proportionate being to be known by uttering the virtually unconditioned yes of reasonable judgment.

It follows that potency, form, and act constitute a unity. For what is experienced is what is understood; and what is understood is what is affirmed. The three levels of cognitional activity yield a single knowing; for experience alone is not human knowing; experience and understanding do not suffice for knowing; only when the unconditioned is reached and affirmation or negation occurs does knowing in the proper meaning of the term arise. In like manner, the contents of the three levels of cognitional activity constitute a unity; one does not know a first proportionate being by experiencing, a second by understanding, and a third by judging; on the contrary, the three contents coalesce into a single known. Hence potency, form, and act, since they are known by experience, understanding, and judgment, are not three proportionate beings but three components in a single proportionate being.

Further, it follows that potency, form, and act not only constitute a unity but also share a common definition or specification. For experience neither defines nor specifies; it merely presents. Again, judgment neither defines nor specifies; it merely affirms or denies what has been defined or specified already. All defining and specifying occur on the level of understanding, and so the unity constituted by potency, form, and act has but a single definition or specification that is reached in knowing form.

Finally, the foregoing account of potency, form, and act will cover any possible scientific explanation. For a scientific explanation is a theory verified in instances; as verified, it refers to act; as theory, it refers to form; as in instances, it refers to potency. Again, as a theory of the classical type, it refers to forms as forms; as a theory of the statistical type, it refers to forms as setting ideal frequencies from which acts do not diverge systematically; as a theory of the genetic type, it refers to the conditions of the emergence of form from potency.

In subsequent sections different types of potency, form, and act will be distinguished, but at once we must draw attention to the fact that, while we employ the names introduced by Aristotle and while we assign them a meaning that Aristotle would recognize as his own, nonetheless Aristotle's ready use of merely descriptive knowledge and our insistence on explanation involve different starting points, different tendencies, and differences in implication. Thus, it is sound Aristotelian doctrine to say that potency stands to form as eye to sight, and that form stands to act as sight to seeing. But it is a far more prominent Aristotelian doctrine to say that potency stands to form as the privation of heat to heat, and that form stands to act as heat to heating. Yet the psychological illustration satisfies our definitions but the physical illustration cannot be reconciled with them.

The psychological illustration satisfies our definitions. For form is what is to be known by insight; but 'sight' is known inasmuch as we understand eyes as organs of sight, or inasmuch as we understand experiences of seeing as grounded in the possession of sight. Again, act is known by the yes of judgment, and we know that a person is seeing, not by a mere inspection of eyes, nor by understanding the inspected eyes as organs of sight, but by affirming that the understood sight is being put to use. Finally, potency is what is to be known by intellectually patterned experience of the empirical residue, and there is such an experience when we inspect eyes in order to understand them.

But the physical illustration cannot be subsumed under our definitions. Form is what is to be known by insight, but Aristotle considered what he named proper sensibles to be forms; such are colors, sounds, heat and cold, the wet and dry, the hard and soft, the heavy and light, etc. At least they are extremely ambiguous forms: in the object they are sensible in potency; in sensation they are sensible in act; as named they are associated with any sufficiently similar quality through an insight that grasps how to employ the name; as objects of inquiry, they enter into a heuristic structure that seeks what is to be known when they will be understood; finally, as explained, they are related to laws that implicitly define conjugate terms. Which of the five is Aristotle's form 'heat'? Again, act is what is to be known by the yes of judgment; but 'heating' is not to be known in this simple manner. To know 'heating' is to know that there are two instances of heat and that one of them is derived causally from the other. Finally, potency is known by intellectually patterned experience of the empirical residue. But the potency to the form 'heat' is the privation of that form; that privation is known, not by merely experiencing the contrary form 'cold' but by understanding it as contrary to heat and excluding heat.[1]

It is easy enough to see how the ambiguities of Aristotle's physical notions made a conflict with Renaissance science humanly inevitable. If the form of heat is what is to be known by understanding heat, then the Aristotelians were bound to approve the scientists' effort to understand. In fact, there was a comedy of errors. The Aristotelians had little grasp

---

1 The historical aspect of the present analysis has been set forth in some detail in my articles on 'The Concept of *Verbum* in the Writings of St. Thomas Aquinas' [see above, p. 9, note 1]. For an excellent outline of these articles, see L.-B. Geiger, O.P., *Bulletin thomiste*, 8:2 (1952) 477–79, § 740. On the intimate relations in both Aristotle and Aquinas between insight and *eidos, forma*, see *Theological Studies* 7 (1946) 360–64 [*Verbum* 12–16]. On the quite common equivalence in Aquinas of *actus, actio, operatio*, in the sense of Aristotle's *energeia*, as distinct from *poiêsis*, see *Theological Studies* 8 (1947) 408–41 passim [*Verbum* 97–137].

In brief, I should say that the present division of being into potency, form, and act is equivalent to Aquinas's affirmations (1) that *ens dividitur per potentiam et actum*, (2) that there are two kinds of *actus*, namely *forma* and *operatio*, and (3) that there are two corresponding kinds of *potentia* of which one is *potentia* to *forma* and the other, identical with *forma*, is *potentia* to *operatio* (see *De potentia*, q. 1, a. 1, and *In metaphysicam Aristotelis commentaria*, lib. IX, lect. 5, §§ 1828–29 [Leonine: *Sentential libri Metaphysicae*]).

Finally, the systematic significance of this triad is evident not merely in the threefold composition of material substance but also in the role played by potency, habit, and act in the sweep of the *Prima secundae* (*Summa theologiae*, 1–2, q. 6, Introductio, and q. 49, Introductio.).

of Aristotle's doctrine of insight into imaginative representations, and they had no notion of the heuristic structure that heads for insight. On the other hand, the scientists did not conceive explaining as knowing inasmuch as one is understanding; their thought was dominated by the notion of objectivity as extroversion; in this sense they denied the proper sensibles to be really 'out there'; and they conceived explanation as the reduction of apparent qualities to the real dimensions of matter in motion. Four centuries ought to suffice for us to learn to see through this set of blunders.

2   Central and Conjugate Forms   [434–37]

The second step in working out the integral heuristic structure of proportionate being will be to distinguish two general cases of potency, form, and act. For while the forms of proportionate being are to be known fully only when full explanation is reached, still the present existence of heuristic techniques can reveal at once that there are different kinds of forms. Moreover, if there are different kinds of forms, there must be different kinds of potency and of act; for potency, form, and act constitute a single known and share a common definition; and the potency and act that share the definition of one kind of form must differ from the potency and act that share the different definition of another kind.

Now at the root of classical method there are two heuristic principles. The first is that similars are understood similarly, that a difference of understanding presupposes a significant difference of data. The second is that the similarities relevant to explanation lie not in the relations of things to our senses but in their relations to one another. Next, when these heuristic principles are applied, there result classifications by sensible similarity, then correlations, and finally the verification of correlations and of systems of correlations. But verified correlations necessarily involve the verification of terms implicitly defined by the correlations; and they do not involve more than such implicitly defined terms as related, for what is verified accurately is not this or that particular proposition but the general and abstract proposition on which ranges of ranges of particular propositions converge. Accordingly, there is a fundamental heuristic structure that leads to the determination of conjugates, that is, of terms defined implicitly by their empirically verified and explanatory relations. Such terms as related are known by understanding, and so they are forms. Let us name them conjugate forms. Since such forms are verified in the empirical residue of experience, they constitute unities with conjugate potencies and conjugate acts. Hence conjugate potency is potency to conjugate form, and conjugate act is act of conjugate form, where potency *to* form and act *of* form mean that the potency, form, and act in question constitute a single unity.

Further, the heuristic structure that leads to knowledge of conjugate forms necessitates another structure that leads to knowledge of central forms. For one reaches explanatory conjugates by considering data as similar to other data; but the data which are similar also are concrete and individual; and as concrete and individual, they are understood inasmuch as one grasps in them a concrete and intelligible unity, identity, whole. Nor can one dispense with this grasp or transcend it. For science advances through the interaction of increasingly accurate descriptions and ever more satisfactory explanations of the same objects. Unless the objects are the same, there is no relation between the description and the explanation, and so no reason why explanation should modify description or description lead to better explanation. But the only object that is the same is the concrete and intelligible unity, identity, whole; for the explanatory conjugates change; and the descriptive or experiential terms undergo modifications and rearrangements. Accordingly, as long as science is developing, the notion of the intelligible unity is indispensable. But in their term no less than in their development, scientific conclusions need to be supported by evidence; the evidence for such conclusions lies in change; and without concrete and intelligible unities there is nothing to change, for change is neither the substitution of one datum for another nor the replacement of one concept by another; it consists in the same concrete, intelligible unity providing the unification for successively different data; and so without the unity there is no change, and without change there is lacking a notable part, if not all, of the evidence for scientific conclusions. Finally, science is applicable to concrete problems; but neither descriptive nor explanatory knowledge can be applied to concrete problems without the use of the demonstrative 'this,' and that demonstrative can be used only inasmuch as there is a link between concepts and data as individual; only the notion of the concrete and intelligible unity of data supplies such a link, and so that notion is necessary for science as applied.

Now concrete and intelligible unities are known by understanding; therefore, they are forms. But they are quite different from conjugate forms, and so there must be recognized another type of form to be named central form; and just as conjugate form implies a conjugate potency and a conjugate act, so also central form implies a central potency and a central act.

The difference between our central form and Aristotle's substantial form is merely nominal. For the Aristotelian substantial form is what is known by grasping an intelligible unity, an *unum per se*. However, since the meaning of the English word 'substance' has been influenced profoundly by Locke, since the Cartesian confusion of 'body' and thing led to an identification of substance and extension and then to the riposte that substance is underneath extension, I have thought it advisable, at least temporarily, to cut myself off from this verbal tangle.

The difference between our conjugate form and Aristotle's accidental form is partly nominal and partly real. The name 'accidental' is misleading, for it suggests the merely incidental. Moreover, the accidental forms of Aristotle's physical theory were, perhaps, sensible qualities as sensed, but we admit no forms that are known apart from understanding. Finally, the name 'conjugate' brings out what we consider the essential feature of intelligible mutual relations that implicitly define conjugate forms.

The distinction between central and conjugate forms leads to the distinction between central and conjugate acts. Central act is existence, for what exists is the intelligible unity. Conjugate act is occurrence, for what occurs is defined explanatorily by appealing to conjugate form.

Similarly, there results a division of the empirical residue between central potency and conjugate potency. Since central form is the intelligible unity of data as individual, central potency may be identified with the individuality of the empirical residue. On the other hand, conjugate forms are verified in spatiotemporal continua, conjunctions, and successions; and so these aspects of the empirical residue are to be deputed to conjugate potency.

To illustrate the meaning of the terms 'central and conjugate potency, form, and act,' let us suppose that mass-velocity is a notion that survives in fully explanatory science. Then the mass-velocity will be a conjugate act; the mass, defined by its intelligible relations to other masses, will be a conjugate form; the space-time continuum of the trajectory will be a conjugate potency; what has the mass will be individual by its central potency, a unity by its central form, and existing by its central act.

3   Explanatory Genera and Species   [437–42]

Genera and species are explanatory if they are derived, not from classifications based on sensible similarities and dissimilarities, but from classifications based upon explanatory knowledge. The general character of such explanatory knowledge has been indicated already in the chapter on 'things,' but perhaps it will not be amiss to recast it in terms of central and conjugate potency, form, and act before asking the twofold question, namely, whether or not that is the structure of explanatory genera and species, and whether or not such a structure will survive in fully explanatory knowledge of proportionate being.

First, then, if there is any explanatory science, then there is a set of conjugate forms, say C_i, defined implicitly by their empirically established and explanatory relations. Different combinations of forms from the set C_i serve to define explanatorily the unities or things T_i, which differ specifically from one another but pertain to the same explanatory genus. Again, different combinations of the verified correlations yield a range of schemes of recurrence S_i, and in the measure such schemes are realized, they make systematic the occurrence of the conjugate acts A_i.

Secondly, either all conjugate acts of the type A_i occur systematically, or some occur systematically in virtue of the schemes S_i, while others occur at random. If there are such random occurrences, then there are instances of the merely empirical residue on the level of conjugate acts. For a manifold of random occurrences offers a much larger range of merely coincidental conjunctions and successions, and such conjunctions and successions pertain to the empirical residue.

Thirdly, there is a further possibility. Besides occurring systematically in virtue of the schemes S_i and occurring at random, conjugate acts of the type A_i may occur quite regularly yet in a manner that cannot be accounted for by any of the schemes S_i. In that case there is the evidence that is necessary and sufficient to affirm the existence of another set of conjugates C_j, defining another genus of things T_j, and yielding another range of schemes S_j that make systematic another type of conjugate acts A_j.

Fourthly, the foregoing possibility is recurrent. Just as a random manifold of conjugate acts A_{ij} is an instance of the empirical residue and so supplies the conjugate potency for the higher systematization by the conjugate forms C_j, so also a random manifold of conjugate acts A_{jk} may be an instance of the empirical residue that supplies the conjugate potency for a still higher systematization by the conjugate forms C_k. Accordingly, there can be a series of genera, T_i, T_j, T_k, . . . and within each genus there can be different species, for the things are defined by their conjugate forms and the conjugate forms differ inasmuch as they systematize differently their different underlying manifolds of lower-order conjugate acts.

Fifthly, in things of any higher genus, there survive lower conjugate potencies, forms, and acts, but there do not survive lower things. The lower conjugates survive, for without them there would be nothing for the higher system of conjugates to systematize. On the other hand, the lower things do not survive within higher things. For a thing is the concrete and intelligible unity of concrete and individual data; the same data from different viewpoints can provide the evidence for different conjugate forms; but the same data under the totality of their aspects cannot be the data for different things. If any datum under all its aspects pertains to one thing, then it does not pertain to any other thing; hence, if there is a higher thing, there are data for affirming it; and the same data are not data for any other thing. It is to be noted, however, that we are speaking not of 'bodies' but of things. Within the 'body' of an animal, there can be many different things; but these different things are not the animal, nor parts of it; they may be foreign 'bodies'; they may live in symbiosis with the animal; but they do not pertain to the animal as do its eyes and other organs.

Sixthly, corresponding to the successive genera, there will be distinct and autonomous empirical sciences. For each genus has its proper range of schemes of recurrence S_i, S_j, S_k, . . . Investigation of these regularities will lead to the discovery of empirically verified correlations and so of implicitly defined sets of conjugates C_i, C_j, C_k, . . . All the terms of the set C_i will be defined by their internal relations; all the terms of the set C_j will be defined by their internal relations; and since the two sets have no terms in common, there will be no logical process from one set to another. Because there is no logical process from one set to another, the several empirical sciences will be distinct and autonomous.

Seventhly, the successive, distinct autonomous sciences will be related as successive higher viewpoints. For the coincidental manifolds of lower conjugate acts, say A_{ij}, can be imagined symbolically. Moreover, as the coincidental manifolds are the conjugate potency for the higher conjugate forms, so the symbolic images provide the materials for insight into the laws relating the higher forms. But there is a higher viewpoint when images of lower-level operations yield insight into the laws governing higher-level operations. Accordingly, the structure of the successive genera runs parallel to the structure of successive higher viewpoints.

Eighthly, this parallel may be stated either as a position or as a counterposition. If one affirms the real to be being and to be known by intelligent grasp and reasonable affirmation, then the real will be existing unities differentiated by conjugate forms of various genera and species. In that case the symbolic images will have a merely heuristic value, for they will serve to facilitate the transition from one science to another and to determine to what extent data are explained or not explained by either science. On the other hand, if one affirms the real to be a subdivision in the 'already out there now,' then the images will be, not heuristic symbols, but representations of things as they really are; the successive intelligible systems will be merely subjective arrangements, for the intelligible cannot be imagined; and so the reality of each higher genus is emptied into the lower until one reaches the image of the lowest; and as the lowest is imagined as too small to be seen, one is left with unverifiable images of the lowest genus as one's extrascientific and pseudometaphysical account of reality.

We have stated our conception of explanatory genera and species, and two questions arise. Is the conception correct? Is it verifiable, not merely in things as they are known now, but also in things as they would be known if they were explained completely?

Perhaps it may be claimed that the conception is uniquely probable. The notion of the succession of higher viewpoints would seem to be the one and only manner in which logically unrelated sciences can be unified. The notion that lower coincidental manifolds of occurrences are systematized by higher forms would seem to be the one and only way in which higher orders of reality can be immanent in lower orders without violating lower classical laws. The two notions are complementary, for the image corresponds to the coincidental manifold, and the insight into the image grasps the forms that systematize the otherwise coincidental manifold. Finally, the two notions satisfy the more general requirements of abstract classical laws, concrete schemes of recurrence, statistical residues, the emergent probability of higher forms and schemes, and the metaphysical structure of central and conjugate potencies, forms, and acts.

Further, the conception rests, not on the present state of empirical sciences, but on the fundamental properties of insight. Insight is into imaginative representations. Insights accumulate into viewpoints. Images that represent viewpoints lead to insights that accumulate into higher viewpoints. This transition can be repeated. Images apart from insight are coincidental manifolds; but images under insight cease to be coincidental, for their elements become related intelligibly. Potency corresponds to the imagined empirical residue. Form corresponds to the insight. Again, direct insight expresses itself in abstract classical laws; this abstractness is an indeterminacy that leaves room for the inverse insights that grasp statistical laws; the compatibility of classical and statistical laws leaves room for the coincidental manifolds that provide the potency for the higher forms. Not only do all these elements mesh together to provide a single coherent account of explanatory genera and species, but the resultant account has no competitors, for to the best of my knowledge, no one else has attempted to work out the pure theory of genera and species, where the genera and species are conceived not descriptively but explanatorily.

Now a conception is uniquely probable if it meets an issue fairly and squarely and there are no available alternative views. Moreover, in the present instance, this probability is of a high order.[b] It regards not an imaginative synthesis of outer events, such as the Ptolemaic or Copernican systems, but the inner ground that is generative of successive imaginative syntheses and systematic unifications. Such syntheses and unifications can rise and fall in endless succession without altering a single element in the fundamental properties of insight, for those fundamental properties are the principle whence the endless succession would spring. Hence the greater one's familiarity with human intelligence and its properties, the clearer it becomes that our development of the notion of the higher viewpoint into a theory of explanatory genera and species has exploited the basic and permanent factors that will hold their ground in subsequent modifications and improvements.

Finally, such unique probability is sufficient for a metaphysical theorem when metaphysics is conceived in accord with the definition of the preceding chapter. For if a metaphysics aims at integrating the empirical sciences and common sense to yield a single view of the universe of proportionate being, then it has to deal with facts. It cannot accept the criteria of a deductivism that is content to affirm the necessary laws of any possible world. It is bound to be nuanced; it may have no doubt about central and conjugate potencies, forms, and acts; yet it can be content with unique probability when it comes to differentiating the explanatory genera and species of forms.

There remains the question of fact. Are there in this universe things that differ specifically and generically, where these differences are conceived not descriptively but explanatorily? A negative answer is dictated by the counterposition, for then reality reduces to imagined and unverifiable entities that differ, not intelligibly, but only in their imaginable determinations. On the other hand, if we appeal to the immemorial convictions of common sense or to the actual division of scientific departments, all the evidence favors the affirmation of different explanatory genera. Finally, we may invoke the testimony of the future and hypothetical reviser of the present affirmation. For if he is to revise that or any other affirmation, he must appeal to experience, understanding, and judgment, and so he will be a concrete and intelligible unity of empirical, intelligent, and rational consciousness. Moreover, he must make his pronouncement, not while he is conscious within the biological, the aesthetic, the artistic, the dramatic, or the practical patterns of experience, but while he is conscious within the intellectual pattern. Still, he will be capable of experience in those other patterns or in some blend or alternation of them, for otherwise he would not be a man. It follows that the hypothetical reviser, if he is a man, will be more than a concrete and intelligible unity of empirical, intelligent, and rational consciousness. What else will he be? One has to invoke at least one other genus of conjugate forms to account for the concrete possibility of other patterns of experience, to account for preconscious and subconscious influences upon consciousness, to account for the fact that the hypothetical reviser eats and breathes and walks on other things besides men. On the other hand, if one's hypothetical reviser is not a man, then one is rather hard put to it to conceive a manner in which the existence of different explanatory genera can be denied.

4   Potency and Limitation   [442–44]

Each higher genus is limited by the preceding lower genus. On the one hand, it must not interfere with the autonomy of the lower order, for if it were to do so, it would destroy its own foundation. On the other hand, the higher genus is a higher systematization of manifolds that would be coincidental on the lower level; and a higher systematization is limited by the manifolds which it systematizes.

Since each higher genus is limited by the preceding lower genus, it follows that the lowest genus provides a principle of limitation for the whole domain of proportionate being.

Moreover, this universal principle of limitation resides in the potency of the lowest genus. For act corresponds to judgment, form to insight, and potency to experience of the empirical residue. But the yes of judgment is restricted to the formulation it affirms; and this formulation results from an insight that is restricted to the pattern of the data to be understood. Accordingly, as judgment is limited by insight, and insight by data, so act is limited by form, and form is limited by potency.

It will be convenient to introduce the name 'prime potency' to denote the potency of the lowest level that provides the principle of limitation for the whole range of proportionate being.

Certain characteristics of prime potency are already familiar. For potency is what is to be known by intellectually patterned experience of the empirical residue. The empirical residue consists in individuality, the continuum, particular place and time, and the nonsystematic divergence from theoretically grounded anticipations. Since all these features of the empirical residue are to be verified in the lowest genus of proportionate being, all are to be attributed to prime potency.

However, one may ask whether, in the light of contemporary science, prime potency has anything to do with energy. In a general fashion one may argue that, since energy may be latent or potential, it is not act. Since it is relevant to mechanics, thermodynamics, electromagnetics, chemistry, and biology, it is not form. Finally, since it functions as a universal principle of limitation, it must be grounded in prime potency.

An investigation of the notion of energy lies outside the scope of the present inquiry, but it may not be amiss to put a few leading questions. In the first place, the notion of energy is reached, not by differentiating, but by integrating. It is not surprising when differentiating, which is an abstractive procedure, yields notions of broad generality. But energy is a notion of extreme generality yet it is reached by integrating. Might one not say that the quantity of energy is the concrete prime potency that is informed mechanically or thermally or electrically as the case may be?

Again, there is the curious fact that the science of mechanics can be developed logically in terms of classical laws and without any mention of energy,[2] yet once the notion of energy is introduced, one can develop Lagrange's method of generalized coordinates and Hamilton's canonical equations, which constitute the most powerful techniques in mechanics. Is one to say that there is a mechanics based on the laws of motion and the conjugate forms which the laws define and that there is another equivalent but more powerful mechanics based upon limitations set by prime potency?

Further, while the notion of a quantity of energy receives its basic formulation in mechanics, still it is not restricted to mechanics. Thermodynamics conceives heat as a form of energy, which it limits by a law of conservation and a law that settles the direction of its changes.[3] M. Planck has worked out Maxwell's electromagnetic equations by beginning from the notion of energy.[4] The Hamiltonian function, which represents total energy, has provided basic clues in quantum mechanics.[5] There is the release and absorption of energy in chemical change, and there is the role of chlorophyll in capturing the energy of radiation. Do these facts refer to prime potency as a universal principle of limitation?

Again, there is an inertia of energy, and there is an equation relating mass and energy. Is one to relate the inertial coefficient of mass to the prime potency it informs, and to conceive mass itself as a conjugate form that is implicitly defined by the laws that relate masses to one another?

Finally, there has been suggested a correlation between the expanding universe and the emergence of additional energy. If this happens to become accepted, is it to be explained because prime potency grounds both the space-time continuum and the quantity of energy, so that an increase of one involves an increase of the other?

What would seem desirable is a single coherent answer to all these questions such that prime potency would be conceived as a ground of quantitative limitation and general heuristic considerations would relate quantitative limitation to the properties that science verifies in the quantity it names energy.

2 Lindsay and Margenau, *Foundations of Physics* 120. [This and notes 3–5 transferred by editors from text.]
3 Ibid. 214–18.
4 Ibid. 315–16.
5 Ibid. 405, 145.

5   Potency and Finality

Being has been conceived heuristically as the objective of the detached and disinterested desire to know, and more precisely as whatever is to be known by intelligent grasp and reasonable affirmation. This heuristic notion has been found to underlie all our knowing, to penetrate all conceptual contents, to go beyond them, to provide a core for all meaning. We have now to formulate a reciprocal notion of equal significance. For it is not only our notion of being that is heuristic, that heads for an objective that can be defined only in terms of the process of knowing it, but also the reality of proportionate being itself exhibits a similar incompleteness and a similar dynamic orientation towards a completeness that becomes determinate only in the process of completion.

Just as intellectually patterned experience heads towards insights and judgments, so potency heads towards forms and acts. Just as cognitional activity mounts through accumulations of insights to higher viewpoints, so objective process involves the information and actuation of prime potency only to uncover a residue of coincidental manifolds and so mount through successive levels of higher systematization. Just as cognitional activity does not know in advance what being is and so has to define it heuristically as whatever is to be known by intelligent grasp and reasonable affirmation, so objective process is not the realization of some blueprint but the cumulation of a conditioned series of things and schemes of recurrence in accord with successive schedules of probabilities. Just as cognitional activity is the becoming known of being, so objective process is the becoming of proportionate being. Indeed, since cognitional activity is itself but a part of this universe, so its heading to being is but the particular instance in which universal striving towards being becomes conscious and intelligent and reasonable.

Such is the meaning we would attach to the name 'finality.' Accordingly, we do not mean by finality some expedient of a lazy intelligence attempting to make amends for the deficiencies in its account of efficient causality. Much less do we mean by finality some pull exerted by the future on the present. By finality we refer to a theorem of the same generality as the notion of being. This theorem affirms a parallelism between the dynamism of the mind and the dynamism of proportionate being. It affirms that the objective universe is not at rest, not static, not fixed in the present, but in process, in tension, fluid. As it regards present reality in its dynamic aspect, so it affirms this dynamism to be open.

As what is to be known becomes determinate only through knowing, so what is to be becomes determinate only through its own becoming. But as present knowing is not just present knowing but also a moment in process towards fuller knowing, so also present reality is not just present reality but also a moment in process to fuller reality.

The objective ground of this open dynamism is potency. For potency is what is to be known by intellectually patterned experience of the empirical residue. But intellectually patterned experience is dynamic; it is experience under some heuristic structure that is derived from the detached and disinterested desire to know; it is experience dominated by that desire. And the dynamic orientation of such experience no less than the experience itself has its counterpart in proportionate being. Indeed, since cognitional activity is itself but a part of this universe, its striving to know being is but the intelligent and reasonable part of a universal striving towards being.

I have been indicating a parallel between incomplete knowing heading towards fuller knowing and an incomplete universe heading towards fuller being, and now I propose to employ the name 'finality' to denote the objective member of the parallel. Against such usage, perhaps, there will be complaints. The imaginative will contend that finality refers to a pull exerted by the future on the present. Abstract deductivists will argue with Scotus that finality should denote a necessary property of every possible world. Concrete deductivists will argue with Spinoza that finality is just a mistake: as premises prove conclusions, so because birds have wings they are able to fly; as premises do not exist in order to prove conclusions, so birds do not have wings in order to be able to fly. Kantians will contend that finality is not a law of nature but a maxim of thought, that it does not reveal a constituent of things but regulates and orders our knowledge of them. In simpler fashion positivists will maintain that, since finality is known by understanding, it does not pertain to the 'already out there now real.' The surviving advocates of scientific monism, finally, will point out that there is no room in their universe for all-pervasive notions such as being and finality, for philosophy has nothing to add to science, and science deals only with the precise concepts proper to particular departments.

In brief, there are as many views of finality as there are philosophies, nor is there any point in repeating here our reasons for the stand we have adopted. Present concern has to be limited to working out the implications of previous conclusions. Because the real is being and being is whatever is to be known by intelligent grasp and reasonable affirmation, finality would not be real if it were known merely as a constituent of the 'already out there now.' Again, because we have conceived metaphysics as the integral heuristic structure of proportionate being, so we must restrict in similar fashion our consideration of finality. Lastly, since analytic principles differ from analytic propositions by the addition of judgments of fact, our knowledge of proportionate being and so our knowledge of finality is knowledge of what in fact is so. Accordingly, our question of finality is simply a question of correctly understanding a fact.

Basically, then, finality is the dynamic aspect of the real. To affirm finality is to disagree with the Eleatic negation of change. It is to deny that this universe is inert, static, finished, complete. It is to affirm movement, fluidity, tension, approximativeness, incompleteness. It is an affirmation that may turn out to have implications for the future, but such implications are a further question, for finality is an affirmation of fact and fact pertains not to the future but to the present and to the past. Finally, the fact in question cannot be denied outright, for our knowing is an event in the universe, and it is not inert, static, finished, complete; on the contrary, insofar as our experience is patterned intellectually, our knowing is in process; it consists in setting questions for intelligence, meeting them by insights, raising further questions to elicit further insights, shifting to critical reflection and judgment only to shift back to further inquiry that will need the control of further critical reflection.

Secondly, finality means not merely dynamism but directed dynamism. It neither denies nor minimizes such facts as entropy, cataclysm, the death that follows every birth, the extinction that threatens every survival. It offers no opinion on the ultimate fate of the universe. But it insists that the negative picture is not the whole picture. For it knows proportionate being as constituted by explanatory genera and species of central and conjugate potencies, forms, and acts. It knows that potency stands in some dynamic direction towards form, that form stands in some dynamic direction to act, that coincidental manifolds of act stand in some connection with potency to higher forms. Just what that dynamic direction may prove to be is a further question. But at least in some sense dynamic direction is to be affirmed. For potency, form, and act constitute a unity; potency is presupposed and complemented by form; form is presupposed and complemented by act; and these relations of presupposition and complementation involve some directing of potency towards form and of form towards act.

Thirdly, the directed dynamism of finality is not deductivist, for deductivism is a mistake. Accurate predictions are possible, but their possibility rests on the survival of schemes of recurrence; that survival is not necessary but probable; and while probability excludes systematic divergence from ideal frequencies, it does not exclude nonsystematic divergence.

Fourthly, the directed dynamism of finality is not determinate in the more obvious meanings of that term. It is not headed to some determinate individual or species or genus of proportionate being. On the contrary, the essential meaning of finality is that it goes beyond such determinations. Potency heads to form, but it also heads beyond it to act; and it heads beyond act to coincidental manifolds of acts, and through them to higher forms and higher coincidental manifolds of acts. Finality goes beyond the myriad individualities of the lowest genus to the fewer individualities of higher genera, and it goes beyond those fewer individualities in perpetual cycles of change. Finality goes beyond lower genera and species to higher genera and species, and if it is halted at some genus, the halt reveals not finality but the limitations which it endeavors to transcend. Even if one cares to assert that finality can go no higher than man, it is clear enough that man's unrestricted desire to know provides concrete evidence that the alleged maximum of possibility is not the maximum of aspiration.

Fifthly, the directed dynamism of finality is an effectively probable realization of possibilities. For potency is an objective possibility of form; form is an objective possibility of act; acts are an objective possibility of higher forms and higher acts. The realization of these possibilities is effectively probable, for on the supposition of sufficient numbers and sufficiently long intervals of time, the realization of any possibility can be assured.

Sixthly, this directed dynamism is realistic. It results from the classical laws that rest on forms, from the statistical laws that rest on acts, from the emergent process that rests on potency. It is not a contrivance added to an incompetent universe to make it work but an unfolding of its immanent implications that is bound to work. Men are apt to judge the universe by anthropomorphic standards. They look for the efficiency of their machines, the economy of their use of materials and power, the security of their comprehensive plans, the absence of disease and death, of violence and pain, of abuse and repression that reflects the desires and the aspirations of their hearts. But human utopias are paper schemes. They postulate in the universe more perfect materials than those with which it builds. They suppose that the building can be some extrinsic activity apart from the universe itself. They forget that they themselves and all their great achievements and all their still greater hopes and dreams are but byproducts of the universe in its proper expansion in accord with its proper intelligibility.

Seventhly, finality is universal. It is no less the sadness of failure than the joy of success. It is to be discerned no less in false starts and in breakdowns than in stability and progress. It is as much the meaning of aberration and corruption and decline as of sanity and honesty and development. For finality is an immanent intelligibility operating through the effective probability of possibility. Effective probability makes no pretense to provide an aseptic universe of chrome and plastic. Its trials will far outnumber its successes, but the trials are no less part of the program than the successes. Again, in human affairs finality does not undertake to run the world along the lines of a kindergarten; it does undertake to enlighten men by allowing their actions to have their consequences, that by this cumulative heaping of evidence men may learn; and if one tribe or culture, one nation or civilization, does not learn, finality will not stoop to coaxing and pleading; it lets things take their course, that eventually tribes and nations, cultures and civilizations may reach the degree of intelligent and rational consciousness necessary to carry forward the task of finality in transcending limitations.

Eighthly, finality is nuanced. It is not some single simple-minded formula. It is as concrete, as differentiated, as various, as are the multitudinous beings of this world. Each has its limitations, its incompleteness, its dynamic aspect, its tension, its thrust towards a fuller future. Just as the notion of being underlies all other contents and penetrates them and goes beyond them, so too does finality underlie and penetrate and head beyond each being that in fact is.

Ninthly, finality is flexible. There is the routine process of the universe, and throughout it the same classical and statistical laws obtain. But routine process is not a rule without exceptions. There also are changes of state; throughout such changes the same classical laws obtain, but statistical laws undergo modification. Nor are changes of state without their significance, for they provide in the long run for the occurrence of emergent trends that begin from one set of classical laws and end with the verifiability of another. Again, the emergent trend is itself flexible. Just as the same lesson can be taught in different manners, just as the same discovery can be made in different ways, so too the emergent process from potency to higher forms may follow different routes. Of this the classical illustration is H. Driesch's experiments with embryonic sea urchins, for, as he found, violent distortions of the early course of cell division were compensated by later and opposite departures from normal development. Finally, as it seems, there is the major flexibility that arises when new coincidental combinations provide the materials for new species and new genera of higher systematization.

We have worked out a notion of finality that attributes to the universe of proportionate being a directed dynamism that parallels the heuristic structure of inquiry and reflection. It is a view that squares with our conception of metaphysics. For if we have appealed to the three levels of our knowing to distinguish potency, form, and act, if we have appealed to individuality and similarity to distinguish central and conjugate forms, if we have appealed to higher viewpoints to set up explanatory genera and species, if we have found in potency a principle of limitation, we also must recognize in heuristic structure itself a clue to the nature of the universe proportionate to our capacities to know. At the root of all heuristic structure is the detached and disinterested desire, and so at the root of universal process we have affirmed a directed dynamism. The pure desire heads for an objective that becomes known only through its own unfolding in understanding and judgment, and so the dynamism of universal process is directed, not to a generically, specifically, or individually determinate goal, but to whatever becomes determinate through the process itself in its effectively probable realization of its possibilities. Finally, as our notion of metaphysics involves not only a major premise affirming an isomorphism between knowing and known and a principal minor premise affirming the structure of knowing but also subsidiary minor premises supplied by empirical science and common sense, so our affirmation of finality rests not simply on an a priori parallel but on that parallel as supported by vast ranges of fact. For our knowing might be much as it is, though the universe were otherwise inert, static, finished, complete, or dynamic but undirected, or dynamic and directed by deductivist necessity, or dynamic and directed naturally or artificially to some determinate goal. But the fact is that this universe is not static but dynamic, not undirected but directed, not deductivist nor inflexible but the effectively probable realization of its own possibilities.

There remains a final point. Is it potency or form or act that provides the objective ground of finality? The answer is not doubtful, if finality is the direction immanent in the dynamism of the real. For the real is dynamic inasmuch as it is incomplete, inasmuch as it is less than it can be. But act constitutes its achievement; form determines what that achievement is; only in potency can one discern the principle that refers determinate achievement to some indeterminate betterment.

It follows that potency is a tension of opposites. As we have seen, it is the ground of universal limitation; as we have just added, it is the ground of the finality that carries proportionate being ever beyond actual limitations. However, this does not mean that potency is a contradictory notion, for contradiction arises only when mutually exclusive predicates are attributed to the same object under the same aspect. In potency there are at least the two aspects of its proper contribution to the constitution of proportionate being and, on the other hand, its relation to the other contributions of form and act. The proper contribution of potency is limitation. But the relation of potency to the other contributions is general and indeterminate, yet dynamic and directed towards such contributions. It is the indeterminacy of that directed dynamism that makes potency the principle of the tendency to transcend limitations.

Lastly, if we have explained what we mean by finality, it may not be out of place to add what we do not mean. In chapter 19 the question of efficient and final causality will be raised. But our present concern is not with such extrinsic causes but with the immanent constituents of proportionate being. Accordingly, if any reader wishes the Aristotelian parallel to our finality, he will find it not in Aristotle's *archê hothen hê kinêsis* nor in his *telos* but in his *physis*.[6] For finality is not *principium motus in alio inquantum aliud*; it is not *id cuius gratia*; it is *principium motus in eo in quo est*.

6   The Notion of Development   [451–58]

Because the notion of development is peculiarly subject to the distorting influence of counterpositions, our account of insight as activity made no attempt to discuss the nature of genetic method. This omission has now to be remedied, and perhaps the simplest procedure will be to begin by stating and illustrating the principles of development.

6 [Aristotle,[c] *Physics*, II, 1, 192b 21–22.]

First, there is the already familiar principle of emergence. Otherwise coincidental manifolds of lower conjugate acts invite the higher integration effected by higher conjugate forms. Thus, in our account of explanatory genera chemical elements and compounds are higher integrations of otherwise coincidental manifolds of subatomic events; organisms are higher integrations of otherwise coincidental manifolds of chemical processes; sensitive consciousness is a higher integration of otherwise coincidental manifolds of changes in neural tissues; and accumulating insights are higher integrations of otherwise coincidental manifolds of images or of data.

Secondly, there is the principle of correspondence. Significantly different underlying manifolds require different higher integrations. Thus, the chemical elements differ by atomic numbers and atomic weights, and these differences are grounded in the underlying manifold. Different aggregates of aggregates of chemical processes involve different organisms. Neural events in the eye and in the ear call forth different conscious experiences. Different data lead to different theories. It is true, of course, that not every difference in the underlying manifold demands a different integration; the same kind of atom can have subatomic components at different energy levels; the same kind of organism admits differences of size, shape, weight; similarities of character and temperament are compatible, probably enough, with neural differences; and the same theory can be reached from different data. Accordingly, the principle of correspondence enjoys a measure of flexibility; within limits the same higher integration will systematize differing manifolds; the point to the principle is that these limits exist and that to transgress them is to eliminate the higher integration.

Thirdly, there is the principle of finality. The underlying manifold is an upwardly but indeterminately directed dynamism towards ever fuller realization of being. Any actual realization will pertain to some determinate genus and species, but this very determinacy is limitation, and every limitation is to finality a barrier to be transcended.

There follows at once a distinction between static and dynamic higher integrations. Every higher integration systematizes an otherwise coincidental manifold, but the systematization may be effected in two different manners. It is static when it dominates the lower manifold with complete success and thereby brings about a notable imperviousness to change. Thus, the inert gases lock coincidental manifolds of subatomic events in remarkably permanent routines. On the other hand, the higher integration is dynamic when it is not content to systematize the underlying manifold but keeps adding to it and modifying it until, by the principle of correspondence, the existing integration is eliminated and, by the principle of emergence, a new integration is introduced.

Fourthly, then, there is the principle of development itself. It is the linked sequence of dynamic higher integrations. An initial coincidental manifold is systematized and modified by a higher integration so as to call forth a second; the second leads to a third; the third to a fourth; and so on, until the possibilities of development along a given line are exhausted and the relative stability of maturity is reached.

Fifthly, the course of development is marked by an increasing explanatory differentiation. The initial integration in the initial manifold pertains to a determinate genus and species; still, exclusive attention to the data on the initial stage would yield little knowledge and less understanding of the relevant genus and species. What is to be known by understanding is what is yet to come, what may be present virtually or potentially but as yet is not present formally or actually. Accordingly, if one attends simply to the data on each successive stage of a development, one finds that the initial integration can be understood only in a generic fashion, that subsequent integrations are increasingly specific intelligibilities, that the specific intelligible differentiation of the ultimate stage attained is generated in the process from the initial stage. Thus, initial single cells of different organisms admit material differences, for example, in the number of chromosomes, but their functioning does not exhibit differences that are comparable to the later differences in functioning. Again, men of widely different temperament and character began, as infants, from instances of sensitive consciousness that not only were remarkably similar but also remarkably undifferentiated; there were sensations, but perceptiveness was undeveloped; there was nothing to remember, and powers of imagination were latent; affects were global affairs of elementary types; and skills were limited to wailing. Finally, intellectual development has its roots in the detached and disinterested desire to know; but the mere desire is not knowledge of anything; it will lead to highly differentiated structures that are masteries of logic, mathematics, natural science, common sense, philosophy, and human science; but these intelligible differentiations are yet to come, and they come only in and through the process of development.

Sixthly, the course of development is capable of a minor flexibility[d] inasmuch as it can pursue the same ultimate goal along different routes.

In other words, the initial manifold with its material differences, though it can evoke no more than the initial integration, nonetheless suffices to determine what the ultimate goal is to be. In virtue of this determination, the course of development can yield to circumstances and so follow any of a set of alternative linked sequences. Thus, a normal sea urchin can result from an embryo subjected to distorting pressures; psychic health can be due to untutored spontaneity or to the ministrations of the psychiatrist; the same science can be taught successfully in accord with different methods; and the same discovery can be made in different manners.

Seventhly, the course of development is capable of a major flexibility that consists in a shift or modification of the ultimate objective. In biology this is the familiar fact of adaptation; in depth psychology it may be illustrated by sublimation; in cognitional activity it appears in the manner in which inquirers, often enough, begin from one problem only to find themselves by the logic of issues forced to engage in the solution of another.

Major flexibility appears to conflict with minor flexibility, for the former involves a shift in the objective while the latter rests on the fixity of the objective. However, this difference is merely descriptive. In minor flexibility there is at work the determination of the development that rests on the initial manifold. This determination exhibits potency as the ground of limitation. But potency is also the ground of finality, and from this viewpoint it heads to ever fuller realizations. Moreover, a higher integration is characterized only partially by its systematization of an underlying manifold; on an adequate account, it is the emergence of a solution to the compound problem of systematizing a coincidental manifold in a given milieu or context; and this solution consists in a set of conjugate forms that are related not only to one another within the integration but also to other instances of the same type outside the integration.

In the light of the foregoing considerations, a development may be defined as a flexible, linked sequence of dynamic and increasingly differentiated higher integrations that meet the tension of successively transformed underlying manifolds through successive applications of the principles of correspondence and emergence. However, lest this prove a mere jumble of words, let us add to the illustration of parts of the definition a few illustrations of the whole.

As there are stable chemical elements that block the road to development, so too there are unstable elements that easily form compounds. The compounds in turn may be more or less unstable, and vast aggregates of them provide a coincidental manifold of processes that in the cell is made systematic. The cell, however, sets up not a static but a dynamic integration. It is ever intussuscepting fresh materials and extruding others that have served their purpose. Nor is it content merely to maintain the balance of this process, but heads towards the duplication of its dynamic pattern, and then it divides. Such a division may be an instance of reproduction or of growth. In the former case, there is the multiplication of life in different instances. In the latter case, there is development. Higher integration is on the move, for growth is not merely an increase in bulk but also an increase in differentiation; the initial manifold is subjected progressively to ever more intricate arrangements and patterns; the principle of correspondence repeatedly forces out earlier integrations, and on each occasion the principle of emergence evokes a more definitely differentiated integration. Eventually, full intelligible differentiation is reached, and development yields place to maturity. Inasmuch as the goal of the genetic sequence is fixed by the initial manifold, only oaks from acorns grow. But in large numbers of instances and over long periods of time, there is an effective probability of different initial manifolds and so of diverse objectives for genetic sequences. However, the attainment of such objectives is conditioned by the prior existence of a suitable environment, and inversely environments change cumulatively with the addition of each new type of organism. There follows a problem of the environment, to be solved by a phylogenetic sequence of different organisms such that each earlier member both can survive in a less developed and can contribute to a more developed environment. In turn, this solution supposes the possibility of major flexibility, for each earlier member has to emerge in one kind of environment, yet if it is to survive, must be able to adapt successively to the cumulative changes produced by later arrivals. Finally, there is to be reached a partial transcendence of environment in the animal that develops in the shelter of the egg or womb, that enjoys parental care, that can move about from one place to another, that is equipped to outwit or to conquer foes.

As there is organic, so also there is psychic development. As the organism in its growth has to assemble and arrange its multitudinous cells, so the animal in its development has to include the genesis and patterned distribution of neural tissues. As the differentiation of material

organs grounds a sequence of integrations of intelligible organic functions, so neural differentiation and structure provide a material basis for
a sequence of increasingly complex forms of sensitive consciousness. As
it is not in the plant but in the animal that the full potentialities of organic diversity are realized, so it is not in the animal but in man that the
full potentialities of a richly diverse and highly integrated sensitive consciousness are attained.

In the single cell there seems to be the irritability that in a generic and
highly rudimentary fashion foreshadows the later sensitivity of touch.
But it is a potentiality that the plant neglects and the animal exploits.
Moreover, such exploitation moves in two different directions. The
multiplication of particularized nerve endings grounds a possibility of
increasingly differentiated sensible impressions and sensitively guided
components of movements. The mounting hierarchy of nerve centers
grounds the possibility of ever more notable integrations of impressions
and ever more diversed coordinations of response. Without the rods and
cones there is no seeing. Without the brain there is no center on which
external influences converge, and there is no base from which integrated
responses emanate. The two types of development are complementary,
and if animals surpass man in keenness of sense or agility of movement,
man surpasses them in powers of integration.

However, neural development merely supplies the underlying manifold for psychic development. The latter is conditioned by the former
but it consists neither in neural tissues nor in neural configurations nor
in neural events but in a sequence of increasingly differentiated and
integrated sets of capacities for perceptiveness, for aggressive or affective
response, for memory, for imaginative projects, and for skilfully and
economically executed performance. While the capacities have a basis in
some neural counterpart of association, still the distinction between the
two is emphasized by the difference between the normal single integration of capacities and the abnormality of multiple personality, in which
a single individual exhibits at different times quite different integrations
of different perceptive, associative, emotive, conative, and operative
characteristics. Just as the single cell is so integrated as to head towards
a duplication of its dynamic pattern and a consequent division, so in a
fashion that is not altogether different the higher integration of sensitive
consciousness can so interact with its neural basis as to generate different
and incompatible integrations.

Perhaps because animal consciousness is dominated by biological purpose, its development is more conspicuous in a comparison of different animals than in contrasts between the behavior of the young and the mature members[e] of the same species, in the effects of training, and in experimentally provoked and charted instances of learning. In any case, it is in man that there are to be observed the greatest diversities of perceptiveness, of imaginative power, of nuanced affects, and of acquired skills. The generic consciousness of the infant becomes differentiated in the process of sensitive living at home, in school, at work, and the traditional laws of the development are the power of example and the maxim that practice makes perfect.

However, the relatively recent science of depth psychology has thrown a great deal of light upon the subject, and it hardly will be amiss to indicate that our definition of development serves to supply a single scheme that unites otherwise unrelated principles. Thus, the notion of finality brings together Freud's wish fulfilment, his somewhat ambiguous sublimation, and Jung's archetypal symbols. The unconscious neural basis neither means nor wishes in the proper senses of those terms, for both meaning and wishing are conscious activities. But the unconscious neural basis is an upwardly directed dynamism seeking fuller realization, first, on the proximate sensitive level, and secondly, beyond its limitations, on higher artistic, dramatic, philosophic, cultural, and religious levels. Hence it is that insight into dream symbols and associated images and affects reveals to the psychologist a grasp of the anticipations and virtualities of higher activities immanent in the underlying unconscious manifold.

A similar phenomenon on a different level is offered by Freud's superego: within consciousness, it is a compound of preceptive symbols and submissive affects; by its finality it anticipates, by its subordination it reflects, by its obsessive and expansive tendencies it caricatures, the judgments of rational consciousness on the conduct of a rational being.

Again, the censor is neither an agent nor an activity but simply a law or rule of the interrelations between successive levels of integration; the constructive censorship is the admission into consciousness of elements that enter into the higher integration; the repressive censorship is the exclusion from consciousness of elements that the higher integration cannot assimilate; the analyst that attempts a retrospective education of his patient is engaged in enlarging potentialities for integration; and the resistance offered by the patient is a byproduct of the higher integration putting its own twist on what it can assimilate and circumventing what it cannot.

Finally, there are three general principles relevant to the possibility of Freud's embryology of sensitive sexual phenomena with their successive stages and their consequent dangers of arrested development, perversion, and retrogression. The first principle is that a developing integration moves from the generic to the specific. The second is that integration cannot precede the unfolding of its underlying manifold; just as the accumulation of insights follows the successive presentations of relevant data, so psychic integration has to follow the stages of development of the organic and neural basis. The third principle is that, so to speak, the degrees of freedom of the sensitive integration decrease as one moves from the highest nerve centers towards the particularized nerve endings; hence one can imagine as one pleases but one cannot both be normal and see as one pleases. It follows that the psychic side of sexual development will be from the generic to the specific, that it will divide into stages imposed by somatic development, that the successive sensitive integrations have to meet increasingly determinate neural demands, and that to meet these demands they must imitate, not the artist or mathematician or philosopher following out the logic of previous positions, but the scientist or man of common sense attending principally to ever larger fields of quite determinate data.

The principal illustration of the notion of development is, of course, human intelligence. An otherwise coincidental manifold of data or images is integrated by insights; the effort to formulate systematically what is grasped by insight, or alternatively the effort to act upon it, gives rise to further questions, directs attention to further data, leads to the emergence of further insights, and so the cycle of development begins another turn. For if one gives free rein to the detached and disinterested desire to know, further questions keep arising. Insights accumulate into viewpoints, and lower viewpoints yield to higher viewpoints. If images are the sole basis of the movement, there develops logic; if images serially related to facts form the basis, the development is mathematical; if data in their bearing on human living determine the circle, there develops common sense; if data in their relations to one another are one's concern, there develops empirical science; finally, if one attends to the circle of development itself and to the structure of what can be known of proportionate being, the development is philosophic. In each of these fields, as in organic growth and in the unfolding of the psyche, development is a flexible, linked sequence of dynamic and increasingly differentiated higher integrations that meet the tension of successively transformed underlying manifolds through successive applications of the principles of correspondence and of emergence.

7   Genetic Method   [458–83]

In our study of insight as activity, we were able to indicate the heuristic structures and procedures of classical and of statistical method. But while we employed genetic method in outlining the development of mathematics, of natural science, and of common sense, still we were forced to refrain from explaining what precisely we were doing. To remedy this defect, to reveal the heuristic significance of the notion of development, and to prepare our statement of the integral heuristic structure that we have named metaphysics, attention must now be directed to genetic method. First, we shall offer our own account of the matter; secondly, we shall clarify this account by contrasting it with other views.

As classical method anticipates an unspecified correlation to be specified, an indeterminate function to be determined, so genetic method finds its heuristic notion in development. In the plant there is the single development of the organism; in the animal there is the twofold development of the organism and the psyche; in man there is the threefold development of the organism, the psyche, and intelligence. Let us make this general statement more precise by recasting it in our metaphysical terms.

7.1   General Notions   [459–63]

First, then, in any plant, animal, or man, there is to be affirmed an individual existing unity. By central potency it is individual; by central form it is a unity, identity, whole; by central act it is existent.

Secondly, besides central potency, form, and act, there are conjugate potencies, forms, and acts. Moreover, the central potency, form, and act are constants throughout the development; it is the same individual and existing unity that develops organically, psychically, intellectually; and so development is to be formulated in terms of conjugate potency, form, and act.

Thirdly, conjugate acts are occurrences, events, functioning. Such are the organic acts of intussusception, assimilation, excretion, the psychic acts of perception, conation, response, the intellectual acts of insight and formulation, reflective understanding and judgment. Further, such acts are recurrent, and their recurrence exhibits a regularity that establishes the relevance of schemes of recurrence. But the regularity in question lacks the fixed and rigid periodicity of the planetary system, and indeed, if the functioning of the organism, the psyche, or intelligence is to be understood, one must think not of some single scheme of recurrence but rather of a flexible circle of ranges of schemes. For the same organism, the same psychic habits and dispositions, the same intellectual development result in widely different operations under different conditions and in accord with different circumstances.

Fourthly, conjugate forms are implicitly defined by empirically established explanatory correlations. Now just as the conjugate form 'mass' was reached by Newton inasmuch as he reduced Kepler's planetary scheme of recurrence to his abstract laws of motion and gravitation, so also the conjugate forms of the organism, the psyche, and intelligence are to be discovered by proceeding from the schemes of organic, psychic, and intellectual recurrence to the underlying correlations. In both cases, one first discerns a regularity of events and then advances to the abstract relation that (1) is verified in the events, (2) implicitly defines the explanatory specification of the events, and (3) fixes by their relations to one another the conjugate forms. Inversely, once correlations are known, it is possible to work out lists of possible schemes of recurrence; from Newton's laws one can proceed to Laplace's account of planetary periodicity; from an understanding of the organism one can conclude to its behavior under given circumstances; from a synthetic account of insight one can set up the procedures of the mathematician, the natural scientist, and the man of common sense.

Fifthly, the foregoing parallel is highly abstract. It rests on the connection between formulation and judgment, law and event, conjugate form and conjugate act. But far more conspicuous than the parallel, there are the differences between physics and, on the other hand, biology, psychology, and intellectual theory. Regular physical events are apt to recur in some single determinate scheme. But organic, psychic, and intellectual events are recurrent, not in single schemes, but in flexible circles of ranges of schemes. Nor is this all. There is the fact of development. In the course of time the conjugate forms advance from generic indeterminacy towards a specific perfection. Concomitantly the flexible circle of schemes of recurrence both shifts and expands. Operations that initially were impossible or extremely awkward and inefficient become possible, spontaneous, economical, rapid, and effective. Masses and electric charges, atoms and molecules are statically systematic; their performance is not a function of their age; there is not a different law of gravitation for each succeeding century. In contrast, organic, psychic, and intellectual development involves a succession of stages; and in that succession the previously impossible becomes possible and the previously awkward and difficult becomes a ready routine. The infant can neither walk nor talk, and once we all were infants. Hence, where the physicist or chemist is out to determine single sets of conjugate forms and consequent schemes of recurrence, the biologist or psychologist or intellectual theorist is out to determine genetic sequences of conjugate forms and consequent sequences of flexible circles of schemes of recurrence.

Sixthly, there follows the outstanding difference between classical and genetic method. Classical method is concerned to reduce regular events to laws. Genetic method is concerned with sequences in which correlations and regularities change. Accordingly, the principal object of genetic method is to master the sequence itself, to understand the development, and thereby to proceed from the correlations and regularities of one stage to those of the next. If a mathematical illustration is helpful and not too much out of place, one might say that genetic method is concerned with a sequence of operators that successively generate further functions from an initial function.

Seventhly, as the heuristic assumption of classical method is the indeterminate function to be determined, so the heuristic assumption of genetic method lies in the notion of development. Again, as classical method determines its functions both by the particular procedures of measuring and curve fitting and by the general procedures of invoking differential equations and principles of invariance and equivalence, so also genetic method determines the course of a development by the scissors-like action of both particular and general procedures.

The general procedures are implicit in the notion of development itself. As has been mentioned already, a development is from generic indeterminacy towards specific perfection. Because of the initial generic indeterminacy, all organic functioning increases in similarity as one mounts to its early stages. Inversely, because of the increasing specific perfection, psychic development is a matter of character becoming set, temperament fixed, skills acquired and perfected. Both the acorn and the oak are alive; both the infant and the adult perceive and respond; but there are vast differences between the earlier and the later living and perceiving, and the differences consist in transitions from generic potentiality to specific determination.

Besides this general direction of development there also is its general mode of operation. The sequence of conjugate forms is a sequence of higher integrations of otherwise coincidental lower manifolds of events. This sequence is intelligible inasmuch as each successive higher integration modifies the lower manifold it systematizes so as to call forth the next higher integration in the sequence. Thus, if the lower manifold of events may be identified with conjugate potency, the mode of operation of development is a circular interaction of potency, form, and act. In the coincidental manifold there emerge corresponding conjugate forms; in accord with the conjugate forms there recur operations in accord with the flexible circle of ranges of schemes made possible and effective by the forms; from the operations there result, not only the higher systematization of the lower manifold, but also its transformation into the materials for the next higher integration in the sequence.

Besides the general direction of development and its general mode of operation, there is the third general consideration, of the field in which it occurs. In metaphysical terms, this field may be described as the finality, the upwardly directed dynamism, of proportionate being. But in terms of the implications of scientific method, the field may be described more precisely as a generalized emergent probability. It is emergent probability that supplies the initial coincidental manifolds of events in which the higher conjugate forms emerge. It is emergent probability that provides the compound conditioned series of things and of schemes of recurrence such that the developing organism or psyche or intelligence will have an environment in which it can function successfully. It is with respect to this field of emergent probability that the genetic sequence enjoys a twofold flexibility: a minor flexibility that reaches the same goal along different routes, and a major flexibility that shifts the goal in adaptation to environmental change. Not only do conjugate forms emerge in coincidental manifolds of lower events; not only do flexible circles of schemes of recurrence result from the conjugate forms; but also operations in accord with the schemes (1) are linked with occurrences outside the organism, the psyche, the intelligence, (2) effect the higher systematization of the lower chemical, neural, or psychic manifold, and (3) so transform the lower manifold as to evoke the emergence of the next conjugate forms that will yield new schemes that will enable the developing subject to function in its environment towards still further development.

Besides the foregoing determinations of development in general, there are the special characteristics of the simple development of the organism, the twofold development in the animal, and the threefold development in man. The physicist cannot reach laws of nature considering only differential equations and principles of invariance and equivalence; he must also invoke the more concrete techniques of measuring and curve fitting. Similarly, the biologist, the psychologist, and the intellectual theorist have to operate not only in the light of a general notion of development but also in accord with more specialized directives.

In this connection our first observation must be negative. The extraordinary success of the physical sciences naturally enough led investigators of the organism, the psyche, and intelligence to a servile rather than an intelligent adoption of the successful procedures. In physics and chemistry, measuring is a basic technique that takes inquiry from the relations of things to our senses to their relations to one another. But when one mounts to the higher integrations of the organism, the psyche, and intelligence, one finds that measuring loses both in significance and in efficacy. It loses in significance, for the higher integration is, within limits, independent of the exact quantities of the lower manifold it systematizes. Moreover, the higher the integration, the greater the independence of lower quantities, so that the meaning of one's dreams is not a function of one's weight, and one's ability in mathematics does not vary with one's height. Besides this loss in significance, there is also a loss in efficacy. Classical method can select among the functions that solve differential equations by appealing to measurements and empirically established curves. What the differential equation is to classical method, the general notion of development is to genetic method. But while the differential equation is mathematical, the general notion of development is not. It follows that, while measurement is an efficacious technique for finding boundary conditions that restrict differential equations, it possesses no assignable efficacy when it comes to particularizing the general notion of development.

7.2 Organic Development   [463–67]

How, then, is a concrete instance of development to be investigated? One has to follow the lead of the successful scientists, the physicists and chemists, but one has to imitate them not slavishly but intelligently. They employ insights of a particular type, namely, the insights of the mathematician and of the curve fitter grasping in an aggregate of measurements a possible law. The student of development also must employ insight, but he must not restrict himself to the particular types relevant to physics and chemistry. On the contrary, he has to work out his own structures of accumulating insights, and indeed different structures for the study of the organism, the psyche, and intelligence itself.

Study of an organism begins from the thing-for-us, from the organism as exhibited to our senses. A first step is a descriptive differentiation of different parts, and since most of the parts are inside, this descriptive preliminary necessitates dissection or anatomy. A second step consists in the accumulation of insights that relate the described parts to organic events, occurrences, operations. By these insights, the parts become known as organs, and the further knowledge constituted by the insights is a grasp of intelligibilities that (1) are immanent in the several parts, (2) refer each part to what it can do and, under determinable conditions, will do, and (3) relate the capacity-for-performance of each part to the capacities-for-performance of the other parts. So physiology follows anatomy. A third step is to effect the transition from the thing-for-us to the thing-itself, from insights that grasp described parts as organs to insights that grasp conjugate forms systematizing otherwise coincidental manifolds of chemical and physical processes. By this transition one links physiology with biochemistry and biophysics. To this end, there have to be invented appropriate symbolic images of the relevant chemical and physical processes; in these images there have to be grasped by insight the laws of the higher system that account for regularities beyond the range of physical and chemical explanation; from these laws there has to be constructed the flexible circle of schemes of recurrence in which the organism functions; finally, this flexible circle of schemes must be coincident with the related set of capacities-for-performance that previously was grasped in sensibly presented organs.

The foregoing three steps of anatomy, physiology, and their transposition to the thing-itself reveal one aspect of the organism as higher system in an underlying manifold of cells, chemical processes, and physical changes. Let us name that aspect the higher system as integrator. The higher system itself is the set of conjugate forms. As integrator, this set is related (1) to inspected organs as the set of functions grasped by the physiologist in sensible data, (2) to the physical, chemical, and cytological manifold as the conjugates implicitly defined by the correlations that account for additional regularities in the otherwise coincidental manifold, and (3) to immanent and transient activities of the organism in its environment as the ground of the flexible circle of ranges of schemes of recurrence. However, the organism grows and develops. Its higher system at any stage of development not only is an integrator but also an operator, that is, it so integrates the underlying manifold as to call forth, by the principles of correspondence and emergence, its own replacement by a more specific and effective integrator.

The difference between the higher system as integrator and as operator may be illustrated rather simply. There is a well-known interlocking of organic parts that enables the biologist to reconstruct an organism by examining, say, its bones. Now this simultaneous interlocking of parts rests on the higher system as integrator: the conjugate forms are related to one another but also are emergent in organic parts; it follows that the parts are related to one another and that through those relations the whole can be reconstructed from the part. But besides the simultaneous interlocking, there also is a successive interlocking. Just as the dinosaur can be reconstructed from the fossil, so a determinate stage in the development of the whole can be made the basis from which earlier or later stages could be reconstructed; and in this reconstruction over time the major premise of the inference is supplied by the higher system as operator.

What is the operator? Obviously, I am not referring to a mathematical entity, though there is an extremely important point to the mathematical analogy. For a mathematical operator changes one function into another; the higher system as integrator corresponds to a set of conjugate forms, of laws of the classical type, of alternative ranges of schemes of recurrence; and the higher system as operator effects the transition from one set of forms, laws, schemes, to another set. Accordingly, while development may be extremely regular, such regularity is not to be confused with the regularity that conforms to classical law; it is the higher regularity of the emergent trend that successively conforms to different sets of classical laws.

Still, what is the operator? In the general case, it is the upwardly directed dynamism of proportionate being that we have named finality. It is conditioned by instability in the underlying manifold, by incompleteness in the higher integration, by imperfection in the correspondence between the two. It is constituted inasmuch as the higher system not merely suffers but provokes the underlying instability; inasmuch as the incompleteness of the higher system consists in a generic, rudimentary, undifferentiated character that can become differentiated, effective, specific; inasmuch as the imperfection of the correspondence is, so to speak, under control and moving towards a limit where the principles of correspondence and emergence result in the replacement of the prior integration by a more developed successor; inasmuch as such operators form a flexible series along which the organism advances from the generic functioning of the initial cell to the flexible circle of ranges of schemes of the mature type.

How is this operator studied? All learning is a matter of data and insight, hypothesis and verification. The difficulty in studying the operator lies in the complexity of its data. We have outlined the procedure (1) of inspecting and describing the dissected parts of an organism, (2) of grasping functions or capacities-to-perform in the parts, (3) of interrelating these functions with one another to determine the flexible circle of ranges of schemes of recurrence, and (4) of replacing the inspected colonies of cells (organs) by their underlying physical and chemical manifolds. Now this procedure can be duplicated with respect to successive stages in the development of the same organism, and the juxtaposition of the twofold set of results illustrates the meaning of comparative study. One compares successive stages of organs, successive capacities of successive organs, successive integrations of capacities, successive physical and chemical manifolds. One goes on to contrast normal and abnormal successions, to note similarities and differences of successions in different subspecies and species, to form an account of the various economies in which some parts develop before others, some are permanent and others transitional; some advance at one rate and others at another. The totality of such information constitutes the data on the operator. The second step is to understand the data. Now understanding is sought methodically through a heuristic structure, and the relevant heuristic structure is 'Specify the operator.' In general, development is higher system on the move. The operator is the higher system known by grasping the interrelated set of capacities-to-perform; but it is this interrelated set, not as the integrator of a given stage, but as the source of the differences that appear in the next stage. But just how is it the source of the concrete differences revealed in comparative study? That question asks for the specification of the operator. It is the question in genetic method that parallels the classical question, How does one determine the indeterminate function?

The matter may be clarified by an illustration. There seems to be a general principle of development that is named the law of effect. It contends that development takes place along lines of successful functioning. Thus, a tree in a forest puts forth branches and leaves not to its sides but at its top. Now such a principle offers a specification of the operator. For the operator is the higher system on the move. The higher system is the ground of the flexible circle of schemes of recurrence in which the organism functions. The law of effect states that the ground of functioning advances to a new ground of functioning where functioning occurs successfully. Clearly, though this specification of the operator is extremely general, it offers some determination of the direction of development. Its application to concrete instances may not only confirm it but also give rise to further questions. The further questions will lead to further insights and so to still further questions. In this fashion, one's understanding of the operator begins to be an instance of higher system on the move in the development of scientific knowledge of development.

7.3 Psychic and Intellectual Development   [467–69]

Essentially the same heuristic structure is applicable to the study of the psyche and of intelligence. But now we are confronted with twofold and threefold developments. In the animal, there is psychic development supervening upon organic development. In man, there is intellectual development supervening upon psychic and psychic supervening upon organic. Moreover, there is an important difference in the accessibility of data. In the organism both the underlying manifold and the higher system are unconscious. In intellectual development both the underlying manifold of sensible presentations and the higher system of insights and formulations are conscious. In psychic development the underlying neural manifold is unconscious and the supervening higher system is conscious. Finally, the higher the level of integration, the greater the freedom from material limitation, the more dominant the dynamic and expansive aspect of the operator, the more significant are the laws[f] of development itself, and consequently the fuller is the development not only on the higher level but also on subordinate levels. Thus, organic differentiation reaches its maximum in animals, and psychic differentiation reaches its maximum in man.

The proximate underlying manifold of psychic development consists in the events and processes of the nervous system. This system involves a central core with afferent and efferent branches. It is at once both a part of the organism and the seat of the manifold of events that have their higher integrations in conscious perceptions and coordinated responses. Psychic development is that higher integration on the move, and the movement is in two different but complementary directions. What may be named the lateral movement is an increasing differentiation of the psychic events in correspondence with particular afferent and efferent nerves. What may be named the vertical movement is an increasing proficiency in integrated perception and in appropriate and coordinated response. The lateral movement has its limit set by the multiplicity and diversity of nerve endings. The vertical movement has its limit set (1) by the operationally significant set of combinations of different nerve endings, and (2) by the existence of higher neural centers at which such combinations can be integrated or coordinated.

The study of animal behavior, of stimulus and response, would reveal at any stage of development a flexible circle of ranges of schemes of recurrence. Implicit in such a circle of schemes, there would be correlations of the classical type. Implicit in such correlations, there would be the conjugate forms that (1) account for habitual perceptiveness of determinate types and habitual modes of aggressive and affective response, and (2) would seem to be emergent in underlying neural configurations or dispositions as insights are emergent in images and functions in organs. While such study would reveal the higher system as integrator at any given stage of development, comparative study of successive stages, of normal and abnormal successions, of similarities and differences of successions in different subspecies, species, and genera, and of the general economy of increasing psychic differentiation would provide the materials to be understood in grasping the nature of the higher system as operator.

With the development of intelligence the reader already possesses some familiarity. The lower, otherwise coincidental manifold is provided by sensible presentations and imaginative representations. In accord with the principle of correspondence, insights emerge to unify and correlate elements in the sensible flow, to ground the formulation of such unifications and correlations in concepts, thoughts, suppositions, considerations, definitions, postulates, hypotheses, theories, and through such conceptual constructions, or their deductive expansions, or their concrete implementation, to give rise sooner or later to further questions. Clearly, as the conceptual construction is the formulated higher system as integrator, so the emergence of the further question effects its transition into the operator. For further questions lead to further insights only to raise still further questions. So insights accumulate into viewpoints, and lower viewpoints lead to higher viewpoints. Such is the circle of the development of understanding, and it occurs in the different departments of logic, mathematics, science, common sense, and philosophy, according to differences in the route of the circle.

Two peculiarities of intellectual development call for attention. On the one hand, there is its exceptional freedom from limitation. The higher system of the organism or of the psyche develops in an underlying material manifold of physical, chemical, cytological events that are subject to their own proper laws. The higher system of intelligence develops not in a material manifold but in the psychic representation of material manifolds. Hence the higher system of intellectual development is primarily the higher integration, not of the man in whom the development occurs, but of the universe that he inspects. Further, along with this freedom from material limitation, intellectual development has an exceptional principle of control. The organism or the psyche justifies the higher system it becomes by its pragmatic success. While the pragmatic criterion is employed by intelligence as well, still its availability commonly is confined to the short run and to superficial issues. The proper criterion of intelligence lies in its own capacity for critical reflection, for grasping the unconditioned, for determining the norms of investigations that are headed towards the unconditioned and therefore probable.

7.4 Human Development   [469–79]

It remains that a word be said on total development in man. Organic, psychic, and intellectual development are not three independent processes. They are interlocked, with the intellectual providing a higher integration of the psychic and the psychic providing a higher integration of the organic. Each level involves its own laws, its flexible circle of schemes of recurrence, its interlocked set of conjugate forms. Each set of forms stands in an emergent correspondence to otherwise coincidental manifolds on the lower levels. Hence a single human action can involve a series of components: physical, chemical, organic, neural, psychic, and intellectual; and the several components occur in accord with the laws and realized schemes of their appropriate levels. However, while physical and chemical laws are static, higher correlations pertain to systems on the move, and quite obviously there results the problem of formulating the heuristic structure of the investigation of this triply compounded development. What the existentialist discovers and talks about, what the ascetic attempts to achieve in himself, what the psychiatrist endeavors to foster in another, what the psychologist aims at understanding completely, the metaphysician outlines in heuristic categories.

First, then, at any stage of his development a man is an individual existing unity differentiated by physical, chemical, organic, psychic, and intellectual conjugates. The organic, psychic, and intellectual conjugate forms ground respective flexible circles of ranges of schemes of recurrence that are revealed in the man's spontaneous and effective behavior, in his bodily movements, in his dealings with persons and things, in the content of his speech and writing. Moreover, if one turns from outward behavior to inner experience, one finds that it shifts into quite different patterns as one engages in different types of activity; absorption in intellectual issues tends to eliminate sensitive emotions and conations, and inversely, mystical absorption tends to eliminate the flow of sensitive presentations and imaginative representations; again, aesthetic experience and the pattern of practical activity tend to be mutually exclusive; finally, while the dramatic pattern of one person dealing with other persons draws upon all one's resources, still it subdivides, like the successive coatings in an onion, into a series of zones from the ego or *moi intime* to the outer rind of the persona, so that one is aloof with strangers, courteous with acquaintances, at ease with one's friends, occasionally unbosoms oneself to intimates, keeps some matters entirely to oneself, and refuses even to face others.

Secondly, man develops. Whatever he is at present, he was not always so, and generally speaking he need not remain so. The flexible circles of ranges of schemes of recurrence shift and expand, for neural, psychic, and intellectual conjugates pertain to systems on the move. The functioning of the higher integration involves changes in the underlying manifold, and the changing manifold evokes a modified higher integration. There obtains the law of effect, for development occurs along the directions in which it succeeds. But there also obtains an anticipated law of effect on the psychic and intellectual levels. Thus, unless one asks the further questions, one remains with the insights one has already, and so intelligence does not develop; inversely, because one wants to develop, one can frequent the lectures and read the books that put the further questions and help one to learn. Again, one develops through functioning, and until one has developed, one's functioning has the lack of poise, of economy, of effectiveness, that betrays as yet undifferentiated potentialities. Unless one is encouraged out of shyness, timidity, pretended indifference, to zest and risk and doing, to humility and laughter, one will not develop but merely foster the objective grounds for one's feeling of inferiority. Rather, one will not develop along a certain more common line; one will seek and find less common fields in which to excel; and there one will be apt to overcompensate for deficiencies elsewhere.

Thirdly, there is a law of integration. The initiative of development may be organic, psychic, intellectual, or external, but the development remains fragmentary until the principle of correspondence between different levels is satisfied. Thus, the initiative may be organic, for the organism is an upwardly directed dynamism, seeking to be more fully, evoking its higher integration by calling forth psychic images and feelings. So man is prompted to waking and sleeping, to eating and drinking, to shade in the summer and the fireside in winter, to loving and begetting children and fending for them; and these psychic, sensitive, corporal activities in their turn call forth the family and technology, the economy and polity, morality and law. Again, the initiative may be psychic, for man's sensitivity not only reflects and integrates its biological basis but also is itself an entity, a value, a living and developing. Intersubjectivity, companionship, play and artistry, the idle hours spent with those with whom one feels at home, the common purpose, labor, achievement, failure, disaster, the sharing of feeling in laughter and lamenting, all are human things, and in them man functions primarily in accord with the development of his perceptiveness, his emotional responses, his sentiments. Thirdly, the initiative may be intellectual; its source is a problem; one is out to understand, to judge, to decide, to choose. Finally, the initiative may spring from a change in one's material circumstances, in the perceptiveness or sentiments of another, in the discoveries of other minds and the decisions of other wills.

Still, the initiation of a development is one thing and its integrated completion is another. If one adapts to external change merely out of deference to material necessity or social pressure, the behavior of the outward persona is modified in a manner that, at best, is tolerated by the inner subject. Again, if one sincerely makes an excellent resolution about one's mode or style of behavior, the resolution is apt to remain sterile if the appropriate perceptiveness and feelings are not forthcoming[g] and one does not know how to evoke them. Inversely, a development can begin in one's perceptiveness and feelings, yet it will remain frustrated if one fails to understand oneself, to plan the strategy, and to execute the tactics that secure congenial companionship or employment. Finally, the nonconscious neural basis can send up its signals that express a starved affectivity or other demands for fuller living, but the signals need an interpreter and the interpreter an intelligent and willing pupil.

The law of integration, then, is a declaration of what is meant by human development. Because man is a unity, his proper development is no more than initiated when a new scheme of recurrence is established in his outward behavior, in his thinking and willing, in his perceptiveness and feeling, in the organic and neural basis of his action. Generally speaking, such an initiation of development invites complementary adjustments and advances, and unless they are effected, either the initiated development recedes and atrophies in favor of the dynamic unity of the subject, or else that unity is sacrificed and deformed to make man a mere dumping ground for unrelated, unintegrated schemes of recurrence and modes of behavior.

Fourthly, there is a law of limitation and transcendence. It is a law of tension. On the one hand, development is in the subject and of the subject; on the other hand, it is from the subject as he is and towards the subject as he is to be.[h] Finality has been conceived as the upwardly but not determinately directed dynamism of proportionate being. Its realization may be regular, but its regularity is not according to law, according to settled spontaneity, according to acquired habit, according to existing schemes of recurrence; on the contrary, it is a change in the law, the spontaneity, the habit, the scheme; it is the process of introducing and establishing a new law, spontaneity, habit, scheme. Its point of departure necessarily is the subject as he happens to be; but its direction is against his remaining as he is; and though its term will involve him in a fresh temptation to inertial repetition and recurrence, that term is to be approached only by breaking away from the inertia of his prior stage.

Now the tension that is inherent in the finality of all proportionate being becomes in man a conscious tension. Present perceptiveness is to be enlarged, and the enlargement is not perceptible to present perceptiveness. Present desires and fears have to be transmuted, and the transmutation is not desirable to present desire but fearful to present fear. Moreover, as has been noted, the organism reaches its highest differentiation under the psychic integration of the animal, and the psyche reaches its highest differentiation under the intellectual integration in man. Because psychic development is so much more extensive and intricate in man than in other animals, it is involved in a more prolonged tension, and it is open to more acute and diversified crises.

There is a further and deeper aspect to the matter. Intellectual development rests upon the dominance of a detached and disinterested desire to know. It reveals to a man a universe of being in which he is but an item, and a universal order in which his desires and fears, his delight and anguish are but infinitesimal components in the history of mankind. It invites man to become intelligent and reasonable not only in his knowing but also in his living, to guide his actions by referring them, not as an animal to a habitat, but as an intelligent being to the intelligible context of some universal order that is or is to be. Still, it is difficult for man, even in knowing, to be dominated simply by the pure desire, and it is far more difficult for him to permit that detachment and disinterestedness to dominate his whole way of life. For the self as perceiving and feeling, as enjoying and suffering, functions as an animal in an environment, as a self-attached and self-interested center within its own narrow world of stimuli and responses. But the same self as inquiring and reflecting, as conceiving intelligently and judging reasonably, is carried by its own higher spontaneity to quite a different mode of operation with the opposite attributes of detachment and disinterestedness. It is confronted with a universe of being in which it finds itself, not the center of reference, but an object coordinated with other objects and, with them, subordinated to some destiny to be discovered or invented, approved or disdained, accepted or repudiated.

Such, then, is the height of the tension of human consciousness. On the side of the object, it is the opposition between the world of sense of man the animal and, on the other hand, the universe of being to be known by intelligent grasp and reasonable affirmation. On the side of the subject, it is the opposition between a center in the world of sense operating self-centeredly and, on the other hand, an entry into an intelligibly ordered universe of being to which one can belong, and in which one can function, only through detachment and disinterestedness. Not only is the opposition complete but also it is ineluctable. As a man cannot divest himself of his animality, so he cannot put off the eros of his mind. To inquire and understand, to reflect and judge, to deliberate and choose are as much an exigence of human nature as waking and sleeping, eating and drinking, talking and loving. Nor is there any escape from the universe of being and its intelligible order by devising some particular type of metaphysics or countermetaphysics. For the universe of being is whatever is intelligently grasped and reasonably affirmed; by its definition it includes an intelligible order; and to set up as a philosopher of any school whatever, one has to claim to understand and pretend to be reasonable.

It is this heightened tension that in human development supplies the content of the compound, antithetical law of limitation and transcendence. All development is development inasmuch as it goes beyond the initial subject, but in man this 'going beyond' is anticipated immanently by the detachment and disinterestedness of the pure desire. Again, all development is development inasmuch as it possesses a point of departure, a concrete material to be transmuted, but in man this concrete material is permanent in the self-centered sensitive psyche content to orientate itself within its visible and palpable environment and to deal with it successfully. Nor are the pure desire and the sensitive psyche two things, one of them 'I' and the other 'It.' They are the unfolding on different levels of a single, individual unity, identity, whole. Both are 'I,' and neither is merely 'It.' If my intelligence is mine, so is my sexuality. If my reasonableness is mine, so are my dreams. If my intelligence and my reasonableness are to be thought more representative of me than my organic and psychic spontaneity, that is only in virtue of the higher integration that in fact my intelligence and reasonableness succeed in imposing on their underlying manifold, or proleptically, in virtue of the development in which the higher integration is to achieve a fuller measure of success. But no matter how full the success, the basic situation within the self is unchanged, for the perfection of the higher integration does not eliminate the integrated or modify the essential opposition between self-centeredness and detachment. The same 'I' on different and related levels of operation retains the opposed characters.

Fifthly, there is a law of genuineness. At first sight it is an obvious matter of simplicity and honesty, of perspicacity and sincerity. But a little probing brings to light a paradox. Insofar as development occurs nonconsciously, there is no relevance to genuineness, for simplicity and honesty, perspicacity and sincerity are qualities of conscious acts. On the other hand, one may argue, the more consciously a development occurs, the less the likelihood that it will be marked by genuineness, for when one speaks of a simple and honest soul, one is not thinking of a person given to deep and prolonged self-scrutiny. What, then, can genuineness be? It does not pertain to nonconscious development, and it seems to stand in conflict with any notable consciousness of development. Is it a property of some twilight development that is neither unconscious nor fully conscious? And if it is, how can there be a general law of genuineness? Such is the paradox.

To meet it, let us say that the requirement of genuineness is conditional and analogous. It is conditional, for it arises only inasmuch as development occurs through consciousness. It is analogous, for the requirement has a different content in different cases. The genuineness of which we think when we speak of a simple and honest soul is the happy fruit of a life in which illusion and pretense have had no place. But there is another genuineness that has to be won back through a self-scrutiny that expels illusion and pretense; and as this enterprise is difficult and its issue doubtful, we do not think of its successful outcome when we cast about for an obvious illustration of genuineness.

In the light of these distinctions, the law of genuineness can be put as follows. Every development involves a starting point in the subject as he is, a term in the subject as he is to be, and a process from the starting point to the term. However, inasmuch as a development is conscious, there is some apprehension of the starting point, the term, and the process. But such apprehensions may be correct or mistaken. If they are correct, the conscious and unconscious components of the development are operating from the same base along the same route to the same goal. If they are mistaken, the conscious and unconscious components, to a greater or less extent, are operating at cross-purposes. Such a conflict is inimical to the development, and so we have the conditional law of genuineness, namely, that if a development is conscious, then its success demands correct apprehensions of its starting point, its process, and its goal.

Further, besides being correct or mistaken, the apprehensions that make a development conscious may be minimal or more or less extensive. They are minimal when they involve little more than the succession of fragmentary and separate acts needed to carry out the successive steps of the development with advertence, intelligence, and reasonableness. They are more or less extensive when one begins to delve into the background, the context, the premises, the interrelations, of the minimal series of conscious acts, and to subsume this understanding of oneself under empirical laws and philosophic theories of development. Now, other things being equal, there is less likelihood of error in the minimal series alone than in the minimal series fitted out with its concrete background and its theoretical explanation; and for this reason we expect genuineness to be more common in the simple and honest soul innocent of introspection and depth psychology. But it very well may be that other things are not equal, that errors have become lodged in the habitual background whence spring our direct and reflective insights, that if we relied upon our virtual and implicit self-knowledge to provide us with concrete guidance through a conscious development, then the minimal series, so far from being probably correct, would be certainly mistaken. Accordingly, the law of genuineness not only is conditional but also is analogous; it becomes relevant insofar as development is conscious; and what it demands will be spontaneous in some cases and in others obtained only through more or less extensive self-scrutiny.

The necessity, then, of genuineness is the necessity of avoiding conflict between the unconscious and the conscious components of a development. But one moves to a deeper grasp of the issue when one asks why conflict should arise. For if one does not have to look far to find a reason, the reason is not without its profundity. As we have seen, all development involves a tension between limitation and transcendence. On the one hand, there is the subject as he is functioning more or less successfully in a flexible circle of ranges of schemes of recurrence. On the other hand, there is the subject as a higher system on the move. One and the same reality is both integrator and operator; but the operator is relentless in transforming the integrator. The integrator resides in successive levels of interrelated conjugate forms that are more familiar under the common name of acquired habits. But habits are inertial. The whole tendency of present perceptiveness, of present affectivity and aggressivity, of present ways of understanding and judging, deliberating and choosing, speaking and doing is for them to remain as they are. Against this solid and salutary conservatism, however, there operate the same principles that gave rise to the acquired habits and now persist in attempting to transform them. Unconsciously operative is the finality that consists in the upwardly but indeterminately directed dynamism of all proportionate being. Consciously operative is the detached and disinterested desire raising ever further questions. Among the topics for questioning are one's own unconscious initiatives, their subsumption under the general order intelligence discovers in the universe of being, their integration in the fabric of one's habitual living. So there emerges into consciousness a concrete apprehension of an obviously practicable and proximate ideal self; but along with it there also emerges the tension between limitation and transcendence; and it is no vague tension between limitation in general and transcendence in general, but an unwelcome invasion of consciousness by opposed apprehensions of oneself as one concretely is and as one concretely is to be.

Genuineness is the admission of that tension into consciousness, and so it is the necessary condition of the harmonious cooperation of the conscious and unconscious components of development. It does not brush questions aside, smother doubts, push problems down, escape to activity, to chatter, to passive entertainment, to sleep, to narcotics. It confronts issues, inspects them, studies their many aspects, works out their various implications, contemplates their concrete consequences in one's own life and in the lives of others. If it respects inertial tendencies as necessary conservative forces, it does not conclude that a defective routine is to be maintained because one has grown accustomed to it. Though it fears the cold plunge into becoming other than one is, it does not dodge the issue, nor pretend bravery, nor act out of bravado. It is capable of assurance and confidence, not only in what has been tried and found successful, but also in what is yet to be tried. It grows weary with the perpetual renewal of further questions to be faced, it longs for rest, it falters and it fails, but it knows its weakness and its failures, and it does not try to rationalize them.

Such genuineness is ideal. It goes far beyond the native endowment of detachment and disinterestedness that we possess in the pure desire to know. For it presupposes the accumulations of direct, introspective, and reflective insights that are needed to discriminate between issues. Some are momentous, some important, some secondary, some minor, some merely silly. Without due perspective and discrimination, the exercise of genuineness, as described above, results only in the earnest person with a remarkable flair for concentrating on the wrong questions. Nor can perspective and discrimination be acquired without asking the significant questions. There is, then, a vicious circle to be broken, for we cannot become wise and discriminating without concentrating on the right questions, and we cannot select those questions unless we already are wise and discriminating.

Still, vicious circles are logical entities, and development is a series of emergent leaps from the logic of one position to the logic of the next. Higher system as on the move, as operator, is not to be deduced from precepts and maxims alone, nor from inner impulses alone, nor from external circumstances alone. It is a creative response that meets the requirements of all three in a concrete intelligible synthesis. Man is alive, sensitive, intelligent, reasonable. Nor is he an isolated monad. His development is a movement from the relative dependence of childhood to the relative autonomy of maturity. And as he develops, the content of the analogous requirement of genuineness-for-him shifts from the simple demand of the pure desire for detachment to an ever more intelligent, more wise, more self-reliant unfolding of that desire.

Finally, there is the sanction of genuineness. To fail in genuineness is not to escape but only to displace the tension between limitation and transcendence. Such a displacement is the root of the dialectical phenomena of scotosis in the individual, of the bias of common sense, of basic philosophical differences, and of their prolongation in natural and human science, in morals and religion, in educational theory and history. But this issue takes us from genetic method to dialectic, and so the present discussion ends.

It has all been, of course, very general. It is meant to be so. A heuristic structure is only the framework in which investigation is to introduce specific laws and particular facts. The question before us is not whether we have dealt adequately with human development. The question before us is not whether we have established the fertility of the heuristic structure or even whether we have explained its precise mode of application. Our topic is genetic method, and the sole question is whether the key idea of the method has been found. Our account takes its stand upon the structure of human knowing. Its basic elements are supplied by the theory of explanatory genera and species, by the consequent analysis of development in general, and by the special characteristics of the triply compounded development of man. It finds that, as classical method rests on the assumption that similars are to be understood similarly, so genetic method rests on the assumption that an understanding of significantly dissimilar individuals is to be reached by subsuming their respective histories under common genetic principles. Again, it finds that as classical method is concerned with laws, so genetic method is concerned with emergent trends, with successions of operators that successively change the laws to which an individual is subject. Further, it finds that, because genetic method is concerned with emergent trends, its object can be formulated only by introducing categories in which the notion of emergence and its implications are set forth adequately and with sufficient generality. Finally, it is for this reason that the account of genetic method had to await the discussion of metaphysics; and within this metaphysical context it has been found possible, I believe, to offer a single integrated view that finds its point of departure in classical method yet embraces biology, the psychology of behavior and depth psychology, existentialist reflection upon man, and fundamental elements in the theory of individual and social history, of morals and asceticism, of education and religion.

7.5 Counterpositions   [479–83]

The complexity of the issues[i] with which we have been dealing has made it impossible for us to weave into our exposition an account of contrary views and our reasons for rejecting them. However, there is a notable addition to clarity that results from such contrasts, and if we are not to invite misinterpretation, we had best attempt some negative indication of our position.

In Ernst Cassirer's *The Problem of Knowledge*,[7] the interested reader will find a well-documented study from the neo-Kantian viewpoint of the biological methods and theories from the time of Linnaeus to the present. By presupposing this exposition of other views, it will be possible for us to set forth compactly the essential contrasts between our position and mechanism, vitalism, organicism, and Kantianism. Finally, we shall indicate the points in which we believe it necessary to develop Aristotle's views.

First, then, our views on reality and objectivity separate us from the mechanists. In our position there is not only room but also relevance for every insight that physics and chemistry can offer to the biologist, for the organism is a higher system of underlying chemical and physical manifolds, and the higher system in no way violates the autonomy of physical and chemical laws. Again, in our position there is a welcome for every discovery of such connections as the conditioned reflex and the tropism, for all such connections are simply parts in the flexible circle of ranges of schemes of recurrence. But we cannot but reject the mechanist belief that reality consists in imaginable elements as imagined, for such

7 Ernst Cassirer, *The Problem of Knowledge: Philosophy, Science, and History since Hegel*, trans. William H. Woglom and Charles W. Hendel, of *Das Erkenntnisproblem in der Philosophie und Wissenschaft der neueren Zeit*, Vierter Band, *Von Hegels Tod bis zur Gegenwart, 1832–1932* (New Haven: Yale University Press, 1950) 118–216; in the German, 127–222. [The English translation was published before any German edition. The first German edition was published in 1957 (Stuttgart: Verlag W. Kohlhammer); we have consulted a reprint of 1973 (Hildesheim: Georg Olms Verlag).]

images as images are unverifiable; and we cannot share the mechanist hope that some day the laws of physics and chemistry will account for all biological phenomena, for the only evidence for that hope is the mechanist belief that reality consists in imaginable elements as imagined.

Secondly, our rejection of mechanism is not an affirmation of vitalism, for we do not believe that vitalism, at least as it commonly is conceived, is sufficiently radical in its rejection of mechanism. For the vitalist seems to accept the mechanist view that reality consists in imaginable elements as imagined but to add that also there are unimaginable, vital entelechies. In contrast, we reject outright the belief that ultimate reality is known by a set of unverifiable images, and if we affirm forms, we affirm them not only in organisms but also in electrons, protons, atoms, and chemical compounds. Nor is such an affirmation to be termed mystery-mongering. For a mystery is what is not understood, but a form is what is to be known inasmuch as one understands correctly. The real mystery is that, while scientists are regarded universally as men of intelligence, nonetheless it is thought outrageous to suggest that they know anything by understanding or that they know better and more adequately when they understand better or more adequately.

Thirdly, while we affirm forms both in atoms and in organisms, while we do so for the same reason in both cases, still we do not affirm that biology deals with the same type of conjugate forms as does chemistry or physics. If one compares the chemical elements, one finds that some, for example, the inert gases, are highly stable, while others move easily and almost endlessly into compounds. Still, both the stable and unstable chemical elements are static systems; carbon of a given weight and number, no matter how large the range of compounds into which it enters, never gives rise to a developing series of instances of carbon of that weight and number. The outstanding characteristic of the organism is that in it instability is matched and balanced by a moving system, that the same individual unity is differentiated by an explanatory sequence of conjugate forms, that these sequences are members of the more comprehensive sequence of ever bolder and more resourceful strategies by which organisms solve the problem of living in an environment.

Fourthly, by our affirmation of central forms we agree with the advocates of holism or organicism. But we affirm not only the intelligible unity to be grasped in data as individual but also the intelligible functions and relations to be grasped in data as of kinds. Moreover, these intelligible relations and functions not only are emergent in the underlying manifolds and determine the flexible circle of ranges of schemes of recurrence but also constitute a moving higher system that so integrates the underlying manifold as to make another and different integration emerge.

Fifthly, we employ the name 'emergence,' but we employ it in a quite determinate meaning to denote a quite unmistakable fact. The prototype of emergence is the insight that arises with respect to an appropriate image: without the insight, the image is a coincidental manifold; by the insight the elements of the image become intelligibly united and related; moreover, accumulations of insights unify and relate ever greater and more diversified ranges of images, and what remains merely coincidental from a lower viewpoint becomes systematic from the accumulation of insights in a higher viewpoint. If the meaning of emergence is thus determinate, so also the fact is unmistakable. There are routine processes, and throughout them one can verify the same classical and statistical laws. There are changes of state, and during them statistical laws are modified but classical laws remain the same. But there also are emergent processes, and the classical laws that can be verified at their inception are not the classical laws that can be verified at their end. There are correlations that can be verified in the adult organism. There are correlations that can be verified in the fertilized ovum. But the two sets of correlations are not identical. In determinate materials, there has occurred a change in what can be grasped by insight, formulated as law, and affirmed as verified. One set of conjugate forms has given place to another. The process from one set to the other is regular. But this regular process is not in accord with classical law, for there are no classical laws about changes of classical laws; nor is it in accord with statistical law, for it is not an indifferent choice between a set of alternative processes; and so one is forced to recognize the fact of a third type of process to be investigated by a third, genetic method.

Sixthly, Kant affirmed a maxim of formal purposiveness as relevant to biological inquiry. Such purposiveness was no part of the reality under investigation, but it was a necessary component of the mind's intelligible ordering of the data. Now we affirm finality in a sense that has been defined already. It is an affirmation of dynamism, of a general directedness to fuller intelligibility and systematization, and of the attainment of ever greater but never complete fulness through an effective probability. A clear example of the exact meaning of such finality is the flexible strategy of the dynamic higher system and, again, of the cumulative succession of ever bolder and richer strategies. Accordingly, our affirmation of finality means no more than what can be grasped intelligently in the data and affirmed reasonably on the basis of the data. But the real is being, and being is what is to be grasped intelligently and affirmed reasonably. On this showing, finality is just as real as anything else. Inasmuch as Kant's formal purposiveness involves a certain anthropocentricity and also a greater determinacy than our notion of finality, we are ready to grant its subjective status, but then we would deny that it possessed any relevance to biological inquiry. Finally, Kant's views in this field are no more than a consequence of his general position, and as has been suggested already, that position has no better foundation than an incomplete rejection of naive views on objectivity along with a failure to find the virtually unconditioned as constitutive of judgment, and thereby to reach the universe of being.

Seventhly, though we are in basic agreement with Aristotle, we differ from him in many positive ways, and it will not be amiss to clarify the matter very briefly. Aristotle acknowledged central and conjugate forms: as sight is to the eye, so soul is to the whole animal. His form is also an end: sight is the intelligibility grasped not only in the developed eye and optic nerve but also proleptically in the developing eye of the fetus. He distinguished between thing-for-us and thing-itself: not only are forms grasped in sensible presentations but also they exist in a prime matter that is sheer potency and so falls short of all categorial[j] description. On the other hand, Aristotle did not grasp the notion of successive higher viewpoints, nor employ it to account for explanatory genera and species. He did not grasp the notion of probability as explanatory, nor conceive an emergent probability, nor think of higher forms as accounting for regularities in underlying otherwise coincidental manifolds. He did not conceive finality as heading beyond every generically and specifically determinate achievement, and his analysis of movement as incomplete act is only a distant approximation to the notion of development as higher system on the move from undifferentiated to fully differentiated perfection. Finally, on his position there is no proximate potentiality to conceive human development as a triply compounded movement of successive higher systems.

8   Summary   [483–87]

Metaphysics has been conceived as the integral heuristic structure of proportionate being. Proportionate being is what is to be known by experience, intelligent grasp, and reasonable affirmation. Integral heuristic structure is the anticipatory outline of what would be known by affirming a complete explanation of experience.

The significance of metaphysics lies not in the future but in the present. It is a matter of indifference to metaphysics whether or not there will be some future date in which complete explanation will in fact be reached. But it is a matter of supreme importance to metaphysics that here and now one reject all obscurantism and so accept in all its implications the effort for complete explanation. Again, the value of an anticipatory outline of a hypothetical complete explanation is not to be measured by the extent to which the future explanation is anticipated. For the metaphysical issue is not the present order of future knowledge but the order immanent in the dynamics of all knowledge whether past, present, or future. Even when science has accounted for all phenomena and common sense has been purged of all bias, there remains the question of the unification of the sciences and of the myriad instances of common sense. As that question never will be met either by science or common sense, so the answer to it can be ascertained at once in its general structural lines; and the point to the answer is not the value of a forecast but the value of a correct order and perspective in present knowledge and present inquiry.

As the significance of metaphysics, so the evidence for it lies in the present. But the uniqueness of metaphysics makes an account of the evidence extremely difficult. Any doctrine can be presented in a set or sets of definitions, postulates, and deductions. But evidence does not lie in the outward vocal or written expression, nor even in the inner assent, but in the prior reflective grasp that compels reasonableness to assent. Once one has accepted definitions and postulates, deduction makes manifest the unconditioned that is to be grasped reflectively. But the definitions and postulates of metaphysics are a manifold of disputed alternatives; the evidence for discriminating between them is as large as the universe on which they pronounce; and a grasp of that evidence lies, not within easy reach of every indolent mind, but only at the term of a long and difficult accumulation of direct and reflective insights.

For this reason a statement of the evidence for a metaphysics has to be in dynamic terms. If a spatial image and a military metaphor may be helpful, the advance of metaphysical evidence is at once a breakthrough, an envelopment, and a confinement. The breakthrough is effected in one's affirmation of oneself as empirically, intelligently, and rationally conscious. The envelopment is effected through the protean notion of being as whatever one intelligently grasps and reasonably affirms. The confinement is effected through the dialectical opposition of twofold notions of the real, of knowing, and of objectivity, so that every attempt to escape is blocked by the awareness that one would be merely substituting some counterposition for a known position, merely deserting the being that can be intelligently grasped and reasonably affirmed, merely distorting the consciousness that is not only empirical but also intelligent and not only intelligent but also reasonable.

Once this foundation is laid and as long as it is retained effectively, one can proceed rapidly with the erection of the integral heuristic structure of proportionate being. In a first moment, dialectical criticism transforms one's commonsense and scientific views to provide the secondary minor premise of the argument. In a second moment, cognitional theory brings to light the four methods of possible inquiry, the condition of their use, and the possibility of their integration, to yield the principal minor premise. In a third moment, metaphysical understanding unites the principal and secondary minor premises, much as a physicist unites a differential equation with empirically ascertained boundary conditions, to obtain the integral heuristic structure relevant to this universe. In a fourth moment, there is invoked the isomorphism of knowing and known: the pattern of relations immanent in the structure of cognitional acts also is to be found in the contents of anticipated acts and still will be found to obtain when the heuristic contents of anticipated acts give place to the actual contents of occurring acts.

To summarize the second moment, one begins by noting that understanding leads to the formulation of systems, and that systems may be supposed either to be constant over time or to change in time. Again, besides the direct understanding that posits systems, there is the inverse understanding that rests on the opposite assumption of defective intelligibility. Accordingly, the anticipation of a constant system to be discovered grounds classical method; the anticipation of an intelligibly related sequence of systems grounds genetic method; the anticipation that data will not conform to system grounds statistical method; and the anticipation that the relations between the successive stages of changing system will not be directly intelligible grounds dialectical method. But data must either conform or not conform to system, and successive systems must be either related or not related in a directly intelligible manner. Accordingly, taken together, the four methods are relevant to any field of data; they do not dictate what data must be; they are able to cope with data no matter what they may prove to be.

However, the use of the methods has a basic condition. For they head to general systems and structures which, despite their generality, must be discovered, verified, and applied in data that are all individual. To link intelligibly the individual data with the general structures, there is needed a further and distinct type of understanding that grasps concrete unities, identities, wholes. Whence it follows that the general structures are concerned with the properties of things, where properties and things are what is to be known by understanding the same data by different but complementary procedures.

Besides their unity by concrete reference, the methods also possess structural unifications. Thus, in a universe in which both classical and statistical methods are relevant, the immanent intelligibility of the order of events can be shown to be an emergent probability. Again, in a universe in which the same things have properties investigated in distinct, autonomous sciences, the notion of successive higher viewpoints is alone capable of intelligibly relating the generically distinct properties of the same thing without violating the autonomy of the sciences. There follows a generalized emergent probability for both things and events, and the heuristic structure of knowing is matched by the finality of being.

To turn now to the fourth moment of the metaphysical argument, there are introduced the notions of central and conjugate potency, form, and act. Proportionate being is what is to be known by experience, intelligent grasp, and reasonable affirmation. The integral heuristic structure of proportionate being is the structure of what is to be known when proportionate being is explained completely. But in that explanatory knowledge there will be affirmation, there will be understanding, and there will be experience of the empirical residue. Let 'act' denote what is known inasmuch as one affirms; let 'form' denote what is known inasmuch as one understands; let 'potency' denote what is known inasmuch as one experiences the empirical residue. From the distinction, relations, and unity of experienced, intelligible, and affirmed contents, there follow the distinction, relations, and unity of potency, form, and act. From the different modes of understanding concrete things and abstract laws, there follows the distinction between central and conjugate forms and, as a corollary, the distinctions between central and conjugate potency and between central and conjugate acts. From the structural unification of the methods by generalized emergent probability, there follow the structural account of the explanatory genera and species and the immanent order of the universe of proportionate being. Such are the elements of metaphysics.[k]

There remains the task, to be opened in the next chapter, of investigating a little more deeply[l] the nature of these elements and their relations. But it may not be amiss to locate once more our position in the history of philosophy. There exists a necessary isomorphism between our knowing and its proportionate known. But that parallel is missed by Spinoza's deductivist *ordo idearum est ordo rerum*. The correct locus of the parallel is to be found in the dynamic structure of our knowing. Inquiry and understanding presuppose and complement experience; reflection and judgment presuppose and complement understanding. But what holds for the activities also holds for their contents. What is known inasmuch as one is understanding presupposes and complements what is known by experiencing; and what is known inasmuch as one is affirming presupposes and complements what is known by understanding. Finally, the contents of cognitional acts either refer to the known or are identical with the known, and so the dynamic structure of knowing is also the structure of proportionate being. This was grasped by Aristotle and more fully by Aquinas, and while the present account of the matter does differ in details from their position, the difference lies in the fact that modern science has made it possible to distinguish very sharply between preliminary description and scientific explanation.

16

Metaphysics as Science[a]

Because we admitted insight to be a fact, we were confronted with a problem of objectivity. Because we were not content to affirm that the fact of insight is merely compatible with objectivity, we have been engaged in showing that our analysis of knowledge implies a method of metaphysics and grounds a deduction of the six metaphysical elements of proportionate being. It remains that the deduced elements give rise to a series of questions, and it will serve both to test the method and to reveal its power if those questions are given answers. Accordingly, the present chapter deals (1) with the notion of distinction and its different kinds, (2) with the notion of relation and the basic problems it generates, (3) with the nature of the metaphysical elements, their reality, their relation to the elements of a logic or grammar, and their technical significance in unified knowledge, (4) with the notion of unity as applied to the universe of proportionate being, to a single concrete being, and to the human compound of matter and spirit, and (5) with the concept of metaphysics as a rigorous department of knowledge.

Though the foregoing issues commonly are treated in manuals of metaphysics, one is not to infer an identity of scope and aim. Our purpose is not to write a treatise on metaphysics but to reveal in concrete fashion the existence and the power of a method.[b] If the method is both valid and powerful, the treatise will follow in due course. It remains that the treatise is a future event and not a present fact, that the present fact is an exploration of method, and that the future event will follow, not as a conclusion deduced by an electronic computer, but as a product of intelligence and reasonableness.

1   Distinctions   [488–90]

In general, any *P* and *Q* are distinct if it is true that *P* is not *Q*. However, this proposition is interpreted differently in accord with different views on reality, knowledge, and objectivity. On the position, knowledge of the distinction between *P* and *Q* is constituted by the negative comparative judgment. On the counterposition, the negative comparative judgment merely expresses previously acquired knowledge of the distinction. On the position, the real is being, and as being is known by affirmative judgments, so distinctions in being are known by negative judgments. On the counterposition, the real has to be known before one can make a judgment; it is known by an ocular or a fictitious intellectual look; and so distinctions are known through the occurrence of different acts of looking that cannot be referred to the same object. We contend, of course, that the counterposition is to be rejected. It is true that prior to judgment there are other components in knowledge, but it is not true that the components of knowledge prior to judgment are complete as knowledge; before one denies that *P* is *Q*, one must have evidence for denying; but having the evidence is one thing, grasping its sufficiency is another, and assenting to the denial is a third. Only in the act of judgment itself does one posit the absolute; only in positing the absolute does one know being.

However, when it is true that *P* is not *Q*, it may or may not be true that *P* is real, and it may or may not be true that *Q* is real. Hence distinctions may be divided into notional, problematic, real, and mixed.

A distinction is notional if it is true that (1) *P* is not *Q*, (2) *P* is merely an object of thought, and (3) *Q* is merely an object of thought. For example, a centaur is not a unicorn.

A distinction is problematic if it is true that (1) *P* is not *Q*, (2) either *P* or *Q* or both have not been explained definitively, and (3) there is the possibility that, when definitive explanation is reached, then *P* or *Q* or both may turn out to be mere objects of thought, or else *P* and *Q* may prove to refer to the same reality.

A distinction is real if it is true that (1) *P* is not *Q*, (2) *P* is real, and (3) *Q* is real.

A distinction is mixed if it is true that (1) P is not Q, (2) one of P and Q is real, and (3) the other is merely notional.

Real distinctions are divided into major and minor; and major real distinctions are subdivided into numerical, specific, and generic. Minor real distinctions are between the elements or constituents of proportionate being, that is, between central and conjugate potency, form, and act. Major real distinctions are between things, which may pertain to different genera or to different species of the same genus or, finally, may be different individuals of the same species.

Again, real distinctions are divided into adequate and inadequate. There is an adequate real distinction between Peter and Paul, between Peter's right hand and his left hand; but there is an inadequate real distinction between Peter and his hands.

In conclusion, it may be noted that the Scotist formal distinction on the side of the object (1) presupposes the counterposition on objectivity, and (2) finds its strongest argument in the field of Trinitarian theory. God the Father is supposed to intuit himself as both God and Father; the object as prior to the intuition cannot exhibit both aspects as completely identical, for otherwise the Son could not be God without also being Father. The fundamental answer is, *Ex falso sequitur quodlibet*; and the supposition of the intuition rests on a mistaken cognitional theory.[1]

2   Relations   [490–97]

In any pair of correlatives one may distinguish between a relation R, its base P, its term Q, the converse relation R', the converse base Q, and the converse term P. Thus, if the relation 'father' has Abraham as its base and Isaac as its term, the converse relation 'son' has Isaac as converse base and Abraham as converse term.

As distinctions, so relations may be notional, problematic, real, or mixed. They are notional if they are merely supposed, merely objects of thought. They are problematic if their affirmation occurs in a description or in a provisional explanation. They are real if their affirmation would survive in a definitive explanatory account of this universe. They are mixed if one correlative is real and the other notional.

---

1 The history of this Scotist distinction has been investigated by Bernhard Jansen, 'Beiträge zur geschichtlichen Entwicklung der Distinctio formalis,' *Zeitschrift für katholische Theologie* 53 (1929) 317–44, 517–44.

The foregoing division has a ground and a consequent. Its ground lies in our view that metaphysics regards proportionate being as explained. Its consequent is the problem of determining which relations survive in a definitive explanation and so pertain to a metaphysical account of reality.

To meet this problem, it is necessary to distinguish in concrete relations between two components, namely, a primary relativity and other, secondary determinations. Thus, if it is true that the size of A is just twice the size of B, then the primary relativity is a proportion and the secondary determinations are the numerical ratio 'twice' and the two observable sizes. Now 'size' is a descriptive notion that may be defined as an aspect of things standing in certain relations to our senses, and so it vanishes from an explanatory account of reality. Again, the numerical ratio 'twice' specifies the proportion between A and B, but it does so only at a given time under given conditions; moreover, this ratio may change, and the change will occur in accord with probabilities; but while probabilities will explain why objects like A and B every so often have sizes in the ratio of two to one, they will not explain why A and B are in fact in that relation here and now; and so the numerical ratio 'twice' is a nonsystematic element in the relation. However, if we ask what a proportion is, we necessarily introduce the abstract notion of quantity, and we make the discovery that quantities and proportions are terms and relations such that the terms fix the relations and the relations fix the terms. For the notion of quantity is not to be confused with a sensitive or imaginative apprehension of a size; a quantity is anything that can serve as a term in a numerical ratio; and inversely, a proportion, in the present context, is a numerically definable ratio between quantities.

The point, then, to our distinction between the primary relativity of a relation and its secondary determinations is that it separates the systematic and the nonsystematic. If A and B are things of determinate kinds, then they must be quantitative; and if they are quantitative, there must be some proportion between their quantities. But just what that proportion will be at any given time will depend on the manifold of factors that form the nonsystematic pattern of a diverging series of conditions, and so there is within the limits of human science no ultimate and fully determinate explanation of why A happens to be just twice B at a given moment.

There is a further point to our distinction. As it separates the systematic and the nonsystematic, so also it separates the relative from its absolute determinations. All that is relative in the notion 'twice' is also found in the notion 'proportion'; the difference between them is that 'twice' is a proportion specified by some pair of quantities such as one and two, or two and four, etc.; and such pairs of quantities, simply as pairs of quantities, prescind from the relations of one to the other.

In this fashion we are brought to conceiving relations as involving two components. One component contains all the relativity of the relation, and it is necessary and permanent inasmuch as it is inseparable from its base in a thing of a determinate kind. The other component, however, is contingent; it is subject to variation in accord with the successive schedules of probabilities in world process; but these variations change, not the primary component, but only the secondary determinations; they modify not the relative but the absolute.

Moreover, this analysis possesses a remarkable generality. For we have found it possible to conceive the universe of proportionate being in terms of central and conjugate potencies, forms, and acts. But conjugate forms are defined implicitly by their explanatory and empirically verified relations to one another. Still, such relations are general laws; they hold in any number of instances; they admit application to the concrete only through the addition of further determinations, and such further determinations pertain to a nonsystematic manifold. There is, then, a primary relativity that is contained in the general law; it is inseparable from its base in the conjugate form which implicitly it defines; and to reach the concrete relation that holds at a given place and time, it is not enough to think about the general law; one has to add further determinations that are contingent from the very fact that they have to be obtained from a nonsystematic manifold.

What holds for the relations of scientific explanation also holds for the relations of metaphysical explanation. As conjugate forms are defined by their relations to one another, so central forms are unities differentiated by their conjugate forms; and central and conjugate potency and act stand to central and conjugate forms as experience and judgment stand to understanding. The whole structure is relational: one cannot conceive the terms without the relations nor the relations without the terms. Both terms and relations constitute a basic framework to be filled out, first, by the advance of the sciences, and secondly, by full information on concrete situations. Moreover, as we have argued metaphysics to be immune from revolutionary change, that framework in its fundamental lines lets us know now the types of relations that would survive in a definitive explanatory account of this universe.

Accordingly, our first problem seems solved. Because we conceived metaphysics as the implementation of integral heuristic structure, we had to affirm that it regarded proportionate being as explained, and so we had also to affirm that real relations are relations that would still be affirmed in a definitive explanatory account of this universe. By distinguishing in concrete relations between their primary relativity and their secondary determinations, it was possible to locate the relative component of the concrete relation entirely within the list of metaphysical elements. Scientific laws and systems are successive approximations to the relations between conjugate forms. Scientific probabilities are approximations to the relations between forms and acts of existence and occurrence. Finally, the emergent processes investigated by genetic and dialectical method contain the relations of successive levels of conjugate forms and the sequences of relations between successive stages in the development of conjugate forms.

Moreover, there follows a clarification of the problem of internal and external relations. Relations are said to be internal when the concept of the relation is intrinsic to the concept of its base; they are external when the base remains essentially the same whether or not the relation accrues to it. Thus, if mass is conceived as a quantity of matter and matter is conceived as whatever satisfies the Kantian scheme of providing a filling for the empty form of time, then the law of inverse squares is external to the notion of mass. On the other hand, if masses are conceived as implicitly defined by their relations to one another and the law of inverse squares is the most fundamental of those relations, then the law is an internal relation, for the denial of the law would involve a change in the concept of mass.

Now at first sight it would seem that on a definitive explanatory account of the universe, all relations would have to be internal. For an explanatory account proceeds from insight; it consists basically of terms and relations, with the terms fixing the relations and the relations fixing the terms; and clearly such relations are internal to the terms. But while this is true of the systems to be reached by classical method, it is not the whole truth. Because classical systems are abstract, because they can be applied to the concrete only by appealing to a nonsystematic manifold of further determinations, there also are statistical method and statistical laws. It follows that classical method reveals the primary relativity without the secondary determinations of concrete relations, that it provides an abstract relational field, say, for the positions and momenta of masses, but it leaves to observation and, in the general case, to probabilities the determination of how many masses with what momenta are at what positions. Again, it is true that statistical laws can be turned to explanatory account when they are coupled with large numbers or with long periods of time; but this explanation does not pin down particulars. It makes it intelligible that things like A and B every so often should be found in the ratio of two to one; but it leaves as mere empirical fact the determination that here and now A and B are in the given ratio. Finally, because that determination is mere empirical fact, A and B remain subject to the same classical laws whether they are found in the ratio of two to one or in the ratio of three to one.

Accordingly, while we must grant that the shift from description to explanation involves a shift from external to internal relations, still we also contend that the internal relations constitute no more than the component of primary relativity, and since in concrete relations there is also a component of contingent secondary determinations, external relations also survive in a definitive explanatory account of our universe.

This issue has an older and slightly different form. Aristotle had advanced that change did not occur primarily in the category of relation, and Aquinas undertook to resolve the consequent paradox that, when a change in the size of Q makes it equal to P, then (1) no reality accrues to P, and yet (2) P becomes the subject of a real relation of equality to Q. Apparently these two propositions are contradictory, but there is no doubt that Aquinas affirmed both. Nor did he fail to offer a reason. P can acquire a real relation of equality without acquiring any new reality, because all along P has possessed the reality of the real relation, so that the change in Q merely provided it with its external term.[2]

However, if one is to agree with Aquinas on the matter, one has to push his analysis further than he did himself. What is the reality of the real relation that is found in P before Q is changed to an equal size? If it is absolute, then the real relation of P to Q is the nothing that comes to P when Q is changed. If it is relative, then what is its term? Such considerations have led the commentators to deny one of the propositions that Aquinas undertook to reconcile, and then to invent distinctions to reconcile their explanation with the text they were explaining. But the present analysis leads us to the opposite procedure of pushing

2 Thomas Aquinas, *In Aristotelis libros Physicorum*, V, lect. 3, §§ 7, 8; see also *De potentia*, q. 7, a. 8; q. 7, a. 9 ad 7m.

Aquinas's thought further on the line he has chosen. The reality of the real relation is in P prior to the change in Q; that reality is relative; it is the primary relativity inseparable from quantity; it involves everything quantitative in some relation of proportion to everything else that is quantitative; but it does not determine just what is the proportion between P and Q, or P and R, or P and S, etc. To settle just what the proportion is in any case, one has to appeal to the secondary determinations, such as the size of P and the size of Q; and because the secondary determinations are found not only in P but also in Q, because variations in P and Q are not functionally related, the determinate proportion of P to Q can change without any change in P.

In other words, concrete relations such as equality and similarity lie in the field of descriptive knowledge. Their metaphysical analysis supposes their transference to the explanatory field. Through such transference it appears that such relations are not simple entities but composite. They involve a component of primary relativity and a component of secondary determinations. The primary relativity is inseparable from its base, and for that reason all change is change in the base and only incidentally and consequently change in the relativity. The secondary determinations are constitutive neither of the relation nor of its reality as relation but simply of the differentiation of concrete relations; and because that differentiation depends, not on the base alone but on the base and term together, it can vary without variation in the base.

There remains a final question. Is the reality of a real relation distinct from the reality of its base? It is one thing to conceive the absolute; it is another to conceive the relative; but is there one reality grounding both concepts, or are there two really distinct realities? To handle this question expeditiously, let us contrast counterpositions with the position.

On the basic counterposition, there is simply no meaning to talk about real relations. The real is a subdivision of the 'already out there now.' That is simply given. All relations arise only through the activities of our understanding. Therefore, no relations are 'already out there now,' and so none are real.

Besides the foregoing counterposition, there is its transposition. Besides the looking that is performed with the eyes, there is also a spiritual looking. It looks at the content of acts of conceiving, thinking, supposing, defining, considering. Such contents are or can be real. But it is one thing to take a spiritual look at an absolute content, and it is quite another to take a spiritual look at a relative content. The two are irreducible.

Therefore, the reality of the absolute base and the reality of the relation must be two really distinct entities.

On the position, the real is being; it is whatever is to be grasped intelligently and affirmed reasonably. Now within the limits of proportionate being, whatever is grasped intelligently is never a term without relations or a relation without terms. To express an insight, one needs several terms and relations, with the terms fixing the relations and the relations fixing the terms. To suppose that there are any terms without relations or any relations without terms is to suppose an oversight. Descriptive terms are no exception, for they express things as related to us. Metaphysical terms are no exception, for they come at least in pairs, such as substance and accident, matter and form, potency and act, essence and existence. On scientific terms we have been sufficiently abundant already. But what cannot be affirmed cannot be. What cannot be conceived cannot be affirmed. But there is no intelligent conception of terms apart from relations or relations apart from terms, and so there is no possibility of their being apart.

It will be said that P and Q can be inseparable and yet be really distinct. But such inseparability would seem to be merely physical. The inseparability in question is not merely physical. It is essential. The basic terms of the sciences and the six elements of metaphysics are defined by their respective relations to one another. To distinguish between the defining relation and the defined term can be no more than a notional operation; and even then it cannot be carried through, for if one prescinds from the defining relation, one no longer is thinking of the term as defined but of some other term that is mistakenly supposed to be absolute. Finally, while there are relations other than such defining relations, still they are not adequately distinct from them; for these other relations are concrete; their primary relativity consists in the defining relations; and their secondary determinations are neither relations nor the reality of relations but the contingent concrete differentiations of the primary relativities.

However, while we maintain that the reality of proportionate being is embraced in its entirety[c] by central and conjugate potencies, forms, and acts, so that there is no further really distinct element named relation, it is to be borne in mind that we are envisaging proportionate being as explained. From a descriptive viewpoint, Aristotle's ten categories retain their obvious validity, and among them the category of relation maintains its distinct place.

3   **The Meaning of the Metaphysical Elements**   [497–509]

3.1 What Are the Metaphysical Elements?   [497–98]

If considerable space has been devoted to the notion and method of metaphysics and to the derivation of the metaphysical elements, it is still possible to be puzzled and to ask just what, after all, are central and conjugate potency, form, and act. In general, one may answer that they are the as yet unspecified *U, V, W* and *X, Y, Z* that are to be specified if proportionate being is to be explained. Again, one may say that they are elements in the articulation of the integral heuristic structure of proportionate being. In all probability, however, more is desired than such a reiteration of an already familiar theme, and so, since the direct answer does not satisfy, various indirect answers must be tried.

First, then, it will not be out of place to recall the conditions of the legitimacy of the question, What is it? One can put the question with regard to data, and the answer will be to name a thing or property; one can repeat the question about the thing or the property and learn that the thing is a unity differentiated by certain properties and that the properties are defined by their relations to one another; one can raise the question once more about the process of explaining data and of defining things and properties, and the answer will tell what knowing is either in concrete instances or in its general structure; finally, one can make the discovery that this structure governs not only the knowing but also the known, and then one can ask what the structure is under the latter aspect. So we arrive at the question, What are the metaphysical elements? Clearly, the answer has to be that the elements do not possess any essence, any 'What is it?' of their own. On the contrary, they express the structure in which one knows what proportionate being is; they outline the mold in which an understanding of proportionate being necessarily will flow; they arise from understanding understanding,[d] and they regard proportionate being, not as understood, but only as to be understood.

There follows an important corollary. If one wants to know just what forms are, the proper procedure is to give up metaphysics and turn to the sciences; for forms become known inasmuch as the sciences approximate towards their ideal of complete explanation; and there is no method apart from scientific method by which one can reach such explanation. However, besides the specialized acts of understanding in which particular types of forms are grasped in their actual intelligibility, there also exist the more general acts of understanding in which one grasps the relations between experience, understanding, and judgment, and the isomorphism of these activities with the constituents of what is to be known. If the metaphysician must leave to the physicist the understanding of physics and to the chemist the understanding of chemistry, he has the task of working out for the physicist and chemist, for the biologist and the psychologist, the dynamic structure that initiates and controls their respective inquiries and, no less, the general characteristics of the goal towards which they head.

In other words, the task of explaining proportionate being leads to a division of labor. Different domains of data fall to different departments of science, and from any given department one is to expect explanation only of the data of its field. But among the data are those that arise from the scientific process itself, from the fact of inquiry, from the division of the undertaking, from the procedures employed, from the results obtained. Such consequent data also admit explanation, and the explanation regards not only investigations and their procedures but also the content of their results. It is on this second level that the cognitional theorist and metaphysician operate, and the content of their results is the general structure of the contents of other results.

The existence of this division of labor means that, while further questions must always be met, still they are not always to be met within a given field of inquiry. Because the metaphysician can assign the general characteristics of proportionate being as explained, it does not follow that he can give detailed answers. On the contrary, he must refer questions of detail to particular departments; and he fails to grasp the limitations of his own subject if, in his hope to meet issues fully, he offers to explain just what various forms are. Inversely, scientists in their several fields can give detailed answers to appropriate questions; but their competence in their own field is conjoined with a failure to grasp its limitations if they attempt to answer the further questions that regard other particular fields or the universe as a whole.

3.2 Cognitional or Ontological Elements?   [499-502]

Secondly, it may be asked whether the metaphysical elements constitute an extrinsic or an intrinsic structure of proportionate being. Are they merely the structure in which proportionate being is known? Or are they the structure immanent in the reality of proportionate being? To put the issue in its traditional form, are the metaphysical elements notionally distinct or really distinct?

The question has to do with the relation between knowing and reality. For central and conjugate potency, form, and act have been defined heuristically in terms of cognitional acts; if there were more or fewer basic types of cognitional acts, there would be more or fewer metaphysical elements. So, as far as their definitions go, the differences of the metaphysical elements are differences in the process of knowing, and unless further evidence is forthcoming, they are not differences in the being to be known. Still, one may expect the further evidence to be available, for the simplest reason why our knowing has its peculiar structure would be that proportionate being has a parallel structure.

A first point, then, is that intelligibility is not extrinsic but intrinsic to being. By intelligibility is meant what is to be known by understanding. By the intrinsic intelligibility of being is meant that being is precisely what is so known or, in negative terms, that being is neither beyond the intelligible nor apart from it nor different from it.

Now if by being one means the objective of the pure desire to know, the goal of intelligent inquiry and critical reflection, the object of intelligent grasp and reasonable affirmation, then one must affirm the intrinsic intelligibility of being. For one defines being by its intelligibility; one claims that being is precisely what is known by understanding correctly; one denies that being is anything apart from the intelligible or beyond it or different from it, for one's definition implies that being is known completely when there are no further questions to be answered.

Further clarification will result from contrast. One might claim that the real is a subdivision in the 'already out there now' or, if one pleases, the 'already in here now.' On that view, intelligent inquiry and critical reflection, however useful or praiseworthy they may be, necessarily are extrinsic to knowing reality, for extroversion or introversion of consciousness is prior to asking questions and independent of answers to questions. Accordingly, by deserting the position on being and reverting to the counterposition, one can form a notion of the real to which intelligibility is extrinsic. Moreover, since such desertion and reversion can take place inadvertently by a mere shift in the pattern of one's experience, it can happen easily enough that the intrinsic intelligibility of being will seem a puzzling or a preposterous view. But once all this is admitted, it becomes still clearer that, if the counterposition is rejected in principle, then in principle being must be intrinsically intelligible, and if in fact one is in the intellectual pattern of experience, then in fact this intrinsic intelligibility sheds its obscurity.

However, a further difficulty can arise. After all, as intelligence, so intelligibility is intrinsic to human cognitional activity. Since by that activity being is to be known, it follows that intelligibility will be intrinsic to being as known. However, the knowing is extrinsic to the being, for the knowing is one thing and the being another. Therefore, what is intrinsic to being as known may be extrinsic to being itself, to being as being.

Now if by being one means an 'already out there now,' it is quite possible to argue that knowing is extrinsic to being. Again, once one has posited an appropriate set of judgments, one again can claim that knowing is extrinsic to certain beings; for example, one will judge that there is a knowing, that there is a known, and that the knowing is not the known; clearly, when the knowing is not the known, it is extrinsic to the known. However, this distinction between knowing and known is within being, and it presupposes the intrinsic intelligibility of being; for without that intrinsic intelligibility our intelligent activities would give us knowledge of the intelligible but not of being, and the distinction between knowing and known would be a distinction within the field of the intelligible but not a distinction of two beings.

Our first point, then, though it has its complexities, at least cuts deeply. It affirms the intrinsic intelligibility of being, and it identifies this affirmation with the affirmation of the possibility of knowledge.

Our second point is that intelligibility is, not all of a piece, but of different kinds. There is the intelligibility that is known inasmuch as one is understanding; it is the formal intelligibility that is the content of the insight and the dominant element in the consequent set of concepts. But our understanding results from inquiry, and as inquiry presupposes something into which we inquire, so our understanding presupposes some presentation of what is to be understood. Such presentations are in some sense intelligible; as materials for inquiry, they are what is to be understood; and when inquiry reaches its term, they become understood. Still, this intelligibility of the presentations is not formal but potential; it is not the intelligibility of the idea, of what is grasped inasmuch as one is understanding; it is the intelligibility of the materials in which the idea is emergent, which the idea unifies and relates. Finally, besides formal and potential intelligibility, there is a third type. It is what is known inasmuch as one grasps the virtually unconditioned; it is the intelligibility of the factual. While the potentially intelligible is what can be understood, and the formally intelligible is what may or may not be, the actually intelligible is restricted to what in fact is.

Now as intelligibility is intrinsic to being, so also the differences of intelligibility are intrinsic to being. In particular, proportionate being is what is to be known by experience, intelligent grasp, and reasonable affirmation. It is not what is known by experience alone, for such knowing falls short of human knowing. It is not what is known by experience and understanding without judgment, for without judgment there is not knowing but merely guesswork. Nor can there be judgment without prior understanding, nor understanding without experience. The proportionate object of human knowing not only is intrinsically intelligible but also is necessarily a compound of three distinct types of intelligibility.

It follows that potency, form, and act assign not merely the structure in which being is known but also the structure immanent in the very reality of being. For intelligibility is intrinsic to that reality, and the intrinsic intelligibility is of three different kinds. Nor are these the only differentiations immanent in being. For there are different formal intelligibilities; conjugate forms are of different kinds; central forms are defined differently from conjugate forms, and they differ from one another by the different conjugates they unite; and potencies and acts share the definitions of the forms with which they constitute unities. For every difference in intelligibility there is a difference intrinsic to the reality of known proportionate being.

So we are swung back to our account of real distinctions. P and Q are really distinct if it is true that P is, Q is, and P is not Q. When P is a thing and Q is a thing, the real distinction is major. When P and Q are metaphysical elements of a thing, the real distinction is minor. When P is a thing and Q is one of its metaphysical elements, the real distinction is inadequate.

Finally, we may note the correctness of our expectation. Why does our knowledge begin with presentations, mount to inquiry, understanding, and formulation, to end with critical reflection and judgment? It is because the proportionate object of our knowing is constituted by combining different types of intelligibility. Insofar as that object is only potentially intelligible, it is to be known by mere experience; insofar as it is formally intelligible, it is to be known inasmuch as we are understanding; insofar as it is actually intelligible, it is to be known inasmuch as we posit the virtually unconditioned yes. Again, experience is of things as potentially intelligible, but through experience alone we do not know what the things are. Understanding is of things as formally intelligible, but through understanding we do not know whether things are what we understand them to be. Judgment is of things as actually intelligible, but through judgment alone we would not know either the nature or the merely empirical differences of what we affirm to be.

3.3 The Nature of Metaphysical Equivalence   [502–507]

We have been endeavoring to clarify from different viewpoints the meaning of the metaphysical elements. First, we considered the question, What are central and conjugate potency, form, and act? Secondly, we asked whether they were merely the structure in which being is known or also the structure in which being is. As a third topic we may ask about the relations between the metaphysical elements, on the one hand, and on the other, the objects of true propositions.

In the first place, then, there is a general community of reference. The object of the true proposition is being, for being is what is known by intelligent grasp and reasonable affirmation; and as we have just seen, the metaphysical elements are components intrinsic to being.

In the second place, true propositions may be analyzed. Grammarians distinguish nouns and verbs, adjectives and adverbs, etc. Logicians distinguish subject, copula, and predicate, terms and relations. In both cases, the analysis is based on a consideration of the end products of cognitional process, of the definitions formed in conception, of the affirmations and negations uttered by reflection. On the other hand, metaphysical analysis has a quite different basis. It takes its stand, not on the end products, but on the dynamic structure of cognitional process. For it, the significant division has nothing to do with nouns and verbs, subjects and predicates, or even terms and relations; it concentrates on the merely empirical residue from which all understanding will abstract, on the content of the act of understanding itself, on the virtually unconditioned grasped in the act that grounds and leads to judgment.

Thirdly, since metaphysical elements and true propositions both refer to being, there must be some correspondence between them. On the other hand, since metaphysical analysis has a quite different basis from grammatical or logical analysis, one must not expect any one-to-one correspondence between metaphysical elements and grammatical or logical elements.

Fourthly, while the foregoing conclusion seems too manifest to be worth mentioning, once one conceives precisely the nature and method of metaphysics, still until such exact conception is reached, metaphysics is apt to languish in a morass of pseudo problems that have no basis apart from a confusion of the metaphysical with the logical and grammatical. Accordingly, even though we do not attempt to offer an exhaustive list of precepts, it may be worth while to set down at least a few obvious rules.

(1) The concepts and names of the metaphysical elements are general: 'potency' can denote any instance of potency. Still, this generality does not involve them in abstractness, for there is nothing to a thing apart from its potencies, forms, and acts. The ground of this generality without abstractness is that the metaphysical elements are defined heuristically; the definition of form does not refer immediately to reality, as does the definition of man or of hydrogen; its immediate reference is to a type of cognitional activity, and only through the occurrence, which is usually hypothetical, of such activity does it refer to being; finally, since the envisaged hypothetical activity is to be full and complete, necessarily it will pertain to knowledge of the concrete.

Accordingly, while 'potency,' 'form,' and 'act' are general concepts and names, their reference is exclusively to concrete potencies, forms, and acts. On the other hand, true propositions may be abstract in their meaning; and then to assign their metaphysical equivalent, they have to be transposed into concrete propositions. Such transposition may be easy or difficult, but insofar as it is found difficult, there also will be found some measure of ignorance taking cover under the abstract expression. It is not the metaphysician's business to remove that ignorance. He fulfils his function by assigning the equivalent metaphysical elements corresponding to true propositions whose concrete meaning is known.

This first principle may be named the rule of concreteness, and its application yields a solution to the problem of individuation. For, in the first place, since potencies, forms, and acts are all concrete, they are all individual, and so there is no problem of their individuation. Secondly, since the problem does not regard the individuality of the metaphysical elements, it has to regard the individuality of beings as referred to in grammatical or logical propositions. Thirdly, the problem does not regard any kind of individuality but solely the individuality that consists in merely empirical difference. Thus, consider two points, A and B, and ask why they are different. One will appeal, perhaps, to the distance between them. Construct, then, an equilateral triangle, ABC, and ask why the distances *AB, BC, CA* differ from one another. It is not because they are unequal, for they are equal. Nor can one say that it is because of their different positions, for then one will be explaining the difference of the distances by the difference of the points and vice versa the difference of the points by the difference of the distances. The only solution is to answer from the start that the points *A* and *B* differ from one another not intelligibly but materially, not for an intrinsically assignable reason but as a pure matter of fact. Such is the meaning of merely empirical difference. It is the object of the problem of individuation. Why is this pea different from that, this Ford from that? Even though the two peas or the two Fords might not be similar in every respect, still they could be absolutely alike and yet different. Such difference would not be grounded in any assignable reason, in anything to be known by a direct act of understanding. It is grounded in what is to be known merely empirically. In other words, its metaphysical ground is potency. Just as the affirmation of the existence of a thing is grounded in central act, just as the affirmation of its unity is grounded in central form, just as the affirmation of its mass is grounded in a conjugate form, just as the affirmation of its momentum is grounded in a conjugate act, so the affirmation of its merely empirical individuality is grounded in potency.

(2) Again, the metaphysical elements are defined through the anticipation of explanatory knowledge. They regard things, not as related to us, not as related to our senses, not as represented in our imaginations, but as understood in their relations to one another. Now true propositions may be merely descriptive; to assign their metaphysical equivalents, they must be transposed into an explanatory form; and until that transposition is effected, formally or virtually, it is useless to attempt to assign the metaphysical grounds of their truth. Accordingly, besides the rule of concreteness, there also is a rule of explanatory formulation.

It is a rule of extreme importance, for the failure to observe it results in the substitution of a pseudometaphysical mythmaking for scientific inquiry. One takes the descriptive conception of sensible contents, and without any effort to understand them one asks for their metaphysical equivalents. One bypasses the scientific theory of color or sound, for after all it is merely a theory and, at best, probable; one insists on the evidence of red, green, and blue, of sharp and flat; and one leaps to a set of objective forms without realizing that the meaning of form is what will be known when the informed object is understood.

Such blind leaping is inimical not only to science but also to philosophy. The scientific effort to understand is blocked by a pretense that one understands already, and indeed in the deep, metaphysical fashion. But philosophy suffers far more, for the absence of at least a virtual transposition from the descriptive to the explanatory commonly is accompanied by counterpositions on reality, knowledge, and objectivity. When one is endeavoring to explain, one is orientated to the universe of being; one is setting up distinctions within being; one is relating distinct beings to one another; and one is relegating all the merely descriptive elements in knowledge to particular instances of the case that arises when some being with senses and imagination is related through his senses and imagination to other beings. But while explanatory knowledge includes descriptive, descriptive knowledge is a part that is prone to fall under the illusion of being the whole. It is a fact that explanatory knowledge is an unattained ideal and that the explanations we have reached are commonly mere opinions. It is also a fact that metaphysics takes its stand on the present existence and functioning of the dynamic structure of explanatory knowledge. But the first fact is far more accessible than the second. There arises a demand for a metaphysics that is grounded, not in the impalpable potentiality of explanation, but in the manifest truth of description. The correct ground of metaphysics is rejected, and instead there is erected a pseudo metaphysics whose elements stand in a happy, if ultimately incoherent, conjunction with sensitive presentations and imaginative representations. Then the real is the 'already out there now,' knowing it is taking a good look, and objectivity begins from the obviousness of extroversion to end in the despair of solipsism.

(3) Even when true propositions have been transposed into a concrete and virtually explanatory formulation, there remain structural differences between logical and metaphysical analysis. True propositions contain affirmations and negations about subjects. Their metaphysical equivalents are positions, distinctions, and relations in the universe of being. If it is true that A is similar to B, then 'similarity to B' is predicated truly of the subject A. But it does not follow that 'similarity to B' is some one of the metaphysical components constitutive of A. For B is not a constitutive component of A, yet without B there is no similarity of A to B. The rule of structural transposition requires a transition from the logical subject A to two beings, A and B. The predicate 'similarity' has its metaphysical ground in the fact that the difference between at least one constitutive component of A and one constitutive component of B is merely empirical.

The foregoing point might have been made in a different manner, for the metaphysical equivalent of a true proposition is also the metaphysical equivalent for all the necessary implications of the true proposition. Since A cannot be similar to B without B being similar to A, one and the same metaphysical equivalent has to provide the ground for both propositions.

Those familiar with traditional metaphysics will recall in this connection the distinctions between intrinsic and extrinsic denomination and between formal cause and formal effect. Intrinsic and extrinsic denomination is a difference in propositions. Denomination or predication is intrinsic to a subject P, when the metaphysical equivalent of the name or predicate is a constituent of the being P. On the other hand, denomination is extrinsic to a subject P, when the metaphysical equivalent of the name or predicate is not a constituent or not entirely a constituent of the being P. Again, the relation between formal cause and formal effect is a less general case of the relation we have named metaphysical equivalence. The formal cause is the metaphysical equivalent in the particular case when that equivalent is a form. The formal effects are the range of objects of true propositions grounded by the formal cause. Formal effects are primary or secondary, absolute or conditioned, intrinsic or extrinsic, according as the true propositions grounded by the formal cause are premises or conclusions, necessary or conditioned conclusions, conclusions about the constituted subject or about other subjects. Thus, if Socrates has a human central form (formal cause), he will be a man (primary formal effect), be capable of understanding (necessary, secondary, intrinsic formal effect), occasionally understand (conditioned, secondary, intrinsic formal effect), have a father (extrinsic formal effect).

3.4 The Significance of Metaphysical Equivalence [507–509]

The significance of metaphysical equivalence is twofold. On the one hand, it provides a critical technique for the precise control of meaning. On the other hand, it is an implement for the development of metaphysics.

'Mean what you say, and say what you mean' is an excellent precept. Obviously, it has to be observed if human communication is to be successful on any but superficial levels. Yet it is a common experience that, as the basic issues in any field are approached, it becomes increasingly difficult to pin down exactly what others mean or, for that matter, what one oneself means. Nor can that fact be surprising to the reader familiar with the distinction between different patterns of human experience, the alternative positions and counterpositions in which may be expressed what one discovers or learns, and the protean character of the notion of being that turns out to mean whatever is to be grasped intelligently and affirmed reasonably.

Now just as the study of human experience, of the philosophies, of the notion of being enables one to grasp in a general fashion the range of the possibilities of meaning, so the use of metaphysical equivalence as a technique enables those who possess such a grasp of possibilities to assign with precision which of possible meanings is their actual meaning. Discussion of this universe is discussion of proportionate being. Proportionate being is one or many, if it is true that there are a P, a Q, an R, . . . and P is or is not Q, P is or is not R, Q is or is not R, . . . Any single being is existent by its central act, one by its central form, individual by its central potency, differentiated from other beings and related to them by its conjugate potencies, forms, and acts. There are generic differences inasmuch as conjugate forms emerge on successive higher levels, and there are specific differences inasmuch as different unities are differentiated by different sets of conjugates. The objects of the several sciences are not an unrelated set of indefinables, such as energy, life, consciousness, intelligence, but a systematically related set of differences in the total object of human inquiry. Nor is this basic unity, this systematic differentiation, to be bought[e] at the price of prejudging scientific issues. It is to be had by recognizing that scientists already are committed to inquiring intelligently and reflecting reasonably, that that commitment has implications, that the implications are coincident with the suppositions of scientific method in its classical, statistical, genetic, and dialectical forms, that it is through that coincidence that metaphysics contains virtually and structurally what the sciences are to discover formally and in detail. Moreover, what is at issue is not merely the luxury of unified science, of distinct and autonomous sciences dealing with a common object in related yet distinct and autonomous fields. There also is at issue the liberation of the sciences from the whirligig of philosophic dialectic; for the counterpositions in which philosophy is involved through the polymorphism of human consciousness automatically spread to the field of scientific thought when, indeed, they do not originate, as Cartesian dualism in Galileo and Kantian criticism in Newton, from scientific failure to reach an adequate account of its assumptions and presuppositions. Finally, while contemporary scientific interest in logic constitutes a recognition of this need, it is not a sufficient remedy for the infection. For logic is static, but science is dynamic. Logic will bring to light the eternal presuppositions and the eternal implications of an absolutely precise account of any position. But the scientist never possesses an absolutely precise account of his present position; for his position is system on the move. It increases in precision inasmuch as it keeps moving from one logical position to another. Its real presuppositions are not a set of propositions but the dynamic structure of the human mind, and its need of liberation arises, not from incautiously formulated sentences, but from the polymorphism of human consciousness.

Metaphysical equivalence possesses a special significance in the human sciences. For man is the being in whom the highest level of integration is, not a static system, nor some dynamic system, but a variable manifold of dynamic systems. For the successive systems that express the development of human understanding are systems that regard the universe of being in all its departments. To that development the human organism and the human psyche have to find appropriate adaptations. In consequence of that development, the range of human skills and techniques, of economies and polities, of sciences and philosophies, of cultures and religions is diversified. Only the broadest possible set of concepts can provide the initial basis and the field of differences that will be adequate to dealing with a variable set of moving systems that regard the universe of being. Only a critical metaphysics that envisages at once positions and counterpositions can hope to present successfully the complex alternatives that arise in the pursuit of the human sciences, in which both the men under inquiry and the men that are inquiring may or may not be involved in the ever possible and ever varied aberrations of polymorphic consciousness.

Finally, there is the inverse aspect of metaphysical equivalence. If the sciences of nature and of man can derive from metaphysics as a technique a common yet systematically and critically differentiated object, so, inversely, metaphysics derives from the sciences the content and enrichment that actual activity brings to a dynamic structure. In human knowledge metaphysics is the initially latent structure that comes to light only through developments in particular fields. It becomes the explicitly transforming and unifying structure that possesses a content, insofar as it has materials to transform and unify. In theory, it is possible for metaphysics to rest solely on the known structure of the human mind. In practice, it is necessary for the metaphysician ever to bear in mind that scientific views are subject to revision. But neither the theoretical possibility nor the practical restraint add up to the conclusion that the metaphysician does well to lose contact with the sciences; for that loss of contact not only means that metaphysics ceases to play its integrating role in the unity of the human mind but also exposes the metaphysician to the ever recurrent danger of discoursing on quiddities without suspecting that quiddity means what is to be known through scientific understanding. Accordingly, just as the scientist has to raise ultimate questions and seek their answers[f] from a metaphysics, so the metaphysician has to raise proximate questions and seek their answers from scientists. In either case, the tool to be employed is metaphysical equivalence, which assigns to true propositions their grounds in the constituents of proportionate being and thereby reveals both what exactly the propositions mean and what the constituents are.

4   The Unity of Proportionate Being   [509–20]

The unity of proportionate being raises three questions, for there is the general question of the unity of this universe, there is the particular question of the unity of any concrete being with its manifold of metaphysical elements grounding its manifold of predicates, and there is the special question of the unity in man in whom both materiality and its opposite seem combined.

4.1 The Unity of the Proportionate Universe   [510]

The unity of the universe of proportionate being is threefold: potential, formal, and actual. Its actual unity is an immanent intelligible order, which we have found reason to identify with a generalized emergent probability. Its formal unity is constituted by its successive levels of conjugate forms, which set up successive intelligible fields. Its potential unity is grounded in conjugate prime potency, in the merely empirical conjunctions and successions that constitute the inexhaustible manifold of the merely coincidental that successive levels of forms and schemes bring under the intelligible control of system. Thus, the merely coincidental becomes space-time through the interrelations of gravitation and electromagnetic theory. This displaces the coincidental to the level of physical events, where it is overcome by the higher unities of the chemical elements and their affinities. There follows its displacement to the level of chemical processes, where it is overcome by the higher system of the cell and by the ontogenetic and phylogenetic sequences of the organism, in which each stage is either adapting to environment or circumventing it. On the psychic level, interrelations are transformed into the developing conjugates governing increasing perceptiveness and ever more nuanced aggressive and affective responses. Finally, on the level of intelligence man's relations to the universe are settled by his grasp of the relations of the universe and by his rational choice of his relation to the universe. The unity of the universe, then, is (1) the possibility and the problem of intelligible relations set by the coincidental, (2) the successive transpositions of the problem to higher levels, where it is met by ever more adjustable and more comprehensive modes of unification, and (3) the realization, in accord with successive schedules of probabilities, of the compound conditioned series of concretely possible solutions.

4.2 The Unity of a Concrete Being   [510–14]

Secondly, there is the unity of any concrete being, and here we meet with a host of difficulties. A first set of difficulties arises when we attempt to imagine not only the concrete being but also its constituent metaphysical elements. These are no sooner overcome than another set arises, because we attempt to think not only of the concrete being as existing and changing but also of the metaphysical constituents as existing and changing. Finally, there are the real difficulties implicit in the fact that the concrete being is one and its metaphysical constituents are many.

Let us begin from the real difficulties. First, then, potency, form, and act are distinct, for intelligibility is intrinsic to being, and potential intelligibility is not formal nor actual, nor is formal intelligibility actual. Still, though they are three, they also are one: for potency is potency to form, and form is the form of act; in other words, potency is capacity to come under law and form is being under law and act is according to law; again, just as one and the same reality is known by experience, understanding, and judgment, so one and the same reality is constituted by potency, form, and act. Nor is there any need for any glue to make potency one with form or form one with act. For if there were any such need, why should it not recur? What would unite the glue with the potency? Its stickiness? Some relativity of function? But relativity is already present in potency, form, and act, which are defined by their relations to one another and by the fact that they constitute a single reality. We can and must dispense, then, with the Suarezian modes; and the argument that potency without form differs from potency as informed is to be met with the distinction between intrinsic and extrinsic denomination.

Secondly, central form differs from conjugate form. Both are intrinsic to the real, and neither is the other. But as they differ, so also they are related. They are to be known inasmuch as the same data are understood (1) as individual, and (2) as similar to other data. When they are grasped by understanding, the central form proves to be a principle of unity that is to be differentiated by further inquiry, and the conjugate forms prove to be principles of differentiation of unities to be determined by further inquiry. Just as potency, form, and act are the many components of a single reality, so central and conjugate forms equally are the many components of a single reality.

Let us now turn to problems of predication. The objects of ordinary discourse are concrete beings: men and women, horses and dogs, hydrogen and oxygen. They exist as individuals with a natural unity. They are differentiated by their capacities for coming under laws, being under laws, acting in accord with laws. The truth of such statements can be assigned its ground in the metaphysical constituents of the concrete beings, for example, that their existing involves a central act, their natural unity a central form, their merely empirical individuality a central potency, and their potential, habitual, and actual behavior conjugate potencies, forms, and acts. But as ordinary discourse speaks of men and women, horses and dogs, hydrogen and oxygen, so metaphysicians speak of central and conjugate potency, form, and act. Now if these elements are real, they exist. Presumably they are unities. In some sense they are individual. Since they can be defined, some laws are relevant to them. Therefore, it would seem to follow that, just as concrete being is composed of central and conjugate potencies, forms, and acts, so each of these elements is so composed; and if the argument works once, then it will work repeatedly, so that not only each element is composite but also the constituents of the elements are composite in turn, and so on indefinitely.

The fallacy, however, in this procedure is apparent. Potency, form, and act are constituents of what is known by experience, understanding, and judgment, where potency corresponds to the experiencing, form to the understanding, and act to the judging. Quite clearly, then, potency itself is not known by experiencing, understanding, and judgment, and so it is not composed of a further potency, form, and act. But if this is so, then there is a profound difference between discourse about horses and dogs and discourse about potency, form, and act; for from the former through the rules of metaphysical equivalence one arrives at constituent potencies, forms, and acts; but from the latter one cannot legitimately proceed to a repetition of the analysis with respect to the elements themselves. It is this difference that is expressed in traditional metaphysics when it is affirmed that, while horses and dogs exist and change, potency, form, and act are, not what exists or changes, but that by which are constituted the beings that exist and change.

There remain the difficulties of the imagination. As we employ sensible names such as potency and form and act, so too we are helped by imagining these constituents of concrete being; and as the images represent the objects, so they give rise to problems about the objects; but it is essential to grasp that such images are merely symbolic and that such problems commonly are to be met by denying their suppositions. For on the one hand, potency, form, and act are not the explanation of anything but the general structure in which occurs the explanation of any proportionate being. On the other hand – and this is the more fundamental point – explaining and explained do not lie within the field of the imaginable, but imaginable and imagining lie within the field of explaining and explained.

This is but another statement of the basic antithesis between positions and counterpositions. A man who understood everything might proceed from his grasp of metaphysical analysis through its determination in appropriate sciences to the nature and occurrence of his own sensations and acts of imagining. Still that all-inclusive act of understanding would account no less for past and future sensations and images than for the experiences of the present; and inasmuch as it accounted for present experiences, it would be independent of the experiencing, for it would consist in assigning laws and probabilities to instances labeled with the ultimate conceptual determinations named 'here' and 'now.' In brief, the relations of things to our senses and imaginations are included within the far broader sweep of the relations of things to one another; but they are not included as sensed nor as imagined nor as described but as explained. Moreover, such explanation is twofold. For there is the dynamic structure of explanatory knowledge, and there is the actuation or filling of that structure through the development of the several departments of science. Only the latter, detailed explaining proximately includes acts of sensing and imagining. Yet the metaphysician is concerned directly only with the general dynamic structure, and so it is only in an extremely remote and general fashion that he can include his own sensitive acts within his explanatory view.

A parallel but complementary point must be made. Just as the metaphysician includes his own capacities and habits and acts of sensing and imagining under the sweeping rubric of conjugate potencies, forms, and acts, so too he includes under the same categories the space and time that, from the viewpoint of sensitive extroversion, contain both the totality of sensible objects and the totality of senses and sensitive acts. This reversal of roles, in which the sensible container becomes the intellectually contained, has already been noted. 'To be' cannot mean 'to be in space' or 'to be in time.' If that were so, and space is or time is, then space would be in space and time would be in time. The further space and time, if real, would also be, and so would demand a still further space and time. The argument could be repeated indefinitely, to yield an infinity of spaces and times. 'To be' then is just 'to be.' Space and time, if real, are determinations within being; and if they are determinations within being, then they are not the containers but the contained. To put the issue more concretely, there are extensions and durations, juxtapositions and successions. Still, such affirmations are descriptive. They have to be transposed into explanatory statements before one may ask legitimately for their metaphysical equivalents; and when that transposition takes place, then from the general nature of explanation it follows that the metaphysical equivalents will be the conjugate potencies, forms, and acts that ground the truth of spatiotemporal laws and frequencies. So it comes about that the extroverted subject visualizing extension and experiencing duration gives place to the subject orientated to the objective of the unrestricted desire to know and affirming beings differentiated by certain conjugate potencies, forms, and acts grounding certain laws and frequencies. It is this shift that gives rise to the antithesis of positions and counterpositions. It is through its acknowledgment of the fact of this shift that a philosophy or metaphysics is critical. It is only by a rigorous confinement of the metaphysician to the intellectual pattern of experience, and of metaphysical objects to the universe of being as explained, that this basic enterprise of human intelligence can free itself from the morass of pseudo problems that otherwise beset it.

The foregoing position must not be confused with any type of Platonism. For if it distinguishes sensible and intelligible, aesthetic and noetic, still it does not distinguish them as being and not-being nor relate them by some theory of participation. One and the same universe of being is sensed, described, understood, affirmed. The same real things are related both to us and to one another. But as affirmed, they just are; as related to one another, they are subject to laws and frequencies; these relations of things to one another include identically all the relations of things to us; but as so included, the relations of things to us are not sensed or described but explained. It is one thing to experience the sensible manifold of juxtapositions and successions, of extensions and durations. It is quite another to understand its laws and frequencies and to postulate as conditions of their possibility noncountable multiplicities of merely empirical differences. For neither the understanding nor the postulation is performed by sensitive activities.

4.3 The Unity of Man   [514–20]

This brings us to our third special question of unity, for man is one yet both material and spiritual. Man is one. No less than electrons and atoms, plants and animals, man is individual by his central potency, one in nature by his central form, existent by his central act. Moreover, this basic unity extends to the distinctive conjugates of human intellectual activity. The conjugate forms of the atom constitute the higher system of the atom's own subatomic events. The conjugate forms of the organism constitute the higher system of the organism's own chemical processes. The conjugate forms of the psyche constitute the higher system of the animal's own organic processes. In like manner, the conjugate forms of human intellectual activity constitute the higher system of man's sensitive living. In each case an otherwise coincidental manifold of lower conjugate acts is rendered systematic by conjugate forms on a higher level.

Still, if we ask in what manner precisely the conjugate forms of human intellectual activity constitute the higher system of man's sensitive living, we are confronted not with a single but with a twofold array of facts. For human intellectual activity provides the higher system for sensitive living both unconsciously and consciously. It does so unconsciously inasmuch as it grounds the pattern in which sensitive experience occurs, and in this respect it is a higher system to sensitive living as sensitive living is a higher system to organic living. But there also is a conscious intellectual control of one's sensitive living, and this differs enormously from the former. For conscious intelligence is engaged primarily in grasping the intelligible systems relevant, not to one's sensitive living, but to the contents of one's sensitive experience. By this shift from subjective acts to objective contents, it is headed towards the systematization, not of the particular animal that I am, but of the whole universe of being. And it is within its knowledge of the universe that knowledge of itself is attained, knowledge of its function in the universe is acquired, and the grounds for willing the execution of that function provided. Finally, it is through willing that conscious intellectual control of sensitive living is effected.

Now if we go to the root of this duality of control over sensitive living, we are brought to the contrast between the intelligible and the intelligent. As has been seen, intelligibility is intrinsic to being. There is in the universe of proportionate being a potential intelligibility that makes experience a necessary component of our knowing, a formal intelligibility that makes understanding a necessary component, and an actual intelligibility that makes judgment a necessary component. But we too are. Besides the potential intelligibility of empirical objects, there is the potential intelligence of the disinterested, detached, unrestricted desire to know. Besides the formal intelligibility of the unity and the laws of things, there is the formal intelligence that consists in insights and grounds conceptions. Besides the actual intelligibility of existences[g] and occurrences, there is the actual intelligence that grasps the unconditioned and posits being as known. Finally, we not only are but also know ourselves. As known to ourselves, we are intelligible, as every other known is.[h] But the intelligibility that is so known is also intelligence and knowing. It has to be distinguished from the intelligibility that can be known but is not intelligent and does not attain to knowledge in the proper human sense of that term. Let us say that intelligibility that is not intelligent is material, and that intelligibility that is intelligent is spiritual. Then, inasmuch as we are material, we are constituted by otherwise coincidental manifolds of conjugate acts that unconsciously and spontaneously are reduced to system by higher conjugate forms. But inasmuch as we are spiritual, we are orientated towards the universe of being, know ourselves as parts within that universe, and guide our living by that knowledge.

Further, inasmuch as the material universe can be understood correctly, there can be a correspondence between the material intelligibility that is understood and the spiritual intelligibility that is understanding. But besides this correspondence, which would seem to consist in some type of similarity, for the latter term is knowledge of the former, there also is difference, for the latter is spiritual and the former is material. Moreover, it seems possible to pin down the precise nature of this difference. For our direct understanding abstracts from the empirical residue. As was noted early in this study, inasmuch as we are understanding, we are grasping the universal apart from its instances, the limit apart from the continuum,[i] the invariant apart from particular places and times, the ideal frequency apart from the nonsystematic divergence of actual frequencies. But just as spiritual intelligibility is apart from the empirical residue, so material intelligibility is not without it. The universal can be thought, but cannot be, without the instance; the limit can be thought, but cannot be, without the continuum; the invariant can be considered, but does not exist, apart from particular places and times; ideal frequencies can be formulated, but cannot be verified, apart from actual frequencies. The empirical residue, then, is at once what spiritual intelligibility excludes and what material intelligibility includes.

Now the metaphysical equivalent of the empirical residue has been found to be prime potency. But since the empirical residue is the ground of materiality, prime potency also is prime matter. There follows the possibility of explaining what matter is and what the material is. Nor is this superfluous. The materialist thinks the nature of matter perfectly obvious: matter is the real, and the real is a subdivision in the 'already out there now.' But we are committed to the view that the real is being and that being is whatever is to be grasped intelligently and affirmed reasonably. So if we are to say that matter is real, we have first to grasp its nature and then find sufficient grounds for our affirmation. But there exist in this universe subatomic entities, chemical elements and compounds, plants and animals. A brief consideration of their functioning reveals not merely that it does not occur, but even that it could not occur, apart from the empirical residue, apart from manifolds of instances in a space-time continuum, and apart from actual frequencies that nonsystematically diverge from ideal frequencies. Accordingly, the material can be defined as whatever is constituted by the empirical residue or is conditioned intrinsically by that residue. It follows that conjugate potencies, forms, and acts on the physical, chemical, organic, and psychic levels are material. Further, since central forms are differentiated by their conjugates, it follows that the corresponding central forms are material. Finally, since act shares the definition of the form with which it constitutes a unity, it follows that the corresponding central acts are material.

If our definition of the material is correct, then it must be possible to say that the spiritual neither is constituted, nor is conditioned intrinsically, by the empirical residue. Certainly, it is not constituted by the empirical residue: for inasmuch as we are understanding, we are abstracting from that residue; and inasmuch as we are grasping the unconditioned, we are attaining the lucid, fully rational factualness that contrasts so violently with the brute factualness with which instances similar in all respects still are different instances, with which the multiplicity of the continuum is noncountable because nonordinable, with which actual frequencies diverge from ideal frequencies in any manner provided it is nonsystematic. But if insight and grasp of the unconditioned are constituted quite differently from the empirical residue, so also are the inquiry and critical reflection that lead to them and the conception and judgment that result from them and express them.

Further, our definition requires that the spiritual be not conditioned intrinsically by the empirical residue. Quite obviously, there is some conditioning. Our inquiry and insight demand something apart from themselves into which we inquire and attain insight; initially and commonly that other is sensible experience, and in it is found the empirical residue. But if sensible experience and so the empirical residue condition inquiry and insight, it is no less plain that that conditioning is extrinsic. Seeing is seeing color, and color is spatial, so that seeing is conditioned intrinsically by the spatial continuum. But insight is an act of understanding, and so far from being conditioned intrinsically by the empirical residue, understanding abstracts from it. Again, to grasp the unconditioned there is a prerequisite of a known fulfilment of conditions; commonly this fulfilment lies in sensible experience; still, the fulfilment is anything but unconditioned; and it is the unconditioned that intrinsically conditions a grasp of the unconditioned.

We have been attempting to define explanatorily the material and the spiritual. Earlier it was shown that intelligibility is intrinsic to being. This intelligibility we have found to be of two kinds, material and spiritual. In the first instance, we distinguished between the two by saying that spiritual intelligibility also was intelligent while material intelligibility was not. In the second place, we moved beyond this descriptive differentiation and determined that material intelligibility either is constituted or is conditioned intrinsically by the empirical residue while spiritual intelligibility neither is constituted nor is conditioned intrinsically by the empirical residue. With these clarifications we may now advance a further step in our study of man's nature.

Man, the concrete being, is both material and spiritual; he is material by his physical, chemical, organic, and sensitive conjugates; he is spiritual by his intellectual conjugates. Still, man is not just an assemblage of conjugates; he is intelligibly one, and that unity has its metaphysical ground in his central form. As was seen in the chapter on self-affirmation, a single knower must be conscious empirically, intelligently, and rationally. Not only is there a unity on the side of the object, inasmuch as the experienced is also understood, and the understood is also affirmed. There is needed the prior unity on the side of the subject, inasmuch as the one that inquires and understands must be identical with the one that experiences, and the one that reflects and grasps the unconditioned must be identical with the one that both experiences and understands. Now it is central form that constitutes the metaphysical ground of the truth of affirming that unity. But are we to say that man's central form is material or spiritual?

The question regards the intelligibility that is the intrinsic constituent of man's being. Such intelligibility may be material or spiritual. As long as the alternatives are merely described, it is possible to straddle the issue. For spiritual intelligibility is intelligent, while material intelligibility is not; and man's central form seems to be the point of transition from the material to the spiritual. As the center of sensitive experience, it is material; as the center of the transformation of sensitive experience by the imposition of an intellectual pattern, and as the origin and ground of inquiry and insight, reflection and grasp of the unconditioned, it emerges as spirit.

However, our explanatory definitions of the material and spiritual are not so accommodating. The metaphysical ground of the empirical residue is prime potency. The material is what is constituted by prime potency or what is conditioned by it intrinsically. The spiritual is what neither is so constituted nor is so conditioned. No central form is constituted by prime potency. But is or is not man's central form conditioned intrinsically by prime potency? Can man exist as a unity without prime potency?

The question is one of possibility. In fact, insight is into sensitive presentations and imaginative representations, but it is no less a fact that what is grasped by insight is not the empirical residue but what is abstracted from the empirical residue, and so insight is not conditioned intrinsically by the empirical residue. In fact, grasp of the unconditioned presupposes a fulfilment of conditions that commonly is obtained by the occurrence of appropriate sensitive experience; still, that occurrence is not the unconditioned that is grasped, unless perhaps one is deciding whether there is occurring a sensitive experience; and there are judgments in which the fulfilment consists, at least proximately, not in any sensitive experience, but in such acts as insight and reflective understanding. Similarly, in fact man exists and functions physically, chemically, organically, and sensitively. But the question is whether the breakdown of his organic and sensitive living necessarily is the end of his identical existence. For if his central form is material, then it is conditioned intrinsically by the prime potency that in turn is bound up with his physical, chemical, organic being. But if his central form is spiritual, then it is not conditioned intrinsically by prime potency; and then, absolutely speaking, his central form could be separated from prime potency without ceasing to ground an existing unity and identity.

A solution seems to result from a simple principle, namely, that material reality cannot perform the role or function of spiritual reality but spiritual reality can perform the role and function of material reality. Were man's central form a material intelligibility, then it could not be intelligent and so could not be the center and ground of man's inquiry and insight, reflection and judgment. Inversely, though man's central form were a spiritual intelligibility, it could be the ground and center of his physical, chemical, organic, and sensitive conjugates; for the spiritual is comprehensive; what can embrace the whole universe through knowledge can provide the center and ground of unity in the material conjugates of a single man.

4.4 Summary   [520]

We have been exploring the traditional metaphysical theme of being and unity. The middle term of our comparison has been intelligibility, for intelligibility is intrinsic to being, and at the same time it is the essence of unity. Potential intelligibility is potency; it is the multiplicity of the empirical residue with the orientation to unity of finality. Formal intelligibility is form; it is the unity of unification or of correlation. Actual intelligibility is act; it is the unity of identity and noncontradiction, which are the basic principles of rational consciousness and judgment. Though potency, form, and act are distinct and three, still they are the distinct components of the same reality. Similarly, though central and conjugate forms are distinct, they too are the distinct components of the same reality; for while it is true that an imaginable whole does not differ imaginably from the sum of its imaginable parts, it also is true that understanding and affirming a central form is quite different from grasping and affirming an aggregate of conjugate forms. Finally, intelligibility may be material or spiritual: material intelligibility either consists in the merely empirical multiplicity and difference of prime potency or else is conditioned intrinsically by it; in contrast, spiritual intelligibility is comprehensive; its reach is the universe of being; and it is in virtue of that reach not only that man can know the universe but also that the universe can bring forth its own unity in the concentrated form of a single intelligent view.

5   Metaphysics as Science   [520–29]

Our study of human intelligence revealed the necessity of distinguishing sharply between ordinary concepts, that express and result from insights, and the notion of being, that has to have quite a different origin and ground. For if the notion of being expressed and resulted from an insight, that insight would have to be an understanding not merely of the whole of the actual universe but also of the total range of possible universes. Such an understanding would be identical with Aquinas's *actus totius entis*, that is, with God.[3] Since man possesses a notion of being yet obviously fails to satisfy Aquinas's concept of God, man's notion cannot result from an act of understanding. Accordingly, we were led to the discovery that the notion of being has its origin and ground in an anticipative desire to understand, in a capacity to inquire and reflect. Further, we were led to conceive metaphysics, which traditionally is the science of being, as an implementation of the integral heuristic structure of the realm of being that coincides with the field of possible experience. From this conception of metaphysics there followed a formulation of a method of metaphysics, and to test this method we have devoted two chapters to the elements of metaphysics and to metaphysics as science.

3 Thomas Aquinas, *Summa theologiae*, 1, q. 79, a. 2 c. [Transferred by editors from text.]

While we have attempted no more than a test, still the test has been, I think, sufficiently basic and extensive to establish the possibility of constructing a complete metaphysical treatise in accord with the method that has been worked out. Moreover, it is not difficult to predict the general character of such a complete treatise, for despite differences in detail the results of applying the method bear an astounding similarity to the doctrines of the Aristotelian and Thomist tradition. There is the contrast between the ten categories and the metaphysical elements of potency, form, and act in central (or substantial) and conjugate (or accidental) orders; there is a hierarchy of grades of being in an objectively ordered universe; there are matter and spirit, with spirit independent in existence and in operation both of matter and of the empirical residue (the *conditiones materiae*); there are distinctions and relations, the immunity of relations from direct change, intrinsic and extrinsic denomination, formal cause and formal effect.

Still, there is a basic novelty, for these results are obtained not by strokes of genius but by method. They are obtained without any appeal to authorities. They are obtained without deductions from principles that claim to be self-evident yet in fact are not self-evident to everybody. They rest on a strategy of breakthrough, encirclement, and confinement. Inquiry and insight, formulation and critical reflection, grasp of the unconditioned and judgment are found to be necessary conditions of our knowing. Without them neither science nor common sense is possible; without them no revision of any view is possible; without them the subject can be neither intelligent nor reasonable, and in fact not only is the subject unable to renounce his intelligence and inquire, or to repudiate his reasonableness and reflect, but also he has a positive and effective inclination both to inquire intelligently and reflect reasonably. From this breakthrough there results encirclement, for despite the protean character of the notion of being (which as protean now is identified with matter and now with idea, now with phenomena and now with essence, now with a transcendent unknowable and now with the things that exist), there is latent and operative prior to all such determinations, the objective of the detached and disinterested desire to know, the objective to be reached through intelligent grasp and reasonable affirmation. Being in this sense is a notion that cannot be controverted; it is assumed in all inquiry and reflection, in all thought and doubt; its acknowledgment is implicit in the breakthrough; and since it embraces all views and their objects, its acknowledgment is an encirclement. Still, if the heuristic notion of being cannot be controverted, it need not be identified with the real; if being is what is to be known by intelligent grasp and reasonable affirmation, then the real may be what is known unquestioningly because it is known before any questions are asked. But at least the antithesis is sharp; it results in the division of philosophic statements into the two classes of positions and counterpositions; it implies that statements of counterpositions cannot be both completely coherent and either intelligent or reasonable; it grounds the account of the dialectical process in which positions invite development and counterpositions invite reversal; and once the subject grasps that, unless he identifies the real with being, his statements are bound to be counterpositions that eventually are due for reversal, confinement has set in.

Nor are the attractions of the method limited to securing a solid foundation for the metaphysical structure. For the very process that erects the foundation also builds upon it. As was noted in examining the methods of natural science, there is a scissors-like action that selects the mathematical expression of physical laws by operating simultaneously from above with differential equations and from below with measurements and empirical correlations. But this procedure was employed in its pure form in reaching the self-affirmation of the knower, when the inevitability of experience, of intelligent inquiry, of critical reflection, and of their unity combined with the subject's awareness of his own subjection to such inevitability, to issue into his affirmation of himself as an individual existing unity differentiated by capacities to experience, to inquire, and to reflect. Now this affirmation of oneself as a knower also is an affirmation of the general structure of any proportionate object of knowledge. Further investigation of the process of knowing can determine in greater detail the structure of the proportionate known. This upper blade of the scissors is matched by the lower blade of common sense and scientific pronouncements, which the philosopher can criticize but cannot replace; for any attempt at replacement would be to desert the method proper to philosophy and to employ the methods proper to science or the procedures proper to common sense. Finally, to close the scissors, there is operative the detached and disinterested desire to know, reinforced by the explicit rejection of all obscurantism, and guided by the critical dialectic that discriminates between positions and counterpositions in the formulation of the results of common sense, of science, and of metaphysics.

If the immediately preceding paragraphs sharpen the outline of our account of method in metaphysics, this and the preceding chapter show that the method can be applied and that it is at once powerful, expeditious, and decisive. For the issues we have raised are neither simple nor secondary nor undisputed. If the answers we have reached are essentially traditional, they have been pulled neatly and effectively out of the compromising orbit of Aristotle's physics, and they have been endowed with new life and vigor by their intimate conjunction with cognitional theory, with the results of possible science, and with the pronouncements of common sense. The surprising dispatch with which the elements of central and conjugate potency, form, and act were established could be followed by an invasion of the new territory of explanatory genera and species and of processes of development.[j] The intricacies of distinctions and relations, of the precise meaning of the metaphysical elements and their function in total human knowledge, and of the unity of the universe, of the single concrete being, of the human compound of spirit and matter could be thrown into a basic perspective with a minimum expenditure of effort.

No doubt, every reader will have his further questions, for our excursion into metaphysics has aimed solely at illustrating and testing the concrete possibility of a method. For that reason, it would be missing the point entirely to put the further questions to me instead of endeavoring to work out the answers oneself. My purpose has been to reveal the nature of insight as knowledge by showing in a concrete fashion that metaphysics can be a science with a sharply defined objective, with strictly imposed limits, and with a criterion that is effective in excluding mere disputation. But the clear-cut proof of possibility is the fact. Accordingly, I have not been content to define metaphysics as the conception and implementation of the integral heuristic structure of our knowing in an endeavor to ground, penetrate, transform, and unify the scattered knowledge of common sense and the sciences. I also have tried to indicate just how that integral heuristic structure could be reached and applied to the task in hand. I have not been content to limit metaphysics to the structure of proportionate being as explained, but repeatedly I have illustrated the meaning and the implications of that limitation. I have not been content to show that the discoveries of human intelligence may be formulated as positions or as counterpositions, but also I have illustrated how that cardinal principle of critical dialectic cuts like a knife through disputes on the nature of the real, of the objective, of development, of distinctions, of relations, of the metaphysical elements, of matter and spirit.

However, the main point is that the method puts an end to mere disputation. It divides the field of possible knowledge of proportionate being into knowledge of things as related to us and knowledge of things as related to one another. It divides the latter field into science that explains and metaphysics that anticipates the general structure of proportionate being as explained. It divides such anticipations into grounded assertions, that possess a factual premise in the utilized structure of our knowing, and empty assertions, that lack such a premise. Finally, it divides grounded assertions into coherent positions that admit development and incoherent counterpositions that invite reversal. Now every disputant has something to say. But what he says either refers to proportionate being or not, either to proportionate beings in their relations to one another or not, either to the anticipated structure of proportionate being as explained or not. If the disputant's statement falls under the negative member of any of these dichotomies, then it is not a metaphysical statement and it is to be disregarded in metaphysics. But if it is a metaphysical statement, then either it possesses a factual premise in the utilized structure of our knowing or it does not; and if it does not, then it is an empty assertion. Finally, if it is a grounded assertion, then either it is a position that admits development or else it is not; and if it is not, then it is a counterposition to be reversed by the simple technique of making it coherent with the statement that it is stated intelligently and reasonably.

The first three disjunctions separate metaphysical assertions from the assertions of common sense, of science, and of theology. The last two disjunctions separate valid metaphysical statements from empty assertions and from counterpositions. Together they serve to define what questions are metaphysical, how correct answers are to be determined, and how they are to be formulated. Moreover, correct answers and correct formulations are selected, not by asking further metaphysical questions, but by investigating issues that pertain to the field of cognitional theory and ultimately prove to be quite determinate questions of concrete cognitional fact. For the metaphysical structure of proportionate being as definitively explained is an object of our knowledge, not through present scientific explanation of the universe, nor through any alleged inspection of the essence of the universe, but through its isomorphism with the utilized structure of our knowing. What the structure of our knowing is, sets a question to be answered by investigation of our cognitional activities. Again, the utilization of that structure sets another question of fact; for the question arises inasmuch as our knowing admits different structural alternatives; and the question can be settled by an appeal to the boundary conditions provided by the broadest certainties of dialectically transformed science and common sense. Finally, correct answers need correct formulations; but the possibility of mistaken formulations has its ground in the polymorphism of human consciousness; and the selection of correct formulations can be effected inasmuch as the incoherence of counterpositions invites their reversal.

Now such a procedure eliminates mere disputation and bestows upon metaphysics the status of a science. I do not mean that it secures automatic solutions for metaphysical issues, or that it annihilates the obscurantist, the obtuse, or the mind fixed in a habitual routine. On the contrary, I regard the automatic solution as a mere myth that springs from a nonrational hankering after a nonrational security, for every solution is to be discovered by intelligence and is to be accepted by reasonableness, and neither the exercise of intelligence nor the exercise of reasonableness is automatic. Again, like the poor of the Gospel, the obscurantist, the obtuse, and the merely routine mind may be expected always to be with us. But however exasperating such minds may be in the short run, in the long run they are negligible; they can block but they cannot initiate; they can manipulate pressures but they cannot lead; and if they denounce you as a fool in your lifetime, their sons will mistake you for a genius when you are dead. For they are indifferent to truth and falsity; they are concerned only with the familiar, which they strive to maintain, and with the unfamiliar, which they strive to oppose; but the mere passage of time makes the unfamiliar familiar, and people that cannot be persuaded by the suddenness of intelligence and reason are easily convinced by the slow but inevitable gradualness of time. So it is in the sciences. For scientific method does not succeed in teaching old dogs new tricks. As Max Planck testified, a new scientific position gains general acceptance, not by making opponents change their minds, but by holding its own until old age has retired them from their professorial chairs.[4]

As in the natural sciences, so also in metaphysics the function of method is to secure a firm orientation and a tendency that in the long run is

4 Max Planck, *Scientific Autobiography and Other Papers*, trans. Frank Gaynor (New York: Philosophical Library, 1949) 33–34. [This book was reprinted in 1968 and 1971 by Greenwood Press of Westport, CT.]

efficacious. As in the natural sciences this goal is attained by requiring a fulfilment in the data of observation and experiment, so that there will exist a possible transition from the conditioned supposition of thought to the virtually unconditioned affirmation of judgment, so too in metaphysics a similar goal is to be attained by requiring a fulfilment in the utilized structure of our knowledge, so that there will exist a possible transition from metaphysical speculation to metaphysical affirmation. Finally, as in the natural sciences, so also in metaphysics, an understanding of the method, its accurate formulation, its acceptance, and its proper use are neither automatically achieved nor automatically efficacious. They are operations of intelligence and reasonableness. They result only from sustained inquiry and sustained reflection. Their power is no more than the power of intelligence and reasonableness, and while that power is great indeed, it is not exercised after the fashion of the steamroller that crushes opposition but through a mounting dialectical tension that makes absurdity ever more evidently absurd until man either rejects it or destroys himself by clinging to it.

The apt illustration of this point lies, of course, in the dialectical demand for method in metaphysics, for it is that demand that arose in the medieval universities, that has remained the basic preoccupation of subsequent philosophies, that is responsible, since it has not been met fairly and squarely, both for the disrepute into which metaphysics has fallen and for the intellectual, moral, and social consequences that in our day so evidently flow from disdain for metaphysics.

The demand for method in metaphysics rose out of medieval theology. The twelfth century was oppressed with an apparently insoluble problem: with the necessity of distinguishing between divine grace and human freedom, and at the same time an inability to conceive either term without implying the other. In the first third of the thirteenth century, there gradually was evolved the notion of two entitative orders so that grace stood above nature, faith above reason, and charity above natural human excellence. With increasing thoroughness this distinction between a natural order and a supervening gratuitous order was carried through by successive theologians, to receive after the middle of the century its complete formulation and its full theological application in the writings of St Thomas Aquinas. Finally, despite the condemnations of Aquinas at Paris and Oxford, despite the aridity of fourteenth-century nominalism and the sterility of its scepticism, despite the worldly contempt of the Renaissance for the schoolmen and the pious contempt of the Reformation for carnal knowledge, despite the semirationalism of a Hermes, a Günther, a Frohschammer, and the agnosticism of modernists, the technically formulated distinction between reason and faith has only grown in importance in the Catholic church since its basic formulation in the thirteenth century. Within his own terms of reference, Aquinas did his work well.

Still, a distinction between reason and faith is a distinction within theology. It pertains to the theologian's delimitation of his own field and to the elaboration of his own methodology. But it possesses implications outside the theological domain. Its meaning is not confined to the erection of distinct and subordinate departments of philosophy and science within theological schools and for the furtherance of theological purposes. For once reason is acknowledged to be distinct from faith, there is issued an invitation to reason to grow in consciousness of its native power, to claim its proper field of inquiry, to work out its departments of investigation, to determine its own methods, to operate on the basis of its own principles and precepts. Such was the underlying significance of the discovery of Aristotle by the medieval age of faith. Such, too, was the open significance of Renaissance humanism, Renaissance philosophy, and Renaissance science.

In Descartes, one finds the problem of philosophic method explicitly envisaged and vigorously explored. But if he could take for granted the legitimacy of pursuing philosophy without bringing his religious faith to bear directly on the issue, he was completely innocent of the notion that science could be pursued with a similar independence of philosophy. For him it was plain that one man had one mind, and to his synthetic grasp it seemed simpler to master the whole of human knowledge than to disentangle one part from the rest and attempt to learn it thoroughly. So, as he deduced the existence of God from the initial certitude of his *Cogito*, he also deduced the conservation of momentum from the immutability of God. Clearly, the distinction between reason and faith had to be followed by a distinction between science and philosophy. As the eleventh-century brilliance of an Anselm had been mistaken in offering necessary reasons for the mysteries of faith, so the seventeenth-century brilliance of Descartes was mistaken in offering philosophic reasons for a theory of mechanics. Yet as theology had been able to work out its method only by distinguishing itself from philosophy and thereby generating a challenge to its preeminence, so philosophy could not formulate its nature and method without distinguishing itself from science and thereby calling forth a challenge to its ambition to rule. And as the challenge to theology emphasized the distinct existence of philosophy, so the challenge to philosophy emphasized the distinct existence of science.

The course of the dialectic is clear enough. As there is a post-Cartesian affirmation of philosophy that rules theology out of court, so there is a post-Kantian affirmation of science that tosses overboard even Kant's modest claims for philosophy, and there is a still later totalitarian violence that with equal impartiality brushes aside theology and philosophy and science. But at that empty conclusion to the sequence of ever less comprehensive syntheses, man still exists and man still is called upon to decide. Archaists urge him to imagine that he lives in an age of liberalism, or rationalism, or faith. Futurists paint for him a utopia that cannot disguise its own mythical features. But the plain fact is that the world lies in pieces before him and pleads to be put together again, to be put together not as it stood before on the careless foundation of assumptions that happened to be unquestioned but on the strong ground of the possibility of questioning and with full awareness of the range of possible answers.

Such, I would submit, is the significance for our time of method in metaphysics. For if I am concerned to meet Kant's demands upon any future metaphysics, if I am impressed by Hume's argument that the central science is the empirical science of man, if I respond to Descartes's aspiration for bold yet methodical initiative, these themes from a past that is over are but overtones in the problem that is our existential situation. If its confusion is to be replaced by intelligible order and its violence by reasonable affirmation, then the nucleus from which this process can begin must include an acknowledgment of detached inquiry and disinterested reflection, a rigorous unfolding of the implications of that acknowledgment, an acceptance not only of the metaphysics that constitutes that unfolding but also of the method that guides it between the Charybdis of asserting too little and the Scylla of asserting too much.

17

Metaphysics as Dialectic[a]

If Descartes has imposed upon subsequent philosophers a requirement of rigorous method, Hegel has obliged them not only to account for their own views but also to explain the existence of contrary convictions and opinions. Accordingly, our appeal has been not only to the isomorphism between the structure of cognitional activity and the structure of proportionate being but also to the polymorphism of human consciousness. From the isomorphism there has followed the account of the six metaphysical elements, of their distinction, relations, unity, and technical significance. From the polymorphism of consciousness there has followed a series of brief but highly effective refutations of contrary views. However, our method possesses still further significance. Not only is it possible to deal piecemeal with opposed opinions but also there is available a general theorem to the effect that any philosophy, whether actual or possible, will rest upon the dynamic structure of cognitional activity either as correctly conceived or as distorted by oversights and by mistaken orientations.

Such a theorem in itself is simple enough but it labors under one considerable difficulty. No one would deny that conclusions follow from premises or that, as our metaphysics has followed from our conception of cognitional activity, other metaphysics or negations of metaphysics would follow from other conceptions. But obviously considerable resistance would meet the claim that the procedure yielded results that were strictly coincident with the views of other philosophers. The most that could be established would be a general similarity of structure and of tendencies, while, commonly enough, philosophers living and dead are not just structures and tendencies but also less general responses to problems peculiar to particular places and times.

To meet this difficulty, it is necessary to transpose the issue from the field of abstract deduction to the field of concrete historical process. Accordingly, instead of asking whether the views of any given philosopher follow from assumptions of a specified type, we propose to ask whether there exists a single base of operations from which any philosophy can be interpreted correctly, and we propose to show that our cognitional analysis provides such a base. In this fashion, the a priori element of cognitional analysis joins hands with the a posteriori element of historical data; attention is turned to the problem of arriving at a heuristic structure for a methodical hermeneutics; and since metaphysics has been defined as the integral heuristic structure of proportionate being, the dialectical aspect of metaphysics is integrated with its scientific aspect by the simple fact that both aspects satisfy a single definition.

The chapter falls into three main parts. In the first there are determined the relations of metaphysics to myth on the one hand and to mystery on the other. In the second there are explored the criterion of truth, the definition of truth, the ontological aspect of truth, the relations between truth and expression, and the appropriation of truth. Finally, in the third section it will prove possible to define the problem of interpretation and to work out the heuristic structure for a methodical hermeneutics.

1   **Metaphysics, Mystery, and Myth**   [531–49]

An account of particular mysteries and myths pertains to the history of religions and of literature. But a genetic account of the radical meaning of mystery and myth, of their significance and function, of the grounds of their emergence, survival, and disappearance can hardly be omitted in a contemporary metaphysics. Myth is a prominent category in Comte's notion of three stages in man's development, in Schelling's later philosophy, in E. Cassirer's *Philosophy of Symbolic Forms*,[1] in P. Tillich's views on religion and theology, in R. Bultmann's principles of New Testament interpretation. Mystery is a notion that plays a fundamental role in the

1 [Ernst Cassirer, *The Philosophy of Symbolic Forms*, 3 vols., trans. Ralph Manheim (New Haven: Yale University Press, 1955).]

philosophy of Gabriel Marcel and in widely different ranges of religious reflection. Finally, while we have been engaged in indicating the character of explicit metaphysics, we also have acknowledged prior stages of latent and of problematic metaphysics; and naturally enough there arises the question whether mystery and myth are cognate to these earlier stages and whether they vanish in the measure that the earlier stages are transcended.

1.1 The Sense of the Unknown [531-34]

First, then, our analysis forces us to recognize the paradoxical category of the 'known unknown.' For we have equated being with the objective of the pure desire to know, with what is to be known through the totality of intelligent and reasonable answers. But in fact our questions outnumber our answers, so that we know of an unknown through our unanswered questions.

Secondly, man's concrete being involves (1) a succession of levels of higher integration, and (2) a principle of correspondence between otherwise coincidental manifolds on each lower level and systematizing forms on the next higher level. Moreover, these higher integrations on the organic, psychic, and intellectual levels are not static but dynamic systems; they are systems on the move; the higher integration is not only an integrator but also an operator; and if developments on different levels are not to conflict, there has to be a correspondence between their respective operators.

Thirdly, on the intellectual level the operator is concretely the detached and disinterested desire to know. It is this desire, not in contemplation of the already known, but headed towards further knowledge, orientated into the known unknown. The principle of dynamic correspondence calls for a harmonious orientation on the psychic level, and from the nature of the case such an orientation would have to consist in some cosmic dimension, in some intimation of unplumbed depths, that accrued to man's feelings, emotions, sentiments. Nor is this merely a theoretical conclusion, as R. Otto's study of the nonrational element in the *Idea of the Holy*[2] rather abundantly indicates.

---

2 [Rudolf Otto, *The Idea of the Holy: An inquiry into the non-rational factor in the idea of the divine and its relation to the rational*, trans. John W. Harvey (London: Oxford University Press, 1920, 1950, 1958).]

Fourthly, such feelings, emotions, sentiments become integrated in the flow of psychic events inasmuch as they are preceded by distinctive sensible presentations or imaginative representations and inasmuch as they issue forth in exclamations and bodily movements, in rites and ceremonies, in song and speech. There results pragmatically a distinction between two spheres of variable content: on the one hand, there is the sphere of reality that is domesticated, familiar, common; on the other hand, there is the sphere of the ulterior unknown, of the unexplored and strange, of the undefined surplus of significance and momentousness. The two spheres are variable, for the first expands with every advance in knowledge of proportionate being. Again, the two spheres may be as separate as Sundays and weekdays or they may interpenetrate so that, as for Wordsworth in his youth, the earth and every common sight take on the glory and the freshness of a dream. Finally, while everyone by the dynamic structure of his being is orientated into the second sphere, it seems reserved to the outer accident of circumstance and the inner accident of temperamental disposition to call forth the more intense experiences that leave one now aghast, now amazed, now entranced.[3]

Fifthly, the primary field of mystery and myth consists in the affect-laden images and names that have to do with this second sphere. However, as the analysis indicates, the primary field is not the only field, and

3 There exist infantile and demonic aspects of mythic consciousness. To account for them, one must advert to the existence of an inverse component of the psychic operator. In other words, development is not only advance into the known unknown but also a flight from anxiety and, in more marked instances, from uncanny feelings of horror, loathing, dread. In this connection I can only refer the reader to the posthumous edition of H.S. Sullivan's lectures under the title *The Interpersonal Theory of Psychiatry*. May I add that Sullivan's work seems to me to possess a remarkable significance from a methodological viewpoint? His adherence to the canon of parsimony has its reward not only in a liberating clarity but even in the achievement of a basic set of genetic concepts. Roughly, Sullivan deals with ranges of intersubjective schemes of recurrence (dynamisms meeting needs), their integrator (the self-system), and their operator (the avoidance of anxiety). From such elements he is in a position to construct any number of fortunate or unfortunate developments from a rather convincing extrapolation to infantile experience, through mischievous children, chums and gangs, early and late adolescence, either to the attainment of psychic maturity, or to the eruption of neurotic malfunctioning, or to the invasion of consciousness by the horrors of the 'not-me' in schizophrenia.

so it will be well to distinguish between the image as image, the image as symbol, and the image as sign. The image as image is the sensible content as operative on the sensitive level; it is the image inasmuch as it functions within the psychic syndrome of associations, affects, exclamations, and articulated speech and actions. The image as symbol or as sign is the image as standing in correspondence with activities or elements on the intellectual level. But as symbol, the image is linked simply with the paradoxical 'known unknown.' As sign, the image is linked with some interpretation that offers to indicate the import of the image.

Sixthly, the interpretations that transform the image into a sign are a vast manifold. Anyone who has glanced through a history of religions will be aware of the enormously divergent attitudes and performances that are jumbled together under that single rubric. But there is no reason for restricting interpretations of the image as sign to the field of religion. The primary field of mystery and myth is both quite general and quite permanent. For inquiry and reflection are both general and permanent; the principle of correspondence between the intellectual and the sensitive is both general and permanent; and so some sensitive awareness and response, symbolic of the known unknown, must be regarded as a generally and permanently recurring feature of human living. Moreover, precisely because of its relation to the known unknown, the image can be interpreted as sign in manners that are as numerous and diverse as human ingenuity and human contrariness. So it is that the full range of interpretations includes not only the whole gamut of religions but also the opposite phenomenon of antireligious feeling and expression, not only antireligious views but also the intense humanistic idealism that characterized liberal display of detachment from all religious concern, not only elevated humanism but also the crudely naturalistic nationalism that exploded in Germany under the fascination exerted by a Hitler, not only such social aberrations but also the individual aberrations that led Jung to declare that very commonly psychoneural disorder is connected with problems of a basically 'religious' character. In brief, there is a dimension to human experience that takes man beyond the domesticated, familiar, common sphere, in which a spade is just a spade. In correspondence with that strange dynamic component of sensitive living, there is the openness of inquiry and reflection and the paradoxical 'known unknown' of unanswered questions. Such directed but, in a sense, indeterminate dynamism is what we have called finality. But whither finality heads is a question that receives countless answers, pragmatic or conceptual, naturalistic, humanistic, or religious, enthusiastically positive or militantly negative.

Seventhly, since metaphysics is restricted to the domain of proportionate being, it will acknowledge the fact of finality and determine its general characteristics. But it would be stepping beyond the limits of its competence if it did not leave to further and distinct inquiries the determination of the precise objective towards which finality may in fact be leading. For there are claims that that goal is transcendent, that it lies outside the realm of proportionate being; and whether or not such claims are justified cannot be settled within the limits of an inquiry that simply prescinds from all questions concerning transcendent being.

Eighthly, it does not follow that metaphysics will have nothing to say on the subject of mystery and myth. For at least in our usage of the term, finality means not a future event but a present fact, not the ultimate result of a tendency but its past and present unfolding. Nor is that unfolding merely a possible topic of metaphysical consideration, for it is interwoven with the very genesis of metaphysics, with the process in which the mind of man moves from a latent through a problematic to an explicit metaphysical view.

1.2 The Genesis of Adequate Self-knowledge[b]   [535–36]

For an explicit and adequate metaphysics is a corollary to explicit and adequate self-knowledge. It follows upon the affirmation of oneself as a unity of empirical, intelligent, and rational consciousness, upon the heuristic definition of being that reveals intelligent and reasonable affirmation to be knowledge of reality, upon the account of objectivity as experiential, normative, absolute, and principal, that strips counterpositions of their apparent plausibility. However, such adequate self-knowledge can be reached by man only at the summit of a long ascent. For self-knowledge involves a self-objectification, and before man can contemplate his own nature in precise but highly difficult concepts, he has to bring the virtualities of that nature into the light of day. In the present work this was achieved by our study of insight as activity, for what we mean by a unity of empirical, intelligent, and rational consciousness has to be gathered from our study of insight in mathematics, in classical and statistical science, in common sense and its fourfold bias, in the ambiguity of things and bodies, and in the reflective understanding that leads to judgment. But such a study would not be possible without the prior development of the sciences and the long clarification of more general issues by philosophic inquiries and debates. Nor would the scientific and philosophic developments themselves have been possible without a prior evolution of language and literature and without the security and leisure generated by technological, economic, and political advance.

Still, this conditioning of metaphysics by self-knowledge and of self-knowledge by human development does not imply that self-knowledge and metaphysics are not attempted until a sufficient human development is attained to ensure their accuracy and adequacy. On the contrary, from the start there is present and operative the latent metaphysics contained in the dynamic structure of all human knowing, which, if it is human, is constituted by experience, by understanding, and by a reflective yes or no. Similarly, from the start there is present and operative the empirically, intelligently, and rationally conscious subject. What is lacking is the appropriate set of conceptual definitions and linguistic expressions in which the triply conscious subject could convey to himself and to others what it is to be a human knower and what such knowing implies in the known. What is lacking is the cultural milieu habituated to the use of abstract concepts and trained in the techniques that safeguard their employment. What is lacking is a critical awareness of the polymorphism of human consciousness, of the alternative formulations of discoveries as positions or as counterpositions, of the momentum of positions for development and of the goal of counterpositions in reversal. Most of all, what is lacking is knowledge of all that is lacking, and only gradually is that knowledge acquired.

So it is that each new venture, each new success and failure, in the history of man provides an objectifying revelation of man's capacities and limitations, a contribution to his self-knowledge, and a premise from which, perhaps, some item of metaphysical import may be gleaned. Man knows himself in the intersubjective community of which he is just a part, in the support and opposition the community finds in its enveloping world of sense, in the tools of its making, in the rites and ceremonies that at once occupy its leisure, vent its psychic awareness of cosmic significance, express its incipient grasp of universal order and its standards of praise and blame. Still, there is a tension between the community and the individual, between the old initiatives that through common acceptance have become inertial routines and, on the other hand, the capacities of individuals constituted by successive higher integrations that are not static systems but systems on the move. And if the proximate effect of this tension is social change, the goal towards which it tends cumulatively is an awareness and an ever more distinct formulation of the nature of the originating subject. So the stories of the gods yield to the more human stories of the heroes; the epic that celebrates a collective past yields to a drama that portrays man's tragic situation; song becomes a more personal lyric; practical techniques open the way to insights into nature; social problems invite social reflection; rhetoricians and sophists call forth logic; and the cosmic whole summons philosophy to venture on its speculative way.

A long history, then, is involved in the genesis of man's self-knowledge. But metaphysics is a corollary to self-knowledge, and so there is a parallel history to the genesis of metaphysics. And as metaphysics is not unconcerned with its own genesis, so it cannot prescind entirely from the historical phenomena of mysteries and myths.

1.3 Mythic Consciousness^c [536-42]

Just as an explicit and adequate metaphysics is to be reached by grasping and formulating the integral heuristic structure of our knowing and its proportionate known, so the hypothetical introduction of blind spots into the structure has the interesting consequence of revealing the categories not only of inadequate philosophies but also, in the limit, of mythic consciousness.

Thus, before the distinction between positions and counterpositions is drawn clearly and distinctly, it is not possible to formulate an accurate and universally applicable criterion of reality and of real distinctness. This lack of a general criterion does not mean that man will be unable to hit things off correctly in particular cases. For as long as man operates intelligently and reasonably, he will succeed in every particular case in determining what is and what is not real and which realities are distinct. But it is not uncommon for other desires to interfere with the unfolding of the detached and disinterested desire to know, and the result of such interference will be error about reality and about real difference. In this fashion, the real sometimes is what is to be known through reasonable affirmation, and sometimes it is what can be really real only if it is 'already out there now.'

On this issue philosophies can straddle, as did Cartesian dualism, or choose one of the alternatives, as did rationalism and empiricism respectively, or reject both, as did Kantian criticism. However, the issue itself is as old as the polymorphism of human consciousness. If it has occupied an extremely prominent position in modern philosophy, it bedeviled medieval thought with problems of universals and of distinctions, and in a still less distinct form it underlay the oppositions between the old Greek nature philosophers and the Pythagoreans, Heraclitus and the Eleatics, Platonists and Aristotelians, atomists and stoics.

If the history of philosophic reflection has been a prolonged clarification of the issue, there occurred human inquiry and reflection before philosophy became a distinct branch of human knowledge. In that still earlier period there could, and in fact did, occur sudden flashes of philosophic acumen and profundity, such as may be illustrated by Ikhnaton's concern with being and its ground. Still, the flashes were no more than flashes for, while man always was intelligent and reasonable, also it always was true that the insights and judgments of the individual can be communicated successfully and permanently to others only in the measure that the community has accumulated the prior, presupposed insights and has developed the techniques for their dissemination and preservation. So it is that prephilosophic mentality tends to straddle unconsciously and confusedly the problem of reality. The real is known by the rational yes; but the real also must be imaginable; and since imagination is ever fluid, the real attains the stability of reality only when it is named. Similarly, real difference is to be known by comparative negations; but mere judgments are not enough; there also must be different images and different names; and inversely, differences in image and in name can result in an acknowledgment of different realities.

This brings us to the confines of mythic consciousness, which operates without the benefit of distinctions that are generated only by the critically reflective process that is aware of myth and goes beyond it. Mythic consciousness experiences and imagines, understands and judges, but it does not distinguish between these activities, and so it is incapable of guiding itself by the rule that the impalpable act of rational assent is the necessary and sufficient condition for knowledge of reality. For it, the real is the object of a sufficiently integrated and a sufficiently intense flow of sensitive representations, feelings, words, and actions. Contrary judgments break the integration, but contrary judgments have a palpable ground only in the sphere of common, familiar, domesticated reality, in which trial and error exercise their pragmatic control. But contrary judgments have no palpable ground when unanalyzed consciousness is orientated into the strange realm of the 'known unknown.' Then there becomes operative, without Kantian reservations, the Kantian scheme of the category of reality, namely, the real is to be affirmed when there occurs a suitable filling of the empty, a priori forms of sensibility. As the uncritical scientist builds for himself a universe constituted by tiny, imaginable knobs or by a sponge-vortex ether, so the mythmaker builds himself a more vital and more impressive world. As for the uncritical scientist, so for the mythmakers, their respective worlds are 'real.' A Kantian would point out that really this reality is only phenomenal, but the possibility of this correction lies on the deeper ground that the criterion of the real is the act of judgment issuing from a grasp of the virtually unconditioned. And the same criterion must be invoked if one cares to argue that the mythmaker or the uncritical scientist did not possess a *suitable* filling for the empty forms of his sensibility.

Next, an adequate metaphysics must distinguish not only positions and counterpositions but also explanation and description. Moreover, the explanatory viewpoint can be adopted only if counterpositions are rejected and positions accepted. For explanation relates things to one another; it includes by a remote and general implication all relations of the sensible to senses and of the imaginable to imaginations under the broad and comparatively undifferentiated category of the relations of things to one another; it drops from consideration the knower as a spectator of the real and makes him an inconspicuous item in the real that is affirmed. But so fine a detachment, so rigorous a disinterestedness, is a sheer leap into the void for the existential subject. His concern is for things as related to him. His explanation has to be explanation of things as related to him.[d] He is quite intelligent; he is eager for insight; but the insight he wants is, not at all the grasp of a system of terms defined by their intelligible relations to one another, but the grasp of intelligibility in the concrete presentations of his own experience.

Now I am no opponent of insight into the concrete presentations of one's own experience. But I would note that all the explaining is done by the insight and that, unless one distinguishes between the insight and the presentations, then one is open to the blunder of attributing an explanatory power to the presentations and even to associated feelings and emotions. One can know exactly the contribution made by the insight by having recourse to concepts, to abstract formulations, to the utterance of terms and relations with the terms fixing the relations and the relations implicitly defining the terms. But if one employs this procedure, one is involved in the explanatory viewpoint; and if one rejects the explanatory viewpoint, one is without any defence against the tendency to regard as explanatory what merely is an item to be explained.

Nor is the danger of such a tendency remote. For what else is at the root of anthropomorphic projections? We have found the abstract intelligibility of space and time to lie in the invariants of the geometry employed in a verified physics. But if one insists that going beyond concrete insights is a desertion of reality, a flight to metaphysical make-believe, then one cannot rise above one's personal spatiotemporal frame of reference, and one cannot distinguish between the intelligibility immanent in that frame and mere sensitive familiarity with directions and with the lapse of time. Without such a distinction, objective space and time are credited not only with the intelligibility of the frame but also with our feelings. As we feel the gravitational field to be directed from above to below, so a man at the antipodes would have to move about like a fly walking on the ceiling of a room. As we make decisions and then produce results, so causes are before effects, and a first cause necessarily and exclusively is first in time. Causality cannot be merely an intelligible relation of dependence; it has to be explained, and the explanation is reached by an appeal to the sensation of muscular effort and to the image of the transmission of effort through contact. So universal causality is a pervasive fate, linking all things at once, keeping the wandering stars to their strange courses and by the same stroke settling for astrologers the destinies of men. Things have properties, but their properties are not conjugates implicitly defined by verified laws, but sensible qualities that can be detached and reassembled to enable alchemists to transform base metals into gold. Besides the properties there are the things, but they are constituted, not so much by their intelligible unity – what could that mean? – but by their capacity to occupy space and endure through time; they are 'bodies.' Finally, one is confronted with the antinomies of nothing less than pure reason when one asks how space and time can be infinite, or if they are not, then what is outside space and what is before time.

There is a complementary fallacy. Just as anthropomorphic projection results from the addition of our feelings to the content of our insights into things, so subjective projection results when we interpret the words and deeds of other men by reconstructing in ourselves their experience and uncritically adding our intellectual viewpoints which they do not share. The error of this procedure promptly comes to light when we have to deal with those whom we interpret in this fashion. The stranger turns out to be strange when we find that his mentality is not the same as our own. A visit to the next village, to the bordering country, to a different continent, leads first to amusement at the oddity of the inhabitants and ultimately to despair over their incomprehensibility. But we cannot travel into the past. So fathers are misunderstood by their sons and each century by the succeeding century. As the data assembled by historical research accumulate, insights are revised continuously in accord with the concrete process of learning. But besides the revisions forced by further data, there also are the revisions due to the advent of new investigators, for history is rewritten not only by each new culture but also by each stage of progress and decline in each culture. Nor is there any escape from such relativism as long as men cling to the descriptive viewpoint. Common sense succeeds in understanding things as related to us only because it is experimental; it deals with things with which it is familiar; its insights are guides in concrete activity; its mistakes promptly come to light in their unpleasant effects. But if one would step beyond the narrow confines in which the procedures of common sense are successful, one has to drop the descriptive viewpoint and adopt a viewpoint that unashamedly is explanatory. No doubt, there can be no history without data, without documents, without the monuments that have survived destruction and decay. But even if one supposes the data to be complete, so that there is available a cinema of past deeds, a soundtrack of past words, an inner reenactment of past feelings, emotions, and sentiments, still there remains to be determined some approximation to the insights and judgments, the beliefs and decisions, that made those words and deeds, those feelings and sentiments, the activities of a more or less intelligent and reasonable being. Interpretation of the past is the recovery of the viewpoint of the past; and that recovery, as opposed to mere subjective projections, can be reached only by grasping exactly what a viewpoint is, how viewpoints develop, what dialectical laws govern their historical unfolding.

If one cannot claim that the explanatory viewpoint is established in the human sciences, if there is a note of optimism in the assertion that its position is secure in the natural sciences, then the incompleteness of our own victory over subjective and anthropomorphic projections should make us understand how rife, almost how inevitable, those fallacies were before science and philosophy existed as distinct forms to give a concrete meaning to the explanatory viewpoint. If counterpositions today lead men to refuse to distinguish sharply between experience and insight, between their own insights and those of others, at least there should be no difficulty in reaching another basic feature of primitive mentality. For the primitive not only lacks examples of successful implementation of the explanatory viewpoint but also lacks the techniques of mastery and control that the study of grammar imparts to the use of words, the study of rhetoric to the use of metaphor,[e] the study of logic to the communication of thought. The primitive cannot begin to distinguish accurately between what he knows by experience and what he knows inasmuch as he understands. His understanding of nature is bound to be anthropomorphic, and his understanding of man is fettered by his inability to conceive other men with a mentality different from his own.

Finally, as an adequate metaphysics demands sharp distinctions between positions and counterpositions and between explanation and description, so also it demands a firm grasp of the heuristic and progressive character of human intelligence. Before man actually understands, he anticipates and seeks to understand. That anticipation implies that there is something to be known by understanding. It is fruitful in the measure that it leads eventually through partial insights and further questions to an adequate grasp of the speculative or practical issue in hand. But the anticipation, instead of being fruitful, may be the source of illusions. Knowledge that there is a nature can be mistaken for knowledge of what the nature is. Socrates' great discovery that he did not know is not without its ambiguities, for it is one thing to understand in a concrete, commonsense fashion, and it is quite another to be able to formulate one's understanding coherently in general terms. The victims of Socrates' persistent questioning could not find an adequate formulation for what they felt they understood; to be embarrassed by the questioning, they must at least have understood how to employ the names of the objects that were under scrutiny; but between an understanding of verbal usage and an understanding of what names denote, there is a large and commonly obscure gap in which the heuristic anticipation of insight can pass muster for the occurrence of insight, and the partial insight for mastery.

It is through this gap that there proudly march the speculative gnostic and the practical magician. They anticipate scientific understanding of what things are and of how[f] results are to be produced. They anticipate the pure scientist's preoccupation with numbers and the applied scientist's preoccupation with tools. They are necessary factors in the dialectical development of human intelligence, for without their appearance and their eventual failure men would not learn the necessity of effective criteria for determining when adequate insight actually has occurred. But because their efforts are prior to the discovery of those criteria, because their pure desire to know is not contrasted with all their other desires, because names and heuristic anticipations can be mistaken for insights, because partial insights have the same generic character as full understanding, because the satisfaction of understanding can be mimicked by an air of profundity, a glow of self-importance, a power to command respectful attention, because the attainment of insight is a hidden event and its content a secret that does not admit communication, because other men worship understanding but are not secure enough in their own possession of it to challenge mistaken claims, the magician and then the gnostic have their day.

1.4 Myth and Metaphysics[8]   [542–43]

As the foregoing analysis implies, mythic consciousness is the absence of self-knowledge, and myth is a consequence of mythic consciousness as metaphysics is a corollary of self-knowledge. Myth, then, and metaphysics are opposites. For myth recedes and metaphysics advances in the measure that the counterpositions are rejected, that the attempt to understand things as related to us gives way to the effort to understand them as related to one another, that effective criteria become available for determining the occurrence and the adequacy of understanding. As myth and metaphysics are opposed, so also they are related dialectically. For myth is the product of an untutored desire to understand and formulate the nature of things. That desire is the root of all science and philosophy. Only by the mistaken unfolding of that desire has man learnt how to avoid the pitfalls, and guard against the dangers, to which its unfolding is exposed. So it is that, by a dialectical relationship of which it is not aware, myth looks forward to its own negation and to the metaphysics that is all the more consciously true because it is also the conscious rejection of error.

Because myth has a permanent basis in the polymorphism of human consciousness, there is a permanent task of overcoming myth by metaphysics, and it takes two forms. On the one hand, philosophic attempts to defend counterpositions cannot but regard the notion of being as the root of myth and the metaphysical analysis of being as an extension of scientific techniques into the domain of myth; for if the real is not being or if being is not the intelligently grasped and reasonably affirmed, then being is mythical, the possibility of metaphysics is precluded, and the conclusions of Dr Tillich unavoidable.[4] On the other hand, outside the field of philosophy, there is the problem of human development that arises with each new generation. Because men do not develop intellectually or, if they do, because they become involved in counterpositions, they cannot be dealt with on the basis of intelligence and reason; but this makes it all the easier to deal with them on the sensitive level, to capture their imaginations, to whip up their emotions, to lead them to action. Power in its highest form is power over men, and the successful maker of myths has that power within his reach and grasp. But, clearly, if an adequate metaphysics can do something to overcome philosophic misinterpretations of the notion of myth, it needs to be extended into a philosophy of education, and the education has to be made effective before there can be exorcized the risk of adventurers climbing to power through sagacious mythmaking.

1.5 Myth and Allegory[h]   [544–46]

In deference to the commonly pejorative meaning attached to the name 'myth,' we have identified mythic consciousness with the counterpositions, with the inability or refusal to go beyond description to explanation, and with the lack or neglect of effective criteria for passing judgments on anticipations and acts of understanding. But this is only part of the picture. Even within a highly developed culture it remains true that, as Quintilian remarked, *paene omne quod dicimus metaphora est.*[i] Not only are words themselves sensible but also their initial meaning commonly is sensible.[5] By an unperceived series of transformations this initial meaning gradually is changed until the primary reference to sensible objects and actions is submerged or forgotten, and from that hidden stem there branch out, often in bewildering variety, a set of other meanings that to a greater or less extent transcend the sensible plane.

However, this process has its conditions. Words are vocal tools of communication. Their use occurs when a speaker or writer communi-

---

4 See Paul Tillich, 'Mythus, begrifflich und religionspsychologisch,' in *Die Religion in Geschichte und Gegenwart: Handwörterbuch für Theologie und Religionswissenschaft,* 2nd ed. (Tübingen: J.C.B. Mohr 1930) 4: 367.

5 An accurate statement on initial meanings would be much more complex. See Susanne K. Langer, *Feeling and Form* 236–57.

cates his thoughts or judgments or decisions to listeners or readers. They are effective tools only in the measure that the speaker or writer correctly estimates the cultural development of listeners or readers and chooses just the words that have a meaning for them. So one can distinguish between a philosophic language,[j] a scientific or mathematical language, a literary language, and a language of the people. One can go on to introduce subdivisions within these categories; for each philosophic school has its own language; different sciences in their successive formulations and different levels of mathematics have different technical terms; literary speech and writing vary in their wealth of overtones of allusion and suggestion, in their consciousness of commonly unconscious metaphor, in their esteem or contempt for univocal meaning and linear discourse; and the language of the people varies with locality, with occupation, with a proud sense of tradition or a vital openness to change.[k]

Now if a philosopher were required to speak to a literary group or a scientist to speak to the people, he would begin by insisting that the task was impossible. He would point out that the proposed audience did not share his interests; he would add that it took him years to learn what he knows and that the process of learning cannot be telescoped; he would complain that, once a philosophic or scientific notion has been communicated successfully, it seems absurd to continue to employ an enormous literary or popular circumlocution instead of introducing a single technical term; he would urge that the process of learning itself is clogged when combinations of technical terms are replaced by combinations of unwieldy circumlocutions. Still, the first philosophers and the first scientists were under the necessity either of remaining silent or of communicating with ordinary people in ordinary language. They had to excite interest and sustain attention. They had to command confidence. They had to impart the notion of learning and obtain willingness to learn. They had to bring about the transformations of meanings that change the reference of words from the sensible to the intelligible and the rational, and they had to do this not only without the aid of grammar and philology, rhetoric and logic, but even without the very names of those disciplines and so without the tools that would enable them to explain to themselves or to others precisely what they were doing.

It would seem, then, that to the contrasts between myth and metaphysics, mythic consciousness and self-knowledge, there must be added a further contrast between mythic expression and developed expression. For just as it is true that nearly all we say is metaphor, so also it is true that metaphor is revised and contracted myth and that myth is anticipated and expanded metaphor. If the philologist can take the words we use and work backwards from our meaning through a series of other meanings to the initial meaning of the root, there must have existed a series of discoveries of new meanings; as long as such discoveries were merely expansions of existing viewpoints, the new meanings could be communicated by employing old words outside their customary contexts;[1] but whenever the discoveries ushered in new viewpoints, a more elaborate procedure was required to effect the communication. So the parables of the Gospels recall the experiences and propound the images that lead to insight into what is meant by the kingdom of God. So Plato in his dialogues introduces myths to convey insights and judgments and evaluations that would seem strange and novel. But the same technique can be employed for the same purpose without the technique itself becoming an object of investigation and analysis, of reflection and evaluation, and then its use is unaccompanied by the announcement that what is said is merely a parable or merely a myth, because it cannot be accompanied by an explanation of what is meant by the mere parable or the mere myth. Then the wise man speaks his riddles, and thoughtful listeners are left to wonder and ponder what he means.

There is, then, an allegorical aspect of myth. It is an aspect that emerges when myth is conceived as a solution to a problem of expression. Moreover, it is an aspect that runs counter to those on which hitherto we have mainly dwelt. For a problem of expression arises inasmuch as the mythmaker is endeavoring to transcend the counterpositions, inasmuch as he is trying to turn attention from the sensible to the intelligible, inasmuch as he has reached a viewpoint that current modes of expression cannot convey. We have described myth as an untutored effort of the desire to know to grasp and formulate the nature of things. In the measure that such an effort tries to free itself from its fetters, myth attains an allegorical significance.

1.6 The Notion of Mystery[m]   [546–49]

Besides myth there is mystery. Man's unanswered questions confront him with a 'known unknown,' and that confrontation may not be dodged. The detached and disinterested desire to know is unrestricted; it flings at us the name of obscurantists if we restrict it by allowing other desire to interfere with its proper unfolding; and while that unfolding can establish that our naturally possible knowledge is restricted, this restriction on possible attainment is not a restriction on the desire itself; on the contrary, the question whether attainment is in all cases possible presupposes the fact that in all cases attainment is desired. Moreover, this unrestricted openness of our intelligence and reasonableness not only is the concrete operator of our intellectual development but also is accompanied by a corresponding operator that deeply and powerfully holds our sensitive integrations open to transforming change. Man by nature is orientated into mystery, and *naturam expellas furca, tamen usque recurret.*[6]

Though the field of mystery is contracted by the advance of knowledge, it cannot be eliminated from human living. There always is the further question. Though metaphysics can grasp the structure of possible science and the ultimate contours of proportionate being, this concentration only serves to put more clearly and distinctly the question of transcendent being. And if that question meets with answers, will not the answers give rise to further questions?

Moreover, the advance of knowledge is through anticipated or achieved explanation. But explanation does not give man a home. It reveals things in their relations to one another through the complex symbols of mathematics, the cumbrous technical terms of science, the bloodless ballet of metaphysical categories. Even if one does not revolt at the very notion that in that fashion man is to contemplate reality as explained, at least one has to admit (1) that the world of pure science and of metaphysics is somehow very different from the world of poetry and of common sense, (2) that the apprehension of explanation stands in opposition and tension with the flow of the sensitive presentations, of the feelings and emotions, of the talking and doing that form the palpable part of our living with persons and our dealing with things, (3) that as explanation is reached through description, so it must be applied concretely by turning from explanation back to the descriptive world of things for us, and therefore (4) that man's explanatory self-knowledge can become effective in his concrete living only if the content of systematic insights, the direction of judgments, the dynamism of decisions can be embodied in images that release feeling and emotion and flow spontaneously into deeds no less than words.

The achievement, then, of full understanding and the attainment even

6 [Horace, *Epistolae*, I, 10, 24.]

of the totality of correct judgments would not free man from the necessity of dynamic images that partly are symbols and partly are signs. This necessity neither supposes nor implies the commonly pejorative meaning of myth, for it remains despite complete and fully conscious rejection of counterpositions, of the attempt to confine explanation within a descriptive mold, of gnosticism and of magic. It is a necessity that has its ground in the very structure of man's being, in which intellectual activity is a higher integration of the sensitive flow and the sensitive flow is a higher integration of organic performance. To such images, then, let us give the name of mysteries. For if that is an ambiguous name, if to some it recalls Eleusis and Samothrace and to others the centuries in which the sayings and deeds of Jesus were the object of preaching and of reverent contemplation, still that very ambiguity is extremely relevant to our topic.

For our inquiry has swung round[n] in a circle. We began from the compound category of mystery and myth. We isolated, first, a pejorative meaning in which mythic consciousness is the lack of self-knowledge and myth the opposite of metaphysics. We noted, secondly, a problem of expression that would arise inevitably in the process from ignorance to knowledge, and there we recognized the possibility of an allegorical aspect of myth. Thirdly, we have found that even adequate self-knowledge and explicit metaphysics may contract, but cannot eliminate, a 'known unknown,' and that they cannot issue into a control of human living without being transposed into dynamic images which make sensible to human sensitivity what human intelligence reaches for or grasps. But this brings us back to the compound category from which we began. Because human understanding and judgment, decision and belief, are the higher integration of sensitive contents and activities, the origin, the expression, and the application of intelligent and rational contents and directives lie in the sensitive field. Because the integrating activities of the intellectual level and the integrated activities of the sensitive level form a dialectical unity in tension, it follows (1) that the intellectual activities are either the proper unfolding of the detached and disinterested desire to know or else a distorted unfolding due to the interference of other desire, and (2) that the sensitive activities from which intellectual contents emerge, and in which they are represented, expressed, and applied, either are involved in the mysteries of the proper unfolding or distort these mysteries into myths. Because man develops in self-knowledge, he distinguishes between his sensitive and intellectual activities with increasing sharpness and exactitude and grasps with ever greater precision their interrelations and interdependence; and so his advance in self-knowledge implies an increasing consciousness and deliberateness and effectiveness in his choice and use of dynamic images, of mottos and slogans. Finally, this advance implies, not any rationalist sublation of both mystery and myth, but simply a displacement of the sensitive representation of spiritual issues. Because counterpositions head to their own reversal and myths are grounded in counterpositions, sooner or later every myth is discredited. Because man cannot renounce intelligence or repudiate reasonableness, every occasion on which a myth is discredited is also an opportunity for man to advance towards a profounder self-knowledge, a more exact grasp of science and metaphysics, and a more conscious use of mystery purified of myth. Because the union of sensitive and intellectual activities is a unity of opposites in tension, because the dominion of the detached and disinterested desire constantly is challenged, the elimination of one myth tends to coincide with the genesis of another, and the advance of science and philosophy implies merely that the later myths will be complemented and defended by appropriate philosophies and made effective through the discoveries of science and the inventions of technology.

So we are brought to the profound disillusionment of modern man and to the focal point of his horror. He had hoped through knowledge to ensure a development that was always progress and never decline. He has discovered that the advance of human knowledge is ambivalent, that it places in man's hands stupendous power without necessarily adding proportionate wisdom and virtue, that the fact of advance and the evidence of power are not guarantees of truth, that myth is the permanent alternative to mystery and mystery is what his hybris rejected.[7]

2   **The Notion of Truth**   [549–62]

The real issue, then, is truth. Though it has concerned us all along, it will not be amiss to bring together at least the main points made on

---

7 Because of their consonance with the present analysis I would draw attention to Mircea Eliade's *Images et symboles* (Paris: Gallimard, 1952) and his more ample *Traité d'histoire des religions* (Paris: Payot, 1948 and 1953). [The first of these works was reprinted in 1980, the second in 1970 and 1987. There is an English translation of each: *Images and Symbols: Studies in Religious Symbolism*, trans. Philip Mairet (New York: Sheed and Ward, 1961) and *Patterns in Comparative Religion*, trans. Rosemary Sheed (New York: Sheed and Ward, 1958).]

different occasions and in different chapters. Accordingly, we distinguish (1) the criterion of truth, (2) the definition of truth, (3) the ontology of truth, (4) truth in expression, (5) the appropriation of truth, and (6) the truth of interpretation.

2.1 The Criterion of Truth   [549–52]

The proximate criterion of truth is reflective grasp of the virtually unconditioned. Because it proceeds by rational necessity from such a grasp, the act of judgment is an actuation of rational consciousness, and the content of judgment has the stamp of the absolute.

Essentially, then, because the content of judgment is unconditioned, it is independent of the judging subject. Essentially, again, rational consciousness is what issues in a product that is independent of itself. Such is the meaning of absolute objectivity, and from it there follows a public or common terrain through which different subjects can and do communicate and agree.

Concretely, however, while reflective understanding grasps the virtually unconditioned, it itself is conditioned by the occurrence of other cognitional acts; and while the content of the judgment is grasped as unconditioned, still that content either demands or rests on the contents of experiences, insights, and other judgments for its full clarification. This concrete inevitability of a context of other acts and a context of other contents is what necessitates the addition of a remote to a proximate criterion of truth.

The remote criterion is the proper unfolding of the detached and disinterested desire to know. In negative terms this proper unfolding is the absence of interference from other desires that inhibit or reinforce, and in either case distort, the guidance given by the pure desire. A more positive account of the matter, perhaps, will be suggested by clarifying the differences between six terms: infallibility and certitude, certainty and probability, ideal and actual frequency.

A frequency is a numerical ratio of occurrences to occasions. An actual frequency is reached by counting both occurrences and occasions. An ideal frequency is a numerical ratio from which actual frequencies diverge but do not do so systematically. Finally, both actual and ideal frequencies may be affirmed or denied, and the affirmation or denial may be certain or probable. It follows that, while judgments are occurrences with actual frequencies, while in principle their ideal frequencies might be estimated or calculated, still the ideal frequency of a judgment is one thing and its probability is another. For certain judgments admit an ideal frequency no less than probable judgments; and if the ideal frequency of the probable judgment were its probability, then the probability of affirming that ideal frequency would be another ideal frequency, so that an infinite regress would result.

Accordingly, the probability of a judgment, like the certainty of a judgment, is a property of its content. If that content coincides with what is grasped as virtually unconditioned, then it is a certainty. But what is grasped as virtually unconditioned may be that a given content heads towards the virtually unconditioned, and then the content is a probability. On this analysis, every judgment rests on a grasp of the virtually unconditioned, and the probability of a probable judgment is a certainty. But the content grasped as virtually unconditioned may be coincident with the content of the judgment or, on the other hand, merely with the approximation of that content towards an ideal content that would be virtually unconditioned.

However, there is a third sense of probability, that is reached by contrasting infallibility with a certitude that admits degrees. A subject may grasp the virtually unconditioned and yet may ask whether that fulfilment of the proximate criterion of truth has been vitiated by subjective bias. Then there arises the question of the remote criterion. The subject becomes more or less secure or anxious about the genuineness of his inquiry and reflection, and further inquiry and reflection will in their turn be open to similar questioning. What is in doubt is the subject himself, and all his efforts to remove the doubt will proceed from the same suspected source.

One component in this situation may be the subject's flight from the personal commitment involved in judgment; another may be a temperamental inclination to anxiety; but the objective issue is the habitual and actual disinterestedness and detachment of the subject in his cognitional activities; and in resolving that issue further considerations come into play.

Thus, one may call upon the judgments of others to support one's own. Detachment and disinterestedness are independent of circumstances, but bias, unless it is general, tends to vary with circumstances. Hence certitudes may be strengthened by the agreement of others, and this strengthening will vary with the numbers of those that agree, the diversity of their circumstances, the consequent virtual elimination of individual and group bias, and the absence of any ground for suspecting general bias.

Again, there are judgments that express the conditions of possible truth or error, certainty and probability, detachment or distortion. To call them into question is to presuppose their validity. To suppose that they will be revised is to postulate a fictitious reviser and to strip the name 'revision' of its current meaning. In such cases the subject is confronted with limiting structures that carry their own guarantee. He may fail in his formulation of the less obvious limiting structures; he may expect others with greater penetration of mind and greater detachment of spirit to improve on the formulation at which he has arrived; but at least he has some grasp of the principle of limiting structures and so some firm foothold against the fear of general bias.

There are, then, degrees of certitude, and their ground lies behind the proximate criterion of the virtually unconditioned in the more obscure region of the remote criterion. Only if this obscure region were to become completely clarified, either in fact, or more radically as a matter of principle, would certitude reach the absolute of infallibility.

2.2 The Definition of Truth [552]

The definition of truth was introduced implicitly in our account of the notion of being. For being was identified with what is to be known through intelligent grasp and reasonable affirmation; but the only reasonable affirmation is the true affirmation; and so being is what is known truly. Inversely, then, knowing is true by its relation to being, and truth is a relation of knowing to being.

What is the relation? In the limiting case, when the knowing is identical with the known, the relation disappears to be replaced by an identity, and then truth consists in the absence of any difference whatever between the knowing and the known being. In the general case, when there is more than one known and one of these is a knower, it is possible to formulate a set of positive and of negative comparative judgments and then to employ this set to define implicitly such terms as 'subject,' 'object,' and 'the principal notion of objectivity.' Within this context there follows the traditional definition of truth as the conformity or correspondence of the subject's affirmations and negations to what is and is not.

2.3 The Ontological Aspect of Truth [552-53]

The identification of being with the possible object of inquiry and reflection places a restriction on what being can be. From this restriction there followed the major premise of metaphysical method, namely, the isomorphism that obtains between the structure of our knowing and the structure of its proportionate known. This isomorphism was elaborated in the chapter on the elements of metaphysics, and it was clarified still further when, in discussing what precisely was meant by the elements, we concluded to the intrinsic intelligibility of being. For what is to be known by intelligence is what is meant by the intelligible; being is what is to be known by intelligence, and so it must be intelligible, and it cannot lie beyond the intelligible or differ from it; moreover, one is confined to this view, for any other view involves one in the counterpositions that become incoherent when supposed to be grasped intelligently and affirmed reasonably.

Ontological truth, then, is the intrinsic intelligibility of being. It is the conformity of being to the conditions of its being known through intelligent inquiry and critical reflection. Moreover, it leads to a distinction between material and spiritual being, between the intrinsically intelligible being that is not intelligent and the intrinsically intelligible being that is intelligent. Since the difference between matter and spirit can be shown to lie in the fact that the material is not intrinsically independent of the merely empirical residue while the spiritual is, there follows a closer determination of the possibility of knowledge in terms of matter and immateriality.

The general theorem is, then, the identification with intrinsic intelligibility of: (1) being, (2) unity, (3) truth in its ontological aspect, and, as will appear in the next chapter, (4) the good.

2.4 Truth and Expression   [553–58]

As knowledge rises on the three levels of experience and imagination, understanding and conception, and reflection and judgment, so in expression there may be distinguished three components. For as affirmative or negative utterance, the expression corresponds to reflection and judgment. As a significant combination of words, the expression corresponds to insight and conception. As an instrumental multiplicity, the expression corresponds to the material multiplicity of experience and imagination.

This isomorphism of knowledge and expression is not to be mistaken for an identity. It is one thing to assert and another to judge, for men can lie. It is one thing to understand experience and another to hit upon the happy and effective combination of phrases and sentences. It is one thing to be rich in experience and another to be fluent with words. To the judgment of knowledge, expression adds an act of willing to speak truthfully or deceitfully. To the insight of knowledge, expression adds a further practical insight that governs the verbal flow towards its end of communication. Finally, the manifold of the presentations of sense and of the representations of imagination is succeeded in expression by the manifold of conventional signs.

If we have emphasized the distinction between knowledge and expression, we have also to take into account their interpenetration. For coming to know is a process; it advances by stages in which inquiry yields insights only to give rise to further questions that lead to further insights and still further questions. At each stage of the process it is helpful to fix what has been reached and to formulate in some fashion what remains to be sought. So expression enters into the very process of learning, and the attainment of knowledge tends to coincide with the attainment of the ability to express it.

The interpenetration of knowledge and expression implies a solidarity, almost a fusion, of the development of knowledge and the development of language. Words are sensible: they support and heighten the resonance of human intersubjectivity; the mere presence of another releases in the dynamism of sensitive consciousness a modification of the flow of feelings and emotions, images and memories, attitudes and sentiments; but words possess their own retinues of associated representations and affects, and so the addition of speech to presence brings about a specialized, directed modification of intersubjective reaction and response. Still, beyond the psychology of words, there is their meaning. They belong together in typical patterns, and learning a language is a matter, first, of grasping such patterns and, secondly, of gradually allowing the insights by which the patterns are grasped to be short-circuited by a sensitive routine that permits the attention of intelligence to concentrate on higher-level controls. Just as the concert pianist is not thinking of the place of middle C, so the speaker or writer is not thinking of the meaning of his words. *Rem tene et verba sequentur.*[8] But these sensitive routines, these typical patterns are able to carry the meaning of words only because initially there occurred the insights that linked words intelligibly

8 [Caius Julius Victor, *Ars Rhetorica* I: Rem tene; verba sequentur.]

not only with one another but also with terms of meaning and with sources of meaning.

The relationship of words to one another is the easiest to formulate. Basic lexicography assigns each word its meaning by quoting from accepted authors the types of sentence in which the word occurs. The mathematician, the scientist, the philosopher employs the technique of implicit definition (or Aristotelian declaration by analogy) to fix the meaning of his fundamental terms and relations. Just as knowledge advances through accumulations of insights to higher viewpoints, so also language advances from a level of elementary meanings through higher viewpoints to ever more compendious vocal gestures. So we speak of Platonism and Aristotelianism, of Christianity and Islam, of Renaissance and Reformation, of Enlightenment and Revolution, of Science and Faith, but to say what we mean by such words would call for volumes of other words.

Were words related only to other words, their meaning would never be more than verbal. But the mere fact that a word can occur in a sentence that is affirmed endows it with a basic reference to the objective of intelligent and rational consciousness, to being. Moreover, this basic reference, which is the core of all meaning, admits differentiation and specialization. There are many words: some are substantival, because they refer to intelligible and concrete unities; some are verbal, because they refer to conjugate acts; some are adjectival or adverbial, because they refer to the regularity or frequency of the occurrence of acts or to potentialities for such regularities or frequencies. Finally, since the development of language fuses with the development of knowledge, the meaning of words depends not only upon the metaphysical matrix of terms of meaning but also upon the experiential sources of meaning. Prior to the explanatory conjugates, defined by their relations to one another, there are the experiential conjugates, that involve a triple correlation of classified experiences, classified contents of experience, and corresponding names. The being to be known as an intelligible unity differentiated by verifiable regularities and frequencies begins by being conceived heuristically, and then its unknown nature is differentiated by experiential conjugates.

We are now, perhaps, in a position to come to grips with our problem, namely, the relation between truth and expression. We began by emphasizing the distinction between knowledge and its expression. But we followed up this contention with no less insistence on the genetic interpenetration of knowledge and language. Because of this interpenetration there arises the conviction that, while knowing and stating are distinct, still they run so much together that they are inseparable. What is known, what is meant, and what is said can be distinguished; but the distinctions point merely to differences of aspect in what inevitably is the same thing.

So it is that efforts to explain what we mean sooner or later, and sooner rather than later, end with the global assertion that what is meant is obvious and neither needs nor admits any explanation. However, it is not difficult to introduce a crucial experiment that reestablishes the gulf between knowledge and expression. For, after all, it is only a matter of common coincidence that this gulf disappears. Commonly it does happen that conversation occurs between people that share the same common sense, that writing is directed to readers that already understand in considerable detail the subject under discussion. But there also is communication between people with different habitual accumulations of insights, between teachers and pupils, between original thinkers and their contemporaries, between the great men of the past and their present readers. And then the greater the gap between the intellectual development of writer and reader, the more stupendous can become the distinction between knowledge and expression.

By way of illustration let us suppose that a writer proposes to communicate some insight A to a reader. Then by an insight B the writer will grasp the reader's habitual accumulation of insights C; by a further insight D he will grasp the deficiencies in insight E^o that must be made up before the reader can grasp the insight A; finally, the writer must reach a practical set of insights F that will govern his verbal flow, the shaping of his sentences, their combination into paragraphs, the sequence of paragraphs in chapters and of chapters in books. Clearly, this practical insight F differs notably from the insight A to be communicated. It is determined by the insight A as its principal objective. But it is also determined by the insight B, which settles both what the writer need not explain and, no less, the resources of language on which he can rely to secure effective communication. Further, it is determined by the insight D, which fixes a subsidiary goal that has to be attained if the principal goal is to be reached. Finally, the expression will be a failure in the measure that insights B and D miscalculate the habitual development C and the relevant deficiencies E of the anticipated reader.

It follows, then, that properly speaking expression is not true or false.

Truth pertains to the judgment inasmuch as it proceeds from a grasp of the virtually unconditioned, inasmuch as it conforms to the being it affirms, and inasmuch as it demands an intrinsic intelligibility in being as a condition of the possibility of knowing. Expressions are instrumental. They are related to the truth of knowledge. Similarly, they are related to the moral truth of the will that communicates knowledge. But in themselves expressions are merely adequate or inadequate.

Moreover, in the general case, the adequacy of expression is not measured exclusively by its correspondence with the knowledge to be communicated. That knowledge sets a principal goal; it defines a central meaning. But besides the principal goal, there can be a subsidiary goal; besides the central meaning, there can be a more or less peripheral meaning. For the speaker may be able to convey what he wishes to say only if he first conveys other insights that in one manner or another enable his hearers to grasp the message with which he is concerned.

Further, adequacy is a variable standard. If one has anything much to say, then one cannot say it all at once. If one has anything very significant to say, then probably one will not be able to express the whole of it except to a rather specialized audience. Such limitations restrict the adequacy with which even one's principal meaning is expressed. But there are further limitations on the adequacy with which subordinate and peripheral meanings are expressed. For one thing leads to another. If insights D must be communicated in order to communicate insight A, other insights G may be needed to communicate insights D; in turn, insights G will need to be preceded by insights H, until one has said all one knows and has discovered, perhaps, a few points that one needed to clear up for oneself. But human expression is never complete expression. It keeps its eye on the central meaning; it expedites subordinate and peripheral meanings by lowering standards of adequacy to a sufficient approximation to the purpose in hand; and, quite clearly, it cannot add in a parenthesis this somewhat involved account of the variable standard of adequate expression.

However, this account of the relation between truth and expression rests on the position that truth resides in the internal act of judgment, of assenting or dissenting. But against every position there stands a counterposition. It can be maintained that truth and falsity reside not in the judgment but in the expression, that if judgments are true or false then that is so because they agree with true or false expressions, that the public or common field through which men can communicate is not an absolute, independent of all subjects because reached through the virtually unconditioned, but simply the atmosphere which, as we breathe it in common, so also we set vibrating in the various manners that carry our words from one to another.

Besides the basic counterpositions, there are minor oppositions. One can grant that truth and falsity reside in the judgment, yet one can conceive the relation between truth and falsity in terms of a mistaken theory of knowledge. Thus, the Scotist view that words correspond to concepts and that concepts are produced in us by the formal aspects of things involves a rigid correlation between knowledge and expression. If its inadequacy is not apparent when communication occurs in the simple case when speaker and hearer share the same intellectual development, it breaks down with a magnificent irrelevance to facts when one recalls the long and fruitless verbal debates of the fourteenth century or the oceans of commentary that ever flow in ever renewed interpretations of the greater works of human intelligence.

Finally, there is the popular fallacy. If often enough the meaning of an expression is simple and obvious, why should it not always be so? Why should honest truth ever hide in the voluminous folds of a lengthy, complicated, and difficult exposition? Perhaps we have done something to meet this objection. Once one has understood, the content of an insight is simple and obvious even though it is expressed poorly. Until one has understood, the content of an insight is as hidden as the far side of the moon. Accordingly, one finds the meaning of expressions simple and obvious when the speaker or writer is communicating what one understands already, and one finds their meaning obscure and difficult when he is stating what one has still to learn. In the latter case no amount of pedagogic and linguistic skill will eliminate the necessity of the effort to learn. For this reason only the man that understands everything already is in a position to demand that all meaning be simple and obvious to him.

2.5 The Appropriation of Truth   [558–62]

To appropriate a truth is to make it one's own. The essential appropriation of truth is cognitional. However, our reasonableness demands consistency between what we know and what we do; and so there is a volitional appropriation of truth that consists in our willingness to live up to it, and a sensitive appropriation of truth that consists in an adaptation of our sensibility to the requirements of our knowledge and our decisions.

The essential appropriation of truth sets a threefold problem. First, there is the problem of learning, of gradually acquiring the accumulation of habitual insights that constitute a viewpoint, and eventually of moving from lower to ever higher viewpoints.

Secondly, there is the problem of identification. By insights one grasps unities and correlations; but besides the unity, there are the elements to be unified; and besides the correlation, there are the elements to be distinguished and related. Until one gets the insight, one has no clue (apart from the directions given by a teacher) for picking out accurately the elements that are to be unified or related. But once the insight is reached, one is able to find in one's own experience just what it is that falls under the insight's grasp and what lies outside it. However, ability is one thing, and performance is another. Identification is performance. Its effect is to make one possess the insight as one's own, to be assured in one's use of it, to be familiar with the range of its relevance. Aristotle remarked, I think, that if one understands, one can teach.[9] But the understanding that enables one to teach adds identification to insight. By that addition one is able to select and arrange and indicate to others the combination of sensible elements that will give rise to the same insight in them. One is able to vary the elements at the demand of circumstances. One is able to put the questions that elicit from the pupil indications of his blind spots, and then to proceed afresh to the task of bringing him to the prior insights he must reach before he can master the present lesson.

Thirdly, there is the problem of orientation. Every discovery can be formulated either as a position or as a counterposition. But counterpositions both seem obvious and yet are destined to ultimate reversal. Inasmuch as we inquire intelligently and reflect critically, we operate under the drive of the detached and disinterested desire to know. But once we have reached the truth, we are prone to find it unreal, to shift from the realm of the intelligible and the unconditioned back into the realm of sense, to turn away from truth and being and settle down like good animals in our palpable environment. In the measure that we fail to orientate ourselves towards truth, we both distort what we know and restrict what we might know. We distort what we know by imposing

9 [See Aristotle, *Metaphysics*, I, 2, 982a 10–19.]

upon it a mistaken notion of reality, a mistaken notion of objectivity, and a mistaken notion of knowledge. We restrict what we might know; for we can justify to ourselves and to others the labor spent in learning only by pointing to the palpable benefits it brings, and the demand satisfied by palpable benefits does not enjoy the unrestricted range of the detached and disinterested desire to know.

The reader will note that the three problems of cognitional appropriation run parallel to the three levels in our knowing. The problem of learning is met on the level of understanding and formulation. The problem of identification is met on the level of experience (where 'experience' is used broadly to denote not only sense experience but also intellectual and rational consciousness). The problem of orientation is met on the level of reflection and judgment when at last we grasp^p (1) that every issue closes when we can say definitively, 'It is so,' or 'It is not so,' (2) that the objective of knowing is being, (3) that, while being is a protean notion, still its content is determined by intelligent grasp and reasonable affirmation and, after affirmation, by nothing else.

We have cast our account of appropriation in terms of problems rather than in terms of results, and this purely dynamic viewpoint is of some importance. For it excludes all fetishism, all mistaking of means for ends. Clear definition, precise language, orderly arrangement, rigorous proof, and all the other paraphernalia of cognitional activity possess their value. They serve to mark clearly the successive stages of advance. They consolidate in masterly fashion what at any given moment appears to be attained solidly and more or less permanently. They provide magnificent expressions of the truth that is to be appropriated. But of their very nature they are static. They shed no light either on the pupil's task of coming to appropriate them or on the investigator's task of going beyond them to the appropriation of further truth. Yet it is precisely that twofold task that an account of appropriation should envisage. The well-formulated system becomes mine insofar as I understand it, insofar as I can identify its empirical elements in my experience, insofar as I grasp the unconditioned or the approximation to the unconditioned that grounds a reasonable affirmation of it, insofar as my orientation permits me to be content with that affirmation as the final increment in my knowledge of the system and does not drive me to seek in the 'already out there now' some imaginative representation of what, after all, it really means. Exactly the same procedure governs efforts to go beyond the well-formulated system and to generate the stresses and strains in knowledge that will lead it to its replacement by a more adequate account of reality.

It may be noted further that the three problems of appropriation are solidary. One cannot go far in understanding without turning to the problem of identification, and without understanding, one is unable to identify. Again, a mistaken orientation gives rise to pseudo problems, but in the limit pseudo problems bring about their own reversal and with it the correction of the mistaken orientation. Thus, contemporary physics finds itself compelled to say that it deals with the entities that satisfy certain types of equations, even though such entities and their processes defy our powers of imagination. Finally, unless one gives oneself to the effort to understand, one has no means of identifying in one's experience what precisely is meant by the proper orientation of the detached and disinterested desire towards the universe of truth and being.

In a somewhat looser fashion, cognitional appropriation of truth is solidary with volitional and with sensitive appropriation. Bad will makes truth unwelcome, and unwelcome truth tends to be overlooked. For the appropriation of truth even in the cognitional field makes demands upon the whole man; his consciousness has to slip into the intellectual pattern of experience, and it has to remain there with the minimum of distractions; his subconsciousness has to throw up the images that lead to insight; his desire to know has to be sufficiently dominant to keep ever further questions complementing and correcting previous insights; his observation and his memory have to contribute spontaneously to the presentation and the recall of relevant data, in which the fulfilment or nonfulfilment of the unconditioned is to be found. Bad will, however, either prevents one from initiating an inquiry or, if that cannot be avoided, from prosecuting it earnestly and effectively. For the collaboration of all our powers towards the grasping of truth, bad will substitutes their conspiracy to bring forth doubts about truth and evidence for error. Inversely, if the attainment of truth demands good will, still good will, as we shall see in the next chapter, is nothing but a willingness to follow the lead of intelligence and truth. So it is that man is boxed in: without the appropriation of truth, his will cannot be positively good; and without good will he cannot proceed to the attainment of truth. On this[q] basic problem something has been said already in the account of genuineness as the operator of human intellectual development; and something more will be added in the chapters to follow.

Human intelligence and reasonableness function as the higher integration of the sensitive flow of percepts and images, emotions and feelings, attitudes and sentiments, words and deeds. It follows that, as the cognitional and volitional appropriations of truth are solidary with each other, so also they condition and are conditioned by adaptations of human sensibility. Here the basic problem is to discover the dynamic images that both correspond to intellectual contents, orientations, and determinations, yet also possess in the sensitive field the power to issue forth not only into words but also into deeds. On this problem we have touched in asserting the necessity of either mysteries or myths; and to it we shall return in attempting to analyze the structure of history.[r] For the moment it must suffice to draw attention to the fact that, as intellectual development occurs through insights into sensible presentations and imaginative representations, so also the intelligent and reasonable control of human living can be effective only in the measure that it has at its disposal the symbols and signs by which it translates its directives to human sensibility. Finally, unless one can carry out in deeds what one knows and wills, then the willing already is a failure, and from failing will to bad will to unconcern for truth there are the easy and, unfortunately, familiar steps.

3   The Truth of Interpretation   [562–94]

3.1 The Problem   [562–64]

The problem of interpretation can best be introduced by distinguishing between expression, simple interpretation, and reflective interpretation.

As has been seen, an expression is a verbal flow governed by a practical insight F that depends upon a principal insight A to be communicated, upon a grasp B of the anticipated audience's habitual intellectual development C, and upon a grasp D of the deficiencies in insight E that have to be overcome if the insight A is to be communicated.

By an interpretation will be meant a second expression addressed to a different audience. Hence, since it is an expression, it will be guided by a practical insight F' that depends upon a principal insight A' to be communicated, upon a grasp B' of the anticipated audience's habitual intellectual development C', and upon a grasp D' of the deficiencies in insight E' that have to be overcome if the principal insight A' is to be communicated.

In the simple interpretation the principal insight A' to be communicated purports to coincide with the principal insight A of the original expression. Hence, differences between the practical insights F and F' depend directly upon differences between the habitual insights B and B', D and D', and remotely upon differences between the habitual developments C and C', and the deficiencies E and E'.

Now the simple interpretation gives rise to further questions. On an elementary level people ask why a faithful interpretation should differ from the original expression. If this issue is met by appealing to the fact that both the original expression and the interpretation are relative to their respective audiences, there arises the problem of settling the differences between the audiences and of incorporating them into the interpretation.

A reflective interpretation, then, is guided by a practical insight F'' that depends upon insights A'', B'', and D''. But now the insight B'' is a grasp of the audience's habitual grasp C'' of its own intellectual development C' and of the difference between that development and the habitual accumulation of the insights C in the initial audience. Similarly, the insight D'' is a grasp of the audience's deficiencies E'' in grasping the differences between the habitual developments C' and C, and so in understanding the differences between the deficiencies E' and E and between the practical insights F' and F. Finally, the principal insight A'' to be communicated will be a grasp of the identity of the insight A communicated in the original expression and of the insight A' communicated in the simple interpretation.

However, the reflective interpretation suffers from two obvious difficulties. In the first place, it is relative to its anticipated audience, and audiences are an ever shifting manifold. Each culture in each of the stages of its progress and decline is divided into a variety of schools, attitudes, orientations, and in each of these varieties there are numerous degrees of intellectual attainment. It would be a matter of considerable difficulty to work out a reflective interpretation that satisfied a single audience; but there is an enormous range of other audiences that will remain to be satisfied; and the single audience one does satisfy will not live forever. In the second place, it is all very well to talk glibly about the habitual intellectual development and the deficiencies of the original and the present audience and the determination of the differences in the practical insights governing the original expression and the simple interpretation. But it is quite another matter to set about the investigation of such obscure objects, to reach something better than a mere guess about them, and to find an appropriate and effective manner of communicating the fruits of one's inquiry. Reflective interpretation is a smart idea, a beautiful object of thought. But is it a practical possibility? Has it ever been achieved?

This brings us to the basic problem of interpretation. It may very well happen that any simple interpretation is correct, that it hits off for a contemporary audience the principal insight communicated by the original document. It may also happen that the interpreter knows his interpretation to be correct, that he grasps the virtually unconditioned, or at least that he grasps the approximation of his interpretation to the virtually unconditioned. For analogous to common sense there is a historical sense. Just as we by common sense can know how our contemporaries would or would not speak or act in any of a series of ordinary and typical situations, so the scholar by a long familiarity with the documents and monuments of another age and by an ever increasing accumulation of complementary insights can arrive at a participation of the common sense of another period, and by this historical sense can tell how the men and women of that time would or would not speak or act in certain types of situation.

However, just as our common sense is open to individual, group, and general bias, so also is the historical sense. Moreover, just as our common sense cannot analyze itself or criticize itself or arrive at an abstract formulation of its central nucleus, so also the historical sense is limited in a similar fashion; both are far more likely to be correct in pronouncing verdicts than in assigning exact and convincing reasons for them. But if interpretation is to be scientific, then the grounds for the interpretation have to be assignable; if interpretation is to be scientific, then there will not be a range of different interpretations due to the individual, group, and general bias of the historical sense of different experts; if interpretation is to be scientific, then it has to discover some method of conceiving and determining the habitual development of all audiences, and it has to invent some technique by which its expression escapes relativity to particular and incidental audiences.

3.2 The Notion of a Universal Viewpoint   [564–68]

By a universal viewpoint will be meant a potential totality of genetically and dialectically ordered viewpoints. Our present concern will be to clarify this notion. Though we believe it to be relevant to the problem of scientific interpretation, its relevance is a further question that can be discussed only later.

First, then, the totality in question is potential. A universal viewpoint is not universal history. It is not a Hegelian dialectic that is complete apart from matters of fact. It is not a Kantian a priori that in itself is determinate and merely awaits imposition upon the raw materials of vicarious experience. It is simply a heuristic structure that contains virtually the various ranges of possible alternatives of interpretations; it can list its own contents only through the stimulus of documents and historical inquiries; it can select between alternatives and differentiate its generalities only by appealing to the accepted norms of historical investigation.

Secondly, the totality is of viewpoints. Hence it is concerned with the principal acts of meaning that lie in insights and judgments, and it reaches these principal acts by directing attention to the experience, the understanding, and the critical reflection of the interpreter. Accordingly, it differs radically from such disciplines as phonetics, comparative grammar, the principles of lexicography, or linguistic and stylistic analysis, for though they ultimately are concerned with meaning, their attention is centered directly upon expression. In contrast, the universal viewpoint is concerned with the interpreter's capacity to grasp meanings; it would open his mind to ideas that do not lie on the surface and to views that diverge enormously from his own; it would enable him to find clues where otherwise he might look but would fail to see; it would equip him with a capacity to transport his thinking to the level and texture of another culture in another epoch. There are the external sources of historical interpretation, and in the main they consist in spatially ordered marks on paper or parchment, papyrus or stone. But there are also sources of interpretation immanent in the historiographer himself, in his ability to distinguish and recombine elements in his own experience, in his ability to work backwards from contemporary to earlier accumulations of insights in human development, in his ability to envisage the protean possibilities of the notion of being, the core of all meaning, which varies in content with the experience, the insights, the judgments, and the habitual orientation of each individual.

Thirdly, the universal viewpoint is an ordered totality of viewpoints. It has its base in an adequate self-knowledge and in the consequent metaphysics. It has a retrospective expansion in the various genetic series of discoveries through which man could advance to his present knowledge. It has a dialectical expansion in the many formulations of discoveries due to the polymorphic consciousness of man, in the invitation issued by positions to further development, and in the implication in counterpositions of their own reversal. Finally, it can reach a concrete presentation of any formulation of any discovery through the identification in personal experience of the elements that, as confused or as distinguished and related, as related under this or that orientation of polymorphic consciousness, could combine to make the position or counterposition humanly convincing.

However, as the totality is potential, so also is the ordering of the viewpoints. The totality is a heuristic structure; its contents are sequences of unknowns; and the relations between the unknowns are determinate not specifically but only generically. Thus, there are genetic sequences, but the same discoveries can be made in different manners. There are dialectically opposed formulations with their contrasting invitations to further development and to reversal; but the dialectical oppositions are not simply the clear-cut identifications of the real either with being or with the 'already out there now,' of the objective either with the intelligent and reasonable or with elementary extroversion, of knowledge either with inquiry and critical reflection or with the look that is prior to all questions; on the contrary, such extremes tend to merge in the ambivalence of the aesthetic, the dramatic, and the practical patterns of experience, to give rise to questions that not only are unsolved but also inadequately conceived, to make their clearest appearance not in the field of knowledge but rather in the volitional tension between moral aspiration and practical living.

Not only is the ordering potential but also what is ordered is itself advancing from the generic to the specific, from the undifferentiated to the differentiated, from the awkward, the global, the spontaneous to the expert, the precise, the methodical. Our distinctions between mathematics, science, common sense, and philosophy are based upon the different manners in which insights can be accumulated. Since the manner in which insights are accumulated is simply a dynamic structure that can be utilized without conscious advertence, it is possible for us to ask whether primitives or children have any interest in mathematical, scientific, or philosophic questions. But even if interests were to be ascribed to primitives or to children, it would be necessary to add not merely that they were uncomplicated by the divisions and subdivisions of later thought but also that they mingled indiscriminately with the questions of common sense and tended both to distort and to be distorted by commonsense procedures.

Fourthly, the universal viewpoint is universal not by abstractness but by potential completeness. It attains its inclusiveness, not by stripping objects of their peculiarities, but by envisaging subjects in their necessities. There are no interpretations without interpreters. There are no interpreters without polymorphic unities of empirical, intelligent, and rational consciousness. There are no expressions to be interpreted without other similar unities of consciousness. Nor has the work of interpreting anything more than a material determinant in the spatially ordered set of marks in documents and monuments. If the interpreter assigns any meaning to the marks, then the experiential component in that meaning will be derived from his experience, the intellectual component will be derived from his intelligence, the rational component will be derived from his critical reflection on the critical reflection of another. Such are the underlying necessities, and from them springs the potential completeness that makes the universal viewpoint universal.

To approach the same issue from another angle, the core of meaning is the notion of being, and that notion is protean. Being is (or is thought to be) whatever is (or is thought to be) grasped intelligently and affirmed reasonably. There is, then, a universe of meanings, and its four dimensions are the full range of possible combinations (1) of experiences and lack of experience, (2) of insights and lack of insight, (3) of judgments and of failures to judge, and (4) of the various orientations of the polymorphic consciousness of man. Now in the measure[s] that one grasps the structure of this protean notion of being, one possesses the base and ground from which one can proceed to the content and context of every meaning. In the measure that one explores human experience, human insights, human reflection,[t] and human polymorphic consciousness, one becomes capable, when provided with the appropriate data, of approximating to the content and context of the meaning of any given expression.

Fifthly, since what we have named the universal viewpoint is simply a corollary of our own philosophic analysis, it will be objected that we are offering not a universal viewpoint but simply the viewpoint of our own philosophy.

To meet this charge, it will be well to begin by distinguishing a universal viewpoint and a universal language. Insofar as we employ names and epithets with laudatory or pejorative implications, such as 'real' and 'illusory,' 'position' and 'counterposition,' 'intelligence' and 'obtuseness,' 'mystery' and 'myth,' it is plain enough that we are not offering a universal language. For anyone that disagreed with our views would prefer a redistribution of the implicit praise and blame. Still, there would be in principle no difficulty in reaching a universal language, for any term that was offensive to anyone could be replaced by some arbitrary name or symbol that was free from all the associations of human imagination and human feeling.

On the other hand, we would contend that there is at least one particular philosophy that could ground a universal viewpoint. For there is a particular philosophy that would take its stand upon the dynamic structure of human cognitional activity, that would distinguish the various elements involved in that structure, that would be able to construct any philosophic position by postulating appropriate and plausible omissions and confusions of the elements, that would reach its own particular views by correcting all omissions and confusions. Now such a philosophy, though particular, would provide a base and ground for a universal viewpoint; for a universal viewpoint is the potential totality of all viewpoints; the potential totality of all viewpoints lies in the dynamic structure of cognitional activity; and the dynamic structure of cognitional activity is the basis of the particular philosophy in question.

Finally, we would argue that the particular philosophy we are offering also is the particular philosophy that can ground a universal viewpoint. By this we do not mean that our views will not be improved vastly by more accurate accounts of experience, of insight and its formulation, of reflection and judgment, and of the polymorphic consciousness of man. Rather our meaning is that such improvements will not involve any radical change in the philosophy, for the philosophy rests, not on the account of experience, of insight, of judgment, and of polymorphic consciousness, but on the defining pattern of relations that bring these four into a single dynamic structure. Again, it is the grasp of that structure that grounds the universal viewpoint since, once the structure is reached, the potential totality of viewpoints is reached. For more refined accounts of the elements in the structure modify, not the potential totality, but the accuracy and completeness with which one can proceed from the universal viewpoint to the reconstruction of particular contents and contexts of meaning.

3.3 Levels and Sequences of Expression   [568–73]

As the notion of the universal viewpoint, so also some account of levels and sequences of expression is, we believe, a necessary preliminary to a treatment of the problem of scientific interpretation. The immediate task will be to classify modes of expression, not in terms of language or of style, but in terms of meanings. Only later shall we attempt to indicate the relevance of such a classification to a science of hermeneutics.

Already distinctions have been drawn between (1) sources, (2) acts, and (3) terms of meaning. Sources of meaning lie in the experiential, intellectual, and rational levels of knowing. Acts of meaning are principal or instrumental; principal acts are formal or full inasmuch as they are constituted by acts of defining, supposing, considering, or by acts of assenting or dissenting; instrumental acts are sensible manifestations of meaning through gestures, speech, and writing. Terms of meaning, finally, are whatever happens to be meant; they form a universe of meanings that includes not only the universe of being but also the totality of terms of suppositions and of false affirmations and negations.

Now the distinction between different levels of expression rests upon a consideration of the sources of meaning both in the speaker or writer and in the hearer or reader. Thus, the expression may have its source (1) simply in the experience of the speaker, as in an exclamation, or (2) in artistically ordered experiential elements, as in a song, or (3) in a reflectively tested intelligent ordering of experiential elements, as in a statement of fact, or (4) in the addition of acts of will, such as wishes and commands, to intellectual and rational knowledge. In turn, the hearer or reader may be intended to respond (1) simply on the experiential level in an intersubjective reproduction of the speaker's feelings, mood, sentiments, images, associations, or (2) both on the level of experience and on the level of insight and consideration, or (3) on the three levels of experience, insight, and judgment, or (4) not only on the three cognitional levels but also in the practical manner that includes an act of will.

The intended response of the hearer or reader may be obscure. But as expression becomes specialized, the differences become more and more manifest. Advertisers and propaganda ministries aim at psychological conditioning; they desire neither adequate insight nor detached reflection nor rational choices but simply the establishment of types of habituation, familiarity, association, automatism, that will dispense with further questions. In contrast, literary writing would convey insights and stimulate reflection, but its mode of operation is indirect. Words are sensible entities; they possess associations with images, memories, and feelings; and the skilful writer is engaged in exploiting the resources of language to attract, hold, and absorb attention. But if there is no frontal attack on the reader's intelligence, there is the insinuation of insights through the images from which they subtly emerge. If there is no methodical summing up of the pros and cons of a judgment, there is an unhurried, almost incidental, display of the evidence without, perhaps, even a suggested question.

Direct concern with the reader's understanding appears in scientific writing. On the introductory level, it aims at provoking insights through illustrations and diagrams. On the advanced level, it becomes the treatise. Then all terms are defined implicitly or explicitly; all basic relations are postulated explicitly; all derived relations are deduced. Thus, the practical insight F that guides the scientific writer's verbal flow is reached by transposing from logic as a science to logic as a technique; the bulk of logic can itself be formulated in a treatise; and the only attention paid to the reader's habitual intellectual development and its deficiencies appears in a prefatory note that indicates the other treatises that must be mastered before tackling the present elucubration.

Direct concern with the reader's judgments emerges in philosophic writing. Just as the author of an introduction to a science uses any images that, he believes, will enable the reader to reach the relevant insights, so the author of an introduction to philosophy appeals to any insights within the reader's intellectual range. For as the scientist is indifferent to the images, as long as the insights are attained, so the philosopher is indifferent to the insights, as long as the reader is made to mount to the level of critical reflection. Further, while advanced scientific writing aims at setting forth clearly and exactly the terms, relations, and implications that proceed from understanding and provide the materials for judgment, advanced philosophic writing is concerned, not to submit ordered materials to a reader's judgment, but to reveal to that judgment the immanent controls to which ineluctably it is subjected. So it is that the philosopher keeps repeating, either on the grand scale of the totality of questions, or with respect to particular issues, the breakthrough that brings to light the empirically, intelligently, and rationally conscious unity of the knower, the encirclement effected by the protean notion of being, and the confinement that results from identifying being with the intelligently grasped and reasonably affirmed.

Such, in outline, is the distinction between the different levels of expression. It envisages the expression as a flow of sensible events that (1) originates in the cognitional and volitional sources of meaning of a speaker or writer, and (2) terminates in a reproduction of sources of meaning in a hearer or reader. It is a distinction that grounds not an actual but a potential classification of expressions, for while the original and terminal sources of meaning are conceived clearly and distinctly, there remains abundant room for the introduction of further differentiations and nuances. Because the classification is potential rather than actual, it does not impose upon the interpreter any a priori Procrustean bed which his documents have to fit, but leaves him free to exercise to the full his ingenuity and subtlety in determining a writer's sources and intention. At the same time, because the differences between experience, understanding, judgment, and will are defined systematically, the determination of the level of expression has systematic implications which, even when they are mere generalities, at least will prevent interpreters and their critics from committing the grosser blunders. There is an intersubjective component to expression that emerges and is transmitted apart from insights and judgments. There is a supervening component of intelligence that admits various degrees of explicitness and deliberateness. There is a still higher component of truth or falsity that may emerge at the term of a series of insights as insight emerges at the term of a series of imaginative representations. Finally, there can be the entry of a volitional component, and its relevance is a fourth variable. To recognize the existence of levels of expression is to eliminate the crude assumptions of the interpreters, and still more of their critics, that take it for granted that all expression lies on a single level, namely, the psychological, literary, scientific, or philosophic level with which they happen to be most familiar.

Besides levels of expression, there also are sequences. Development in general is a process from the undifferentiated to the differentiated, from the generic to the specific, from the global and awkward to the expert and precise. It would simplify enormously the task of the interpreter if, from the beginning of human speech and writing, there existed and were recognized the full range of specialized modes of expression. But the fact is that the specializations had to be invented, and the use of the inventions presupposes a corresponding development or education of prospective audiences or readers. Some early Greek philosophers wrote verse; Plato employed a highly literary dialogue; Aristotle proceeded in the manner of descriptive science; the medieval writers, in their *quaestiones*, developed a compound of the dialogue and the dogmatic decision; Spinoza and Kant molded philosophy in the form of the scientific treatise; Hegelian dialectic seems the initial essay in philosophic writing that envisaged the totality of possible positions. If there is any truth in this hurried and rough indication of the evolution of philosophic expression, then there will be a complementary truth inasmuch as scientific writing will pass through a period in which its difference from philosophy will be obscure (so Newton's main work was entitled *Principia mathematica philosophiae naturalis*) and, similarly, literary writing will have its period of fusion or confusion with scientific and philosophic concerns.

However, our affirmation of sequences of expression must be confined to its proper generality. The one point that we wish to make is that specialized modes of expression have to be evolved. Thus, at the present time a narrative that opens with the words 'Once upon a time ...' may be expected to be a fairy story, to offer a certain stimulus to imagination and feeling, and to be exempt from reasonable criticism on the part of scientific intelligence and of philosophic reflection. In similar fashion, there exist other correlations between fields of meaning and modes of expression, but such correlations are not to be conceived as components of static systems, such as are illustrated by physical and chemical theories, but as components of dynamic systems, such as are illustrated by the genetic theories of biology, psychology, and cognitional analysis.

It follows that the problem of working out types of expression (*genera litteraria*) is to be met, not by assigning some static classification that claims validity for all time, but by determining the operators that relate the classifications relevant to one level of development to the classifications relevant to the next. Moreover, the most significant element in the theory of types of expression will be the operators. For the great difficulties of interpretation arise when the new wine of literary, scientific, and philosophic leaders cannot but be poured into the old bottles of established modes of expression. In such cases the type of expression, so far from providing a sure index to the level of meaning, originally was an impediment which the writer's thought could not shake off, and now easily can become a misleading signpost for the unwary interpreter.

3.4 *Limitations of the Treatise* [573–77]

A little learning is a dangerous thing, and the adage has, perhaps, its most abundant illustrations from the application of logic to the tasks of interpretation. A familiarity with the elements of logic can be obtained by a very modest effort and in a very short time. Until one has made notable progress in cognitional analysis, one is constantly tempted to mistake the rules of logic for the laws of thought. And as all reading involves interpreting, there follows automatically the imposition upon documents of meanings and implications that 'logically' they must possess but in fact do not bear.

It will serve (1) to bring home this point, (2) to illustrate in a particular case the significance of levels and sequences of expression, and (3) to indicate the relativity to an audience that commonly afflicts expression, if we add to our preliminary considerations a note on the limitations of the treatise. For the treatise is subjected legitimately to logical analysis and extension; it undertakes to define all its terms implicitly or explicitly, to prove all its conclusions, and to accept every conclusion that follows logically from its premises. Again, the treatise stands precisely and unambiguously upon a single level of expression, for its function primarily is to present clearly, exactly, and fully the content and the implications of a determinate and coherent set of insights. Finally, the treatise approximates to freedom from relativity to an audience, for the practical insight that governs its verbal flow is an application of logic, and this practical insight depends simply on the principal insight to be communicated, since the treatise mercilessly disregards the habitual intellectual development and the anticipated deficiencies in insight of its readers.

The first limitation of the treatise appears in the expression of logic itself. For it seems that the introduction and the first approximation to one's basic definitions and rules have to be expressed in ordinary language. Once one begins to operate under the guidance of the definitions and rules, everything will proceed automatically with perfect exactitude and rigor. But one has to take one's initial steps into this realm of automatic security without perfect exactitude and without perfect rigor through expression that is relative to an audience and successful when the audience happens to be sized up correctly.

The second limitation of the treatise appears in the field of mathematics. Any department of mathematics can be cast in the form of a treatise by the method of logical formalization. But as Gödel's theorem implies, for every set of mathematical definitions and axioms there is also a set of further questions that arise, but cannot be answered, on the basis of the definitions and axioms. Hence mathematics cannot be included within a single treatise, and no matter how long one's series of treatises may be, there always will be occasion for further discoveries and further treatises.

Further limitations appear when one turns from mathematics to such sciences as physics and chemistry. A logic of terms and relations, universals and particulars, is no longer adequate. There are needed distinctions between terms that specify experiential conjugates, explanatory conjugates, events, and things; there are needed relations between experiential conjugates, between explanatory conjugates, between things and such relations, and between conjugates, frequencies, and events. Moreover, the greater logical complexity is only the minor difficulty. For while static system constitutes the intelligibility of physics and chemistry, still our knowledge of such system is on the move. Its more or less definitive acquisitions can be cast quite usefully in the form of a treatise; but the contemporary state of the question in any science never consists simply in such more or less definitive acquisitions; there also are tentative solutions, tendencies, and unsolved problems that point to the lines of future development yet would be quite misrepresented if expressed in the form of the treatise. Accordingly, while the historical development of physics, chemistry, and allied sciences can be indicated by an unfinished series of treatises in each subject, still the series of treatises cannot represent adequately the series of states of knowledge in the subjects.

The limitations of the treatise become painfully evident when one shifts from the static systems of physics and chemistry to the dynamic systems of biology and psychology. Besides the previous limitations imposed by the more complex logic and by the development of our knowledge, there now appears a still further difficulty. For the treatise expresses system, and each biological species and, on the human level, each individual psyche is system on the move. Unfortunately, treatises cannot move; definitions and postulates have the eternal quality of Plato's Ideas; their implications are perpetually the same; but the growth of an organism or the development of a psyche is a movement from a generic, rudimentary, undifferentiated system to a specific, expert, differentiated system; and the proper concern of the scientist in the field of genetics is not the several stages of the dynamic system but rather the operators that bring about the successive transformations from each stage to the next. Nor is one to entertain the hope that some day when such operators are well known there may be developed a more complicated logic that will handle the operators with the exactitude, the rigor, and the automatic security that now is enjoyed by the mathematical treatise.[u] For neither the organism nor the psyche develops exactly, rigorously, and securely; it advances tentatively; it adapts to a nonsystematic manifold of circumstance; it is what it is because exactitude, rigor, and automatic security are irrelevant to the problems that are to be solved only vitally and by consciousness.

Still further limitations of the treatise make their appearance when one turns to the human level. To the complexities of genetic method there have now to be added the graver complexities of dialectical method. For the sake of simplicity we have worked out our philosophic position in terms of simple contrasts: either the real is being or it is a subdivision in the 'already out there now'; either objectivity is reached by intelligent inquiry and critical reflection or else it is a matter of taking a good look at what is 'out there'; either knowing is mounting up the levels of experience, of understanding and formulation, of reflective grasp and judgment, or else it is the ineffable confrontation that makes the known present to the knower. Still, these contrasts stand between extremes. Men live their lives not in the intellectual pattern of experience nor again in the elementary pattern of experience but, for the most part, in some alternation and fusion of the aesthetic, the dramatic, and the practical patterns. In this middle way they oscillate between tendencies to emphasize now the intellectual orientation and now the elementary; commonly they never settle outright for either view; their minds remain ambivalent, and that ambivalence mocks all attempts to practice Socrates' maieutic art of definition in the hope of bringing them to clear and distinct knowledge of what they happen to mean. Not only must the treatise on human meanings dispense with precise terms, it also has to get along without definable relations. For, as we have seen, common sense consists in a basic nucleus of insights that never is utilized without the addition of at least one further insight into the situation at hand. Not only does this nucleus vary with occupation, social group, place, and time, but essentially it is something incomplete; its content is not relations between things but a more or less invariant element in variable relations; and that invariant element is not only without precise terms through which it might be defined, but also without verifiability through which it might be fixed by its correspondence with concrete situations.

Such, then, are the limitations of the treatise, and they reveal rather convincingly the importance of the distinction between logic as a science and logic as a technique. Logic as a science may be deduced from cognitional analysis. Just as metaphysics rests on the major premise of the isomorphism of the structures of knowing and of proportionate being, so logic rests on the major premise of the parallel between the conditions of knowing and the conditions of possible terms of meaning. Thus, terms of possible meaning are subject to principles of identity and noncontradiction, because judgment is an intrinsically rational act that affirms or denies. Again, terms of possible meaning are subject to the principle of excluded middle as long as the terms are regarded as acceptable; for if one is to employ the terms, one has no third alternative to affirming or denying them; but, of course, one commonly can anticipate the occurrence of further insights, a consequent modification of present terms, and so an elimination of the present alternatives and their replacement by other alternatives. Again, while the principles of identity, noncontradiction, and excluded middle primarily regard the act of judging and its full terms of meaning, still the act of thinking, supposing, defining, considering is preparatory to judgment and anticipatorily submits to its laws; and so the basic principles of logic hold for formal as well as full terms of meaning. Again, a study of the various kinds of insight provides the ground for the logical theory of universals and particulars, experiential and explanatory conjugates, descriptive and explanatory genera and species of things, and Aristotle's explanatory syllogism. Finally, the ground of judgment in the reflective grasp of the virtually unconditioned reveals the quite different basis of valid inference, which is of the form 'If A, then B; but A; therefore B,' where A and B are propositions or sets of propositions.

However, while logic as a science is quite well established, it owes its universality and its rigor to the simple fact that it deals with unspecified concepts and problems. Hence it differs in an essential fashion from logic as an applied technique for, as an applied technique, logic deals not with indeterminate acts and contents of conceiving and judging but with the more or less accurately determined contents of some department of human knowledge at some stage of its development. On the supposition that the knowledge of that department at that stage is both fully determinate and completely coherent, logic as a technique can be applied successfully. But in fact human knowledge commonly is in process of development, and to a notable extent the objects of human knowledge also are in process of development. As long as they are developing, they are heading for the determinacy and the coherence that will legitimate the application of logic as a technique; but until that legitimacy becomes a fact, the utility of the technique consists simply in its capacity to demonstrate the commonly admitted view that further progress remains to be made.

3.5 Interpretation and Method   [577-79]

Let us begin by recalling the structure of classical empirical method. It operates as a pair of scissors. Its upper blade consists in a heuristic structure: thus, the nature to be known will be expressed by some function; this function will satisfy differential equations that can be reached from quite general considerations; moreover, the function will satisfy a canon of invariance and, in the case of full abstraction from observers, a canon of equivalence as well. The upper blade, then, is a set of generalities demanding specific determination, and such determination comes from the lower blade of working hypotheses, precise measurements, empirical correlations, deductions of their implications, experiments to test the deduced conclusions, revisions of the hypothesis, and so *da capo*.

Now with appropriate modifications the same method can be applied to the problem of interpretation. For the possibility of any interpretation whatever implies an upper blade of generalities; and the existing techniques of scholars supply a lower blade by which the generalities can be determined with ever greater accuracy. Moreover, the introduction of such a method meets the problem of relativism. For the relativism with which hermeneutics has been afflicted arises, not because scholars have been neglecting the lower blade that consists in the extraordinary array of techniques for dealing with the documents and monuments of the past, but because there has not been available an appropriate upper blade. In consequence they either labored under the delusion that their inquiry was *voraussetzungslos* or else operated on the basis of assumptions^v that did not square with the single legitimate assumption, namely, that in principle and under appropriate reservations a correct interpretation is possible.

What, then, is the upper blade? It has two components, which respectively regard meaning and expression. Both components are concretely universal, for they regard the potential totality of meanings and the potential totality of modes of expression. For the totality of meanings, the upper blade is the assertion that the protean notion of being is differentiated by a series of genetically and dialectically related unknowns.

For the totality of modes of expression, the upper blade is the assertion that there is a genetic process in which modes of expression move towards their specialization and differentiation on sharply distinguishable levels.

In general, the meaning and the grounds of these two assertions have been indicated in the sections on the universal viewpoint and on levels and sequences of expression. But one may ask whether the content of those sections can be inferred from the necessary assumption mentioned above, namely, that in principle and under appropriate reservations a correct interpretation is possible. In favor of an affirmative answer, the following argument may be adduced. Since interpretation has no more than a material determinant in the spatially ordered marks found in documents, the experiential, intellectual, and rational components of the interpretation have their proximate source in the interpreter's experience, understanding, and judgment. Hence, if a correct interpretation is possible, it has to be possible (1) for interpreters to proceed from their own experience, understanding, and judgment to the range of possible meanings of documents, and (2) for them to determine which of the possible meanings are to be assigned to each of the documents. Unless they can envisage the range of possible meanings, they will exclude a priori some meanings that are possible; and such exclusion runs counter to the possibility of correct interpretation. Again, unless they can connect possible meanings with actual documents, interpretation again becomes impossible. But the possibility of envisaging the full range of possible meaning lies in the universal viewpoint, and the possibility of connecting possible meanings with particular documents lies in the genetic sequence that extrapolates from present to past correlations between meaning and mode of expression.

However, one may grant readily enough that meanings form a genetically and dialectically related sequence of unknowns and that expressions develop from the undifferentiated to the specialized. The two basic assertions are sound, but where do they lead? Though the actual implementation of a method cannot be tucked into the corner of a chapter on a more general topic, still some sketch seems desirable. To meet this reasonable demand, let us first envisage in summary fashion the ultimate results that may be anticipated, let us secondly confront the counterpositions that distort interpretation, and thirdly let us endeavor to indicate the canons of a methodical hermeneutics on the analogy of the canons of empirical method in such a science as physics.

3.6 The Sketch [579–81]

The science of mathematics provides the physicist with a sharply defined field of sequences and relations and thereby enables him to anticipate the general nature of any physical theory. The purpose of the present sketch will be to perform an analogous service, not indeed for the actual task of interpretation, but at least for a consideration of the method to be employed in performing that task.

First, then, envisage the materials. They consist in the totality of documents and monuments. The documents may be divided into primary, secondary, and tertiary, where original communications are primary, interpretations of primary documents are secondary, and critical studies of interpretations are tertiary. Again, all the monuments and some of the documents are artistic; they provide materials or occasions from which we can reach insights; but they do not attempt to formulate insights after the fashion of the scientific treatise. Finally, in view of the limitations of the treatise, there are numerous gradations of documents from the purely artistic to ever more conscious and deliberate efforts to communicate a particular or universal viewpoint exactly.

Secondly, there are the immanent sources of meaning. They consist (1) in approximately reproducible human experience on all its levels, (2) orientated under approximately reproducible blends and mixtures of the elementary, the aesthetic, the dramatic, the practical, the intellectual, and the mystical patterns of experience, (3) informed by the unities, distinctions, and relations grasped by accumulations of insights, and (4) actuated by sets of certain and probable acts of assent and dissent.

Thirdly, there are the pure formulations. They proceed from the immanent sources of meaning to determinate[w] differentiations of the protean notion of being. Such differentiations may be either the contents of single judgments or the contexts constituted by more or less coherent aggregates of judgments. In either case they are pure formulations if they proceed from an interpreter that grasps the universal viewpoint and if they are addressed to an audience that similarly grasps the universal viewpoint.

Fourthly, there are the hypothetical expressions. Suppose P to be interpreting Q. From his immanent sources of meaning P will work out a hypothetical pure formulation of Q's context and of the content of Q's message. But the pure formulation of the content of Q's message proceeds from a universal viewpoint. It has to be transposed into an equivalent content that would proceed from Q's particular viewpoint. That particular viewpoint is assigned in the pure formulation of Q's context. Finally, inasmuch as this transposition is effected under the limitations of the resources of language and of the channels of communication available for Q, there results the hypothetical expression.

Fifthly, there is the control, and it is threefold. The totality of hypothetical expressions has to stand in a one-to-one correspondence with the totality of documents. The totality of pure formulations of contexts has to exhibit the sequence of developing human insights, the tendency of positions to unmodified survival, and the pressure on counterpositions to shift their ground or to accept their own reversal. Finally, the totality of assumptions on available resources of language and channels of communication has to exhibit the genetic sequence of modes of expression from the undifferentiated to the specialized.

Though this sketch claims to be no more enlightening than the assertion that physics is a mathematization of sensible data, it will serve to bring out the significance of the upper blade of method. For that upper blade forces out into the open the fact that the proximate sources of meaning lie in the interpreter's own experience, understanding, and judgment. It involves an explicit acknowledgment of the dangers of merely relative interpretation and a systematic procedure for circumventing such relativity by ascending to the universal viewpoint. It calls for a clear distinction between the interpreter's account of Q's context, his account of Q's content, his assumptions regarding Q's resources of expression, his inferred account of the manner in which Q would express his content in the light of his context through his resources of expression, and finally Q's actual expression. It introduces multiple verification:[x] not only must hypothetical expression square with actual expression, but the totality of assumptions regarding resources of expression has to satisfy the genetic sequence, and the totality of pure formulations of contexts has to satisfy a genetic and dialectical unfolding of human intelligence.

3.7 Counterpositions   [581–86]

The foregoing sketch will call forth rather vigorous resistance, and it is of some importance to distinguish between different sources of opposition. The introduction into physics of tensor fields and eigenfunctions raised a barrier between the theoretical physicists that grasped the mathematics but possessed no great skill in handling laboratory equipment and, on the other hand, the experts in experimental work for whom the recondite mathematics was sheer mystery. In similar fashion one may expect the diligent authors of highly specialized monographs to be somewhat bewildered and dismayed when they find that instead of singly following the bent of their genius, their aptitudes, and their acquired skills, they are to collaborate in the light of common but abstruse principles and to have their individual results checked by general requirements that envisage simultaneously the totality of results. Still, this is the minor resistance, and it should cause no greater difficulty in the field of interpretation than its analogue does in physics.

Major resistance will spring from the counterpositions, from the conviction that the real is a subdivision of the 'already out there now,' that objectivity is a matter of elementary extroversion, and that knowing another's knowledge is reenacting it.

One of our basic assertions was that interpretation aims at differentiating the protean notion of being by a set of genetically and dialectically related determinations. But if the position calls for determinations of being by an explanatorily[y] related set of terms, the counterpositions call for the exact opposite. If the real is the 'out there' and knowing it is taking a look, then the ideal of interpretation has to be as close an approximation as possible to a reconstruction of the cinema of what was done, of the soundtrack of what was said, and even of the Huxleyan 'feelie' of the emotions and sentiments of the participants in the drama of the past. Fortunately, counterpositions bring about their own reversal. Just as Descartes's vortices violated the canon of parsimony[z] that obliges the scientist to add nothing to the data except the content of verifiable insights, so the ideal of the cinema and soundtrack is the ideal not of historical science but of historical fiction. There is no verifiable cinema of the past nor any verifiable soundtrack of its speech. The available evidence lies in spatially ordered marks in documents and on monuments, and the interpreter's business is not to create nonexistent evidence but to understand the evidence that exists. Finally, if his understanding is correct, it will provide a differentiation of the protean notion of being, and it will provide no more. The artist and the teacher, no doubt, will endeavor to reconstitute the sights and sounds, the feelings and sentiments, that help us to recapture the past; but such recapture is educative; it makes ascent to the universal viewpoint possible; it prepares us for an understanding, an appreciation, an execution, of scientific interpretation; but in itself it is not science.

Secondly, as the counterpositions lead to a misconception of the goal of interpretation, so also they lead to blunders about the procedures of interpreters. If objectivity is a matter of elementary extroversion, then the objective interpreter has to have more to look at than spatially ordered marks on paper; not only the marks but also the meanings have to be 'out there'; and the difference between an objective interpreter and one that is merely subjective is that the objective interpreter observes simply the meanings that are obviously 'out there,' while the merely subjective interpreter 'reads' his own ideas 'into' statements that obviously possess quite a different meaning. But the plain fact is that there is nothing 'out there' except spatially ordered marks; to appeal to dictionaries and to grammars, to linguistic and stylistic studies, is to appeal to more marks. The proximate source of the whole experiential component in the meaning of both objective and subjective interpreters lies in their own experience; the proximate source of the whole intellectual component lies in their own insights; the proximate source of the whole reflective component lies in their own critical reflection. If the criterion of objectivity is the 'obviously out there,' then there is no objective interpretation whatever; there is only gaping at ordered marks, and the only order is spatial. But if the criterion of objectivity lies in intelligent inquiry, critical reflection, and grasp of the virtually unconditioned, then the humbug about the 'out there' and the simulated indignation about 'reading into' are rather convincing evidence that one has very little notion of what objectivity is.

Thirdly, from the viewpoint of the counterpositions the introduction of the universal viewpoint will be denounced as a pretentious appeal to vain and empty theorizing. Even if some possible utility is conceded to this abstruse procedure, at least it will be asserted roundly and confidently that its value is highly hypothetical and its implications quite unreliable, unless of course they are confirmed in some independent fashion. Now, no doubt, this view is very reasonable if meanings are 'obviously out there.' But if the proximate sources of all meanings are immanent, then either those sources make the universal viewpoint possible or not, and either that possibility is exploited or not. If they do not make the universal viewpoint possible, then objective interpretation of another's meaning is impossible; for if there is no possible universal viewpoint, there is no general possibility of rising above one's personal views and reaching without bias what the personal views of another are. Again, if the possibility of the universal viewpoint exists but is not exploited, then objective interpretation is possible but does not occur. Finally, since scientific objectivity is to be reached only through the universal viewpoint, there is no question of a confirmation that is independent of the universal viewpoint.

Fourthly, commonly it is contended that an author has to be interpreted in his own terms. Plato is to be interpreted by Plato, Aquinas by Aquinas, Kant by Kant. This common contention possesses three indisputable excellences. In the first place, it implements the lexicographical principle that the meanings of words emerge from the sentences in which they occur, so that the meaning of an author's words has to be settled by appealing, at least proximately, to his own usage. In the second place, it implements the epistemological principle that an explanation forms a closed system; if one understands, then the content of one's understanding can be formulated only through a set of mutually determining and determined terms and relations; accordingly, if one understands Plato or Aquinas or Kant or anyone else, then the formulation of one's understanding will be some closed system, and both the elements of the system and the relations between the elements can be found in the original author's own statements. In the third place, the rule that an author must be allowed to speak for himself tends to exclude the intrusion of another's mentality into his meaning. Inasmuch as the author's usage determines his meanings, other meanings are excluded; and inasmuch as the author's system determines the relations between his meanings, other systems are excluded.

Nonetheless, Plato and Aquinas and Kant keep on speaking for themselves each in several widely different manners when they are allowed to do so by different interpreters. Nor is this surprising, for they are long dead, and their speaking for themselves is just a metaphor. Despite its excellences the rule contains an obvious piece of humbug, and the root of the humbug is the counterposition. A Platonic avatar and a repetition of the dialogues might solve some textual problems, but by and large it would leave the understanding of Plato exactly where it was. The proximate sources of every interpretation are immanent in the interpreter, and there is nothing to be gained by clouding the fact or obscuring the issue. On the contrary, a methodical hermeneutics demands an open acknowledgment by the interpreter of his immanent sources of interpretation, of his formulation from a universal viewpoint of his hypothesis on the context and content of another's meaning, of his process from that pure formulation to the hypothetical expression, and of the introduction of multiple controls that check interpretations not only individually against documents but also as members of a totality with common or interrelated assumptions.

Fifthly, the counterpositions not only lead to misconceptions of the goal of interpretation and to blunders about the means to reach the goal; they also involve interpreters in systematic distortions of the authors that are to be interpreted. If one identifies the real with being, one can acknowledge the reality of the various blends and mixtures of the patterns of human experience, and one can grasp how these blends and mixtures generate confusion and error on the notions of reality, objectivity, and knowledge. Through that grasp one reaches the protean notion of being: just as being is the intelligently grasped and reasonably affirmed, so what anyone happens to think is grasped intelligently and affirmed reasonably will be coincident with what he happens to think is being; and as human utterance, as distinct from gibberish, proceeds from putative intelligence and reasonableness, a grasp of the protean notion of being gives access to the universe of possible meanings.

But clearly enough the counterpositions block the identification of the real with being, of being with the intelligently grasped and reasonably affirmed, and of the protean notion of being with the objects of putative intelligent grasp and reasonable affirmation. It follows that the counterpositions bar the way to the universal viewpoint and to an unbiased interpretation of an author with different views from the interpreter's.

Thus,[aa] if one agrees with the logical positivists that meaning refers to sensible data or to signs that refer to sensible data, then one must conclude that the majority of philosophers have been indulging in nonsense; it will follow that a history of philosophy is engaged mainly in cataloguing and comparing different brands of nonsense; and it will be a matter of small moment just how much nonsense of what brand is attributed to this or that philosopher.

If one agrees with existentialist opinion, then one has no choice but to accept R. Bultmann's program of singling out the existential elements in the New Testament and of naming the rest of its content myth.

If one takes one's stand on the ambivalence of average common sense that lives in some blend of the aesthetic, dramatic, and practical patterns of experience with occasional forays into the biological and intellectual patterns, then one can obtain a base of operations for entering into the mentality of another age and interpreting its documents only by some putative reenactment in oneself of its ambivalent blend of the aesthetic, dramatic, and practical patterns and of its forays into the biological and intellectual patterns. So there arise the problems[bb] of determining, not differentiations of the protean notion of being, but imaginative and emotive reconstructions of the Nature Religions, of the Greek mysteries, of Eschatology and Apocalyptic, of traditional and Hellenistic Judaism, of the Christian *Urgemeinde* and Paulinism. So the many solutions to these problems give rise to problems of quite a new order: for within the protean notion of being the transition from one differentiation to another is the quite determinate and determinable process of changing patterns of experience, accumulations of insights, and sets of judgments; but the transition from one imaginative and emotive reconstruction to another is condemned by its very nature to be a mere transmogrification; people begin by perceiving and feeling in one manner; they end by perceiving and feeling in another; and there are no imaginable percepts or reproducible revulsions of feeling that could link verifiably their beginning to their end.

Finally, if one agrees with Scotus that words correspond to concepts, and that concepts are the contents of fictitious spiritual acts of looking at the formally distinct aspects of things, then the meanings of words cannot vary without a corresponding variation in concepts, and concepts cannot vary without a corresponding variation in things. It follows that basic problems of interpretation simply cannot exist. One has only to define enough words clearly and exactly to arrive at the exact meaning of anyone else's words. The uniformity of nature guarantees the uniformity of concepts; the uniformity of concepts guarantees the uniformity of verbal meanings. All that is needed is a good dose of controversy, and then all honest men will hold exactly similar opinions.

3.8 Some Canons for a Methodical Hermeneutics   [586–94]

An interpretation is the expression of the meaning of another expression. It may be literary or scientific. A literary interpretation offers the images and associations from which a reader can reach the insights and form the judgments that the interpreter believes to correspond to the content of the original expression. A scientific interpretation is concerned to formulate the relevant insights and judgments, and to do so in a manner that is consonant with scientific collaboration and scientific control.

A methodical hermeneutics necessarily is limited to scientific interpretations, and so the canons to be suggested will not be of interest to interpreters that cast the results of their investigations in literary form. Inversely, there can be no valid objections against the canons on the score that they are not compatible with literary procedures, with the needs of the average reader, with the demand of the publishing trade for books that sell, and so forth.

There is a further limitation on the scope of the canons. Our problem has been the relativity of interpretations, and our solution has been to appeal to the upper blade of an empirical method. For this reason the canons will aim simply at summarizing the conclusions that already have been reached. Obviously enough, a complete method cannot be outlined in a subsection of a chapter that deals with a quite different topic, and so no effort will be made to specify the numerous and complicated techniques of the lower blade of a methodical hermeneutics.

First, then, there is a canon of relevance. It demands that the interpreter begin from the universal viewpoint and that his interpretation convey some differentiation of the protean notion of being. By beginning from the universal viewpoint there is eliminated the relativity not only of the interpreter to his prospective audience but also of both interpreter and audience to places and times, schools and sects. By placing the meaning of the interpretation within the protean notion of being there are secured (1) a common field for all possible interpretations, (2) the possibility of an exact statement of the differences between opposed interpretations, and (3) a reasonable hope that such oppositions will be eliminated by further appeals to the available data.

Secondly, there is a canon of explanation. The interpreter's differentiation of the protean notion of being must be not descriptive but explanatory. It will aim at relating, not to us, but to one another, the contents and contexts of the totality of documents and interpretations. As long as interpretation remains on the descriptive level, it may happen to be correct but it cannot escape the relativity of a manifold of interpretations to a manifold of audiences; in turn, this relativity excludes the possibility of scientific collaboration, scientific control, and scientific advance towards commonly accepted results.

The explanatory differentiation of the protean notion of being involves three elements. First, there is the genetic sequence in which insights gradually are accumulated by man. Secondly, there are the dialectical alternatives in which accumulated insights are formulated, with positions inviting further development and counterpositions shifting their ground to avoid the reversal they demand. Thirdly, with the advance of culture and of effective education, there arises the possibility of the differentiation and specialization of modes of expression; and since this development conditions not only the exact communication of insights but also the discoverer's own grasp of his discovery, since such grasp and its exact communication intimately are connected with the advance of positions and the reversal of counterpositions, the three elements in the explanatory differentiation of the protean notion of being fuse into a single explanation.

To avoid confusion and misunderstanding, it will not be amiss to draw attention to the possibility of an explanatory interpretation of a nonexplanatory meaning. The original writer's meaning may have its source in insights into things as related to him, and in all probability he will have neither a clear notion of what is meant by insight nor any distinct advertence to the occurrence of his insights. Still, *ex hypothesi*, he had the insights and they provided a source of his meaning; moreover, the insights he had were or were not different from the insights of other earlier, contemporary, and later writers; and if they were different, then they stood in some genetic and dialectical relations with those other sets. Now it is through these genetic and dialectical relations that interpretation is explanatory. It is through these genetic and dialectical relations that explanatory interpretation conceives, defines, reaches the insights of a given writer. Accordingly, it in no way involves the imputation of explanatory knowledge to a mind that possessed only descriptive knowledge. It is concerned to reach, as exactly as possible, the descriptive knowledge of the writers $P, Q, R, \ldots$, and it attempts to do so, not by offering an unverifiable inventory of the insights enjoyed respectively by $P, Q, R, \ldots$, but by establishing the verifiable differences between $P, Q, R, \ldots$ Because it approaches terms through differences, because the differences can be explained genetically and dialectically, the interpretation of nonexplanatory meaning is itself explanatory.

Thirdly, there is a canon of successive approximations. The totality of documents cannot be interpreted scientifically by a single interpreter or even by a single generation of interpreters. There must be a division of labor, and the labor must be cumulative. Accordingly, the fundamental need is for reliable principles of criticism that will select what is satisfactory and will correct what is unsatisfactory in any contributions that are made. With such principles the end of even a stupendous task is already somehow in sight. On the other hand, without such principles, even enormous and indefinitely prolonged labors may merely move around in an inconclusive circle.

A first principle of criticism is supplied by the demand for a universal viewpoint. Moreover, this demand possesses the requisite dynamic character. For though a contributor fails to present his results in terms of the protean notion of being, a critic can proceed from that notion to a determination of the contributor's particular viewpoint, he can indicate how the particularism probably would not invalidate the contributor's work, and, on the other hand, he can suggest to others working in the contributor's special field the points on which his work may need revision.

A second principle of criticism is supplied by the conditions of the extrapolation of meaning. Proximate sources of meaning are immanent in the interpreter, and from them he has to reach the meaning of some other writer. The first condition of such an extrapolation is an adequate self-knowledge. Is he sufficiently aware of the diverse elements of human experience, of the different manners in which insights accumulate, of the nature of reflection and judgment, of the various patterns of human experience and the consequent varieties of philosophic views and prephilosophic orientations? The second condition of the extrapolation is that it is to the meaning of a man at a different stage of human development. Because it is to the meaning of a man, there must be recognized some general orientation in living, some measure of critical reflection, some insight, some flow of experience. Because it is to a meaning at a different stage of human development, there can be invoked a merging of the clear and distinct into the obscure and undifferentiated. Because all stages of development are linked genetically and dialectically, it should be possible to retrace through intervening documents the series of developments and reversals that bridge the gap from the past to the universal viewpoint.[cc]

A third principle of criticism results from the genetic sequence of modes of expression and the recurrent gap between meaning and expression. For expression is an instrumental act of meaning; it results from principal acts of conception and judgment; the principal acts follow from the immanent sources of meaning; and so, once sources have been tapped, it is only a matter of normal ingenuity to develop appropriate modes of expression. It follows that, once any stage in the development of meaning has become propagated and established in a cultural milieu, there will result an appropriate mode of expression to bear witness to its existence. But it also follows that new meanings can be expressed only by transforming old modes of expression, that the greater the novelty, the less prepared the audience, the less malleable the previous mode of expression, then the greater will be the initial gap between meaning and expression and the more prolonged will be the period of experimentation in which the new ideas are forging the tools for their own exteriorization.

A fourth principle of criticism is to be derived from the goal. It is truth, and the criterion of truth is the virtually unconditioned. Because the proximate sources of interpretation are immanent in the interpreter, every interpretation is, at first, no more than a hypothesis. Because initially it is no more than a hypothesis, it can become probable or certain only by approximating to the virtually unconditioned or by reaching it. The question, then, is not how many people say it is obvious, nor how great is their authority and renown, but simply what is the evidence. Nor is evidence some peculiar sheen or convincing glamor. It supposes the coherence of the hypothesis with the universal viewpoint, with the genetic and dialectical relations between successive stages of meaning, with the genetic sequence of modes of expression and the recurrent gaps between meaning and expression. It consists in the fulfilment offered by the data of documents and monuments for this wide-ranging and multiply interlocked coherence.

Fourthly, there is a canon of parsimony, and it has two aspects. On its negative side, it excludes from consideration the unverifiable. The cinema of what was done and the soundtrack of what was said can be imagined but cannot be verified. They pertain not to science but to fiction. On its positive side, the canon of parsimony invokes the resources of critical reflection. Because the relativist fails to distinguish between the formally and the virtually unconditioned, he demands a complete explanation of everything before passing any judgment on anything. On the other hand, precisely because a distinction is to be drawn between the formally and the virtually unconditioned, it is both possible and salutary to illuminate with intermediate certitudes the long way to complete explanation. When sufficient evidence is not forthcoming for the more detailed interpretation, it may be available for a less ambitious pronouncement. When a positive conclusion cannot be substantiated, a number of negative conclusions may be possible, and they will serve to bracket the locus of future successful inquiry. Moreover, in the measure that the universal viewpoint is reached, radical surprises are excluded;

in the measure that extrapolation is not to future but to past meanings, the relevant insights do not call for the discoveries of genius but simply for the thoroughness of painstaking and intelligent analysis; in the measure that eventually there was closed the gap that once existed between original meaning and available resources of expression, it is possible to begin from the later, more adequate expression and remount to the origin of the ideas in the initial, transforming stresses and strains in linguistic usage.

Fifthly, there is a canon of residues. Just as the field of physics contains a nonsystematic component, so also do the fields of meaning, of expression as related to meaning, of expression as grounded in dynamic constellations of the writer's psyche, and of documents in their origins, their production, and their survival. Just as the physicist deals with the nonsystematic by combining inverse with direct insights, so also must the interpreter. Finally, just as the actual frequencies of physical events are to be known only by observation and counting, so also the interpreter has to acknowledge a residue of mere matters of fact.

On the level of meaning it is important not to confuse the genetic with the dialectical. An intelligent writer advances in insight as he writes. At times, his fresh insights will be so basic that he is forced to destroy what he has written and to begin afresh. So it comes about that paragraphs, sections, chapters, series of chapters, even volumes are rewritten. But there is a limit to human endurance, and so it also happens that the rewriting is not done,[dd] that the shift in viewpoint is unnoticed, or that it is noticed but corrected inadequately. Again, the intelligent reader advances in insight as he reads, and this advance of the reader may be anticipated by the writer. So the present work has been written from a moving viewpoint: earlier sections and chapters do not presuppose what can be treated only later; but later sections and chapters do presuppose what has been presented in the successive, ever broadening stages that precede.

Now from the viewpoint of the electronic computer, which coincides with the viewpoint of logic as a technique, such a procedure is illegitimate. System has to be static system. System on the move has to be outlawed. The dynamism of life and of intelligence may be facts but the facts are not to be recognized. If it is indisputable that the same author has written in the light of a moving accumulation of insights, then he is to be named not intelligent but incoherent. On the other hand, if the identity of the author is not indisputable, then in the name of logic as a technique the alleged incoherences are to be removed, and the one author is to be divided up into a number of different men. Plainly, with such conclusions we are not inclined to agree. As was argued in the section on the limitations of the treatise, the relevance of logic as a technique is extremely restricted. What the interpreter has to grasp is the meaning of a man, and in the measure that men are intelligent, in that measure they can be expected, unless the contrary is demonstrated, both to write in the light of ever accumulating insights and to address intelligent readers.

Not only does human meaning have its source in a moving system but also it is subject to the stress and distortion of the counterpositions and, in the limit, of mythic consciousness. It is here that the interpreter has to deal with the dialectical, with the intrusion of the nonsystematic into moving system, with the ambivalent tendency of the counterposition and the mythical either to bring about its own reversal or to attempt to save itself by perpetually shifting its ground. But on this aspect of the problem of interpretation enough has been said already in insisting upon the universal viewpoint and in defining the work of interpreting as differentiating the protean notion of being.

When one turns from meaning to expression of meaning, similar problems arise. There is a genetic absence of static system in expression when new ideas have to be exteriorized through a gradual transformation of prior modes of expression. Then the tension between meaning and expression will be at its maximum at the beginning of the movement: images and words that previously bore an established significance appear in strange collocations; they struggle under a burden of meaning that they do not succeed in conveying; quite suddenly they pass out of currency to be replaced by fresh efforts, and these in turn may have their day only to yield, so to speak, to a third generation of words and images; finally, if the movement endures, the transformations of language do not end until a technical vocabulary on an explanatory basis is established. In contrast with the foregoing genetic process, there is the ambivalence of allegory: the intelligible is being communicated through the sensible; the known unknown of intellect is manifested through the images and feelings associated with the operator on the sensitive level. But from the nature of the case, critical reflection is hampered, and so, while the basic content of the allegory may be mystery, very easily it is mingled with myth. Thus, the Iranian contrast of light and darkness corresponds to our own contrast between the detached and disinterested desire to know and the interference of other desire; but while the Iranian allegory expands into the personification of a cosmic dualism, into a pantheon, and into an extrinsicist[ee] theory of history, our corresponding contrast has led to a conflict immanent in the dramatic individual and expanding into a dialectic of social and cultural life. So it is that Iranian thought may be said to begin in mystery only to end in myth.

Expression not only is an instrument of the principal acts of meaning that reside in conception and judgment but also a prolongation of the psychic flow from percepts, memories, images, and feelings into the shaping of the countenance, the movement of the hands, and the utterance of the words. In childhood we learnt to speak; in youth we were trained in letters; but in neither procedure did we come to grasp just where our words come from or why they are just what they happen to be. In brief, our speech and writing are basically automatisms, and our conscious control supervenes only to order, to select, to revise, or to reject. It follows that expression bears the signature not only of the controlling meaning but also of the underlying psychic flow, and that painstaking study will reveal in the automatic part of composition the recurrence of characteristic patterns to which their author, in all probability, never adverted.

Now this fact possesses its significance, but its proper appreciation calls for a distinction between the systematic, the genetic, and the incidental. There is a systematic component inasmuch as expression proceeds automatically from the dynamic structures of the psyche. There is a genetic component inasmuch as the dynamic structures of the psyche satisfy not a static system but a system on the move. Finally, there is an incidental component inasmuch as the sensitive automatism may be interrupted at any moment by the intervention of the principal acts of meaning, and for reasons that cannot be reconstructed and still less verified, give rise to a different usage or an unexpected turn of phrase. To illustrate these points, one may take Lutoslawski's well-known study of Plato[10] and observe that the systematic component grounds the possibility of the investigation, the genetic component grounds the concluded relative chronology of the dialogues, and the incidental component requires that the argument should be based, not on rigid criteria, but on relative actual frequencies.

10 [Wincenty Lutoslawski, *The Origin and Growth of Plato's Logic* (London: Longmans, Green, and Co., 1897).]

Finally, there are nonsystematic residues on the level of the documents themselves. An unverifiable host of accidents can enter into the decisions that led to their production, into the circumstances under which they were composed, into the arbitrariness that governs their survival. Much that is obscure, ambiguous, unexplained would be illuminated, were it not for the lamented hand of destructive time, were we more familiar with former modes of compilation and composition, were our information on authors and origins more complete. Much that is unknown to us may yet be discovered. But perhaps it will not be amiss to recall that a profound difference exists between general and particular hypotheses. For the general hypothesis has general presuppositions and implications, and so it can be tested in a variety of manners; in contrast, the particular hypothesis is an ad hoc construction; it might be true but it also might be mere fiction; and, unfortunately, there is not available the evidence[ff] that would enable one to decide which of these alternatives is correct. It follows from the canon of parsimony, which restricts scientific pronouncements to the verifiable, that holes in their evidence at times force interpreters to prefer a frank confession of ignorance to plausible guesses that head beyond the confines of science.

3.9 Conclusion   [594]

As our study of insight began from an analysis of the procedures of mathematics and of the natural sciences, so the present endeavor has been to draw upon the consequent theories of objectivity and meaning to outline the possibility of a general heuristic structure for a methodical hermeneutics. While the practical significance of such a structure can hardly appear before it is complemented with the array of concrete techniques familiar to the historical inquirer, at least it is at once apparent that the present account of insight into the insights of others possesses peculiar relevance at a time when theoretical differences of a philosophic character so frequently constitute the principal cause of divergence not only in the conclusions reached but also in the methods employed by otherwise competent investigators. However, while readers perhaps will be more interested in such possible applications of the proposed method, it will not be amiss for us to draw attention once more to the fact that our primary intention is somewhat different. Metaphysics has been defined as the integral heuristic structure of proportionate being, and so the existence of a heuristic structure for interpretation brings under metaphysics the interpretation not only of less general utterances but also of every possible philosophy and metaphysics. A similar claim would be made, of course, by Hegelianism, but between the Hegelian view and our own there exists the important difference that the idealist position with its alleged dialectical necessity has to pretend to be complete independently of nonsystematic matters of fact, while our realism permits us not only to respect but even to include every valid conclusion of empirical human science.

18

The Possibility of Ethics[a]

Metaphysics was conceived as the implementation of the integral heuristic structure of proportionate being. The fundamental question of the present chapter is whether ethics can be conceived in the same fashion. Our answer, which prolongs the discussion of questions raised in the chapters on common sense and in the study of human development, meets the issue in three steps.

First, an attempt is made to work out such notions as the good, will, value, obligation. From this effort there follow a method of ethics that parallels the method of metaphysics and, at the same time, a cosmic or ontological account of the good.

Secondly, the possibility of ethics is envisaged from the viewpoint of freedom and responsibility. The relevance of the canon of statistical residues is considered. The nature of practical insight, practical reflection, and the act of decision is outlined. The fact of man's essential freedom and responsibility is concluded.

Thirdly, the possibility of ethics is investigated from the further viewpoint of effective freedom. Is an ethics possible in the sense that it can be observed? Is man condemned to moral frustration? Is there a need for a moral liberation if human development is to escape the cycle of alternating progress and decline?

Finally, it may be well to note that our concern is not to draw up a code of ethics but rather to meet the relevant prior questions. The present chapter, then, sets forth not precepts but the general form of precepts. Perhaps there is no need to insist that the transition from such a

general form to the specialized precepts of particular domains of human
activity can take place only through an understanding of these activities.
It follows that if an electronic computer were supplied with premises
from this chapter, it could not conclude to any specialized precepts.
However, I am writing not for electronic computers but for men, and
as complete moral obtuseness is very rare, I feel justified in expecting
critics to suppose that readers of this book will be able to make the transition from the remote possibility of ethics, which is established, to the
proximate possibility, which the exigent may demand.

1   The Notion of the Good   [596–607]

As being is intelligible and one, so also it is good. But while the intelligibility and unity of being follow spontaneously from the fact that being
is whatever is to be grasped intelligently and affirmed reasonably, the
goodness of being comes to light only by considering the extension of
intellectual activity that we name deliberation and decision, choice and
will.

1.1 Levels of the Good   [596–98]

On an elementary level, the good is the object of desire, and when it is
attained it is experienced as pleasant, enjoyable, satisfying. But man
experiences aversion no less than desire, pain no less than pleasure; and
so, on this elementary, empirical level, the good is coupled with its opposite, the bad.

However, among men's many desires, there is one that is unique. It
is the detached, disinterested, unrestricted desire to know. As other
desire, it has its satisfaction. But unlike other desire, it is not content
with satisfaction. Of itself, it heads beyond one's own joy in one's own
insight to the further question whether one's own insight is correct. It
is a desire to know, and its immanent criterion is the attainment of an
unconditioned that, by the fact that it is unconditioned, is independent
of the individual's likes and dislikes, of his wishful and his anxious
thinking.

Now through this desire and the knowledge it generates, there comes
to light a second meaning of the good. Besides the good that is simply
object of desire, there is the good of order. Such is the polity, the economy, the family as an institution. It is not the object of any single desire,

for it stands to single desires as system to systematized, as universal condition to particulars that are conditioned, as scheme of recurrence that supervenes upon the materials of desires and the efforts to meet them and, at the price of limited restrictions, through the fertility of intelligent control, secures an otherwise unattainable abundance of satisfactions.

The good of order is dynamic, not merely in the sense that it orders the dynamic unfolding of desires and aversions, but also in the sense that it itself is system on the move. It possesses its own normative line of development, inasmuch as elements of the idea of order are grasped by insight into concrete situations, are formulated in proposals, are accepted by explicit or tacit agreements, and are put into execution only to change the situation and give rise to still further insights. Still, this normative line provides no more than a first approximation to the actual course of social development. The planets would move in straight lines if there were no gravitation, but in fact they move in perturbed ellipses. In like manner, social development would be simply a matter of intellectual development, if the human psyche were without its contribution; but in fact man's sensitive nature constitutes both the dynamic materials to be ordered and the subjective conditions under which the order is discovered, communicated, accepted, and executed. So it is that social order finds in the desires and aversions of individuals and intersubjective groups both an enormously powerful ally and a permanent source of egoistic and class deviation. The deviation not only constitutes a change in the main channel of development but also gives rise to secondary channels in which men are engaged in working out ever more efficacious countermoves to protect themselves against the effects of deviations initiated by others, to correct the deviators, and in the ideal case to attack deviation at its root. However, as has been seen, concern with this ideal involves a transposition of the issue from the level of the policeman and the court, of diplomacy and war, to the level of culture and morality. Nor in the long run is common sense equal to this task since, besides its individual and group aberrations, it is subject to a general bias against concern with ultimate issues and ultimate results.

This brings us to the third aspect of the good, which is value. For the good of order is linked, not only with the manifold manifestations of spontaneous desires and aversions which it orders, but also with a third type of good, which emerges on the level of reflection and judgment, of deliberation and choice. As the data of experience, so also sensitive desires and aversions are prior to questions and insights, reflections and judgments. In contrast, the good of order, while it is anticipated and reflected by spontaneous intersubjectivity, essentially is a formal intelligibility that is to be discovered only by raising questions, grasped only through accumulating insights, formulated only in conceptions. Nonetheless, though the good of order lies totally outside the field of sensitive appetition, it is in itself an object of human devotion. Individualism and socialism are neither food nor drink, neither clothes nor shelter, neither health nor wealth. They are constructions of human intelligence, possible systems for ordering the satisfaction of human desires. Still, men can embrace one system and reject others. They can do so with all the ardor of their being, though the issue regard neither their own individual advantage nor that of their relatives, friends, acquaintances, countrymen. Nor is this fact surprising. For human intelligence is not only speculative but also practical. So far from being content to determine the unities and correlations in things as they are, it is constantly on the watch to discern the possibilities that reveal things as they might be. But such possibilities are manifold. In large part they are mutually exclusive. The inventiveness of practical intelligence can issue in practical results only if there exist the conjugate potency, form, and act of will, willingness, and willing, with the function of singling out some possibilities from the manifold and by that decision and choice initiating and grounding the transition from the intellectual conception of a possible order to its concrete realization.

1.2 The Notion of Will   [598–600]

Will, then, is intellectual or spiritual appetite. As capacity for sensitive hunger stands to sensible food, so will stands to objects presented by intellect. As a bare capacity, will extends to every intellectual object, and so both to every possible order and to every concrete object as subsumed under some possible order. But besides the bare capacity that is will, there is the habitual inclination, specialized in particular directions, that constitutes the willingness and unwillingness with which individuals antecedently are disposed to making decisions and choices of determinate kinds. Just as a person that has not learnt a subject must go through a laborious process to acquire mastery, yet once mastery is acquired can grasp readily the solution to any problem that arises in the field, so too a person that has not acquired willingness needs to be persuaded before he will will, yet once willingness is acquired leaps to willing without any need of persuasion. Finally, besides the capacity 'will' and the habit 'willingness' there is the act 'willing.' It is the event, and so it alone is revealed directly. To know willingness, one must study the frequencies with which various objects are chosen by a given individual over a given period; and to know will, one must study the changes in such frequencies over a lifetime.

Further, willing is rational and so moral. The detached, disinterested, unrestricted desire to know grasps intelligently and affirms reasonably not only the facts of the universe of being but also its practical possibilities. Such practical possibilities include intelligent transformations not only of the environment in which man lives but also of man's own spontaneous living. For that living exhibits an otherwise coincidental manifold into which man can introduce a higher system by his own understanding of himself and his own deliberate choices. So it is that the detached and disinterested desire extends its sphere of influence from the field of cognitional activities through the field of knowledge into the field of deliberate human acts. So it is that the empirically, intelligently, rationally conscious subject of self-affirmation becomes a morally self-conscious subject. Man is not only a knower but also a doer; the same intelligent and rational consciousness grounds the doing as well as the knowing; and from that identity of consciousness there springs inevitably an exigence for self-consistency in knowing and doing.

How can that exigence be met? It is difficult enough for purely cognitional activities to be dominated by the detached and disinterested desire to know. How are such detachment and disinterestedness to be extended over human living? No doubt, moral living is difficult; even theologians admit a sense in which it is impossible; but our present concern is with the fact of the exigence, and not a little of the evidence for the fact lies in the efforts of men to dodge it. The first and most common escape is to avoid self-consciousness. The precept of the sage was 'Know thyself.' But the precept at least was needed. How finely tempered must one's sincerity be if one is to know oneself as one is, to know not a character sketch that explains one in terms of ancestry and environment, but a moral analysis of one's deeds, one's words, one's mixed motives. How much simpler to pour oneself out in 'worthwhile' external activity and, if praise and blame must be administered, then administer them not to oneself but to others. The second escape is rationalization. Inconsistency between knowing and doing can be removed by revising one's knowing into harmony with one's doing. Such a revision is, of course, a bold step. Not a little ingenuity is needed to transpose inconsistency between knowing and doing into inconsistency within knowing itself. The average mind can invent lies about matters of fact; it can trump up excuses; it can allege extenuating circumstances that mingle fact with fiction. But hypocrisy is no more than the tribute paid by vice to virtue. It falls far short of the genuine rationalization that argues vice to be virtue, that meets the charge of inconsistency not by denying the minor premise of fact but by denying the major premise of principle. But the revision of major premises is a tricky business; it is playing fast and loose with the pure desire to know in its immediate domain of cognitional activity; and so the majority of men, instead of attempting rationalization themselves, are content to create an effective demand, a welcoming market, for more or less consistently developed counterpositions presented in myths and in philosophies. The third escape is moral renunciation. *Video meliora proboque, deteriora autem sequor.*[1] It is without the illusion generated by fleeing self-consciousness. It is without the deceit generated by rationalization. But it is content with a speculative acknowledgment of the aspiration to make one's own living intelligent and reasonable. It is ready to confess its wrongdoing, but it has given up any hope of amending its ways. If you please, it is very human; yet it also is incompletely human, for the demand for consistency between knowing and doing is dynamic; it asks to be operative; it seeks to extend detachment and disinterestedness into living, and it is not satisfied with a merely speculative acknowledgment of its existence.

As will be noted, we have been considering moral self-consciousness in its complete generality. According to the proverb there is honor among thieves. In different strata of society, in different epochs, in different cultures and civilizations, one meets with different moral codes. But the content of the moral code is one thing, and the dynamic function that demands its observance is another. Our consideration has centered on that dynamic function, on the operative exigence for self-consistency in self-consciousness, and since contrast is luminous, on the threefold escape of fleeing self-consciousness, of mitigating the moral code by rationalization, and of giving up hope in the struggle. In brief, we have been dealing with the question, Is there a meaning to the

---

1 [Ovid, *Metamorphoses* 7, 21: 'Video. meliora proboque, Deteriora sequor.']

word 'ought'? Our answer differs from the Kantian answer, for if we agree in affirming a categorical imperative, we disagree inasmuch as we derive it wholly from speculative intelligence and reason. Again, our answer differs from the views at least popularly associated with Freud's name for, while we grant that moral self-consciousness has a concomitant in moral emotions and moral sentiments, and while we agree that these emotions and sentiments have a psychoneural basis and are subject to psychoneural aberration, we contend that it is a blunder to confuse these concomitants with moral self-consciousness itself. When Freud decided eventually to publish his *Traumdeutung*, he was overcoming emotions and sentiments and following what he considered the only intelligent and reasonable course of action; and such following is what we mean by obeying moral conscience.

1.3   The Notion of Value   [601–602]

Now it is in rational, moral self-consciousness that the good as value comes to light, for the value is the good as the possible object of rational choice. Just as the objects of desire fall under schemes of recurrence to give rise to the good of order grasped by intelligence, so also the good of order with its concrete contents is a possible object of rational choice and so a value.

There follows at once a triple cross-division of values. They are true insofar as the possible choice is rational, but false insofar as the possibility of the choice results from a flight from self-consciousness, or from rationalization, or from moral renunciation. They are terminal inasmuch as they are objects for possible choices, but they are originating inasmuch as directly and explicitly or indirectly and implicitly the fact that they are chosen modifies our habitual willingness, our effective orientation in the universe, and so our contribution to the dialectical process of progress or decline. Finally, they are actual, or in process, or in prospect, according as they have been realized already, or are in course of being realized, or merely are under consideration.

Further, values are hierarchic. Objects of desire are values only inasmuch as they fall under some intelligible order, for the value is the possible object of choice, choice is an act of will, and the will is intellectual appetite that regards directly only the intelligible good. Again, terminal values are subordinate to originating values, for the originating values ground good will, and good will grounds the realization of the terminal values. Finally, within terminal values themselves there is a hierarchy; for each is an intelligible order, but some of these orders include others, some are conditioning and others conditioned, some conditions are more general and others less.

Now the division and the hierarchy of values reveal how the dynamic exigence of rational self-consciousness for self-consistency unfolds into a body of moral precepts concretely operative in a moral consciousness. For sensitive desires and aversions arise spontaneously; their objects cannot be willed until they are subsumed under some intelligible order; intelligible orders are linked one with another in mutual dependence, or as condition and conditioned, or as part and whole; and prior to becoming engaged of one's own choice, one already is engaged in the process by the fact of one's desires and aversions, by one's intelligent grasp of the intelligible orders under which they can be satisfied, and by one's self-consciousness of oneself as an actually rational knower and a potentially rational doer. For 'not to choose' is not the object of a possible choice, and while one's choices can be reasonable or not, while they can be more reasonable or less, still one's own rational consciousness is an accomplished fact in the field of knowing, and it demands in the name of its own consistency its extension into the field of doing. Such is the dynamic exigence, the operative moral imperative. But as it concretely exists and functions in consciousness, it is immanent in its own concrete presuppositions and implications. It demands, not consistency in the abstract, but consistency in my consciousness, not the superficial consistency purchased by the flight from self-consciousness nor the illusory consistency obtained by self-deception and rationalization nor the inadequate consistency that is content to be no worse than the next fellow, but the penetrating, honest, complete consistency that alone meets the requirements of the detached, disinterested, unrestricted desire to know. Nor is this all, for in the concrete, consistency means consistent terminal objects. But if there are to be terminal objects, there must be intelligible orders; their intelligibility must be genuine, and not the mere seeming that results from the scotosis of the dramatic subject or from the individual, group, or general bias of common sense. If the terminal objects are to be consistent, then there is no room for choosing the part and repudiating the whole, for choosing the conditioned and repudiating the condition, for choosing the antecedent and repudiating the consequent. Finally, intelligible orders include concrete objects of desire and exclude concrete objects of aversion, and so from the dynamic exigence of rational self-consciousness, by the simple process of asking what in fact that exigence concretely is, there can be determined a body of ethical principles.

1.4 The Method of Ethics   [602–604]

There follows a conclusion of fundamental importance, namely, the parallel and interpenetration of metaphysics and ethics. For just as the dynamic structure of our knowing grounds a metaphysics, so the prolongation of that structure into human doing grounds an ethics. Just as the universe of proportionate being is a compound of potency, form, and act, because it is to be known through experience, understanding, and judgment, so the universe of man's proportionate good is a compound of objects of desire, intelligible orders, and values, because the good that man does intelligently and rationally is a manifold in the field of experience, ordered by intelligence, and rationally chosen. Just as metaphysics is a set of positions opposed by sets of counterpositions that arise from the incomplete domination in knowing of the detached and disinterested desire to know, so also values are true and false, orders are troubled by disorders, and desires are unnecessarily frustrated, because the detachment and disinterestedness of the pure desire easily fails to develop into fully rational self-consciousness. Just as the counterpositions of metaphysics invite their own reversal by their inconsistency with intelligent and reasonable affirmation, so the basically similar counterpositions of the ethical order, through the shorter and longer cycles of the dialectic of progress and decline, either enforce their own reversal or destroy their carriers. Just as the heuristic structure of our knowing couples with the generalized emergent probability of the proportionate universe, to reveal an upwardly directed dynamism of finality towards ever fuller being, so the obligatory structure of our rational self-consciousness (1) finds its materials and its basis in the products of universal finality, (2) is itself finality on the level of intelligent and rational consciousness, and (3) is finality confronted with the alternative of choosing either development and progress or decline and extinction.

The theme of the parallel and interpenetration of metaphysics and ethics cannot be expanded further in the present context, but at least something must be said on its methodological ground. We refused to conceive metaphysical method either as an abstract or as a concrete or as a transcendental deduction, not because we denied the exposition of a metaphysics to make use of the deductive form, but because we placed the principles of metaphysics neither in sentences nor in propositions nor in judgments but in the very structure of our knowing. Because that structure is latent and operative in everyone's knowing, it is universal on the side of the subject; and because that structure can be distorted by the interference of alien desires, it grounds a dialectical criticism of subjects. Again, because that structure is employed in every instance of knowing, it is universal on the side of the proportionate object; and because the structure remains dynamic until all questions are answered, it regards every proportionate object concretely. Accordingly, metaphysical method can take subjects as they are, invoke dialectical criticism to bring their fundamental orientations into agreement, and apply this agreement to the whole domain of proportionate being in its concreteness. But essentially the same method is available for ethics. Deductivism is brushed aside, not because there are no universally valid precepts, nor because conclusions do not follow from them,[b] but because the most basic precepts with all their conclusions fail to go to the root of the matter. For the root of ethics, as the root of metaphysics, lies neither in sentences nor in propositions nor in judgments but in the dynamic structure of rational self-consciousness. Because that structure is latent and operative in everyone's choosing, it is universal on the side of the subject; because that structure can be dodged, it grounds a dialectical criticism of subjects. Again, because that structure is recurrent in every act of choice, it is universal on the side of the object;[c] and because its universality consists not in abstraction but in inevitable recurrence, it also is concrete. Accordingly, ethical method, as metaphysical, can take subjects as they are; it can correct any aberration in their views by a dialectical criticism; and it can apply these corrected views to the totality of concrete objects of choice. Such a method not only sets forth precepts but also bases them on their real principles, which are not propositions or judgments but existing persons; it not only sets forth correct precepts but also provides a radical criticism for mistaken precepts; it is not content to appeal to logic for the application of precepts, for it can criticize situations as well as subjects, and it can invoke dialectical analysis to reveal how situations are to be corrected; finally, because such a method clearly grasps an unchanging dynamic structure immanent in developing subjects that deal with changing situations in correspondingly changing manners, it can steer a sane course between the relativism of mere concreteness and the legalism of remote and static generalities; and it can do so, not by good luck nor by vaguely postulating prudence, but methodically, because it takes its stand on the ever recurrent dynamic generality that is the structure of rational self-consciousness.

1.5 The Ontology of the Good [604–607]

So far our analysis has been concerned with the good in a human sense, with objects of desire, intelligible orders, terminal and originating values. But as the close relations between metaphysics and ethics suggest, it should be possible to generalize this notion and, indeed, to conceive the good as identical with the intelligibility that is intrinsic to being.

The main lines of the generalization are grasped easily enough. Instead of speaking of objects of desire, the intelligible orders within which desires are satisfied, and the terminal and originating values involved in choosing such orders and their contents, we propose to speak of a potential, formal, and actual good, where the potential good is identical with potential intelligibility and so includes but also extends beyond objects of desire, where the formal good is identical with formal intelligibility and so includes but also extends beyond human intelligible orders, where the actual good is identical with actual intelligibilities and so includes but also may extend beyond human values.

The justification of this generalization of the notion of the good is that it is already implicit in the narrower notion. Objects of desire are manifold, but they are not an isolated manifold. They are existents and events that in their concrete possibility and in their realization are bound inextricably through natural laws and actual frequencies with the total manifold of the universe of proportionate being. If objects of desire are instances of the good because of the satisfactions they yield, then the rest of the manifold of existents and events also are a good, because desires are satisfied not in some dreamland but only in the concrete universe. Again, the intelligible orders that are invented, implemented, adjusted, and improved by men are but further exploitations of prehuman intelligible orders; moreover, they fall within the universal order of generalized emergent probability, both as consequents of its fertility and as ruled by its more inclusive sweep. If the intelligible orders of human invention are a good because they systematically assure the satisfaction of desires, then so also are the intelligible orders that underlie, condition, precede, and include man's invention. Finally, intelligible orders and their contents, as possible objects of rational choice, are values; but the universal order which is generalized emergent probability conditions and penetrates, corrects and develops every particular order; and rational self-consciousness cannot consistently choose the conditioned and reject the condition, choose the part and reject the whole, choose the consequent and reject the antecedent. Accordingly, since man is involved in choosing, and since every consistent choice, at least implicitly, is a choice of universal order, the realization of universal order is a true value.

It will be noted that the third part of the argument includes the other two. For the actual good of value presupposes the formal good of order, and the formal good of order presupposes the potential good of a manifold to be ordered. Moreover, the realization of universal order is the realization of all existents and all events; universal order includes all intelligibilities as its constituent parts, whether they are unities or conjugates, frequencies or the operators of development; and universal order presupposes all manifolds that are ordered or to be ordered. So the good is identified with the intelligibility intrinsic to being.

To carry out so broad a generalization is far easier than to state exactly the range of its implications. Ignorance of implications, in turn, gives rise to the suspicion that one is being tricked into an easy optimism that denies the rather evident fact of evil in this universe. Accordingly, it will not be amiss to assert emphatically that the identification of being and the good bypasses human feelings and sentiments to take its stand exclusively upon intelligible order and rational value.

Feelings and sentiments are bypassed for, though one begins from objects of desire, one finds the potential good not in them alone but in the total manifold of the universe. This step does not suppose the discovery of some calculus to measure pleasure and pain, nor does it introduce any claim that the pleasure outweighs the pain. Quite simply it notes that objects of desire are manifold, that this manifold, so far from being isolated, is part and parcel of the total manifold, and that it is in the total manifold that concretely and effectively the potential good resides. Now it is to this first step that the hedonist or sentimentalist must object. He must claim that the meaning of the term 'good' is settled on the unquestioning and unquestionable level of experience, that the good has to be the good as experienced, and that opposite to the good there is the no less real category of evil as experienced. Moreover, the foregoing is a quite coherent position, as long as no claim is made that it is either intelligent or reasonable. The trouble is that the claim cannot be avoided, and once it is made the contradiction becomes obvious; for it is only by excluding the relevance of questions for intelligence and reflection that the good can be identified with objects of desire; and if such questions are excluded, then intelligence and reasonableness are excluded. On the other hand, if the determination of the notion of the good is a matter of intelligent inquiry and critical reflection, then critical reflection's affirmation will be knowledge of the actual component of the good, intelligent inquiry's explanation will be knowledge[d] of the formal component of the good, the manifold of objects of desire can be no more than a potential good, and the way is open to the discovery that the manifold of indifferent objects and even the manifold of objects of aversion also are a potential good. Finally, to throw in the obvious methodological note, the positions and counterpositions of metaphysics not only have their prolongations into ethics but also these prolongations respectively invite development or invite reversal by the same dialectical procedures as the metaphysical originals.

As the identification of the good with being in no manner denies or attempts to minimize pain or suffering, so it has not the slightest implication of a denial of unordered manifolds, of disorder, or of false values. For the middle term in the identification of the good with being is intelligibility. The intelligibility of this universe is to be grasped not only by direct but also by inverse insights; it is to be reached not by a single method but by the fourfold battery of classical and genetic, statistical and dialectical methods. Insofar as the intelligibility of this universe is statistical, its goodness consists potentially in unordered manifolds, formally in the effective probability of the emergence of order, and actually in the eventual emergence. Insofar as the intelligibility of this universe is genetic, its goodness consists potentially in the incompleteness and awkwardness of earlier stages of development, formally in the sequence of operators that would replace generic incompleteness by specific perfection, and actually in the attainment of that perfection. Insofar as the intelligibility of this universe is dialectical, its goodness consists potentially in the failures and refusals of autonomous self-consciousness to be consistently reasonable, formally in the inner and outer tensions through which such failures and refusals bring about either the choice of their own reversal or the elimination of those that obstinately refuse the reversal, and actually in the consequent removal of disorders and false values. To identify the good with the intelligibility of being is to identify it, not with the ideal intelligibility of some postulated utopia, but with the ascertainable intelligibility of the universe that exists.

2   The Notion of Freedom   [607–19]

Further clarification of the notions of will and choice introduced in the preceding section demands a consideration of the nature of human freedom.

2.1   The Significance of Statistical Residues   [607–608]

In our account of the canon of statistical residues it was argued that, while any physical event Z is implicit in a spatially and temporally scattered set of antecedents $P, Q, R, \ldots$, nonetheless this implication does not admit systematic formulation. For the implication is constituted by the combination of a major and a minor premise; and while the major premise resides in laws and systematic unifications of laws, the minor premise lies in the concrete pattern of a diverging series of conditions that cannot be determined systematically. Accordingly, the objective significance of statistical laws is, not that physical events occur freely, nor even that under special circumstances, such as schemes of recurrence, they cannot be predicted with a qualified certainty, but that in general they cannot be predicted in virtue of any systematic deduction.

However, the existence of statistical residues is the possibility of higher integrations. There can be autonomous sciences of physics, chemistry, biology, and psychology, because on each earlier level of systematization there are statistical residues that constitute the merely coincidental manifolds to be systematized on the next level. It follows that higher laws and higher schemes of recurrence cannot be deduced from lower laws and lower schemes of recurrence, for the higher is engaged in regulating what the lower leaves as merely coincidental. Moreover, since there are statistical residues on every level, it follows that events on any given level cannot be deduced in systematic fashion from the combination of all the laws and all the schemes of recurrence of that and of all prior levels.

Accordingly, the significance of the canon of statistical residues is not that it implies the freedom of our choices. Its significance lies in the fact that it makes possible an account of the autonomy of the successive departments of science, that this autonomy excludes a determinism of the higher by the lower, and that the canon of statistical residues itself excludes a deductive determinism in either the lower or the higher. Undoubtedly, these exclusions make it far easier to dispose of arguments against the possibility of freedom, and they narrow down the field in which impediments to freedom can be found. Still, they are only exclusions. A positive account of freedom must arise from an examination of the act of will and of its intellectual antecedents.

2.2 The Underlying Sensitive Flow [608–609]

In such a positive account there are four main elements, namely, the underlying sensitive flow, the practical insight, the process of reflection, and the decision.

The underlying sensitive flow consists of sensible presentations and imaginative representations, of affective and aggressive feelings, of conscious bodily movements, etc. In this flow the sensitive psychologist can discern various laws and can work out consequent schemes of recurrence; he can compare such a flow at earlier and later stages of psychic development and move to the discovery of the operators that explanatorily relate the laws effective at one time to the laws effective at another. However, if his statement of his results is intelligent and reasonable, then his statement is not simply a product of the laws and schemes operative in his own psyche. On the contrary, precisely insofar as his statement is intelligent and reasonable, it consists in the imposition of higher integrations upon what is merely coincidental as far as the laws and schemes of his psyche go. Moreover, this possibility of imposing higher integrations upon lower coincidental manifolds is not restricted to psychological investigators; it is a general possibility; and it is only insofar as this possibility has been realized that there arises the question of any free choice.

There follows an important corollary. If it happens that we discover the existence of free acts of will, at least it will not happen that we discover all the acts of all men to be free. For from the outset we are excluding from consideration any act that occurs through mere sensitive routine and that can be accounted for without appealing to the introduction of some higher integration by intelligence.

2.3 The Practical Insight [609–10]

The second element to be considered is the practical insight. As any direct insight, it results from inquiry and it emerges upon the sensitive flow, in which it grasps some intelligible unity or correlation. Again, as in any direct insight, the mere fact of grasping the unity or correlation does not imply that the unity exists or that the correlation governs actual events. For beyond the question for intelligence that is met by insight, there is always the question for reflection. However, while the speculative or factual insight is followed by the question whether the unity exists or whether the correlation governs events, the practical insight is followed by the question whether the unity is going to be made to exist or whether the correlation is going to be made to govern events. In other words, while speculative and factual insights are concerned to lead to knowledge of being, practical insights are concerned to lead to the making of being. Their objective is not what is but what is to be done. They reveal, not the unities and relations of things as they are, but the unities and relations of possible courses of action.

There follows another important corollary. When speculative or factual insight is correct, reflective understanding can grasp a relevant virtually unconditioned. But when practical insight is correct, then reflective understanding cannot grasp a relevant virtually unconditioned; for if it could, the content of the insight already would be a fact; and if it were already a fact, then it would not be a possible course of action which, as yet, is not a fact but just a possibility.

2.4 Practical Reflection   [610–12]

The third element to be considered is reflection. For the grasp of a possible course of action need not result automatically and blindly in its execution. Further questions can be raised, and commonly their number varies with our familiarity with the situation in hand, with the seriousness of the consequences of the proposed course of action, with the uncertainties and the risks it involves, with our antecedent willingness or unwillingness to assume responsibility for the consequences and to run the risks. But the essence of the reflection does not consist in the number of questions asked or in the length of time spent in reaching answers. For further questions may regard the object; then one asks oneself just what the proposed course of action is, what are its successive steps, what alternatives it admits, what it excludes, what consequences it will have, whether the whole proposal is really possible, just how probable or certain are its various features. But in a familiar situation one may already know the answers to all these questions, and then there is no need to inquire into the object of the act; like the master of a science, one has only to advert to the issue to reach a full grasp of it and of its implications. Again, further questions may regard motives for the course of action. Would its execution be agreeable? Are there other features to compensate for its disagreeableness? What is its utility? How desirable are the goals to which it is useful? From the greater or less satisfaction of more or fewer desires one can turn to the consideration of intelligible order and then of value. Does the proposed act come under the accepted order? If not, is it merely egoistic, or is it a contribution to the initiation of an improvement in the accepted order? Or if it does come under the accepted order, is not that order in need of improvement? Is not this the time to begin improving things? Finally, all such questions may be superfluous. There is no need to marshal motives in the given instance, because willingness to perform such an act has become habitual. Still, is that willingness right or wrong, good or bad? The world's work would be never done unless we acted largely out of habit. But might not my habits be improved? Are the values to which they commit me true or false? Am I intelligent and reasonable enough in the short run, only to be blind to the larger implications of my way of living? Or if I advert to such larger implications, am I doing what I can to be helpful to others in this respect?

There follows a set of corollaries. First of all, the reflection consists in an actuation of rational self-consciousness. I am empirically conscious inasmuch as I am experiencing, intellectually conscious inasmuch as I am inquiring or formulating intelligently, rationally conscious inasmuch as I am seeking to grasp the virtually unconditioned or judging on the basis of such a grasp. But I become rationally self-conscious inasmuch as I am concerned with reasons for my own acts, and this occurs when I scrutinize the object and investigate the motives of a possible course of action.

Secondly, though the reflection heads beyond knowing to doing, still it consists simply in knowing. Thus, it may reveal that the proposed action is concretely possible, clearly effective, highly agreeable, quite useful, morally obligatory, etc. But it is one thing to know exactly what could be done and all the reasons for doing it. It is quite another for such knowledge to issue in doing.

Thirdly, the reflection has no internal term, no capacity of its own to come to an end. For it is a knowing that leads to doing. Insofar as it is a knowing, it can reach an internal term, for one can grasp the virtually unconditioned and thereby attain certitude on the possibility of a proposed course of action, on its agreeableness, on its utility, on its obligatoriness. But insofar as this knowing is practical, insofar as its concern is with something to be done and with the reasons for doing it, the reflection has not an internal but an external term; for the reflection is just knowing, but the term is an ulterior deciding and doing.

Fourthly, because the reflection has no internal term, it can expand more or less indefinitely. The proposed action can be examined in enormous detail; its certain, probable, and possible consequences can be followed far into the future; motives can be submitted to fine analysis; the variation in their appeal at different times can be noted and studied; from concrete questions one can shift to general philosophic issues, to return to the concrete with inquiries about one's orientation in life and the influence upon one of unconscious factors. So the native hue of resolution is sicklied over with the pale cast of thought.

Fifthly, one can advert to the possibility of reflection expanding indefinitely, to the incompatibility between such expansion and the business of living, and to the unreasonableness of the expansion. Still such advertence is simply a transposition of the issue. Reflection on a course of action is replaced by reflection on reflection. As the former heads beyond itself to a decision, so the latter heads beyond itself to a decision to decide. As the former yields the conclusion that I should act or not act in a given manner, so the latter yields the conclusion that I should decide to decide or not decide in that manner. But it is one thing to know what I should do, and it is another to do it.

Sixthly, while there is a normal duration for the reflection, it is not reflection but decision that enforces the norm. Reflection occurs because rational self-consciousness demands knowledge of what one proposes to do and of the reasons one has for doing it. Its normal duration is the length of time needed to learn the nature of the object of the proposed act and to persuade oneself to willingness to perform the act. Accordingly, the normal duration is a variable that is inverse to one's antecedent knowledge and willingness. But it is neither the normal duration itself nor reflection upon it that ends the process of reflecting. For that process has no internal term, no capacity to bring itself to an end. What ends the reflection is the decision. As long as I am reflecting, I have not decided yet. Until I have decided, the reflection can be prolonged by further questions. But once I have decided and as long as I remain decided, the reflection is over and done with. The proposed course of action has ceased to be a mere possibility; it has begun to be an actuality.

There remains to be considered the fourth element in our analysis. It is the decision, and one will do well to distinguish between the decision itself and its manifestation whether in execution, or in knowledge, or in expression of that knowledge. For the decision itself is an act of willing. It possesses the internal alternatives of either consenting or refusing. It may also possess external alternatives, when different courses of action are considered simultaneously, and then consent to one and refusal of the others constitute a choice.

The fundamental nature of decision is best revealed by comparing it with judgment. Decision, then, resembles judgment inasmuch as both select one member of a pair of contradictories; as judgment either affirms or denies, so decision either consents or refuses. Again, both decision and judgment are concerned with actuality; but judgment is concerned to complete one's knowledge of an actuality that already exists, while decision is concerned to confer actuality upon a course of action that otherwise will not exist. Finally, both decision and judgment are rational, for both deal with objects apprehended by insight, and both occur because of a reflective grasp of reasons.

However, there is a radical difference between the rationality of judgment and the rationality of decision. Judgment is an act of rational consciousness, but decision is an act of rational self-consciousness. The rationality of judgment emerges in the unfolding of the detached and disinterested desire to know in the process towards knowledge of the universe of being. But the rationality of decision emerges in the demand of the rationally conscious subject for consistency between his knowing and his deciding and doing. Again, the rationality of judgment emerges if in fact a reasonable judgment occurs, but the rationality of decision emerges if in fact a reasonable decision occurs. Finally, the effective rationality of the subject of rational consciousness is radically negative, for then the subject is effectively rational if he does not allow other desire to interfere with the functioning of the pure desire to know; but the effective rationality of the subject of rational self-consciousness is radically positive, for then the subject is effectively rational only if his demand for consistency between knowing and doing is followed by his deciding and doing in a manner consistent with his knowing.

In other words, there is a succession of enlargements of consciousness, a succession of transformations of what consciousness means. Waking replaces dreaming. Intelligent inquiry emerges in waking to compound intelligent with empirical consciousness. Critical reflection follows understanding and formulation to add rational consciousness to intelligent and empirical consciousness. But the final enlargement and transformation of consciousness consists in the empirically, intelligently, and rationally conscious subject (1) demanding conformity of his doing to his knowing, and (2) acceding to that demand by deciding reasonably.

Again, a set of corollaries is to be noted. For, in the first place, it is now possible to explain why practical reflection lacks an internal term. If it were concerned simply with knowing what the proposed course of action is and what are the motives in its favor, it would be an activity of rational consciousness and would possess an internal term in certain judgments upon the object and the motives of the proposed action. But practical reflection is concerned with knowing only in order to guide doing. It is an activity that involves an enlarging transformation of consciousness. In that enlarged consciousness the term is not judgment but decision. Consequently, practical reflection does not come to an end once the object and motives of a proposed action are known; it comes to an end when one decides either in favor of the proposal or against it.

Secondly, the same enlarging transformation of consciousness illuminates both the meaning and the frequent inefficacy of obligation. It is possible for practical reflection to reach with certitude the conclusion that a proposed course of action is obligatory, that either I decide in favor of the proposal or else I surrender consistency between my knowing and my doing. Now in such instances it is apparent that the emergence of an obligation is the emergence of a rational necessity in rational consciousness. I cannot prevent questions for reflection from arising; once they arise, I cannot set aside the demand of my rationality that I assent if, and only if, I grasp the virtually unconditioned; and once I judge that I ought to act in a determinate manner, that I cannot both be reasonable and act otherwise, then my reasonableness is bound to the act by a link of necessity. Such is the meaning of obligation.

Yet the fact remains that I can fail to fulfil my known obligations, that the iron link of necessity can prove to be a wisp of straw. How can this be? How can necessity turn out to be contingence? The answer lies in the enlarging transformation of consciousness. The rationality that imposes an obligation is not conditioned internally by an act of will. The rationality that carries out an obligation is conditioned internally by the occurrence of a reasonable act of will. To repeat the point in other words, the rational subject as imposing an obligation upon himself is just a knower, and his rationality consists radically in not allowing other desire to interfere with the unfolding of the detached and disinterested desire to know. But the rational subject as carrying out an obligation is not just a knower but also a doer, and his rationality consists not merely in excluding interference with cognitional process but also in extending the rationality of his knowing into the field of doing. But that extension does not occur simply by knowing one's obligations. It occurs just inasmuch as one wills to meet one's obligations.

How then does necessity turn out to be contingence? Clearly, there is no change in the necessity itself, but there occurs a change in the context. Rational consciousness is being transformed into rational self-consciousness. What in the context of rational consciousness is a rational necessity, in the context of rational self-consciousness becomes a rational exigence. If a proposed action is obligatory, then one cannot be a rational knower and deny the obligation, and one cannot be a rational doer and not fulfil the obligation. But one can be a rational knower without an act of willing, and one cannot be a rational doer without an act of willing. It is the addition of the further constitutive requirement of an act of will that (1) marks the shift from rational consciousness to rational self-consciousness, and (2) changes what is rational necessity in the field of knowing into rational exigence in the larger field of both knowing and doing.

Thirdly, the same enlarging transformation throws light upon the difference between the acknowledgment of actuality in judgment and the bestowal of actuality by decision. As has been seen, both judgment and decision are concerned with actuality; but judgment merely acknowledges an actuality that already exists; while decision confers actuality upon a course of action that otherwise is merely possible.

Now actuality has peculiar characteristics. It is known primarily by grasping the virtually unconditioned, the conditioned that happens to have its conditions fulfilled. Because it is unconditioned, it ranks high in the field of intelligibility. Still, it merely happens to have its conditions fulfilled, and so it merely happens to be an unconditioned. Though unconditioned, it also is contingent. And this contingence appears (1) in its being, (2) in its being known, and (3) in its being willed.

It is apparent in its being. For actuality as act is existence or occurrence, and actuality as of the actuated supposes at least existence and also at times occurrence. But there is no systematic deduction of existence or occurrence. The most that understanding can do is set up ideal frequencies from which actual frequencies of existence and occurrence do not diverge systematically. But actual frequencies can and do diverge nonsystematically from the ideal, and so in every instance actuality is just what happens to be.

Again, contingence is apparent in actuality as known. For it is known by grasping the virtually unconditioned. The virtually unconditioned can be grasped if fulfilment of its conditions happens to be given. And the fulfilment can never be more than what happens, for the fulfilment consists in the occurrence of relevant data, and the occurrence of data, like all occurrence, is contingent. For it merely happens that I exist, that I experience in such and such a manner, etc.

Finally, the possible courses of action invented by intelligence, motivated by reason, and executed by willing are contingent in their actuality. For the insights that reveal possible courses of action also reveal that they are not necessities but mere possibilities in need of reflective evaluation. Reflective evaluation in turn brings to light not what must be so but merely what for such and such reasons may be chosen or rejected. Lastly, even when reflective evaluation reveals only one course of action to be reasonable, there still is needed the reasonableness of actual willing; and as the reasonableness of human acts of will is not a natural endowment but an ever uncertain personal achievement, there is a third and final contingence to the actuality of courses of action. In particular, one should note the fallacy in every argument from determinate knowing to determinate willing. For every argument of that type must postulate a conformity between knowing and willing. But such conformity exists only when in fact willing actually is reasonable. Hence, to deduce the determinate act of will one must postulate the conformity; and to verify the postulate one must already have the determinate willing that one is out to demonstrate.

2.6 Freedom   [616–19]

Further consideration of the contingence of the act of will brings us to the notion of freedom. As this is our main topic, it may not be amiss to resume what has been said. Proportionate being, then, involves a number of explanatory genera, so that there is a series of levels of operation with each higher level making systematic what otherwise would have been merely coincidental on the previous level. It follows that there can be distinct, autonomous, yet related departments of science: distinct, because they deal with different levels of proportionate being; autonomous, because defining relations on any level constitute a closed system; related, because each higher level finds its materials in the coincidental manifold of the previous level, and each lower level supplies a coincidental manifold for the next higher level.

While this analysis goes beyond determinism by its acknowledgment of statistical laws and of autonomous sciences, it does not imply freedom. Though classical laws are abstract, they retain their universality, so that occurrence is always according to law. Though the application of abstract laws to concrete situations involves an appeal to a nonsystematic manifold of further determinations, this merely means that there can be no general procedure for establishing concrete premises of the type 'If P, Q, R, . . . occur, then Z must occur.' But it is not impossible to formulate such premises in particular instances, notably in the special situations created in laboratories. Nor is it impossible to make accurate predictions of the distant future, when schemes of recurrence exist and their survival is supposed.

Accordingly, an account of freedom has to turn to a study of intellect and will. In the coincidental manifolds of sensible presentations, practical insights grasp possible courses of action that are examined by reflection, decided upon by acts of willing, and thereby either are or are not realized in the underlying sensitive flow. In this process there is to be discerned the emergence of elements of higher integration. For the higher integration effected on the level of human living consists of sets of courses of action, and these actions emerge inasmuch as they are understood by intelligent consciousness, evaluated by rational consciousness, and willed by rational self-consciousness.

To grasp the significance of this emergence, one must revert to the point already made that intelligibility is intrinsic to being and that it is either spiritual or material, either an intelligibility that also is intelligent or else an intelligibility that is not also intelligent. For the distinction between the spiritual and the material emphasizes the fact that the intelligent and rational emergence of courses of action stands to the level of distinctively human operations as dynamic systems on the move stand to the psychic and organic levels and as static systems stand to the chemical and physical orders of events. In other words, practical insight, reflection, and decision are a legislative function; instead of being subject to laws, as are physical and chemical events, they are what make the laws of the distinctively human level of operations. Where material reality is subject to law and thereby intelligible, spiritual reality has intelligibility, not through subjection to law, but by its native intelligence; and while spiritual reality is manifested through the higher systematization or order it imposes on lower levels of being, still that systematization or order is not imposed upon spiritual reality, as the law of inverse squares upon masses, but is generated by practical insights, rational reflection, and decision.

At this point, however, there crops up the ambiguity of the notion of law. There are, then, the laws of matter and the laws of spirit.[e] The laws of matter are investigated by empirical scientists, and when spirit is said to be legislative, one means that spirit originates intelligible orders that are parallel to the intelligibilities investigated by empirical scientists. On the other hand, the laws of spirit are the principles and norms that govern spirit in the exercise of its legislative function; and they differ radically from the laws of matter, not only in their higher point of application, but also in their nature and content. As has been seen, the laws of matter are abstract, and they can be applied concretely only by the addition of further determinations from a nonsystematic manifold. But the laws of spirit reside in the dynamic structure of its cognitional and volitional operations, and their concrete application is effected through spirit's own operations within that dynamic structure. Thus, in working out the notion of the good, we discovered in the rationally self-conscious subject an exigence for consistency between his knowing and his doing, and we saw how a body of ethical precepts could be derived simply by asking what concretely was implicit in that exigence. As metaphysics is a corollary to the structure of knowing, so ethics is a corollary to the structure of knowing and doing; and as ethics resides in the structure, so the concrete applications of ethics are worked out by spirit inasmuch as it operates within the structure to reflect and decide upon the possible courses of action that it grasps.

It follows that there is a radical difference between the contingence of the act of willing and the general contingence of existence and occurrence in the rest of the domain of proportionate being. The latter contingence falls short of strict intelligible necessity, not because it is free, but because it is involved in the nonsystematic character of material multiplicity, continuity, and frequency. But the contingence of the act of will,[f] so far from resulting from the nonsystematic, arises in the imposition of further intelligible order upon otherwise merely coincidental manifolds. Moreover, that imposition of further intelligible order is the work of intelligence, of rational reflection, and of ethically guided will. Nonetheless, that imposition of intelligible order is contingent. For, on the one hand, even when possibility is unique, so that rational consciousness has no alternative, still the unique possibility is not realized necessarily. To claim that the sole reasonable course of action is realized necessarily is to claim that willing is necessarily consistent with knowing. But that claim is preposterous, for it contradicts the common experience of a divergence between what one does and what one knows one ought to do. Nor is it preposterous merely in fact but also in principle, for actual consistency between knowing and deciding is the result of deciding reasonably, and what results from deciding reasonably cannot be erected into a universal principle that proves all decisions to be necessarily reasonable.

Freedom, then, is a special kind of contingence. It is contingence that arises, not from the empirical residue that grounds materiality and the nonsystematic, but in the order of spirit, of intelligent grasp, rational reflection, and morally guided will. It has the twofold basis that its object is merely a possibility and that its agent is contingent not only in his existence but also in the extension of his rational consciousness into rational self-consciousness. For it is one and the same act of willing that both decides in favor of the object or against it and that constitutes the subject as deciding reasonably or unreasonably, as succeeding or failing in the extension of rational consciousness into an effectively rational self-consciousness.

Accordingly, freedom possesses not only the negative aspect of excluding necessity but also the positive aspect of responsibility. Intelligent grasp of a possible course of action need not result automatically in its execution, for critical reflection can intervene to scrutinize the object and evaluate the motives. Critical reflection cannot execute the proposed action, for it is simply a knowing. Knowing cannot necessitate the decision, for consistency between knowing and willing becomes an actuality only through the willing. The decision, then, is not a consequent but a new emergence that both realizes the course of action or rejects it, and realizes an effectively rational self-consciousness or fails to do so. Nonetheless, though the act of will is a contingent emergence, it also is an act of the subject; the measure of the freedom with which the act occurs also is the measure of his responsibility for it.

3   **The Problem of Liberation** ~   [619–33]

3.1 Essential and Effective Freedom   [619–22]

The difference between essential and effective freedom is the difference between a dynamic structure and its operational range. Man is free essentially inasmuch as possible courses of action are grasped by practical insight, motivated by reflection, and executed by decision. But man is free effectively to a greater or less extent inasmuch as this dynamic structure is open to grasping, motivating, and executing a broad or a narrow range of otherwise possible courses of action. Thus, one may be essentially but not effectively free to give up smoking.

A consideration of effective freedom is meaningless, unless essential freedom exists. Nonetheless, the negation of full effective freedom may appear a negation of essential freedom if the proper grounds of the latter are not grasped clearly and distinctly. Accordingly, it hardly will be amiss to recall briefly the main points that already have been made.

First, then, all formal intelligibility within the domain of proportionate being is contingent. It is not what of itself must be but merely what in fact happens to be. Hence, species are not realizations of static descriptive concepts but intelligible solutions to the concrete problems of generalized emergent probability and so subject to variation with variation of the problems. Again, natural laws are not to be determined by pure speculation but solely by an empirical method in which what is grasped by insight is mere hypothesis until confirmed by verification. Finally, the possible courses of action grasped by practical insight are merely possible until they are motivated by reflection and executed by decision.

Secondly, not only are possible courses of action contingent but also they constitute a manifold of alternatives. The sensitive flow of a man's percepts and images, feelings and conations offers an otherwise coincidental manifold for higher systematization. In fact, that higher systematization is effected in different manners, whether one considers the same individual at different times, or different individuals, or aggregates of individuals in different environments or different epochs or different cultures.

Thirdly, not only are possible courses of action a manifold, but man is aware of the alternatives. He does not suffer from the illusion that because a course of action is possible therefore it also is necessary. The possibilities that he grasps are submitted to reflective examination, and such examination commonly leads to a grasp of further possibilities. Nor does the examination come to an end out of its own resources but only through the intervention of the will's decision.

Fourthly, the will's decision is not determined by its antecedents. For the remote antecedents lie on the levels of physics, chemistry, biology, and sensitive psychology; and events on such lower levels determine merely the materials that admit a manifold of alternative higher systematizations. On the other hand, the proximate antecedents merely define and motivate the alternative higher systematizations; they present no more than a projected formal intelligibility, which, so far from necessitating its own actuality, can attain actuality only if the will decides in its favor.

Fifthly, the most obvious bit of evidence for the freedom of man's decisions lies in the possibility of inconsistency between human knowing and doing; for if such inconsistency is possible, then there cannot be any valid argument from determinate knowing to determinate willing and doing. However, one is not to mistake the obvious for the essential. Man is not free because he can be unreasonable in his choices. Rather the root of freedom lies in the contingence of the formal intelligibility of proportionate being. Because such intelligibility is contingent, it cannot guarantee its own existence or occurrence. Again, because it is contingent, it is not unique but a manifold of alternatives. Further, because it is contingent, it is known as merely possible, as in need of motivation, as needing motivation because it will exist or occur only if decision is forthcoming. Finally, because it is contingent, there cannot be valid motives for it that necessitate decision in its favor.

To put the point in another manner, any practical insight can be formulated in a proposition of the type 'Under such and such circumstances the intelligent thing to do is to make such and such a decision.' Let the totality of circumstances be denoted by P and the decision by Q. Then the content of the practical insight will be the inferential relation 'If P, then Q.' But such an inferential relation ceases to be a mere supposition about what might be or should be and becomes a true statement of what is, only when the act of will Q occurs. But any attempt to show that the act of will is necessitated by its proximate antecedents must suppose the truth of the inferential relation 'If P, then Q.' Therefore, it must suppose that the act of will is occurring. And so it is involved in a *petitio principii* or, if you prefer, in a simple appeal to the principle of identity, namely, If the act Q is occurring, then it must be occurring.

Sixthly, though the act of will is free, it is not arbitrary. A course of action is intelligent and intelligible if it is grasped by a practical insight. It is reasonable if it is motivated favorably by rational reflection. The act of will has the function of conferring actuality upon an intelligible, intelligent, and reasonable course of action; and what is intelligible, intelligent, and reasonable is not arbitrary.

Seventhly, the analysis is quite general. For while there is presupposed a sensitive flow that receives a higher integration, still intelligent grasp, reflection, and decision rise from the flow as content, and that content may be not representative but symbolic. Thus, one can make decisions about deciding by having the sensitive flow present the relevant words.

3.2 Conditions of Effective Freedom [622–24]

Conditions of effective freedom may be listed under the four headings of (1) external circumstance, (2) the subject as sensitive, (3) the subject as intelligent, and (4) the subject as antecedently willing.

Everyone is familiar with the limitations placed upon effective freedom by external constraint. But just as the prisoner is not free to go and come as he pleases, so the Eskimo is not free to mount a camel or the desert nomad to go fishing in a kayak. Whatever one's external circumstances may be, they offer only a limited range of concretely possible alternatives and only limited resources for bringing about the enlargement of that range.

In the second place, there are the limitations that arise from one's psychoneural state. It is the proximate source of the otherwise coincidental manifold that receives its higher integration from intelligence and will. In the normal state, there is a spontaneous adaptation and adjustment between the orientations of intellectual and of psychoneural[g] development. But even perfect adjustment does not dispense one from the necessity of acquiring sensitive skills and habits, and until they are acquired, one is not free to speak a foreign language or to play the violin merely by taking thought. Moreover, perfect adjustment may be lacking; scotosis can result in a conflict between the operators of intellectual and of psychoneural development; and then the sensitive subject is invaded by anxiety, by obsessions, and by other neurotic phenomena that restrict his capacity for effective deliberation and choice.

Thirdly, there are the limitations of intellectual development. Once one has understood, one can reproduce almost at will the act of understanding. But until one has understood, one has to struggle through the process of learning. Moreover, the greater one's accumulation of insights, the broader is the base from which one can move towards still further insights and, perhaps, the greater is the facility with which one can reach them. Now the same laws hold for the occurrence of practical insights as for insights generally, and so it is that the greater the development of one's practical intelligence, the greater the range of possible courses of action one can grasp and consider. Inversely, the less the development of one's practical intelligence, the less the range of possible courses of action that here and now will occur to one.

Fourthly, we have distinguished already between the conjugate potency 'will,' the conjugate form 'willingness,' and the conjugate act 'willing.' Will is the bare capacity to make decisions. Willingness is the state in which persuasion is not needed to bring one to a decision. Willing, finally, is the act of deciding.

Now the function of willingness runs parallel to the function of the habitual accumulation of insights. What one does not understand yet, one can learn; but learning takes time, and until that time is devoted to learning, otherwise possible courses of action are excluded. Similarly, when antecedent willingness is lacking, persuasion can be invoked; but persuasion takes time, and until that time is devoted to persuading oneself or to being persuaded by others, one remains closed to otherwise possible courses of action.

There is a further aspect to the matter. For genetically one mounts from empirical to intellectual consciousness, from intellectual to rational consciousness, and from rational consciousness to rational self-consciousness. As long as one is moving towards full self-possession, the detached and disinterested desire to know tends to be in control. But once one is in the state of rational self-consciousness, then one's decisions are in control, for they set the objective of one's total activity and select the actions that are to lead to the goal. So it is that a person, caught as it were unawares, may be ready for any scheme or exploit but, on the second thoughts of rational self-consciousness, settles back into the narrow routine defined by his antecedent willingness. For unless one's antecedent willingness has the height and breadth and depth of the unrestricted desire to know, the emergence of rational self-consciousness involves the addition of a restriction upon one's effective freedom.

In brief, effective freedom itself has to be won. The key point is to reach a willingness to persuade oneself and to submit to the persuasion of others. For then one can be persuaded to a universal willingness; so one becomes antecedently willing to learn all there is to be learnt about willing and learning and about the enlargement of one's freedom from external constraints and psychoneural interferences. But to reach the universal willingness that matches the unrestricted desire to know is indeed a high achievement, for it consists not in the mere recognition of an ideal norm but in the adoption of an attitude towards the universe of being, not in the adoption of an affective attitude that would desire but not perform but in the adoption of an effective attitude in which performance matches aspiration.

Finally, if effective freedom is to be won, it is not to be won easily. Just as the pure desire to know is the possibility but not in itself the attainment of the scientist's settled habit of constant inquiry, so the potency 'will' is the possibility but not in itself the attainment of the genuine person's complete openness to reflection and to rational persuasion. Clearly, this confronts us with a paradox. How is one to be persuaded to genuineness and openness, when one is not yet open to persuasion?

3.3 Possible Functions of Satire and Humor   [624–26]

Kierkegaardian thought draws attention to an aesthetic, an ethical, and a religious sphere of existential subjectivity, and it finds in irony the means of effecting the transition from the first to the second, and in humor the means for development from the second to the third.

The aesthetic and the ethical spheres would seem to stand to the whole man, to the existential subject, as the counterpositions and the positions stand to the cognitional subject. Inasmuch as one accepts the counterpositions, one thinks of the real as a subdivision in the 'already out there now,' of objectivity as extroversion, and of knowing as taking a good look; similarly, on the counterpositions, the good is identified with objects of desire while the intelligible good of order and the rational good of value are regarded as so much ideological superstructure that can claim to be good only inasmuch as it furthers the attainment of objects of desire. On the other hand, by accepting the positions, one identifies the real with being, objectivity with intelligent inquiry and rational reflection, and knowledge with the cumulative process that rises from experience through understanding to judgment; similarly, one lumps objects of desire along with objects of aversion as instances of the potential good, subordinates both to the formal good of order, and selects between alternative orders by appealing to the rational criteria that are the sources of the meaning of the name 'value.'

However, if the ethical sphere stands to the aesthetic as the positions to the counterpositions, it would be a mistake to identify the ethical sphere with acceptance of the positions and the aesthetic sphere with acceptance of the counterpositions. For the spheres are existential, but the positions and counterpositions are defined sharply. One might claim that Marxism satisfies the definition of the counterpositions, for Marxism is a philosophy. One could not claim that Marx satisfied the same definition, for Marx was not a theory but a man.

The fact of the matter would seem to be that men commonly live in some blend or mixture of the artistic, dramatic, and practical patterns of experience, that they tend to the positions in enouncing their principles and to the counterpositions in living their lives, and that they reveal little inclination to a rigidly consistent adherence to the claims either of pure reason or of pure animality. As contemporary existentialism would put it, *L'homme se définit par une exigence.*[h] Man develops biologically to develop psychically, and he develops psychically to develop intellectually and rationally. The higher integrations suffer the disadvantage of emerging later. They are the demands of finality upon us before they are realities in us. They are manifested more commonly in aspiration and in dissatisfaction with oneself than in the rounded achievement of complete genuineness, perfect openness, universal willingness. Finally, even that rounded achievement is itself not a goal but a means to a goal; for genuineness and openness and willingness name, not acts, but conditions for acts of correct understanding and good willing.

The concrete being of man, then, is being in process. His existing lies in developing. His unrestricted desire to know heads him ever towards a known unknown. His sensitivity matches the operator of his intellectual advance with a capacity and a need to respond to a further reality than meets the eye and to grope his way towards it. Still, this basic, indeterminately directed dynamism has its ground in potency; it is without the settled assurance and efficacy of form; it tends to be shouldered out of the busy day, to make its force felt in the tranquility of darkness, in the solitude of loneliness, in the shattering upheavals of personal or social disaster.

It is in this context that the profound significance of satire and of humor comes to light. For satire breaks in upon the busy day. It puts printers to work, competes on the glossy page of advertisement, challenges even the enclaves of bright chatter. It enters not by argument but by laughter. For argument would presuppose premises, and premises that would be accepted easily also would be mistaken. But laughter supposes only human nature, and men there are. Moreover, as it is without logical presuppositions, so it occurs with apparent purposelessness; and that too is highly important for, if men are afraid to think, they may not be afraid to laugh. Yet proofless, purposeless laughter can dissolve honored pretence; it can disrupt conventional humbug; it can disillusion man of his most cherished illusions, for it is in league with the detached, disinterested, unrestricted desire to know.

Satire laughs *at*, humor laughs *with*. Satire would depict the counterpositions in their current concrete features, and by that serene act of cool objectification it would hurry them to their destiny of bringing about their own reversal. In contrast, humor keeps the positions in contact with human limitations and human infirmity. It listens with sincere respect to the Stoic description of the Wise Man, and then requests an introduction. It has an honest admiration for the blueprints of Utopia, but it also has a vivid imagination that puts a familiar Tom and Dick and Harry in the unfamiliar roles. It questions neither aspirations nor ideals nor high seriousness nor earnest purpose nor self-sacrificing generosity; but it knows the difference between promise and fulfilment, and it refuses to calculate without men as they are, without me as I am. For if satire becomes red with indignation, humor blushes with humility.

But the significance of satire and humor is, I suggest, out of proportion to their efficacy. Because counterpositions commonly keep shifting their ground, the satirist is likely to clip one head off the monster he attacks only to witness another sprout out in its place. Again, because the point of humor is transcendent, it is apt to be missed. But if satire and humor are weighed, not by the results they obtain, but by the potentialities they reveal, then theirs is the signal importance of marking with a chortle the chasms that divide successive orientations of man's polymorphic consciousness. For as satire can help man swing out of the self-centeredness of an animal in a habitat to the universal viewpoint of an intelligent and reasonable being, so humor can aid him to the discovery of the complex problem of grasping and holding the nettle of a restricted effective freedom.

3.4 Moral Impotence   [627–30]

To assert moral impotence is to assert that man's effective freedom is restricted, not in the superficial fashion that results from external circumstance or psychic abnormality, but in the profound fashion that follows from incomplete intellectual and volitional development. For when that development is incomplete, there are practical insights that could be had if a man took time out to acquire the necessary preparatory insights, and there are courses of action that would be chosen if a man took time out to persuade himself to willingness. There follows a gap between the proximate effective freedom he actually possesses and, on the other hand, the remote and hypothetical effective freedom that he would possess if certain conditions happened to be fulfilled. Now this gap measures one's moral impotence. For complete self-development is a long and difficult process. During that process one has to live and make decisions in the light of one's undeveloped intelligence and under the guidance of one's incomplete willingness. And the less developed one is, the less one appreciates the need of development and the less one is willing to take time out for one's intellectual and moral education.

Moreover, as the scotosis of the dramatic subject, so the moral impotence of the essentially free subject is neither grasped with perfect clarity nor totally unconscious.[i] For if one were to represent a man's field of freedom as a circular area, then one would distinguish a luminous central region in which he was effectively free, a surrounding penumbra in which his uneasy conscience keeps suggesting that he could do better if only he would make up his mind, and finally an outer shadow to which he barely if ever adverts. Further, these areas are not fixed; as he develops, the penumbra penetrates into the shadow and the luminous area into the penumbra while, inversely, moral decline is a contraction of the luminous area and of the penumbra. Finally, this consciousness of moral impotence not only heightens the tension between limitation and transcendence but also can provide ambivalent materials for reflection; correctly interpreted, it brings home to man the fact that his living is a developing, that he is not to be discouraged by his failures, that rather he is to profit by them both as lessons on his personal weaknesses and as a stimulus to greater efforts; but the same data can also be regarded as evidence that there is no use trying, that moral codes ask the impossible, that one has to be content with oneself as one is.

This inner tension and its ambivalence are reflected and heightened in the social sphere. For rational self-consciousness demands consistency between knowing and doing not only in the individual but also in the common concerns of the group. To the ethics of the individual conscience there is added an ethical transformation of the home, of the technological expansion, of the economy, and of the polity. But just as individual intelligence and individual reasonableness lead to the individual decisions that may be right or wrong, so too common intelligence and common reasonableness lead to common decisions that may be right or wrong. Moreover, in both cases, decisions are right not because they are the pronouncements of the individual conscience, nor because they proceed from this or that type of social mechanism for reaching common decisions, but because they are in the concrete situation intelligent and reasonable. Again, in both cases, decisions are wrong, not because of their private or public origin, but because they diverge from the dictates of intelligence and reasonableness.

Now, as has been seen, common sense is subject to a threefold bias. Accordingly, we can expect that individual decisions will be likely to suffer from individual bias, that common decisions will be likely to suffer from the various types of group bias, and that all decisions will be likely to suffer from general bias. There will result conflicts between the individual and the group, between economic and national groups within the state, and between states. But far more significant than these relatively superficial and overt conflicts will be the underlying opposition that general bias sets up between the decisions that intelligence and reasonableness would demand and the actual decisions, individual and common, that are made. For this opposition is both profound and unnoticed. As individuals, so societies fail to distinguish sharply and accurately between positions and counterpositions. As individuals, so societies fail to reach the universal willingness that reflects and sustains the detachment and disinterestedness of the unrestricted desire to know. More or less automatically and unconsciously, each successive batch of possible and practical courses of action is screened to eliminate as unpractical whatever does not seem practical to an intelligence and a willingness that not only are developed imperfectly but also suffer from bias. But the social situation is the cumulative product of individual and group decisions, and as these decisions depart from the demands of intelligence and reasonableness, so the social situation becomes, like the complex number, a compound of the rational and irrational. Then if it is to be understood, it must be met by a parallel compound of direct and inverse insights, of direct insights that grasp its intelligibility and of inverse insights that grasp its lack of intelligibility. Nor is it enough to understand the situation; it must also be managed. Its intelligible components have to be encouraged towards fuller development; and its unintelligible components have to be hurried to their reversal.

Still, this is only the outer aspect of the problem. Just as the social situation with its objective surd proceeds from minds and wills that oscillate between the positions and the counterpositions, so too it constitutes the materials for their practical insights, the conditions to be taken into account in their reflection, the reality to be maintained and developed by their decisions. Just as there are philosophies that take their stand upon the positions and urge the development of the intelligible components in the situation and the reversal of the unintelligible components, so too there are counterphilosophies that take their stand upon the counterpositions, that welcome the unintelligible components in the situation as objective facts that provide the empirical proof of their views, that demand the further expansion of the objective surd, and that clamor for the complete elimination of the intelligible components that they regard as wicked survivals of antiquated attitudes. But philosophies and counterphilosophies are for the few. Like Mercutio, the average man imprecates a plague on both their houses. What he wants is peace and prosperity. By his own light he selects what he believes is the intelligent and reasonable but practical course of action; and as that practicality is the root of the trouble, the civilization drifts through successive less comprehensive syntheses to the sterility of the objectively unintelligible situation and to the coercion of economic pressures, political forces, and psychological conditioning.

Clearly, both the outward conditions and the inner mentality prevalent in social decline intensify to the point of desperation the tension, inherent in all development but conscious in man, between limitation and transcendence. One can agree with Christian praise of charity, with Kant's affirmation that the unqualified good is the good will, with existentialist exhortations to genuineness. But good will is never better than the intelligence and reasonableness that it implements. Indeed, when proposals and programs only putatively are intelligent and reasonable, then the good will that executes them so faithfully and energetically is engaged really in the systematic imposition of ever further evils on the already weary shoulders of mankind. And who will tell which proposals and programs truly are intelligent and reasonable, and which are not? For the only transition from the analytic proposition to the analytic principle is through concrete judgments of fact, and alas, the facts are ambivalent. The objective situation is all fact, but partly it is the product of intelligence and reasonableness, and partly it is the product of aberration from them. The whole of man is all fact, but it also is malleable, polymorphic fact. No doubt, a subtle and protracted analysis can bring to light the components in that polymorphic fact and proceed to a dialectical criticism of any proposal or program. But to whom does it bring the light? To how many? How clearly and how effectively? Are philosophers to be kings or kings to learn philosophy? Are they to rule in the name of wisdom subjects judged incapable of wisdom? Are all the members of our democracies to be philosophers? Is there to be a provisional dictatorship while they are learning philosophy?

3.5 The Problem of Liberation [630–33]

The elements in the problem are basically simple. Man's intelligence, reasonableness, and willingness (1) proceed from a detached, disinterested, unrestricted desire to know, (2) are potentialities in process of development towards a full effective freedom, (3) supply the higher integration for otherwise coincidental manifolds on successively underlying psychic, organic, chemical, and physical levels, (4) stand in opposition and tension with sensitive and intersubjective attachment, interest, and exclusiveness, and (5) suffer from that tension a cumulative bias that increasingly distorts immanent development, its outward products, and the outer conditions under which the immanent development occurs.

Essentially the problem lies in an incapacity for sustained development. The tension divides and disorientates cognitional activity by the conflict of positions and counterpositions. This conflict issues into contrary views of the good, which in turn make good will appear misdirected, and misdirected will appear good. There follows the confounding of the social situation with the social surd to provide misleading inspiration for further insights, deceptive evidence for further judgments, and illusory causes to fascinate unwary wills.

The problem is radical, for it is a problem in the very dynamic structure of cognitional, volitional, and social activity. It is not a question of error on this or that general or particular issue. It is a question of orientation, approach, procedure, method. It affects concretely every issue, both general and particular, for it recurs with every use of the dynamic structure.

The problem is permanent. It vanishes if one supposes man's intelligence, reasonableness, and willingness not to be potentialities in process of development but already in possession of the insights that make learning superfluous, of the reasonableness that makes judgments correct, of the willingness that makes persuasion unnecessary. Again, it vanishes if one supposes the elimination of the tension and opposition between the detached, disinterested, unrestricted desire to know and, on the other hand, attached, interested, and narrow sensitivity and intersubjectivity. But in fact both development and tension pertain to the very nature of man, and as long as they exist the problem remains in full force.

The problem is independent of the underlying manifolds. No doubt, if the underlying manifolds were different, the higher cognitional and volitional integration would differ in its content. But such a change of content would leave the dynamic structure of the higher integration unmodified; and it is in the structure that the problem resides. It follows that neither physics nor chemistry nor biology nor sensitive psychology can bring forth devices that go to the root of the trouble.

The problem is not primarily social. It results in the social surd. It receives from the social surd its continuity, its aggravation, its cumulative character. But its root is elsewhere. Hence it is that a revolution can sweep away old evils and initiate a fresh effort; but the fresh effort will occur through the same dynamic structure as the old effort and lead to essentially the same results.

The problem is not to discover a correct philosophy, ethics, or human science. For such discoveries are quite compatible with the continued existence of the problem. The correct philosophy can be but one of many philosophies, the correct ethics one of many ethical systems, the correct human science an old or new view among many views. But precisely because they are correct, they will not appear correct to minds disorientated by the conflict between positions and counterpositions. Precisely because they are correct, they will not appear workable to wills with restricted ranges of effective freedom. Precisely because they are correct, they will be weak competitors for serious attention in the realm of practical affairs.

The problem is not met by setting up a benevolent despotism to enforce a correct philosophy, ethics, or human science. No doubt, if there is to be the appeal to force, then it is better that the force be directed by wisdom than by folly, by benevolence than by malevolence. But the appeal to force is a counsel of despair. So far from solving the problem, it regards the problem as insoluble. For if men are intelligent, reasonable, and willing, they do not have to be forced. Only in the measure that men are unintelligent, unreasonable, unwilling, does force enter into human affairs. Finally, if force can be used by the group against the wayward individual and by the larger group against the smaller, it does not follow that it can be used to correct the general bias of common sense. For the general bias of common sense is the bias of all men, and to a notable extent it consists in the notion that ideas are negligible unless they are reinforced by sensitive desires and fears. Is everyone to use force against everyone to convince everyone that force is beside the point?

The problem is real. In the present work it has been reached in the compendious fashion that operates through the integral heuristic structure of proportionate being and the consequent ethics. But the expeditiousness of the procedure must not be allowed to engender the mistake that the problem resides in some theoretical realm. On the contrary, its dimensions are the dimensions of human history, and the fourth, fifth, and sixth volumes of Arnold Toynbee's *Study of History* illustrate abundantly and rather relevantly the failure of self-determination, the schism in the body social, and the schism in the soul that follow from an incapacity for sustained development.

The solution has to be a still higher integration of human living. For the problem is radical and permanent; it is independent of the underlying physical, chemical, organic, and psychic manifolds; it is not met by revolutionary change, nor by human discovery, nor by the enforced implementation of discovery; it is as large as human living and human history. Further, the solution has to take people just as they are. If it is to be a solution and not a mere suppression of the problem, it has to acknowledge and respect and work through man's intelligence and reasonableness and freedom. It may eliminate neither development nor tension yet it must be able to replace incapacity by capacity for sustained development. Only a still higher integration can meet such requirements. For only a higher integration leaves underlying manifolds with their autonomy yet succeeds in introducing a higher systematization into their nonsystematic coincidences. And only a still higher integration than any that so far has been considered can deal with the dialectical manifold immanent in human subjects and the human situation.

There is needed, then, a further manifestation of finality, of the upwardly but indeterminately directed dynamism of generalized emergent probability. Earlier, in the chapter on common sense as object, it was concluded that a viewpoint higher than the viewpoint of common sense was needed; moreover, that X was given the name 'cosmopolis,' and some of its aspects and functions were indicated. But the subsequent argument has revealed that, besides higher viewpoints in the mind, there are higher integrations in the realm of being; and both the initial and subsequent argument have left it abundantly clear that the needed higher viewpoint is a concrete possibility only as a consequence of an actual higher integration.

Finally, whether the needed higher integration has emerged or is yet to emerge is a question of fact. Similarly, its nature is an object not for speculation but for empirical inquiry. Still, what can that empirical inquiry be? Since our metaphysics and ethics have been developed under a restriction to proportionate being, we have to raise the question of transcendent knowledge before we can attempt an investigation of the ulterior finality of man.

19

General Transcendent
Knowledge

If there is or if there is to be a higher integration of human living, then it will be known only through a knowledge that goes beyond the various types that hitherto have engaged our attention. But if the new knowledge is to be continuous with the old, then it will conform to the basic characteristics with which we have become familiar.

Perhaps the most fundamental of these characteristics appears in the distinction between a heuristic structure and its determination. The simple fact that man knows through intelligent inquiry and rational reflection enables him to determine in advance certain general attributes of the object under investigation. So the methods of the empirical sciences rest on the anticipation of systems of laws, of ideal frequencies, of genetic operators, of dialectical tensions. So the metaphysics of proportionate being has been conceived as an implementation of the integrated heuristic structures[a] of empirical science. So the present chapter on general transcendent knowledge is concerned to determine what we can and do know about transcendent being prior to the attainment of an act of understanding that grasps what any transcendent being is. To employ the terms that will be more familiar to many, the present chapter is concerned with the knowledge of God that, according to St Thomas Aquinas, consists in knowing that he is but not what he is.

1   **The Notion of Transcendence**   [634–36]

Commonly transcendence is opposed to immanence, and then the simplest way to understand the opposition is to begin from the ordinary view that knowing consists in looking. For on that view the fact of error is somewhat disconcerting: either error consists in seeing what is not there or else it consists in not seeing what is there. But if the first look is erroneous, the second, third, fourth, or nth may err in the same or in some different fashion. Which is to be trusted? Is any to be trusted? Does not certitude require the possibility of some super-look in which one can compare the object to be looked at and the object as seen? Would not the super-look be open to exactly the same difficulty? Obviously it would, and so one is brought to the conclusion that knowing is immanent not simply in the ontological sense that knowing occurs within the knower but also in the epistemological sense that nothing is known except the content immanent within the act of knowing.

A first step towards transcendence, then, is to reject the mistaken supposition that knowing consists in taking a look. After all, even the above argument for immanence is not a matter of looking but a matter of understanding and judging, and so anyone that appeals to the above argument to affirm epistemological immanence might better appeal to the fact that he argues and so be led to reject the major premise of the argument. Counterpositions invite their own reversal.

In a more general sense, transcendence means 'going beyond.' So inquiry, insight, and formulation do not merely reproduce the content of sensible experience but go beyond it. So reflection, grasp of the unconditioned, and judgment are not content with mere objects of supposing, defining, considering, but go beyond them to the universe of facts, of being, of what truly is affirmed and really is. Moreover, one can rest content with knowing things as related to us, or one can go beyond that to join the scientists in searching for knowledge of things as related to one another. One can go beyond both common sense and present science, to grasp the dynamic structure of our rational knowing and doing, and then formulate a metaphysics and an ethics. Finally, one can ask whether human knowledge is confined to the universe of proportionate being or goes beyond it to the realm of transcendent being; and this transcendent realm may be conceived either relatively or absolutely, either as beyond man or as the ultimate in the whole process of going beyond.

Clearly, despite the imposing name, transcendence is the elementary matter of raising further questions. Thus, the present work has been written from a moving viewpoint. It began from insight as an interesting event in human consciousness. It went on to insight as a central event in the genesis of mathematical knowledge. It went beyond mathematics to study the role of insight in classical and statistical investigations. It went beyond the reproducible insights of scientists to the more complex functioning of intelligence in common sense, in its relations to its psychoneural basis, and in its historical expansion in the development of technology, economies, and polities. It went beyond all such direct and inverse insights to the reflective grasp that grounds judgment. It went beyond all insights as activities, to consider them as elements in knowledge. It went beyond actual knowledge to its permanent dynamic structure, to construct an explicit metaphysics and add the general form of an ethics. It has found man involved and engaged in developing, in going beyond what he happens to be, and it has been confronted both with man's incapacity for sustained development and with his need to go beyond the hitherto considered procedures of his endeavor to go beyond.

Transcendence, then, at the present juncture, means a development in man's knowledge relevant to a development in man's being. Hitherto we have been content with knowledge of proportionate being. But man is in process of development. Inasmuch as he is intelligent and reasonable, free and responsible, he has to grasp and affirm, accept and execute his own developing. But can he? To grasp his own developing is for man to understand it, to extrapolate from his past through the present to the alternative ranges of the future. It is to extrapolate not only horizontally but also vertically, not only to future recurrences of past events, but also to future higher integrations of contemporary unsystematized manifolds. More fundamentally, it is to grasp the principles that govern possible extrapolations; for while possibilities are many and difficult to determine, principles may be few and ascertainable. Moreover, since finality is an upwardly but indeterminately directed dynamism and since man is free, the real issue lies not in the many possibilities but in the few principles on which man may rely in working out his destiny.

2   The Immanent Source of Transcendence   [636–39]

The immanent source of transcendence in man is his detached, disinterested, unrestricted desire to know. As it is the origin of all his questions, it is the origin of the radical further questions that take him beyond the defined limits of particular issues. Nor is it solely the operator of his cognitional development. For its detachment and disinterestedness set it in opposition to his attached and interested sensitivity and intersubjectivity; and the knowledge it yields demands of his will the endeavor to develop in willingness and so make his doing consistent with his knowing.

Still, if this tension is too manifest for the existence of the pure desire to be doubted, the claim that it is an unrestricted desire seems so extravagant as to cause misgivings even in those that already accept all its implications. Accordingly, it will be well to clarify once more this point before attempting to advance further in our inquiry.

The desire in question, then, is a desire to understand correctly. To affirm that the desire is unrestricted is not to affirm that man's understanding is unrestricted or that the correctness of his understanding is unrestricted. For the desire is prior to understanding, and it is compatible with not understanding. Were it not, the effort and process of inquiry would be impossible; for inquiry is a manifestation of a desire to understand, and it occurs before one does understand.

Secondly, to affirm that the desire is unrestricted is not to affirm that the attainment of understanding will be unrestricted. For the transition from the desire to the attainment has conditions that are distinct from desiring. It is to help fulfil such conditions that scientific and philosophic methods exist. Hence, to affirm an unrestricted desire to understand is to affirm the fulfilment of only one of many conditions for the attainment of unrestricted understanding. So far from stating that the other conditions will be fulfilled, it does not attempt to determine what the other conditions might be.

Thirdly, to affirm that the desire is unrestricted is not to affirm that, in a wisely ordered universe, the attainment of understanding ought to be unrestricted. Such an affirmation would follow from the premise 'In every wisely ordered universe desire for attainment entails exigence for attainment.' But the premise is obviously false: a desire to commit murder does not entail a duty to commit murder, and least of all does it do so in a wisely ordered universe. It may be contended, however, that the premise is correct when the desire is good, natural, spontaneous. But this contention has its own suppositions. In a universe of static horizontal strata, such as is envisaged by autonomous abstract physics, autonomous abstract chemistry, autonomous abstract biology, and so forth, the tendencies and desires natural and spontaneous on any level would have to be confined to that level; because they were confined to their own level, they could and would be fulfilled on their own level; and because they could and would be fulfilled on their own level, it would be true to claim that in a wisely regulated universe of static horizontal strata desire for attainment entailed exigence for attainment. It remains to be shown, however, that this universe corresponds to a set of abstract, unrelated sciences and so consists in a set of static horizontal strata. The fact seems to be that this universe is concrete and that logically unrelated sciences are related intelligently by a succession of higher viewpoints. Accordingly, besides the tendencies and desires confined to any given level, there are the tendencies and desires that go beyond any given level; they are the reality of finality conceived as an upwardly but indeterminately directed dynamism; and since this dynamism of finality attains its successive goals statistically, since probabilities decrease as attainment increases, the implication of unrestricted attainment in unrestricted desire is neither necessity nor exigence but, at most, negligible probability.

If one has to labor to clarify what the unrestricted desire is not, it is relatively simple to reveal what it is. Man wants to understand completely. As the desire to understand is the opposite of total obscurantism, so the unrestricted desire to understand is the opposite of any and every partial obscurantism no matter how slight. The rejection of total obscurantism is the demand that some questions, at least, are not to be met with an arbitrary exclamation, 'Let's forget it!' The rejection of any and every partial obscurantism is the demand that no question whatever is to be met arbitrarily, that every question is to be submitted to the process of intelligent grasp and critical reflection. Negatively, then, the unrestricted desire excludes the unintelligent and uncritical rejection of any question, and positively the unrestricted desire demands the intelligent and critical handling of every question.

Nor is the existence of this unrestricted desire doubtful. Neither centuries of inquiry nor enormous libraries of answers have revealed any tendency for the stream of further questions to diminish. Philosophies and counterphilosophies have been multiplied, but whether intellectualist or antiintellectualist, whether they proclaim the rule of reason or advocate thinking with the blood, they do not exclude any field of inquiry without first arguing that the effort is useless or enervating or misleading or illusory. And in this respect we may be confident that the future will resemble the past, for unless someone comes forth to speak in the name of stupidity and silliness, he will not be able to claim that some questions, specified or unspecified, are to be brushed aside though there is no reason whatever for doing so.

Analysis yields the same conclusion. For apart from being there is nothing. The proposition is analytic, for it cannot be denied without internal contradiction. If apart from being there were something, that something would be; and if that something were, it would be another instance of being and so not apart from being. Moreover, being is the objective of the detached and disinterested desire to know; for that desire grounds inquiry and reflection; inquiry leads to understanding, reflection leads to affirmation; and being is whatever can be grasped intelligently and affirmed reasonably. But being is unrestricted, for apart from it there is nothing. Therefore the objective of the detached and disinterested desire is unrestricted. But a desire with an unrestricted objective is an unrestricted desire, and so the desire to know is unrestricted.

Introspective reflection brings us once more to the same affirmation. For whatever may be true about the cognitional aspirations of others, might not my own be radically limited? Might not my desire to understand correctly suffer from some immanent and hidden restriction and bias, so that there could be real things that lay quite beyond its utmost horizon? Might not that be so? Yet if I ask the question, it is in virtue of my desire to know; and as the question itself reveals, my desire to know concerns itself with what lies quite beyond a suspected limited horizon. Even my desire seems unrestricted.

3   The Notion of Transcendent Knowledge   [639–41]

Man's unrestricted desire to know is mated to a limited capacity to attain knowledge. From this paradox there follow both a fact and a requirement. The fact is that the range of possible questions is larger than the range of possible answers. The requirement is a critical survey of possible questions. For it is only through such a critical survey that man can provide himself with intelligent and reasonable grounds both for setting aside the questions that cannot be answered and for limiting his attention to the questions to which answers are possible.

This critical undertaking is not as simple as has been supposed. For while the issue is formulated in terms of possibility and impossibility, it can be answered only in terms of fact. In the first place, the question of possibility is regressive. If any less general inquiry has to be preceded by a critical inquiry on its possibility, then critical inquiry has to be preceded by a precritical inquiry on the possibility of critical inquiry, the precritical needs a pre-precritical inquiry, and so on indefinitely. In the second place, questions of possibility and impossibility can be settled only

by appealing to judgments of fact. For while there are analytic propositions and while they can be established ad libitum by postulating syntactical rules and defining terms subject to the rules, analytic principles are
to be had only by meeting the further requirement that both the terms
and the relations of the analytic propositions occur in concrete judgments of fact.

The paramount issue, then, in determining the possibility of knowledge is always the fact of knowledge. The argument always will be that
knowledge is possible if in fact knowledge of that kind occurs. It follows
that the critical issue can be tackled only piecemeal. Facts have to be
settled one after another, and it is only in the grand strategy that guides
the seriation of the facts that the answer to the critical issue appears.

In our own procedure four main stages may be distinguished. First,
we centered attention on cognitional activity as activity and endeavored
to grasp the key occurrences in learning mathematics, advancing science,
developing common sense, and forming judgments in these fields. Secondly, we turned to cognitional activity as cognitional and began with the
particular case of self-affirmation to show that self-affirmation occurred,
that it is knowledge if knowing is knowing being, and that it is objective
in certain determinable meanings of objectivity. Thirdly, we turned to
the general case of knowledge of proportionate being, and because
self-affirmation was a key act, we were able to set up a general dialectical
theorem that divided the formulations of the discoveries of human intelligence into positions and counterpositions and that showed positions to
invite development and counterpositions to invite reversal. On this basis
it was shown to be possible to set up a metaphysics of proportionate
being and a consequent ethics.

The fourth stage of the argument is concerned with human knowledge of transcendent being. The bare bones of the procedure are simple
enough. Being is whatever can be grasped intelligently and affirmed
reasonably. Being is proportionate or transcendent according as it lies
within or without the domain of man's outer and inner experience. The
possibility of transcendent knowledge, then, is the possibility of grasping
intelligently and affirming reasonably a transcendent being. And the
proof of the possibility lies in the fact that such intelligent grasp and
reasonable affirmation occur.

But, as has been observed, so general an outline cannot reveal whether
or not the procedure possesses critical significance. For such significance
lies, not in the proof of possibility from fact, but in the strategic choice

and seriation of the facts. For the moment, then, all that can be said is that the fourth stage of the argument will contribute to a determination of the power and of the limitations of the human mind in the measure that intelligent grasp and reasonable affirmation of transcendent being prove to be the inevitable culmination of our whole account of understanding and of judgment.

Finally, it may not be amiss to note that this section on the notion of transcendent knowledge calls for no comment on the views of positivists and Kantians. For though both groups are loud in their negations of the possibility of transcendent knowledge, their failure to give an adequate account of proportionate knowledge has forced us to register our differences at a more elementary stage of the argument. Unless one considers Comte's mythic religion of humanity to be positive, positivism has nothing positive to add to the counterpositions as illustrated by materialism, empiricism, sensism, phenomenalism, solipsism, pragmatism, modernism, and existentialism. In contrast, Kantian thought is rich and fertile in the problems it raises. But its transcendental aesthetic has been mauled by more recent work in geometry and in physics, and the transcendental logic suffers from an incoherence that seems irremediable. For the transcendental dialectic rests its affirmation of a transcendental illusion on the ground that the unconditioned is not a constituent factor in judgment but simply a regulative ideal of pure reason. However, the schematism of the categories provides the link between sense and the pure categories of the understanding; such a link is prior to judgment and a constituent factor in judgment as concrete. Finally, while Kant does not notice that the schematism is simply an application of the virtually unconditioned (e.g., if there is a filling of the empty form of Time, there is an instance of the Real; the filling occurs; hence, there is an instance of the Real), the fact remains that the unconditioned grounds the schematism and so grounds concrete judgment on Kant's own showing.

4   Preliminaries to Conceiving the Transcendent Idea   [641–44]

Knowledge of transcendent being involves both intelligent grasp and reasonable affirmation. But before we can affirm reasonably, we must grasp intelligently; and before we can grasp transcendent being intelligently, we have to extrapolate from proportionate being. The present section, then, is concerned with that extrapolation.

The nature of the extrapolation may best be illustrated by comparing it with mathematics. For the mathematician differs both from the logician and from the scientist. He differs from the logician inasmuch as he cannot grant all the terms and relations he employs to be mere objects of thought. He differs from the scientist inasmuch as he is not bound to repudiate every object of thought that lacks verification. In somewhat similar fashion, the present effort to conceive the transcendent idea is concerned simply with concepts, with objects of supposing, defining, considering, and therefore no question of existence or occurrence arises. Nonetheless, the extrapolation to the transcendent, though conceptual, operates from the real basis of proportionate being, so that some elements in the transcendent idea will be verifiable just as some of the positive integers are verifiable.

The question that leads to the extrapolation has been raised already but not answered. For we have identified the real with being but we have not ventured to say just what being is. What, then, is being?

Let us begin by taking our bearings. One may distinguish[b] (1) the pure notion of being, (2) the heuristic notion of being, (3) restricted acts of understanding, conceiving, and affirming being, and (4) the unrestricted act of understanding being.

The pure notion of being is the detached, disinterested, unrestricted desire to know. It is prior to understanding and affirming, but it heads to them for it is the ground of intelligent inquiry and critical reflection. Moreover, this heading towards knowing is itself a notion, for it heads not unconsciously, as the seed to the plant, nor sensitively, as hunger for food, but intelligently and reasonably, as the radical *noêsis* towards every *noêma*, the basic *pensée pensante* towards every *pensée pensée*, the initiating *intentio intendens* towards every *intentio intenta*.

Secondly, since the pure notion of being unfolds through understanding and judgment, there can be formulated a heuristic notion of being as whatever is to be grasped intelligently and affirmed reasonably.

Thirdly, though the pure notion is unrestricted desire, still it is intelligent and reasonable desire. Hence it is content to restrict itself provisionally, to ask one question at a time, to prescind from other questions while working towards the solution of the issue in hand. From such prescinding, which anticipates comparative negative judgments, as the notion of nature or essence or universal anticipates the content of intelligent definition, there follow restricted inquiries, restricted acts of understanding and conceiving, reflection on such conceptions, and judgments about particular beings and particular domains of being.

Fourthly, none of the foregoing activities enables one to answer the question, What is being? The pure notion of being raises all questions but answers none. The heuristic notion envisages all answers but determines none. Particular inquiries solve some questions but not all. Only an unrestricted act of understanding can meet the issue. For being is completely universal and completely concrete; apart from it, there is nothing; and so knowledge of what being is cannot be had in anything less than an act of understanding everything about everything. Correlative to an unrestricted desire to understand, there may be posited either an indefinite process of development or an unrestricted act of understanding. But the content of developing understanding never is the idea of being, for as long as understanding is developing, there are further questions to be answered. Only the content of the unrestricted act of understanding can be the idea of being, for it is only on the supposition of an unrestricted act that everything about everything is understood.

It follows that the idea of being is absolutely transcendent. For it is the content of an act of unrestricted understanding. But such an act not only takes us beyond all human achievement but also assigns the ultimate limit to the whole process of going beyond. Insights and viewpoints can be transcended as long as further questions can be asked. But once all about all is understood, there is no room for further questions.

We have extrapolated from the question, What is being? to the absolutely transcendent idea of being, and obviously the critical question arises. Because man's desire to know is unrestricted while his capacity to know is limited, one does not have to be a fool to ask more questions than a wise man can answer. Certainly men ask, What is being? Indeed, ever since we identified the real with being we have been laboring to stave off that question until we could tackle it properly. But though the question arises very naturally, it does not follow that man's natural resources suffice to answer it. Clearly, man cannot answer it by enjoying an unrestricted act of understanding, for then his capacity to know would not be limited, and he would have no need for critical investigations. But it seems equally clear that man can answer the question by working out the conclusion that the idea of being is the content of an unrestricted act of understanding; for the fact proves possibility; and we have reached that conclusion. Moreover, what we have determined already in a highly general fashion may be determined in a more detailed fashion. For, on the one hand, we have worked out the outlines of a metaphysic of proportionate being, and so we have at our command at least one segment in the total range of the idea of being. On the other hand, we have been engaged throughout the present work in determining the nature of understanding in mathematics, in common sense, in the sciences, and in philosophy; and so we have at our disposal a body of evidence that provides some determinations for the notion of an unrestricted act of understanding. Accordingly, we are led to the conclusion that, while man cannot enjoy an unrestricted act of understanding and so answer the question, What is being? still he can determine a number of features of the answer by proceeding on the side of the subject from restricted to unrestricted understanding and on the side of the object from the structure of proportionate being to the transcendent idea of being.

Indeed, such a procedure not only is possible but also imperative. For the pure desire excludes not only the total obscurantism which arbitrarily brushes aside every intelligent and reasonable question, but also the partial obscurantism which arbitrarily brushes aside this or that part of the range of intelligent and reasonable questions that admit determinate answers. Just as the mathematician legitimately and fruitfully extrapolates from the existent to series of the nonexistent, just as the physicist profits from mathematical knowledge and adds such extrapolations of his own as the absolute zero of temperature, so an exploration of the idea of being is necessary if one is to measure the power and the limitations of the human mind.

5   The Idea of Being   [644-46]

An idea is the content of an act of understanding. As a sense datum is the content of an act of sensing, as an image is the content of an act of imagining, as a percept is the content of an act of perceiving, as a concept is the content of an act of conceiving, defining, supposing, considering, as a judgment is the content of an act of judging, so an idea is the content of an act of understanding.

Being is the objective of the unrestricted desire to know. Therefore, the idea of being is the content of an unrestricted act of understanding.

Again, apart from being there is nothing. Therefore, the idea of being is the content of an act of understanding that leaves nothing to be understood, no further questions to be asked. But one cannot go beyond an act of understanding that leaves no questions to be asked, and so the idea of being is absolutely transcendent.

Again, being is completely universal and completely concrete. Therefore, the idea of being is the content of an act of understanding that grasps everything about everything. Moreover, since that understanding leaves no questions to be asked, no part of its content can be implicit or obscure or indistinct.

Again, being is intrinsically intelligible. Therefore, the idea of being is the idea of the total range of intelligibility.

Again, the good is identical with the intelligible. Therefore, the idea of being is the idea of the good.

Again, the unrestricted act of understanding is one act. Otherwise, it would be an aggregate or a succession of acts. If none of these acts was the understanding of everything about everything, then the denial of unity would be the denial of unrestricted understanding. If any of these acts was the understanding of everything about everything, then at least that unrestricted act would be a single act.

Again, the idea of being is one idea. For if it were many, then either the many would be related intelligibly or not. If they were related intelligibly, the alleged many would be intelligibly one, and so there would be one idea. If they were not related intelligibly, then either there would not be one act or the one act would not be an act of understanding.

Again, the idea of being is one but of many. Similarly, it is immaterial but of the material, nontemporal but of the temporal, nonspatial but of the spatial. For it has been shown that the idea is one, yet it is the content of an unrestricted act that understands at least the many beings that there are in all their aspects and details. Again, it is the content of an act of understanding, and understanding has been shown to be intrinsically independent of the empirical residue; but what is intrinsically independent of the empirical residue can be neither material nor temporal nor spatial, for these all depend intrinsically on the empirical residue; at the same time, the act of understanding in question is unrestricted; it understands perfectly all the beings that there are, and some of them, at least, are material, temporal, and spatial.

Again, there is no paradox in affirming that the idea of being is one, immaterial, nontemporal, and nonspatial, yet of the many, the material, the temporal, and the spatial. For what is possible in the content of restricted acts of understanding is not beyond the attainment of unrestricted understanding. But our understanding is one yet of many, for in a single act we understand the whole series of positive integers. Similarly, it is immaterial, for it abstracts from the empirical residue, yet of the material, for it advances in understanding of this universe. Again, while it is involved in an ordinal time, for it develops, it is not involved in the continuous time of local motion, for its development is not through a sequence of noncountable stages. Finally, while it pertains to a spatially conditioned subject, it is nonspatial, for it deals with the noncountable multiplicity of space through invariants that are independent of particular spatial standpoints.

Again, in the idea of being a distinction is to be drawn between a primary and a secondary component. For the one is not identical with the many, nor the immaterial with the material, nor the nontemporal with the temporal, nor the nonspatial with the spatial. But in the one idea there are to be grasped many beings; in the immaterial, nontemporal, nonspatial idea there are grasped the material, the temporal, and the spatial. There must be, then, a primary component grasped inasmuch as there is a single act of understanding, and a secondary component that is understood inasmuch as the primary component is grasped. For just as the infinite series of positive integers is understood inasmuch as the generative principle of the series is grasped, so the total range of beings is understood inasmuch as the one idea of being is grasped.

6   The Primary Component in the Idea of Being   [646–48]

The idea of being has been defined as the content of an unrestricted act of understanding;· and in that content a distinction has been established between a primary and a secondary component. Naturally one asks just what is the primary component, and the answer will be that the primary component is identical with the unrestricted act. It will follow that, as the primary component consists in the unrestricted act's understanding of itself, so the secondary component consists in the unrestricted act's understanding of everything else because it understands itself.

However, certain preliminary clarifications are in order. On the counterposition there is an ultimate duality between knower and known; for objectivity is conceived on the analogy of extroversion; and so knowing is essentially a looking, gazing, intuiting, beholding, while the known has to be something else that is looked at, gazed upon, intuited, beheld. On the position, such a duality is rejected; knowing is knowing being; in any given case the knowing and the known being may be the same or different; and whether or nor they are the same or different is to be determined by making the relevant correct judgments.

Further, the adjective 'intelligible' may be employed in two quite different senses. Ordinarily, it denotes what is or can be understood, and in that sense the content of every act of conceiving is intelligible. More profoundly, it denotes the primary component in an idea; it is what is grasped inasmuch as one is understanding; it is the intelligible ground or root or key from which results intelligibility in the ordinary sense. Moreover, there is a simple test for distinguishing between the ordinary and the profounder meaning of the name 'intelligible.' For the intelligible in the ordinary sense can be understood without understanding what it is to understand; but the intelligible in the profounder sense is identical with the understanding, and so it cannot be understood without understanding what understanding is.

For example, the positive integers are an infinite series of intelligibly related terms. Both the terms and the relations are understood by anyone who can do arithmetic, and one can do arithmetic without understanding what it is to understand. But besides the terms and their relations there is the generative principle of the series; inasmuch as that generative principle is grasped, one grasps the ground of an infinity of distinct concepts. Still, what is the generative principle? It is intelligible, for it is grasped, understood. But it cannot be conceived without conceiving what an insight is, for the real generative principle of the series is the insight; and only those ready to speak about insight are capable of asking and answering the question, How does one know the infinite remainder of positive integers denoted by the 'and so forth'?

There follows a needed clarification of the notion of the spiritual. A distinction was drawn between the intelligible that is also intelligent and the intelligible that is not. Again, a distinction was drawn between what intrinsically is independent of the empirical residue and what intrinsically is not independent of the empirical residue. The spiritual was identified both with the intelligible that is intelligent and with what is independent intrinsically of the empirical residue. However, a difficulty arises when one asks whether an essence as conceived is or is not spiritual. For an essence as conceived is abstracted from the empirical residue, but it is not intelligent and it does not understand. A solution is to be had by appealing to the two meanings of the term 'intelligible.' If there is an intelligible in the profounder sense, there also is an act of understanding with which it is identical; and then the intelligible is spiritual both in the sense that it is identical with understanding and in the sense that it is intrinsically independent of the empirical residue. On the other hand, if there is an intelligible in the ordinary sense, then it is not identical with an act of understanding; but it may be abstracted from the empirical residue inasmuch as it results from a spiritual act; and so essences as conceived are spiritual in the sense that they are products of spirit but not in the sense that they are intelligent intelligibles.

With these clarifications, we may return to our problem. The idea of being is the content of the unrestricted act of understanding, and that content relentlessly divides into a primary component, which is one, immaterial, nontemporal, and nonspatial, and a secondary component, which is many and includes the material, the temporal, and the spatial. What, then, is the primary component? It is the unrestricted act of understanding.

For if an act of understanding is unrestricted, it understands understanding; it understands not only restricted acts but also the unrestricted act; understanding the unrestricted act it must understand its content, otherwise the understanding of the unrestricted act would be restricted; but the content of the unrestricted act is the idea of being, and so if the unrestricted act understands itself, it thereby also understands everything else.

It follows that the unrestricted act of understanding is itself the primary component in the idea of being. For the primary component is the immaterial, nontemporal, nonspatial unity such that, if it is grasped, everything about everything else is grasped. But the unrestricted act satisfies this definition. For it is one act; it is spiritual, and so it is immaterial, nontemporal, and nonspatial; and it has just been shown that, if it is grasped, then everything about everything else also will be grasped.

Accordingly, instead of speaking of primary and secondary components in the idea of being, we may distinguish between a primary intelligible and secondary intelligibles. The primary intelligible is by identity the unrestricted act of understanding. It is intelligible in the profounder sense, for it is an intelligible that is identical with intelligence in act. It is a unique intelligible, for it is identical with the unique act of unrestricted understanding. On the other hand, the secondary intelligibles are what are also grasped inasmuch as the unrestricted act understands itself. They are intelligible in the ordinary sense, for they are understood; but they are not intelligible in the profounder sense, for the unrestricted act is one understanding of many intelligibles, and only the unique, primary intelligible is identical with the unrestricted act.

7   The Secondary Component in the Idea of Being   [649–51]

Because it understands itself, the unrestricted act of understanding understands in consequence everything about everything else. But is this consequence possible? After all, we have found the existing universe of being to include a nonsystematic component. Moreover, at each instant in the unfolding of this universe, there are a number of probable alternatives and a far larger number of possible alternatives. There is, then, an enormous aggregate of similar possible universes, and in each of them there would be a similar nonsystematic component. Now the nonsystematic is the absence of intelligible rule or law; elements are determinate; relations between elements are determinate; but there is no possibility of a single formula that is satisfied by the sequence of determinate relations. It seems to follow that the nonsystematic component in the actual universe and in other possible and even more probable universes^c excludes the possibility of an unrestricted act that understands everything about everything.

Such is the problem of the secondary intelligibles in the idea of being, and our solution will be that, from the viewpoint of unrestricted understanding, the nonsystematic vanishes. But first we must recall how the notion of the nonsystematic arises, for otherwise its exact implications cannot be determined.

Our analysis, then, acknowledged the possibility of complete knowledge of all systems of laws but held such systems to be abstract and so to be in need of further determinations if they were to be applied to the concrete. It inferred that such further determinations could not be related systematically to one another, for complete knowledge of all laws would include complete knowledge of all systematic relations. However, it did not deny the further determinations to be related intelligibly to one another. On the contrary, it acknowledged the existence of schemes of recurrence in which a happy combination of abstract laws and concrete circumstances makes typical further determinations recurrent, and so brings them under the domination of intelligence. Moreover, it acknowledged that concrete patterns of diverging series of conditions are intelligible; granted both the requisite information and mastery of the systematic laws, it is possible in principle to work from any physical event Z, through as many prior stages of its diverging and scattering conditions as one pleases; and it is this intelligibility of concrete patterns that grounds the conviction of determinists such as Albert Einstein that statistical laws fall short of what there is to be known.

However, we agree with the indeterminists inasmuch as they deny in the general case the possibility of deduction and prediction. For while each concrete pattern of diverging conditions is intelligible, still its intelligibility lies not on the level of the abstract understanding that grasps systems of laws but on the level of the concrete understanding that deals with particular situations. Moreover, such concrete patterns form an enormous manifold that cannot be handled by abstract systematizing intelligence, for the excellent reason that their intelligibility in each case is concrete. There results the peculiar type of impossibility that arises from mutual conditioning. Granted complete information on a totality of events, one could work out from knowledge of all laws the concrete pattern in which the laws related the events in the totality. Again, granted knowledge of the concrete pattern, one could use it as a guide to obtain information on a totality of relevant events. But the proviso of the first statement is the conclusion of the second; the proviso of the second statement is the conclusion of the first; and so both conclusions are merely theoretical possibilities. For the concrete patterns form a nonsystematic aggregate, and so it is only by appealing to the totality of relevant events that one can select the correct pattern; on the other hand, the relevant totality of events is scattered, and so they can be selected for observation and measurement only if the relevant pattern is known already.

Still, if there is an unrestricted act of understanding, then it will understand everything about everything, with no further questions to be asked. But concrete patterns of diverging series of scattering conditions are each intelligible, and so an unrestricted act will understand each of them. Moreover, to understand each concrete pattern entails knowledge of the totality of events relevant for each pattern, for the concrete pattern includes all the determinations and circumstances of each event. Nor does this conclusion contradict our prior conclusion. For the unrestricted act of understanding proceeds, not from a grasp of abstract systems of laws, but from a grasp of itself; it does not attempt the impossible task of relating through an abstract system the concrete patterns but grasps the lot of them in a single view inasmuch as it understands itself. It does not offer either to deduce or to predict events, for it has neither need nor use for deduction or prediction, since in a single view it grasps the totality of concrete patterns and in each pattern the totality of its relevant events.

To resume the argument, deduction and prediction in the general case are impossible. They are impossible for man's limited understanding, because limited understanding could master the manifold of concrete patterns of diverging series of scattering conditions only if that manifold could be systematized; and it cannot be systematized. On the other hand, though for a different reason, deduction and prediction are impossible for the unrestricted act of understanding; for it could deduce only if it advanced in knowledge either by transforming one abstract premise into another or by combining abstract premises with concrete information; but unrestricted understanding does not advance in knowledge, for it already knows everything. Again, unrestricted understanding could predict only if some events were present relative to it and other events were future relative to it; but unrestricted understanding is nontemporal; it is, so to speak, outside the totality of temporal sequences, for that totality is part of the everything about everything else that it grasps in understanding itself; and as it grasps everything about everything else in a single view, so it grasps the totality of temporal sequences in a single view.

8 Causality   [651–57]

By asking what being is, we have been led to conceive an unrestricted act of understanding. If now we ask what causality is, we shall be led to affirm that there is such an unrestricted act.

In general, causality denotes the objective and real counterpart of the questions and further questions raised by the detached, disinterested, and unrestricted desire to know. As such questions are of various kinds, distinctions are to be drawn between different types of causes.

The basic division is between external and internal causes. Internal causes are the central and conjugate potency, form, and act which already have been examined. External causes are efficient, final, and exemplary, and they may be considered in three manners; namely, in concrete instances, in principle, and in the fulness that results from applying the principles. Thus, in some concrete instance, a community may be divided by a river and see in a bridge the solution to many of its problems; an engineer will examine the site and design an appropriate structure; finally, contractors will assemble laborers and materials to build it. The final cause in this case will be the use to which the bridge is put by the community; the efficient cause will be the work of building it; the exemplary cause will be the design grasped and conceived by the engineer. However, one may not assume that the universe is just like a bridge, and so if one is to affirm efficient, final, and exemplary causality as generally valid principles, one must go to the root of these notions and determine whether or not they are of general validity. Finally, if such general validity is affirmed, then since efficient, final, and exemplary causes are external, one will be led sooner or later to conceive and affirm a first agent, a last end, a primary exemplar of the universe of proportionate being; and then the principle of causality will acquire a significance and fulness that it lacked as long as its concrete implications had not been ascertained.

Our first task, accordingly, is to investigate the transition from familiar but anthropomorphic notions of external causality to their root in a universally applicable principle. We assume that exemplary causality is a fact illustrated by inventions, that efficient causality is a fact illustrated by industry, and that final causality is a fact illustrated by the use to which the products of invention and industry are put. We ask whether such facts are instances of a principle capable of bearing human knowledge from the realm of proportionate being to that of transcendent being. Our answer will be affirmative, and the reasons for it run as follows.

In the first place, being is intelligible. It is neither beyond nor apart nor different from the intelligible. It is what is to be known by intelligent grasp and reasonable affirmation. It is the objective of the detached and disinterested desire to inquire intelligently and to reflect critically; and that desire is unrestricted. On the other hand, what is apart from being is nothing, and so what is apart from intelligibility is nothing. It follows that to talk about mere matters of fact that admit no explanation is to talk about nothing. If existence is mere matter of fact, it is nothing. If occurrence is mere matter of fact, it is nothing. If it is a mere matter of fact that we know and that there are to be known classical and statistical laws, genetic operators and their dialectical perturbations, explanatory genera and species, emergent probability and upward finalistic dynamism, then both the knowing and the known are nothing. This is rude and harsh, and one may be tempted to take flight into the counterpositions, to refuse to identify the real with being, confuse objectivity with extroversion, mistake mere experiencing for human knowing. But any such escape is only temporary. Despite their pullulating variety and perennial vitality, the counterpositions bring about their own reversal the moment they claim to be grasped intelligently and affirmed reasonably.

Since the claim cannot be avoided by an intelligent and reasonable subject, the reversal cannot be avoided; and since the reversal cannot be avoided, ultimately one will be back to affirm that being is intelligible and that the mere matter of fact without explanation is apart from being.

In the second place, one cannot confine human knowledge within the domain of proportionate being without condemning it to mere matters of fact without explanation and so stripping it of knowledge not only of transcendent but also of proportionate being. In other words, every positivism is involved essentially in the counterpositions.

For we do not know until we judge; our judgments rest on a grasp of the virtually unconditioned; and the virtually unconditioned is a conditioned that happens to have its conditions fulfilled. Thus every judgment raises a further question; it reveals a conditioned to be virtually unconditioned, and by that very stroke it reveals conditions that happen to be fulfilled; that happening is a matter of fact, and if it is not to be a mere matter of fact without explanation, a further question arises.

But proportionate being is being proportionate to our knowing. As our judgments rest on a grasp of the virtually unconditioned, so every proportionate being in its every aspect is a virtually unconditioned. As a matter of fact, it is, and so it is unconditioned. But it is unconditioned, not formally in the sense that it has no conditions whatever, but only virtually in the sense that its conditions happen to be fulfilled. To regard that happening as ultimate is to affirm a mere matter of fact without any explanation. To account for one happening by appealing to another is to change the topic without meeting the issue, for if the other happening is regarded as mere matter of fact without any explanation then either it is not being or else being is not the intelligible.

Such is the nerve of the argument, and it can be given as many distinct applications as there are distinct features of proportionate being.

If nothing existed, there would be no one to ask questions and nothing to ask questions about. The most fundamental of all questions, then, asks about existence, yet neither empirical science nor a methodically restricted philosophy can have an adequate answer. Statistical laws assign the frequencies with which things exist, and the explanation of statistical laws will account for the respective numbers of different kinds of things. But the number of existents is one thing, and their existing is another. Again, in particular cases, the scientist can deduce one existent from others, but not even in particular cases can he account for the existence of the others to which he appeals for his premises. As far as empirical science goes, existence is just a matter of fact. Nor is the methodically restricted philosophy better off. So far from accounting for existence, the philosopher can establish that it cannot be accounted for within the limits of proportionate being. For every proportionate being that exists, exists conditionally; it exists inasmuch as the conditions of its existence happen to be fulfilled; and the contingence of that happening cannot be eliminated by appealing to another happening that equally is contingent.

What is true of existence is no less true of occurrence. Both questions and answers occur, and so without occurrences there would be neither questions nor answers. Statistical laws assign the respective numbers of different kinds of occurrences, but their numbers are one thing and their occurring is another. In particular cases, the scientist can deduce some occurrences from others, but the others are no less conditioned than those that are deduced. Without initial premises, there is no deduction; and without conditions that happen to be fulfilled, there are no initial premises. As far as empirical science goes, occurrence is just a matter of fact; and a methodically restricted philosophy can repeat the argument about existence to show that occurrence too must be regarded as mere matter of fact as long as one remains within the realm of proportionate being.

Further, everything that is to be known by empirical science and by restricted philosophy is penetrated by the contingence of existence and occurrence. Classical laws are not what must be; they are empirical; they are what in fact is so. Genetic operators enjoy both a minor and a major flexibility, and so in each concrete case the operator is what in fact it happens to be. Explanatory genera and species are not avatars of Plato's eternal Ideas; they are more or less successful solutions to contingent problems set by contingent situations. The actual course of generalized emergent probability is but one among a large number of other probable courses, and the probable courses are a minority among possible courses; the actual course, then, is what in fact it happens to be. So far from eliminating such contingence, the scientist is restricted by his method to ascertaining what in fact are the classical laws and genetic operators, what in fact are the explanatory genera and species, what in fact is the actual course of generalized emergent probability. Nor can a philosopher[d] restricted to proportionate being offer more than an account of what in fact the structure of this universe is, nor can he base this account on more than what in fact the structure of human knowing is.

Our first step was to affirm the intelligibility of being and the nothingness of the mere matter of fact that admitted no explanation. Our second step was to affirm that, if one remained within the limits of proportionate being, one was confronted at every turn with mere matters of fact with no possible explanation. There follows at once the negative conclusion that knowledge of transcendent being cannot be excluded if there is proportionate being and being is intelligible. And this conclusion gives rise to the further question, In what does our knowledge of transcendent being consist?

In the third place, then, a transcendent being relevant to our problem must possess two basic attributes. On the one hand, it must not be contingent in any respect, for if it were, once more we would be confronted with the mere matter of fact that we have to avoid. On the other hand, besides being self-explanatory, the transcendent being must be capable of grounding the explanation of everything about everything else; for without this second attribute, the transcendent being would leave unsolved our problem of contingence in proportionate being.

The foregoing requirements may be expressed in another manner. Every proportionate being is a conditioned that happens to have its conditions fulfilled. But being is intelligible, and so there is no mere happening, no contingence, that is ultimate. Still, proportionate being both exists and exists contingently; therefore, it is not ultimate; therefore, some other being is ultimate, and it is not contingent. Moreover, the ultimate being not only must be self-explanatory itself but also it must be capable of explaining everything else; for otherwise proportionate being would remain a conditioned that merely happened to have its conditions fulfilled; in its every aspect it would be mere matter of fact; and as mere matter of fact is nothing, it would be nothing.

To put the same point in still another fashion, one has only to formulate correctly the already acknowledged facts of final, exemplary, and efficient causality.

For one misses the real point to efficient causality if one supposes that it consists simply in the necessity that conditioned being becomes virtually unconditioned only if its conditions are fulfilled. On that formulation, efficient causality would be satisfied by an infinite regress in which each conditioned has its conditions fulfilled by a prior conditioned or, perhaps more realistically, by a circle illustrated by the scheme of recurrence. However, the real requirement is that, if conditioned being is being, it has to be intelligible; it cannot be or exist or occur merely as a matter of fact for which no explanation is to be asked or expected, for the nonintelligible is apart from being. Now both the infinite regress and the circle are simply aggregates of mere matters of fact; they fail to provide for the intelligibility of conditioned being; and so they do not succeed in assigning an efficient cause for being that is intelligible yet conditioned. Nor can an efficient cause be assigned, until one affirms a being that both is itself without any conditions and can ground the fulfilment of conditions for anything else that can be.

Again, if there are conditioned beings, there also is the fulfilling of their conditions; and if there are no mere matters of fact that remain ultimately unexplained, then no conditions are fulfilled simply at random. But if no conditions are fulfilled simply at random, then all^e are fulfilled in accord with some exemplar; and so there must be an exemplary cause that can ground the intelligibility of the pattern in which are or would be fulfilled all conditions that are or would be fulfilled.

Again, because being is intelligible, it also is good. As potentially intelligible, it is a manifold, and this manifold is good inasmuch as it can stand under the formal good of order. But possible orders are many; they include incompatible alternatives; they develop but do so flexibly in a variety of manners; they can fail at any stage in many different ways to bring forth their dialectical correction. If, then, in any universe there is one actual order, if that actual order lies within being and so is not mere matter of fact, then the order must be a value and its selection due to rational choice. Similarly, if in every possible universe being is intelligible and the intelligible is good, then the possibility of every universe is the possibility of its being selected by an ultimate rational choice.

This may seem too rapid, and so it may be well to go back over the argument. First, the universe of proportionate being is shot through with contingence. Secondly, mere contingence is apart from being, and so there must be an ultimate ground for the universe, and that ground cannot be contingent. Thirdly, the necessary ultimate ground cannot be necessitated in grounding a contingent universe, and it cannot be arbitrary in grounding an intelligible and good universe. It cannot be necessitated, for what follows necessarily from the necessary is equally necessary. It cannot be arbitrary, for what results arbitrarily from the necessary results as a mere matter of fact without any possible explanation. But what is neither necessary nor arbitrary yet intelligible and a value is what proceeds freely from the reasonable choice of a rational consciousness.

The final cause, then, is the ground of value, and it is the ultimate cause of causes for it overcomes contingence at its deepest level. Being cannot be arbitrary, and contingent being cannot be necessary. It follows that contingent being must be[f] a reasonably realized possibility. Its possibility is grounded in the exemplary cause, its realization in the efficient cause, but its reasonableness in the final cause. Without that reasonableness, it would be arbitrary, and so it would be apart from being; but what is apart from being is not possible; and what is not possible cannot be realized.

Such, then, is the transition from efficient, exemplary, and final causality as facts within the domain of proportionate being to universal principles that bear our knowing into the domain of transcendent being.

The reader, perhaps, will feel that the transition has failed to free these notions of causality from their anthropomorphic quality. So far from getting away from man, they lead rather obviously to the affirmation of an unconditioned intelligent and rational consciousness that freely grounds the universe in much the same fashion as the conditioned intelligent and rational consciousness of man grounds freely his own actions and products. Our answer is twofold. On the one hand, the specifically human, the anthropomorphic, is not a pure intelligent and rational consciousness but a consciousness in tension between the pure desire and other desire. On the other hand, insofar as one considers in man solely his intelligent and rational consciousness, one cannot but deal with what is related intimately to the universe and its ultimate ground. For what is the universe and its ground but the objective of man's detached, disinterested, unrestricted desire to know?

9   The Notion of God   [657–69]

If God is a being, he is to be known by intelligent grasp and reasonable affirmation. Accordingly, two questions arise, namely, what God is and whether God is. But by asking what being is, already we have been led to the conclusion that the idea of being would be the content of an unrestricted act of understanding that primarily understood itself and consequently grasped every other intelligibility. Now, as will appear, our concept of an unrestricted act of understanding has a number of implications, and when they are worked out, it becomes manifest that it is one and the same thing to understand what being is and to understand what God is. The present section, accordingly, is concerned exclusively with the formulation of the notion of God; whether this notion refers to

681   General Transcendent Knowledge

existent reality is a further question to be considered in the section that follows on the affirmation of God.[g]

First, then, if there is an unrestricted act of understanding, there is by identity a primary intelligible. For the unrestricted act understands itself.

Secondly, because the act is unrestricted, there would be no possibility of correction, or revision, or improvement, and so the unrestricted act would be invulnerable as understanding. Moreover, since it knew itself, it would know it was unrestricted and so invulnerable. Accordingly, by identity, it would be a reflective act of understanding grasping itself as unconditioned and therefore correct and true; and so, by identity, the primary intelligible would be also the primary truth.

Thirdly, what is known by correct and true understanding is being; so the primary intelligible would be also the primary being; and the primary being would be spiritual in the full sense of the identity of the intelligent and intelligible.

Fourthly, the primary being would be without any defect or lack or imperfection. For were there any defect or lack or imperfection, at least unrestricted understanding would grasp what was missing. But the consequent is impossible, and so the antecedent must be false. For the primary being is identical with the unrestricted act, and so a grasp of what was missing in the primary being would be a grasp of a restriction in the unrestricted act.[h]

Fifthly, the good is identical with intelligible being, and so the primary intelligible and completely perfect primary being also is the primary good.

Sixthly, as the perfection of the spiritual requires that the intelligible also be intelligent, so too it requires that affirmable truth be affirmed and the lovable good be loved. But the primary intelligible also is the primary truth and the primary good; and so in a completely perfect spiritual being the primary intelligible is identical not only with an unrestricted act of understanding but also with a completely perfect act of affirming the primary truth and a completely perfect act of loving the primary good. Moreover, the act of affirming is not a second act distinct from the unrestricted act of understanding, nor the act of loving a third act distinct from the understanding and the affirming. For if they were, then the primary being would be incomplete and imperfect and in need of further acts of affirming and loving to be completed and perfected. Hence, one and the same reality is at once unrestricted understanding and the primary intelligible, reflective understanding and the unconditioned, perfect affirming and the primary truth, perfect loving and the primary good.

Seventhly, the primary intelligible is self-explanatory. For if it were not, it would be incomplete in intelligibility; and we have already shown any defect or lack or imperfection to be incompatible with unrestricted understanding.

Eighthly, the primary being is unconditioned.[i] For the primary being is identical with the primary intelligible; and the primary intelligible must be unconditioned, for if it depended on anything else, it would not be self-explanatory. Finally, it is impossible for the primary intelligible to be completely independent and the primary being identical with it to be dependent on something else.

Ninthly, the primary being either is necessary or impossible. For it cannot be contingent, since the contingent is not self-explanatory. Hence, if it exists, it exists of necessity and without any conditions; and if it does not exist, then it is impossible, for there is no condition from which it could result. But whether it exists or not is a question that does not pertain to the idea of being or to the notion of God.

Tenthly, there is only one primary being. For *entia non sunt multiplicanda praeter necessitatem*, and there is no necessity for more than one. Moreover, if there was more than one primary being, then each would or would not be identical with an unrestricted act of understanding. If not, then the intelligibles identical with restricted acts of understanding would not be primary beings.[j] If so, there would be several primary beings similar in all respects; for unrestricted acts cannot grasp different objects without one or more failing to grasp what another grasps and so ceasing to be unrestricted acts. But there cannot be several primary beings similar in all respects, for then they would differ merely empirically; and the merely empirical is not self-explanatory. Accordingly, there can be only one primary being.

In the eleventh place, the primary being is simple. For the primary being is a single act that at once is unrestricted understanding and perfect affirming and perfect loving; and it is identical with the primary intelligible and the primary truth and the primary good.

It does not admit the compositeness of central and conjugate forms. For there are no other beings of the same order with which it could be conjugate; and as it is but a single act, it has no need of a unifying central form.

Nor does it admit the compositeness of potency and form. For it is a spiritual being beyond all development, and potency has been identified either with a capacity to develop or with the empirical residue and materiality.

Nor does it admit the compositeness of distinct form and act. For if it exists, it exists necessarily. Moreover, if the primary intelligible and primary being and primary good are named form or essence, and the unrestricted act of understanding, affirming, loving are named act or existence or occurrence, still they are not distinct but identical.

In the twelfth place, the primary being is timeless. It is without continuous time, for it is spiritual while continuous time presupposes the empirical residue and materiality. And it is without ordinal time, for it does not develop.

In the thirteenth place, if the primary being exists, it is eternal. For it is timeless, and eternity is timeless existence.

However, besides the primary intelligible, there are to be considered the secondary intelligibles; for the unrestricted act of understanding, inasmuch as it understands itself, also grasps everything about everything else.

In the fourteenth place, then, the secondary intelligibles are conditioned. For they are what is to be understood if the primary intelligible is understood.

It follows that they are distinct from the primary intelligible, for they are conditioned and it is unconditioned.

Still, though the secondary intelligibles are distinct from the primary, they need not be distinct realities. For knowing does not consist in taking a look at something else, and so, though the secondary intelligibles are known, they need not be something else to be looked at. Moreover, the primary being is without any lack or defect or imperfection; but it would be imperfect if further realities were needed for the unrestricted act of understanding to be unrestricted.

Finally, the secondary intelligibles may be mere objects of thought. For they are grasped as distinct from the primary intelligible, yet they need not be distinct realities. Thus, the infinity of positive integers is grasped by us in the insight that is the generative principle of the relations and the terms of the series.

In the fifteenth place, the primary being is the omnipotent efficient cause. For the primary being would be imperfect if it could ground all possible universes as objects of thought but not as realities; similarly, the primary good would be imperfect if it was good in itself but not the source of other instances of the good. But the primary being and primary good is without any imperfection; and so it can ground any possible universe and originate any other instance of the good.

In the sixteenth place, the primary being is the omniscient exemplary cause. For it is the idea of being, and in itself it grasps the intelligible order of every possible universe of beings in their every component and aspect and detail.

In the seventeenth place, the primary being is free. For the secondary intelligibles are contingent: they need not be distinct realities; they can be merely objects of thought; they are not unconditioned either in intelligibility or in goodness, and so they are not unconditioned in being, which is not apart from intelligibility and goodness. But contingent being as contingent cannot be necessary and as being cannot be arbitrary; it remains that, if contingent beings exist, they exist in virtue of the freedom of unrestricted understanding and perfect affirming and perfect loving.

In the eighteenth place, because man develops, every additional element of understanding and affirming and willing is a further act and reality in him. But the perfect primary being does not develop, for it is without defect or lack or imperfection; and so the unrestricted act understands and affirms and wills contingent beings to be, without any increment or change in its reality.

There follow a number of conclusions of considerable importance. Though often enough they are supposed to be extremely difficult, the only difficulty lies in grasping the differences that separate grammar, logic, and metaphysics. Grammar is concerned with words and sentences; logic is concerned with concepts and judgments; but metaphysics is concerned with the enumeration of the necessary and sufficient realities on the supposition that judgments are true.

The first corollary is that every contingent predication concerning God also is an extrinsic denomination. In other words, God is intrinsically the same whether or not he understands, affirms, wills, causes this or that universe to be. If he does not, then God exists and nothing else exists. If he does, God exists and the universe in question exists; the two existences suffice for the truth of the judgments that God understands, affirms, wills, effects the universe; for God is unlimited in perfection, and what is unlimited in perfection must understand, affirm, will, effect whatever else is.

The second corollary is that, though the extrinsic denominator is temporal, the contingent predication concerning God can be eternal. For an eternal act is timeless; in it all instants are one and the same instant; and so what is true at any instant is true at every instant. Hence, if at any instant it is true that God understands, affirms, wills the existence of Alexander's horse Bucephalus, then the metaphysical conditions of the truth are the existence of God and the existence of Bucephalus; moreover, though Bucephalus exists only for a short period, still God eternally understands, affirms, and wills Bucephalus to exist for that short period.

The third corollary is divine efficacy. It is impossible for it to be true that God understands, affirms, wills, effects anything to exist or occur without it being true that the thing exists or the event occurs exactly as God understands, affirms, or wills it. For one and the same metaphysical condition is needed for the truth of both propositions, namely, the relevant contingent existence or occurrence.

The fourth corollary is inverse to the third, namely, that divine efficacy does not impose necessity upon its consequents. In the light of divine efficacy it is quite true that if God understands or affirms or wills or effects this or that to exist or occur, then it is impossible for the this or that not to exist or not to occur. Still, the existence or occurrence is a metaphysical condition of the truth of the antecedent, and so the consequence merely enunciates the principle of identity, namely, if there is the existence or occurrence, then there is the existence or occurrence. To recall Aquinas's repeated illustration, *Socrates, dum sedet, necessario sedet, necessitate tamen non absoluta sed conditionata.*

The fifth corollary is the *scientia media*. Since the divine act of understanding is unrestricted and true, it grasps not only every possible world order but also the foregoing four corollaries. Hence, independently of any free decision (*in signo antecedente omnem actum voluntatis*) God knows that if he were to will any world order, then that order would be realized in every aspect and detail; but every world order is a single intelligible pattern of completely determinate existents and events; and so quite apart from any divine decision, God knows exactly what every free will would choose in each successive set of circumstances contained in each possible world order.

The foregoing *scientia media* includes Molina's notion of divine wisdom grasping the order of every possible universe, but it does not include Molina's tendency to speak of the conditioned futurables as entities at which God looks for guidance. Again, it rests neither on Molina's super-comprehension of the human will nor on Suarez's unexplained objective truth but on Aquinas's familiar contentions on the immutability of God and the conditioned necessity of what God knows or wills or causes. Finally, it is radically opposed to Scotist voluntarism and to the voluntaristic *decreta hypothetice praedeterminantia*.

In the nineteenth place, God would be the creator. For if God's efficient causality presupposed the existence of some matter and was limited to fashioning and ordering it, then the existence of this matter would be unexplained; but what ultimately is unexplained does not pertain to being; and so the alleged matter would prove to be nothing.

It may be said that, in fact, there is in this universe a merely empirical residue that is unexplained. But one may answer that the empirical residue of individuality, of the continuum, of particular places and times, and of the nonsystematic divergence of actual frequencies, while unexplained by the particular sciences, partly are understood in cognitional theory and metaphysics and ultimately are accounted for by God's creative decision. For the prime potency of individuality is the condition of the possibility of universal knowledge and common natures; the prime potency of the space-time continuum is the condition of the possibility of abstract and invariant laws, of concrete probabilities, and of their cumulation into a world order of emergent probability; the nonsystematic, finally, is transcended by an unrestricted act of understanding. Moreover, the empirical residue grounds the manifold of the potential good, and inasmuch as it stands under world order, it possesses the value that accrues to the contingent through the reasonableness of the freedom of a completely wise and good being.

In the twentieth place, God would be the conserver. His efficient causality would not produce a universe and then leave it to its own devices but, on the contrary, would be exercised as long as the universe or any of its parts existed. For the metaphysical condition of the truth of the proposition that A causes B is the reality of a relation of dependence (*ut a quo*) in B with respect to A. It is not, as the counterpositions would have it, an imaginable 'influence' occupying the space intermediate between A and B. It is not a change in A, for the fire does not change when it ceases to cook the potatoes and begins to cook the steak. It is B as emerging or existing or occurring in intelligible dependence on A. But no contingent being is self-explanatory, and so every contingent being, as long as it is, is in intelligible dependence on the self-explanatory being.

In the twenty-first place, God would be the first agent of every event, every development, every emergent. For every such occurrence is conditioned, and either the conditions diverge and scatter throughout the universe or else they form a scheme of recurrence which, however, emerges and survives only on conditions that diverge and scatter throughout the universe. It follows that only the cause of the order of the universe can be the sufficient ground for the occurrence of any event; further, since every development and every emergence depends upon a complex of events, only the cause of the order of the universe can be the sufficient ground for any development or emergence.

It follows, further, that God applies every contingent agent to its operation. For the agent operates in accord with the pattern of world order when the conditions of the operation are fulfilled; but the conditions are fulfilled when other events occur; and God is the first agent of each of those occurrences. Moreover, it follows that every created agent is an instrument in executing the divine plan; for its operation is the fulfilment of a condition for other events; and so it is used by a higher agent for an ulterior end. Finally, it follows that God by his intelligence moves all things to their proper ends; for God causes every event and applies every agent and uses every operation inasmuch as he is the cause of the order of the universe.

It will be noted that this account of divine control of events differs from the accounts of both Bañez and Molina. For they ascribe divine control of all events to the fact that God by a peculiar activity controls each. But on the above analysis God controls each event because he controls all, and he controls all because he alone can be the cause of the order of the universe on which every event depends. Moreover, though our analysis is cast in contemporary terms, one has only to replace modern by Aristotelian physics to arrive, I believe, at the thought and expression of Aquinas.[1]

In the twenty-second place, God would be the ultimate final cause of any universe, the ground of its value, and the ultimate objective of all finalistic striving. For, as we have seen, the primary intelligible would be incomplete if in it were not to be grasped every other intelligible; the primary being would be imperfect in being if it could not originate other being; and the primary good would be lacking in goodness if it were sterile and could not be the source of other instances of the good. In-

---

1 See my article 'St. Thomas' Theory of Operation,' *Theological Studies* 3 (1942) 387–91 (*Grace and Freedom* 76–80 [CWL 1]).

versely, then, the secondary intelligibles are intelligible because of the completeness of the primary; contingent beings are possible because of the perfection of primary being; and other instances of the good can arise because of the excellence of the primary good. But what is possible because of the perfection and excellence of another also will be actual because of that perfection and excellence; and so God's perfection and excellence must be the final cause of everything else.

Moreover, a value is a possible object of reasonable choice, and so the ground of value is the ground of possibility in objects and of reasonableness in choosing. But every possible world order is grasped in the primary intelligible and derived from it; and any actual world order is chosen by a willing that not merely accords with unrestricted understanding but is identical with it. Hence God would be the ground of the value of any world order and, indeed, a ground that is identical with the standard of what true value is.

Further, it has been seen that the immanent order of this universe is a compound conditioned series of things and schemes of recurrence realized in accord with successive schedules of probabilities; and it has been added that, from the viewpoint of unrestricted understanding, the nonsystematic vanishes to yield place to a fully determinate and absolutely efficacious plan and intention. It follows that finality is to be conceived more accurately. Instead of an upward but indeterminately directed dynamism, there is the intended ordination of each potency for the form it receives, of each form for the act it receives, of each manifold of lower acts for the higher unities and integrations under which they are subsumed. So it is that every tendency and force, every movement and change, every desire and striving is designed^k to bring about the order of the universe in the manner in which in fact they contribute to it; and since the order of the universe itself has been shown to be because of the perfection and excellence of the primary being and good, so all that is for the order of the universe is headed ultimately to the perfection and excellence that is its primary source and ground.

In the twenty-third place, there follows a transformation of metaphysics as we have conceived it. For the metaphysics of proportionate being becomes a subordinate part of a more general metaphysics that envisages the transcendent idea of being.

In the twenty-fourth place, there follows a transformation of the ethics based on restricted metaphysics. For that ethics was concerned with the consistency of knowing and doing within the individual's rational self-consciousness. But now it is clear that true knowledge not only is true but also is an apprehension of the divinely ordained order of the universe, and that doing consistent with knowing not merely is consistent with knowing but also is man's cooperation with God in the realization of the order of the universe. Inversely, error becomes a deviation not only from truth but also from God, and wrongdoing takes on the character of sin against God.

In the twenty-fifth place, something must be said about evil and sin. For it would seem that, since God is the efficacious cause of everything in the universe, he must be the author of all its evils and responsible for all its sins. But before leaping to that conclusion, let us distinguish between physical evil, moral evil, and basic sin.

By basic sin I shall mean the failure of free will to choose a morally obligatory course of action or its failure to reject a morally reprehensible course of action. Thus basic sin is the root of the irrational in man's rational self-consciousness. As intelligently and rationally conscious, man grasps and affirms what he ought to do and what he ought not to do; but knowing is one thing and doing is another; if he wills, he does what he ought; if he wills, he diverts his attention from proposals to do what he ought not; but if he fails to will, then the obligatory course of action is not executed; again, if he fails to will, his attention remains on illicit proposals; the incompleteness of their intelligibility and the incoherence of their apparent reasonableness are disregarded; and in this contraction of consciousness, which is the basic sin, there occurs the wrong action, which is more conspicuous but really derivative.

Next, by moral evils I shall mean the consequences of basic sins. From the basic sin of not willing what one ought to will, there follow moral evils of omission and a heightening of the temptation in oneself or others to further basic sins. From the basic sin of not setting aside illicit proposals, there follows their execution and a more positive heightening of tension and temptation in oneself or in one's social milieu.

Finally, by physical evils I shall mean all the shortcomings of a world order that consists, insofar as we understand it, in a generalized emergent probability. For in such an order the unordered manifold is prior to the formal good of higher unities and higher orders; the undeveloped is prior to the developed; there are false starts, breakdowns, failures; advance is at the price of risk; security is mated with sterility; and the life of man is guided by an intelligence that has to develop and a willingness that has to be acquired.

Now it is not difficult to grasp the relevance of this threefold distinction to our problem. For a problem is a question for intelligence; it defines an intelligibility to be grasped; and clearly intelligence cannot lump together basic sins, moral evils, and physical ills.

In the first place, all that intelligence can grasp with respect to basic sins is that there is no intelligibility to be grasped. What is basic sin? It is the irrational. Why does it occur? If there were a reason, it would not be sin. There may be excuses; there may be extenuating circumstances; but there cannot be a reason, for basic sin consists, not in yielding to reasons and reasonableness, but in failing to yield to them; it consists not in inadvertent failure but in advertence to and in acknowledgment of obligation that nonetheless is not followed by reasonable response.

Now if basic sin is simply irrational, if understanding it consists in grasping that it has no intelligibility, then clearly it cannot be in intelligible dependence on anything else. But what cannot be in intelligible dependence on anything else cannot have a cause; for cause is correlative with effect; and an effect is what is in intelligible dependence on something else. Finally, if basic sins cannot have a cause, God cannot be their cause. Nor does this conclusion contradict our earlier affirmation that every event is caused by God. For basic sin is not an event; it is not something that positively occurs; on the contrary, it consists in a failure of occurrence, in the absence in the will of a reasonable response to an obligatory motive.

Further, when a problem contains the irrational, it can be handled correctly only in a highly complex and critical fashion. If the mathematician attributed to imaginary numbers exactly the same properties as he finds in real numbers, then certainly he would blunder. A graver but no less inevitable blunder awaits anyone that fails to draw the distinctions and follow the rules necessitated by the irrationality of basic sin. For the familiar disjunction of the principle of excluded middle (Either *A* or not *A*) must be replaced by a trichotomy. Besides what is positively and what simply is not, there is the irrational constituted by what could and ought to be but is not. Besides the being that God causes, and the nonbeing that God does not cause, there is the irrational that God neither causes nor does not cause but permits others to perpetrate. Besides the actual good that God wills and the unrealized good that God does not will, there are the basic sins that he neither wills nor does not will but forbids.

Clearly, it is not evil but good to create a being so excellent that it possesses rational self-consciousness whence freedom naturally follows.

It is not evil but good to leave that freedom intact, to command good indeed and to forbid evil, but to refrain from an interference that would reduce freedom to an illusory appearance. Consequently, it is not evil but good to conceive and choose and effect a world order, even though basic sins will and do occur; for it is only fallacy to argue that basic sins are either entities or nonentities and that, if they are entities, they must be due to God's universal causality, or if they are nonentities, they must be due to God's unwillingness to cause the opposite entities.

There remain physical and moral evils. Now if the criteria of good and evil are sensitive pleasure and pain, then clearly physical and moral evils are ultimately evil. But the proper criterion of the good is intelligibility, and in this universe everything but basic sin can be understood and so is good. For the imperfection of the lower is the potentiality for the higher; the undeveloped is for the developed; and even moral evils through the dialectical tension they generate head either to their own elimination or to a reinforcement of the moral good. So it is that a generalized emergent probability can be grasped even by our limited understanding as an immanently and highly intelligible order embracing everything in our universe.

In the twenty-sixth place, God is personal. Though we began from the highly impersonal question, What is being? though we have been working out the implications of an unrestricted act of understanding in itself and in its relations to the universe, though we have been speaking of an object of thought which, if it exists, will be known as an object of affirmation in the objective domain of being, still the notion at which we have arrived is the notion of a personal being. As man, so God is a rational self-consciousness, for man was made in the image and likeness of God. But what man is through unrestricted desire and limited attainment, God is as unrestricted act. But an unrestricted act of rational self-consciousness, however objectively and impersonally it has been conceived, clearly satisfies all that is meant by the subject, the person, the other with an intelligence and a reasonableness and a willing that is his own.

Moreover, as the idea of being is the notion of a personal God, so too it implies a personalist view of the order of the universe. For that order is not a blueprint such as might be drawn up by an architect for a building, nor is it a plan such as might be imposed by a government given to social engineering, but it is an intelligibility that is to be grasped only by compounding classical and statistical, genetic and dialectical methods, that includes the commands and prohibitions that express the willing of one about the willing of others, that has room for the forbearance with which even omnipotent will refuses to interfere with the will of other persons, that contains the apparent anomaly of the trichotomy that goes beyond the principle of excluded middle to make place for the surd of basic sin.

10   The Affirmation of God   [669–77]

Our knowledge of being is by intelligent grasp and reasonable affirmation. By asking what being is, we have been led to grasp and conceive what God is. Since it has been shown that being is the core of all meaning, it follows that our grasp and conception of the notion of God is the most meaningful of all possible objects of our thought. Still, every object of thought raises a further question; for once the activity of intelligent consciousness is completed, the activity of reflective consciousness begins. Is God then merely an object of thought? Or is God real? Is he an object of reasonable affirmation? Does he exist?

These four further questions are one and the same. For the real is being, and apart from being there is nothing. Being is not known without reasonable affirmation, and existence is the respect in which being is known precisely inasmuch as it is affirmed reasonably. Hence it is one and the same thing to say that God is real, that he is an object of reasonable affirmation, and that he exists.

Again, to affirm that God exists is not to ascribe to him the *Existenz* or the subtly drawn *Dasein* of existentialist thought. For such existence is the existence of man, not as intelligently grasped and reasonably affirmed, but as experiencing, inquiring, and reflecting, yet not obtaining any definitive answers to his questions about himself.

Further, while both the existence of any proportionate being and the existence of God are to be known through a rationally posited yes, it does not follow that both the existences are the same. For the meaning of the yes varies with the question that it answers. If one asks whether a contingent being exists, an affirmative answer means a contingent existence. But if one asks whether a self-explanatory being exists, an affirmative answer means a self-explanatory existence.

Again, in the self-knowledge of a self-explanatory being it would be one and the same thing for him to know what he is and whether he is. For his knowledge of what he is would consist in a grasp of the formally unconditioned, and as the grasp answers the question, What? so the unconditioned answers the question, Whether?

But it does not follow that the two questions have a single answer in our knowledge. For when we grasp what God is, our grasp is not an unrestricted act of understanding but a restricted understanding that extrapolates from itself to an unrestricted act and by asking ever further questions arrives at a list of attributes of the unrestricted act. Accordingly, what is grasped is not the unrestricted act but the extrapolation that proceeds from the properties of a restricted act to the properties of the unrestricted act. Hence, when the extrapolation is completed, there remains the further question whether the unrestricted act is just an object of thought or a reality.

It follows that all forms of the ontological argument are fallacious. For they argue from the conception of God to his existence. But our conceptions yield no more than analytic propositions. And, as has been seen, one can effect the transition from the analytic proposition to the analytic principle only inasmuch as the terms and relations of the proposition occur in concrete judgments of fact. Hence, while there is no difficulty in so conceiving God that the denial of his existence would be a contradiction in terms, still that conception yields no more than an analytic proposition; and the proposition in question can become an analytic principle only if we can affirm in a concrete judgment of fact that God does exist.

The Anselmian argument, then, is to be met by distinguishing the premise *Deus est quo maius cogitari nequit*. One grants that by appropriate definitions and syntactical rules it can be made into an analytic proposition. But one asks for the evidence that the terms as defined occur in concrete judgments of fact.

The Cartesian argument seems to be from the concept to the existence of a perfect being. This would be valid if conceiving were looking and looking were knowing. But that view involves the counterpositions; and when one shifts to the positions, one finds that conceptions become knowing only through reflective grasp of the unconditioned.

The Leibnizian argument is from the possibility to the actuality of God. As we have seen, God is either necessary or impossible. But he is not impossible, for the notion of God is not a contradiction in terms. Therefore, he exists necessarily. But the major is only an analytic proposition, and so the conclusion can be no more than an analytic proposition. Further, the reason offered for the minor calls for a distinction. If there is an omnipotent God, and if omnipotence consists in the power to produce whatever does not involve an internal contradiction, then the absence of internal contradiction proves possibility. But if one does not presuppose the existence of divine omnipotence, then the absence of internal contradiction proves no more than the coherence of an object of thought.

However, if the ontological argument is to be regarded as fallacious, it may seem that there is no possibility of affirming rationally the existence of God. For our distinction between analytic propositions and analytic principles is equivalent to the verification principle of the logical positivists. But there seems no possibility of verifying an unrestricted act of understanding either in our external or in our internal experience. And even if the experience were possible, still there would be needed the fact before the existence of God could be affirmed reasonably.

This objection, however, rests on an identification of the notions of verification and of experience. Yet clearly, if the law of falling bodies is verified, it is not experienced. All that is experienced is a large aggregate of contents of acts of observing. It is not experience but understanding that unifies the aggregate by referring them to a hypothetical law of falling bodies. It is not experience but critical reflection that asks whether the data correspond to the law and whether the correspondence suffices for an affirmation of the law. It is not experience but a reflective grasp of the fulfilment of the conditions for a probable affirmation that constitutes the only act of verifying that exists for the law of falling bodies; and similarly it is a reflective grasp of the unconditioned that grounds every other judgment.

Moreover, the point to the demand for a transition from analytic propositions to analytic judgments primarily is a distinction between different types of unconditioned, and only secondarily does it involve a resemblance to the verification principle. There is a virtually unconditioned that has its conditions fulfilled solely by acts of defining and postulating; such is the analytic proposition. To this virtually unconditioned there can accrue a further fulfilment inasmuch as what it defines and what it postulates also prove to be virtually unconditioned; such is the analytic principle. This further fulfilment arises in concrete judgments of fact, such as occur in the process of verification; and so our position resembles that of the logical positivists. But resemblance need not be identity. For unlike the logical positivists, we are completely disillusioned of the notion that knowing the real is somehow looking at what is already out there now. Unlike them, we have much to say about the unconditioned, and indeed it is in the unconditioned that we place the whole meaning and force of verification.

On the one hand, then, the ontological argument is to be rejected, for conception alone is an insufficient ground for judgment. On the other hand, what has to be added to mere conception is, not an experience of God, but a grasp of the unconditioned. Affirming is an intrinsically rational act; it proceeds with rational necessity from grasp of the unconditioned; and the unconditioned to be grasped is, not the formally unconditioned that God is and that unrestricted understanding grasps, but the virtually unconditioned that consists in inferring God's existence from premises that are true. There remains but one more preliminary. Already we have remarked, but again we must repeat, that proof is not some automatic process that results in a judgment, as taking an aspirin relieves a headache, or as turning on a switch sets the digital computer on its unerring way. All that can be set down in these pages is a set of signs. The signs can represent a relevant virtually unconditioned. But grasping it and making the consequent judgment is an immanent act of rational consciousness that each has to perform for himself and no one else can perform for him.

The existence of God, then, is known as the conclusion to an argument, and while such arguments are many, all of them, I believe, are included in the following general form.

If the real is completely intelligible, God exists. But the real is completely intelligible. Therefore, God exists.

To begin from the minor premise, one argues that being is completely intelligible, that the real is being, and that therefore the real is completely intelligible.

Now being is completely intelligible. For being is the objective of the detached, disinterested, unrestricted desire to know; this desire consists in intelligent inquiry and critical reflection; it results in partial knowledge inasmuch as intelligent inquiry yields understanding and critical reflection grasps understanding to be correct; but it reaches its objective, which is being, only when every intelligent question has been given an intelligent answer and that answer has been found to be correct. Being, then, is intelligible, for it is what is to be known by correct understanding; and it is completely intelligible, for being is known completely only when all intelligent questions are answered correctly.

Moreover, the real is being. For the real is what is meant by the name 'real.' But all that is meant is either a mere object of thought or else both an object of thought and an object of affirmation. The real is not merely an object of thought; and so it is both an object of thought and an object of affirmation. Nor is the real merely some of the objects of both thought and affirmation but all of them. And similarly, being is all that is to be known by intelligent grasp and reasonable affirmation.

If this coincidence of the real and being presupposes an acceptance of the positions and a rejection of the counterpositions, the reader will not expect at this stage of the argument any repetition of the basic points that have been made over and over again in the preceding pages of this work. To accept the positions is to accept one's own intelligence and reasonableness and to stand by that acceptance. To reject the counterpositions is to reject the interference of other desire with the proper functioning of the detached, disinterested, and unrestricted desire to know. Hence every counterposition leads to its own reversal; for it is involved in incoherence as soon as the claim is made that it is grasped intelligently and affirmed reasonably; and an intelligent and reasonable subject cannot avoid making that claim.

There remains the major premise, namely, If the real is completely intelligible, then God exists. The argument may be cast as follows.

If the real is completely intelligible, then complete intelligibility exists. If complete intelligibility exists, the idea of being exists. If the idea of being exists, then God exists. Therefore, if the real is completely intelligible, God exists.

Let us comment on each of the premises in turn.

First, if the real is completely intelligible, then complete intelligibility exists. For just as the real could not be intelligible if intelligibility were nonexistent, so the real could not be completely intelligible if complete intelligibility were nonexistent. In other words, to affirm the complete intelligibility of the real is to affirm the complete intelligibility of all that is to be affirmed. But one cannot affirm the complete intelligibility of all that is to be affirmed without affirming complete intelligibility. And to affirm complete intelligibility is to know its existence.

Secondly, if complete intelligibility exists, the idea of being exists. For intelligibility either is material or spiritual or abstract: it is material in the objects of physics, chemistry, biology, and sensitive psychology; it is spiritual when it is identical with understanding; and it is abstract in concepts of unities, laws, ideal frequencies, genetic operators, dialectical tensions and conflicts. But abstract intelligibility necessarily is incomplete, for it arises only in the self-expression of spiritual intelligibility. Again, spiritual intelligibility is incomplete as long as it can inquire. Finally, material intelligibility necessarily is incomplete, for it is contingent in its existence and in its occurrences, in its genera and species, in its classical and statistical laws, in its genetic operators and the actual course of its emergent probability; moreover, it includes a merely empirical residue of individuality, noncountable infinities, particular places and times, and for systematic knowledge a nonsystematic divergence. It follows that the only possibility of complete intelligibility lies in a spiritual intelligibility that cannot inquire because it understands everything about everything. And such unrestricted understanding is the idea of being.

Thirdly, if the idea of being exists, God exists. For if the idea of being exists, at least its primary component exists. But the primary component has been shown to possess all the attributes of God. Therefore, if the idea of being exists, God exists.

Such, then, is the argument. As a set of signs printed in a book, it can do no more than indicate the materials for a reflective grasp of the virtually unconditioned. To elicit such an act is the work that the reader has to perform for himself. Further, inasmuch as any reader has been impressed by the widely diffused contemporary view that the existence of God cannot be proved, he will be wondering just where the fallacy lies, just when the unjustified step was taken, in the foregoing endeavor to accomplish the reputedly impossible. Let us join him in his reflection.

Certainly, there would have to be some fallacy in the argument if it did not presuppose a complete break with the various currents of modern thought that insist on atheism or agnosticism. But such a complete break does exist in the rejection, root and branch, of the counterpositions and in a complete acceptance of the positions. Granted that the real is being, granted that being is known by intelligent grasp and reasonable affirmation, then God is a reality if he is a being, and he is a being if intelligent grasp conceives him and reasonableness affirms what intelligence conceives. Again, granted the exclusion of all obscurantism, intelligence is committed to the effort to conceive a notion of God; for if the real is being, then one must face the question, What is being? and as has been seen, the answer to that question includes the answer to the question, What is God? But the answer to a question for intelligence necessarily raises the corresponding question for reflection, and the exclusion of obscurantism once more commits us to an effort to answer. If the answer is negative, atheism is correct. If no answer is possible, agnosticism is correct. If the answer is affirmative, theism is correct. The only issue is to decide which of the three is the answer to be given by the unity of empirical, intelligent, and rational consciousness that I happen to be. Finally, if I am operating in the intellectual pattern of experience, if I am genuine in my acceptance of the domination of the detached, disinterested, unrestricted desire to inquire intelligently and reflect reasonably, then I have no just grounds for surprise if I find myself unable to deny either that there is a reality or that the real is being or that being is completely intelligible or that complete intelligibility is unrestricted understanding or that unrestricted understanding is God.

Still, a conclusion can contain no more than its premises. If at the start one does not know that God exists, at least that knowledge must emerge in the process if it is to be present at its end. Where, then, in the process does knowledge of God's existence make its implicit entry?

It is a fair question, but to answer it a distinction has to be drawn between (1) affirming a link between other existence and God's and (2) affirming the other existence that is linked to God's existence. The second element lies in the affirmation of some reality: it took place in the chapter on self-affirmation, and it was expanded to the universe of proportionate being in subsequent chapters. The first element is the process that identifies the real with being, then identifies being with complete intelligibility, and finally identifies complete intelligibility with the unrestricted act of understanding that possesses the properties of God and accounts for everything else. In this process the expansive moment is the first: for if the real is being, the real is the objective of an unrestricted desire to understand correctly; to be such an objective, the real has to be completely intelligible, for what is not intelligible is not the objective of a desire to understand, and what is not completely intelligible is the objective, not of an unrestricted desire to understand correctly, but of such a desire judiciously blended with an obscurantist refusal to understand. Once this expansive moment is achieved, the rest follows. The real cannot be completely intelligible if complete intelligibility is unreal. Nor can complete intelligibility be real if the unrestricted act of understanding is merely an object of thought. For the intelligibility of the merely conceived is not real; the intelligibility of material reality is dependent on a merely empirical residue, and so it is incomplete; the intelligibility of inquiring and developing intelligence is seeking its own completion and thereby proclaiming its incompleteness; and so the only possibility of an intelligibility that is at once complete and real is the unrestricted act of understanding.

Yet who are we to pretend to knowledge of every possibility? Might not there be some further alternative? Might not intelligibility be both real and complete in some quite different fashion that lies beyond the narrow confines of our comprehension? There might be, if we were ready to take refuge in the counterpositions or to give way to our tendencies to obscurantism. But the presupposition is that we are not. And if we are not, then the possible is possible being, being is intrinsically intelligible, and the intelligible either is identical with understanding or else related to it as something that could be understood. But intelligibility of the latter type is incomplete, for it is conditioned in its very intelligibility by its relation to something else. Nor is inquiring and developing understanding complete. So there remains only the unrestricted act of understanding. Nor is there any paradox in our claiming to envisage all possible alternatives; for if we can know that our attainment is extremely limited, we can do so because our knowledge springs from an unrestricted desire to understand correctly; and so it is one and the same unrestricted desire that both reveals to us the vastness of the range of possibilities and, by the same stroke, defines the basic conditions that every possibility must satisfy.

Finally, it may be objected that, for all we know, an unrestricted act of understanding may be a contradiction in terms. But at least an unrestricted desire to understand correctly is not a contradiction, for it is a fact. Nor has contradiction any other origin but the existence of different acts of understanding with respect to the same object. Nor does contradiction imply impossibility unless reality is completely intelligible. But the unrestricted act of understanding is a single act, so that contradiction cannot originate from it; and only because the unrestricted act grounds all that is and would ground all that could be, is it true that the contradictory cannot be.

11   Comparisons and Contrasts   [677–86]

It has been argued that our metaphysics of proportionate being supplies a universal viewpoint, and now that that metaphysics has been transformed to include transcendent being, we must ask whether the universal viewpoint remains.

First, then, our conception of God as the unrestricted act of understanding coincides with Aristotle's conception of the unmoved mover as *noêsis noêseôs*, if *noêsis* has the same meaning as *noein* in the famous statement on insight in the *De anima* that forms are grasped by mind in images.[2] Nor is there anything fanciful about such an interpretation. As Aristotle's metaphysics of matter and form corresponds to a psychology of sense and insight, so Aristotle's separate forms are, not Platonic Ideas without intelligence, but identities of intelligibility in act with intelligence in act.

Secondly, the series of attributes we have found in the unrestricted act of understanding reveal the identity of our conception with Aquinas's conception of God as *ipsum intelligere, ipsum esse, summum bonum*, the exemplar, efficient cause, first agent, and last end of all else that is or could be. Among Thomists, however, there is a dispute whether *ipsum intelligere* or *ipsum esse subsistens* is logically first among divine attributes. As has been seen in the section on the notion of God, all other divine attributes follow from the notion of an unrestricted act of understanding. Moreover, since we define being by its relation to intelligence, necessarily our ultimate is not being but intelligence.

Thirdly, as Aquinas, so have we rejected the ontological argument and every other claim to immediate knowledge of God. However, as we have argued mediately from the reality of creatures to the reality of God, so we have made explicit the implication of this procedure by distinguishing two levels in metaphysics. For if creatures are known by us before God is known, then there is in our knowledge a metaphysics of proportionate being that is true as a matter of fact and as a matter of fact reveals the ontological structure of the proportionate universe. But mere matters of fact cannot be ultimate for intelligence, and so from proportionate metaphysics we are led from contingence through causality to being as at once transcendent idea and transcendent reality.

Fourthly, the five ways in which Aquinas proves the existence of God are so many particular cases of the general statement that the proportionate universe is incompletely intelligible and that complete intelligibility is demanded. Thus, there is an argument from motion, because the transition from potency to act is conditioned, and an unlimited aggregate of conditioned transitions does not add up to complete intelligibility. There is an argument from efficient causality, for the intelligible dependence of effect on cause becomes completely intelligible only if there is a cause that is intelligible without being dependent. There is an

2 [Aristotle, *De anima*, III, 7, 431b 2 – a statement quoted in the Greek on Lonergan's title page. The MSS give the Greek here, but Lonergan changed it at the proof stage to English (see below our note to the title page).]

argument from contingence, for the contingent is as a matter of fact, and the matter of fact is not completely intelligible. There is an argument from the several levels of being, for the many can be completely intelligible only by being related to the one and unique. There is an argument from the order of the universe, for the intelligibility of an order is conditioned in its intelligibility by its relation to an intelligence.

Fifthly, besides Aquinas's five ways, there are as many other proofs of the existence of God as there are aspects of incomplete intelligibility in the universe of proportionate being. In particular, attention must be drawn to the epistemological problem. For as nothing in the proportionate universe is a complete intelligibility, so our knowing is not. Inversely, unless we know some reality, there is no possibility of deducing the existence of God. It follows that first we must establish that as a matter of fact we know and that as a matter of fact there is some reality proportionate to our knowing. For only after the facts are known can we entertain any hope of reaching an explanation of the possibility of a correspondence between our inquiry and understanding, our reflection and judgment, and, on the other hand, the real as it really is.

Accordingly, we are led to disagree with what seems to have been Schleiermacher's procedure. Correctly he maintained that our knowing is possible only if ultimately there is an identity of *Denken* and *Sein*. But it does not follow that in our knowledge such an identity must be genetically first. And so it does not follow that the whole of our knowing rests on a belief, prompted by religious feeling, in the ultimate identity. As has been seen, our own unrestricted desire to know defines for us what we must mean when we speak of being; in the light of that notion we can settle by intelligent grasp and reasonable affirmation what in fact is and what in fact is not; and while this procedure does not explain why every possible and actual reality must be intelligible, it does settle what in fact already is known to be true, and at the same time it gives rise to the further question that asks for complete explanation and complete intelligibility.

Sixthly, as the metaphysics of proportionate being rests on the isomorphism of the proportionate known to the knower, so the transition to the transcendent is effected by proceeding from the contingent subject's unrestricted desire to know to the transcendent subject's unrestricted act of understanding. Again, as the structure of proportionate being can be deduced from the structure of the contingent subject, so certain general properties of any possible universe can be deduced from the attributes of the transcendent subject. However, while the metaphysics of proportionate being can be developed by appealing to common sense and to the empirical sciences, the general properties of any possible universe are bound to remain generalities in our knowledge, for we have no empirical knowledge of universes other than the one in which we exist.

There follows a corollary of considerable theological importance, namely, that our knowledge of possible worlds is, in general, no more than an inference from our knowledge of God. Thus, because God is omnipotent, one can infer that every noncontradictory statement would be true in some possible world. Because divine wisdom equals divine power, one can say that every possible world would be ordered in accord with infinite wisdom. Because divine goodness accords with divine wisdom, one can say that any possible world would be worthy of infinite goodness. But because our understanding is not the unrestricted act, we are not in a position to go into details. Briefly, we are committed to the sobriety of Aquinas in the twenty-fifth question of the first part of his *Summa theologiae,* and we are led to reject as methodologically unsound the Scotist view that a question becomes scientific when it is raised with respect to all possible worlds. The fact is that a question then usually becomes indeterminable, and to no small extent the sterility of later scholasticism seems attributable to its mistaken conceptions on the nature of scientific knowledge.

Seventhly, if our account of the notion and the affirmation of God may be placed within the Aristotelian and Thomist tradition, it also meets the requirement of explaining the existence of other views. For though we have gone beyond the metaphysics of proportionate being to the transcendent idea and transcendent reality of being, still our base of operations has remained the same. We raised the question of the notion of God by asking what being is. We answered the question whether God exists by affirming that the real is being and that being is the completely intelligible objective of an unrestricted desire to understand correctly. Nor was it obscure at any decisive point in the process that we were reaching our answers by remaining true to the positions and by rejecting the counterpositions. But the polymorphism of human consciousness is not suppressed by the mere fact that a man is asking what and whether God is. Accordingly, just as our notion and affirmation of God result from the positions, so other views on the divinity may be reached by supposing different stages in the development of the positions and in the aberration of the counterpositions.

It follows that the universal viewpoint of proportionate metaphysics has been preserved yet expanded. For a viewpoint is universal in the measure that (1) it is one and coherent, (2) it raises issues too basic to be dodged, and (3) its analysis of the evidence is penetrating enough to explain the existence of every other view as well as to establish its own. But the notion and affirmation of God is one, for God is one; it is coherent, for coherence results from the unity of a single act of understanding, and God is a single, unrestricted act of understanding. Again, to ask what being is and whether the real is being is to raise questions that are too basic to be dodged. Finally, as our answer results from the positions at the present stage of their development, so other answers (at least if we prescind for the moment from the mystic's affirmation of the ineffable and the believer's affirmation of a divine revelation) can be derived by assigning different values to the variables in man's polymorphic consciousness.

To illustrate this conclusion briefly, the positions develop primarily inasmuch as sense is distinguished from understanding and both sense and understanding from judgment, and they develop secondarily inasmuch as the positions are distinguished sharply and effectively from the counterpositions. Pythagoras and Parmenides, Plato and Aristotle, Augustine and Aquinas are the great names in the primary process, while the breakdown of medieval scholasticism and the methodological efforts of modern philosophy set the problem of the secondary development, and the advance of mathematics and empirical science provides the precise information needed to effect it.

In the measure that the primary and secondary developments have not occurred or are not assimilated, not only is human consciousness polymorphic but its various components are unresolved. Man affirms the divine, and obscurely he knows what he means. As best he can, he expresses his meaning, but his resources for expression are unequal to the task. He can give God a name, but there are many tongues, and so there are many names. He can indicate divine attributes by analogy, but he cannot disassociate[1] the analogies he employs from their imperfections. To make God a cause is also to relegate him to the past; to make him an end is to postpone him to the future; to insist upon his immediacy and relevance to the world and to human living is to involve him in the hearth and the family, in the emphases of patriarchal and matriarchal arrangements, in the concerns of hunters and fishers, of agriculturalists, craftsmen, and nomads, in the interests of property and the state, in the occupations of peace and war. The fourfold bias of the dramatic and practical subject[m] of common sense reappears in the conception of the divine, and by this reinforcement and sanction it heads, first, to an ever fuller expansion but, ultimately, to its own reversal. So the empires of the Mediterranean basin gathered the gods of their peoples into pantheons; syncretists reduced their numbers; allegorists gave new meanings to their exploits; and philosophers discovered and preached the primacy of the Intelligible and of the One.

Still, the emergence of philosophy as a distinct field of inquiry merely transposes the issue. The many gods give place to the many philosophies. The intellectualism of a Plato and an Aristotle is opposed by the atomism of a Leucippus and Democritus. Time divides the Old, the Middle, and the New Academies. The Lyceum deserts the fifty-odd unmoved movers of Aristotelian cosmology to settle down to empirical research. Philosophy itself becomes practical in the primarily ethical concern of Cynic and Cyrenaic, of Epicurean and Stoic, and the brilliant speculation of a Plotinus ends in the more effective oddities of a Proclus and Iamblichus.

Again, if the sustained monotheism of the Hebraic and Christian traditions and of some of their offshoots can be argued to exhibit a historical singularity, it cannot be said to have exorcized the polymorphism of human consciousness. Besides the true believers, there have been the heretics. The apparently monolithic front of medieval scholasticism, on closer inspection, splinters into schools, and within each school men dispute about their special orthodoxy. Behind the certitudes of a common faith, there arise the doubts and denials about the independent range and value of human reason. The Cartesian rebirth is followed by the opposition of rationalism and empiricism. The Kantian compromise is deserted for idealism on the one hand and for irrationalism on the other. To fill the increasing vacuum, science becomes scientism to proclaim that as the earth is just one of the planets, so man is just one of the brutes, God is just a projection from the psychological depths, and religion is just a façade for economic and social interests.

Now if the notion and affirmation of God pertain to the positions, not in any incidental fashion, but as necessary answers to the inevitable questions about the idea of being and the identity of being with the real, it follows that the counterpositions, ever sustained by the polymorphism of human consciousness, will involve prephilosophic notions of the divine in the mythical, will generate counterphilosophic misconceptions, doubts, and denials, and will tend to corrupt even correct notions and affirmations if they are unsupported by an effective criticism of the influences that rise from the unconscious into human sensitivity and intersubjectivity and that invade the realm of truth at the demand of tribal, national, economic, and political necessity and utility.

If, then, the procedure of the present chapter in conceiving the nature and affirming the reality of God appears to be excessively laborious, complex, and difficult, it would be unfair to overlook the fact that our concern has been, not to select the easiest approach to the notion of God, not to offer the simplest proof of his existence, but so to advance from proportionate to transcendent being that the universal viewpoint, attained in the earlier stages of the argument, might be preserved as well as expanded. It is an old saying that *veritas est una et error multiplex*, but even truth changes its appearance as human understanding develops, and it is not a negligible advantage to be able to account from a single base not only for the changing face of truth, not only for the multiplicity of error, but also for the worst of enemies, the one in a man's own household, that so spontaneously and so naturally tends to adjust and color the truth one knows to the exigences of one's sociocultural milieu and to the hue of one's temperament.

Eighthly, because it is difficult to know what our knowing is, it also is difficult to know what our knowledge of God is. But just as our knowing is prior to an analysis of knowledge and far easier than it, so too our knowledge of God is both earlier and easier than any attempt to give it formal expression. For without any formulation of the notion of being, we use it whenever we inquire and understand, reflect and judge. Without any explicit repudiation of obscurantism, we ask questions and further questions in our search for the intelligible and unconditioned. But all that we know and can know about ourselves and about the world around us raises the same further question; for it is known to be just as a matter of fact through a reflective grasp of the virtually unconditioned; and the ubiquitous and incessant further question admits only one answer, namely, an intelligibility that formally is unconditioned. So it is that, just as all men understand what they mean by the 'nature of ...' though they are at a loss to say what they mean, similarly they all understand what they mean by God though they are at a loss when asked to explain so basic and familiar a notion. Again, just as every inquirer knows something when he knows that there is a nature to be known though he still has to discover what the nature is, similarly everyone knows something when he knows that there is a God even though he entertains no hope of ever reaching an unrestricted act of understanding and so knowing what God is. Again, just as the notion of nature can be misused by the gnostic and the magician, yet, if used properly, provides the dynamic base on which the whole of scientific knowledge is erected, so too the notion of God can be corrupted by mythical consciousness and distorted by misplaced practicality, yet, if used properly, it supplies the dynamic base on which rise not only the whole of intelligent and rational knowing but also the whole of intelligent and rational living. Finally, just as misuse of the notion of nature makes it ridiculous in the eyes of those most eager to know what is to be known by understanding, so too misconception and misuse of the notion of God lead to its rejection by the very men that are most insistent in denouncing obscurantism, in demanding judgments to rest on the unconditioned, and in calling for consistency between knowing and doing. But if one is eager to know what is to be known by understanding, one can ridicule the notion of nature only because one does not know what the name means; and if one is genuine in denouncing obscurantism and in demanding the unconditioned, either one already adores God without naming him or else one has not far to go to reach him.

Ninthly, we have admitted the existence of a critical problem because man's unrestricted desire asks more questions than man's limited attainment can answer; we have contended that a solution to the problem must be piecemeal because questions of possibility are to be settled only by appealing to facts; and we have pointed out that the piecemeal solution becomes methodical in the measure that it executes a comprehensive and effective strategy in selecting the facts to which it successively appeals. Earlier elements in the strategy which we have been following already are familiar to the reader; but it remains to be shown that the fact that we can conceive God as the transcendent idea and affirm him as the transcendent reality of being not only is continuous with all that has gone before but also is its culmination.

Our subject has been the act of insight or understanding, and God is the unrestricted act of understanding, the eternal rapture glimpsed in every Archimedean cry of 'Eureka.' Understanding meets questions for intelligence and questions for reflection. The unrestricted act meets all at once; for it understands understanding and all the intelligibility based on it; and it understands its own understanding as unrestricted, invulnerable, true. What is known by true understanding is being, and the being known by unrestricted understanding's self-knowledge is primary being, self-explanatory, unconditioned, necessary, without any lack or defect.

The good is the intelligible, and so the primary being also is the primary good. As intelligibility without intelligence would be defective, so also would truth without affirming, or the good without loving; but God is without defect, not because the act of understanding is complemented by further acts, but by a single act that at once is understanding and intelligible, truth and affirming, goodness and loving, being and omnipotence.

Our subject has been understanding in its genesis. It arises in intelligent and rational consciousness, but before it arises it is anticipated, and that anticipation is the spontaneous ground that, when reflectively enucleated, becomes the methods of science and the integral heuristic structure implemented in the metaphysics of proportionate being. But the fundamental anticipation is the detached, disinterested, unrestricted desire to understand correctly; the fundamental assumption is that the real is coincident with the grounded intelligibility to be known by correct understanding; the fundamental reflective enucleation of all intelligent and rational anticipation and assumption is to conceive the idea of being, and thereby the notion of God, and to affirm that the real is being, and thereby to affirm the reality of God.

Our subject has been the flight from understanding in the scotosis of the dramatic subject, in the threefold bias of common sense, in the murkiness of mythical consciousness, in the aberrations of the counter-philosophies. But it is not the spirit of inquiry that refuses to ask what being is, nor critical reflection that ignores the question whether being and only being is the real. It is not flight from understanding that forms the notion of an unrestricted act of understanding, nor the demand of rational consciousness for the unconditioned that draws back in alarm when there arises a demand for the formally unconditioned. It is by the positions that the notion of God is developed and the affirmation of God is sustained, and it is by the counterpositions that the issues are misconceived and confused.

Kant spoke of a transcendental illusion, and if what he meant has been shown to be a mistake, the expression survives to generate distrust. But it is not the detached and disinterested desire to understand correctly that can be named an illusion, for it is interference with that desire that is at the root of all error. Nor can the unrestricted desire be named a transcendental illusion, for there has to exist some illusion before it can be either immanental or transcendental. Nor can one say that the pure desire exists, that it is not illusory, yet in fact it is not unrestricted. After all, Kantians and positivists are not deluded but merely mistaken when they endeavor to restrict human inquiry within bounds that everyone naturally and spontaneously transcends.

What, then, is critical method? It is method with respect to the ultimate, method applied to the most basic issues. Now it has been seen that the method of the empirical sciences rests on the heuristic structure of man's desire and capacity to understand data correctly. In similar fashion the method of metaphysics consisted in integrating and implementing classical and statistical, genetic and dialectical methods. Critical method differs from other methods only in its subject matter. As they, so it takes its stand on the detached, disinterested, unrestricted desire to understand correctly.[n] As they, so it grasps and affirms an object correlative to the desire. As they, so it insists both that general statements can be made about the object before it actually is understood and that such statements, though valid and true and useful, fall far short of what is to be known if understanding is attained. In brief, critical method neither is nor can be the bland procedure of consigning transcendental issues to oblivion. Just as scientific method does not repudiate the notion of nature but makes it explicit and precise as the indeterminate function to be determined, as the ideal frequency from which actual frequencies cannot diverge systematically, as the genetic operator, as the dialectical tension and opposition between the pure desire and human sensitivity, so critical method does not repudiate the notion of God but formulates it as the unrestricted act of understanding and works out its general attributes. Just as scientific method does not confuse knowledge of method with its fruits, so critical method does not confuse our formulation of unrestricted understanding with a claim that we understand everything about everything. Just as the scientist is ready to abandon every scientific hypothesis and theory without losing confidence in the correctness of scientific method, so the metaphysician affirms the reality of what the scientist seeks to know, and the critical thinker does not allow developments in the notion of God to generate any doubt that it is one and the same being to which all men refer whether they are more or less successful in conceiving him, whether correctly they affirm his existence or mistakenly they deny it.

20

Special Transcendent Knowledge[a]

Knowledge is transcendent, in our present usage, inasmuch as it goes beyond the domain of proportionate being.

General transcendent knowledge is the knowledge of God that answers the basic questions raised by proportionate being, namely, what being is and whether being is the real.

Still, there is a fact of evil, and man is inclined to argue from that fact to a denial of the intelligence or the power or the goodness of God. Even though it is agreed that the evil of objects of aversion is, from an intellectualist viewpoint, a potential good, even though it is agreed that the evil of disorder is an absence of intelligibility that is to be understood only by the inverse insight that grasps its lack of intelligibility, there remains the concrete fact of evil and the practical problem of determining what one is to do about it.

Indeed, since God is the first agent of every event and emergence and development, the question really is what God is or has been doing about the fact of evil. The answer to that question we shall name special transcendent knowledge, and our discussion will fall under four main heads, namely, the fact of evil, the existence of a solution, the heuristic structure of the properties of the possible solutions, and the identification of the solution that exists.

To these main topics we are forced to add a lengthy excursus on the notion of belief. For among the evils that afflict man, none is graver than the erroneous beliefs which at once distort his mind and make systematic the aberrations of his conduct. Yet, despite its potentialities for evil, belief is inevitable in human collaboration, and the policy of believing nothing is as illusory as the Cartesian program of doubting everything that can be doubted. So we are compelled to determine just what is the necessity of belief, what precisely occurs when one believes, and what one can do to free oneself from false beliefs.

The relation between the central theme and the excursus is, of course, dialectical. Were there not a problem of evil, there would exist neither the mass of erroneous beliefs nor the consequent errors about the nature of belief. Were there not a solution to the problem of evil, there would be little point either in determining correctly the notion of belief or in working out a practicable method for freeing oneself from false beliefs. Finally, because the heuristic structure of the solution to the problem of evil involves beliefs of its own, we have placed our excursus where the issue arises. Nonetheless, we cannot but admit that this yielding to the inner structure of the issue involves an extensive break in the argument, and accordingly we forthwith advise readers disinclined to gulping excessively long parentheses either to read section 4 (p. 725) at once or to skip it on a first reading.

1   The Problem   [688–93]

The cult of progress has suffered an eclipse, not because man does not develop, nor because development does not imply a revision of what has been, but because development does imply that perfection belongs not to the present but to the future. Had that implication of present shortcomings not been overlooked with such abandon, had the apostles of progress not mistaken their basic views for premature attainments of future perfection, then the disillusionment of the twentieth century could hardly have been at once so unexpected, so bitter, and so complete.

Yet as things are, in the aftermath of economic and political upheavals, amidst the fears of worse evils to come, the thesis of progress needs to be affirmed again. For the very structure of man's being is dynamic. His knowing and willing rest on inquiry, and inquiry is unrestricted. His knowing consists in understanding, and every act of understanding not only raises further questions but also opens the way to further answers. His good will is consistent with his knowledge, and as his knowledge develops, he can be persuaded effectively to an ever fuller willingness. His sensitivity and his intersubjectivity are, like his knowledge and willingness, systems on the move; if their adaptation to spiritual advance is slow, at least it tends to endure; and so the accepted manners and customs of an earlier time can become abominations, at once incredible and repulsive, to a later age.

But if the thesis of progress must be affirmed, it must be taken to imply, not only a contrast with the past, but also a contrast with its goal. An unrestricted desire to understand correctly heads towards an unrestricted act of understanding, towards God. A will that is good by its consistency with knowledge is headed towards an antecedent willingness that matches the desire to know both in its essential detachment from the sensitive subject and in its unrestricted commitment to complete intelligibility, to God. A sensitivity and an intersubjectivity that have their higher integration in knowing and willing are headed towards objects and activities that can be no more than symbols and signs of what they cannot comprehend or appreciate. The whole world of sense is to be, then, a token, a mystery, of God, for the desire of intelligence is for God, and the goodness of will is the love of God.

There is a further implication. As the thesis of progress never places man on the pinnacle of perfection, it ever asserts that his knowledge is incomplete, that his willingness is imperfect, that his sensitivity and intersubjectivity still need to be adapted. Knowledge comes by the apparently random process of discovery, and it is disseminated by the laborious process of teaching and learning, writing and reading. Willingness to live consistently with knowledge has to be acquired by persuading oneself or by being persuaded by others. Sensitivity and intersubjectivity need time to become at ease with new ways. So it is that the present is ever a pattern of lags. No one can postpone his living until he has learnt, until he has become willing, until his sensitivity has been adapted. To learn, to be persuaded, to become adapted, occur within living and through living. The living is ever now, but the knowledge to guide living, the willingness to follow knowledge, the sensitive adaptation that vigorously and joyously executes the will's decisions, these belong to the future, and when the future is present, there will be beyond it a further future with steeper demands.

Now, inasmuch as the courses of action that men choose reflect either their ignorance or their bad will or their ineffectual self-control, there results the social surd. Then, to understand his concrete situation, man has to invoke not only the direct insights that grasp intelligibility but also the inverse insights that acknowledge the absence of intelligibility. Still, this subtle procedure has to be discovered, taught, learnt. Until the discovery is made and disseminated and accepted, man tends to regard his situation as a homogeneous array of intelligible facts. The social surd, which should be discounted as mere proof of aberration, is regarded as evidence in favor of error. Man becomes a realist. The dictates of intelligence and reasonableness are found irrelevant to concrete living. The facts have to be faced, and facing them means the adjustment of theory to practice. But every adjustment makes the incidental sins of the past into the commonly accepted rule of the present; the social surd expands; and its expansion demands a further adjustment.

If this succession of ever less comprehensive syntheses can be deduced from man's failure to understand himself and his situation dialectically, if, historically, evidence for the failure and its consequences is forthcoming both in the distant and in the recent past, still it is far too general a theorem to unravel at a stroke the tangled skein of intelligibility and absurdity in concrete situations. Its generality has to be mediated by a vast accumulation of direct and inverse insights and by a long series of judgments of truth and of value, before any concrete judgments can be made. And on what Galahad shall we call to do the understanding and to make the judgments? For the social surd resides least of all in outer things and most of all in the minds and wills of men. Without an unbiased judge, the truth would not be reached; and if an unbiased judge were found, would the biased remainder of mankind acknowledge the rectitude of his decisions and effectively abide by them?

It was to this point that we were brought by our study of common sense and by its revelation of the scotosis of the dramatic subject and of the threefold bias of the practical subject. Then we appealed to a higher viewpoint, to an X named cosmopolis; and we indicated some of its features. But if the need of some cosmopolis makes manifest the inadequacy of common sense to deal with the issue, on a deeper level it makes manifest the inadequacy of man. For the possibility of a cosmopolis is conditioned by the possibility of a critical human science, and a critical human science is conditioned by the possibility of a correct and accepted philosophy.

However, as the intervening chapters have attempted to explain, and as the history of philosophy rather abundantly confirms, the polymorphism of human consciousness loses none of its ambivalence because men have turned to philosophy. On the contrary, the many philosophies are but the adequate expression of the inner polymorphic fact. For every human discovery can be formulated either as a position or as a counter-position. The positions invite development, and in the measure that they are developed they are expressed in many ways. Initially each may appear singly. Then it is joined with further antithetical questions. Then positions begin to coalesce, first in more numerous but lesser syntheses, later in fewer but more comprehensive unities. Besides the many expressions of the positions, there are the counterpositions, and they invite reversal. But the reversal that could come from a single penetrating stroke more commonly is delayed. The counterposition expands by the unfolding of its logical implications; it recognizes its fellows and unites with them in a common cause; together they foresee the impending danger of reversal, not in its root, but in some particular manifestation; and then they shift their ground and avoid the menaced attack. So the counterpositions multiply; they occupy a vast territory from high-minded incoherence to simple-minded opportunism and violence; and if the worst of the counterpositions has no truck with any position, if the most perfect expression of the positions happens to be free from any taint of the counterpositions, still philosophers are men, and the vast majority of them cling to some blend of both.

This conclusion may sound like scepticism. But certainly I would be the last to deny the possibility of working out a philosophy on the basis of the polymorphism of human consciousness and of the dialectical opposition between positions and counterpositions. After all, one does not deem impossible what one labors to achieve. Yet, if I fancy that I have made some contribution towards a philosophy of philosophies, I cannot dream so complex a transposition to end multiplicity; I cannot but suppose that those that will accept my conclusions also will endeavor to improve upon them, while those that disagree, if ever they cease to believe silence the more efficacious weapon, will labor manfully to reverse my views. Moreover, in the measure that this work and subsequent improvements upon it possess concrete and practical implications, in that measure not only human intelligence and reasonableness but also human will and the established routines of human sensitivity and intersubjectivity are involved. So the Babel of men's minds passes into the conflict of their wills, and the conflict of wills reaches for its panoply of image and emotion, sound and passion.

Now if philosophy speaks with so many voices that a correct philosophy must be too complicated to pierce the din, should one not appeal directly to men of good will? Indeed one should, provided one can find them. But there must be no illusions. One is not to define good will by its resemblance to one's own will, or even by its resemblance to the will one would like to possess but does not. Will is good by its conformity to intelligence. It is good in the measure that antecedently and without persuasion it matches the pure desire both in its detachment from the sensitive subject and in its incessant dedication to complete intelligibility. A will less good than that is less than genuine; it is ready for the obnubilation that takes flight from self-knowledge; it is inclined to the rationalization that makes out wrong to be right; it is infected with the renunciation that approves the good yet knows itself to be evil. In brief, as man's intelligence has to be developed, so also must his will. But progress in willingness is effected by persuasion, persuasion rests upon intelligent grasp and reasonable judgment, and so the failure of intellect to develop entails the failure of the will.

There is a deeper level to the problem. In an earlier paragraph it was concluded that the pure desire of the mind is a desire of God, that the goodness of man's will consists in a consuming love of God, that the world of sense is, more than all else, a mystery that signifies God as we know him and symbolizes the further depths that lie beyond our comprehension. There is a theological dimension that must be added to our detached analysis of the compounding of man's progress with man's decline. Bad will is not merely the inconsistency of rational self-consciousness; it also is sin against God. The hopeless tangle of the social surd, of the impotence of common sense, of the endlessly multiplied philosophies, is not merely a *cul-de-sac* for human progress; it also is a reign of sin, a despotism of darkness; and men are its slaves.

No doubt, men are free. Were they not free, there would be no question of their sinning. But their essential freedom is one thing, and their effective freedom is another. Their essential freedom lies in the dynamic structure of rational self-consciousness; it is a higher integration of lower manifolds that can be integrated in many different manners; each element in that higher integration appears, first, as a possible course of action revealed by insight, secondly, as a value to be weighed by reflection, and thirdly, as an actuality only if it is chosen. No single course of action is necessary. If insight grasps only one at a time, still the insight raises the further question that leads to reflection, and the reflection leads to the further insights that reveal the alternative possibilities of the concrete situation. Again, reflection can pronounce one course of action preferable to all others, but that pronouncement has its suppositions, and the suppositions are not all that necessarily is so, but at least in part merely what one chooses or has chosen to prefer. Finally, reflection never settles the issue; it can determine that a given course is valuable or pleasurable or useful; but only the decision makes the course actual; nor does the decision follow because the reflection ends, but the reflection ends because the decision is made. Because man determines himself, he is responsible; because the course of action determined upon and the process of determining are both contingent, man is free.

Effective freedom supposes essential freedom, as statistical law supposes classical law. Essential freedom is an intrinsic property of acts of a determinate class; but effective freedom regards the relative frequencies of different kinds of acts within the class. Essential freedom is concerned with the manner in which acts occur; but effective freedom asks what acts are to be expected to occur.

The reign of sin, then, is the expectation of sin. On a primary level, it is the priority of living to learning how to live, to acquiring the willingness to live rightly, to developing the adaptation that makes right living habitual. On a second level, it is man's awareness of his plight and his self-surrender to it; on each occasion, he could reflect and through reflection avoid sinning; but he cannot bear the burden of perpetual reflection; and long before that burden has mounted to the limit of physical impossibility, he chooses the easy way out. On both the primary and the second levels, there is the transposition of the inner issue into the outer social milieu; concrete situations become infected with the social surd; they are intractable without dialectical analysis; and the intractability is taken as evidence that only in an increasingly limited fashion can intelligence and reasonableness and good will have any real bearing upon the conduct of human affairs. Finally, dialectical analysis can transpose the issue, but it cannot do so effectively. It goes beyond common sense to a critical human science that supposes a correct and accepted philosophy; but a correct philosophy will be but one of many philosophies, and precisely because it is correct it will be too complicated to be commonly accessible and too alien to sinful man to be widely accepted.

2 The Existence of a Solution   [693–96]

There is a fact of evil. It is not an incidental waywardness that provides the exceptions to prove a rule of goodness. Rather it is a rule. If it is not a necessary but only a statistical rule, it is no less a fact, and indeed it is a worse fact. Were the rule necessary, it would exclude freedom; were freedom excluded, there would be no sin. But the rule is statistical; freedom remains essentially intact; and so effectively man's rational self-consciousness is frustrated with the burden of responsibility for sins it could avoid but does not.

But is there also a problem of evil? There can be a problem only if there is an intelligibility to be grasped. But what intelligibility and as well what lack of intelligibility there are in man's condition and situation have been grasped already. There are intelligible possibilities of intelligent and reasonable and good courses of action. There is the intelligibility of the frequencies with which they are and are not executed. There is the intelligibility of actual choices that are good. There is the surd of sin, and it is understood inasmuch as one grasps its lack of intelligibility. Nor are there further questions, as long as one directs one's attention to man; for while intelligence can grasp what man might do, it also grasps that man will not do it.

Nonetheless, there is a problem of evil, for besides man there also is God. The order of this universe in all its aspects and details has been shown to be the product of unrestricted understanding, of unlimited power, of complete goodness. Because God is omniscient, he knows man's plight. Because he is omnipotent, he can remedy it. Because he is good, he wills to do so. The fact of evil is not the whole story. It also is a problem. Because God exists, there is a further intelligibility to be grasped.

Certain remarks are in order. First of all, I have employed the name 'problem' in a technical sense, so that it is meaningless to speak of a problem for which no solution exists. But the argument does not depend upon the definition of terms. No matter how one cares to phrase it, the point seems to remain that evil is, not a mere fact, but a problem, only if one attempts to reconcile it with the goodness of God; and if God is good then there is not only a problem of evil but also a solution.

In the second place, since a solution exists, our account of man's moral impotence and of the limitations on[b] his effective freedom cannot be the whole story. There is a further component in the actual universe that as yet has not been mentioned. Because it has not been mentioned, our statements on man's plight are true as far as they go, but they are not the whole truth. They are true hypothetically inasmuch as they tell what would be did the further component not exist; but they are not true absolutely, for they prescind from a further component that both exists and is relevant to the issue.

In the third place, because this book has been written from a moving viewpoint, we have mentioned first a problem and only later its solution. But it would be an anthropomorphic blunder to transfer this succession to God. There are no divine afterthoughts. The unrestricted act of understanding grasps the total range of possible world orders; each is a consequence and manifestation of divine intelligence and wisdom, of divine reality and truth, of divine goodness and love; since all are worthy of God, any can be chosen, and that choice will be intelligent and wise, good and loving. Moreover, as has been seen already, the good is potential or formal or actual; but the problem under consideration is potentially good, for it is the potency to the solution; the solution as a further order is formally good and as a possible object of choice is a value or actual good in prospect or in process or in its term. It follows that the problem and its solution are related both from the viewpoint of intelligence and from the viewpoint of the good; and so once more there appears the absurdity of thinking of the problem without its solution.

In the fourth place, it is important not to confuse the intelligible unity of the actual world order including both its problem and its solution and, on the other hand, the possibility that the things of this world order might exist in any of a range of other orders. The root of this confusion is conceptualism,[c] which places conception before understanding and things before their orders; in consequence, it divides the order of things into two parts, of which the first is necessitated by the things that are ordered and the second is an arbitrary complement added by a voluntaristically conceived divine will. It follows that the conceptualist cannot argue from the intelligible unity of this world order, for he acknowledges no such unity but merely a compound of the necessary and the arbitrary. Again, it follows that, if the conceptualist argues at all, then he argues from the natures of the things that are ordered, and so he can conclude only to what is necessary.

On the other hand, the intellectualist, as he rejects the conceptualist's suppositions, so he is not hampered by their limitations. For him, understanding is first. The unrestricted act grasps in itself the total range of possible world orders, and it is within the orders that the things are known. Since every instance of possibility is included within the total range of possible orders, since every instance of the noncontradictory is possible, since the same things admit many possible but mutually incompatible predicates, it follows that the same things recur in many different orders. But this recurrence of the same things within different orders is by no means opposed to the intelligible unity of each order. For necessarily every order is worthy of God, intelligent and wise, good and loving, just and merciful. Moreover, this necessity is not a restriction on possibility defined as internal coherence; for as one and the same reality is at once divine intelligence and wisdom, divine reality and power, divine goodness and love, so all that divine power can do, divine wisdom can do wisely and divine goodness can do well.[1]

3   The Heuristic Structure of the Solution   [696–703]

We have affirmed the existence both of a problem and of its solution within the intelligible unity of the actual order of the universe. But this implies the existence of a heuristic structure. For there is a heuristic structure whenever the object of an inquiry admits antecedent determinations; and the solution that we are seeking is an object of inquiry that satisfies the intelligible unity of the actual world order and that solves the problem defined above.

Now it would seem that this heuristic structure is worth investigating. For even when such a structure fails to determine a single answer, at least it offers a set of alternative answers; and then through an appeal to the facts it becomes possible to settle which of the alternatives is correct.

First, then, the solution will be one. For there is one God, one world order, and one problem that is both individual and social.

Secondly, the solution will be universally accessible and permanent. For the problem is not restricted to men of a particular class or of a particular time; and the solution has to meet the problem.

Thirdly, the solution will be a harmonious continuation of the actual order of this universe. For there are no divine afterthoughts.

Fourthly, the solution will not consist in the addition of central forms of a new genus or species. For the solution is to a human problem; the problem has to be solved for men, and it would merely be dodged by introducing a new genus or species.

Fifthly, the solution can consist in the introduction of new conjugate forms in man's intellect, will, and sensitivity. For such forms are habits.

1 See Thomas Aquinas, *Summa theologiae*, 1, q. 25, aa. 3 and 5.

But man's intellect is an unrestricted potency, and so it can receive habits of any kind; man's will is good insofar as it follows intellect, and so it can receive habits that correspond to the habits received in intellect; finally, man's sensitivity is a lower manifold under the higher integration of intellectual and volitional acts, and so it can be adapted habitually to the acts that occur.

Sixthly, the solution will include the introduction of such conjugate forms. For the problem arises from the nature of development; because man's living is prior to learning and being persuaded, it is without the guidance of knowledge and without the direction of effective good will; as long as that priority remains, the problem remains. The solution, then, must reverse the priority, and it does so inasmuch as it provides intellect, will, and sensitivity with forms or habits that are operative throughout living.

Seventhly, the relevant conjugate forms will be in some sense transcendent or supernatural. For what arises from nature is the problem. The forms that solve the problem, then, do not arise from nature; they are not the result of accumulated insights, for such accumulation takes time, and the problem arises because man has to live during the interval in which insights are being accumulated. Moreover, the understanding that[d] man acquires in this fashion, the judgments that he forms, and the willingness that he obtains all suffer from the fourfold bias of the dramatic and practical subject and from the tendency of speculative thought to the counterpositions.

Eighthly, since the solution is a harmonious continuation of the actual order of the universe, and since that order involves the successive emergence of higher integrations that systematize the nonsystematic residues on lower levels, it follows that the relatively transcendent conjugate forms will constitute a new and higher integration of human activity and that that higher integration will solve the problem by controlling elements that otherwise are nonsystematic or irrational.

Ninthly, these higher conjugate forms will pertain not to static system but to system on the move. For they have their place in a harmonious continuation of the actual order of the universe, and in that order the lower static systems of physics and chemistry are succeeded by the higher dynamic systems of biology, sensitive psychology, and human intellectual activity. Moreover, the higher conjugate forms have to meet a problem that varies as man develops and declines, and so they too must be capable of some development and adaptation.

Tenthly, since higher integrations leave intact the natures and laws of the underlying manifold, and since man is intelligent and rational, free and responsible, it follows that the solution will come to men through their apprehension and with their consent.

Eleventhly, since the solution is a harmonious continuation of the actual order of the universe, and since that order is an emergent probability, it follows that the emergence of the solution and its propagation will be in accord with the probabilities. It is to be borne in mind, however, that emergent probability has the same meaning here as in the earlier chapters of this work; it does not denote any sort of efficient cause; it refers to the immanent intelligibility of the design or order in which things exist and events occur.

Twelfthly, the relevant probabilities are those that regard the occurrence of man's intelligent and rational apprehension of the solution and his free and responsible consent to it. But there are stages in human development when there is no probability that men will apprehend and consent to a universally accessible and permanent solution that meets the basic problem of human nature. Moreover, all human development has been seen to be compounded with decline, and so it fails to prepare men directly and positively to apprehend and consent to the solution. Accordingly, it seems necessary to distinguish between the realization of the full solution and, on the other hand, the emergent trend in which the full solution becomes effectively probable.

From the cosmic and metaphysical aspects of the solution, we now turn to a closer determination of the appropriate higher conjugate forms.

In the thirteenth place, then, the appropriate willingness will be some type or species of charity.

For good will follows intellect, and so it matches the detached, disinterested, unrestricted desire of intellect for complete understanding; but complete understanding is the unrestricted act that is God; and so the good that is willed by good will is God. Moreover, to will the good of a person is to love the person; but God is a person, for he is intelligent and free; and so good will is the love of God. Further, good will matches the detachment and disinterestedness of the pure desire to know, and so good will is a love of God that is prompted not by a hope of one's own advantage but simply by God's goodness.

Again, a man or woman knows that he or she is in love by making the discovery that all spontaneous and deliberate tendencies and actions regard the beloved. Now as the arm rises spontaneously to protect the head, so all the parts of each thing conspire to the good of the whole, and all things in all their operations proceed to the realization of the order of the universe. But the order of this universe is actual, and the orders of all other universes are possible, because of the completeness of the intelligibility, the power of the reality, and the perfection of the goodness and love of God. It follows that, apart from the surd of sin, the universe is in love with God; and good will is the opposite of the irrationality of sin; accordingly, the man of good will is in love with God.

Again, the actual order of the universe is a good and value chosen by God for the manifestation of the perfection of God. Moreover, it grounds the emergence, and includes the excellence, of every other good within the universe, so that to will any other good is to will the order of the universe. But good will follows intellect, and so, as intellect apprehends, so it wills, every other good because of the order of the universe, and the order of the universe because of God.

Again, the order of the universe includes all the good that all persons in the universe are or enjoy or possess. But to will the good of a person is to love the person; and so to will the order of the universe because of one's love of God is to love all persons in the universe because of one's love of God.

Again, the order of the universe is its intelligibility to be grasped by following the appropriate classical or statistical or genetic or dialectical method. Hence, to will the order of the universe is not to will the clock-work perfection of mechanist thought but the emergent probability of the universe that exists. It is not to demand that all things be perfect in their inception but to expect and will that they grow and develop. It is not to exclude from man's world the possibility of the social surd, nor to ignore it (for it is a fact), nor to mistake it for an intelligibility and so systematize and perpetuate it, but to acknowledge it as a problem and to embrace its solution.

Now the will can contribute to the solution of the problem of the social surd inasmuch as it adopts a dialectical attitude that parallels the dialectical method of intellect. The dialectical method of intellect consists in grasping that the social surd neither is intelligible nor is to be treated as intelligible. The corresponding dialectical attitude of will is to return good for evil. For it is only inasmuch as men are willing to meet evil with good, to love their enemies, to pray for those that persecute and calumniate them, that the social surd is a potential good. It follows that love of God above all and in all so embraces the order of the universe as to love all men with a self-sacrificing love.

Again, self-sacrificing love of God and of one's neighbor is repentant. For man's rational self-consciousness exists over time. If it develops and becomes good, it has been less good and perhaps evil. If it approves its past, it thereby reverts to its past. If it would remain as it is, it must disapprove its own past; and if it would become still better, it must disapprove its present. So rational self-consciousness deplores and regrets the scotosis of its dramatic bias and its involvement in the individual, group, and general bias of common sense; it repents its flight from self-knowledge, its rationalization of wrong, its surrender to evil; it detests its commitment to the counterpositions, its contribution to man's decline through the successive adjustments of theory to ever worse practice, its share in the genesis and the propagation of the myths that confer on appearance the strength and power and passion that are the due of reality.

Such repentance is not a merely sensitive feeling of guilt. It is an act of good will following the insights of intelligence and the pronouncements of reasonableness. It is apart from the vagaries of mere feelings, and when they go astray it disapproves them, curbs them, and may seek aid in controlling them.

Further, such repentance does not stop short at the limited viewpoint of our chapter on the possibility of ethics. For as intellect rises to knowledge of God, the will is called to love of God, and then evil is revealed to be not merely a human wrong but also sin, revolt against God, an abuse of his goodness and love, a pragmatic calumny that hides from oneself and from others the absolute goodness and perfect love that through the universe and through men expresses itself to men. So repentance becomes sorrow. A relation between stages in one's living is transformed into a personal relation to the one loved above all and in all.

Finally, good will is joyful. For it is love of God above all and in all, and love is joy. Its repentance and sorrow regard the past. Its present sacrifices look to the future. It is at one with the universe in being in love with God, and it shares its dynamic resilience and expectancy. As emergent probability, it ever rises above past achievement. As genetic process, it develops generic potentiality to its specific perfection. As dialectic, it overcomes evil both by meeting it with good and by using it to reinforce the good. But good will wills the order of the universe, and so it wills with that order's dynamic joy and zeal.

In the fourteenth place, besides the charity by which the will itself is made good, there will be the hope by which the will makes the intellect good.

For intellect functions properly inasmuch as the detached and disinterested desire to know is dominant in cognitional operations. Still, this desire is merely spontaneous. It is the root of intelligent and rational self-consciousness, and it operates prior to our insights, our judgments, and our decisions. Now if this desire is to be maintained in its purity, if it is not to suffer from the competition of the attached and interested desires of man's sensitivity and intersubjectivity, if it is not to be overruled by the will's connivance with rationalizations, then it must be aided, supported, reinforced, by a deliberate decision and a habitual determination of the will itself.

Now such a decision and determination of the will can have as its object only the proper good of intellect. But the proper good of intellect is the attainment of the objective of the detached, disinterested, unrestricted desire to know; and the attainment of that objective is knowledge of God, who is at once the transcendent idea of being and the transcendent reality of being. It follows that, as intellect spontaneously desires knowledge of God, so the will deliberately desires attainment of that knowledge. Moreover, since the act of will is an act of rational self-consciousness, it will not be a mere repetition of the intellect's desire but also will take issue with conflicting tendencies and considerations. On the one hand, then, it will be a decision against man's despair, for the secret of the counterpositions is not the superficial confusion generated by the polymorphism of human consciousness but the deeper hopelessness that allows man's spirit to surrender the legitimate aspirations of the unrestricted desire and to seek comfort in the all too human ambitions of the Kantian and the positivist. On the other hand, it will be a decision against presumption no less than against despair. The objective of an unrestricted desire to understand correctly lies beyond the reach of empirical science, of common sense, of their unification in metaphysics, of the transcendent knowledge by which we know that God exists and that he is the unrestricted act of understanding. That objective is some attainment by knowledge of God who is the unrestricted act. The fulfilment of the conditions for that attainment lie not with man but with God, whose wisdom designed the order of the universe and whose goodness brings a solution to man's problem of evil. Now a desire that excludes both despair and presumption is a confident hope, and so the conjugate form of willingness that aids and supports and reinforces the pure desire is a confident hope that God will bring man's intellect to a knowledge, participation, possession of the unrestricted act of understanding.

However, the range of divine wisdom is as large as the range of divine omnipotence. As there are many possible solutions to man's problem of evil, so there are many manners in which God could communicate to man a knowledge that manifested the answer to all questions and so provided the will's love of God with an irresistible source and ground in man's own knowledge. Now in the present section we are concerned to work out the heuristic structure of all solutions possible within the framework of the actual order of the universe. Accordingly, we must remain content to affirm hope only in a generic fashion. What specifically is man's hope in the actual order of things is to be settled later by an appeal to facts.

In the fifteenth place, there is to be considered the appropriate, relatively transcendent conjugate form that a realization of the solution to the problem of evil would involve in man's intellect. For if hope aids and supports the pure desire by striving for its goal, still hope is not knowledge but only an expectation of knowledge. It is not the knowledge that we hope for but the knowledge we possess that will supply the will's hope with its object and assurance and the will's charity with its motives. There is needed in the present a universally accessible and permanently effective manner of pulling men's minds out of the counterpositions, of fixing them in the positions, of securing for them certitude that God exists and that he has provided a solution which they are to acknowledge and to accept.

However, at first sight, this seems an impossibility within the limits of the problem. For the problem arises inasmuch as human knowledge bogs down in the counterpositions; and the solution has to be received by man not merely as intelligent and rational, free and responsible, but also as operating within a harmonious continuation of the present order of the universe. Not only is there demanded a leap from the counterpositions, but also it is expected that its occurrence will be probable not in a few cases but in a general and permanent fashion.

This argument, however, can be met with a distinction. For there are two ways in which men reach truth and certitude. If one asks a mathematician what is the logarithm of the square root of minus one, he will set down the relevant definitions and postulates and then proceed to deduce the answer. But if you ask a non-mathematician, he will turn and ask the mathematicians, and in the measure he is confident of their ability and sincerity he will have no doubt that the answer they give is correct. In both cases truth and certitude are attained, but in the first case it is generated immanently, while in the second case it is obtained through communication with those whom one knows to know. Now the argument outlined above goes to prove that there is no probability of men generally moving from the counterpositions to the positions by immanently generated knowledge. On the other hand, as far as the argument goes, it reveals no obstacles to the attainment of truth through the communication of reliable knowledge.

Still, one has only to notice the similarity between such communicated knowledge and belief to be aware that this proposal bristles with difficulties. For on the subject of belief the counterpositions have been both abundant and eloquent, and until it can be shown that there is a possibility of conceiving belief as an intelligent and reasonable procedure, there is no use attempting to continue the present account of the heuristic structure of the solution to the human problem of evil.

4   The Notion of Belief   [703–18]

The account to be offered of the notion of belief falls into four main parts. First, there will be outlined the general context of the procedure named believing. Secondly, the procedure itself will be analyzed. Thirdly, the method of eliminating mistaken beliefs will be explained. Fourthly, certain technical questions raised by the analysis will be discussed.

It is to be noted that the whole of the present section is simply an explanatory note that interrupts the exposition of the heuristic structure of the solution. To that exposition we return in the next section.

4.1 The General Context of Belief   [703–706]

The general context of belief is the collaboration of mankind in the advancement and the dissemination of knowledge. For if there is such a collaboration, then men not only contribute to a common fund of knowledge but also receive from it. But while they contribute in virtue of their own experience, understanding, and judgment, they receive not an immanently generated but a reliably communicated knowledge. That reception is belief, and our immediate concern is its general context.

Already the reader is familiar with the distinctions between empirical, intelligent, and rational consciousness, and the further enlargement that we have named rational self-consciousness. One is empirically conscious inasmuch as one is aware of data into which one can inquire. One is intelligently conscious inasmuch as one inquires, understands, formulates, and raises further questions for intelligence. One is rationally conscious inasmuch as one puts questions for reflection, grasps the unconditioned, and passes judgment. But one becomes rationally self-conscious inasmuch as one adverts to the self-affirming unity, grasps the different courses of action it can pursue, reflects upon their value, utility, or agreeableness, and proceeds to a free and responsible decision.

Now just as the pure desire to know, which is spontaneous, can be aided, supported, reinforced, by a free decision of the will in which one determines to be quite genuine in all one's investigations and judgments, so also the spontaneous procedures of the mind can be submitted to introspective analysis, formulated as methods, and reinforced by free decisions in which one wills to be faithful to methodological precepts.

But a fundamental methodological issue is whether each man should confine his assents to what he knows in virtue of his personal experience, his personal insights, and his personal grasp of the virtually unconditioned or, on the other hand, there can and should be a collaboration in the advancement and dissemination of knowledge.

In fact, the collaboration exists. Our senses are limited to an extremely narrow strip of space-time, and unless we are ready to rely on the senses of others, we must leave blank all other places and times or, as is more likely, fill them with our conjectures and then explain our conjectures with myths. Again, the personal contribution of any individual to the advance of human understanding is never large. We may be astounded by men of genius; but the way for their discoveries was prepared by many others in a long succession; and if they took enormous strides, commonly it was because the logic of their circumstances left them no opportunity to take shorter ones. But without collaboration each successive generation, instead of beginning where its predecessor left off, would have to begin at the very beginning and so could never advance beyond the most rudimentary of primitive levels.

Some collaboration, then, is inevitable. But once it begins, it spreads. Mathematicians expedite their calculations by having the recurrent parts of their work done once for all and then published in tables of various kinds. Again, the departments of mathematics multiply, and as it becomes obvious that no one can master all, it follows that each begins to rely on others for results obtained in branches in which he himself is not competent. What holds for mathematics also holds in a broader manner for the empirical sciences. Not only must each physicist and chemist rely on the reports of his predecessors and colleagues, not only are the further questions set by an objective and general process of advance rather than by the individual's desire to learn, but even the verification of each hypothesis really lies not in the confirmation that any one man's work can bring but rather in the cumulative evidence that is provided by the whole scientific tradition.

It is true, of course, that if the engineer suspects his tables, if the mathematician doubts the theorems propounded in a different branch, if the empirical scientist has reason to challenge accepted views, then it is not only possible but also highly laudable for them to labor to bring about a revision. But if this possibility and encouragement offer a necessary safeguard, they must not blind us to the actual facts. Engineers tend to feel their duty has been done when they learn how to use a slide rule, and no one would dream of imposing upon their intellectual consciences[e] the obligation of working out independently the trigonometric functions and the logarithmic tables. When it is claimed that any engineer could have immanently generated knowledge of the correctness of his slide rule, it is not to be forgotten that all engineers merely believe slide rules to be correct and that none of them has any intention of seeking to establish the matter by carrying out for himself the endless computations that the slide rule so compactly summarizes. When it is claimed that each scientist could repeat and check the results of any experiment, it is not to be forgotten that no scientist has any intention of repeating and checking all the experiments which his thinking presupposes. Nor is this all, for empirical science is a collective enterprise to so radical an extent that no scientist can have immanently generated knowledge of the evidence that really counts; for the evidence that really counts for any theory or hypothesis is the common testimony of all scientists that the implications of the theory or hypothesis have been verified in their separate and diverse investigations. In plainer language, the evidence that really counts is the evidence for a belief.

Because collaboration is a fact, because it is inevitable, because it spreads into a highly differentiated network of interdependent specialties, the mentality of any individual becomes a composite product in which it is impossible to separate immanently generated knowledge and belief. As was seen in the chapter on the notion of judgment, there stands in the habitual background of our minds a host of previous judgments and assents that serve to clarify and define, to explain and defend, to qualify and limit, the prospective judgment that one is about to make. But if this host is submitted to scrutiny, one finds that one's beliefs are no less operative than one's immanently generated knowledge; and if one pursues the examination, one is forced to the conclusion that, as no belief is independent of some items of immanently generated knowledge, so there are extraordinarily few items of immanently generated knowledge that are totally independent of beliefs. One does not simply know that England is an island.[f] Neither does one merely believe it. Perhaps no one has immanently generated knowledge that general relativity is more accurate than Newtonian theory on the perihelion of Mercury. But it does not follow that for everyone it is purely a matter of belief. The development of the human mind is by the self-correcting process of learning, and in that process personal knowledge and belief practice an unrelenting symbiosis. The broadening of individual experience includes hearing the opinions and the convictions of others. The deepening of individual understanding includes the exploration of many viewpoints. The formation of individual judgment is a process of differentiation, clarification, and revision, in which the shock of contradictory judgments is as relevant as one's own observation and memory, one's own intelligent inquiry and critical reflection. So each of us advances from the nescience of infancy to the fixed mentality of old age, and however large and determinate the contributions of belief to the shaping of our minds, still every belief and all its implications have been submitted to the endlessly repeated, if unnoticed, test of fresh experiences, of further questions and new insights, of clarifying and qualifying revisions of judgment.

The general context of belief, then, is a sustained collaboration of many instances of rational self-consciousness in the attainment and the dissemination of knowledge. The alternative to the collaboration is a primitive ignorance. But the consequence of the collaboration is a symbiosis of knowledge and belief. What, then, is the process of believing?

4.2 The Analysis of Belief   [707–13]

The analysis of belief presupposes a theorem and outlines a typical process.

The theorem regards the logical possibility of belief, and it may be divided into two parts, one remote and general, the other proximate and concrete.

The remote and general part of the theorem argues from the criterion of truth. As has been seen, when a proposition is grasped as virtually unconditioned, there arises a rational necessity that leads us to affirm or deny the proposition as certainly or probably true. Hence, while truth is a property immanent in rationally conscious acts of assent or dissent, still it rests on the unconditioned. But the unconditioned is independent not only of particular places and times but also of the particular mind that happens to be its subject. Accordingly, there is to any truth an essential detachability from the mind in which it happened to be generated, and an essential communicability, for the unconditioned cannot but be independent of processes of transmission from one place and time to another and from one mind to another.

The proximate and concrete part of the theorem is involved in a question of fact. There can and to some extent there does exist a collaboration of men in the advancement and the dissemination of knowledge. On that collaboration there rest the invention and development of languages, the erection of schools and universities, the use of scientific methods and the publication of scientific journals, our domestic, economic, and political institutions, and the whole network of communications of the civilized world with their implicit, and often explicit, reprobation of perjury, deceit, and propaganda. Now insofar as this collaboration is conducted properly, there is an implementation of the essential detachability and communicability of truth. To a common fund each may contribute inasmuch as he grasps the virtually unconditioned; to that common fund each does contribute inasmuch as he expresses exactly the unconditioned that he grasps; and from the common fund each may make his own appropriations inasmuch as intelligently and critically he believes the truths which others have grasped.

Just how one is to discriminate between the properly and the improperly conducted parts of the collaboration raises a complex question that had best be reserved to the next subsection (4.3). Our immediate concern is with the outline of the typical process of true belief, say, an acceptance of a table of logarithms as true. Five stages are to be distinguished, namely, (1) preliminary judgments on the value of belief in general, on the reliability of the source for this belief, and on the accuracy of the communication from the source, (2) a reflective act of understanding that, in virtue of the preliminary judgments, grasps as virtually unconditioned the value of deciding to believe some particular proposition, (3) the consequent judgment of value, (4) the consequent decision of the will, and (5) the assent that is the act of believing.

In this sequence the key act is the second. For it is the goal towards which the preliminary judgments head and in which they are resumed; and at the same time it anticipates the subsequent three acts and constitutes the guarantee of their validity and of their rationality. Accordingly, it will be well to begin with a brief consideration of the other acts so that we may know both what the central act has to support and what it may presuppose.

The third act, then, is a judgment on the value of deciding to believe with certitude or with probability that some proposition certainly or probably is true or false. As any judgment, it proceeds with rational necessity from one's own grasp of the virtually unconditioned, and it posits precisely what is grasped as unconditioned. As any judgment, it may be true or false, for the investigation leading up to the judgment may or may not have been free from the undue influence of desires other than the pure desire to know, and again, one may or may not be insufficiently or excessively exigent in determining the presence of the virtually unconditioned. However, it differs from judgments of fact and from theoretical judgments, for it settles a question of value; and it differs from other judgments of value, for it is concerned not with the good of the senses nor with the good of the will nor with the good of the whole man nor with the good of society but simply and solely with the good of intellect. Moreover, it is concerned not with the good of intellect in general but with a particular belief. Accordingly, it presupposes that it is good for intellect to reach the unconditioned through its own inquiry and reflection, that it is good for intellect to communicate to others the unconditioned that it has reached, and that it is good for intellect to accept from others the unconditioned that they have reached. But the judgment of value now under discussion goes beyond these generalities to pronounce upon the value of accepting from others in a determinate instance what they communicate as unconditioned.

The fourth act follows upon the third. It is a free and responsible decision of the will to believe a given proposition as probably or certainly true or false. It is a reasonable act of the will, if it is preceded by a sincere and favorable judgment on the value of deciding to believe the proposition in question. It is a good act of the will, if the sincere and favorable judgment of value also is correct. Moreover, in its antecedents, the decision to believe may be said to resemble any other decision; for it presupposes the occurrence of an insight in which one grasps believing as a possible course of action, and further, it presupposes the occurrence of rational reflection in which the course of action is evaluated favorably. But in its consequents, the decision to believe differs from other decisions of the will; for other decisions initiate or continue integrated sequences of bodily movements, or they modify the flow of images and consequent affects, or they regard the will itself by deciding to decide; but the decision to believe is a decision to produce in intellect the act of assenting to a proposition or dissenting from it.

The fifth act is the act of believing. It is an act of rational self-consciousness that occurs within the general program of a collaboration of minds in the advancement and in the dissemination of knowledge of truth. It resembles the act of judgment in object and in mode, but it differs from it in motive and in origin. It resembles judgment in its object, for it affirms or denies a proposition to be true. It resembles judgment in its mode, for it is a rational utterance of a yes or no that may be pronounced with certitude or with probability. But while judgment is motivated by one's own grasp of the unconditioned, the assent or dissent of belief is motivated by a decision to profit by a human collaboration in the pursuit of truth. And while judgment results with rational necessity from reflective grasp of the unconditioned, the assent or dissent of belief results with natural necessity from a free and responsible decision to believe.

The third, fourth, and fifth acts form a sequence. The judgment is on the value of deciding to believe. The act of will is a decision to believe because of the value. The assent or dissent of belief is the value that one affirms and decides to accept. Now as the act of believing depends upon the decision, and the decision depends upon the judgment of value, so all three acts are anticipated by the reflective act of understanding; for in that reflective act the conditioned that is grasped as virtually unconditioned is the value of deciding to believe a given proposition. Accordingly, if the reflective act occurs, there will follow with rational necessity the judgment of value, with free responsibility the decision to believe, and with natural necessity the act of believing. However, if the reflective act is to occur, there must be (1) a conditioned, (2) a link between the conditioned and its conditions, and (3) the fulfilment of the conditions.

The conditioned in question is the value of deciding to believe a determinate proposition.

The link between the conditions and the conditioned is that, if the proposition has been grasped as unconditioned in a manner that satisfies the criterion of truth, then there exists a value in deciding to believe the proposition.

Finally, the conditions are fulfilled in the measure that one knows (1) that the proposition has been communicated accurately from its source, and (2) that the source uttered the proposition, uttered it as true, uttered it truthfully, and was not mistaken.

Since knowledge of the fulfilment of the conditions commonly consists in judgments or assents, the unconditioned can be expressed as a syllogism in which the link supplies the major premise and the fulfilment of the conditions supplies the minor premise. However, as has been seen already, the function of syllogistic expression is not to eliminate but to facilitate the occurrence of the reflective act of understanding. A parrot or an electronic computer can send forth signs in a syllogistic pattern; but neither can grasp the virtually unconditioned; and neither can be subjected to the rational necessity that results in a judgment. Inversely, when a man pronounces a judgment on the value of deciding to believe, it is not because of a syllogism nor even because he accepts the premises of a syllogism but only because the syllogism has helped him grasp the virtually unconditioned in his acceptance of the premises.

It remains that something be said on the preliminary judgments. For if we have considered already their theoretical elements, such as the essential communicability of the unconditioned and the value of implementing this communicability in a human collaboration, there also are involved such concrete elements as the reliability of a given source and the accuracy of a given communication.

Here the fundamental observation is, of course, the ultimate insufficiency of any set of general rules. For the concrete goes beyond all generalities, and the relevant concrete judgment of fact will vary not only with beliefs but also with sources, with communications, and with the circumstances and knowledge of prospective believers. Intelligent inquiry and critical reflection have to deploy all their resources both to exclude the numerous possibilities of error and inaccuracy and to discover and assemble the equally varied indications and confirmations of truth. Finally, as has been seen, while an analysis can indicate the general lines along which man's intellect proceeds to the concrete judgment of fact, it can never do justice to the full range of its resources and to the delicacy of its discernment.

But if one cannot hope to present concrete judgments in general terms, at least one can distinguish certain broad differences. For one can reach the unconditioned grasped by another mind either in a personal interview or through a series of intermediaries. One can rely on personal knowledge of an individual's abilities and character or on the testimony of others whose ability and character are known. One can exclude error by appealing to ability, and deceit by scrutinizing motives, or one can argue in the opposite fashion as in Professor Collingwood's detective story, in which all the witnesses were lying and all the clues were planted. One can move beyond the whole range of personal considerations to base one's case on the constitutive laws of a human collaboration that not only in its intent but also in its functioning is constructed to reduce error and inaccuracy to a minimum and, sooner rather than later, to extrude even the minimum that incidentally arises. But whatever the procedure, the only general rule is to be alertly intelligent and critically reflective; and however intelligent and critical one may be, the result is to be named not knowledge but belief, for one ends with an assent to a proposition that one could not oneself grasp to be unconditioned.

There is a final observation, and it is that the scrutiny of the reasons for almost any belief will reveal that it rests on other beliefs. This is only to be expected, since in fact men collaborate in the pursuit of knowledge and since each judgment they make rests on their prior judgments and assents. But it will not be amiss to illustrate the point, and we shall take a scientific example both because science is so clearly a collective enterprise and because there exists a widespread blunder that contrasts science with belief.

Let us ask, then, whether the general theory of relativity reduces the error of 43 seconds of arc per century that arises in the Newtonian calculation of the perihelion of Mercury. An affirmative answer would presuppose (1) a number of different and quite accurate observations, (2) the principles and inferences introduced in constructing, mounting, and using the astronomical instruments, (3) the principles and lengthy calculations needed to determine the Newtonian expectations, and (4) the validity of the tensor calculus and the correctness with which it is employed to reach the Einsteinian approximation. But to secure the relevant observations, there is needed a succession of trained observers and the knowledge or belief that they were trained successfully, that they were conscientious, and that they obtained the results that are attributed to them. A long range of scientific issues is involved in the design and construction, the erection and use, of the astronomical instruments; the principles on which each of these issues was solved, if established scientifically, were established by a human collaboration that operates through belief; and whether or not the principles were applied correctly in the case of each instrument is a matter of further belief for all for whom the applications were not a matter of immanently generated knowledge. What is meant by Newtonian theory and by the general theory of relativity may be read in a variety of books that ultimately acknowledge Newton and Einstein as their sources; but not only the readers of the books but also most of the authors did not know but believed that Newton and Einstein were the sources. Finally, while one may know both Newtonian mechanics and the tensor calculus, one may be a bit hesitant about trusting one's own unsupported judgment on the correctness of the Einsteinian approximation, or one may shrink from the labor of working out for oneself the relevant Newtonian calculations, or at least one will draw the line at undertaking a fresh and independent computation of the mathematical tables that facilitate the calculations; and so one would be led to add still further beliefs to ground one's belief in the superiority of the theory of relativity.

Nonetheless, however numerous the beliefs involved, one will console oneself with the thought that one is believing scientists. They possess a high reputation for intellectual integrity. Moreover, it is rather difficult for them to avoid meriting their reputation, for not only are they subjected to strong motives for avoiding all error[g] and inaccuracy but also each of them possesses both the incentives and the facilities for making public any error or inaccuracy that escaped the notice of his colleagues. Like the Constitution of the United States of America, scientific collaboration is a system of checks and balances in which everyone is out to avoid mistakes and alert to spot the mistakes of others. But while everyone can grasp this general principle, it is another matter to have some experience of the way it works out in practice. Scientists themselves have such experience, and it both yields knowledge of their individual case and supports belief in the operativeness of the same pressures upon other scientists. Yet the question is whether these pressures were in fact operative on the individual scientists positively or negatively responsible for the expression of the precise proposition to be believed here and now. If they were, the longer the time in which the proposition remains unchallenged, the greater becomes the approximation to certitude. If they were not, if other equally efficacious pressures or motives were not operative, then modern science could hardly have succeeded in effecting its profound transformation of modern living. And so the dependence of belief on other beliefs moves from the field of science to the field of history, for the profound transformation of modern living by modern science is a truth that we accept without immanently generating knowledge of the whole of it by our personal experience, personal inquiry, and personal grasp of the unconditioned.

4.3 The Critique of Beliefs [713–18]

In principle, belief is possible because the criterion of truth is the unconditioned. In practice, belief is as intelligent and reasonable as is the collaboration of men in the advancement and in the dissemination of knowledge. In fact, if the collaboration in the field of natural science enjoys enormous prestige, it does not merit the same high praise in other fields. Mistaken beliefs exist, and the function of an analysis of belief is overlooked if it fails to explain how mistaken beliefs arise and how they are to be eliminated.

Fortunately, the present question raises no new issues. Already there has been carried through a general critique of error, and, as error in general, so mistaken beliefs have their roots in the scotosis of the dramatic subject, in the individual, group, and general bias of the practical subject, in the counterpositions of philosophy, and in their ethical implications and consequences. In belief as in personal thought and judgment, men go wrong when they have to understand and to judge either themselves or other things in relation to themselves. The serenity and surefootedness of the mathematician, the physicist, the chemist are not independent of the remoteness of these fields from human living. If in the past physicists and chemists have been prominent in propagating an erroneous mechanist determinism,[h] still it was a single sweeping mistake, it had its origin in the polymorphism of human consciousness, and it has been corrected by the abstractness of relativity and the indeterminism of quantum mechanics. If Haeckel offers an instance of scientific fraudulence, it also is true that his deception was in the interest not of biology but of a materialist philosophy. On the other hand, when it comes to the study of life, of the psychological depths, of human institutions, of the history of nations, cultures, and religions, then diversity multiplies, differences become irreconcilable, and the name of science can be invoked with plausibility only by introducing methodological conventions that exclude from scientific consideration the heart of the matter. The life of man on earth lies under the shadow of a problem of evil; the evil invades his mind; and as it distorts his immanently generated knowledge, so also it distorts his beliefs.

If the determination of the origin of mistaken beliefs raises no new issues, neither does the problem of eliminating from one's own mind the rubbish that may have settled there in a lifelong symbiosis of personal inquiry and of believing. For learning one's errors is but a particular case of learning. It takes as its starting point and clue the discovery of some precise issue on which undoubtedly one was mistaken. It advances by inquiring into the sources that may have contributed to that error and, perhaps, contributed to other errors as well. It asks about the motives and the supporting judgments that, as they once confirmed one in that error, may still be holding one in others. It investigates the consequences of the view one now rejects, and it seeks to determine whether or not they too are to be rejected. The process is cumulative. The discovery of one error is exploited to lead to the discovery of others; and the discovery of the others provides a still larger base to proceed to the discovery of still more. Moreover, this cumulative process not only takes advantage of the mind's native process of learning, in which one insight leads on to other insights that open the way to still further insights, but it also exploits the insistence of rational consciousness on consistency; for just as our love of consistency, once we have made one mistake, leads us to make others, so the same love of consistency leads us to reject other mistakes when one is rejected, and at the same time it provides us with abundant clues for finding the others that are to be rejected.

If our general principles enable us to be brief both on the origin of mistaken beliefs and on the method of eliminating them, there is not to be overlooked the clarification that comes from contrast.

In the first place, the critique rests on a systematically formulated notion of belief. There exists a human collaboration in the pursuit and the dissemination of truth. It implies that in the mentality of any individual there exists in principle a distinction between his judgments, which rest on immanently generated knowledge, and his other assents, which owe their existence to his participation in the collaboration. Without some immanently generated knowledge, there would be no contributions to the collaboration. Without some beliefs, there would be no one that profited by the collaboration. It follows, further, that immanently generated knowledge and belief differ, not in their object or their modes, but in their motives and their origin. Thus, the same proposition, say $E = mc^2$, may be known by some and believed by others; it may be known or believed as more or less probable; but if it is known, the proposition itself is grasped as unconditioned; and if it is believed rationally, then the unconditioned that is grasped is the value of being willing to profit by the intellectual labors of others. Hence, because the object of belief is the same as the object of immanently generated knowledge, we have to disagree with all the views that attribute belief to the psychological depths or to desire or fear or to sentiment or to mere will. On the other hand, because even an intellectual collaboration is conditioned by decisions of the will, we also disagree with all the views that admit any belief to be simply a matter of cognitional activity.

In the second place, though there exists in principle a distinction between immanently generated knowledge and belief, it does not follow that there exist two compartments in anyone's mind and that he can retain what he knows and throw out what he believes. On the contrary, the external collaboration is matched by an internal symbiosis, and the counsel that one should drop all belief has the same ludicrous consequences as the Cartesian philosophic criterion of indubitability. For the counsel can be followed only if one has a quite inaccurate notion of the nature and the extent of belief; it leads to the rejection of all beliefs that, on erroneous suppositions, are taken[i] to be beliefs; and so not only are true beliefs rejected, which is not an act of devotion to truth, but also there arises the absurd conviction that one's mistaken but covert beliefs must be named either science or sound common sense or philosophy.

No doubt there are mistaken beliefs. No doubt mistaken beliefs are to be eliminated. But the first step is to know what a belief is. It is to make the discovery, perhaps startling to many today, that a report over the radio of the latest scientific discovery adds, not to one's scientific knowledge, but to one's beliefs. The second step, no less necessary than the first, is to grasp the method to be followed in eliminating mistaken beliefs. For if one fails to hit upon the right method, one gets nowhere. The elimination of mistaken beliefs is not a matter of taking up a book and of believing the author when he proceeds to enumerate your mistaken beliefs; for that procedure adds to your beliefs; the addition varies with the author that you happen to read; it is extremely unlikely that he will hit off with any accuracy your personal list of mistaken beliefs; and it is not improbable that your mistaken beliefs will determine which author you prefer and so covertly govern your critique of belief by belief. Again, the elimination of mistaken beliefs is not a matter of attempting to assign explicitly the grounds for each of your beliefs and of rejecting those for which adequate explicit grounds are not available. For inquiry into the grounds of any belief soon brings to light that it depends on, say, ten other beliefs; each of the ten, in turn, will be found to depend on ten others; one's neglect of method now has one attempting to test at once one hundred and eleven beliefs, and they will be found not only to be linked together in an organic interdependence of mutual conditioning but also to raise still further considerations that partly are matters of immanently generated knowledge and partly matters of further belief. The simple fact is that a man cannot reconstruct his mind by the process of explicit analysis; for explicit analysis takes more time than the spontaneous procedures of the mind; it has taken each of us our lifetime to reach by spontaneous procedures the mentalities we now possess; and so if it were necessary for us to submit our mentalities to a total explicit analysis, it would also be necessary for us to have twofold lives: a life to live, and another, longer life in which to analyze the life that is lived.

In contrast, the method offered by our critique asks no one to believe that he subscribes to mistaken beliefs. Without undue optimism it expects people of even moderate intelligence to be able to discover for themselves at least one mistaken belief. Again, the proposed method does not offer anyone a putative list of his mistaken beliefs; it does not even offer a list of alternative lists, as the clothing industry offers a range of ready-made suits of different sizes. Rather it aims at the perfect fit, and so it is content to point out the far-reaching significance of the discovery of even one mistaken belief. For that discovery enables one to set in reverse the same spontaneous and cumulative process that gave rise to one's mistaken beliefs. So one secures at a stroke the procedure that is both economical and efficacious: it is economical, for it wastes no time examining beliefs that are true; and it is efficacious, for it begins from the conviction that one has made one bad mistake, and it proceeds along the structural lines of one's own mentality and through the spontaneous and cumulative operations of the mind that alone can deal successfully with concrete issues.

In the third place, though we claim the method to be efficacious against mistaken beliefs, we do not claim that it goes to the root of the problem. For the basic problem lies not in mistaken beliefs but in the mistaken believer. Far more than they, he is at fault. Until his fault is corrected, until his bias is attacked and extirpated, he will have little heart in applying an efficacious method, little zeal in prosecuting the lesser culprits, little rigor in pronouncing sentence upon them, little patience with the prospect of ferreting out and examining and condemning still further offenders. A critique of mistaken beliefs is a human contrivance, and a human contrivance cannot exorcize the problem of human evil. If man's will matched the detachment and the unrestricted devotion of the pure desire to know, the problem of evil would not arise. Inversely, as long as will fails to match the desire of intellect, intellect may devise its efficacious methods but the will fails to give them the cooperation they demand. Still, this pessimism is only hypothetical. It acknowledges a problem of evil, yet it prescinds from the existence of a solution. The solution does exist, and so no one can assure himself that its realization has not begun in him. And if in him that realization has begun, then his discovery and rejection of one mistaken belief can lead him on to the discovery and the rejection of as many more as the God of truth demands of him.

4.4 A Logical Note[j] [718]

The possibility and fact of belief enlarges the notion of truth to include not only the content of judgments resulting from reflective grasp of the unconditioned but also the content of assents that proceed proximately from decisions of the will and remotely from someone else's grasp of the unconditioned.

However, it remains that 'known to be true' and 'believed to be true' are quite distinct, and it follows that one will be inviting fallacy if one ignores the distinction and speaks without qualification of what is 'true.'

Further, while analysis can reveal a typical process from knowledge of a truth to belief in the same truth, this process, however reasonable, is not to be confused with inference. For inference moves from knowledge of premises to knowledge of a conclusion in the same mind. But the typical process of belief is from knowledge in one mind to belief in the same truth in another mind.

Finally, just as one should distinguish between (1) the general validity of syllogistic inference, (2) the conformity of a particular instance to the general type, (3) grasping the general validity, (4) grasping the conformity of a particular instance, and (5) affirming the conclusion that follows in that instance, so also one should distinguish between (1) the general validity of an analysis of belief, (2) the conformity of a particular process of believing to the general type, (3) acknowledging the validity of the general analysis, (4) acknowledging its validity in a particular instance, and (5) personally believing in that instance.

5   Resumption of the Heuristic Structure of the Solution [718–29]

The foregoing account of belief interrupted a larger discussion. For the present chapter began with the affirmation both of a problem of evil[k] and of the existence of a solution. Moreover, though it was clear that many solutions lie within the reach of divine omnipotence, it was seen to be possible to determine the general characteristics common to all solutions. Thus, any solution would be one; it would be universally accessible and permanent; it would be some harmonious continuation of the actual order of the universe; it would consist in some reversal of the priority of living over the knowledge needed to guide life and over the good will needed to follow knowledge; this reversal would be effected through conjugate forms that in some sense would transcend human nature, that would constitute a new and higher integration[l] of human activity, that would pertain not to static system but to system on the move, that would be realized with man's apprehension and consent and in accord with the probabilities of world order. Finally, it was seen that these conjugate forms would be some type of charity, of hope, and of belief.

Now that the nature of belief has been clarified, it is possible to resume our investigation of the heuristic structure; and to emphasize the continuity of the present fifth section with the earlier third section, it may not be amiss to carry over the numbering of the successive assertions.

In the sixteenth place, then, the solution in its cognitional aspect will consist in a new and higher collaboration of men in the pursuit of truth. For it has been seen that the solution meets a problem of error and sin through a higher integration that, though in some sense transcendent, nonetheless is a harmonious continuation of the actual order of the universe. Now in the actual order of the universe man's intellectual development occurs within a collaboration which men maintain by their truthfulness and accuracy, in which they participate by their beliefs, and to which they contribute by the addition of their immanently generated knowledge. Accordingly, because the solution is a harmonious continuation of the actual order, it too will be a collaboration that involves belief, truthfulness, accuracy, and immanently generated knowledge. Again, because the solution is a higher integration, it will be a new and higher collaboration. Finally, because the solution meets a problem of error and sin, the new and higher collaboration in the pursuit of truth will provide an antidote to the errors to which man is inclined.

In the seventeenth place, the new and higher collaboration will be, not simply a collaboration of men with one another, but basically man's cooperation with God in solving man's problem of evil. For if men could collaborate successfully in the pursuit of the truth that regards human living, there would be no problem, and so there would be no need of a solution. But the problem exists, and the existence of a solution is affirmed because of divine wisdom, divine goodness, and divine omnipotence. It follows that the new and higher collaboration is, not the work of man alone, but principally the work of God.

In the eighteenth place, man's entry into the new and higher collaboration and his participation of its fruits will be some species of faith.

By faith is meant the requisite conjugate form that the solution brings to man's intellect. By some species of faith is meant any of the conjugate forms that perfect intellect in any of the series of possible solutions within the reach of divine omnipotence.

Moreover, it can be shown that this faith will be a transcendent belief. For the solution is to be universally accessible, yet it is not to violate the probabilities of the actual order of the universe. But belief and only belief is universally accessible within a harmonious continuation of the existing order. Moreover, the relevant belief will be transcendent; for it makes a man a participant in the new and higher collaboration in which God is the initiator and the principal agent.

In the nineteenth place, with regard to faith three stages have to be distinguished. For it has been seen that the solution introduces into man's will a hope of knowledge of God that reinforces the pure desire to know. There is, then, a final stage when the attainment of knowledge supplants faith and realizes the object of hope. Moreover, it has been seen that the solution itself divides into two parts, with first an emergent trend, and only secondly its full realization. Accordingly, there will be an introductory faith and collaboration in the emergent trend towards the solution, and there will be a full faith and collaboration in the full realization of the solution.

In the twentieth place, because faith is a transcendent belief operative within a new and higher collaboration of man with God, the act of faith will be an assent of intellect to truths transmitted through the collaboration, and it will be motivated by man's reliance on the truthfulness of God. For, as a belief, the act of faith will be an assent of intellect to an object and because of a motive. As a belief within a new and higher collaboration, the object of faith will be the truths transmitted by the collaboration. Because it is a belief within a collaboration of man with God as initiator and principal agent, the motive of faith will be the omniscience, goodness, and omnipotence of God originating and preserving the collaboration.

In the twenty-first place, the act of faith as specified by its object will include an affirmation of man's spiritual nature, of his freedom, responsibility, and sinfulness, of God's existence and nature, and of the transcendent solution God provides for man's problem of evil. It will include the basic truths about man and about God, not because the ordinary collaboration of men cannot arrive at them, but because it invariably fails to reach unanimity upon them. It will include an announcement and an account of the solution because, as has been seen, though man cannot originate the solution nor preserve it, still he must be intelligent and reasonable in his acknowledgment of it and his acceptance of it.

In the twenty-second place, man will be intelligent and reasonable in his acknowledgment of the solution inasmuch as (1) he grasps the existence of the problem of evil and, in particular, of man's inability to cope with it, (2) he infers that divine wisdom must know many possible solutions, that divine omnipotence can effect any of them, and that divine goodness must have effected some one of them, (3) he recognizes that, in fact, there has been in human history, first an emergent trend, and later the full realization of a solution that possesses all the characteristics determined or to be determined in such a heuristic structure as the present.

In the twenty-third place, man will be intelligent and reasonable in his acceptance of the solution inasmuch as the foregoing judgments enable him to grasp as unconditioned the value of deciding to assent to the truths of the new and higher collaboration because of the initiating and preserving truthfulness of God. For from that grasp of the unconditioned there will follow with rational necessity a judgment on the value of deciding to assent, with free responsibility a decision to assent, and with conditioned natural necessity the act of assent itself.

In the twenty-fourth place, since the solution is a harmonious continuation of the actual order of the universe, man will not only acknowledge and accept the solution but also will collaborate with it. Accordingly, because the solution is for all men and universally accessible, there will be the collaboration that consists in making known to others the good news of the solution and its nature. Again, because the solution is permanent, there will be the collaboration that consists in transmitting it from each generation to the next. Again, because human expression is relative to its audience, there will be the collaboration that consists in recasting the expression of the solution into the equivalent expressions of different places, times, classes, and cultures. Again, because man can arrive at a universal viewpoint, there will be the collaboration that consists in conceiving and expressing the solution in terms of the universal viewpoint. Finally, because the solution regards man's problem of evil, there will be the collaboration that consists in grasping and formulating the manner in which the solution is relevant and effective in each of the successive situations of individuals, classes, national groups, and of men generally.

In the twenty-fifth place, as the problem of evil exists because God respects man's freedom, so the existence of the solution leaves human freedom intact. Accordingly, one is to expect not only that man's collaboration in the solution will be marked by deficiencies and failures but also that these indications of aberration will be marked by their human origin. The scotosis of the dramatic subject will betray itself both by excessively spiritual pretensions and by excessive interest in the sensible. Individual bias will forget that man's basic role in the collaboration is faith and that the contributions he can make are limited to grasping and clarifying and expressing the significance, the implications, and the applications of the truths of faith. Group bias will replace a single, universally accessible solution by a multiplicity of solutions for different classes and different nations. General bias will introduce the counterpositions. For in virtue of its failure to grasp that the real is being and that being is known by a rationally uttered yes, it will account the truths of faith to be mere words or mere symbols, and it will insist that man contacts reality only on the level of the experience that is prior to all questions and all answers. In turn, once the counterpositions become operative, whether fully as in modernism or in some mitigated form, the new and higher collaboration of men under God is stripped of its meaning; its implementing procedures and institutions are denied validity and competence; and the hope and charity that would reinforce man's pure desire and transform his willingness are left without the motivation and guidance of an intelligently formulated and reasonably accepted faith.

In the twenty-sixth place, if faith does not exclude the possibility and the fact of heresy because the solution is a harmonious continuation of the actual order of the universe, still heresy cannot eliminate the solution and restore an unchallenged reign of sin. For the solution is principally the work of God, who is omniscient and omnipotent and goodness itself. It follows, then, that the new and higher collaboration will survive the inroads of heresy. Moreover, this survival and preservation, though principally the work of God, will be effected through human channels and in accord with the probabilities, for the new collaboration is part and parcel of the actual order of the universe. But the one human means of keeping a collaboration true to its purpose and united in its efforts is to set up an organization that possesses institutions capable of making necessary judgments and decisions that are binding on all. Accordingly, it follows that God will secure the preservation of faith against heresy through some appropriate institutional organization of the new and higher collaboration.

In the twenty-seventh place, though the solution as a higher integration will be implemented principally in man's intellect and will through conjugate forms of faith and hope and charity, it must also penetrate to the sensitive level and envelop it. For, in the main, human consciousness flows in some blend of the dramatic and practical patterns of experience, and as the solution harmoniously continues the actual order of the universe, it can be successful only if it captures man's sensitivity and intersubjectivity. Moreover, as has been seen, all exercise of human intelligence presupposes a suitable flow of sensitive and imaginative presentations, and again, inasmuch as intelligence and reasonableness and will issue into human words matched with deeds, they need at their disposal images so charged with affects that they succeed both in guiding and in propelling action. Again, besides the image that is a sign of intelligible and rational contents and the image that is a psychic force, there is the image that symbolizes man's orientation into the known unknown; and since faith gives more truth than understanding comprehends, since hope reinforces the detached, disinterested, unrestricted desire to know, man's sensitivity needs symbols that unlock its transforming dynamism and bring it into harmony with the vast but impalpable pressures of the pure desire, of hope, and of self-sacrificing charity.

It follows that the solution will be not only a renovation of will that matches intellectual detachment and aspiration, not only a new and higher collaboration of intellects through faith in God, but also a mystery that is at once symbol of the uncomprehended and sign of what is grasped and psychic force that sweeps living human bodies, linked in charity, to the joyful, courageous, wholehearted, yet intelligently controlled performance of the tasks set by a world order in which the problem of evil is not suppressed but transcended.

Further, since mystery is a permanent need of man's sensitivity and intersubjectivity, while myth is an aberration not only of mystery but also of intellect and will, the mystery that is the solution as sensible must be not fiction but fact, not a story but history. It follows, then, that the emergent trend and the full realization of the solution must include the sensible data that are demanded by man's sensitive nature and that will command his attention, nourish his imagination, stimulate his intelligence and will, release his affectivity, control his aggressivity, and, as central features of the world of sense, intimate its finality, its yearning for God.

In the twenty-eighth place, the solution will be effective in the sense that it meets the problem of evil not by suppressing the consequences of man's waywardness but by introducing a new and higher integration that enables man, if he will, to rise above the consequences, to halt and reverse the sequence of ever less comprehensive syntheses in which theory keeps surrendering to practice, to provide a new and more solid base on which man's intellectual and social development can rise to heights undreamed of, and perpetually to overcome the objective surd of social situations by meeting abundant evil with a more generous good.

In the twenty-ninth place, the solution will have a nature and content and significance and power of its own. For if we have approached the solution through the problem of evil, and consequently have emphasized the aspects in which it is related to the problem, nonetheless the solution will be a new and higher integration, a new level on which human living develops and rejoices. However, many different solutions are possible to divine omnipotence, and a heuristic structure necessarily is confined to determining the generalities that are common to all solutions. Accordingly, for a specific account of the new and higher integration, of the content of its faith, of the object of its hope, of the intimacy of its charity, of the mystery of its transformed humanism, it is necessary to proceed from the heuristic structure of the solution to its identification in the facts of human living and human history.

In the thirtieth place, while every solution is transcendent in the sense that it involves a new and higher integration, while every solution is religious inasmuch as it is constituted by a faith and hope and love that look primarily to God, still in the measure that the higher integration goes beyond the minimal essentials of every solution, in that measure there will be revealed to faith truths that man never could discover for himself nor, even when he assented to them, could he understand them in an adequate fashion. For the greater the proper perfection and significance of the higher integration, the more it will lie beyond man's familiar range, and the more it will be grounded in the absolutely transcendent excellence of the unrestricted act of understanding.

Accordingly, if we specialize the general heuristic structure by adding further alternative hypotheses, we are led to distinguish between natural solutions, relatively supernatural[2] solutions, and absolutely supernatural solutions. All three types would have the common feature that they provide solutions to man's problem of evil. But the natural solutions would not offer to faith any truths that man could not discover for himself through the development of his own understanding; they would not offer to hope more than the natural immortality that can be deduced from the spirituality of the human soul, and the knowledge of God that is consequent upon the separation of the immortal soul from the mortal body; they would not offer to charity more than the perfection of a total, self-sacrificing love in a creature for his or her creator. In the relatively supernatural solutions, man's natural capacities cease to set a limiting rule; the object of faith includes truths that man could not reach through the development of his understanding; the object of hope is a knowledge of God beyond the appropriate attainment of an immortal soul; and charity is the more abundant response to a more indulgent beneficence. Still, all such solutions are only relatively supernatural, for though they go beyond the measure set by human nature, still there are other possible creatures more excellent than man for whom they would be natural solutions. Finally, there are the absolutely supernatural solutions. Conceived negatively, they are absolutely supernatural, because there is no possible creature for which they would be the natural so-

---

2 I should explain that I use the word 'supernatural' not in its current meaning, but as the English equivalent to the medieval theologians' *supernaturale*. It was a technical term that referred to the entitative disproportion between nature and grace, reason and faith, good will and charity, human esteem and merit before God.

lutions. Conceived positively, they are absolutely supernatural, because their sole ground and measure is the divine nature itself. Then faith includes objects beyond the natural reach of any finite understanding. Then hope is for a vision of God that exhausts the unrestricted desire of intelligence. Then charity is the transport, the ecstasy and unbounded intimacy that result from the communication of the absolute love that is God himself and alone can respond to the vision of God.

In the thirty-first place, if the solution which in fact is provided for man happens to be supernatural, and in particular if it happens to be absolutely supernatural, there will result a heightening of the tension that, as we have seen, arises whenever the limitations of lower levels are transcended. Moreover, when the higher integration is emergent in consciousness, not only is the tension itself conscious as an inner opposition and struggle but also it is objectified socially and culturally in the dialectical unfolding of human living and human history.

For the supernatural solution not only meets a human need but also goes beyond it to transform it into the point of insertion into human life of truths beyond human comprehension, of values beyond human estimation, of an alliance and a love that, so to speak, brings God too close to man. No doubt, once man was established within the supernatural solution, all would be well. For such a solution would be a higher integration; of its very nature it would respect and indeed foster the proper unfolding of all human capacities; and just as the organism attains the height of its complexity and versatility under the higher integration of animal consciousness, just as the psyche reaches the wealth and fulness of its apprehensions and responses under the higher integration of human intelligence, so also would human excellence enjoy a vast expansion of its effective potentialities under the higher integration of the supernatural solution. Still, generalities can be very misleading. It is not to be forgotten that the solution is a harmonious continuation of the present order of the universe, that it is constituted through conjugate forms that develop, and that its realization and development occur through acts of human acknowledgment and consent that accord with probability schedules. The assent of faith is the starting point for an ever fuller understanding of its meaning, its implications, and its applications. The antecedent willingness of hope has to advance from a generic reinforcement of the pure desire to an adapted and specialized auxiliary ever ready to offset every interference either with intellect's unrestricted finality or with its essential detachment and disinterestedness. The antecedent willingness of charity has to mount from an affective to an effective determination to discover and to implement in all things the intelligibility of universal order that is God's concept and choice. Accordingly, even in those in whom the solution is realized, there are endless gradations in the measure in which it is realized, and by a necessary consequence there are endless degrees in which those that profess to know and embrace the solution can fail to bring forth the fruits it promises in their individual lives and in the human situations of which those lives are part.

But the point I would make is that in solutions of the supernatural type these difficulties are augmented. Even of natural solutions it would be probable that universal accessibility would not ensure universal acceptance, that intellectual collaboration would develop down the ages, that the faith and hope and charity of successive generations of members more commonly would hover about intermediate values than reach maxima of intensity and efficacy. Still, natural solutions would not exceed the bounds of humanism. Their faith would be not only believing to understand (*crede ut intelligas*) but also believing what man in this life eventually could understand. Their hope would reinforce the pure desire without introducing a displacement away from human concerns. Their charity would be a self-sacrificing love of God that bore no appearance of a contempt for human values. In contrast, the supernatural solution involves a transcendence of humanism, and the imperfect realization of the supernatural solution is apt to oscillate between an emphasis on the supernatural and an emphasis on the solution. Imperfect faith can insist on believing to the neglect of the understanding that makes faith an effective factor in human living and human history; and an even less perfect faith can endanger the general collaboration in its hurry to show forth its social and cultural fruits. Imperfect hope can so expect the New Jerusalem as to oppose any foretaste of intellectual bliss and union in this life; and an even less perfect hope can forget that a supernatural solution involves a real displacement of the center of human concerns. Imperfect charity lacks the resources needed to combine both true loving and the true transformation of loving. It can be absorbed in the union of the family, in the intersubjectivity of comrades in work and in adventure, in the common cause of fellows in nationality and in citizenship, in the common aspiration of associates in scientific, cultural, and humanitarian pursuits. On the other hand, it can withdraw from home and country, from human cares and human ambitions, from the clamor of the senses and the entanglement of the social surd, to fix its gaze upon the unseen ultimate, to respond to an impalpable presence, to grow inwardly to the stature of eternity. But imperfect charity, inasmuch as it is imperfect, will not realize at once the opposed facets of its perfection; if it is in the world, it ever risks being of the world; and if it withdraws from the world, the human basis of its ascent to God risks a contraction and an atrophy.

Moreover, the heightened tension which would result from a supernatural solution would not lack its objectification in the dialectical succession of human situations. Hitherto, the dialectic has been conceived to rest on a bipolar conjunction and opposition. Within each man there are both the attachment and interestedness of sensitivity and intersubjectivity and, on the other hand, the detachment and disinterestedness of the pure desire to know. From this conjunction of opposites there follow (1) the interference of the lower level with the unfolding of inquiry and reflection, of deliberation and decision, (2) the consequent unintelligibility of situations, and (3) the increasing irrelevance of intelligence and reasonableness to the real problem of human living. But when this problem of evil is met by a supernatural solution, human perfection itself becomes a limit to be transcended, and then the dialectic is transformed from a bipolar to a tripolar conjunction and opposition. The humanist viewpoint loses its primacy, not by some extrinsicist invasion, but by submitting to its own immanent necessities. For if the humanist is to stand by the exigences[m] of his own unrestricted desire, if he is to yield to the demands for openness set by every further question, then he will discover the limitations that imply man's incapacity for sustained development, he will acknowledge and consent to the one solution that exists, and if that solution is supernatural, his very humanism will lead beyond itself.

At the same time, because the supernatural solution is realized in accord with probability schedules, because it is accepted by some and rejected by others, because acceptance is no more than the base and beginning for further development, because the undeveloped is imperfect and the imperfection of the supernatural solution misses the higher synthesis of human living, there will be a humanism in revolt against the proffered supernatural solution. It will ignore the problem of evil; it will contest the fact of a solution; it will condemn mystery as myth; it will demand reason and exclude faith; it will repudiate hope and labor passionately to build the city of man with the hands of man; it will be ready to love God in song and dance, in human feasting and human sorrow, with human intelligence and human good will, but only so. For a time it may base its case upon the shortcomings of those that profess the solution but live it imperfectly or intermittently or not at all. But this incidental argument sooner or later will give place to its real basis. For it rests on man's proud content to be just a man, and its tragedy is that, on the present supposition of a supernatural solution, to be just a man is what man cannot be. If he would be truly a man, he would submit to the unrestricted desire and discover the problem of evil and affirm the existence of a solution and accept the solution that exists. But if he would be only a man, he has to be less. He has to forsake the openness of the pure desire; he has to take refuge in the counterpositions; he has to develop what counterphilosophies he can to save his dwindling humanism from further losses; and there will not be lacking men clear-sighted enough to grasp that the issue is between God and man, logical enough to grant that intelligence and reason are orientated towards God, ruthless enough to summon to their aid the dark forces of passion and of violence.

6   The Identification of the Solution   [729–30]

There remains the problem of identifying the solution that exists. For if possible solutions are many, the existent solution is one, universally accessible and permanent, continuous with the actual order of the universe, and realized through human acts of acknowledgment and consent that occur in accordance with the probabilities; it is a divinely sponsored collaboration in the transmission and application of the truths of the solution; it is a mystery in the threefold sense of psychic force, of sign, and of symbol; it moves from an initial emergent trend through a basic realization and consequent development to the attainment of an ulterior goal; it is operative through conjugate forms of faith, hope, and charity that enable man to achieve sustained development on the human level inasmuch as they reverse the priority of living over the knowledge needed to guide life and over the good will needed to follow knowledge; it is a new and higher integration of human activity that, in any case, involves some transcendence of human ways and, possibly, complicates the dialectic by adding to the inner conflict between attachment and detachment in man the necessity of man's going quite beyond his humanity to save himself from disfiguring and distorting it.

The task of identifying the solution is not the same for all. Already many have acknowledged and accepted it, and their problem lies in bringing forth fruits worthy of their faith, hope, and charity. But the existence of a problem of error and sin implies that others will have notable difficulty in recognizing the solution. For further insights depend upon one's past accumulation of insights, and further judgments depend upon the context of habitual judgments that favor some new affirmations and are hostile to others. Nonetheless, there is available the critique of erroneous beliefs that has been outlined. Anyone that has found himself in error on one point can initiate a scrutiny that cumulatively will bring to light any other errors in which he happens to be involved. Nor will he labor alone in the purification of his own mind, for the realization of the solution and its development in each of us is principally the work of God, who illuminates our intellects to understand what we had not understood and to grasp as unconditioned what we had reputed error, who breaks the bonds of our habitual unwillingness to be utterly genuine in intelligent inquiry and critical reflection by inspiring the hope that reinforces the detached, disinterested, unrestricted desire to know and by infusing the charity, the love, that bestows on intelligence the fulness of life.[n]

Epilogue

It might be thought that, at the end of this long book, the long-suffering reader was entitled to a concluding summary. For many matters have been treated in isolation; others have been handled in a series of disparate contexts; still others have been partly developed but left unfinished.

Yet if the justice of the claim is not to be disputed, the difficulty of meeting it is not to be overlooked. As was stated in the introduction, this work has been written from a moving viewpoint. Successive contexts have been formed only to provide the base and the need for forming a further, fuller context; and as is clear from our final chapter, even several hundred pages have not brought us to the end of the process. If I have written as a humanist, as one dominated by the desire not only to understand but also, through understanding understanding,[a] to reach a grasp of the main lines of all there is to be understood, still the very shape of things as they are has compelled me to end with a question at once too basic and too detailed to admit a brief answer. The self-appropriation of one's own intellectual and rational self-consciousness begins as cognitional theory, expands into a metaphysics and an ethics, mounts to a conception and an affirmation of God, only to be confronted with a problem of evil that demands the transformation of self-reliant intelligence into an *intellectus quaerens fidem*. Only at the term of that search for faith, for the new and higher collaboration of minds that has God as its author and its guide, could the desired summary and completion be undertaken; and then, I believe, it would prove to be, not some brief appendage to the present work, but the inception of a far larger one.[1]

So it is that I am forced to be content with the inner logic of the plan with which I began. From a succession of lower contexts there was gradually to emerge an upper context. The lower contexts were to be subject to further additions and to indefinite revision. The upper context was to be constituted (1) by the invariant structures of experiencing, inquiring, and reflecting, (2) by the consequent isomorphic structures of all there is to be known of the universe of proportionate being, (3) by the fuller invariant structure that adds reasonable choice and action to intelligent and reasonable knowing, (4) by the profounder structure of knowing and known to be reached by acknowledging the full significance of the detached, disinterested, unrestricted desire to know, and (5) by the structure of the process in which the existential situation sets human intelligence the problem of rising above its native resources and seeking the divine solution to man's incapacity for sustained development.

Still, if the inner logic of this work is a process that admits no concluding summary, it is possible to view that process, not in itself, but in its ulterior significance, and to ask whether it has any contributions to offer to the higher collaboration which it has envisaged and to which it leads. To this question the remaining paragraphs of this epilogue will be devoted, and as the reader already has surmised, they will be written, not from the moving viewpoint whose exigences, I trust, I have been observing honestly and sincerely, but from the terminal viewpoint of a believer, a Catholic, and, it happens, a professor of dogmatic theology.

First, then, there is a contribution to the introduction to theology or, as more commonly it is named, to apologetics. The Catholic admits neither the exclusive rationalism of the Enlightenment nor, on the other hand, the various irrationalist tendencies that can be traced from the medieval period through the Reformation to their sharp manifestation in Kierkegaard's reaction to Hegelianism and in contemporary dialectical and existentialist trends. But this twofold negation involves a positive commitment. If one is not to affirm reason at the expense of faith or faith at the expense of reason, one is called upon both to produce a

---

1 Since I believe personal relations[b] can be studied adequately only in this larger and more concrete context, the skimpy treatment accorded them in the present work is not to be taken as a denial of their singular importance in human living.

synthesis that unites two orders of truth and to give evidence of a successful symbiosis of two principles of knowledge. Clearly, this positive commitment goes beyond the assertion that irreligious rationalism and irrationalist religiosity are not the contradictories that exclude a third possibility. For there is a broad jump from a logical possibility to a concrete achievement, and there would be an unpleasant ambiguity to an assertion of principle that was not coupled with the evidence of fact.

But if Catholics have endeavored to establish the synthesis of the objects and the symbiosis of the principles of reason and faith, it also is true that their effort has been embarrassed continually by the instability of the pronouncements of scientific reason. From the nature of the case the initiative seemed permanently in the hands of those who invoked science against religion, and if it mattered little to them that at any given moment the issue had shifted from physics to Semitic literature, from Semitic literature to biology, from biology to economics, or from economics to depth psychology, the defenders were left in the unenviable position of always arriving on the scene a little breathlessly and a little late.[c]

Now inasmuch as the difficulty has arisen from an insufficiently supple and detailed cognitional theory, a remedy may be not too far distant. For if we have begun with a complete deference to the positive element in rationalism, we have had no difficulty in ending with a reversal of its opposition between the exigences of intelligence and the claims of religion. Again, while we have stressed the de facto limitations of purely human development, we have been so far from making any concession to irrationalism that the self-transcendence of man in the final chapter has the same type of structure as empirical science and, indeed, a structure that reveals how one may cut short the investigations that, in his *Concluding Unscientific Postscript*, Kierkegaard argued to be interminably long.[2] Finally, something has been done to redress the balance of the initiative in the alleged conflicts between science and religion. For our sketch of metaphysics makes it the invariant form for which the sciences provide the variable matter, and our dialectical analysis provides a technique that systematically discriminates between the genuine discoveries that science ever brings forth and the counterpositions in which they may happen to be formulated.

2 [*Kierkegaard's Concluding Unscientific Postscript*, trans. David F. Swenson, completed and provided with introduction and notes by Walter Lowrie (Princeton: Princeton University Press, 1941).]

In the second place, there is a contribution to the method of theology itself, and though this contribution is remote, it may prove to be nonetheless fruitful.

For the opposition that has been worked out between positions and counterpositions possesses a threefold theological significance. It lays bare the roots of the revolt of pietists and modernists against dogma, for as the philosophic counterpositions appeal to experience generally against the yes of rational consciousness, so they appeal to religious experience against the yes of articulate faith. Secondly, the same dialectical technique that cuts short the disputed questions of metaphysicians will contribute at least indirectly to the systematic demise of not a few disputed questions of theologians. Finally, the clarification we have effected of the role of understanding in knowledge recalls to mind the impressive statements of the Vatican Council on the role of understanding in faith; and a firm grasp of what it is to understand can hardly fail to promote the limited but most fruitful understanding of the Christian mysteries that results both from the analogy of nature and from the inner coherence of the mysteries themselves.

To move to more technical matters, there has been worked out what seems to me a very relevant distinction between the more detailed metaphysics of proportionate being and the generalities that alone are available a priori on other possible worlds and on supernatural elements in this world. For, on the one hand, this distinction allows the theologian to elaborate his understanding of this world without undertaking to offer an explanatory account of other worlds. On the other hand, it reveals that the theologian is under no necessity of reducing to the metaphysical elements, which suffice for an account of this world, such supernatural realities as the incarnation, the indwelling of the Holy Spirit, and the beatific vision.

Again, a reasoned answer is provided for the question whether there can be more than one true metaphysics.

In its contemporary presentation the question arises from the analogy of mathematics. To cite but one of a number of examples that kept multiplying until mathematicians grew tired of the novelty, the pattern of relations constitutive of the theoretical content of Euclidean geometry was formulated with complete logical rigor, first by Hilbert in terms of 'point,' 'line,' and 'between,' and then by Huntington in terms of 'sphere' and 'inclusion.' Hence it is argued that, since the same geometry admits different yet equivalent conceptualizations and expressions, there is no reason to expect the conceptualization of the true metaphysics to be unique. Further, in confirmation, it is pointed out that a metaphysics in terms of potency, form, and act is indigenous to Mediterranean and Western thought; but is it not to be expected that, once we overcome the parochialism of our outlook and come to understand the mentality of the East, then we shall have to acknowledge a plurality of different yet true and so equivalent metaphysics? Finally, it may be contended that in an ontologically structured metaphysics the ultimate *causa essendi* in terms of which all else is explained is God; but according to Aquinas we know that God is and what he is not; we do not know positively what God is; and so we do not know how many different positive aspects of the ultimate *causa essendi* can provide a complete account of whatever else is.

I do not believe that this question can be answered by appealing to the principle of contradiction. Those that envisage the possibility of a plurality of metaphysics need not envisage the possibility of contradictory propositions being both true. On the contrary, their point can be that each of the several metaphysics would have its own distinct set of basic terms, so that contradiction would be impossible.

Again, I do not believe that an answer to the question is independent of the precise manner in which metaphysics happens to be conceived. But I would contend that the conception of metaphysics that has been implemented in the present work yields unique results. For potency, form, and act have been defined, not solely by their relations to one another, but also by their relations to human knowing. The argument is that (1) if a man is in the intellectual pattern of experience, and (2) if he is knowing an object within the domain of proportionate being, then his knowing will consist in experiencing, understanding, and judging, and the known will be a compound of potency, form, and act, where potency, form, and act are related as the experienced, the understood, and the affirmed, and where they possess no meaning other than what has to be presupposed if there is inquiry, what is known inasmuch as there is understanding, and what is known inasmuch as judgment results from a grasp of the virtually unconditioned. The only manner in which this basic theorem could be modified would be to modify its factual supposition that knowing consists in experiencing, understanding, and judging; and it has been argued that that fact is not open to revision in any concrete meaning of the term 'revision.' For any human reviser would appeal to experience, understanding, and judgment; and there is no use arguing that men might be other than they are, because it is equally true that the universe might be other than it is, and the issue lies, not in the possibility of a different metaphysics in a different universe, but in the possibility of a different metaphysics in this universe.

Hence I do not find the mathematical analogy compelling. What that analogy establishes is that the same field of abstract relations can be deduced from different initial sets of definitions and postulates. But the totality of fields of explanatory relations is included under our single term 'form.' Moreover, the triad 'potency, form, and act' is not an arbitrary triad; it has the intrinsic unity of (1) what inquiring intelligence must presuppose, (2) what it grasps, and (3) what it demands of what it grasps. Finally, the basic theorem of potency, form, and act is not a starting point to be expanded deductively but a nucleus to be enriched by recurrences of the same basic procedure; so one advances from potency, form, and act to the distinction between central and conjugate forms, to the relations between successive levels of conjugates, and to the theory of development.

Again, the argument from the cultural differences of East and West does not seem to touch our position. For while those differences are profound and manifest, they are not differences that lie within the intellectual pattern of experience. A man can unfold his detached, disinterested, unrestricted desire to know by asking and answering questions, and then he operates in the intellectual pattern of experience; again, he can reflect that asking questions can never lead to more than mere answers, that his intellectual desire demands more than mere answers, and then he will endeavor to enter into the mystical pattern of experience. Both procedures have the same origin and both have the same ultimate goal. Both yield their different and basically equivalent accounts of ultimate reality. But both do not yield a metaphysics in the sense in which metaphysics has been conceived in this work; for metaphysics, as it has been conceived, arises in the intellectual pattern of experience, and when an Easterner inquires and understands, reflects and judges, he performs the same operations as a Westerner.

Finally,[d] it is true that the human mind cannot plumb the reality of God, but there does not follow the possibility of a plurality of aspects of God grounding a plurality of different but equivalent metaphysics. For it is not metaphysics but the particular departments of science that deal with parts or aspects of reality. Metaphysics deals with the whole, for it is the science of being, and apart from being there is nothing.

Closely related to the question of the unicity of metaphysics is the question of changeless concepts. It is an enormous issue, but perhaps we may claim to have provided a basis from which a solution proportionate to the complexity of the problem may be developed. In any case, the following points may be noted towards the formulation of a first approximation.

Inasmuch as there is change in the things that are conceived, there is necessitated a change from earlier to later concepts (1) if the concepts are correct, and (2) if they are completely accurate. But it is not to be thought that all concepts aim at complete accuracy. Thus, the motorcars of 1953 differ greatly from those of 1913, but the differences lie in the manner in which the same function of transportation is fulfilled. Attention to the manner leads to an affirmation of conceptual variation; but attention to the function leads to an affirmation of conceptual constancy.

Again, things may not change, but man's understanding of them may develop. Now a change of understanding involves a change in explanatory conception, for the explanatory concept may be defined as an expression of the content of the understanding. Yet here there is an important distinction between heuristic and explanatory concepts. Fire was conceived by Aristotle as an element, by Lavoisier's predecessors as a manifestation of phlogiston, and by later chemists as a type of oxydization. But though the explanations differed, the object to be explained was conceived uniformly as the 'nature of' a familiar phenomenon, and without this uniformity it would be incorrect to say that Aristotle had an incorrect explanation of what he meant and we mean by fire.

Again, while the identity of the heuristic concept forms the unifying principle in a series of successive explanations, still there can be a development in heuristic concepts themselves. Thus, the discovery of the significance of measurement led to a shift from the vague 'nature of ...' to the precise 'indeterminate function to be determined.' Further, classical method has been complemented by statistical, and both may be complemented by genetic and by dialectical methods. Still, these changes are not radical. As the very name 'method' suggests, they are not determinations of a new goal but determinations of a new procedure or technique for reaching the goal that already was envisaged, though hardly attained, when men referred to what was to be known by understanding as the 'nature of ...'

Again, as there is a development in heuristic structures, so also there is a development in explicit metaphysics. Thus, if I agree with Aristotle that potency, form, and act are related as eye, sight, and seeing, I also agree with Aquinas who added to Aristotle's metaphysical elements the substantial act of *esse* or existence. Further, agreement with Aquinas on the basic elements does not preclude a development[e] of his thought to provide a metaphysical analysis of explanatory genera and species and of development itself. But besides explicit metaphysics, there is the latent metaphysics that is immanent and operative in all human minds and that yields uniform conceptions not only when the process of conceiving is not explained but even when it is explained mistakenly. Thus, I believe that Parmenides and Plato, Aristotle and Avicenna, Scotus and Hegel were mistaken in their formulations of the notion of being; but I do not believe that such mistaken formulations have the power of changing the structure of one's mind; nor do I suppose it would be difficult to show how the writings of these thinkers reveal an awareness of the objective of the detached, disinterested, unrestricted desire to know. Again, I have based the notion of the thing upon a grasp of unity and identity in data as individual; but though I am not aware that anyone else has expressed the matter in precisely this fashion, I would be prepared to contend that their spontaneous use of the notion of thing satisfied my account.

Finally, though there is a latent metaphysics common to all minds, there also is common a variable interference with the proper functioning of the pure desire to know, and consequently there also is common a distortion of the latent metaphysics. So it is that the *philosophia perennis* is flanked by no less perennial counterphilosophies. But as the detached, disinterested, unrestricted desire to know is a constant,[f] so too are the principles that interfere with its unfolding. However much at variance with one another positions and counterpositions may be, a dialectical analysis based upon a sufficiently accurate cognitional theory can proceed to a universal viewpoint that embraces at once (1) the positions in the contemporary stage of their development, (2) the positions at each prior stage of their development, and (3) the successive counterpositions of the past and present with their essential incoherence with the claim that they are grasped intelligently and affirmed reasonably.

In brief, concepts change inasmuch as things change, inasmuch as human understanding develops, and inasmuch as that development is formulated coherently or incoherently. But behind every change there is an underlying unity, and that unity may be formulated explicitly on the level of heuristic anticipation or of consciously adopted method or of a dialectical metaphysics. Hence it follows that changes in conceptualization do not imply any ultimate multiplicity and that behind any conceptual variation there is a conceptual constant that can be formulated from a universal viewpoint. Finally, while the notion of the universal viewpoint was worked out on the level of a dialectical metaphysics of proportionate being, it is to be borne in mind that it receives further determinations from our final chapters on transcendent knowledge. For general transcendent knowledge is concerned with the ultimate condition of the possibility of the positions, and special transcendent knowledge is concerned with the de facto condition of the possibility of man's fidelity to the positions.

There is still another manner in which the present work may be construed as a remote contribution to the method of theology. For in successive statements the Vatican Council insisted (1) that divine revelation was to be regarded, not as a human invention to be perfected by human ingenuity, but as a permanent deposit confided to the church and by the church to be preserved and defended, and (2) that every group and every period should advance in the understanding, knowledge, and wisdom by which the same doctrine with the same meaning was to be apprehended ever more fully. Now this affirmation of identity not only in difference but also in development confers a relevance both on our analysis of development and on our discussion of the truth of interpretation.

For the discussion of interpretation envisaged (1) initial statements addressed to particular audiences, (2) their successive recasting for sequences of other particular audiences, (3) the ascent to a universal viewpoint to express the initial statements in a form accessible to any sufficiently cultured audience, and (4) the explanatory unification from the universal viewpoint of the initial statements and all their subsequent reexpressions. But isomorphic with this interpretative process, there is the Catholic fact of (1) an initial divine revelation, (2) the work of teachers and preachers communicating and applying the initial message to a succession of different audiences, (3) the work of the speculative theologian seeking a universal formulation of the truths of faith, and (4) the work of the historical theologian revealing the doctrinal identity in the verbal and conceptual differences of (1), (2), and (3).

While this parallel is not to be pushed in any a priori manner, it does serve to bring together within a single frame of reference a large number of otherwise unrelated aspects of the Catholic position. As true interpretations, so also Catholic teaching presents the same doctrine and the same meaning through a diversity of conceptualizations and expressions. As true interpretation has to mount to a universal viewpoint, so the church takes advantage of the *philosophia perennis* and its expansion into a speculative theology. As there is a difference between interpretations adapted to particular audiences or particular times and the interpretation from the universal viewpoint, so also the church distinguishes between authoritative pronouncements that call for dutiful submission and definitive pronouncements that the church itself cannot contradict. As historical interpretation may be based simply on a historical sense or may operate in the light of the universal viewpoint, so too the nontheological interpreter may recapture the mentality for which the books of the Old and New Testament were written or the spirit of the age in which a heresy arose and was condemned, but the theological interpreter has to operate from the firmer and broader base that includes the theologically transformed universal viewpoint; and so it is that in a preeminent and unique manner the dogmatic decision is, and the technical thesis of the dogmatic theologian can be, the true interpretation of scriptural texts, patristic teaching, and traditional utterances.

If the parallel with the interpretative process emphasizes identity and continuity, there also is development, though its complexity can be no more than sketched in an epilogue.

In general, development occurs inasmuch as higher conjugate forms not only integrate their underlying manifold but also through conjugate acts so transform it as to call forth the next higher forms of the process.

In man, there are three levels of development, namely, the biological, the psychic, and the intellectual. So one may consider (1) any level in itself, (2) any level in its relations to other levels, (3) the harmonious or conflicting process of development on all three levels in any individual, and (4) the cumulative historical process of development in a multiplicity and succession of individuals. Clearly, the only complete consideration is the fourth.

The advent of the absolutely supernatural solution to man's problem of evil adds to man's biological, psychic, and intellectual levels of development a fourth level that includes the higher conjugate forms of faith, hope, and charity. It follows that now the four considerations regard not three but four levels of development.

Considered in themselves, faith, hope, and charity constitute an absolutely supernatural living that advances towards an absolutely supernatural goal under the action of divine grace.

Considered in their relation to other human intellectual and volitional activities, (1) they are anticipated inasmuch as rational self-consciousness adverts to its need for the divine solution of its problem of evil, (2) they constitute a dialectical higher integration inasmuch as they make possible the sustained development of rational self-consciousness by reversing counterpositions through faith and by overcoming evil through the firmness of hope and through the generosity of charity, and (3) they call forth their own development inasmuch as they give rise to an advance of the understanding, knowledge, and wisdom by which man apprehends, appreciates, and applies the divine solution to human living in all its aspects.

Considered in their relation to man's sensitivity and intersubjectivity, (1) they are announced through the signs that communicate the Gospel, (2) they constitute a new psychic integration through affective contemplation of the mystery of Christ and his church, and (3) they call forth their own development inasmuch as they intensify man's intersubjective awareness of the sufferings and the needs of mankind.

It is to be noted that this transformation of sensitivity and intersubjectivity penetrates to the physiological level though the clear instances appear only in the intensity of mystical experience.

To these considerations there is to be added the alternative of harmony or conflict in a development that proceeds on four levels of successive higher integration.

Finally, to the foregoing considerations that regard any individual that has embraced God's solution, there is to be added the consideration of the cumulative historical development, first of the chosen people and then of the Catholic church, both in themselves and in their role in the unfolding of all human history and in the order of the universe.

It may be asked in what department of theology the historical aspect of development might be treated, and I would like to suggest that it may possess peculiar relevance to a treatise on the mystical body of Christ.[g] For in any theological treatise a distinction may be drawn between a material and a formal element: the material element is supplied by scriptural and patristic texts and by dogmatic pronouncements; the formal element, that makes a treatise a treatise, consists in the pattern of terms and relations through which the materials may be embraced in a single coherent view. Thus, the formal element in the treatise on grace consists in theorems on the supernatural, and the formal element in the treatise on the Blessed Trinity consists in theorems on the notions of procession, relation, and person. Now while the scriptural, patristic, and dogmatic materials for a treatise on the mystical body have been assembled, I would incline to the opinion that its formal element remains incomplete as long as it fails to draw upon a theory of history. It was at the fulness of time that there came into the world the Light of the world. It was the advent not only of the light that directs but also of the grace that gives good will and good performance. It was the advent of a light and a grace to be propagated, not only through the inner mystery of individual conversion, but also through the outer channels of human communication. If its principal function was to carry the seeds of eternal life, still it could not bear its fruits without effecting a transfiguration of human living, and in turn that transfiguration contains the solution not only to man's individual but also to his social problem of evil. So it is that the Pauline thesis of the moral impotence of Jew and Gentile alike was due to be complemented by the Augustinian analysis of history in terms of the city of God and the city of this world. So it is that the profound and penetrating influence of liberal, Hegelian, Marxist, and romantic theories of history has been met by a firmer affirmation of the organic structure and functions of the church, by a long series of social encyclicals, by calls to Catholic action, by a fuller advertence to collective responsibility, and by a deep and widespread interest in the doctrine of the mystical body. So too it may be that the contemporary crisis of human living and human values demands of the theologian, in addition to treatises on the unique and to treatises on the universal common to many instances, a treatise on the concrete universal that is mankind in the concrete and cumulative consequences of the acceptance or rejection of the message of the Gospel. And as the remote possibility of thought on the concrete universal lies in the insight that grasps the intelligible in the sensible, so its proximate possibility resides in a theory of development that can envisage not only natural and intelligent progress but also sinful decline, and not only progress and decline but also supernatural recovery.

We have been asking whether our essay in aid of personal appropriation of one's own rational self-consciousness may possess any significance for theology, and we have been listing a number of potential, though remote, contributions to apologetic and to the method of theology. But there remains a third topic, for theology is accounted traditionally *regina scientiarum,* and the relation of theology to other sciences is a matter of more than apologetic interest.

Commonly it is recognized that St Thomas Aquinas took over the Aristotelian synthesis of philosophy and science to construct the larger Christian view that includes theology. But it is, perhaps, less commonly appreciated that the development of empirical human sciences has created a fundamentally new problem. For these sciences consider man in his concrete performance, and that performance is a manifestation not only of human nature but also of human sin, not only of nature and sin but also of a de facto need of divine grace, not only of a need of grace but also of its reception and of its acceptance or rejection. It follows that an empirical human science cannot analyze successfully the elements in its object without an appeal to theology. Inversely, it follows that if theology is to be queen of the sciences, not only by right but also in fact, then theologians have to take a professional interest in the human sciences and make a positive contribution to their methodology. Finally, insofar as philosophy itself becomes existentialist, it stands in the same relation to theology as the empirical human sciences.

Now it is this problem that in a large measure has dictated the structure of the present work. For the Catholic thinker has to meet a twofold exigence. On the one hand, he believes Christ to be the sign of contradiction, and he accepts Christ's statement that he that is not with me is against me and he that gathereth not scattereth; and from this belief and acceptance it follows that theology has a universal relevance. Yet on the other hand, he must also acknowledge that by the natural light of human reason man can know with certitude the existence of God; and from this acknowledgment it follows that there can and do exist independent inquiries that can reach valid conclusions out of their own resources.

It was to give concrete expression to the sincerity of Catholic thought in affirming the essential independence of other fields that our first eighteen chapters were written solely in the light of human intelligence and reasonableness and without any presupposition of God's existence, without any appeal to the authority of the church, and without any explicit deference to the genius of St Thomas Aquinas. At the same time, our first eighteen chapters were followed by a nineteenth and twentieth that revealed the inevitability with which the affirmation of God and the search of intellect for faith arise out of a sincere acceptance of scientific presuppositions and precepts.

In other words, it is the inner dynamism of inquiry that provides the reconciliation, both completely general and completely concrete, of the independence of other fields and of the universal relevance of theology. In principle, other fields alone are competent to answer their proper questions. In fact, men in other fields do not triumph over all the various types of bias to which polymorphic human consciousness is subject, unless they raise and answer successfully the further questions that belong to ever further fields. So it is that against the bias of the subject there can be set the expansive dynamism of the object. So it is that we have endeavored to promote the fruitful interaction of subject and object by inviting subjects to a personal appropriation of their own rational self-consciousness. And if we began from the minimal context of the meaning of the name 'insight,' if we were portentously slow in advancing to a metaphysics even of proportionate being, it is not to be forgotten that we do not live in the medieval period, in which a thinker could presuppose his faith and proceed to the development of theology, nor in the sixteenth century, in which he could presuppose the validity of human reason and proceed to develop a philosophy, but, to employ Professor Sorokin's phrase,[h] we live in the midst of a sensate culture, in which very many men, insofar as they acknowledge any hegemony of truth, give their allegiance not to a divine revelation, nor to a theology, nor to a philosophy, nor even to an intellectualist science, but to science interpreted in a positivistic and pragmatic fashion. Indeed, even were this attitude not so prevalent, even were ninety-nine percent of English readers not only devout Catholics but also convinced Thomists, the parable of the lost sheep would retain its significance and its relevance.

In this epilogue, however, in which we have shifted from the moving viewpoint that advances towards faith and theology and have adopted the terminal viewpoint of the theologian, perhaps the following suggestions may be made.

First, theology possesses a twofold relevance to empirical human science. On the one hand, it is relevant to the scientist as a scientist inasmuch as the untrammeled unfolding of his detached, disinterested, and unrestricted desire to understand his own field correctly is open to a variety of interferences that ultimately can be surmounted only by accepting the ultimate implications of the unrestricted desire. On the other hand, it is relevant to the possibility of a correct interpretation of the results of empirical human science. For let us suppose some such science to be so highly developed that it has ascertained the classical laws that hold at relevant stages of human development, the genetic operators that relate successive stages, the dialectical analysis that envisages differ-

ent sets of consequences following respectively on reasonable and unreasonable human choices, and the statistical laws that indicate the probable
frequencies of both types of choice. Still, such human science would
offer, not an adequate understanding of its proper aspect of human
activity, but only the measure of understanding possible from the scientific viewpoint. For an adequate understanding reveals the manner in
which man can remedy the evil in his situation. But the solution to man's
problem of evil has been seen to lie, not in a human initiative, but in an
acceptance of the solution that God has provided; and while empirical
human science can lead on to the further context of the solution, the
systematic treatment of the solution itself is theological. In a word, empirical human science can become practical only through theology, and
the relentless modern drift to social engineering and totalitarian controls
is the fruit of man's effort to make human science practical though he
prescinds from God and from the solution God provides for man's
problem.

My second suggestion is the obverse of the first. Grace perfects nature
both in the sense that it adds a perfection beyond nature and in the
sense that it confers on nature the effective freedom to attain its own
perfection. But grace is not a substitute for nature, and theology is not
a substitute for empirical human science. It is a fuller viewpoint that
both reinforces the scientist's detached, disinterested, unrestricted desire
to know and reveals the concrete possibility of intelligent and reasonable
solutions to human problems. Still, this possibility revealed by theology
is not intrinsic but extrinsic. It is not the theologian operating in his own
field that reaches the accumulation of insights to be formulated in the
classical laws and genetic operators constitutive of a theoretical science
of physiology or psychology, of economics or sociology. Nor again is it
the theologian that would add to such theory the enumeration of the
dialectical alternatives it offers or the probable frequencies with which
different alternatives would in fact be chosen. Nor clearly, can the theologian supply the knowhow of the technician, the analyst, the economic
consultant, or the social worker.

Yet if the theologian cannot contribute directly either to the abstract
theory or to the concrete relevance or to the awareness of the material
circumstances of empirical human science, it does not follow that his
influence is not of paramount importance. For inasmuch as he knows
that the detached, disinterested, unrestricted desire to know is a key
instance of the universal law that *omnia Deum appetunt,* he is in a position

not only to encourage scientists to complete fidelity in their calling but also to teach nonscientists the high office of the scientific spirit; and in this fashion he can hope not only to promote scientific willingness to undertake fundamental research but also to mitigate the pressures that are exerted by so-called practicality and that ever seek to turn scientists away from their proper tasks and to direct their energies to projects with a significance that, because it is minimal, easily is understood.

Again, though the theologian does not carry out the precepts of classical, genetic, dialectical, and statistical method in empirical human science, he can hasten the day when adherence to counterpositions ceases to block scientific apprehension and appreciation of those methods. No less than the physicists, the human scientist has to learn the inadequacy of mechanist determinism. No less than the biologists, he has to formulate a genetic method based on universally valid principles. Above all, he has to make the discovery that the guinea pigs of his theories read his theories and exploit his knowledge to circumvent what they dislike in his conclusions and predictions; and so he needs a dialectical method that will take into account the variable of more or less enlightened and reasonable choice.

Finally, once an empirical human science is developed sufficiently to be relevant to practical applications, there arises the supreme danger that the scientist will despair of human intelligence and reasonableness and will ambition the role of consultant in the policy-making of the ever more paternalistic state. Then it is that the theologian needs the alliance of fully enlightened scientists. For the drift to totalitarianism can be stopped only in the measure that human scientists work out intelligent and reasonable solutions to human problems and theologians succeed in convincing hardheaded practical men, on the one hand, that by God's grace intelligent and reasonable solutions can work and, on the other hand, that the desertion of intelligent and reasonable solutions for 'realist' policies is the operative principle in the breakdown and the disintegration of civilizations.

In conclusion, I would add that I believe this work to contribute to the program *vetera novis augere et perficere* initiated by the encyclical *Aeterni Patris* of His Holiness Pope Leo XIII.

Some eighty years have elapsed since scholars began to apply the methods of historical research to the products of medieval thought. Their labors have given us texts. They have informed us about sources and chronology. They have supplied a stream of monographs upon doctrinal issues. Above all, they have created a climate of opinion that has made it increasingly difficult to substitute rhetoric for history, fancy for fact, abstract argument for textual evidence.

But however indispensable this work, it is in vain unless it is complemented by a further labor. To penetrate to the mind of a medieval thinker is to go beyond his words and phrases. It is to effect an advance in depth that is proportionate to the broadening influence of historical research. It is to grasp questions as once they were grasped. It is to take the *opera omnia* of such a writer as St Thomas Aquinas and to follow through successive works the variations and developments of his views. It is to study the concomitance of such variations and developments and to arrive at a grasp of their motives and causes. It is to discover for oneself that the intellect of Aquinas, more rapidly on some points, more slowly on others, reached a position of dynamic equilibrium without ever ceasing to drive towards fuller and more nuanced synthesis, without ever halting complacently in some finished mental edifice, as though his mind had become dull, or his brain exhausted, or his judgment had lapsed into the error of those that forget man to be potency in the realm of intelligence.

Nor is this labor of penetration enough, for I have tried it. After spending years reaching up to the mind of Aquinas, I came to a twofold conclusion. On the one hand, that reaching had changed me profoundly. On the other hand, that change was the essential benefit. For not only did it make me capable of grasping what, in the light of my conclusions, the *vetera* really were, but also it opened challenging vistas on what the *nova* could be.

So it is that my detailed investigations of the thought of Aquinas on *gratia operans* and on *verbum* have been followed by the present essay in aid of a personal appropriation of one's own rational self-consciousness. No doubt, it would be better if I could satisfy in a single work both those that want abundant quotations from St Thomas and those that want an independently elaborated system of thought. But perhaps I shall be excused by those who enjoy enough energy to read both my historical studies and the present book, for they, I think, will agree that either task by itself is sufficiently difficult and complex.

In the introduction I stated a program. Thoroughly understand what it is to understand, and not only will you understand the broad lines of all there is to be understood but also you will possess a fixed base, an invariant pattern, opening upon all further developments of understanding. If I may end by adding the present context to that assertion, then I would say that it is only through a personal appropriation of one's own rational self-consciousness that one can hope to reach the mind of Aquinas, and once that mind is reached, then it is difficult not to import his compelling genius to the problems of this later day.

Lexicon of Latin and Greek Words and Phrases

The purpose of the lexicon is not to contribute to Latin and Greek scholarship, but to assist readers of *Insight* who may not be familiar with those languages; translations may therefore be freely adapted to that purpose. Occasionally we are able to provide Lonergan's own translation (signified by 'L'), which may be likewise free. Phrases ordinarily found in English dictionaries are omitted.

Latin Words and Phrases

actio: action, activity
actus: act, activity, reality
actus totius entis: the act of total being
an sit?: is it?

causa essendi: the cause of being
causa cognoscendi: the cause of knowing
cogito, ergo sum: I think, therefore I am
conditiones materiae: the conditions (of being) of anything material (space and time)
crede ut intelligas: believe that you may understand

decreta hypothetice praedeterminantia: decrees that hypothetically predetermine
Deus est quo maius cogitari nequit: God is (the Being, the One) than which nothing greater can be conceived

ens: being, a being

ens dividitur per potentiam et actum: being is divided by potency and act

entia non sunt multiplicanda praeter necessitatem: beings (entities) are not to be unnecessarily multiplied

esse: to be, to exist, being

esse viventium est vivere: 'the being of living things is being alive' (L)

essentia dicitur secundum quod per eam et in ea ens habet esse: 'It is in and through essences that being has existence' (L)

Ethica ordine geometrico demonstrata: Ethics Demonstrated in Geometrical Order

ex falso sequitur quodlibet: from a false (premise) anything follows

ex hypothesi: by hypothesis

forma: form

genera litteraria: literary genre (L: 'types of expression')

gratia operans: operative grace

id cuius gratia: that for the sake of which

in signo antecedente omnem actum voluntatis: prior in an ordered sequence to every act of will (L: 'independently of any free decision')

intellectus quaerens fidem: understanding seeking faith

intentio intendens: intending intention

intentio intenta: intended intention

ipsum esse: being itself

ipsum esse subsistens: subsistent being itself

ipsum intelligere: understanding itself

materiae dispositae advenit forma: form comes to matter disposed (to receive it)

naturam expellas furca, tamen usque recurret: you can drive nature out with a pitchfork, but it will always return

nova: new things

omnia Deum appetunt: all things desire God

operatio: operation, action, activity

ordo idearum est ordo rerum: the order of ideas is (the same as) the order of things

paene omne quod dicimus metaphora est: almost every word we use (everything we say) is a metaphor

philosophia perennis: the perennial philosophy

potens omnia facere et fieri: able to make all things and to become all things
potens omnia fieri: able to become all things
Principia mathematica philosophiae naturalis: Mathematical Principles of Natural Philosophy
principium motus in alio inquantum aliud: the principle of movement in another thing insofar as it is other
principium motus in eo in quo est: a principle of movement within the thing itself (in that in which the principle too has being)

quaestiones: questions
quid sit?: what is it?

regina scientiarum: the queen of the sciences
Regulae ad directionem ingenii: Rules for the Direction of the Mind (of Intelligence)
rem tene et verba sequentur: get hold of the idea, and the words will take care of themselves (grasp the reality and the words will follow)
res cogitans: the thinking being
res extensa: the extended being

scientia media: middle knowledge
Socrates, dum sedet, necessario sedet, necessitate tamen non absoluta sed conditionata: when Socrates is sitting, necessarily he is sitting; the necessity, however, is not absolute, but conditional
summum bonum: the supreme good

unum per se: a thing that is per se one
ut a quo: that from which

verbum: word
veritas: truth (Augustine's reality)
veritas est una et error multiplex: truth is one and error multiple
vetera: old things
vetera novis augere et perficere: to add to and perfect the old by means of the new
video meliora proboque, deteriora autem sequor: I see what is better, and approve of it, but I follow what is less honorable
vis materiae insita: a force resident in matter

Greek Words and Phrases

archê hothen hê kinêsis: the source of movement (L: regularly 'movement' rather than 'motion')

eidos: form
energeia: 'operation' (L)
eureka: I have found (it)

noein: to grasp, to understand (L: to have an insight)
nomos: law
noêma: the understood (object)
noêsis: (the act of) understanding
noêsis noêseôs: understanding of understanding

physis: nature
poiêsis: making (L: 'production')

telos: end, purpose

Editorial Notes
R.M. Doran and F.E. Crowe

These research notes, besides accounting for changes from the text of the 1958 edition and providing information on *Insight*'s genesis, set some of its particular ideas in the broader context of Lonergan's life and work.

The number in square brackets at the beginning of each note gives the page of this edition to which the note refers. References to Lonergan's other works are abbreviated, but full data follow below in Works of Lonergan Referred to in Editors' Preface and Editorial Notes.

We use 'MSA' for Lonergan's autograph, 'MSB' for the professionally typed manuscript, and 'PT' for the published text (specifying the edition when that is relevant). 'MSA corr. MSB' means the autograph correcting the professionally typed manuscript, 'MSS corr. PT' means the two manuscripts correcting the published text, 'eds corr. PT' means editors correcting the published text, etc.

Title page

MSA has no title page, but the title is given at the top of the table of contents; here, and in a letter written during its composition (1952–55: letter, December 23, 1952), the subtitle is 'A Study of Human Intelligence.' In MSB the title is again found at the top of the table of contents, and now the subtitle is 'An Essay in Aid of Personal Appropriation of One's Own Rational Self-Consciousness.' Some time later, however, a title page was added to MSB with the subtitle actually used in PT: 'A Study of Human Understanding.' Echoes of the intermediate form of the subtitle appear passim in the introduction and epilogue of *Insight*; for example: 'our essay in aid of personal appropriation of one's own rational self-consciousness' (764 – see also 13, 16, 769).

The last change and third subtitle is also part of an undated list, headed

Further corrections, that Lonergan apparently drew up in the fall of 1954 and sent to Eric O'Connor for insertion into the second carbon of MSB (we will refer to this list again [note *a* to chapter 3, note *k* to chapter 7]).

In the same 1954 list of changes Lonergan corrected the quotation from Aristotle; likely written from memory it had first read *kai voei ho nous ta eidê en tois phantasmasi,* and the source was given simply as Aristotle, without reference to work or Bekker number. The same Greek occurs in the MSS for chapter 19, but there it was deleted at the proof stage, and Lonergan's English translation substituted: 'forms are grasped by mind in images' (see 699–700 above). In 'Isomorphism of Thomist and Scientific Thought,' first published in 1955, Lonergan translates in more scholastic terms: 'the faculty of understanding grasps the forms in images' (1988: 133–41, at 138).

We note here that the artist (Stein) responsible for the book's dustjacket figure clearly meant to suggest Rodin's famous sculpture, though Lonergan says in his first chapter that insights do not occur in the posture 'that a sculptor would select to portray "The Thinker"' (29).

Contents

The first edition did not use the MSB table of contents, but an abbreviated one drawn up, presumably, by the publisher. It does not columnize the chapter contents, sometimes gives just the main subdivisions, sometimes rewords them, sometimes omits one, sometimes includes some subdivisions (elevating them to equal status with the main ones) while omitting others.

The second edition gives the full table of MSB in columns. This created a problem of pagination: instead of v to vii as in the first edition, the table would need v to xi; but the preface started on page ix! The solution was to remove page numbers from the whole table – the preface is still numbered ix, though it is really xiii.

Discrepancies on particular points between the table and the actual text will be considered at the appropriate place in the book.

Preface

a [3] **Preface:** This is a new preface, written in the summer of 1954 (which Lonergan spent in England), conversations with T. Michael Longman during July having persuaded him to make the change; a letter dated August 26 acknowledges receipt of it at Longmans. For the story see *METHOD: Journal of Lonergan Studies* 3:1 (March 1985) 1–3; for the original preface as found in MSA and sent to Longmans in May 1954, ibid. 3–7. But for some reason it was only in the fall of 1954 that Lonergan sent the new preface to Canada to be substituted in the second carbon of MSA for the original (1952–55: letter of October 16, 1954).

b [7] **What practical good:** Lonergan gave serious thought to this question; a much longer answer (over six paragraphs) is found crossed out in MSA.

c [8] **progress and decline:** a central pair of terms for Lonergan early in life, as became clear from his 1973 paper '*Insight* Revisited' (1974: 263–78, at 271–72), and was verified by his student writings (1933–38) discovered after his death. His concern to relate it to the present context shows up in MSA, where an earlier account is crossed out and the present two paragraphs substituted.

d [9] **twenty-eight years:** calculated from 1926, the year he began the study of philosophy at Heythrop College, England.

e [9] **benefactors:** Lonergan was professor at the Collège de l'Immaculée-Conception in Montreal from the summer of 1940 to Christmas of 1946. His friendship with Fr R. Eric O'Connor developed in this period, and his debt to O'Connor was often acknowledged – for example in his obituary tribute, *Lonergan Studies Newsletter* 2 (1981) 2. Fr Jos. Wulftange studied philosophy in Toronto, 1949–50, and lived in Lonergan's Jesuit community that year. The history of the input of Fr Joseph Clark and Fr Norris Clarke is interesting: both were professors in the Jesuit school of philosophy, Plattsburg, NY, when Lonergan went there to consult them, apparently in the summer of 1953; he took his MS with him, they would read a chapter in the morning, go to the pool afternoons, and discuss the chapter evenings – combining holiday and study. Frs Crowe, Copleston, and Godin read the MS when it was already completed, the latter two in Rome, where they were professors at the Gregorian University when Lonergan arrived there in the fall of 1953. The first draft of the original preface recorded his thanks also to Patrick Plunkett 'who labored (to my shame, rather vainly) to reduce the solecisms of my style,' and 'to a friend that was in a position to insist on anonymity for the long labor of typing out my manuscript' (Beatrice Kelly); further, in a note on the galleys he expressed his thanks to 'T. Michael Longman and his associates' (crossed out, reinstated with a *stet*, but not published).

f [9] **compiling an index:** there follows in the first version of the discarded preface an exact reference to the period he spent writing the book, 'June 1949 to September 1953'; MSB was in fact complete in early August 1953 (personal memory of F. Crowe), though tidying up may have continued into September.

A note at the end of the preface lists revisions made for the second edition. It reads: 'I have recast the last fifteen lines on page 66, the first two on page 67, lines 15 to 31 on page 98, the first twelve lines on page 111, and the passage running from line 24 page 340 to line 12 page 341' (the lines recast on page 98 are in fact 5 to 31). All these changes will be indicated where they occur below, with the first-edition reading given in these notes.

Further, the second edition corrected many misprints of the first (Lonergan accepting some of them from a perhaps too finical reader). For the record we list the main ones by page and line of the PT (minus sign means 'count up'). 22, 22: later *for* latter; 98, 2: of *for* o; 108, −12: of contributing *for* in contributing; 118, −1: exists *for* exist; 121, 7: occurs *for* occur; 130, 1: successive *for* succesive; 159, 16: aether *for* ether; 160, −10: sensibility *for* the sensibility; 171, 17: still it is applied *for* still is applied; 193, 7: intelligence *for* intellegence; 199, 4: proscription *for* prescription; 259, −15: jugates *for* ugates; 282, 2: syllogisms *for* syllogism; 287, 18: and many *for* and the many; 289, −16: lies *for* lie; 300, 14: constitutes *for* constitues; 335, −10: account of *for* account or; 335, −6: notion of *for* notion or; 341, −16: inflexibility *for* flexibility; 359, −8: is to be *for* are to be; 364, 17: unchangeable *for* unchangable; 405, 12: *question mark for period*; 413, 19: qualities *for* qualitites; 424, 10: as mere ignorance *for* a mere ignorance; 436, −6: an *unum for* a *unum*; 446, −18: known *for* grasped; 464, 15: for-performance *for* for performance; 473, 3: his remaining *for* him remaining; 488, −11: infer *for* infer to; 499, −1: on being *for* of being; 507, 13: others mean or *for* others or; 517, −2: be not *for* is not; 538, −13: aether *for* ether; 540, 13: antinomies *for* antimonies; 542, 5: ledge *for* lege; 601, −12: conditions are more *for* conditions more; 604, 13: universal on the side of the object *for* universal; 617, 1: acknowledgement *for* acknowledgment; 642, 18: critical *for* cricital; 667, 16: advertence to *for* advertence; 682, −15: the demand of *for* demand of; 709, 7: preceded *for* proceeded; 721, 6: arrive *for* arive.

Introduction

a [15] **the name 'body':** we have not located a passage in which Augustine says this in so many words, but in the *Confessions* he repeatedly speaks of conceiving a being without a body (4, 16; 6, 3; 6, 4; 7, 1; and passim), adding, 'I saw clearly only later' (6, 4).

Eugène Portalié, *A Guide to the Thought of Saint Augustine* (Chicago: Henry Regnery Company, 1960), tells of Augustine learning from the Platonists, who understood that God is not a body, and had the ability to conceive a being without a body (99). Lonergan had seen Portalié's study in the original French ('Augustin, Saint,' *Dictionnaire de Théologie*

Catholique [Paris: Letouzey, 1902; reprinted 1923], tome I, col. 2268–2472), and refers to it (but in another context) in his unpublished paper *Pantôn Anakephalaiôsis* (1935b: 8). Whether Portalié or personal reading was Lonergan's source remains a question. See also his remark in chapter 14 (437 below) on the help Augustine got from the neo-Platonists in this matter.

b [15] **generically:** MSA corr. MSB and PT 'generally.'

c [15] **the experiment of history:** the reference may be to *The Unity of Philosophical Experience* (New York: Charles Scribner's Sons, 1948), in which Gilson calls the philosophies he studies there 'a series of concrete philosophical experiments' (p. vii and passim in the volume). See Lonergan's *Verbum*, in which he considers inviting 'some historian of the stature of M. Gilson to describe the historical experiment of understanding understanding and thinking thought' (1967: 219); also his review of Gilson's *Being and Some Philosophers*, where Lonergan speaks of those 'who can learn a lesson from the experiments conducted by history' (1949: 10).

d [16] **scientific thought:** a passage crossed out here in MSA has four philosophical experiments that fall 'into the unity of a single perspective when formulated as heuristic structure'; three of the six in MSB and PT (later in the same paragraph) coincide roughly with the deleted four.

e [16] **intellectualist ... conceptualist:** Lonergan's classic treatment of this pair occurs in *Verbum* (1967: index under Conceptualist); on abstraction see chapter 4 of that book.

f [16] **the question ... the question:** a neat twofold question, with a neat corresponding division in the book. But ten years later Lonergan conceived *Insight* as answering 'three linked questions: What am I doing when I am knowing? Why is doing that knowing? What do I know when I do it?' (1974: 37, in the 1967 paper 'Theories of Inquiry: Responses to a Symposium' 33–42). How would the book be divided in this new conception? His answer to that varies a bit, but one way was to assign chapters 9–13 to the middle question (1973); this gives an emphasis and unity to those five chapters that they certainly had in the composition (see our preface above). The three questions are related to the division found earlier in *De intellectu et methodo* (1959a: 48): sciences of the subject, sciences of objectification, sciences of the object.

g [19] **Nor is this all:** here Lonergan wrote and crossed out the sentence, 'Nor is this all, for I have not been able to reach within these pages the ultimate statements that govern the meaning of my last statements' – possibly a reference to the theological positions the original plan of the book would call for.

h [19] **Gödel's theorem:** Gödel's theorem was published in Vienna in

1931 (J. van Heijenoort, 'Gödel's Theorem,' Paul Edwards [Editor in Chief], *The Encyclopedia of Philosophy* 3 [New York: Macmillan and Free Press, 1967] 348–57). Though soon accepted (Max Black could say in 1940 that Gödel's results were 'no longer in dispute' [*Mind* 49: 244]), it was still recent when Lonergan referred to it. Subsequent history seems to have confirmed his endorsement: J.L. Bell, reviewing *Collected Works of Gödel, Vol. I,* calls him 'the greatest logician of this century, and perhaps of all time' (*The Philosophical Quarterly* 37 [1987] 216).

i [19] **definitive:** MSS corr. PT 'definite.'

j [21] **enough has been said:** a long paragraph deleted from MSA spoke here of the logical, the prelogical, and the way 'the genetic order of developing insights differs from the logical order of defining thought.' The genetic and logical orders are related to the *ordo inventionis* and *ordo doctrinae* that were beginning to structure Lonergan's theology at the time of writing (1988: 120–22, 123–27 – in 'Theology and Understanding,' first published in 1954).

k [21] **To turn ... to metaphysical considerations:** another long paragraph, deleted from MSA, discussed Lonergan's approach to metaphysics; it is followed by an even longer discussion not crossed out in MSA, though it does not appear in MSB or PT. Both the MSA paragraphs are on the *causa essendi/cognoscendi* distinction. A passage in the epilogue that referred back to these paragraphs was also deleted from MSA (see note *d* to epilogue below).

l [21] **I am far from certain:** this paragraph is not found in the MSS; it was apparently substituted at the time of proofreading for a long paragraph (crossed out in the proofs) dealing with the effort in 'the three centuries since Descartes and, particularly, in the century and a half since Kant,' to work out 'a metaphysically inspired epistemology.'

m [22] **appropriation of ... rational self-consciousness ... is not an end in itself:** a statement useful for perspective on Lonergan's long-range strategy; the point is made again in *Method in Theology,* 'The withdrawal into interiority is not an end in itself' (1972: 83), and 'withdrawal is for return' (ibid. 342).

n [23] **the historian ... the interpreter:** an interest more characteristic of *Method in Theology* (1972: chapters 7–9), but already present here and treated passim, esp. in chapter 17.

1   **Elements**

a [27] **A Dramatic Instance:** MSA has several attempts at telling the story of Archimedes, all crossed out except the one found in PT. They indicate that the example is offered to show 'the psychological resonance of the occurrence of an insight,' and is invested with 'the over-emphasis that aids clarity.'

b [29] **'I've got it!':** this phrase, as used by a student whacking his desk as she came to a lecture on Thought and Reality (1945–46), was reassuring for Lonergan as he began his book; he often repeated the story (see our preface to this edition, note 1).

c [30] **insight pivots:** compare *Verbum*, 'insight is the grasp of the object in an inward aspect such that the mind, pivoting on the insight, is able to conceive, not without labor, the philosophic concept of form and matter' (1967: 25).

d [30] **geometers use diagrams:** MSA has this clause, MSB has the crossed-out clause 'teachers use diagrams'; our hypothesis is that the latter was a typist's error made under the influence of 'teachers' occurring a line below, and that Lonergan then deleted the whole clause rather than write in the correct one; we restore it knowing how important the role of the diagram is in insight – see 'The Form of Mathematical Inference' (1928: 134–35), also *Caring* (1982: 2), and note *c* to chapter 2 below).

e [33] **The Image:** Lonergan's copy of *Insight* (1970 edition, as in other references in this context) has the annotation here 'De An III 7 431a 14–17, b 2' – 'b 2' is the locus of the phrase from Aristotle used as the book's motto (see above, our note to the title page).

f [33] **The Question:** the same copy has the annotation here 'Met VII 17 1041a 20 ff' – a passage in which Aristotle deals with 'why?' as seeking the cause.

g [35] **Nominal and Explanatory Definition:** another key pair of terms, also called 'nominal and essential'; see 'A Note on Geometrical Possibility' (1988: 92–107, at 93–98, and note *c*, ibid. 272); also note *m* to chapter 2 below). Lonergan's marked copy of *Insight* sidelines the first four lines of the last paragraph of this section ('Still, this yields ...'), and annotates as follows: 'cf. "ordinary language" [–] "generative grammar".'

h [37] **Implicit Definition:** Lonergan's copy of *Insight* has the annotation (apparently referring to this section 2.8) 'Met. VII, 10 f' – Aristotle deals there with definitions of the parts and definition of the whole.

i [38] **studied in high school:** we follow the MSS instead of PT here; the proofs are badly marked, perhaps by the publisher, and it is difficult to determine what corrections Lonergan intended.

j [38] **etc., etc., etc.:** the marked copy of *Insight* annotates this section, 'last + one = next.' This brings out the basic insight and excludes ambiguity; otherwise one might run one's eye *down* the first column where 2 comes after 1, without noticing that the 2 of the second line was generated at the end ('last') of the previous line (P. McShane).

k [41] **any of the operations:** the same marked copy has the annotation here, 'group $\sqrt{-1}$.' We interpret this to refer to the preceding paragraph, in which Lonergan highlighted the first sentence ('What are the new rules?') and parts of the last sentence. – For some light on the complex questions involved, P. McShane suggests Garrett Birkhoff and Saunders MacLane, *A Survey of Modern Algebra* (Macmillan and Co., 1941 [4th ed., 1977] – Lonergan has a scribbled reference to it in his archival papers), or for still greater complexity, Eric Temple Bell, *The Development of Mathematics* (New York: McGraw-Hill Book Co., 1940), Chapter 10: 'Arithmetic Generalized.'

Lonergan's keen interest in group theory appears in his Philosophy of Education lectures (1959b: as found in mathematics, 5th day of lectures; as found in Piaget's psychology, 8th day); it had appeared already in his own metaphysics – see note *k* to chapter 5 below, and the references given there.

l [43] **Inverse Insight:** this section and the following (§ 5. The Empirical Residue), along with parts of chapters 2, 3, and 5, were rewritten between late October 1954, when Lonergan received from T. Michael Longman the substance of a critique by Professor George Temple (1952–55: letter of October 26, 1954), and early spring 1955, when final reports on the resulting revisions are dated (ibid.: letter of April 2, 1955, reporting Eric O'Connor's agreement with the revisions; there is also a note dated March 24, 1955, which O'Connor sent to F. Crowe along with the revisions). The revised sections are approximately the same length as the original.

Prior to the revisions the present § 4 had subdivisions as follows: 4.1 Surds, 4.2 Non-Countable Infinity, 4.3 Functions and Limits, 4.4 Abstraction; 5.1 Individuality, 5.2 Continuity, 5.3 Place and Time, 5.4 Actual Frequency, 5.5 The Significance of the Empirical Residue. Lonergan's later references sometimes include the omitted topics, for example, p. 468: 'The empirical residue consists in individuality, the continuum, particular place and time, and ... nonsystematic divergence ...'; sometimes they are modified to correspond to the omissions (see note *a* to chapter 4 below); sometimes the omission is overlooked, resulting in minor inconsistencies (see note *e* to chapter 2, and note *i* to chapter 16).

Lonergan's marked copy of *Insight* has next to this heading of § 4 the annotation 'Specific postulates,' possibly in connection with his references in this section to 'the basic postulate' of relativity theory.

m [46] **real:** MSS corr. omission of this word in PT.

n [46] **in that interval:** both Lonergan's MS (as rewritten after Temple's critique) and the PT have two asterisks for the footnote we numbered 4; the second was located here at the end of the paragraph.

At the bottom of p. 21 of the PT in his marked copy he drew a diagram of axes and transverse diagonal, with the annotation 'Diagonal theorem.' It is not clear what it is on p. 21 that the note refers to; the page begins 'Essentially the question' (p. 45 in the present edition), and ends 'not on the action of external forces but on the absence' (46).

o [49] **infracategorial:** MSS corr. 'infracategorical' of PT.

p [50] **The Empirical Residue:** Lonergan's marked copy has next to this heading the annotation, 'General method.'

q [51] **exceptional significance:** this sentence (and the next, which makes a parallel statement on the empirical residue) has raised a question for many, since Lonergan had just stated that 'inverse insights ... seem regularly to be connected with ideas or principles or methods or techniques of quite exceptional significance.' Does he contradict himself, first affirming that connection and then denying it?

Apart from the unlikelihood of a blatant contradiction within a page, analysis seems to remove the difficulty. For Lonergan what 'characterizes' inverse insight and what may be 'connected' with it are two different questions. He did indeed affirm the *connection*, but he did not list it among the *characteristics* of inverse insight; these are three: 'there is the positive object ... There is a negation ... Finally, this negation ... runs counter to the spontaneous anticipations of human intelligence' (46; see also 78 and note *l* to chapter 2).

It may be relevant that this section on the empirical residue and the section on inverse insight in chapter 2 (§ 4.2) were both written in Rome after Lonergan received the Temple critique.

2   Heuristic Structures of Empirical Method

a [57] **Mathematical and Scientific Insights Compared:** this title, obviously appropriate, appears in the PT table of contents, both first and second editions, but curiously in neither the proofs nor the PT of the text of chapter 2; nor is it found in the MSS.

b [59] **no less than mathematical premises do:** 'do' is an editorial addition.

c [60, note 1] **the solution ... is facilitated by drawing a diagram:** a characteristic remark about a characteristic practice; students of Lonergan remember his diagrams even for cognitional theory and metaphysics (see also note *d* to chapter 1 above).

d [61] **similarities:** MSS corr. PT 'the similarities.'

e [62] **Accordingly, we recall:** what Lonergan is recalling here is what he wrote in his 1953 version of §5 of chapter 1, where §5.1 was on Individuality and §5.2 on Continuity; but the latter section was dropped in the revisions that followed Temple's critique (see note *l* to chapter 1 above, and the references given there).

f [63] **f(x, y, z, ...):** the MSS and PT added '= 0' to give the form of an equation, not a simple function; the error was noticed by Hugh MacPhee, professor of mathematics and physics at Loyola College, Montreal, (letter of E. O'Connor to F. Crowe, November 25, 1972, confirmed by letter from H. MacPhee, August 31, 1984). A list of *corrigenda* in Lonergan's papers and notations in his marked copy of *Insight* show that he accepted the correction, as he did those of notes *i* and *j* below, also due to Fr MacPhee. Other occurrences of 'function' for 'equation' (e.g., p. 169) are left as Lonergan wrote them.

g [63] **vanishing:** PT has 'vanishing into gas'; we follow MSB where 'into gas' is deleted by hand. Why did the deletion fail to reach the print stage? Perhaps because Lonergan failed to make the correction on the copy that went to the publisher, perhaps because the typesetter failed to notice the correction, perhaps for some other reason; this kind of question keeps recurring, and we shall regularly refer back to this note.
   At the top of p. 39 in Lonergan's marked copy of *Insight* there is an annotation which seems to refer to the paragraph with the equation for a fluid in motion: $\Delta R = \partial^2 R/\partial x^2 + \partial^2 R/\partial y^2 + \partial^2 R/\partial z^2 = 0$. ($\Delta R$ seems a double slip of the pen for $\nabla^2 R$. – P. McShane.)

h [63] **What is happening?:** this paragraph and the rest of the chapter were rewritten after the Temple critique; the original subtitles were: 2.5 Restricted Invariance, 2.6 Equivalence, 3.0 Statistical Heuristic Structure, 3.1 The Non-Systematic [marked for deletion, perhaps by Eric O'Connor], 3.2 [without title, but on actual frequency], 3.3 A Generic Notion of Probability, 3.4 Specific Differences, 3.5 Summary.

i [63] **Let the equation:** corrected from PT 'Let the function' (see note *f* above).

j [67] **force with rate of change:** corrected from PT 'force with change' (see note *f* above).

k [76] **Statistical Heuristic Structures:** MSA corr. MSB and PT singular (the table of contents of the second edition had the correct plural).

l [78] **three characteristics:** the three are the same here as on p. 46, and in neither case is 'a connection with ideas, principles, methods, or techniques of exceptional significance' listed with the three (see note *q* to ch. 1). This section too was rewritten after the Temple critique.

m [81] **to grasp the meaning of the name is to reach an explanatory definition:** 'meaning' here seems to refer to the full meaning – the intelligibility of the object named. This differs from Lonergan's regular usage, which sharply distinguishes nominal and explanatory definitions: 'Nominal definitions tell us about the correct usage of names. Explanatory definitions include something further' (35 above, and see note *g* to chapter 1); also: 'between an understanding of verbal usage and an understanding of what names denote, there is a large and commonly obscure gap' (565, and see *Collection* [1988: 94] on nominal and essential definitions).

n [87] **or of relative actual frequencies:** 'or' added to PT from the MSS.

o [89] **foundations:** the next two paragraphs ('I shall be asked ...' and 'However, if ...') were written for the second edition to replace the following passage of the first.

In particular there will be noticed a certain looseness in the notions of state and probability. But it is not indeliberate. The intelligent formulation of any notion is the fruit of an insight, and insights grasp not only necessities but also mere possibilities. There is an insight that leads to the definition of the circle, but it does not prove that circles exist. There is a cluster of insights that are formulated in Euclidean geometry, but they do not prove the existence of Euclidean space. Similarly, there is a rather complex insight that leads to a notion of probability, and there is a cluster of insights expressed in a calculus of probabilities. But the excellence of the insights and the intellectual satisfaction they yield do not establish their correspondence with the specific content of verifiable probabilities and verifiable relations between probabilities. At least, I do not see my way to excluding on the general level of this inquiry the possibility that a range of different fields of relations between probabilities may be formulated and that statistical science may have the task of selecting one of these fields of relations and the type of probability they define implicitly.

3   **The Canons of Empirical Method**

a [93] **The Canons of Empirical Method:** in the lectures on Intelligence and Reality these were called 'principles' instead of 'canons,' and there were only two: the principle of exclusion, and the principle of relevance (1951a: 7; see also note *d* to chapter 10 below).

Here in *Insight*, in the overview of the second paragraph ('Six canons will be presented ...'), the MSB sentence on the canon of complete explanation was recast before publication (Lonergan's list of revisions, fall of 1954 – see our editorial note to title page above).

b [94] **procedures:** MSA corr. MSB and PT singular.

c [97] **to this fact the scientist alludes:** Lonergan wrote this in (on the second try) in MSB, crossing out 'is a difference'; the correction was lost on the way to printing and the deleted phrase appears in PT (see note *g* to chapter 2 above).

d [101] **binomial:** MSA corr. MSB and PT 'binominal.'

e [102] **are unverifiable:** MSA had two tries at the next section; the first (not named a new section) is crossed out, but began (we quote with omissions), 'Next, what is verified is the formulation, and all formulations may be reduced to terms and relations. Further ... relations are of two kinds ... of things to our senses ... of things to one another. But all definition is some sort of relation. It follows that ... there will be two types of terms ...' The second try is the one we have in MSB and PT.

f [104] **thing:** MSA corr. MSB and PT 'things.'

g [106] **grasp the relations:** MSA has almost half a page crossed out here – 'There are questions for intelligence and questions for reflection ... questions for reflection can be pure or mixed ... mixed, if what is to be affirmed or denied is the answer to some question for intelligence ... pure [when] I am asking about occurrence or existence ... pure fact.'

h [110] **only inasmuch:** MSS corr. PT 'only and inasmuch.'

i [112] **to be abstract:** the reading of both MSS as typed was, 'Accordingly, it is in this sense that we affirm classical laws to be abstract, and it is in this sense that a canon of statistical residues cuts a middle path between determinism and indeterminism. So far ...' In each MS this is changed by hand, but not to the form that appears in the published text, rather to: 'Accordingly, it is in this sense that we affirm classical laws to be abstract, and it is in this sense that a canon of statistical residues transposes the issue of determinism or indeterminism. So far ...' Presumably, Lonergan after two tries was still unhappy with the second half of the sentence and simply deleted it from the copy that went to the publisher.

j [115] **of world process:** MSA corr. MSB and PT 'of the world process.'

k [119] **and nonoccurrences:** MSA corr. MSB and PT 'and the nonoccurrences.'

l [119] **traverses ... with equal speeds:** the MSS both read '... traverses either different distances with equal speeds or unequal distances with equal speeds'; so do the proofs, which are not corrected on this point; we have no data to indicate how and when the change was made (see note *g* to chapter 1 above).

m [119] **relevant:** MSA and MSB have '... would not know which observations to assemble into the conditions at some *n*th remove for some specific event'; the change here was made in the rewriting described in the next note.

n [119] **The Nonsystematic Aggregate of Diverging Series:** this whole section, along with §6.6 to line 2 of §6.6.1 (exactly two pages, 96–97, as it happens, in the PT), was rewritten after Lonergan received the reports of the Longmans readers; §6.6.2 picks up the MSA text again. In the deleted section the subtitles were: 6.53 The Non-Systematic Aggregates of Diverging Series, 6.54 Summary, 6.55 The Possibility of Accurate Prediction, 6.56 The Indeterminacy of the Abstract, 6.57 A Mathematical Analogy, 6.6 The General Character of Statistical Theories, 6.61 Events.

o [120] **from 2 to *n*:** in his 1954–55 revisions Lonergan wrote 'from 1 to *n*'; there is no corresponding passage in MSA or MSB with which to compare the phrase, nor is there any indication when the change was made to the PT 'from 2 to *n*' (see note *g* to chapter 2 above); but it shows Lonergan juggling for a precise expression (P. McShane).

p [121] **6.6.3:** this subsection and the one following (6.6.4) is a revision made for the second edition; the first edition had read as follows.

6.6.3 *Observable Events.* Thirdly, statistical theories will deal only with observable events. For the canon of parsimony restricts scientific utterance to the verifiable. And only the frequencies of observable events are verifiable. Hence, if one were to suppose that some type of event occurred nine times on every ten occasions yet only one of the nine occurrences and only seven of the ten occasions were observable, then the correct frequency would be, not 9/10, but 1/7. For the scientist is restricted to the verifiable, and so he defines his frequencies in terms, not of events in general, but of observable events.

6.6.4 *Special not General Relativity.* Accordingly, there will be a formal opposition between a statistical theory and, on the other hand, a classical theory satisfying the principle of equivalence.

For the principle of equivalence abstracts from the relations of things to us to determine the relations of things to one another.

But statistical theory necessarily deals with only observable events and so must include the relations of things to our senses.

It is to be noted that this formal opposition excludes the possibility of a contradiction between such theories. For contradictory statements must regard not only the same things but also the same aspects of things. But the formal opposition excludes the possibility of statistical theory and fully invariant classical theory referring to the same aspects of the same things.

It is to be recalled that we based the invariance of Special Relativity, not on the fully general principle of equivalence, but on the same grounds as Newton's First Law of Motion. Hence, the formal opposition between the principle of equivalence and statistical theory does not preclude the use of Special Relativity in Quantum Mechanics.

q [123] **so that to deny them:** 'that' is editorial addition.

r [123] **fully concrete:** MSA has written corrections to make the passage read: 'But an axiomatic structure for statistical laws would be a set of systematic premises. Its implications would reach to the concrete, for statistical laws deal with events, and events are always fully concrete.' The correction may be E. O'Connor's; if Lonergan's, it was lost on the way to MSB and printing (see note g to chapter 2 above).

s [124] **are reached:** again MSA has handwritten corrections (lost on the way to printing – see again note g to chapter 2) to make the passage read: 'Therefore the axiomatic structure for statistical laws must have some means of cutting short its implications before the full determinacy of the concrete is reached.'

t [124] **On this analysis:** the whole passage from here to the end of the chapter was rewritten in Rome after September 1953 – why and exactly when is unknown; it is not among the corrections due to the Temple critique, but it was sent to Eric O'Connor, who copied it by hand into MSA (the typed pages going, presumably, to Philosophical Library).

4   **The Complementarity of Classical and Statistical Investigations**

a [126] **Finally:** MSA reads, 'Finally, from an examination of infinities and of limits, there was effected ...'; in MSB the phrase 'from ... limits' is crossed out by hand, possibly because the revisions after the Temple critique omitted a lengthier discussion of infinities and limits (see note l to chapter 1 above).

b [134] **On the other hand:** the rest of this paragraph is a revision made for the second edition; the first edition had read as follows.

statistical laws deal, not simply with occasions and events, but with observable occasions and observable events. They are not, in principle, independent of the relations of things to our senses, and they cannot be subjected to a full principle of equivalence. There follows the already-mentioned formal opposition between Quantum Mechanics, interpreted statistically, and General Relativity; the two theories may deal with the same things, but they deal with them from radically different viewpoints; they are complementary in so far as General Relativity is concerned with things as independent of their relations to our senses while Quantum Mechanics views things in a manner that includes those relations.

c [146] **on:** MSA, in agreement with 136, −3, corr. MSB and PT 'in.'

d [147] **was:** MSA, in agreement with 'was' two lines below, corr. MSB and PT 'is.'

e [150] **breakdown:** MSA, in agreement with 'breakdown' two lines below, corr. MSB and PT plural.

f [150] **Moreover:** this and the two following paragraphs are part of the twelfth property of world process, as is clear from indentations in the MSS. PT indented only the first paragraph; our edition does not indent any of the twelve points.

g [154] **had been dominant:** eds corr. PT 'has been dominant.'

h [157] **nineteenth-century science:** the preceding paragraph does not appear in either MSA or MSB; instead there is a slightly longer paragraph which got as far as the proofs but is marked for deletion there; presumably Lonergan inserted the new paragraph at that time.

i [157] *Indeterminism:* MSA has an earlier version of 3.4. It is too long to transcribe here, but begins (we quote with omissions), 'Nineteenth century physicists were prone to regard Darwinism as the triumph, in the field of biology, of their own mechanistic view of world order ... In this fashion the crisis in the world view, immanent in scientific methodology, was postponed from the nineteenth century to the twentieth ...'

j [161] **Conclusion:** the subtitle is lacking in both MSS and PT, but appears in the table of contents of the second edition.

5   **Space and Time**

a [165] **invariant tense that abstracts from particular times:** this point had come up and been worked out in Lonergan's Latin theology at the very time he was writing *Insight*; in the context of the *simul esse* of God with things he wrote, ' "est" duo significat; primo et semper significat ens et verum, et ita non differt ab "erat" vel "erit"; deinde connotat comparationem inter tempus rei et tempus iudicantis, et ita differt ab "erat" et "erit".' After further discussion he concluded, ' "simul esse" sequitur ipsam rationem entis nisi praedicamentum "quando" impedit' (1950: §3, De comparatione entis aeterni et temporalis; see also §3.4 below, Simultaneity).

b [165] **Since the laws:** MSA corr. MSB and PT 'Since laws.'

c [167] **further extension ... further duration:** another idea related to the Latin theology of this time, for the role of the imagination in relating us across space and time to Christ – 'non tamen ad ... Iesum ... acceditur nisi hic locus hocque tempus sensibus innotescunt et per imaginationem continuantur donec ad Palestinam ... ante duo millia annorum perveniatur' (1956: 19).

d [172] **experiences:** MSS corr. PT singular.

e [174] **principles and laws:** MSA adds a paragraph here that has 'a further corollary' on verifiable geometries; but it was then crossed out – possibly because the idea was promoted in MSB to a full section (§ 3.2).

f [182] **one local motion:** we follow MSA here; though MSB and PT have, 'Time must be one, and so he appealed to the *primum mobile*, the outermost sphere, and it had only one local motion,' the state of MSA is such that an error in typing MSB would be easy.

g [183] **The Principle at Issue:** this subtitle is found (handwritten) in both MSS; it was missing from the text in PT but was included in the table of contents of the second edition as 'Principles at Issue.'

h [184] **any values:** both MSS read 'any number of values'; 'number of' was crossed out in the proofs.

i [185] **The Elementary Paradox:** this whole section (§ 4.1) was revised after the critiques of the Longmans readers.

j [192] **Now the transition:** the rest of § 4, as we have it in PT, was substituted for the much longer original version after the same critiques.

k [195] **emergent probability is the immanent form or intelligibility:** in the lectures on Intelligence and Reality Lonergan has nine metaphysical elements, adding to the familiar six (central and conjugate potency, form, and act) three others – group potency, group form, and group act (1951a: 24–25); the relation of these three to the other six can be studied at length in chapter 15 below and is briefly indicated in the epilogue – 'agreement with Aquinas on the basic elements does not preclude a development of his thought to provide a metaphysical analysis of explanatory genera and species and of development itself' (760) – but pieces in this fascinating puzzle of the nine and the six begin with this last sentence of chapter 5 (see also note *a* to chapter 9 below, notes *a* and *k* to chapter 15, notes *c* and *j* to chapter 16, and note *e* to the epilogue).

6   Common Sense and Its Subject

a [196] **Common Sense and Its Subject:** it is clear from the MSS that the two chapters on common sense were originally one chapter in three parts; it was to have the following introduction: 'The present chapter falls into three main sections. In the first the parallel between empirical science and common sense is examined. In the second and third, attention is drawn to fundamental differences.' The second part became The Subjective Field of Common Sense (§ 2 in chapter 6), and the third became the present chapter 7. Certain passages in later chapters, not corrected after the change, reflect the original plan (see note *l* to chapter 7 below).

b [198] **From spontaneous inquiry:** MSS corr. PT 'From a spontaneous inquiry'; the 'a' was typed in MSB but crossed out by hand.

c [201] **with things:** MSA corr. MSB and PT 'with the things.'

d [203] **the differentiations of common sense:** MSA, in agreement with last sentence of § 1, corr. singular of MSB and PT. In later years, speaking of the differentiations of consciousness, Lonergan will call common sense undifferentiated, and will speak of 'brands,' etc., for its varieties (see 1972: 84–85, 272–73, 276).

e [204] **science:** MSA corr. MSB and PT 'sciences.'

f [207] **over against:** MSA corr. MSB and PT 'ever against.'

g [208] **unfolding situations and actions of fiction:** an idea exploited some years later in discussion of mutual self-mediation; 'Mutual self-mediation proves the inexhaustible theme of dramatists and novelists' (1984: 13).

Here in *Insight* the footnote reference to Susanne K. Langer may suggest that this section, The Aesthetic Pattern of Experience, was based on her book; but the note was added to MSB after Lonergan's arrival in Rome – Langer's work was confirmatory for him of what he had already written.

h [208] **also are symbolic:** MSA corr. MSB and PT omission of 'also.'

i [208] **Art then becomes symbolic:** MSA corr. MSB and PT insertion of commas around 'then'; commas change the sense of 'then' from 'in that case' (our interpretation) to 'therefore.'

j [209] **to these questions:** MSA corr. MSB 'to those questions.'

k [211] **Style is the man:** MSA corr. MSB and PT 'Style is in the man'; Lonergan is surely alluding to the phrase, 'Le style est l'homme même' (Buffon).

l [212] **an artistic transformation:** instead of 'transformation,' MSA had written and then crossed out 'sublimation.' In chapter 15 (482 below) Lonergan refers to Freud's 'somewhat ambiguous sublimation'; perhaps he changed the text here in order to avoid a similar ambiguity.

m [213] **release them:** MSA used learning to walk as its first example, picking up the present text again at 'initial plasticity' – especially interesting because a few years later Lonergan will discover Piaget and develop these ideas in reference to him.

n [214] **Nor has such a bias ... isolated effect:** MSA corr. MSB omission of this sentence – presumably a typing oversight.

o [217] **a diffident shadow:** here the MSS add (though it is crossed out in MSB), 'It would seem to be ultimately the same phenomena that are named ambivalence by the Freudians, bipolarity by Stekel, and an alternation of opposites by Adler.'

p [218] **wasting my time**: MSA had underlined 'my,' but this was changed in MSB – the emphasis would have removed the effect of the 'Freudian slip.'

In MSA Lonergan followed this paragraph with several sentences subsequently crossed out, in which he indicated he was now moving from the problems discussed in Freud's *Psychopathology of Everyday Life* to those treated in *The Interpretation of Dreams*.

q [220] **the immanent direction**: MSS corr. PT 'the direction.'

r [223] **his moral feelings**: the word 'moral' is found in the proofs but not in the MSS – added, presumably, to the MS copy that went to the publisher (see note g to chapter 2 above).

s [223] **A Piece of Evidence**: for the first paragraph of this subsection the MSS and the proofs have the following.

In his *History of the Psychoanalytic Movement*, Freud prefaced his indict-ment of the secessionists, Adler and Jung, with the statement that he had always asserted that repressions and the sustaining resistance might involve a suspension of understanding. But where Freud recognized a consequence, we have seen an antecedent. Our study of the dramatic bias begins from the flight from insight and, rather systematically, it has led us to repression and inhibition, the slips of waking consciousness and the function of dreams, the aberrations of religions and morality and, as a limit, the psychoneuroses. Naturally, there arises the question whether any specialists in the field of abnormal disorders provide us with confirmatory evidence on the connection between repression and a refusal to understand.

An affirmative answer is offered by Dr. Wilhelm Stekel's *Technique of Analytic Psychotherapy* (The Bodley Head, London, 1939). The work ...

All this was crossed out at the proofs stage. Lonergan's new text reflects a movement toward speaking of a functional correlation rather than roots, antecedents, or causal origins (see the next note).

t [224] **the disorder is linked with a refusal**: both MSS have 'the root of the disorder is a refusal'; the correction to the PT reading was made in the proofs, presumably in line with Lonergan's purpose (just stated: 223) 'to prescind from all questions of causal origins and to view our account ... as a functional correlation.'

u [226] **regular**: both MSS have 'genetic'; the correction was made in the proofs, probably for the reason mentioned in the two preceding notes.

v [227 note 9] **a communication of insights**: this whole footnote was added in Rome when the book was already complete; the references are therefore not sources for Lonergan but confirmations of his ideas (see also note *g* above).

w [229] **Still, whatever ... Freud's involvement:** the five paragraphs from here to the end of the chapter were written in Rome, where Lonergan had made new contacts. For example, 'A. Godin ... put me on the track of H.S. Sullivan's Interpersonal Theory of Psychiatry' (1952–55: letter of May 5, 1954). It may be that Godin influenced Lonergan's decision to speak of a functional correlation rather than causal origins (see notes *s*, *t*, and *u* above).

7   Common Sense as Object

a [233] **but also practical:** MSA corr. MSB and PT omission of 'also.'

b [233] **only to suggest:** MSA corr. MSB and PT omission of 'only.'

c [236] **communication, persuasion, agreement:** MSA corr. MSB and PT omission of 'persuasion.'

d [238] **basis in intersubjectivity:** MSA corr. MSB and PT 'basis of intersubjectivity.'

e [244] **satisfactions:** MSS corr. PT singular.

f [249] **Group bias, however:** MSB and PT start a new paragraph here; we prefer the single paragraph of MSA.

g [250] **a full development:** MSA corr. MSB and PT omission of article.

h [251] **the concrete and particular:** MSA corr. MSB and PT 'the concrete and the particular.'

i [251] **It easily is led:** MSS corr. PT 'It is easily led' – a trivial matter, but a characteristic of Lonergan's style was lost in the PT.

j [267] **Cosmopolis ... from Babel:** both MSS have this sentence, lacking in the proofs; somewhere on the way it disappeared without trace (see note *g* to chapter 2 above).

k [268] **succeed ... dialectic of his history:** these lines appear as follows in the MSS, 'succeed in hitting off the thought of the average man, as would Newman, the problem of his affects, as would Freud, and the dialectic of his history, as would a higher synthesis of liberal and Marxist thought'; the three 'as would' clauses are crossed out by hand in Lonergan's MSB (first carbon), and the correction is one in the list Lonergan sent from Rome in the fall of 1954 for revising the second carbon (see our editorial note to the title page above).

l [268] **In the present chapter:** a remnant of the time when the present chapters 6 and 7 were only one; in the last paragraph of chapter 7 MSB has the plural, 'the present chapters ... are'; MSA had 'the present chapter ... is,' but corrected it by hand to the plural.

8   Things

a [285] ***Materiae dispositae advenit forma:*** an axiom found in Thomas
Aquinas, at least in substance; see *Summa contra gentes* 2, 19, 'Quando
materia iam perfecte disposita est ad formam, eam recipit in instanti';
also *Summa theologiae* 1–2, q. 112, a. 3, obj. 3: 'cum igitur forma
naturalis ex necessitate adveniat materiae dispositae.'

b [291] **into:** MSA corr. MSB and PT 'in.'

9   The Notion of Judgment

a [298] **Hitherto ... diverge:** the three questions of this paragraph are
related to the three sets of metaphysical elements listed in the lectures
on Intelligence and Reality (1951a: 24–25); 'what' to central potency-
form-act, 'why' to the conjugate set, 'how often' to what in the lectures
he had called 'group' potency-form-act (see note *k* to chapter 5 above,
and the references given there).

b [298] **chapter on common sense:** the first reading of the MSS was 'This
prior level was described in the section on data, images, and percepts';
MSA changed this by hand to 'This prior level consists in data, images,
and percepts'; MSB changed it by hand to 'This prior level was described in the chapters on common sense.' (PT followed MSB, but with
'chapter' curiously in the singular.) It seems that when Lonergan wrote
chapter 9 he expected to describe the prior level more formally in a
chapter on common sense (perhaps already drafted); chapter 6 comes
closest to realizing this, but there is really no formal exposition. There
was a formal exposition in the Intelligence and Reality lectures, where
we have a page with the heading: Data, Images, Percepts (1951a: 9);
this may have been in his mind as he wrote chapter 9; significantly, it is
followed in the lectures by pages on Things (10) and Analysis of Judgment (11) – corresponding to chapters 8 and 9 of the book.

10   Reflective Understanding

a [314] **Though some repetition will be involved:** this and the phrase a
few lines later, 'If I may repeat myself,' were not part of the original
MSS (both are added by hand to MSB), a further indication that chapter
6 was not written when Lonergan typed the present chapter; in fact,
then, it is not chapter 10 that repeats chapter 6, but chapter 6 (see
197–98 above) that repeats chapter 10.

b [319] **experiential conjugates:** MSA had 'immediate conjugates' and
'mediated conjugates' for, respectively, 'explanatory conjugates' and

'experiential conjugates.' The lectures on Intelligence and Reality spoke of 'descriptive, heuristic, terminal, and dialectical categories' (1951a: 23); the first and third now become 'experiential' and 'explanatory' (see also note *e* below).

c [327] **to the establishment:** MSA corr. MSB and PT 'to be the establishment.'

d [328] **the canon of selection:** MSA, and MSB as typed, have 'principle of exclusion' (corrected by hand in MSB to the PT reading); this is probably a carry-over from the Intelligence and Reality lectures, where instead of six canons there were two principles, one of them the principle of exclusion (1951a: 7; see also note *a* to chapter 3 above).

e [329] **elements or categories:** MSA has (typed) 'what will be named the terminal categories' but changed 'terminal' to 'explanatory' (by hand); MSB retains 'the terminal categories' in the typing, but this was changed by hand to 'the elements or categories' (see note *b* to this chapter above).

f [329] **A proposition:** twenty-three lines at the beginning of §7 (down to the sentence, 'The definitions of its partial terms ...') are a new page, substituted after Lonergan went to Rome (the carbon is on Gregorian University stationery); MSA has a marginal note, perhaps in Eric O'Connor's hand, 'made a little neater in revision,' but in fact the revision differs considerably from MSA.

g [329] **source of meaning:** chapter 12, §5, will distinguish sources, acts, terms, and core of meaning; adding, 'Any element of knowledge may serve as a source of meaning.'

h [339] **one can distinguish:** numbers for the three divisions are an editorial addition.

11   Self-affirmation of the Knower

a [345] **would be as unconscious as:** MSA corr. MSB and PT 'would be unconscious as'; the correction had been made in the proofs but was lost on the way to print.

b [346] **Empirical ... Consciousness:** MSA has no subheading here (or anywhere in the chapter); it begins, 'Thirdly, by consciousness is meant ...'; MSB adds subtitles by hand and crosses out 'Thirdly.'

c [351] **By such experiential fulfilment:** the first three sentences of this paragraph restore what we consider the correct reading; they are found in MSA but the state of the MS is such that the typist of MSB could easily miss them; with their omission 'such' had to be changed to 'an' – as was done at the proof stage.

d [360] **definitively:** MSA corr. MSB and PT 'definitely.'

e [360] **definitively:** MSA corr. MSB and PT 'definitely.'

f [362] **Contrast with Kantian Analysis:** Lonergan's marked copy of *Insight* (1970 edition) has a note at the bottom of page 339: 'synthetic a priori principles vs. Hume → verifiable possibilities Collection 208'; he may have meant it to indicate schematically the process from Hume through Kant to his own position, though 'Collection 208' (1988: 194) speaks only of Kant.

g [365] **to know knowledge:** the twenty-six preceding lines (starting at 'In any case ...' in the previous paragraph) are a revision made for the second edition; the first edition had read as follows.

What he was trying to get hold of was, perhaps, the reflective process of checking, of verifying, of bringing the merely conceived and the merely given into unity. In fact, that process is far more complicated and far more versatile than Kantian analysis would lead one to suspect. Verifying supposes a vast array of hypothetical propositions that state what would be experienced under precisely defined conditions. Verifying consists in having those experiences, all of them, and none but them, under the defined conditions. Moreover, what is verified, is what is conceived, formulated, supposed. It need have no imaginable counterpart, and so one can speak of verifying the theory of relativity or the affirmations of quantum mechanics. Indeed, as we have shown at length, there is a single formula that covers the immediate ground of all our judgments; it is the grasp of the virtually unconditioned. So far was Kant from positing the unconditioned as the immediate ground of every judgment, that he described it as an Ideal of Pure Reason, an ideal that becomes operative in our knowing, not prior to judgment and as a condition of judgment, but subsequently inasmuch as each judgment rests on an infinite regress of prosyllogisms. As the reader familiar with Kant will note, our assertion of a demand for the unconditioned as a prior ground for judgment not merely implies that the Kantian analytic is seriously incomplete but also involves in utter ruin the Kantian dialectic. For the dialectic has but a single premise, namely, that since the demand for the unconditioned is not a necessary ground for judgment, therefore, it is a transcendental illusion; in other words, since the unconditioned is not constitutive of knowing an object in the sense of making a judgment, therefore, it has a purely regulative function in our knowing. On our showing, the unconditioned is prior and constitutive; to affirm a fact is to affirm an unconditioned.

h [366] **exactly as it ought to be:** MSA corr. MSB and PT omission of 'exactly.'

i [368] **definitively:** MSA corr. MSB and PT 'definitely.'

12   The Notion of Being

a [376] **an answer:** MSA, in agreement with 'a formulation' in the same sentence, corr. MSB and PT 'the answer.'

b [376] **the right answers:** following this paragraph MSA starts another as follows. 'Again, it may be objected that the really real is being, and that is to be known not by inquiry and reflection but by some ordinary or mystical experience or intuition. The objection formulates, I think, a difficulty that will be treated when we come to discuss objectivity. But as it stands' – here the passage breaks off.

c [376] **whatever we ask about:** for this sentence MSB (and the proofs, except for a comma change) had, 'For we ask whether it might be; and the being we are talking about, is the being we ask about'; Lonergan corrected the proofs to the PT wording.

d [378] **not yet the knowing:** MSA corr. MSB and PT 'not yet knowing.'

e [380] **through that content:** MSA, in agreement with the next line, corr. MSB and PT 'through the content.'

f [381] **the core of meaning:** MSA first had 'the meaning of meaning,' corrected by hand to 'the core of meaning'; further, the paragraph a few lines later that begins 'Now the all-inclusive term' began in MSA by saying 'The meaning of meaning is the intention of being.' Despite its deletion here 'the meaning of meaning' remains a focal phrase for Lonergan; see his preface, 'insight into insight includes the apprehension of the meaning of meaning' (5 above), and 'insight into ... flight from understanding will explain ... aberrant views on the meaning of meaning' (6 above).

g [382] **function:** MSS corr. PT 'fraction.'

h [386] **all-inclusive:** in MSA the rest of this paragraph, and the remaining three paragraphs of 'Seventhly,' are not crossed out but sidelined with the notation 'omit'; then handwritten at the top of the page is the following: 'However, while the notion of being is always concrete, every human consideration of being is abstract. For we consider when we ask questions; we ask only one question at a time; and in asking that one, we prescind from all others to center attention upon some part or aspect of being and to abstract from the rest.' One begins to appreciate the intelligence and fidelity of the typist in dealing with the text submitted, especially in these chapters 9 to 13, but it is sometimes difficult to determine what Lonergan's final choice was; to add to the confusion there was in MSA a false start, thoroughly crossed out, after 'all-inclusive.'

i [386] **differences:** MSA, in agreement with next sentence, corr. MSB and PT singular.

j [387] **cognitional:** thus MSA; the typist of MSB made it 'conditional,' which Lonergan changed by hand to 'unconditioned'; the return to MSA seems truer to his intention.

k [389] **neither ... nor ... nor ... is being, and so all three:** eds corr. MSS and PT 'neither ... nor ... not ... are being, and so they.'

l [389] **element:** MSA corr. MSB and PT plural.

m [396] **would he insist:** MSA corr. MSB and PT 'would insist.'

n [398, note 21] **my attitude towards Hegel:** this remark is not just an afterthought – letters and papers from Lonergan's student days, especially File 713 (1933–38) and the letter of January 1935 to his Provincial (1935a: 5), show a focal interest in Hegel and Marx, and that early interest is surely the basis for Lonergan's remarks on history in *Insight* (see 258–59, 260, 266, etc., above).

13   The Notion of Objectivity

a [401] **On the other hand:** the preceding twelve words were omitted in the typing of MSB; in proofreading Lonergan noticed the lack of sequence, first wrote 'On the other hand' in the margin, but then compromised by deleting 'and then' and inserting 'Further' to start a new sentence and give the PT reading; we have restored the text as it is found in MSA.

b [402] **conditioning and conditioned terms:** both MSS had typed 'conditions and conditioneds'; MSA crossed this out and wrote in the margin 'conditioning and conditioned terms' – which we take as probably correct, though MSB wrote 'conditioning and conditions' and then crossed out the 's.'

c [407] **a still deeper reason:** MSA corr. MSB and PT 'still a deeper reason.'

d [408] **what really is objective:** MSA corr. MSB and PT 'what is objective.'

14   The Method of Metaphysics

a [410] **The Underlying Problem:** in MSA the chapter title is The Dialectic of Philosophy; this is the running head throughout the chapter in both MSS, and seems to have been the title still when Lonergan came to this point on April 21, 1953, in his Regis College lectures (1952–53: 77); further, instead of The Underlying Problem the first subheading in the chapter is Ground of the Dialectic. The changes to what became the PT readings were made by hand in MSB, but interesting carry-overs from the original chapter title remain; for example, 'So too we began to talk about the dialectic of philosophy' (423 below).

The last sentence of this introductory section, 'In subsequent chapters ...' (414–15), was added later to MSA (but before it went to the typist); evidently, when Lonergan started chapter 14, the 'subsequent chapters' had not yet come to mind in the form they eventually assumed.

b [412] **method:** MSA has 'dialectic,' changed by hand in MSB to the PT 'method.'

c [413] **and:** the MSS and proofs had 'or' – corrected in the proofs to this PT reading.

d [415] **principles:** MSA corr. MSB and PT singular.

e [422] **People as they are cannot:** thus MSA; MSB omitted 'are,' and Lonergan's remedy was to cross out 'as they' to give the PT reading.

f [426] **The Dialectic of Method in Metaphysics:** the reading of proofs and PT, and Lonergan's choice, it seems, though MSB changed this subtitle by hand to A Critique of Some Methods in Metaphysics (see note *o* below).

g [427] **differences:** MSA corr. MSB and PT singular.

h [428] **through a concrete judgment:** MSA corr. MSB and PT 'through concrete judgment.'

i [429] **is concluded to:** eds corr. MSS and PT omission of 'to.'

j [431] **an a priori synthesis:** MSS corr. PT omission of 'synthesis.'

k [432] **prior to the judgment:** MSA corr. MSB and PT omission of 'the.'

l [432] **Thomist cognitional theory:** MSS corr. PT 'the Thomist's cognitional theory.'

m [434] **the subject as prior:** MSA corr. MSB and PT omission of 'as.'

n [441] **is a variable:** MSA corr. MSB and PT 'is variable.'

o [446] *Hegelian Dialectic:* the subtitle in MSS is simply Dialectic – clashing somewhat with the general title, The Dialectic of Method in Metaphysics; possibly Lonergan first thought of changing the latter (see note *f* above), then decided to change this subtitle instead.

p [448] **elementary knowing:** MSA had 'human knowing and the realism of the *res extensa et talis* for animal knowing'; MSB omitted a line between the first 'knowing' and the second; when Lonergan corrected it by hand he omitted '*et talis*' and changed 'animal' to 'elementary.'

q [449] **satisfied commonly enough:** thus MSA; MSB omitted 'commonly' and Lonergan remedied the situation by crossing out 'enough' as well.

r [450] **Now there is ... but there is:** thus MSA; the typist missed 'but' in typing MSB; rather than reinsert it Lonergan added 'if' after 'Now' to give PT 'Now if there is no use ... there is a point ...'

15   Elements of Metaphysics

a [456] **There are six of them:** chapter 15 is central for the relation of these six metaphysical elements to the nine of Intelligence and Reality (1951a: 24–25; for pieces in the puzzle see note *k* to chapter 5 above, and the references given there).

b [466] **of a high order:** MSA and Lonergan's hand on MSB corr. PT 'of a higher order.'

c [476 note 6] **Aristotle:** Lonergan's personal copy of *The Basic Works of Aristotle* (ed. Richard McKeon, New York: Random House, 1941) is sidelined at *Physics*, II, 1, 192b 21–22, *'nature is a source or cause of being moved and of being at rest ...'*; he was still exploiting this notion in his 1977 paper, Natural Right and Historical Mindedness (1985b: 169–83, at 172 – but correct the reference in note 6, p. 183, of that printing; for 195b read 192b).

d [478] **of a minor flexibility:** MSA corr. MSB and PT 'of minor flexibility.'

e [482] **members:** MSA corr. MSB and PT singular.

f [492] **are the laws:** 'are' is editorial addition to suggest the point of transition in the series of comparative phrases – English lacks the Latin 'quo ... eo' and the German 'je ... desto' that would fix the point clearly.

g [496] **resolution ... sterile if ... feelings ... not forthcoming:** an early recognition of the role of feelings which is given such importance in the *Method* period; see An Interview with Fr. Bernard Lonergan, S.J. (1974: 209–230, at 221), 'Without feelings this experience, understanding, judgment is paper-thin. The whole mass and momentum of living is in feeling.'

h [497] **towards the subject as he is to be:** see the existentialism lectures on the gap between the subject that I am and the subject that I should be (1957: 22).

i [504] **issues:** MSA corr. MSB and PT singular.

j [507] **categorial:** MSA corr. MSB and PT 'categorical.'

k [511] **Such are the elements of metaphysics:** the sentence preceding this ('From the structural ...') is particularly relevant to the question of 'group' potency-form-act of the Intelligence and Reality lectures (see note *k* to chapter 5 above and the references given there).

l [511] **more deeply:** a verbal reminder of Lonergan's original title for the next chapter (see also note *a* to chapter 16 below).

16   Metaphysics as Science

a [512] **Metaphysics as Science:** running heads on all but the first page of MSA (obviously a revised page) show that this chapter was once called Deepening of Metaphysics.

b [512] **existence and ... power of a method:** Lonergan's purpose from
the start was to write on method for theology, though he had to round
off his work when called to Rome in 1953; on arriving there his first
graduate course at the Gregorian University was called *De methodis in
universim* but was in fact a course on the (still unpublished) *Insight*
(1952–55: letters, September 9, October 16, November 9, 1954).

c [520] **the reality of proportionate being ... in its entirety:** more data
here for the puzzle of the nine metaphysical elements of Intelligence
and Reality and the six of chapter 15 of *Insight* (see note *k* to chapter 5,
and the references given there).

d [521] **understanding understanding:** MSA corr. MSB and PT omission of
the noun object 'understanding.'

e [531] **bought:** MSA corr. MSB and PT 'sought.'

f [533] **seek their answers:** MSS corr. PT 'seek the answers.'

g [539] **existences:** MSS corr. PT singular.

h [539] **as every other known is:** 'is' is ed. addition.

i [540] **the limit apart from the continuum:** this example no longer
belongs in the list of ideas noted 'early in this study'; it was omitted
when the whole passage was revised (see note *l* to chapter 1 above, and
the references given there).

j [547] **the new territory of explanatory genera and species and of
processes of development:** the new territory is that of the 'group'
potency-form-act of the lectures on Intelligence and Reality (see note *k*
to chapter 5 above, and the references given there).

17   Metaphysics as Dialectic

a [553] **Metaphysics as Dialectic:** the running head in MSA remains the
same as it was for chapter 16, Deepening of Metaphysics; at that time
the two chapters were one (the two pages introducing chapter 17 were
written later).

b [558] ***The Genesis of Adequate Self-knowledge:*** this subtitle was added to
MSB by hand; so were others passim in the volume, but we note the fact
here where the section starts with a conjunction – less surprising in the
original running sequence of paragraphs.

c [560] ***Mythic Consciousness:*** again, the subtitle was added by hand, and
the 'Ninthly' which began the paragraph was crossed out; the change
may be due to the long interval since 'Eighthly' (see also notes *g*, *h*, and
m below).

d [562] **His explanation ... related to him:** this whole sentence, missed in
MSB, is supplied from MSA.

e [565] **the study of rhetoric to the use of metaphor:** a phrase found in

MSA but missed in MSB (to remedy the omission 'and' was written in before the following phrase).

f [565] **and of how:** MSA corr. MSB and PT omission of 'of.'

g [566] ***Myth and Metaphysics:*** this heading was added by hand, and the 'Tenthly' that began the paragraph crossed out (see note *c* above).

h [567] ***Myth and Allegory:*** the subtitle was added by hand; the first paragraph had begun 'In the eleventh place, in deference' (see note *c* above).

i [567] ***paene omne quod dicimus metaphora est:*** a possible source for this is Ernst Cassirer, *Language and Myth*, trans. Susanne K. Langer (New York: Harper & Brothers, 1946) 95, where Quintilian is quoted as having said *paene quidquid loquimur metaphora est*. For Quintilian himself, see *Institutio oratoria* IX, 1, 12: '... in quo ita loquimur, tamquam omnis sermo habeat figuram ... quare ... nihil non figuratum est.' Also IX, 3, 1: 'paene iam quidquid loquimur figura est.'

j [568] **between a philosophic language:** MSA corr. MSB and PT 'between philosophical language'; Lonergan regularly wrote 'philosophic.'

k [568] **or a vital openness to change:** MSA corr. MSB and PT 'or with a vital openness to change.'

l [569] **contexts:** MSS corr. PT 'context.'

m [569] ***The Notion of Mystery:*** the subtitle was added by hand, with correction of 'In the twelfth place, besides myth' (see note *c* above).

n [571] **swung round:** MSA corr. MSB and PT 'swung around.'

o [579] **deficiencies in insight E:** this ambiguous phrase occurs several times (see also §3.1), the context making it clear that Lonergan is not speaking of insight *E* but of deficiencies *E*.

p [583] **we grasp:** addition of numbers '(1) ... (2) ... (3)' is editorial.

q [584] **On this:** MSS corr. PT 'On his.'

r [585] **the structure of history:** where does Lonergan fulfil this promise to analyze the structure of history? Evidently, though there is no formal announcement, in chapter 20; see '*Insight* Revisited': 'The whole idea [of history] was presented in chapter twenty of *Insight*' (1974: 272). One table of contents sketched while he was writing the book shows a final chapter with this very title (Archives, Batch 4, Folder 2); that, it seems, was still his plan as he wrote chapter 17.

s [590] **Now in the measure:** MSS corr. paragraphing of PT (Lonergan's way of listing the four dimensions misled the typesetter).

t [590] **reflection:** MSA corr. MSB and PT plural.

u [598] **treatise:** MSA corr. MSB and PT plural.

v [600] **on the basis of assumptions:** MSA corr. MSB and PT omission of 'basis of.'

w [602] **to determinate:** MSS corr. PT 'determine.'

x [603] **verification:** MSA corr. MSB and PT plural.

y [604] **explanatorily:** MSS corr. PT 'explanatory.'

z [604] **Descartes's vortices violated the canon of parsimony:** eds corr. 'canon of relevance'; see p. 93 above where Descartes's vortices are said to conflict with the canon of parsimony.

aa [607] **Thus:** in MSA Lonergan had inserted the paragraph sign; the editors have made a new paragraph also at 'If one agree,' to give four paragraphs for the four views Lonergan would dispute.

bb [608] **there arise the problems:** following MSA; MSB made the verb singular, the noun plural; PT made the noun singular.

cc [611] **to the universal viewpoint:** restoring the original wording of MSA; MSB had omitted a line ('intervening ... that bridge') and Lonergan patched up the resulting fault to give the PT 'retrace the steps that lead from the past to the present.'

dd [613] **the rewriting is not done:** Lonergan himself wrote and rewrote (see our preface to this edition); still there was a limit to his endurance – as he once said when asked why he left a certain passage in conflict with another: 'I didn't have a word processor. When is a work done? When you are sick and tired of correcting it.'

ee [615] **into an extrinsicist:** MSS corr. PT omission of 'an.'

ff [616] **there is not available the evidence:** MSA has 'there is not the available the evidence'; the typist deleted the second 'the,' but it seems more in Lonergan's style to delete the first.

18   The Possibility of Ethics

a [618] **The Possibility of Ethics:** this chapter too began as a continuation of Deepening of Metaphysics, which is the running head for forty-one pages of MSA after the two pages of introduction.

b [627] **conclusions do not follow from them:** MSB omitted the clause 'not because there are no universally valid precepts,' requiring the change (by hand) of 'them' to 'premises.'

c [627] **on the side of the object:** a phrase found neither in the MSS nor in the PT of 1957; it is one of the corrections made for the 1958 edition. MSA shows a struggle here between 'universal' and 'virtually universal,' with the former winning out.

d [630] **will be knowledge:** MSA corr. MSB and PT 'will be the knowledge.'

e [641] **laws of matter ... laws of spirit:** relevant here are *Verbum*'s 'three differences between natural process and the procession of an inner word' (1967: 33–34).

f [641] **act of will:** MSA corr. MSB and PT 'act of the will.'

g [645] **and of psychoneural:** MSA, in agreement with the second sentence after this, corr. MSB and PT 'and psychoneural.'

h [648] *L'homme se définit par une exigence:* the phrase occurs in *Understanding and Being* (1990: 99 n. 11) and in the 1957 lectures on existentialism (1957: 5), in each case without exact reference.

i [650] **nor totally unconscious:** thus MSA; Lonergan changed MSB to 'nor is it totally unconscious,' but his first way seems better.

19   General Transcendent Knowledge

a [657] **of the integrated heuristic structures:** MSA corr. MSB and PT omission of 'the.'

b [665] **One may distinguish:** in *La notion de verbe dans les écrits de saint Thomas d'Aquin* Lonergan states, 'Je distinguerais maintenant: (1) notion, (2) concept implicite, (3) connaissance, (4) idée et (5) théorie de l'être,' and gives several lines of explanation (1966: 44 n. 196); the 'maintenant' indicates a development in his thought, and this was confirmed in conversation at the time. A letter provided by Timothy Lynch states that 'we have a notion of "being" but knowledge of "beings." The notion is a component within cognitional process but of itself it is not a full instance of coming-to-know' (1977: letter).

Here in *Insight* Lonergan's two paragraphs on the fourth heading (666: 'Fourthly ...' and 'It follows ...') are a revision obviously made after he went to Rome in 1953: a new page typed on Gregorian University stationery has been substituted in MSB for the original one.

c [672] **in other possible and even more probable universes:** did Lonergan get the order wrong in his 'possible ... probable'? The third sentence of the paragraph, 'a number of probable alternatives and a far larger number of possible alternatives,' suggests that. But it is at least possible that the focus of 'even more' is not on the number of universes but on the likelihood of the consequence in 'It seems to follow ...'

d [677] **a philosopher:** editorial change from 'a philosophy,' to agree with the following 'he.'

e [679] **then all:** the words, 'But if no conditions are fulfilled simply at random, then,' are added from MSA, corr. MSB and PT omission.

f [680] **contingent being must be:** the words, 'cannot be necessary ... contingent being,' are added from MSA, corr. MSB and PT omission.

g [681] **affirmation of God:** this sentence ('The present section ... affirmation of God') was added at the proof stage.

h [681] **in the unrestricted act:** the MSS read here, 'For the primary being is identical with what is grasped by the unrestricted act, and so the primary being has all the perfection grasped by the unrestricted act.' Lonergan wrote the revision into the proofs.

i [682] **unconditioned:** MSS corr. PT 'unconditional.'

j [682] **would not be primary beings:** MSS corr. PT omission of 'not.' Someone canceled the 'not' in the proofs; if it was Lonergan himself, there must have been a slip of attention on his part, for 'not' is required by the sense, and in a thorough discussion with Giovanni Sala he insisted on the 'not' (1970: interview 337–38); further, in his marked copy of the first edition he inserts the 'not' marginally – perhaps at the time of the Sala interview.

k [688] **is designed:** the MSS have 'are'; the 'is' of the proofs and PT could be the preference of the Longmans editor.

l [703] **disassociate:** MSS corr. PT 'dissociate.'

m [704] **the dramatic and practical subject:** MSB and PT have 'the' also before 'practical'; so did MSA originally, but there it is crossed it out by hand.

n [708] **As they, so it ... desire to understand correctly:** this whole sentence (the first of three 'As they, so it ...' sentences), missing from MSB and PT, is supplied from MSA.

20   Special Transcendent Knowledge

a [709] **Special Transcendent Knowledge:** in an early plan that Lonergan sketched, the material in this chapter was to come under the heading, The Structure of History (see note r to chapter 17 above).

The introduction to this chapter (up to § 1, The Problem) was originally much shorter; at the proof stage Lonergan inserted the two last paragraphs, 'To these main topics ...,' and 'The relation between ...'

b [716] **limitations on:** MSA corr. MSB and PT 'limitations of.'

c [717] **conceptualism:** the conceptualist view of world order is discussed at length in The Natural Desire to See God, first published in 1949 (1988: 81–91, see esp. 84–86).

d [719] **the understanding that:** 'that' is an editorial addition.

e [727] **consciences:** MSA corr. MSB and PT singular.

f [728] **England is an island:** an allusion, surely, to Newman's example, but a slip on Lonergan's part; Newman was more accurate: Great Britain is an island (*An Essay in Aid of a Grammar of Assent* [London: Longmans, Green and Co., 1930] 294 and passim).

g [734] **avoiding all error:** MSA corr. MSB and PT omission of 'all.'

h [735] **mechanist determinism:** editorial change of 'mechanist determination.'

i [737] **are taken:** the MSS reading, 'are known,' appeared in the proofs, where it was corrected to 'are taken.'

j [739] *A Logical Note:* this was much longer in the MSS – almost a whole galley (six pages of typescript in MSB) was deleted after the first paragraph in the proofs and the three paragraphs beginning 'However, it remains' substituted.

k [740] **both of a problem of evil:** MSS corr. PT omission of 'both.'

l [740] **a new and higher integration:** MSA corr. MSB and PT omission of 'and'; the editors make the same change (which accords with 'a new and higher collaboration') elsewhere in this section also.

m [749] **exigences:** MSA corr. MSB and PT 'exigencies'; Lonergan rather regularly used the MSA form of this term – a technical one in his thinking.

n [751] **the love ... fulness of life:** for this last line of the PT the MSS and the proofs have 'the dispassionate, unrelenting at-oneness with all the true, the real, the good, that outlasts the fire-ball of the atom bomb and immeasurably exceeds its power to change the living of man'; this was not deleted from the galleys – presumably the change was made at the stage of page proofs.

Epilogue

a [753] **through understanding understanding:** MSS corr. PT omission of second 'understanding.'

b [754, note 1] **personal relations:** this footnote was added at the proof-reading stage; the larger concrete context in which Lonergan would study personal relations is illustrated in his Latin theology at the time of writing (1964: not only caput III on the relations within the Trinity but also such passages as quaestio XXXII on the divine Three inhabiting the just – the first edition of this volume was published in 1957, at about the same time as *Insight*).

c [755] **a little breathlessly and a little late:** we draw attention to the wording of this phrase, so often misquoted; the original context in MSA (crossed out there, and not found in MSB) was a reference to Demosthenes' 'untutored boxer that raised his hands, not to block the adversary's blow, but to cover the spot that had been hit.'

d [758] **Finally:** the MSS have a different paragraph at this point (most of it crossed out in the proofs); it was related to material on the *causa essendi/cognoscendi* that the MSS have in the introduction to the book, material that was deleted before publication (see note *k* to the introduction above).

e [760] **agreement ... on the basic elements does not preclude a development:** a window on the way Lonergan relates the six (basic) metaphysical elements to the list of nine in Intelligence and Reality (see note *k* to chapter 5 above, and the references given there).

f [760] **is a constant:** MSA corr. MSB and PT 'is constant.'

g [763] **the mystical body of Christ:** important in Lonergan's early thinking (1933–38: passim; 1941; 1951b; 1988: see the index at Mystical body).

h [766] **Professor Sorokin's phrase:** Lonergan came back to Sorokin, with more detail, in his lectures of 1958 and 1959 at Halifax and Cincinnati respectively (1988: 221; 1959b: lectures of the 2nd and 8th days).

Works of Lonergan Referred to in Editors' Preface and Editorial Notes

This is not a list of all Lonergan's works but only of those referred to editorially in this volume, and the code used (year, with letter where necessary) applies only to this volume. Some of these works are published, some are in the semipublished state of notes issued for students, some are not published in any sense, but are available in the Library and/or Archives of the Lonergan Research Institute, Toronto; for all of these we have indicated the number (anticipated or actual) of the volumes of the Collected Works (CWL) in which they do or should appear. A few of Lonergan's letters shedding light on the history of *Insight* are also listed here.

1928 'The Form of Mathematical Inference.' *Blandyke Papers*, No. 283 (January), 126–37 (CWL 17).

1933–38 Papers in File 713, Lonergan Archives (CWL 21).

1935a Letter, January 22 (to Henry Keane) (CWL 21).

1935b *PANTÔN ANAKEPHALAIÔSIS: A Theory of Human Solidarity, A Metaphysic for the Interpretation of St Paul, A Theology for the Social Order, Catholic Action, And the Kingship of Christ, IN INCIPIENT OUTLINE.* Lonergan Archives paper (in 'File 713 History') dated 'Dominica in Albis' [= April 28] (CWL 21). See 1991a below.

1941 'The Mystical Body and the Sacraments.' *The Canadian League* (The Catholic Women's League of Canada), March 8–10, 32 (CWL 17).

1945–46 Thought and Reality. Notes taken by J. Martin O'Hara from lectures at the Thomas More Institute, Montreal (CWL 21).

1949 Review of Etienne Gilson, *Being and Some Philosophers. The Ensign* (Montreal), May 28, p. 10 (CWL 17).

1950 *De scientia atque voluntate Dei: Supplementum schematicum.* Notes for students. Regis College (at that time Christ the King Seminary), Toronto (CWL 16).

1951a Intelligence and Reality. Notes for lectures at the Thomas More Institute, Montreal, March–May (CWL 21).

1951b The Mystical Body of Christ. A 'domestic exhortation.' Regis College (Christ the King Seminary), Toronto, November (CWL 17).

1952–53 Lectures on *Insight* in preparation, November 11 to April 21. Notes taken by Thomas O'D. Hanley.

1952–55 Letters to F. Crowe.

1956 *De constitutione Christi ontologica et psychologica.* Rome: Gregorian University Press (CWL 7).

1957 Existentialism. Notes for lectures, Boston College (our references: from counting pages in typescript made at Thomas More Institute, Montreal [CWL 18]).

1959a *De intellectu et methodo.* Notes by students of theology course, Gregorian University (CWL 19).

1959b The Philosophy of Education. Lectures at Xavier University, Cincinnati, August 3–14. There is an edited transcription, made by James Quinn and John Quinn (1979), of the tape-recording. A new edition of the lectures will appear under the title *Topics in Education* (CWL 10).

1964 *De Deo trino.* Vol. 2, 3rd ed. (much of the material appeared in the first edition in 1957). Rome: Gregorian University Press (CWL 9).

1966 *La notion de verbe dans les écrits de Saint Thomas d'Aquin.* French translation of *Verbum* (1967). Paris: Beauchesne.

1967 *Verbum: Word and Idea in Aquinas* (ed. David B. Burrell). Notre Dame: University of Notre Dame Press (CWL 2).

1970 Interview with Bernard Lonergan (Conversazioni con BL) by Giovanni Sala, March 11–18.

1971 *Grace and Freedom: Operative Grace in the Thought of St. Thomas Aquinas* (ed. J. Patout Burns). London: Darton, Longman & Todd (CWL 1).

1972 *Method in Theology.* London: Darton, Longman & Todd (CWL 12).

1973 Insight. Notes for a lecture on the book of that title, University of Guelph, November 27.

1974 *A Second Collection: Papers by Bernard J.F. Lonergan, S.J.* (eds William F.J. Ryan and Bernard J. Tyrrell). London: Darton, Longman & Todd (CWL 11).

1977 Letter, September 14, to Timothy Lynch.

1982 *Caring about Meaning: Patterns in the Life of Bernard Lonergan.* Eds Pierrot Lambert, Charlotte Tansey, Cathleen Going. Montreal: Thomas More Institute Papers/82.

1984 'The Mediation of Christ in Prayer.' *METHOD: Journal of Lonergan Studies* 2:1, 1–20 (CWL 6).

1985a 'The Original Preface of *INSIGHT.*' *METHOD: Journal of Lonergan Studies* 3:1, 3–7.

1985b *A Third Collection: Papers by Bernard J.F. Lonergan, S.J.* (ed. Frederick E. Crowe). New York: Paulist (CWL 13).

1988 *Collection* (2nd edition). Eds Frederick E. Crowe and Robert M. Doran. Toronto: University of Toronto Press (CWL 4).

1990 *Understanding and Being.* Edited by Elizabeth A. Morelli and Mark D. Morelli. Revised and augmented by Frederick E. Crowe with the collaboration of Elizabeth Morelli, Mark Morelli, Robert M. Doran, and Thomas V. Daly. Toronto: University of Toronto Press (CWL 5).

1991a '*Pantôn Anakephalaiôsis.*' *METHOD: Journal of Lonergan Studies* 9:2, 139–72. (1935b above, with 'Editors' Preface' by F. Crowe and R. Doran, pp. 134–38.)

1991b 'Lonergan's Own Account of *Insight.*' *Lonergan Studies Newsletter* 12, 22–24.

Lonergan's Lectures on *Insight*

This list does not include Lonergan's courses and seminars in the academic programs of colleges or universities where he was professor, nor does it include many talks and interviews in which exposition of *Insight* was a main topic. But, insofar as records are available, it will provide some leads to the most reliable commentaries there are on a most difficult book. The list starts with publication of the book in 1957.

1957 Thomas More Institute, Montreal: lecture in the course, Insight, September 26.

1958 American Catholic Philosophical Association, annual convention, Detroit: paper (in absentia), *Insight*: Preface to a Discussion, April 9.

– Saint Mary's University, Halifax: institute of twenty lectures, August 4–15. (Published as *Understanding and Being.*)

– Department of Psychiatry, Victoria General Hospital, Halifax: single lecture some time in August.

– Community of Sacred Heart Convent, Halifax: two lectures, September 2–3.

– University of Ottawa: four lectures, September 17–20.

– Xavier University, Cincinnati: two lectures, September 22–23.

1958–59 North American College, Rome: series of monthly lectures.

1959 Heythrop College, England: lecture to the academic community, April 17.

– Thomas More Institute: lecture in the course, Insight: A Dialectical Inquiry, September 25.

1961 Collegio Bellarmino, Rome: four or five lectures in the spring term.
- Irish Jesuit philosophate, Tullamore: lecture under the title, Insight into Phantasm, May 20.
- St Mary's College, Moraga, CA: forty lectures under the title, Philosophic and Scientific Knowledge, July 10 to August 4.

1963 North American College, Rome: lecture, March 4.

1964 Loyola University, Los Angeles: three lectures under the titles, The Nature of Insight, Self-Appropriation, and Being and Objectivity, September 21–23.

1967 American Catholic Philosophical Association, annual convention, University of Notre Dame: response to papers of Andrew Reck, Michael Novak, David Burrell, March 29 (probable date).
- University of Chicago Divinity School: lecture under the requested title, The General Character of the Natural Theology Contained in My Book, *Insight*, March 30 (probable date).

1971 Loyola College, Montreal: seminar session with students, November.

1973 Jesuit Philosophical Association, annual convention, Brebeuf College, Montreal: paper under the title, *Insight* Revisited, April 23.
- Department of Philosophy, University of Guelph: lecture to faculty and students, November 17.

1974 Canadian Philosophical Association, annual convention, Toronto: lecture under the title, Introduction to *Insight*, May 30.

Index

A priori: canons of method an, 128; conditions for judgment of fact, 360–62; God's knowledge is, 394; heuristic structures an, 128; insight and a p. synthesis, 5, 6, 431; Kant's, 178, 181, 363, 365, 439, 448; synthetic premises in deductivist metaphysics, 430–31

Aberration: of censor, 215–16; of insight, *see* Bias (*also* Flight, from insight, from rational self-consciousness; Scotosis); myth as a. of mystery, 614–15, 745; psychic a. and psychic health, 230

Absolute: component of relative, 515–16; frequency, 77; Hegelian, 447; of infallibility, 575; in measurement, 193; objectivity, 402–4; space, 176–79, 184, 403; time, 181, 184, 403; transcendence, 666

Abstract: deductivist metaphysics, 427–29; heuristic definitions general but not, 527; intelligibility of space and time, 172–84; laws, indeterminacy of, 117–25; material, spiritual, and a. types of intel-

ligibility, 696–97; propositions, invariance a property of, 165, 183–84; propositions and reference to being, 387–88 (*see also* Analytic principles); system and particular cases, 110; universal and 153–54, 198–99

Abstract and concrete: application of a. to c., 70–71, 110–11, 112, 117–18, 120–21, 570; in insight, 30; propositions, 164–65; in space and time, 194–95; in things, 271; in unrestricted act of understanding the universe, 672–74; as yielding two complementary types of insight (into laws, into things), 270–71, 510–11. *See also* Abstract; Nonsystematic; Systematic

Abstraction: complementary modes of in classical and statistical, 87–88, 133–34; from continuum, 87–88; and empirical residue, 53–55, 87–88, 336 (*see also* Empirical residue); enriching and impoverishing, 111–12, 336 (yet concrete insight has fuller object than ab-

mediary between explanation and data, 368–69; relativism of, 564; scientific and common sense, 201–2, 317; the tweezers holding thing for explanation, 316; as unchanging, 321

Description and explanation, 273, 316–17, 320–21, 368–69, 440, 461, 528, 562, 570; and Husserl, 440; in interpretation, 609–10; in metaphysics, 419–20; in relations, 516–18; same object of, 316–17; and self-affirmation, 357–59; transition from d. to e. necessary for metaphysical equivalence, 528. *See also* Relations of things to us, to one another

Desire and the good, 237, 619

Desire to know: detached, disinterested, pure, unrestricted, 5, 9, 28–29, 34, 97, 245–47, 372–75, 404–5, 573, 619, 622–23, 646–47, 659–62, 665, 707, 723–24, 760 (vs. attached and interested sensitivity, 659–60); dynamism of, *see* Dynamism (*also* Eros of mind); and hope, 723–24; immanent source of transcendence, 659–62; an instance of *omnia appetunt Deum*, 767–68; and logic, 404–5; and method, 404–5; a normative structure, 420; operator of cognitional development, 555, 659; provisionally restricted, 665; is pure notion of being, 377–80; restraint on, 202–3, 245–47; and universal willing, 646–47; as unrestricted, 375–76, 659–62

Despair, 723

Destiny, 253

Deterioration. *See* Wheel of progress; Decline, and progress

Determinacy of concept vs. indeterminacy of data, 158

Determinate: and being, 374; and notion of being, 385

Determination, heuristic structure vs. its, 657

Determinism: of event and random differences, 78, 84; and finality, 473; and freedom, 644; and Freud, 227–31; vs. indeterminism, 78, 120, 125, 161, 631, 672–73; mechanist, 154, 227–29, 280, 449–50; vs. statistical laws, 78, 124–25, 631

Development: defined, 479; and differentiation, 478; as emergence of higher viewpoint, 37–43; and emergent probability, 487; and environment, 480; of expression, 592–95 (operator of, 595); flexibility (minor, major) of, 479; and Hegel's sublation, 447; the heuristic assumption of genetic method, 486; of history (and theology), 763–64; human, *see* Development, human; human existence essentially in, 648; incapacity for sustained, essential problem of liberation, 653–54; incomplete (and flight from insight, 5–6; ground of moral impotence, 650); intellectual, 37–38, 251, 483–84, 485–86, 492 (communal, 197–98; desire to know, question, openness of intellect, operator of, 493–94, 555, 569–70, 659–60; freedom of, 361, 494; formulation of integrator of, 493–94; lag in, 251; and logic, 599–600); intelligence as illustration of, 483–84; of knowledge and language linked, 578; of language, 592–95; law of effect in, 491–92,

Insight: abstract and concrete yield
two types of (laws or conjugates,
and things), 270–71, 510–11; and
act of abstraction, 111–12; accumulation of, *see* Accumulation; as
activity, 4, 16, chs. 1–9, 558; in
algebra, 60; and application of
laws, 70, 75, 109–10, 120, 127; as
a priori synthesis, 5, 6, 431; in
Aristotle, Thomas Aquinas,
431–32, 699–700; in arithmetic,
38–40; in art, 207–9; basic, 36; a
beginning, 29; and being, 384;
characteristics of, 27–31, 357; and
clear and distinct ideas, 4, 6; and
clues, 3, 31, 34, 60 (*see also* Heuristic); of common sense, 3–4,
196–204 (incompleteness of,
197–98); communication of,
579–80 (*see also* Teaching); and
concepts, 35, 39, 332, 447 (*see also*
Concepts, and insight); into concrete situation, 30, 70, 75, 161,
308–12; constructive, 71, 75; and
decline, 8; and diagrams, 60; dialectical alternatives of formulation
of, 609; direct, introspective,
43–44, 298, 299, 304; factual,
speculative, practical, 622, 632–33;
as fixing terms and relations, 36,
417, 460–61; flight from, aberrations of, *see* Flight, from insight,
and Scotosis; into form, 112, 300,
391, 458–59, 699–700 (*see also*
Abstraction); and frames of reference, 52; habits of, 30–31, 302 (*see
also* Accumulation); human, vs.
non-human, 121; and image, 33,
34, 41, 42–43, 58–59; infallibility
of, 432; into insight (understanding of understanding), 3–4, 22,
398, 671, 706 (into insights of

others, 616); intelligibility the content of direct, 44; inverse, 43–50,
50–51, 78–81, 83, 198, 260–61,
412, 466, 509, 613, 709, 711 (and
common sense, 198–99; devaluated, 78; and empirical residue, 51;
and evil, 709, 711; and interpretation, 613; and philosophy, 412;
and statistical inquiry, 78–81);
invulnerable and vulnerable,
309–10, 433; judgment of correctness of, 309, 335, 340; as knowledge, 4, 16, chs. 11–20; into language, 35, 565; in mathematics,
3–4, 57–59, 336; and meaning, 5,
6, 611–12; as mediator, 30; and
metaphysics, philosophy, 5, 6,
412–13; and nonsystematic, 72,
74, 81–82; and notion of being,
384; and oversights, 5, 8, 21; a
perennial source of higher system,
291; and polity, 234; and the practical, 7–8, 70, 632–33; and problems, 4, 28; and progress, 8; and
psychotherapy, 223–227; as reflective understanding, 306, 332–33
(reflective understanding pronounces on, 332–33); and relations, 4–5, 36, 417, 460; reproducible vs. others, 659; rules for, 29;
vs. sensation, 29; into sensible present form, 30, 60; and similarities,
61; and surds, 45–46, 651–52 (*see
also* Insight, inverse); and symbolism, 43, 59, 116; and teaching, *see*
Teaching; and understanding,
366–67; as unifying data, 4–5,
506; as unifying field of knowledge, 4, 5–6; and velocity, 46–50;
and verification, 5
Instances: ferreted out by memory,
209; particular, 53–56, 109–11,

sical (relations, 339; inquiry,
61–62); of structure of cognitional
process and structure of universe,
456–57
'It': bare, 361; and 'I' as unity, 499.
See also Ego
'I've got it,' 29, 348. *See also* Eureka

Jansen, Bernhard, 514
Jones, Ernest, 229
Joule, James P., 77
Judgment(s), 16–17, ch. 9 (ch. 11
gives first concrete judgment, from
logical point of view, of author);
abstract and reference to existence,
331–32, 334–39, 387–88; an
affirmation, 296; assent of belief
compared with, 731; being known
in, 377; certitude of, 574; as commitment (limited, 368; personal,
297, 574); of common sense,
314–24 (common sense encourages j., 444–45); concrete of fact,
306–8, 331 (in belief, 732; conditions for, 360–62; means of transition from analytic propositions to
analytic principles, 364, 694; rules
for, 732; self-affirmation and
possibility of, 360–62; and universal doubt, 433–35); conditioned
element in, 305–6; content of
(proper and borrowed, direct and
indirect), 300–1; contextual aspect
of (logic and dialectic), 301–3,
399–400; of correctness of
insights, 309, 334–35, 340; and
decision compared, 636, 638; as
defining objectivity, 399–400,
408–9; evidence for, 304, 305,
333–34; existential, *see* Judgment,
concrete of fact, *and* Analytic principles; serially existential, 334–36;

formal inference differs from, 599;
and generalizations, 312–14;
groundedness of, 346–48,
379–80; with guarantee included,
575; habits of and insight, 30,
302–3; as increment (total) in
cognitional process, 301–3; infallibility of, 575; as level of cognitional
process, *see* Experience – understanding – reflection; mathematical, 334–39; necessary and universal, 363–64; and Plato, 389–90; as
positing synthesis, 390; privileged
(self-affirmation), 365–66; probability as property of, 90, 298, 574;
probable, 324–29, 574–76; and
propositions, 296; and questions,
297; rash, 309, 312; and reflective
understanding, 304; and relativity,
402; responsibility in, 297, 299;
revision of, 574; strategic of various philosophies, 386; and thought
(knowing and thinking), 377–78,
382, 387; totality of true, 374, 386;
totalities of possible, 386; true and
false, 382; truth, falsity formally in,
298, 579–80, 580; of value of
belief, 730
Jung, Carl, 217, 223, 482, 557; and
archetypal symbols, 482; and ego,
217; and shadow, 217, 218–19,
221

Kant, Immanuel, 5, 12, 15, 16, 153,
178, 181, 184, 228, 277, 279, 293,
300, 362–66, 397, 411, 431, 433,
437, 438–39, 447–48, 471, 504,
507, 531, 552, 560, 562, 588, 595,
606, 624, 652, 664, 704, 707, 723;
and a priori, 178, 181, 362, 365,
439, 448; and apperception, 365;
and categories, 364–65; and dia-

Mass: and energy, 469; and form, 462–63; notion of, 103, 358–59; and velocity, 462

Materiae dispositae advenit forma, 285. *See also* Emergent probability

Material: causality, 100; conditions dominated by immanent intelligibility, 289; defined, 540–41; and spiritual intelligibility, and empirical residue, 538–43; and spiritual, abstract intelligibility, 696–97; vs. spiritual (intelligible vs. intelligent), 537–43, 640, 670–71; as subject to law vs. spirit as legislative, 640–41; and understanding, 668–69, 670 (*see also* Abstraction; Empirical residue)

Materialism, dialectical, 242, 260

Mathematical: analogy to show plurality of metaphysics not compelling, 756–57; differentiation as abstraction, 468; formalizations not free expressions of intelligence, 336, 338; function, *see* Function; integration and energy, 468; judgments (serially existential), 334–36; limit, 82–83; matter, 336–37; method, circuit of, 59, 93, 99; operations, numbers, rules, 40, 335; and physical isomorphic (in relations, 339; in inquiry, 61–62); and scientific insights, 3–4, 57–60, 335–36; surds, 45–46

Mathematics: conceptualist vs. intellectualist in, 338; and empirical residue, 335; group theory in, 41; higher viewpoints in, 335–36; invariance in, *see* Invariance, in expressions of mathematics; and logic, 339, 664–65; material and formal elements in, 336; relevance of to *Insight*, 14–16; and science,

664–65; symbolism in, 42–43; and treatise, 596–97

'Mathesis,' 339

Matter: mathematical, 337; prime, 540 (*see also* Potency); subject to law vs. legislative spirit, 640–42; viewpoint that only m. exists, 386

Maturity. *See* Development, maturity as term of

Maxwell, James Clerk, 49, 69, 77, 91, 103, 469

Meaning(s): acts (formal, full, instrumental, ostensive, principal) of, 329–30, 381, 588, 589–90, 592, 611; and being, 381–83, 590; of common sense, 200; control of, 564–65, 568, 577, 585–86, 593, 602–3 (vs. automatisms in expression, 615; by metaphysical equivalence, 530–32); core of (and conflict between intention and meaning, 382; and intention of being, 382); dialectical factor in, 613–14; and expression (e. as instrument of, 576–77, 580, 611, 614; recurrent gap between, 612; tension of, 614); extrapolation of, 611; and falsity, 382; formulations of, 602, 606; genetic sequence in and expression, 594–95, 611–12, 613–16; and insight, 4, 6, 613; isomorphism of conditions of knowing and conditions of possible terms of, 599; for lexicon, for universal viewpoint, 588; of meaning, 4–5, 6; nonsystematic in field of, 613–16; obvious, no further discussion, 579; as 'out there,' 605; rules of, 330, 331; seen in usage, 332; sources of, 329, 381, 592; terms (all-inclusive, existential, formal, full, partial) of, 329–31,

No and yes. *See* Yes and no, significance of
Noesis, vs. *noema*, 19–20, 665. *See also*
Act vs. content
Nominal vs. explanatory definition,
35–36, 37. *See also* Names
Nomos and *physis*, 238
Noncountable multitude, 46, 538, 669
Nonscientific knowledge of God,
705–6
Nonsystematic: in diverging series of
conditions, 119–20; and documents, 616; existence as, 638–39;
in expression, field of meaning,
514–18; and indeterminacy,
124–25; insight and intelligibility
in, 71–74, 81–85, 269; and interpretation, 613–16; on levels of
psyche, 229–30; and measurement, 515; occurrence, 72–80,
121–22, 463; and prediction, 74;
and probability, 81–85; process,
72–77, 80, 122 (irreversibility of,
75); in relations, 515–18; and
successive levels of science,
229–30; and systematic, *see* Classical and statistical; vanishes for
unrestricted act of understanding,
672–74, 688, 697; the womb of
novelty, 74. *See also* Abstract and
concrete; Random; Systematic
Nonverbal communication, 200
Normative: criticism, 260–61; vs.
Hegelian dialectic, 446; objectivity,
404–5; science, 260–61; structure
of cognitional process, 420
'Not-me' (Sullivan), 556
Nothing and notion of being,
396–97
Notion, 378–79, 665
Notion of being, God, good, etc. *See*
those terms

Noumenon and phenomenon, 363
Novelty and nonsystematic, 74
Numbers: algebraic, 45–46; and
distribution of data, 136–37; fixed
by operations in mathematics, 41,
336; irrational, 45–46; significance
of large n. in world process,
136–37, 146, 149–50
Numerical difference and universal
knowledge, 53–56

Object: of description and explanation the same, 316–17; of inquiry
and reflection is being, 575,
661–62, 675; of practical insight
the to-be-done, 632–33; and subject and the problem of transcendence, 399–402; of true propositions and metaphysical elements,
526–30
Objectification: of absolute space and
time, 184; of inner tension, 747,
749; self-o. and self-knowledge,
558–60
Objectivity: absolute, 402–4; commonsense notion of, 408; defined
by judgments, 399–400, 408; and
Descartes, 413–14; experiential,
405–7; extroversion as model of,
410, 414, 431, 437–41, 447–48,
449–50, 604–6 (*see also* Knowing,
and looking); and imaginable, 15,
154, 158, 404, 465, 583–84 (*see also*
Verification, and images); and
knowing, *see* Knowing – objectivity
– reality – truth; normative,
404–5; notion of, ch. 13 (compatible with any philosophy, 408; and
notion of being, 401; principal,
399–402); vs. subjectivity, 407
Obligation: meaning of, 637; necessity, contingence in, 637–39

Samples, representative, 82, 88

Satire and humor, possible functions of, 647–49

Satisfaction, and desire, 619

Scattering of conditions, 119

Scepticism, incoherence of, 353–54, 356

Schelling, Friedrich Wilhelm, 554

Schemes: Kantian, 364, 439, 562, 664; of recurrence, see Recurrence, schemes of

Schilpp, Paul Arthur, 194

Schizophrenia, 556

Schleiermacher, Friedrich Ernst, 701

Scholar, 587, 600

Scholastic, Schoolmen, 21, 242, 391, 440, 448, 550, 595, 702, 703, 704

Schrödinger, Erwin, 91, 160

Science(s): applied vs. pure, 93, 99–100, 321 (see also Canon of relevance); and art, 208; autonomy and distinction of, 281, 464, 640 (see also Sciences, succession of higher); and central forms, 461; and common sense, 198–204, 318–24; critical, normative, 260–61; generalizations of, 52, 199, 327; human, 357 (servile imitation of natural science, 488); knowledge of form in and in metaphysics, 521–22; language of vs. that of philosophy, 451–52, 568; and logic, 281–82, 464, 465, 532; logic as technique and as, 598–99; of man (critical, normative), 260–61, 532; and mathematics, 665; measurement and higher, 488; mechanical, physical, chemical, biological, 101, 229, 230, 234–35, 236, 280–83, 287–90, 294, 477, 479–80, 488–92, 494, 495, 503, 504–5, 522, 538–39,

540, 542, 543, 631, 644, 654, 660–61; metaphysics as, ch. 16, esp. 544–52; and philosophy, 483, 551; precision of, 14, 196, 321; provide variable matter for invariant form of metaphysics, 755; role of belief in, 452–53, 726, 734–35; s. as specialized understanding, metaphysics as general, 521–22; statistical not impossible, 76; succession of higher, 229–30, 280–82, 464–65, 631, 639–40 (and logic, 280–81, 464–65; and nonsystematic, 230); symbolism in, 158; theology, queen of, 764–68; traditionalist mentality in, 452–53; unification of, 3, 5, 23, 454–55, 465; is of universals, 153–54, 198–99, 202. (Note: the term 'science' is often interchangeable with the term 'empirical science,' q.v.)

Scientia media, 685–86

Scientific: collaboration, see Collaboration, of scientists; explanation is theory verified in instances, 458; insight, 3–4, 57–60; interpretation vs. literary, 609; method, see Empirical method; monism, 449–50; observation, 94–98, 121–22, 228; progress, 107, 328–29 (and deduction, 190); thought and things, 272–73; writing, objective of, 593

Scientist: existence and occurrence mere matter of fact for, 677; and philosopher, reasonableness of, 453–54. See also Collaboration, of scientists

Scissors-action, of heuristic method. See Heuristic method

Scotosis, scotoma, 215–27, 625, 722

Scotus, 391–92, 395, 396, 397, 427, 431, 433, 437, 438, 471, 514, 581,

Suffering, 410

Sufficient reason. *See* Reason, sufficient

Sullivan, Harry Stack, 227, 279, 556

Superego, 482

Superlook, 658

Supernatural: bipolar dialectic becomes tripolar with, 749; conjugate forms, *see* Charity (*also* Faith; Hope); and higher integrations, *see* Integrations, higher; and metaphysical elements, 757; vs. natural, 550–51, 746–50, 767; solution to problem of evil as (relatively or absolutely), 719, 746–47; tension between and humanism, 747–50; s. transformation of physiological, sensitive, and intersubjective, 744, 763; truth and value, 747

Superstructures, 321

Suppositions, 32, 329–30, 358, 434, 435; and levels of cognitional activity, *see* Experience – understanding – reflection; and universal doubt, 434–35

Surds. *See* Insight, and surds; Mathematical surds; Sin, surd of; Social surd

Surrender, of disinterested intellect, 255–57. *See also* Obscurantism; Rationalization

Survival, of schemes of recurrence. *See* Recurrence, schemes of

Syllogism, 732, 739–40. *See also* Inference

Symbiosis, of knowledge and belief, 728, 735–36, 737, 754–55

Symbol(s): archetypal (Jung), 482; and art, 208; in calculus, 42; dream, 482; as heuristic, 43, 283, 323, 465; and human living, 585; and image, sign, *see* Image; and

insight, 43, 59, 116; and invariance, 43; invariant mathematical, 170–71; in mathematics, 42–43; and mystery, 556–57, 571, 744–45; in science, 158; and solution to problem of evil, 744–45

Synchronization of clocks, 182, 192

Synthesis: a priori, *see* A priori; imaginative, 114–17; insight as a priori, 5, 6, 431; judgment as positing, 390

System(s): freely developing, 361; Hegel's, 397; as hypothetical, 359; vs. law, 98–99, 110, 114–15, 140; understanding of vs. understanding of concrete unity, 270–71, 510

System(s), higher, 98–99, 229–30; good as, 622–23; insight a perennial source of, 291–92; as integrator of intellectual development, 494; in known, *see* Genera (*also* Species; Integrations); in knowing, *see* Viewpoint, higher

System(s), moving (operator), 491, 495, 501, 502, 507, 555, 597–98, 615; good as, 619; and logic, 532; solution to problem of evil as, 719; and static treatise, 597–98

Systematic: and nonsystematic occurrence, 72–79 passim, 463 (*see also* Classical and statistical); and prediction, 71; process, 72; reversibility of, 75; s. unification vs. imaginative, 114–17. *See also* Abstract and concrete; Nonsystematic

Taboo, and morality, 222

Talking: art of, 198, 315; automatisms in, 615

Tautology, 331

Teaching: and insight, 29, 197–98,

Weather prediction, 74
Western vs. Eastern philosophy,
  756–58
Wheel: insight, action, new situation,
  new insight, 248–49, 251, 710; of
  progress (inverse of deterioration),
  254, 328 (*see also* Feedback); in
  reverse, 8
Whittaker, Edmund Taylor, 115
Whole. *See* Unity – identity – whole
'Why?' 34, 197. *See also* Desire to
  know; Inquiry; Questions
Will: as appetite, 621; and belief,
  726; contingence of act of, 639;
  dialectic in, 631; and experience –
  understanding – reflection, 594,
  653; free, and grace, 550, 767;
  God's, 681, 684–86, 688, 689–91;
  indeterminacy of, 643–44; and
  intellect (*see* Will and intellect);
  notion of, 621–24; transcendent
  conjugate forms in (charity, hope),
  719, 720–22; and willingness and
  willing as potency – form – act,
  621–22, 646
Will, four elements in, 632 (underlying, sensitive flow, 632; practical
  insight, 632–33; practical reflection, 633–35; decision, 636–39)
Will and intellect: relations of, 720,
  723, 739; in belief, 726, 730–31
William of Ockham, 427–28
Willing: and persuasion, 646–47;
  rational and moral, not arbitrary,
  622, 645, 679
Willingness: antecedent, as limitation
  of effective freedom, 646–47; as
  form, habitual inclination in, 621,
  634, 646; parallel to habitual accumulation of insights, 646; unrestricted desire to know and universal w., 646–47

Wisdom, 331, 432; and omnipotence
  of God have equal range, 724;
  prior to metaphysics, 446
Wish fulfilment, 219, 482
Woglom, William H., 504
Wolter, Allan B., 392
Woman, and intersubjectivity,
  237–38
Wonder, 34, 196–97, 208, 354, 367,
  380 (as pure desire to know is
  always about something, about the
  given, 34); and art, 208; emergence of, 34; and inquiry, 367. *See
  also* Desire to know; Dynamism;
  Inquiry; Questions
Words: meaning of, 567, 578; psychology of, 577, 592–93; Scotist
  theory of, 608
Wordsworth, William, 556
World(s): Light of the, 764; possible,
  702; process, *see* World process; of
  science, metaphysics, poetry, and
  common sense, 570; of sense a
  mystery of God, 711, 714; situations (basic, initial), 143, 149–50,
  155. *See also* Universe
World process, order, 76, 115, 120,
  149–50, 195; blind alleys and
  breakdowns in, 150; and conceptualist vs. intellectualist, 717–18;
  cycles in, *see* Recurrence, schemes
  of; and effective probability, 474;
  and evil, 716–18; and finality,
  471–76; generalized equilibrium
  of, 141, 146; intelligibility of, 151,
  473–74; isomorphic with cognitional activity, 470–71, 475; and
  nonsystematic, 76; significance of
  large numbers and long intervals
  of time in, 136–37, 146, 150; as
  teaching, 474
World view(s): of Aristotle, Galileo,

The Series

Collected Works of

Bernard Lonergan

was designed by

ANTJE LINGNER

of University of

Toronto Press